Encyclopedia of
Women Social Reformers

Encyclopedia of
Women Social Reformers

Helen Rappaport

A B C CLIO

Santa Barbara, California   Denver, Colorado   Oxford, England

Library of Congress Cataloging-in-Publication Data

Rappaport, Helen.
   Encyclopedia of women social reformers / Helen Rappaport.
      p. cm.
   Includes bibliographical references and index.
   ISBN 1-57607-101-4 (hardcover : alk. paper) ; 1-57607-581-8 (e-book)
   1. Women social reformers—Encyclopedias. 2. Women political
activists—Encyclopedias. 3. Women's rights—Encyclopedias. I. Title.
   HQ1236 .R29 2001
   303.48'4'03—dc21

                                    2001005601

06 05 04 03 02 01   10 9 8 7 6 5 4 3 2 1

This book is also available on the World Wide Web as an e-book.
Visit abc-clio.com for details.

ABC-CLIO, Inc.
130 Cremona Drive, P.O. Box 1911
Santa Barbara, California 93116–1911

This book is printed on acid-free paper ∞.

Manufactured in the United States of America

Contents

Foreword, Marian Wright Edelman, xv
Preface, xvii
Acknowledgments, xxi
Women Social Reformers by Country, xxiii
Women Social Reformers by Cause, xxix

Encyclopedia of Women Social Reformers

Contents

Contents

Volume 2: M–Z

Contents

Contents

M

Maathai, Wangari Muta
(1940–)
Kenya

The Kenyan environmentalist, human rights activist, and scholar Maathai Wangari has been in the forefront of a campaign since the late 1970s to preserve Africa's disappearing forests. As founder of the Green Belt Movement in 1977, she has seen her organization grow into a pan-African movement that has inspired other Third World activists to fight for the preservation of their own natural ecologies and wildlife.

Wangari was born in Nyeri, Kenya, in a farming community and studied for a B.S. in biology at Mount St. Scholastica College in Kansas. In 1971 she was the first woman from East and Central Africa to acquire a master's degree in biological science, awarded by the University of Pittsburgh. In 1971 she returned to Africa to study for her Ph.D. at the University of Nairobi, which later appointed her to a professorship.

She was first alerted to the problems of deforestation in Kenya when she noticed mothers feeding their children on processed bread and other manufactured foods because they could no longer acquire sufficient firewood to prepare their own native foods. On the campaign trail in support of her husband's candidacy for parliament, she became further alarmed at the rate of desertification and deforestation in Kenya and saw tree planting as a way of providing work for the impoverished. In 1977 she founded the Green Belt Movement, with the object of encouraging peasants and farmers (the great majority of them women) to join in community tree-planting schemes that favored local species such as baobab, acacia, blue gum, and fig. With the endorsement of the United Nations and for-

eign governments, the help of private sponsors, and the money provided by fund-raising activities, the movement bought thousands of trees and established nurseries to cultivate saplings. Its workers began replanting areas that had been razed by unscrupulous developers (many of whom had been unlawfully allocated the land by an equally unscrupulous government), in the process providing work for many poor and unemployed women. The movement also developed an education program among poor women to teach them better nutrition, birth control, and hygiene.

Throughout the 1980s, Wangari continued her fight against government malpractice in the allocation of protected forests. She also launched a protest campaign in 1989 against the construction of a sixty-story office block in Nairobi that would have destroyed green space and pushed the country into massive debt (the project would have cost $200 million). Thanks to her group's lobbying, with support from the World Bank and the U.S. government, the building project was abandoned.

In 1991 Wangari was awarded the Africa Prize for Leadership for the Sustainable End of Hunger and spoke at the Earth Summit in Rio de Janeiro in 1992. Also in that year, she declined to be nominated as a presidential candidate, in the hope that she could do better work uniting Kenya's disparate political groups against President Daniel Arap Moi's African National Union. After Moi was returned to power and in light of increasing clashes between activists and government, she withdrew from the political scene.

Throughout her years of campaigning, Wangari has paid a high price for her stubborn commitment to her beliefs. Derision and government hostility to her activities caused her marriage to a Kenyan politician to break down. In 1999 she decided to stand in the presidential elections as a Liberal Party candidate for the Tetu constituency, with a program on environmental protection and schemes to combat poverty, disease, and the exploitation of poor farmers. That same year she launched another major campaign against the destruction of virgin forest in Kenya's Karura region.

A recipient of fourteen international and environmental awards, including a Woman of the Year Award in 1983 and a Woman of the World Award in 1989, Maathai is also a member of the National Council of Women and the Forum for the Restoration of Democracy. She has served as director of the Kenyan Red Cross Society. The Green Belt Movement can be found at www.geocities.com/gbm0001.

References and Further Reading

Wallace, Aubrey, and David Gancher. 1993. *Eco-heroes: Twelve Tales of Environmental Victory.* San Francisco: Mercury House.

Wangari, Maathai. 1994. *The Bottom Is Heavy Too: Even with the Green Belt Movement.* Edinburgh: Edinburgh University Press.

Machel, Graça Simbine
(1946–)
Mozambique

With her marriage in July 1998 to South African president Nelson Mandela, Graça Machel attracted international media attention. For many years previously, however, she had been diligently campaigning as an educator and for the rights of children in the Third World in her home country of Mozambique. Before marrying Mandela, she was the wife of Mozambique's former president, Samora Machel, who died in a plane crash in 1986.

In 1975, when the war of independence spearheaded by the Front for the Liberation of Mozambique (FRELIMO) ended with the foundation of an independent people's republic, Graça, who had studied languages at Portugal's Lisbon University, was appointed minister of education and culture. Soon after, she married Samora Machel, who had founded FRELIMO in 1964. Graça Machel remained in her post until 1989, during which time she set out to fulfill FRELIMO's objective of universal education. Between 1975 and 1985, the percentage of children enrolling for school rose from 40 percent to 90 percent (male) and to 75 percent (female) of those of school age, and literacy levels were considerably improved.

During attempts (supported by South Africa) to destabilize the Mozambican government, Machel sought reconciliation and fostered Mozambique's first grant-making organization, the Foundation for Community Development, which sought to improve living standards for ordinary Mozambicans by providing training and access to credit. Her work for the National Organization of Children of Mozambique also played a crucial role in the rehabilitation of children displaced and orphaned by the years of unrest. She later served as president of the National Commission of the United Nations Educational, Scientific, and Cultural Organization in Mozambique, was a member of the steering committee of the 1990 World Conference on Education for All, and has also led the Forum for African Women Educationists in its work for women's education in Mozambique.

In 1994, in support of the UN Convention on the Rights of the Child, Machel supervised a two-year study on the impact of armed conflict on children, which took her on field trips to Angola, Cambodia, Colombia, Northern Ireland, Lebanon, Rwanda, Sierra Leone, and the former Yugoslavia. Her report, submitted to the UN Committee on the Rights of the Child and to the General Assembly, described the tragic deaths of 2 million children over a period of ten years as a result of armed conflict and tribal vendettas and drew attention to the plight of child soldiers in Africa and children permanently disabled by land mines worldwide. Such firsthand testimony only reinforced Machel's belief in the protection of children as a fundamental responsibility of every civil society. Her concern resulted in the 1995 award of the Nansen Medal for her work for refugee children.

In 1997 Machel opened the third CIVITAS conference in Pretoria on civic education, stressing the importance of African cultural identity. The time had come, she felt, for Africans to "decolonize" their minds in the quest for a new kind of democracy based on indigenous family values, which could only be achieved by winning the battle for the hearts and minds of Africa's future generations—the children. In 1998 Machel married Nelson Mandela, who had long been an admirer of her work in Mozambique and with whom she had been corresponding since he wrote to her from his prison cell on Robben Island after the death of her husband. The couple met for the first time after Mandela's release in 1990. Since Nelson Mandela's retirement from government in June 1999, Machel's public profile as an international campaigner has not diminished. She has retained her commitment to the Foundation for Community Development in Mozambique and is a member of numerous international humanitarian organizations. In October 2000 she was the keynote speaker at the Tenth Anniversary Global Summit of Women, held in Johannesburg. Machel's report, *Impact of Armed Conflict on Children,* can be read on the Internet at www. unicef.org/graca/graright.

References and Further Reading

Current Biography. 1997. New York: H. W. Wilson.

Hacker, Carlotta. 1999. *Humanitarians.* New York: Crabtree.

Kidder, Rushworth M. 1994. *Shared Values for a Troubled World: Conversations with Men and Women of Conscience.* San Francisco: Jossey-Bass Publishers.

Machel, Graça. 1996. *Impact of Armed Conflict on Children: Report of Graça Machel: Selected Highlights.* New York: United National Department of Public Information: UNICEF, United Nations Children's Fund.

———. 1998. *The Graça Machel/UN Study on the Effects of War on Children.* Mahwah, NJ: Erlbaum Associates.

MacMillan, Chrystal
(1871–1937)
United Kingdom

One of the outstanding figures in the women's peace movement in the early twentieth century and a prime mover in attempts to engage world leaders in peace mediation during World War I, Scottish suffragist Chrystal MacMillan refused to compromise her pacifism, which would bring her frequent disappointments. As an equal rights feminist, she endorsed the objectives of the Six Point Group and Open Door Council during the interwar years.

MacMillan was born into a prominent Edinburgh family. After attending St. Leonard's School in St. Andrews, she turned down a scholarship to Girton College at Cambridge University, opting instead to study at Edinburgh University (1892–1896), where she gained a first-class degree in mathematics and natural philosophy. After a year's study in Berlin in 1900, she became honorary secretary of the Committee of Women Graduates of the Scottish Universities. In November 1908 she became the first woman to plead before the bar of the House of Lords, when she argued her right to vote, as a graduate, for candidates standing for the Scottish Universities seat in the general election. She based her case on the interpretation of the word "person" in previous legislation on voting rights referring to both women and men—a tactic that had also been tried in the past by suffragists in the United States. Although she lost her case, it gave valuable publicity to the suffrage cause.

As a member of the Edinburgh Ladies' Debating Society since 1902, MacMillan became an accomplished speaker. She chose to join the more moderate National Union of Women's Suffrage Societies (NUWSS), later serving as vice president of its Edinburgh branch. She rose through the ranks of the NUWSS to become a member of the national executive committee, serving throughout World War I, and by 1915 was also chair of the Scottish Federation of the NUWSS. Her publications on suffrage at this time included "The Struggle for Political Liberty" (1909), "Facts versus Fancies on Women's Suffrage" (1914), and "Woman Suffrage in Practice, 1913–23."

After 1911, MacMillan was increasingly active in the international women's movement. She attended the sixth congress of the International Woman Suffrage Association (IWSA) in Stockholm and the seventh in 1913 in Budapest. During her years as vice president of the IWSA from 1913 to 1923, she contributed regular reports on British suffrage to the organization's publication, *Jus Suffragii* (later *International Woman Suffrage News*). Her international connections brought her increasingly into contact with other European pacifists who, in 1914, with war imminent, were lobbying their governments to avert the outbreak of war. Together with Millicent Garrett Fawcett and Mary Sheepshanks, MacMillan composed an "International Manifesto of Women" calling for peace mediation and presented it to the British government, but to no avail. The response of MacMillan and her fellow pacifists was to organize a conference of women in The Hague in 1915, which she attended with Kate Courtney (only three women from Britain were able to attend) and where the International Committee of Women for Permanent Peace was formed. Afterward, MacMillan embarked on peace missions to Russia and the United States as a member of the committee.

During World War I, MacMillan was vice chair of the International Women's Relief Committee, which organized relief supplies for Belgian refugees. At war's end, she was again at the center of the drive to reestablish a women's peace movement, becoming secretary of the Women's International Congress in Zurich 1919 at which the Women's International League for Peace and Freedom was established as a successor to the committee formed in The Hague in 1915.

In the postwar years, MacMillan became a specialist in the legal status of women after being called to the bar of the Middle Temple in 1924, although she never practiced as a barrister. In 1923 she cofounded the Open Door Council for the repeal of the legal restraints on women and in support of equal opportunities for them in the workplace. After the winning of women's suffrage in 1918, the NUWSS was renamed the National Union of Societies for Equal Citizenship in 1924, but MacMillan resigned from the executive in disagreement over its support for protective legislation for women workers. In 1929 she was also a founding member of the Open Door International for the Economic Emancipation of the Woman Worker, which she served as president until her death.

During the early 1930s, MacMillan used her legal expertise to come to the defense of women who, having married foreign nationals, were not allowed to retain their British citizenship. She was active on various committees and wrote pamphlets on the subject during 1930–1933. She stood, unsuccessfully, as a Liberal candidate for Edinburgh in the 1935 election. She was also active in the interwar campaign against the white slave traffic, through her membership in the Association for Moral and Social Hygiene, led by Alison Neilans.

See also Courtney, Kathleen D'Olier; Fawcett, Millicent Garrett; Neilans, Alison.

References and Further Reading

Banks, Olive, ed. 1985, 1990. *The Biographical Dictionary of British Feminists*, vol. 1, *1800–1930*; vol. 2, *1900–1945*. Brighton: Harvester Wheatsheaf.

Crawford, Elizabeth. 1999. *The Women's Suffrage Movement, 1866–1928: A Reference Guide.* London: University College of London Press.

Holton, Sandra Stanley. 1986. *Feminism and Democracy: Women's Suffrage and Reform Politics in Britain, 1900–1918.* Cambridge: Cambridge University Press.

Jus Suffragii, October 1937. Obituary notice.

Leneman, Lori. 1995. *"A Guid Cause": The Women's Suffrage Movement in Scotland.* Rev. ed. Edinburgh: Mercat Press.

Oldfield, Sybil. 1984. *Spinsters of This Parish: The Life and Times of F. M. Mayor and Mary Sheepshanks.* London: Virago.

Pierson, Ruth Roach, ed. 1987. *Woman and Peace: Theoretical, Historical and Practical Perspectives.* London: Croom Helm.

Whittick, A., with Frederick Muller. 1979. *Woman into Citizen.* London: Atheneum.

Wiltsher, Anne. 1985. *Most Dangerous Women: Feminist Peace Campaigners of the Great War.* London: Pandora, and Westport, CT: Greenwood Press.

MacPhail, Agnes
(1890–1954)
Canada

The first woman to enter the Canadian Parliament in 1921, Agnes MacPhail remained its only woman member for seventeen of her nineteen years there. She was also a noted international pacifist, an advocate of disarmament, and a supporter of the work of the League of Nations Society in Canada.

Born in Proton Township, Grey County, Ontario, MacPhail was educated at Stratford Normal College in Ontario. She took up teaching in southwestern Ontario and Alberta from 1910 to 1921.

A supporter of agrarian reform, MacPhail successfully stood in the first national elections to which women were admitted in Canada. She served as member for South-East Grey, representing the United Farmers of Ontario, and remained until 1940, during which time she wrote regular columns in the *Farmers' Sun*. She was also a leading advocate of prison reform during her tenure and was instrumental in setting up a royal commission in 1936 to examine the Canadian penal system, as a result of which prison conditions were improved. After her defeat in the federal elections in 1940, MacPhail turned to provincial politics. Still taking a keen interest in rural affairs, she wrote a regular column on agricultural issues for Toronto's *Globe and Mail* (1941–1942). Originally a member of the Progressive Party (of which the United Farmers was a part), she had left it in 1924 after it fell into disarray to cofound the "Ginger Group." This organization in turn established the Cooperative Commonwealth Federation of Canada in 1932, a social democratic group that elected MacPhail president. In 1943 she was elected as its member for York East in the Ontario legislature, serving until 1945 and again from 1948 to 1951. During her political career, MacPhail toured extensively in Canada and the United States.

Beyond national politics, MacPhail was a lifelong pacifist who became prominent in the international movement as a member of the Women's International League for Peace and Freedom, founded in 1919. Like her compatriot Nellie McClung, she was a staunch maternal feminist who believed in the healing and conciliatory role of women in wartime. During the 1920s, she promoted this role at numerous international peace conferences geared to encouraging peace mediation and collective security. In 1929 she was the first woman member of a Canadian peace delegation to the League of Nations and became involved in the work of the World Disarmament Committee. She lobbied in Parliament for reductions in defense spending, and just as she had opposed conscription in World War I, so during the 1930s she objected to the militarization of Canadian youth through cadet training in schools. As another war loomed in 1939, she urged the Canadian government to keep the country out of the war, despite its membership in the British Commonwealth, and align more closely with its natural ally and neighbor, the United States, in maintaining a neutral position. In the end, she was reluctantly forced to endorse Canada's limited commitment to the war effort, in the belief that it was a just one against the evil of Nazism.

MacPhail retired from the Ontario legislature in 1951, although at the time of her death there was talk of her being appointed to the Canadian Senate. In 1999 the New Democratic Party of Ontario established an Agnes MacPhail Award to honor women's work for the party and other women's issues.

See also McClung, Nellie.

References and Further Reading

Benson, Eugene, and William Toye, eds. 1997. *Oxford Companion to Canadian Literature.* 2d ed. Oxford: Oxford University Press.

Cleverdon, Catherine Lyle. 1950. *The Woman Suffrage Movement in Canada.* Toronto: University of Toronto Press.

Crowley, Terence Allan. 1990. *Agnes MacPhail and the Politics of Equality.* Toronto: J. Lorimer.

Innis, M. Q., ed. 1959. *The Clear Spirit: Twenty Canadian Women and Their Times.* Toronto: University of Toronto Press.

Josephson, Harold, Sandi Cooper, and Steven C. Hause et al., eds. 1985. *Biographical Dictionary of Modern Peace Leaders.* Westport, CT: Greenwood Press.

Pennington, Doris. 1989. *Agnes MacPhail, Reformer: Canada's First Female MP.* Toronto: Simon and Pierre.

Stewart, M., and D. French. 1959. *Ask No Quarter: A Biography of Agnes MacPhail.* Toronto: Longman's Green.

Strong-Boag, Veronica. 1987. "Peace-Making Women: Canada 1919–1939." In Ruth Roach Pierson, ed., *Woman and Peace: Theoretical, Historical and Practical Perspectives.* London: Croom Helm.

Malkowska, Olga
(1888–1979)
Poland

Olga Malkowska is a revered figure in Polish twentieth-century history. She was the founder of the Polish Girl Guide Movement (1911) prior to Poland regaining independence in 1918 after 150 years of partition among the Austro-Hungarian Empire, Prussia, and Russia. As the chief guide of Poland, she was also a founding member of the World Association of Girl Guides and Girl Scouts in 1928.

Malkowska was born Olga Drahonowska at Krzeszowice, which was then under Austro-Hungarian rule. She studied music at Lwów (modern-day Lvov) Conservatoire, where she was active in the Eleusis patriotic movement. After so many years of foreign rule and several insurrections, many freethinking Poles before World War I were not only looking for ways to win an independent Poland but also were preparing the next generation for life within it, and Olga fervently supported this ideal. At Eleusis meetings, she met Andrzej Malkowski, who had translated Robert

Baden-Powell's 1908 classic *Scouting for Boys* and went on to found Polish Scouting in 1910. They married in 1913.

The Scouting and Guiding movement helped Polish youth to develop common goals and national aspirations and by the outbreak of war in 1914, had trained thousands of young people. The Malkowskis imbued their charges with a strong sense of patriotism and self-help, placing an emphasis on the wholeness of body, psyche, and intellect. Many were soon conscripted in the partitioning powers' respective armies and forced to fight in World War I, often against Poles from other partitions. At the same time, many Poles were also working to create a Polish Free Army in a free and sovereign Poland. Many Scouts and Guides joined and supported Marshal Józef Pilsudski's "Legions," the armed independence movement, which took advantage of the upheavals of World War I to make its own bid for Polish freedom, and went on to fight the Bolsheviks and drive them out of Poland in 1920.

Because of their nationalist activities, Olga and Andrzej were soon personae non grata in their home country. They fled to Switzerland in 1914 and then to the United States, where their son was born. Andrzej joined the Canadian army as an officer, subsequently losing his life in 1919 while on a diplomatic mission for General Józef Haller of the Polish Free Army in Odessa. Meanwhile, Olga had returned to Europe in 1917, where she worked with the Polish independence leader, concert pianist, and later prime minister Ignacy Paderewski and with the Dutch painter Laurence Alma Tadema, running a school in London for Polish refugee children. Upon her return to an independent Poland in 1921, she created the first Girl Guide boarding school, Yew Manor (Dworek Cisowy), in the Pieniny mountains in southern Poland.

Malkowska's school flourished from its founding in 1924 until the Nazi invasion in 1939, producing some of the leading Polish women intellectuals and activists of their generation. Under the leadership of Malkowska and others who followed her into the movement, Polish Scouting and Guiding was a major force in modernizing the Polish nation between 1920 and 1939, after its long period of occupation. The movement was notable for its self-empowering philosophy and its system of values broadly based on the ethical notion of duty to God, country, and community. Based closely on the system created by Robert Baden-Powell in England but with an extra-patriotic cast, the Polish version of Guiding was instrumental in reconnecting the newly independent Poland with the rest of the world at a time when the Guiding movement was becoming highly influential and popular around the world.

Keeping to a ten-point law and a lifelong promise, each guide pledged to work for her own development and that of her society. Although Guiding was always intended to be a great game, its rules and methods were such that they inspired each guide to take on very serious and real responsibilities. Everything she did mattered. She was required to monitor her every action, be continuously self-aware, and be ready to challenge her own shortcomings in striving for continuous self-improvement. She was expected to develop her talents, show initiative, think critically, and work with others while also attending to her spiritual life and physical prowess.

Yew Manor was a radical, experimental girls' school. In addition to regular courses, girls were required to develop their own program of study based on their passions and interests, all undertaken in an environment of fresh air, vegetarian food, and healthy exercise. The school was wholly staffed by Guiding women, who both taught the girls and lived with them. Physical health was achieved by frequent walks and outdoor work and play; the school produced its own food, and all the members of the school, from youngest to oldest, shared in its day-to-day maintenance and upkeep. It was situated in a remote part of rural Poland, and so it provided local services, including a drop-in medical surgery for local villagers, courses for village children in everything from cooking to radio communications, and cultural events. It also helped to modernize local agriculture by introducing new seed varieties and enlightened methods of husbandry. The school ethos included a respect for the natural environment many years ahead of its time.

Beyond its core curriculum and methods, the school was unique in being a twenty-four-hour Guiding experience: day-to-day life took place within the patrol system, and the aesthetic and ceremonies of the Guiding path, including outdoor activities, were an integral part of school life. Plays, readings, concerts, and folk art, all drawn from Poland's rich cultural heritage, were given space, and the school owned its own train coach, which could be attached to trains on the national network, thus enabling geography field studies to take place regularly.

For its time, Yew Manor was unique, and, with Malkowska enjoying a reputation for her work throughout Poland and beyond, it had an influence far beyond its own sphere in promoting the empowerment of girls and women, both as a training center for Guiding women and by offering a home for a worldwide Guiding family. Those whom Malkowska educated at Yew Manor went on to fight alongside thousands of other Guides and Scouts against the Nazis and the Soviets in World War II as part of the Resistance movement. Of those who survived, many entered the core of Poland's postwar reconstruction, and became some of the leading artists and thinkers of their generation. A number of them outlived communism with their values intact to be revered as elders of the nation in the Solidarity movement and the postcommunist era.

Malkowska represented Poland at many international conferences during the interwar years. As Chief Guide of Poland (whose movement was now the third largest in the world), she became a key figure in 1931 when the international Guiding movement conformed to the League of Nations' Childrens' Section. In 1932 she hosted an international Guiding congress in Poland; the following year she welcomed to Poland an international Guiding delegation, including Olave Baden-Powell. In 1935 she led the first international jamboree in Poland. She was a regular contributor to such English Guiding journals as *The Council Fire* and worked with the children's writer Arthur Mee, contributing, among others, to his *Children's Newspaper*.

After escaping the Nazi invasion of Poland at the outbreak of World War II, Malkowska arrived in London, where she was awarded the Bronze Cross by Queen Elizabeth (now the queen mother). She spent the war years running an orphanage at Castlemains, Lord Home's country seat in Scotland, for displaced, orphaned, or refugee Polish children. She gave hundreds of lectures on the situation in Eastern Europe throughout Britain; ran the London-based Polish Guiding and Scouting headquarters, and liaised with the London-based Polish government. She also founded and ran the Guides International Service, which brought aid to children and families in some of the worst-hit areas of Europe.

Farther afield, it was the Guides who recognized the plight of the hundreds of thousands of orphaned, displaced, and dispossessed Polish children scattered across wartime Europe and beyond. Guiding and Scouting was organized at every stage of evacuation and resettlement. Even in the German concentration camps, such as Bergen Belsen, where Anne Frank died, clandestine Guide and Scout troops sprang up, helping build morale and a sense of purpose and optimism, even in conditions of unimaginable cruelty and bleakness. Malkowska offered unstinting support for the whole Guiding and Scouting Polish family throughout the war. Letters written to Malkowska by Girl Guides in the Polish resistance also described how they applied the Guide Laws as a way of surviving Gestapo torture. But after the failure of the Warsaw Uprising in 1944 and Poland's subsequent transformation into a communist state, her health suffered badly.

Some years later, when she was nearing sixty, she began again, creating a new Polish Children's Home in Devon, which she ran from 1949 to 1961. Returning to Poland in 1961, Malkowska gave Yew Manor to the nation and retired to a modest mountain house in the nearby spa town of Zakopane, where she was respected by all Poles, irrespective of their political allegiances and affiliations. During the 1960s and 1970s, when communism made allegiance to patriotic values illegal, and the Guiding and Scouting movement was transformed into a communist youth organization, Malkowska quietly supported those youth leaders who maintained the real values of the movement and of Poland.

Malkowska died in 1979, at the age of ninety-one, just a year before the trade union Solidarity began the process of breaking the communist stranglehold on Eastern Europe. Simultaneously with the founding of Solidarity, a revitalized Polish Scouting and Guiding movement openly opposed to Soviet influence sprang up and adopted Olga and Andrzej Malkowski as its role models. In the teeth of the greatest difficulties and persecution, the Malkowskis' story was compiled by their followers and their writings preserved. They now form the basis of the system of values for postcommunist Girl Guides and Girl Scouts in Poland.

Olga Malkowska was an inspiring leader and a captain to many. Highly gifted, imaginative, intuitive, naturally charming, and noted for her beauty, she was also self-disciplined, independent, a clear and systematic thinker, physically fit, and fervently patriotic. Together with her husband Andrzej, she was overt and systematic in instilling patriotic values, high ideals, and the utmost self-discipline in the youth with whom she worked and whom she was preparing to take a role in a free and independent Poland. Under her leadership, the aim of the Girl Guide movement in Poland was nothing less than to transform the world. As Walt Whitman once exhorted: "Produce great Persons, the rest follows." Eight books have been published in Polish about Olga and Andrzej Malkowski since her death, many running into several editions. A museum dedicated to their work has now been opened in Zakopane.

References and Further Reading

Baden-Powell, Olave. 1973. *Window on My Heart: The Autobiography of Olave, Lady Baden-Powell.* London: Hodder and Stoughton.

Davies, Norman. 1981. *God's Playground: A History of Poland.* 2 vols. Oxford: Clarendon Press.

Kerr, Rose. 1937. *The Story of a Million Girls: Guiding and Girl Scouting round the World.* London: The Girl Guides Association.

Liddell, Alix. 1970. *The Girl Guides 1910–70.* London: Frederick Muller.

Manuchehrian, Mehrangiz
(c. 1915–?)
Iran

An accomplished lawyer and campaigner for women's and children's welfare and legal rights, Manuchehrian is looked upon by many Iranian feminists as one of the "founding mothers" of the movement for female emancipation since the 1950s. After being one of the first female students to enter Tehran University in 1936, Manuchehrian did her legal postgraduate studies in Europe and in U.S. juvenile courts. She was finally awarded a doctorate in law by Tehran University in 1947 for her work on juvenile delinquency and went into practice as the first Iranian woman lawyer, for the next twenty-one years (1947–1968) making an important contribution to the review and reform of Iranian penal law.

She also acted as a legal adviser to the National Council of Women in Iran and took an active part in Iranian women's organizations that called for the political equality of women with men.

Manuchehrian was appointed professor of psychology and philosophy at Tehran University during the 1950s and professor of penal law at Tehran University (1964–1968). In 1964 she became one of the first two women to be appointed to the Iranian senate.

As a founding member of the Iranian Federation of Women Lawyers, which in 1961 proposed extensive reforms in Iran, Manuchehrian worked on a draft proposal for the abolition of certain aspects of the civil code that discriminated against women, such as polygamy. The proposal also called for equal political rights and greater fairness to women with regard to divorce, child custody, and the inheritance of property gained in marriage. It was also proposed that women should be given equal rights of employment and the ability to work outside the home. Although the Iranian Family Protection Law of 1967 that resulted from these proposals was limited in scope, it is clear that Manuchehrian contributed significantly to its enactment.

Aside from her legal work, Manuchehrian has remained active in welfare and charitable projects, working for the Red Lion and Sun Society (the Iranian Red Cross). She has served as a legal adviser to the National Association for the Protection of Children, as well as being a leading light of the Federation of Iranian Women's Organizations. This latter collaborates with the Iranian Association of Women Lawyers to achieve advances in the social and economic welfare of women and improvement in their health care.

In 1968 Manuchehrian's work on human rights was commended by the United Nations. In the mid-1970s, she proposed reform of the law under which women had to have the written permission of their husbands to be issued a passport, and the law was changed in 1976. During her distinguished legal and academic career, Manuchehrian has published books on aesthetics and education, as well as on the law. Most notable among these is *Criticism of the Constitutional, Civil and Criminal Law of Iran in Regard to Women,* a treatise inspired by the tenets of the U.S. Bill of Rights. In 1987 her book, *The Inequalities between Men and Women's Rights in Iran,* questioned the validity of certain aspects of shari'ah (i.e., Islamic law) relating to women. A woman of considerable status in her time for her pioneer legal work in Iran, Manuchehrian became a member of the International Association of Women Lawyers, of which she was elected president. It has not been possible, however, to trace her recent activities in Iran, although she is known to have contributed regular articles on women's legal rights to the journal *Woman (Zanan)*, established in 1992.

References and Further Reading

Moghissi, Haideh. 1994. *Populism and Feminism in Iran*. Women's Studies at York. London: St. Martin's Press.

Manus, Rosa
(1880–1942)
Netherlands

The Dutch feminist and suffragist Rosa Manus was a leading member of the International Woman Suffrage Alliance (IWSA) during the interwar years and worked closely with U.S. suffrage leader Carrie Chapman Catt (to whom she was devoted like a daughter to a mother) and her successor Margery Corbett Ashby. She also served as vice president of IWSA's successor, the International Alliance of Women for Suffrage and Equal Citizenship and is best remembered for her brave, self-sacrificing work for Jewish refugees during World War II.

A Jew who was the daughter of a businessman, Manus was ambivalent about her religious background all her life. Active as a young suffragist from the 1900s, she became a leading figure in the Dutch feminist movement prior to World War I. She became Aletta Jacobs's devoted friend and assistant in organizing women's consciousness-raising in the Netherlands, beginning with an exhibition, "Woman 1813–1913," which she staged in Amsterdam to provide an opportunity for women to celebrate their achievements and gain a sense of their common cause.

During World War I, Manus and Jacobs organized the 1915 women's peace conference at The Hague, where the attendees established the International Committee of Women for Permanent Peace (later changed to the Women's International League for Peace and Freedom). Manus served as its first secretary during the war, helping Jacobs coordinate the activities of member countries, dealing with the huge correspondence from around the world, and keeping members abreast of news and developments in pacifist attempts at mediation. Manus was central to the postwar activities of the IWSA after its 1920 congress in Geneva. She garnered a reputation as an excellent organizer, as being even-tempered and enthusiastic, and as a person who worked hard to raise the profile of the IWSA's peace committee by taking on fund-raising and running conferences. She retained close links with the peace movement and helped organize pacifist conferences in Dresden and Berlin, and, when visiting Carrie Chapman Catt in the United States in 1928, attended a conference of the Committee on the Cause and Cure of War. In 1936 she was appointed honorary organizing secretary of a major peace conference held in Brussels. By the 1930s Manus was a revered figure in the Netherlands. She was made an extraordinary member of the Amsterdam Soroptimist Club, the only member of this club for business and professional women who was accorded this honor, in recognition of her long years of work on behalf of women. A higher honor followed in 1940, when Queen Wilhelmina presented her with the Order of Orange Nassau for her work as chair of the Holland Committee for Refugees.

It was in 1908 that Manus had become a close friend of the U.S. suffrage leader Carrie Chapman Catt, after meeting her at the IWSA congress held in Amsterdam that year. When Catt took on a punishing tour of Europe in 1922, Manus acted as companion-cum-nurse as they toured women's organizations, gauging the level of suffrage activities in Rome, Budapest, Vienna, Prague, and Berlin. Then in November, they undertook the long journey to South America, where they toured six republics, attended a congress of women of Brazil organized by Bertha Lutz, and met members of Argentina's and Chile's National Councils of Women, before returning to Rome for the 1923 congress of the IWSA.

By 1933, with the rise of fascism in Adolf Hitler's Germany now relentless, Manus's level of alarm about the safety of German Jews was running high. When she visited Catt in the United States that year, she reported on the increasing atmosphere of anti-Semitism in Europe. Meanwhile, she had taken the chair of a women's committee set up in the Netherlands to help Jewish refugees from Germany. She never mentioned fears for her own personal safety as a Jew, nor did she discuss her Jewishness, although she found the experiences of anti-Semitism that she had witnessed in Hungary in 1922 harrowing. During her visit to Catt in 1933, Manus approached the International Congress of Women in Chicago and sought further advice from Jewish leaders on a rescue program for the Jews of Germany. Catt reinforced her appeal by founding the Protest Committee of Non-Jewish Women Against the Persecution of Jews in Germany, which gathered a 9,000-signature petition for submission to the German government. In 1936 Manus was appointed honorary organizing secretary of a major peace conference in Brussels. A year later, she attended an International Alliance of Women for Suffrage and Equal Citizenship study conference in Zurich.

Manus's fears about fascism were no doubt in the back of her mind when in 1935 she was instrumental in setting up the International Archives for the Women's Movement in rooms provided by the International Institute of Social History in Amsterdam. Manus collaborated with Dutch historian Johanna Naber and feminist Wilemijn Posthumus-van der Groot (she also received valuable support from the Hungarian feminist Rosika Schwimmer). Appointed president of the archive, Manus made the first donation—of the books and papers of Aletta Jacobs, who had died in 1929—and they were housed in premises made available at the International Institute of Social History in Amsterdam. Using her wide international contacts in the women's movement, she gathered other important documents, periodicals, and photographs. But in July 1940 the Germans occupied the Netherlands and soon after confiscated the entire archive. Fifty-two years later, a Dutch historian discovered some of the lost material languishing in the Osobyi Archive in Moscow and was able to microfilm it.

In 1939 Manus went to the United States for Catt's eightieth birthday celebrations as a representative of the IWSA. Although she had repeatedly been urged by Catt to leave the Netherlands, Manus courageously refused. As a patriot, she would not leave her country or give up her refugee relief work. In June 1939, at the annual IWSA congress, held in Copenhagen, she announced her retirement, having never missed a congress since 1904. When the Germans occupied Amsterdam, Manus went into hiding at a hospital for a year, before being arrested by the Gestapo in August 1941. She spent several months in a succession of concentration camps, first at Scheveningen, a camp near Berlin, then Ravensbruck, and finally Auschwitz, where she died on 29 May 1942. It was many months before the news of her death finally reached her friends in the international women's movement.

See also Ashby, Margery Corbett; Catt, Carrie Chapman; Jacobs, Aletta; Lutz, Bertha; Schwimmer, Rosika.

References and Further Reading

Bosch, Mineke. 1990. *Politics and Friendship: Letters from the International Woman Suffrage Alliance, 1902–42.* Columbus: Ohio State University Press.

Jacobs, Aletta. 1996. *Memories: My Life as an International Leader in Health, Suffrage, and Peace.* New York: Feminist Press.

Van Voris, Jacqueline. 1987. *Carrie Chapman Catt: A Public Life.* New York: Feminist Press.

Markievicz, Constance de
(1868–1927)
Ireland

The Irish feminist, suffragist, and militant nationalist Constance de Markievicz was romantically named the "Rebel Countess" by her admirers, a sobriquet that denotes her status as one of the most flamboyant figures in the Irish movement for independence. She came from the privileged background of a wealthy but enlightened family of the Anglo-Irish gentry. For the first part of her life, she was a leading society figure; at the age of forty she embraced Irish nationalism.

Constance and her sister Eva Gore-Booth grew up on the idyllically beautiful family estate at Lissadell in County Sligo. Both learned philanthropy at the knee of their father, Sir Henry Gore-Booth, a humane landowner who had ensured that his poor tenants were provided for in times of need, such as the 1879–1880 famine, when he handed out food from his own stores.

The two sisters were great beauties, much admired and cosseted, who enjoyed all the privileges of their status. Constance was presented at court in 1887, but she was no conventional bored socialite. A natural bohemian, she soon became restless and dissatisfied with the social round and moved to London to study at the Slade School of Art in 1893. During 1898–1900 she studied art in Paris, where she met and married the Polish artist and playwright Count Casimir de Markiewicz (*sic*). After living briefly in Paris and on the Markiewicz estate in Ukraine, they settled in Dublin. There Constance threw herself into cultural and artistic circles, lending her support to the Gaelic League and the new Abbey Theatre, where she performed in several plays. But such a sybaritic lifestyle left her discontented. Having witnessed the poverty of the poor farmers on the family estate in Sligo, she could not ignore the misery and deprivation existing in the poor quarters of Dublin. She also became increasingly drawn into both the suffrage and nationalist causes.

In 1908 she joined Maud Gonne's women's organization, the Daughters of Ireland, and later contributed to its magazine the *Irish Woman,* in which she urged women to take up the nationalist cause. Markievicz's commitment to suffrage was soon sidelined by a conflict of interests, however, for she became convinced that women's enfranchisement could only follow the achievement of Irish independence. She joined Sinn Féin in 1908, and a year later, taking as her inspiration the English Boy Scout movement, Markievicz founded Fianna na hÉireann—a Boy Scout organization that was used as a cover for training young men in the cause of Irish nationalism. Renowned herself as a good shot, Markievicz taught her recruits marksmanship, signaling, and army drills—a far cry from the cozy campfires of the English movement.

In her support for the rights of Irish workers, Markievicz joined with trade union leaders to organize protests against poor working conditions and low wages. In 1913, during a six-month lockout of trade union members (at a time when Dublin employers were resisting the growing muscle of the Irish National Transport and General Workers' Union), Markievicz collected money and set up and staffed a soup kitchen in Dublin for workers. By that time, because of her association with nationalists and trade union leaders such as Jim Larkin and James Connolly, she was under surveillance by the police. And not without justification, for by this time she and her boys in the Fianna na hÉireann had become in-

Constance de Markievicz (Archive Photos)

volved in the activities of the Irish Volunteers, unloading consignments of guns smuggled in from Germany and hiding them in her cottage in the mountains. Meanwhile, her home in Dublin had become the covert headquarters of the Irish Citizen Army.

In 1913 Markievicz and her husband separated on amicable terms, and he returned to his estate in the Ukraine and served in the tsarist army during World War I. Markievicz became deeply embroiled in the militant activities of Irish Republicans leading up to the Easter Rising of 1916. Not surprisingly, she rose to the full theatricality of the moment, as a staff lieutenant commanding a detachment of 120 Irish Citizen Army volunteers. On the day of the rising, she was much in evidence, wielding a gun at the College of Surgeons on St. Stephen's Green, wearing the green uniform of the Irish Citizen Army, and sporting her own improvised plumed hat. The rising involved about 1,500 Republican fighters (including about ninety women), and during its course Markievicz claimed to have shot several

British soldiers. After a week, however, she was forced to surrender, another theatrical moment that she performed with flair and disdain. She was held in Kilmainham jail before being court-martialed (as an officer) and sentenced to death. Unlike the rest of the leaders of the rising, however, she was not shot, because of her sex and also because the British authorities did not want to execute a woman in the wake of the 1915 execution by the Germans of Edith Cavell. Sentenced to penal servitude for life, Markievicz was sent to Aylesbury prison in England. There she made use of her time writing many letters and catching up on her reading. As she averred, "Jail is the only place where one gets time to read" (Coxhead 1965, 108).

Markievicz was released in the general amnesty of 1917, after thirteen months in prison, on the orders of British prime minister Lloyd George, who was anxious to reassure his allies in the war effort that Britain was making serious efforts to address the issue of Irish independence. She became a member of the executive council of Sinn Féin and traveled the country lecturing on the cause. She was rearrested in May 1918 and sent to Holloway jail along with Maud Gonne for their suspected involvement in a German plot against the British government and their vocal opposition to the conscription of Irish men for the British war effort. While she was still in prison, the passing of the Representation of the People Act in the British Parliament gave women over thirty the vote and the right to stand as candidates in general elections. Markievicz stood as the Sinn Féin candidate for the St. Patrick's division of Dublin, a seat to which she was elected while still in jail. Indeed, she was the first and only woman candidate who was successful in the 1918 general election, but along with the other seventy-two elected Sinn Féin members of Parliament, she did not take up her seat in the House of Commons because they all refused to cooperate with the British government. In January 1919, she became instead a member of the Dáil Éireann (which was not recognized by the British government) and was made minister of labor by Eamon de Valera. Her uncalled-for response, however, was to speak out on the Dáil's insufficient attention to the rights of working people.

Markievicz was arrested yet again in September 1920 and was court-martialed for her involvement in organizing and training Fianna na hÉireann recruits. Sentenced to two years' hard labor at Mountjoy prison in Dublin, in a letter to her sister she wryly observed that, in contrast, Robert Baden-Powell had been made a baronet in England for founding the Boy Scouts. After the truce in the civil war in Ireland, Markiewicz was released, but as part of her opposition to the 1921 Anglo-Irish treaty, she toured the United States on a fund-raising mission and campaigned against the terms of the treaty. The U.S. press noted her revolutionary fervor and passionate commitment, but as ever, there was no getting away from her inherently aristocratic, upper-class manner. In 1917 Markievicz had converted to Catholicism in her desire to feel closer to the Irish cause, and her concerns were genuine enough, despite her attention-seeking manner. In 1923 she was elected to the Dáil as a member for Dublin Borough South but did not take up her seat, preferring instead to continue working with the Dublin poor and sick—often supporting her charitable acts from her own funds.

Later that year, she petitioned for the release of Republicans still being held in jail. Arrested in November, she went on a hunger strike in detention camp and after her release resumed her work looking after the needy. During the coal strike of 1926, she transported coal to deprived families in the slums. As a member of the Rathmines Urban District Council, she also became involved in issues relating to local housing, public health, welfare, and pensions.

In 1926 Markievicz joined de Valera's new Fianna Fáil party. She was reelected to Dublin Borough South in 1927 but not long after became sick. She died of peritonitis after an appendix operation, at her own insistence being nursed in the public ward of a Dublin hospital. Thousands filed past her coffin as it lay in state for two days—and like all good Fenians, she was buried in a Republican plot in the Glasnevin cemetery.

Although Markievicz has often unfairly been accused of abandoning the cause of suffrage and women's rights for the glamour of republicanism, an unshakable and outspoken sense of social justice and compassion lay at the root of all her activism. She and Maud Gonne together have earned the accolade, as Coxhead expresses it, of being named "the Anglo-Irish Valkyries of [Irish] national resurgence" (1965, 121).

See also Gonne, Maud; Gore-Booth, Eva.
References and Further Reading
Coxhead, Elizabeth. 1965. *Daughters of Erin: Five Women of the Irish Renascence*. London: Secker and Warburg.
Markievicz, Constance de. 1934. *Prison Letters of Countess Markievicz*. London: Longman's Green.
Marreco, Anne. 1967. *The Rebel Countess*. London: Weidenfeld and Nicolson.
Norman, D. 1987. *Terrible Beauty: The Life of Constance Markievicz*. London: Hodder and Stoughton.
Ó Céirín, Kit, and Cyril Ó Céirín, eds. 1996. *Women of Ireland: A Biographic Dictionary*. Kinvara, County Galway: Tír Eolás.
O'Faoláin, Sean. 1954. *Constance Markievicz*. London: Cape.
Van Voris, Jacqueline. 1967. *Constance Markievicz in the Cause of Ireland*. Amherst: University of Massachusetts Press.

Marshall, Catherine
(1880–1964)
United Kingdom

A leading interwar pacifist with Chrystal MacMillan and Kathleen Courtney, Catherine Marshall was also a staunch, nonmilitant suffragist and member of the Independent Labour Party. The daughter of a mathematics teacher and housemaster at the boys' public school at Harrow, Marshall was educated at home and at St. Leonard's girls' school in St. Andrews, Scotland, where she proved to be talented in music and languages and was self-taught in economics. With her mother, Caroline, she was a member of the Women's Liberal Association in Harrow from 1904 and maintained her work for the Liberal Party after the family moved to the Lake District. By 1908 she had become a keen suffragist and along with her mother founded the Keswick branch of the National Union of Women's Suffrage Societies (NUWSS), organizing a suffrage campaign across Westmoreland and Cumberland during the general election of 1910.

Marshall's commitment to women's suffrage caused her to spend more and more time in London after 1910, where she was active in the press office of the NUWSS and also a member of the London Society for Women's Suffrage. In March 1912 she became honorary assistant parliamentary secretary of the NUWSS and showed herself to be a most talented and energetic political or-

ganizer. In light of the failure of the Liberal government to get a suffrage bill through the House of Commons, she became convinced, along with NUWSS leader Millicent Garrett Fawcett, that the NUWSS should align itself with the Independent Labour Party (ILP), which endorsed women's suffrage. With this in mind, she applied her diplomatic talents to winning over other Liberal women in the NUWSS. After being appointed secretary of the NUWSS's Election Fighting Fund to promote the campaigns of ILP candidates sympathetic to women's suffrage, Marshall threw herself into the new strategy of arousing wider support for suffrage among the electorate at large. She still remained active in the Liberal Party, but by the outbreak of war in 1914 her disillusion with its failure to officially support women's suffrage prompted her final defection to the ILP.

In 1911 Marshall had been a delegate to the Stockholm conference of the International Women's Suffrage Alliance (IWSA), at which she had established numerous feminist contacts around the world. In the prewar years, she was increasingly sensitive to the militancy of the suffrage movement, disliking the tactics of the Women's Social and Political Union and believing that violence was not the answer in furthering any political cause. Thus, when World War I broke out, she was inevitably drawn into the peace movement through her international connections and opposed the NUWSS's temporary suspension of activities in support of the war effort. In 1915, she was one of several British women involved in organizing a women's peace congress, held in The Hague in April, in an attempt to promote peace mediation and produced a pamphlet, "Women and War." Her efforts led to a split in the ranks of the NUWSS, and Marshall resigned her seat on its executive, in September becoming secretary of the British section of the International Committee of Women for Permanent Peace, which had been founded at the congress. She joined the British branch of the No-Conscription Fellowship for conscientious objectors in 1916, serving as secretary until 1919, and keeping the organization going when many of its male leaders were imprisoned.

In 1917, however, overwork led to a breakdown, and thereafter Marshall was incapacitated by poor health. She resumed her pacifist work in

1919, attending the women's international congress in Zurich, at which the committee established in The Hague in 1915 reorganized as the Women's International League for Peace and Freedom (WILPF). She served the WILPF in various capacities until 1941, spending 1920–1921 at its headquarters in Geneva. Marshall was one of many who opposed the draconian war reparations demanded of the Germans in the 1919 Versailles Treaty, and she visited Germany in 1923 when the Germans resisted the French occupation of the industrial region of the Ruhr. She also upheld the work of the League of Nations in peace mediation during the interwar years. In the 1920–1921 famine in Bolshevik Russia, she was a League of Nations representative on the Red Cross's International Relief Commission, which organized supplies. During the 1930s, she was staunchly antifascist and assisted Jewish refugees from Czechoslovakia as a member of the Czech Refugee Committee (1938–1943), offering some of them asylum at her home in the Lake District.

See also Courtney, Kathleen D'Olier; Fawcett, Millicent Garrett; MacMillan, Chrystal.

References and Further Reading
Alberti, Johanna. 1989. *Beyond Suffrage: Feminists in War and Peace, 1914–1928*. London: Macmillan.
Bussey, Gertrude, and Margaret Tims. 1980 [1960]. *Pioneers for Peace: Women's International League for Peace and Freedom 1915–1965*. Reprint, London: George Allen and Unwin.
Crawford, Elizabeth. 1999. *The Women's Suffrage Movement, 1866–1928: A Reference Guide*. London: University College of London Press.
Holton, Sandra Stanley. 1986. *Feminism and Democracy: Women's Suffrage and Reform Politics in Britain, 1900–1918*. Cambridge: Cambridge University Press.
Josephson, Harold, Sandi Cooper, and Steven C. Hause et al., eds. 1985. *Biographical Dictionary of Modern Peace Leaders*. Westport, CT: Greenwood Press.
Kamester, Margaret, and Jo Vellacott, eds. 1987. *Militarism and Feminism: Writings on Women and War: Catherine Marshall, C. K. Ogden and Mary Sargant Florence*. London: Virago.
Kennedy, Thomas C. 1981. *The Hound of Conscience: A History of the No-Conscription Fellowship 1914–1919*. Fayetteville: University of Arkansas Press.
McDonald, Lynn, ed. 1998. *Women Theorists on Society and Politics*. Waterloo, ON: Wilfrid Laurier University Press.
Oldfield, Sybil. 2001. *Women Humanitarians: A Biographical Dictionary of British Women Active between 1900 and 1950*. London: Continuum.
Pierson, Ruth Roach, ed. 1987. *Woman and Peace: Theoretical, Historical and Practical Perspectives*. London: Croom Helm.
Vellacott, Jo. 1993. *From Liberal to Labour with Women's Suffrage: The Story of Catherine Marshall*. Montreal: McGill-Queen's University Press.
Wiltsher, Anne. 1985. *Most Dangerous Women: Feminist Peace Campaigners of the Great War*. London: Pandora, and Westport, CT: Greenwood Press.

Marson, Una
(1905–1965)
Jamaica

Jamaican feminist and social activist Una Marson is one of many women of color overlooked in standard biographical reference sources. Although she is known primarily as a poet and playwright, her liberal activism and humanism place Marson in the forefront of social reform in Jamaica, in arousing a sense of national and cultural pride among Jamaicans, both at home and in emigration. Marson did valuable work for the promotion of West Indian arts and culture in Britain during the 1930s and 1940s, when she was active in the League of Coloured Peoples (LCP), and during her work for BBC Radio, as one of the first voices of black feminism ever to be heard in Britain.

Marson was born at a rural mission house in St. Elizabeth, Jamaica, where her father was a Baptist preacher. She was educated at the predominantly white Hampton School for Girls on a scholarship from 1915 to 1922 and then moved to Kingston, where she took up social work with the Salvation Army and the Young Women's Christian Association (YWCA), supporting herself with a part-time secretarial job on the sociopolitical journal *Jamaica Critic*. In the mid-1920s, she started writing poetry and in 1928 founded a magazine, the *Cosmopolitan*. It served as the official journal of the Jamaica Stenographers' Association, representing women in the Jamaican civil service and in business. In it, Marson discussed women's employment and raised local issues such as irrigation, street lighting, housing, and the development of local industry. The journal was also the first women's publication in Jamaica offering articles on feminist issues as well as promoting the work of Jamaican poets and short-story writers.

Marson published two collections of poetry, *Tropic Reveries* (1930) and *Heights and Depths* (1931), and a play, *At What Price* (1931), before deciding to go to England. Arriving in July 1932, she lived in the then-small immigrant Caribbean black community of Peckham, in south London, and stayed with Harold Moody, a doctor who had that year established the League of Coloured Peoples, Britain's "first significant black-led organization" (Jarrett-Macauley 1998, 47). She joined in LCP activities, although these were mainly social rather than political functions, and became its unpaid assistant secretary. Soon she had her first taste of racial harassment, being verbally abused on the street, and coming up against the color bar when she tried to get secretarial work. After meeting a visiting African king in 1933, Sir Nana Ofori Atta Omanhene, Marson's pan-Africanist sensitivities were aroused, and she became interested in African culture and the problems of English colonialism.

As a feminist, Marson soon became active in the international women's movement, in 1934 attending the conference of the Women's International League for Peace and Freedom in London, where she spoke on "Social and Political Equality in Jamaica." Marson was inevitably looked upon as something of a novelty by women activists in Britain, for it would be twenty years before black immigrants would begin arriving in any significant numbers from the West Indies. She was, nevertheless, valued for her unique perspective on black culture and civil rights and received many requests to speak to various women's organizations. By 1936 Marson had established a network of friends in the Women's Freedom League, the Women's Peace Crusade, the International Alliance of Women for Suffrage and Equal Citizenship, and the British Commonwealth League, lecturing regularly on women's lives in Jamaica and the position of black women in England and throughout the Commonwealth. She was particularly impressed with the feminist writer and advocate of multiracialism Winifred Holtby, whom she met in 1934, and admired Holtby's work for black South African trade unionists in Cape Town. She was also an associate of the writer and civil rights activist Nancy Cunard, who in-

terviewed her about her work for the Associated Negro Press.

In 1935 Marson attracted a good deal of attention when she attended the twelfth congress of the International Alliance of Women for Suffrage and Equal Citizenship, which was held in Istanbul. Alliance president Margery Corbett Ashby noted that Marson was "the first woman of African race—Negro" to attend a conference (Jarrett-Macauley 1998, 88). Marson impressed the delegates with her speech, "East and West in Cooperation," in which she described her experiences of racial discrimination in England and the difficulties black immigrants experienced there in obtaining housing. By the time she decided to return to Jamaica in 1936, Marson had become the "leading black feminist activist in London," according to Macauley-Jarrett (1998, 78).

Back in Kingston, she continued to promote her own brand of cultural nationalism through her journalism and tried to encourage feminist activities. In 1937 she founded the Readers and Writers Club and the Kingston Dramatic Club, which in 1938 staged her play *Pocomania*. Written in Creole dialect, it charts the voyage of self-discovery of a black middle-class Jamaican woman seeking to uncover her African roots, with Marson contrasting tribal African traditions with the imposed colonial conditioning of Christianity and drawing upon her own Baptist upbringing. She also published two more volumes of poetry: *The Moth and the Star* (1937) and *Towards the Stars* (1945).

Marson returned to England in 1938, fundraising with a Jamaican colleague, Amy Bailey, for a Jamaican branch of the Save the Children Fund, for which she continued to work for many years. Her campaigning on behalf of impoverished Jamaican children led her in 1938 to testify to the West India Royal Commission on Jamaica, when she posited the idea of a tax on single men to support fatherless children in Jamaica.

During World War II, Marson spent time in Britain, where in 1941 she took a post on the Empire Service of BBC Radio, producing a program entitled *Calling the West Indies,* which offered a valued public voice for Caribbean people in Britain and Europe, and later an arts program entitled *Caribbean Voices,* which promoted West Indian writing. After her return to Jamaica in 1945, she suffered a nervous breakdown and was thereafter plagued by ill health. In 1949, in a move to produce affordable books by Jamaican authors, she established the Pioneer Press. She continued to promote local social and cultural projects, working for Jamsave and the YWCA and also was one of the first to confront local prejudice against Rastafarians. In March 1965 she was awarded a grant by the British Council to research social development in Jamaica since 1915 but died of a heart attack soon after.

See also Ashby, Margery Corbett; Cunard, Nancy; Holtby, Winifred.

References and Further Reading

Bush, Barbara. 1998. "'Britain's Conscience on Africa': White Women, Race, and Imperial Politics in Inter-war Britain." In Clare Midgley, ed., *Gender and Imperialism*. Manchester: Manchester University Press.

Campbell, Elaine. 1998. *The Whistling Bird: Women Writers of the Caribbean*. Boulder, CO: Lynne Rienner.

Jarrett-Macauley, Delia. 1996. "Exemplary Women." In Jarrett-Macauley, ed., *Reconstructing Womanhood, Reconstructing Feminism*. London: Routledge.

———. 1998. *The Life of Una Marson, 1905–1965.* Manchester: Manchester University Press.

Smilowitz, Erika Sollish. 1983. "Una Marson: Woman before Her Time." *Jamaica Journal* (May): 29–30.

———. 1986. *Expatriate Women Writers from Former British Colonies: A Bio-critical Study of Katherine Mansfield, Jean Rhys, and Una Marson.* Unpublished thesis.

Smith, Honor Ford, ed. 1986. *Una Marson: Black Nationalist and Feminist Writer.* Kingston, Jamaica: Sistren Publications.

Martineau, Harriet
(1802–1876)
United Kingdom

The social economist, journalist, and feminist Harriet Martineau was one of the most widely read women writers of her era and a leading intellectual whose economic theories and liberal ideas in particular were taken seriously even in Parliament. In a classic account of her travels in the United States, she voiced her objections to slavery and noted similar parallels in the constraints placed by society upon women. As a regular commentator on the social and political status of women and a supporter of women's education and employment rights, Martineau viewed women's confinement to the purely domestic sphere as training them for only one objective in life—marriage. Martineau also collaborated with leading women reformers of her day, including Josephine Butler, in the campaign for the repeal of the Contagious Diseases Acts, and in the wake of the Crimean War, with Florence Nightingale, in her calls for sanitary reforms in the British army at home and in India.

Martineau's family was descended from French Huguenot refugees who had settled in Norwich in the seventeenth century. One of eight children of a fabric manufacturer, she grew up in a Unitarian environment of piety but was provided with a sound education at school in Norwich and also had tuition from the Unitarian educator Dr. Lant Carpenter (the father of social reformer Mary Carpenter) in Bristol. But her primary intellectual stimulus came from her brothers at home, most particularly her adored brother James, with whom she later quarreled. She was a sickly child, who suffered from increasing deafness from her early teens and also lost her senses of taste and smell. Denied the intellectual outlet of university studies accorded to her brothers, she became intensely pious and published her first work in 1823, three essays in the Unitarian *Monthly Repository* in which, among other issues, she discussed the rights of girls to equal standards of education with boys. Her first published book was the suitably sober *Devotional Exercises: Consisting of Reflections and Prayers for the Use of Young Persons,* also in 1823.

Martineau's circumstances changed dramatically after her father died in 1826 and his business collapsed three years later, leaving the family without an income. Martineau was briefly engaged in 1826, but her fiancé died soon after. With little prospect of marriage and, in fact, looking upon her changes in fortune as liberating her from a life of "small means, sewing, and economizing, and growing narrower every year" (Martineau 1877, vol. 1, 143), she began using her writing skills to support herself, contributing further articles to the *Monthly Repository* and entering essay-writing competitions. Needing to find a much more regular means of support, she set about writing a major series of populist moral tales, based on the thinking on political economy of men such as Adam Smith, Jeremy Bentham, Thomas Malthus, and David Ricardo and aimed at enlightening ordinary people. Martineau was acutely aware of the economic problems posed by a rapidly industrializing society and the widespread poverty and social deprivation of urban living. In particular, she sympathized with the plight of low-paid agricultural workers and those in the textile industry whose labor was being supplanted by machinery. Her work was also partly prompted by the example of Swiss writer Jane Marcet (with whom she later became close friends), who had produced a series of simple, didactic texts accessible to ordinary working people in *Conversations on Political Economy* (1816).

Writing in a similar vein, Martineau produced a stream of such anecdotal and homiletic writings and dialogues, covering direct taxation, laissez-faire, and other economic issues, and published them monthly during 1832–1834. They were collected in twenty-five volumes as *Illustrations of Political Economy* and were later translated into French and German. They enjoyed such unprecedented popular success that Martineau's fame and fortune were secured, with printruns of individual tales often being as large as 10,000. Two further sequences of tales, which in their depiction of contemporary issues helped to set the trend for the social-problem novels of the 1840s by Charles Dickens and Elizabeth Gaskell, were produced by Martineau for Brougham's Society for the Diffusion of Useful Knowledge: the ten-volume *Poor Laws and Paupers* (1833) and the five-volume *Illustrations of Taxation* (1834).

Such a prodigious output might have exhausted the most energetic of writers, but Martineau had now earned enough to finance a visit to the United States. She embarked on the perilous sea voyage across the Atlantic in 1834, during which she passed the time by writing *How to Observe Morals and Manners* (1838), an early prototype in the methodology of social observation. She spent the next two years touring the United States with a female companion (a necessity both socially and in view of her deafness). American society was upset by her later critiques, published as *Society in America* (1837) and *A Retrospect of Western Travel* (1838). Having witnessed slave auctions and visited southern plantations during her trip, Martineau was disturbed by slavery but convinced that its demise was inevitable, pointing out that the slave system flew in the face of the basic principles of the Dec-

laration of Independence. She was also heavily critical of the very marked sexual inequality she had perceived in the United States. Describing the widespread indifference to women's rights among male politicians and the indolent, enclosed lives of American women in a famous chapter entitled "The Political Non-existence of Women" in *Society in America,* she drew comparisons between the enslavement of blacks and the domestic enslavement of women. Asserting the freedom of the individual and the importance of women's education, which she argued enhanced rather than detracted from their domestic roles, she lamented what she perceived as the legal prostitution of marriage and the passivity and subservience of American women.

In 1839 Martineau was forced by illness (an ovarian cyst) to stop writing. Turning down the offer of a pension from the prime minister, Lord Melbourne, she retired to her sickbed, spending the next five years mainly recumbent on a sofa (as she later recalled in her *Autobiography*) while recuperating at Tynemouth on the northeastern coast. While there, she wrote a novel of provincial life, *Deerbrook* (1839), that in content predates the work of Gaskell and George Eliot, and *The Hour and the Man* (1840), a novel based on the story of the rebel slave leader Toussaint-Louverture. A number of children's stories were collected in 1841 as *The Playfellow*. During this time, Martineau continued to search for medical treatment for her condition and eventually submitted herself to the new fringe cure of hypnosis. She was so impressed with her recovery that she became a passionate convert to mesmerism, describing its efficacy in *Life in the Sick Room* (1843) and *Letters on Mesmerism* (1845). These works and Martineau's increasing obsession with mysticism after she rejected her Unitarian faith caused considerable embarrassment to her friends and family, particularly her theologian brother James.

In 1844 Martineau moved to Clappergate in the Lake District, where she built a house with royalties from her writing and became friendly with the poet William Wordsworth and his sister Dorothy. Reinvigorated since her recovery from illness, she decided to go on an investigative trip to Egypt and Palestine, the product of which—*Eastern Life, Past and Present* (1848)—contains a discussion of the development of non-Christian religions and a critique of harems and the practice of polygamy. She produced two heavyweight works in later life: the major radical study *A History of England during the Thirty Years' Peace*, A.D. *1816–1846* (1849–1850), and an antitheological, rationalist work written with H. G. Atkinson, *Letters on the Laws of Man's Social Nature and Development* (1841). The agnosticism of the latter work further alienated her friends and supporters. Martineau's most scholarly work was a translation of Auguste Comte's six-volume philosophical writings, edited down as *The Positive Philosophy of Auguste Comte, Freely Translated and Condensed* (1853). A further example of her belief in making intellectual writing more accessible to the reader, it contributed greatly to the dissemination of Comte's ideas in Britain.

Martineau's social and feminist concerns were many and were expressed in 1,642 articles contributed to the liberal newspaper, the *Daily News,* between 1852 and 1866, as well as others on women's role, published in the *Edinburgh Review.* Her article "Female Industry," published there in 1859, prompted the establishment of the Society for Promoting the Employment of Women by Jessie Boucherett and women of the Langham Place Circle. Martineau wrote on political economy, abolition and the work of pioneer abolitionists, women's employment, her support for a Married Women's Property Bill (the petition for which, organized by Barbara Bodichon, she had signed in 1856), licensed prostitution, and women's suffrage (she was also a signatory of Bodichon's 1866 petition).

Martineau lent much moral and written support to Josephine Butler's campaign for repeal of the Contagious Diseases Acts. In 1864, after the passage of the first of these acts, she published four important "letters from an Englishwoman" in the *Daily News,* in which she decried the state regulation of prostitution. She argued for preventive measures to control vice and the men who solicited the services of prostitutes rather than infringing on the civil liberties of the prostitutes themselves through enforced medical examinations. In 1869 she drafted a "Solemn Protest" against the acts for Butler's Ladies' National Association for the Repeal of the Contagious Diseases Acts, which was published again in the *Daily News* (31 December), and followed this with her 1870 *The Contagious Diseases Acts, as Applied to Garrison Towns and Naval Stations.* Her moral support for the campaign was still ap-

parent in an 1871 letter, in which she wryly commented on the sexual double standard and noted the "phenomenon of innocent wickedness—educational and conventional—of the upper and middle classes—men who go to church on Sundays and call themselves Christians, who set out from the supposition that men's passions must be gratified, and that, if women are ruined in that process it is simply necessary and a matter of course" (McDonald 1998, 164).

Martineau also worked closely with Florence Nightingale, endorsing her work for improved medical care in the British army and collaborating with her on *England and Her Soldiers* (1859). Nightingale had insisted that her contribution remain anonymous, although she funded publication of the book. In it, Martineau drew on Nightingale's reports on hospital conditions in the Crimea and demystified the image of the "lady with the lamp" in an exposé (with Nightingale's full collusion) of the bad ventilation and sanitation that had been the cause of the high death rate in Nightingale's Barrack Hospital at Scutari. Martineau shared Nightingale's interests in sanitary reform and from 1859 onward also published numerous articles in the *Daily News* on improvements in sanitation in army barracks in India after an inquiry by a royal commission. She also advocated political and economic reform in India, suggesting more efficient ways of raising taxes.

Suffering from what she thought was incurable heart disease from 1855, Martineau settled down to die but kept up her professional life for another ten years or so before spending the remainder of her days at her home in the Lake District. She wrote her autobiography in three months (1856) but vetoed its publication until after her death. Now one of her most admired works, the three-volume *Autobiography* appeared eventually in 1877, edited by her friend, the American abolitionist Maria Weston Chapman. In it, Martineau averred she was "very thankful" for never having married and thus never having "suffered anything at all in relation to that matter which is held to be all important to women, love and marriage" (Martineau 1877, I: 66). A website containing links to several articles on Martineau can be found at http://cepa. newschool.edu/het/profiles/ martineau.htm.

See also Bodichon, Barbara; Boucherett, Jessie;

Butler, Josephine; Carpenter, Mary; Gaskell, Elizabeth; Nightingale, Florence.

References and Further Reading

Cranstoun Nevill, John. 1976. *Harriet Martineau.* Norwood, PA: Norwood Editions.

David, Dierdre. 1987. *Intellectual Woman and Victorian Patriarchy: Harriet Martineau, Elizabeth Barrett Browning and George Eliot.* Ithaca: Cornell University Press.

Hoecker-Drysdale, Susan. 1993. *Harriet Martineau: First Woman Sociologist.* Oxford: Berg.

Martineau, Harriet. 1983 [1877]. *Autobiography, with Memorials by Maria Weston Chapman.* Reprint, London: Virago.

McDonald, Lynn, ed. 1998. *Women Theorists on Society and Politics.* Waterloo, ON: Wilfrid Laurier University Press.

Midgely, Clare. 1992. *Women against Slavery: The British Campaigns 1780–1870.* London: Routledge.

Pichanick, Valerie K. 1980. *Harriet Martineau: The Woman and Her Work 1802–1876.* Ann Arbor: University of Michigan Press.

Walters, Margaret. 1976. "The Rights and Wrongs of Women: Mary Wollstonecraft, Harriet Martineau, Simone de Beauvoir." In Juliet Mitchell and Ann Oakley, eds., *The Rights and Wrongs of Women.* Harmondsworth: Penguin.

Webb, R. K. 1960. *Harriet Martineau: A Radical Victorian.* London: Heinemann.

Weiner, Gaby. 1983. "Harriet Martineau: A Reassessment (1802–1876)." In Dale Spender, ed., *Feminist Theorists: Three Centuries of Women's Intellectual Traditions.* London: Women's Press.

Wheatley, Vera. 1957. *Life and Work of Harriet Martineau.* London: Secker and Warburg.

Masarykova, Alice
(1879–1966)
Czechoslovakia

As the daughter of Tomáš Masaryk, the founder and first president of the newly created state of Czechoslovakia in 1918, Alice Masarykova was born into a deeply patriotic and reformist family. Her American feminist mother, Charlotte Garrigue (who had been born in Brooklyn of Huguenot ancestry), had met her husband while studying music in Leipzig.

Masarykova was born in 1879 in Vienna, where her father was a lecturer at the university. When Alice was three years old, the family moved to Prague, where her father took the chair of philosophy at Charles University. She attended a girls' high school in Prague, also studying music, Russian, French, and English at home, and went on to study medicine at Charles University. Forced by her extreme nearsightedness to give up this dream, she switched to philosophy, history, and sociology. She completed her studies at the University of Berlin, where in 1903 she gained her Ph.D. with a thesis on the Magna Carta, and in 1903–1904 she did postdoctorate studies in history and economics in Leipzig.

In 1904, Mary McDowell, the director of the University of Chicago Settlement on Gross Avenue (an institution that worked closely with Jane Addams's Hull House, concentrating on the stockyard area) invited Masarykova to observe and take part in its social work among immigrants in the neighborhood, many of whom were Czech. Masarykova stayed in Chicago for two years, from there visiting Czech communities in Iowa, Nebraska, Cleveland, and New York. She visited the stockyards themselves, where the plight of many poor immigrants from Bohemia, Slovakia, and Poland made her weep. She met with immigrants in the meatpacking industry and aided delegates from the Union of Packing House Women in organizing support for women workers in the yards; she backed a strike by these workers for higher wages and the slowing of the assembly lines and helped in a cleanup of the area's litter-strewn vacant lots and yards. She also met and discussed the horrific conditions she found with the writer Upton Sinclair, whose powerful 1906 exposé of the Chicago meatpacking industry, *The Jungle,* went some way to draw attention to the miseries endured by poor immigrants.

Masarykova returned to Prague in 1906 and took a post in a girls' lycée in Ceské, where she aroused the interest of her pupils in women's emancipation, health and hygiene, and the rights of the poor. She persuaded a local dentist to treat poor girls free of charge and encouraged a daily intake of milk and physical exercise. In 1910 she transferred to a girls' lycée in Prague, where she taught history and pedagogy, again emphasizing to her pupils the importance of women's role in society, and infusing them with a sense of national pride. Masarykova became increasingly interested in educational theory and was a great admirer of the work of Helen Keller, about whom she published a book in 1915 under the pen name Jan Skála.

In 1915, by which time her father had become involved in the Czech and Slovak independence movement, Masarykova was arrested for demonstrating against the war. She was held in prison in Vienna for eight months, during which time her mother's regular letters kept her going, and Jane Addams and her other friends and supporters in the United States campaigned for her release, which came in July 1916. She was not allowed to return to her old job at the lycée and turned instead to making plans for training professional social workers. In 1911, while still teaching, Masarykova had raised the question of a sociological section being attached to the university in the firm belief that a better understanding of social problems would aid doctors, lawyers, theologians, and teachers in their work. The section, when established, offered lectures on nutrition, venereal disease, alcoholism, housing, and the stresses and strains experienced by working people, but it had been discontinued after Masarykova's arrest in 1915. After her release, Masarykova had to resort to inviting interested women to her home, where she taught them methods of social investigation and casework in secret and discussed the principles for a proper school of social work. This school finally opened in the autumn of 1918 at the lycée in Prague where Masarykova had taught.

Throughout this period, the Masaryk family had been systematically persecuted by the authorities until their homeland was finally given its independence in June 1918, with Tomáš Masaryk its first elected president. Alice Masarykova was, in April 1920, one of the first sixteen women elected as deputies to the new National Assembly. In 1919, after teams from the American Red Cross and the Young Women's Christian Association (YWCA) visited Czechoslovakia to give help and advice, she had also been appointed president of the newly established Czech Red Cross and director of social service activities, facing a huge challenge in dealing with many pressing social problems resulting from four years of war. The most urgent were malnourishment, the spread of tuberculosis and other contagious diseases such as typhus and cholera, and the high rate of infant mortality. Masarykova initiated important work in welfare, food aid, and other projects for the postwar reconstruction of Czechoslovakia, funded by aid from Herbert Hoover's mission for relief in Europe and the Rockefeller Foundation. In addition, she was the guiding force behind a survey of social conditions in Prague, a summer training scheme for social workers, a first aid organization, public nursing, and a system for teaching social hygiene under the auspices of a central board. The work of these welfare bodies was coordinated through a Directory of Social Organizations set up by Masarykova, who also devised the curriculum for its summer school.

In organizing the Czech Red Cross, Masarykova faced huge shortages of food, clothes, and medical supplies. But she set to the task not just with the short-term view of administering immediate welfare to the victims of war but also looking to the Red Cross's wider social role as a moral guide and proponent of world peace, emphasizing its crucial role in maintaining standards of health in peacetime. Over a period of eighteen months, she developed a peacetime program in which volunteer services coordinated their welfare efforts in conjunction with the work of the ministries of health, social welfare, and education. A Red Cross hospital was built at Hust and a children's hospital established in a castle in Slovakia, and Masarykova also planned a modern Red Cross hospital and a nurses' home. During 1919–1921, she established hospitals for infectious diseases where medical students were able to vaccinate thousands of people and initiated mobile "health trains" to travel to outlying regions with vaccination and other programs. There was also the enormous problem of Russian refugees who had fled the communist regime, and Masarykova again oversaw the establishment of three health camps that looked after 100 refugee children each. She even found time to organize Czech aid to Russian scholars in Petrograd in need of food and clothing (under the aegis of the Committee for the Aid of Russian Scholars established by the eminent writer Maxim Gorky). By 1921 the Czech Red Cross under Masarykova's leadership had 200,000 members active in 340 local branches. Masarykova's suggestion to the League of Nations that an international emergency organization should oversee relief aid for people in Russia and Ukraine affected by famine in 1920–1921 also gave her a role in the deliberations of the committee of the Nansen Commission that in 1921 coordinated forty-eight Red Cross organizations to send food aid to these stricken areas.

During the 1920s, after her mother fell ill, Masarykova took over the role of surrogate first lady and helped run her father's official household. She was chosen to serve as chair of the organizing committee of the American and British Conferences of Social Work and presided over the First International Conference of Social Work in Paris in 1928. Her book *The Czechoslovak Red Cross* was published in 1935. In 1937, the year Tomáš Masaryk died, Czechoslovakia was once again facing crisis with the growing threat from Adolf Hitler's Germany. After the German army invaded, Masarykova's brother Jan went into exile in Britain, where he acted as foreign minister of the government in exile. Masarykova herself fled to the United States, where, anxious to raise the consciousness of the American public about the oppression of Czechoslovakia, she went on an exhausting lecture tour and also raised funds for Czech refugees. But the punishing schedule made her ill, and she had to spend two years in a sanatorium in New York before she was able to return to Prague in 1945 at the end of the war, where she once again took up her work for the Czech Red Cross and for international peace.

Further tragedy followed after the communist takeover of Czechoslovakia in February 1948, when her brother Jan was found dead under suspicious circumstances (probably murdered by Soviet agents). Once again, Masarykova was forced to flee her beloved country and went to Geneva, to England, and then on to the United States, arriving in December 1948. There she was welcomed into New York's émigré Czech community and lived in an apartment provided by the YWCA. She broadcast to Czechoslovakia on Radio Free Europe and wrote *Memories of Childhood and Youth* (1960). In 1951 the Charlotte G. Masaryk Society (established in 1910) made her an honorary member, and that same year Masarykova received a Woman of Achievement Award at the Twenty-eighth World's International Exposition.

In 1954 Masarykova was granted U.S. residency and set up a Masaryk Publications Trust with her sister Olga to publish and promote the extensive writings on social and political theory of their father Tomáš —works that were banned by the communist government in Czechoslovakia. Despite her outstanding achievements, Masarykova's work has gone almost entirely unnoticed outside her home country.

See also Addams, Jane; Keller, Helen.
References and Further Reading
Masarykova, Alice. 1980. *Alice Masarykova 1879–1966: Her Life as Recorded in Her Own Words*. Pittsburgh: University Center for International Studies.

Maxeke, Charlotte Manye
(1874–1939)
South Africa

As a probation officer, educator, and civil rights campaigner in the eastern Cape who also took a particular interest in the plight of African women in the townships, Charlotte Maxeke earned a considerable reputation and a wide range of experience, unique in her time for a black woman in South Africa. To many Africans she became known as "the mother of African freedom."

Born in Ramokgopa in the Pietersburg district of what was then the Northern Transvaal, of Bantu and Xhosa parents, Maxeke was educated in mission schools at Uitenhage and Port Elizabeth. After training as a teacher, she took a post in Kimberley. Her good singing voice led to her taking two tours abroad—to England, Canada, and the United States—as a member of an African choir. At the end of the tour in New York, she was offered a scholarship to study at the Wilberforce University, a segregated college in Ohio affiliated with the African Methodist Episcopal Church. Maxeke returned to South Africa in 1905, having become the first black South African woman to gain a university degree.

As a member of the African Methodist Episcopal Church, which had established a base in South Africa, Maxeke worked as an evangelist-teacher and helped run a succession of schools with her husband, the Reverend M. M. Maxeke (whom she had met at Wilberforce). Their most successful was a training college in Pietersburg, which they relocated to Evaton in the Witwatersrand, where as the Wilberforce Institution, it became a leading establishment for higher education.

The couple later moved to Johannesburg, where Maxeke, like her husband, became an early member of the executive committee of the South African Native National Congress (SANNC), established in 1912 (and which in 1925 became the African National Congress, or ANC). In 1918 Maxeke inaugurated the Bantu Women's League, an adjunct of the SANNC that had developed out of the participation of women in the 1912–1913 protest campaign against the Native Land Act, which sought to impose stringent pass laws for African women on the same basis as men. In 1918 Maxeke led a women's deputation from the Bantu League to prime minister Louis Botha to argue against amendments to the law. Women's protest continued throughout 1919, and in 1920 Maxeke gave evidence at an interdepartmental committee of inquiry into passes.

At this time, Maxeke's activities also extended to support for black workers protesting low wages in the Witwatersrand, and she was involved in setting up the Industrial and Commercial Workers' Union. She also retained an interest in social welfare, the temperance movement, and her work for the church. When her husband died, she tackled the problem of her own economic independence by founding a women's employment bureau in Johannesburg. But her work was interrupted by a request to take on the role of native probation officer at the Magistrates' Court in Johannesburg.

This important role involved Maxeke, as the first black woman to serve in this capacity, in offering counseling and support for poor black women and girls from the Witwatersrand, many of whom had been drawn into crime and prostitution. She visited them in prison and helped them find work and accommodation upon their release, as well as making recommendations for the appointment of women magistrates and special juvenile courts. By the 1920s, Maxeke's reputation had attracted the attention of even white South African suffragists, who in 1921 invited her to speak at a meeting held by the Women's Enfranchisement Association of the Union at the Women's Reform Club in Pretoria, the first and only black woman to do so. In her speech, Maxeke outlined her experience working for the probation service and the hardships encountered by black women in the townships. She reiterated her own personal support of African women in their struggle to preserve the stability of their families when so many of their menfolk migrated elsewhere to work, and voiced her support for women in their traditional roles as mothers.

In 1928 Maxeke returned to the United States to represent the African Methodist Episcopal Church at a conference. For a few years afterward, she remained a regular speaker at church and other Christian and African conferences, as well as continuing her association with the ANC in its campaign against the pass laws. In 1935 Maxeke's Bantu Women's League was superseded by the National Council of African Women at the All-African Convention held in Bloemfontein, with Maxeke becoming its first president. In 1980, at a time when the activities of the ANC were banned in South Africa, its women's section named a nursery the Charlotte Maxeke Child Care Centre at its headquarters in Tanzania.

References and Further Reading

Gollack, Georgina A. 1932. *Daughters of Africa.* London: Longman's Green.
Ofosu-Appiah, L. A., ed. 1977. *Encyclopaedia Africana,* vol. 3, *Dictionary of African Biography.* Algonac, MI: Reference Publications.
Uerwey, E. J., ed. 1995. *New Dictionary of South African Biography.* Pretoria: HSRC Publishers.
Uweche, Raph, ed. 1996. *Makers of Modern Africa.* 3d ed. London: Africa Books.
Walker, Cheryl. 1991. *Women and Resistance in South Africa.* 2d ed. Cape Town: David Philip.

Mayreder, Rosa
(1858–1938)
Austria

A feminist essayist, poet, artist, and pacifist, Rosa Mayreder was a leading radical intellectual active in the General Austrian Women's Association from 1893. She challenged male arguments against women's emancipation in her classic work, *A Survey of the Woman Problem,* published in 1905. It was her guiding belief that women, as the more pacific sex, had a mission to civilize male-dominated society.

Mayreder was a talented painter who had exhibited in Vienna and at the World's Fair in Chicago in 1893. She became a leading figure in Viennese artistic and intellectual circles at the end of the nineteenth century, cofounding an art school for women in Vienna in 1897. In 1893 she cofounded the General Austrian Women's Association and served as vice president until 1903, dominating what was a relatively small, middle-class women's movement within this part of the Austro-Hungarian Empire. She also encouraged women to take physical exercise and welcomed the invention of the lady's bicycle as liberating.

In 1894, after becoming a member of the Vienna Ethical Society, in which the leading women's peace campaigner Bertha von Suttner was active, Mayreder joined Suttner's Austrian Peace Society (founded in 1891), and in 1903 she left the women's association to concentrate on work for pacifism. From 1915 she took an active role in the Austrian branch of the International Committee of Women for Permanent Peace (which became the Women's International League and changed its name in 1919 to the Women's International League for Peace and Freedom, or WILPF). She wrote articles such as "Women in War" and gave lectures, such as "Women and Internationalism" in 1916, in which she underlined women's creative role as peacemakers in contrast to that of men as aggressive warmongers. At the end of World War I, Mayreder became vice president of the Austrian branch of the WILPF and in 1921 helped organize an international peace conference in Vienna.

In 1899–1900 Mayreder coedited the radical Austrian journal *Women's Documents* and in 1905 entered the debate over the cultural position of women and motherhood in her book, *A Survey of the Woman Problem* (the original title was *To Critics of Femininity*). In this major contribution to emergent feminist theory, which was published in English in 1913, she demolished the misogynist writings of the Austrian philosopher Otto Weiniger, who had argued that the feminine element in society was amoral and unproductive. She also challenged the old chestnut, so often offered up by men hostile to feminism, that women were intellectually inferior to them. She urged women to reject the notion that men were greater achievers than they, stating: "The woman who omits to develop any talent of her own, because of her belief that it is possible to develop it in her son will, in ninety-nine out of a hundred cases, be grievously cheated" (Smith 1989, 350). The *Survey* also emphasized the individuality of women and sought to liberate them from the anodyne uniformity of their sole feminine role as wives and mothers, allowing for their natural right to freedom of choice in lifestyle. Her 1923 work *Gender and Culture* underlined the individual talents of men and women that were not dependent on their sexuality.

Mayreder produced a versatile body of work on pacifism, sociology, and "Christian-evolutionist theodicy" and wrote novels, poetry, and drama. As president of the Austrian branch of the WILPF for ten years, she warned against militarism and the dangers of man's attempt to master nature. She also wrote the libretto for an opera by Hugo Wolf, later publishing *Remembrances of Hugo Wolf*. After her diaries were finally published in Germany in 1988, she entered the German-language pantheon as a leading feminist thinker.

See also Suttner, Bertha Félice Sophie von.

References and Further Reading

Anderson, Harriet. 1992. *Utopian Feminism: Women's Movements in Fin-de-Siècle Vienna*. New Haven, CT: Yale University Press.

Buck, Claire, ed. 1992. *Bloomsbury Guide to Women's Literature*. London: Bloomsbury.

Josephson, Harold, Sandi Cooper, and Steven C. Hause et al., eds. 1985. *Biographical Dictionary of Modern Peace Leaders*. Westport, CT: Greenwood Press.

Mayreder, Rosa. 1913. *A Survey of the Woman Problem*. Translated by Herman Scheffauer. London: Heinemann.

Smith, Bonnie G. 1989. *Changing Lives: Women in European History since 1700*. Lexington, MA: D. C. Heath.

Uglow, Jennifer, ed. *Macmillan Dictionary of Women's Biography*. London: Macmillan.

McAuley, Catherine
(1778–1841)
Ireland

Catherine McAuley, the founder of the Irish Sisters of Mercy, initiated a Roman Catholic order that later spread its activities to India, where it did much to help the underprivileged through the work of Mother Teresa. The original House of Our Blessed Lady of Mercy, founded by McAuley in 1827 in Dublin, would eventually be joined by eleven other convents, and McAuley would do much to encourage primary and secondary education as well as practical and vocational training for girls.

McAuley grew up in Glasnevin, Dublin. After the death of her father, her mother's mismanagement of finances left the family in straitened circumstances. When she died in 1789, Catherine was brought up by authoritarian Protestant relatives before going, at the age of eighteen, to live with William and Catherine Callaghan as their adoptive daughter. As the live-in companion to this wealthy couple, who were friends of her family, for the next twenty years McAuley lived quietly, devoting herself to good works among the poor, teaching the family servants, and retaining her devout Catholic faith within a nonpracticing household.

After the death of the Callaghans, in 1822 Catherine found herself the beneficiary of the substantial fortune of £25,000. She began to use this money to fund her work in a parochial poor school in Middle Abbey Street, Dublin, and funded various other schemes for girls' education by visiting local poor schools, where she gave away food and clothing and taught handicrafts. But she had for long nurtured a desire to set up her own permanent home for poor working girls so that she could offer them protection and education and training of some kind.

In 1824, despite family disapproval and opposition from local residents, who believed that such an institution would devalue property in the area, McAuley took over the lease of a site in Lower Baggot Street, a fashionable area of Dublin, and paid for a home for the relief of the poor to be built there. Meanwhile, she began to make a serious study of Irish and French educational methods. In September 1827 McAuley opened her school—the House of Our Blessed Lady of Mercy—and by 1828, 500 poor girls had enrolled there. She later extended the premises to include a home for young servant girls, providing full board for those who lived there, teaching them needlework and handicrafts (which she sold to her rich friends to raise funds), and serving meals daily to the local poor. With twelve female followers, McAuley began to undertake the care of the local sick and elderly, particularly at the Hospital for Incurables at Donnybrook and the Lying-in-Hospital in the Coombe.

McAuley's group of women helpers had been originally established on a semireligious basis but was not controlled by the Catholic Church, although it adopted the dress and understated manner of a religious order. However, from the inception of the Baggott Street premises, pressure was put on McAuley to opt for official status as a religious order. She found herself constantly faced with the church's and society's moral opposition to laywomen undertaking philanthropic work among the lower classes. When Archbishop Daniel Murray threatened to give her lay work among the poor to the Sisters of Charity, McAuley was finally forced to concede and agreed to set up an order that would be based on simple religious vows but would not be cloistered. She hated elitism in religious practice and would always emphasize the democratic nature of her order, as one that invited neither privilege, nor precedence, nor any kind of hierarchy.

In 1830 McAuley and two of her colleagues entered the novitiate in Dublin and fifteen months later took their vows, thus establishing the Order of the Sisters of Mercy. The order set out to be a refuge for poor and destitute girls, to offer education and living accommodations, and to care for the sick. In 1837, having for long been aware of the lack of secondary and intermediate education for girls, McAuley established a "pension school," which for a fee trained middle-class girls in McAuley's particular sense of social responsibility. The sisters of McAuley's establishment in Cork also served as prison visitors and teachers, and in Dublin her sisters nursed the sick in the city's major workhouse.

Nine further convents were added to the order before McAuley's death in 1841, during which time she tirelessly traveled between convents, invited local people to take an interest in the work of the order, and recruited new members. By the 1850s the congregation had spread around the world, and its nurses eventually served in the Crimean War, the Civil War in the United States, and the Boer War, contributing in no small way to the early history of military nursing.

After her death in November 1841, McAuley was given the kind of simple funeral she had insisted on—one befitting the poor. Such an insistence was characteristic of her dignity and modesty and her firm belief in equality of rich and poor alike. Her order has since grown to become one of the largest Catholic religious congregations and one that, through the later work of women such as Mother Teresa in India, has remained dedicated to providing social welfare to the underprivileged. In 1990 McAuley was proclaimed "venerable" by a solemn decree of the Catholic Church—the first Irishwoman to be accorded this honor.

See also Mother Teresa.

References and Further Reading

Bolster, Angela. 1990. *Catherine McAuley: Venerable for Mercy.* Dublin: Dominican.

Breault, William. 1986. *The Lady from Dublin.* Boston: Quinlan.

Ó Céirín, Kit, and Cyril Ó Céirín, eds. 1996. *Women

of Ireland: A Biographic Dictionary. Kinvara, Co. Galway: Tír Eolás.

Regan, M. Joanna, and Isabella Keiss. 1988. *Tender Courage: A Reflection of the Life and Spirit of Catherine McAuley, First Sister of Mercy.* Chicago: Franciscan Herald.

Sullivan, Mary C. 1995. *Catherine McAuley and the Tradition of Mercy.* Notre Dame: University of Indiana Press.

McClung, Nellie
(1873–1951)
Canada

One of Canada's outstanding feminist leaders and social activists, Nellie McClung was also the author of sixteen novels and many short stories. She was central to the women's suffrage campaign in the prairies of western Canada, helping women in Manitoba win the provincial vote in 1916, the first Canadian province to achieve this goal.

Born in Owen Sound, Ontario, McClung was the daughter of Irish immigrants. The family moved to Manitoba in 1879, where she grew up on a farmstead near Wawanesa, in the Tiger Hills at Brandon. She had no formal education until the age of ten, but after moving to Winnipeg to study at its Normal School, she took a teacher's certificate six years later. She taught in a rural school in Manitou until 1896, when she married Robert Wesley McClung. He came from a family heavily involved in the temperance movement, and his mother, an ardent suffragist, inspired Nellie to become active in the temperance movement in Manitoba, which also advocated women's suffrage. In between the birth of five children, McClung became a leading campaigner, much admired for her skill and wit as a public speaker.

As a woman of deep Methodist faith who was desirous of communicating her strong social ideals, McClung also took up writing. Her first published novel, *Sowing Seeds in Danny* (1908), was a great success, selling over 100,000 copies. Like subsequent novels, it was a celebration of pioneer life in the prairies of the Canadian west and of the tough, resourceful women who were the mainstay both of family life and of rural farming communities. McClung saw women's activism as providing them with an opportunity to display their natural instincts for social justice and public service. She was unequivocal in her view of them as the superior sex, destined to pick up the pieces in a man's world full of social injustices. Society, she felt, suffered from too much "masculinity," and women were as much to blame as men for this situation for having so little self-esteem and allowing men to dominate. McClung's strong sense of maternal feminism was reflected in all her speeches and political writings, and novels such as *The Second Chance* (1910) and *Purple Springs* (1921) would feature feisty suffragist heroines.

In 1911 the McClungs moved to Winnipeg. She took a leading role there in the Woman's Christian Temperance Union and also lobbied for safer conditions in factories. Branching into journalism for Canadian and U.S. magazines, she became a member of the Canadian Women's Press Club. A year later, McClung was at the center of a new suffrage group, the Manitoba Political Equality League, and became one of its most popular speakers during the provincial election campaigns of 1914 and 1915. Many of McClung's suffrage campaign speeches from this period were collected in a 1915 anthology, *In Times Like These* (reprinted in 1972). With her ready wit, she became a thorn in the side of conservative premier Sir Rodmond Roblin, a rampant antisuffragist whom she parodied unmercifully. By 1914 the league had gained considerable political ground across Manitoba. During the campaign, McClung had moved to Edmonton, Alberta, where her husband had set up a pharmacy, but she returned to Manitoba in the summer of 1915 to help the provincial suffrage campaign there achieve its goal. The vote was granted for women early the following year and with it their right to hold public office.

Back in Alberta, McClung threw her energies into achieving provincial suffrage there through the Edmonton Equal Franchise League, and success followed shortly after that in Manitoba and Saskatchewan, with royal assent being given in April. In the summer of 1914, World War I broke out in Europe. McClung, a passionate nationalist, supported the Canadian national effort but condemned men for making wars and lauded women, by nature more conciliatory and willing to compromise, as having the special qualities of peacemakers. As she put it, "Men make wounds and women bind them up" (Strong-Boag 1987, 170). She admired these qualities in fellow countrywoman Agnes MacPhail and the British pacifist and preacher Maude Royden. In 1918 McClung was a delegate to the Women's War Conference in Ottawa.

McClung successfully stood for the Alberta provincial government elections in 1921 and entered the legislature as a member of the Liberal Party. But she served only for a single term, finding she disliked the cut and thrust of party politics. During her term, which lasted until 1926, she lobbied on her favorite causes in the legislature and through her regular news column in the *Calgary Albertan,* "Nellie McClung Chats with Albertan Readers." McClung's social reform interests were many: she supported the introduction of old-age pensions, mother's allowances, free health and dental care for children, a system of public health nursing, and improvements in factory conditions—especially in sweatshops. She also wanted women to have easier access to methods of birth control and called for legal reforms that would protect women's property rights and make divorce easier for them. After leaving Parliament and now living in Calgary, she continued to support prohibition and write on social reform and women's rights issues, publishing articles in the *Canadian Home Journal, Maclean's Magazine,* and others. Her regular columns in the press were collected as *Be Good to Yourself* (1930), *Flowers for the Living* (1931), and *Leaves from Lantern Lane* (1936).

McClung's name was once more in the headlines in 1927, when she became involved in a celebrated court case as one of the "famous five," joining with Emily Murphy and three other Albertan women in challenging the interpretation of the word *persons* in Section 24 of the British North America Act of 1867. Under a court ruling two years later in the British Court of Appeal, the word *persons* was deemed to infer women and thus recognized their eligibility for appointment to the Senate of Canada. This historic case was commemorated in 1999 with the raising of a statue in Calgary's Olympic Plaza.

In 1932 McClung moved again, to Victoria, British Columbia. In between speaking tours in Canada, the United States, and England, she was also involved in the foundation of the Federated Women's Institutes of Canada and was the first woman to join the board of the Canadian Broadcasting Corporation (1936–1942). She was the sole female Canadian delegate to the League of Nations in 1938. McClung published two volumes of autobiography, *Clearing in the West* (1935) and *The Stream Runs Fast* (1945); her short story collections include *The Black Creek Stopping-House and Other Stories* (1912) and *When Christmas Crossed "The Peace"* (1923). Her 1925 novel *Painted Fires* discussed the particular problems of immigrants to Canada. A website with links to numerous other sources on McClung can be found at www.nellie.epsb.net/pages/nmclinks. htm.

See also MacPhail, Agnes; Murphy, Emily Gowan; Royden; Maude.

References and Further Reading

Benham, Mary Lile. 1975. *Nellie McClung.* Toronto: Fitzhenry and Whiteside.

Benson, Eugene, and William Toye, eds. 1997. *Oxford Companion to Canadian Literature.* 2d ed. Oxford: Oxford University Press.

Cleverdon, Catherine Lyle. 1950. *The Woman Suffrage Movement in Canada.* Toronto: University of Toronto Press.

Hallett, Mary E., and Marilyn Davis. 1993. *Firing the Heather: The Life and Times of Nellie McClung.* Saskatoon: Fifth House.

Josephson, Harold, Sandi Cooper, and Steven C. Hause et al., eds. 1985. *Biographical Dictionary of Modern Peace Leaders.* Westport, CT: Greenwood Press.

McClung, Nellie. 1972 [1915]. *In Times Like These.* Reprint, Toronto: University of Toronto Press.

Millar, Nancy. 1999. *The Famous Five, or Emily Murphy and the Case of the Missing Persons.* Cochrane: Western Heritage Centre.

Savage, Candace. *Our Nell: A Scrapbook Biography of Nellie L. McClung.* Saskatoon: Western Producer Prairie Books.

Strong-Boag, Veronica. 1987. "Peace-Making Women: Canada 1919–1939." In Ruth Roach Pierson, ed., *Woman and Peace: Theoretical, Historical and Practical Perspectives.* London: Croom Helm.

Warne, Randi R. 1993. *Literature as Pulpit: The Christian Social Activism of Nellie L. McClung.* Waterloo: Wilfred Laurier University Press.

McDowell, Mary
(1854–1936)
United States

Mary McDowell was one of a generation of outstanding social reformers in Chicago who devoted their lives to pioneering the settlement house movement. In her work among the city's largely immigrant community and in support of the trade union representation of stockyard workers, McDowell garnered considerable respect and the epithet "the Angel of the Stockyards." She also lobbied for improvements to public health as commissioner of the Department of Public Welfare in Chicago, a body that she turned into "the eyes of the city" (Davis 1967, 233).

McDowell was born in Cincinnati, and her family moved to Chicago after the Civil War, where her father (a lay preacher) set up a steel-rolling mill. As a young girl, her education was repeatedly interrupted when she had to take over the care of her five younger siblings from her invalid mother. McDowell and her father had rejected the Episcopalian church for Methodism, and during the great fire in Chicago in 1871, she joined with other Methodists, led by her father, in organizing relief work. After moving to the suburb of Evanston in the 1880s, McDowell began teaching Sunday school. At this time, she met the reformer and temperance campaigner Frances Willard and joined her organization, the Woman's Christian Temperance Union, acting as a national organizer for its young women's division and later taking on the leadership of its kindergarten department.

After training to run a kindergarten, McDowell taught for a while in New York before returning to Chicago in 1890 to join Jane Addams's Hull House, where she set up a kindergarten. During the 1894 strike by Pullman railroad workers, McDowell encountered the dark side of worker exploitation and resolved to pioneer social work among Chicago's huge immigrant laboring community. She and a group of associates from Chicago University therefore set up a new settlement house in one of the most insalubrious parts of Chicago, close to the stockyards, an area populated by workers employed in the huge Chicago meatpacking industry. For the next twenty-five years, McDowell dedicated herself to working in the area known as "back of the yards," where she soon set up a day nursery for workers' children, recreational clubs, literacy classes, programs on nutrition and hygiene, handicraft classes, and events such as summer outings and concerts. In 1906 the community moved into a new, more spacious building on Gross Avenue (renamed McDowell Avenue after McDowell's death).

It is hard to conceive now of the filth and pollution of the square mile of Packingtown, the area in which McDowell chose to make her life's work. The combined smell and effluent from the nearby stockyards, the railroad complex that served them—bringing in livestock daily from all over the United States—and the noxious fumes from a local rubbish dump became intolerable during the heat of the summer. Everywhere one went in this district, the visible signs and smells of filth, sewage, offal, and effluent from the stockyards and local industries could be seen overflowing into the nearby tributary of the Chicago River. It had been euphemistically dubbed "Bubbly Creek" by the local community (a reference to the bubbling of the water caused by carbonic waste from nearby factories). Appalled by the threat to public health, McDowell initiated a cleanup campaign (in so doing earning herself other nicknames, such as the "Garbage Lady," "Mary the Magnificent," and the "Duchess of Bubbly Creek"). She lobbied municipal officials and the management of the stockyards to improve public health standards and to establish a community park, library, and public bathhouse. With members of the Woman's City Club, she launched a campaign to investigate better means of waste disposal and even went on a trip to Europe to study the methods used there. In 1913 McDowell's lobbying finally secured the establishment of a City Waste Commission, which eventually closed down the offensive public rubbish dumps in favor of more efficient methods, and constructed a new sewer, and, finally, filled in the stagnant waters of the Bubbly Creek.

In addition to her cleanup of the environment around the stockyards, McDowell was closely involved in the burgeoning labor movement among stockyard workers. In 1901 she and Michael Donnelly, the president of the packing-house unions, cofounded the Illinois Women's Trade Union League, which in 1903 became a branch of the Women's Trade Union League. Also in 1903, she was a key figure in the highly charged Chicago stockyard strike, when unskilled laborers demanded implementation of a 25-cents-an-hour agreement on pay. When the management reneged on this and reduced their offer to 16 cents, 20,000 workers came out on strike. McDowell, loathe to see the strike escalate and cause more hardship, encouraged arbitration, fund-raised for the families of strikers, and made speeches about working conditions in the meatpacking houses. She also helped immigrant female workers, many of them Irish, build their modest Maud Gonne Club (named after the famous patriot) into the Local 183 branch of the Amalgamated Meat Cutters and Butcher Workmen of North America. Eventually, the stockyard strike was broken by the employers, despite McDowell's attempts at conciliation, but the meatpacking union had by then at least won official recognition.

In the wake of the strike, the American socialist Upton Sinclair produced a coruscating exposé of the terrible working conditions in the stockyards and the miserable lives endured by immigrant workers in Chicago. In what was a most disturbing and at times nauseating catalog of the uses and abuses of both animals and workers, the 1906 novel *The Jungle* finally brought the disreputable practices of the meatpacking industry to the attention of an outraged American public. McDowell wrote to President Theodore Roosevelt calling for urgent reform of the industry and was summoned to Washington for a meeting with him. There, while conceding that Sinclair had exaggerated some aspects of the situation, she confirmed that the novel in general was largely accurate in its depiction of the particularly unpleasant working conditions that underpaid immigrant labor endured and also in its exposé of the widespread adulteration of foodstuffs in the industry. A federal investigation of the stockyards was set up, to which McDowell later provided testimony in the form of a report entitled "Government Inspection of Products of Packing Plants," just one of many articles on the industry that she would write.

McDowell continued to lobby for improved working conditions for women in industry, in 1907 again appealing to Roosevelt, this time to set up a federal investigation of the exploitation of women and child workers and calling for the limitation of the working day and improved working conditions. The detailed findings of her investigation were published in several volumes four years later. Frequently collaborating with other reformers in the University of Chicago settlement movement, such as Edith Abbott and Sophonisba Breckinridge, McDowell fought for the rights of women workers for many years. During World War I, she served as a watchdog on safety for women working in the munitions and other wartime industries, and in 1920 she was instrumental in the establishment of the Women's Bureau in the Department of Labor.

Throughout the Progressive era, McDowell also supported social work among Chicago's immigrant communities through her membership in the Urban League of Chicago and the Immigrants' Protective League. After witnessing the violence of the Chicago race riots of 1919, she fought for racial equality, suggesting that a Commission on Interracial Cooperation of eighty women's clubs be established to monitor legislation and continue the campaign for racial equality. She would go on to become a member of the National Association for the Advancement of Colored People and in Chicago encouraged a higher profile for black culture through exhibitions staged at the Chicago Art Institute.

In 1923 McDowell's preeminence as a social worker was recognized when she was appointed commissioner of public welfare in Chicago, in which capacity for the next five years she oversaw the work of numerous social agencies and research projects. In the 1920s she supported the work of the League of Women Voters, the League of Nations, and the international peace movement until her retirement in 1929.

McDowell's original settlement house on Gross Avenue finally closed in 1973, but a documentary record of its achievements is preserved in the three-volume work *Mary McDowell and the University of Chicago Settlement,* published by the Archives of the Chicago Historical Society, which also holds material relating to McDowell. In 1980 a new Mary McDowell Settlement House was established in Chicago to carry on work in the community begun by McDowell ninety years earlier. It offers a wide range of community and self-help programs, as well as heading campaigns to prevent violence, monitor adolescent welfare and health care, and offer advice on employment. Although in McDowell's day, her work was largely conducted among immigrant groups from Europe—Irish, Poles, Lithuanians, Czechs, and Slovaks—83 percent of the new settlement house's work is now with the underprivileged black community that replaced them. For information on McDowell's original settlement house, go to http://www.chicagohs.org/. For information on the programs of the new Mary McDowell Settlement House, go to http://www.chicagocommons.org/mary/.

See also Abbott, Edith; Addams, Jane; Bloor, Ella Reeve; Gonne, Maud; Masarykova, Alice; Willard, Frances.

References and Further Reading

Barrett, James. 1987. *Work and Community in the Jungle: Chicago's Packinghouse Workers, 1894–1922.* Urbana: University of Illinois Press.

Chambers, Clarke A. 1963. *Seedtime of Reform: American Social Service and Social Action, 1918–1933.* Minneapolis: University of Minnesota Press.

Davis, Allen F. 1967. *Spearheads for Reform: The Social Settlements and the Progressive Movement 1890–1914.* New York: Oxford University Press.

Hill, Caroline M., ed. 1938 *Mary McDowell and Municipal Housekeeping.* Chicago: Millar Publishing.

Marchand, C. Roland. 1972. *The American Peace Movement and Social Reform, 1898–1918.* Princeton: Princeton University Press.

Sinclair, Upton. 1986 [1906]. *The Jungle.* Reprint, Harmondsworth: Penguin Books.

Tyler, Helen E. *Where Prayer and Purpose Meet: The WCTU Story, 1874–1949.* Evanston, IL: Signal Press.

Wilson, Howard E. 1928. *Mary McDowell, Neighbor.* Chicago: University of Chicago Press.

McMillan, Margaret
(1860–1931)
United Kingdom

The nursery school pioneer Margaret McMillan sought to improve the poor standards of health care for schoolchildren in Britain's deprived and industrial districts and lobbied for the introduction of free school meals. She afterward devoted her life to her Deptford Open Air Nursery School, where she created a healthier and happier environment for that district's underprivileged and often sickly preschool children. Her principles on nursery school care, like those of her contemporary, Maria Montessori, were taken up in many countries around the world. In her persistence and dedication to social justice, she was, in the writer J. B. Priestley's phrase, the "Nuisance Who Worked Miracles" (Bradburn 1989, 165).

McMillan was born in West Chester County, New York, after her Scottish parents emigrated to the United States. But the family was forced to return to Inverness, Scotland, when they became impoverished after her father's death in 1865. After studying at Inverness High School and the Royal Academy in Inverness, she continued her education in Europe, studying music in Frank-furt am Main (1878) and languages in Geneva and Lausanne (1881–1883). Initially resigned to the idea of having to become a governess or a lady's companion, she pursued such work for the next six years. In 1889, while living with her sister Rachel (1859–1917) in Bloomsbury, she took up voluntary work for the labor movement and became a follower of Christian socialism. McMillan's religious beliefs, strong sense of social justice, and high moral ideals, inspired in part by her close friend, the socialist leader Keir Hardie, lay at the root of all her later work.

Obliged once more to find a job, she became the paid companion to a Lady Meux in London's upmarket Park Lane (1889–1892). Her continuing involvement with socialist activities, distributing leaflets during the dock strike of 1889 and making her first public speech in Hyde Park in 1892, eventually prompted McMillan to give up her job. As an early member of the Independent Labour Party (ILP) after its establishment in 1893, she headed north to Bradford, where she once again lived with her sister and took up unpaid lecturing and writing on behalf of the ILP. McMillan's desire as a devout Christian for active public service was initially fulfilled by her becoming a member of the Bradford Local School Board in 1894 (which she served till 1902). It was in this northern industrial heartland that she first became aware of how much schoolchildren's health and psychological state suffered as a result of deprivation, poor health care, and lack of even the most basic of essentials—regular washing. She began undertaking unofficial medical inspections of local elementary schools with Dr. James Kerr, encountering all too often rickets, scurvy, anemia, and curvature of the spine in malnourished schoolchildren, not to mention their infestation with head lice. She revealed her findings at a public meeting held in Bradford and began campaigning for the establishment of public baths. Beginning in 1899, she undertook regular, official medical checks of children in Bradford's elementary schools, urging their adoption of better ventilation and hygiene. In 1900 McMillan published a study of child development, *Early Childhood*. A 1907 act would eventually institute health inspections throughout Britain's schools, with the first school clinic opening in Bradford. McMillan was also a prime mover in the campaign of the Cinderella Clubs to provide nutritious food for slum children, and she called for the provision of free school meals for needy children, a goal that was achieved with the 1906 Education Act.

After moving to her sister's home in Kent in 1902, McMillan lived with Rachel, who was now a trained sanitary inspector and teaching hygiene. McMillan spent the next three years developing her ideas on the physiological and emotional development of the child, publishing *Education through the Imagination* (1904), *The Economic Aspects of Child Labour and Education* (1905), and *Labour and Childhood* (1907). In the latter, she argued forcefully against the common practice of poor schoolchildren engaging in part-time labor as being detrimental to their well-being. Together with Rachel, she opened the first children's health clinic in London (at Bow in the East End) in 1908, but it was short-lived because of lack of funds. The sisters then set up another in Deptford in 1910, which proved extremely successful and was awarded grants by the London County Council to offer dental, eye, and ear treatment. When a local benefactor offered the use of a house and garden in Evelyn Street, they also set up night camps—open-air dormitories for slum children offering recreation and washing facilities and a change of clothes—one for girls at Evelyn House and, later, another for boys at St. Nicholas's churchyard. These ventures were described by McMillan in *The Camp School* (1917).

In 1913, in the belief that the first five years were crucial to the physical and mental development of the child, the McMillan sisters founded an innovative open-air nursery school on a rented site in the East Ward of Deptford for children under five, guided by Rachel's training in hygiene and health care and with Margaret emphasizing a healthy mix of rest, play, and fresh air in promoting physical and mental development and well-being. In as dirty and polluted an environment as the poorest part of Deptford then was, with its cattle markets and the detritus from its slaughterhouses overflowing into the nearby streets, the McMillans sought to create a pleasant garden full of sweet-smelling flowers to offset these and other industrial odors. The school, McMillan believed, should be an extension of family life, and with so many working-class homes hopelessly overcrowded, the Deptford nursery offered a welcome nine hours–a–day respite from slum life for many deprived children. It also provided invaluable assistance to mothers engaged in war work during the years 1914–1918. When the Deptford Open Air Nursery School was finally completed in 1917, it was officially named the Rachel McMillan Open Air Nursery School, but sadly, Rachel died prematurely that year.

After Rachel's death, Margaret oversaw the establishment of the Rachel McMillan Training Centre (from the end of 1929 known as the Rachel McMillan College) in her memory, to promote the training of nursery and infant teachers. As principal, McMillan laid down a three-year training program recommended for teachers of children between the ages of three and six, which had a far-reaching influence on the establishment of preschool and primary education in Britain. Many McMillan-trained teachers went out to work in the British Commonwealth and also in the United States. McMillan's ideas on the care and education of the young were also endorsed by the pioneering Italian educationist Maria Montessori.

McMillan described many of her ideas on child development and nursery education in *The Child and the State* (1912) and *The Nursery School* (1919); she also published a biography of her sister, *The Life of Rachel McMillan*, in 1927. She was active in the antivivisection movement and signed a petition calling for its end that was compiled in 1896 by the Humanitarian League. She was briefly active in the suffrage movement after 1912 and suffered injuries after being trampled during a demonstration against the cruel practice of the Cat and Mouse Act, under which suffragettes on hunger strike in prison were repeatedly released and rearrested. She was honored for her work by being made a Commander of the Order of the British Empire (CBE) in 1917 and a Companion of Honour in 1930.

See also Montessori, Maria.

References and Further Reading

Bradburn, Elizabeth. 1989. *Margaret McMillan: Portrait of a Pioneer.* London: Routledge.

Cresswell, Walter D'Arcy. 1948. *Margaret McMillan: A Memoir.* London: Hutchinson.

Lowndes, George. 1960. *Margaret McMillan, "The Children's Champion."* London: Museum Press.

Mansbridge, Albert. 1932. *Margaret McMillan, Prophet and Pioneer: Her Life and Work.* London: J. M. Dent.

Steedman, Carolyn. 1990. *Childhood, Culture and*

Class in Britain: Margaret McMillan 1860–1931.
London: Virago.

Vicinus, Martha. 1985. *Independent Women, Work
and Community for Single Women, 1850–1920.*
London: Virago.

Menchú Tum, Rigoberta
(1959–)
Guatemala

From the moment of its publication in 1984, her acclaimed autobiography *I, Rigoberta Menchú,* catapulted the humble Quiché native to the status of high-profile civil rights activist, in which guise she led an international campaign to draw attention to the abuse of Guatemala's indigenous peoples by successive right-wing military juntas. Menchú was awarded the Nobel Peace Prize in 1992, the year of the five hundredth anniversary of the "discovery" of the Americas by Christopher Columbus, when she had led opposition to the celebration of an event that she perceived as having inaugurated the mass destruction and exploitation of the continent's indigenous peoples.

At the time there seemed no more fitting recognition of the struggle of indigenous peoples everywhere against political and economic oppression than Menchú's peace prize, and she was embraced by the political left as a symbol of how indigenous people could finally gain moral ascendancy over their oppressors. Menchú soon capitalized politically on the huge international interest in her story, which became required reading for anyone studying Latin American history and society, and as a representative of the United Nations was influential not only in the peace negotiations between government and insurgents in Guatemala but as a human rights observer around the world.

But in 1999 a book entitled *Rigoberta Menchú and the Story of All Poor Guatemalans* discredited her for falsifying some of the details of her life story. Its author, the U.S. anthropologist David Stoll, after conducting exhaustive research over many years, alleged that Menchú had falsified her own "humble" origins and had elaborated on some of the more horrific elements of her family's story during a period of violent peasant-backed guerrilla insurgency for land rights. The scene was set for a fierce debate over the nature of biographical authenticity and the validity of Menchú's

Rigoberta Menchú Tum (Reuters/Oswaldo Jimenez/ Archive Photos)

subsequent work. For there was no denying that, by this time, whatever the demerits of her "embellished" story, Menchú had become a prominent campaigner whose genuine concerns and energetic campaigning had extended far beyond her work for Guatemala's Quiché and Mayans.

The true facts of Menchú's life would appear to be that she was the sixth of nine children of Vicente Menchú and his wife, a local midwife and healer. She was born in the remote Quiché village of Chimel in the northwestern highlands of Guatemala. Her father, a local farmer and activist, had been recruited into the Peasant Unity Committee that fought for land rights from the 1970s. Far from being uneducated, disadvantaged, and unable to speak Spanish as she had claimed, Menchú attended a Catholic boarding school, learned Spanish, and never had to labor in the coffee fields from dawn till dusk. It would be her contention, however, that such a life of hardship—deprived of education and forced to work for low wages—was the experience of many Guatemalans and that her book was merely a synthesis of the everyday experience of Guatemala's twenty or more indigenous peoples.

In any event, in 1979 Menchú and her brothers became involved in the organization by the

Peasant Unity Committee of local resistance to the government expropriation of Maya land in Quiché, after military action was launched against unrest there. It was a conflict that would result in many deaths, including those of her brother Petrocinio and father, although again, the true circumstances in which they died, according to Stoll, were other than how Menchú described them. Vicente Menchú died in a fire that broke out after left-wing insurgents, in protesting human rights abuses by the Guatemalan army, mounted an armed takeover of the Spanish Embassy in Guatemala City on 31 January 1980. Thirty-six people died and immediately became martyrs to the cause, Vicente Menchú included, although the fire may well have been started by the rebels themselves. Nevertheless, Vicente Menchú's wife and his son later perished in military reprisals for acts of terrorism during the continuing no-win conflict with the military that would blight Guatemala for many years.

Menchú herself escaped to Mexico City in 1981, where she was taken in by members of the Guatemalan Church in Exile and cofounded the "31 January Popular Front." Working as a cook in safe houses run by radicals, she set out to raise awareness of the situation in Guatemala, acting as official mouthpiece for the United Representation of the Guatemalan Opposition in Latin America and later joining a UN Working Group on Indigenous Populations. In 1982 she went to Paris, where she became involved in the activities of the Guerrilla Army of the Poor, the radical wing of the Cuban-backed guerrillas in Guatemala that had been involved in the bitter fighting in Quiché province. In Paris Menchú was assisted in the writing of her autobiography by the Venezuelan communist Elisabeth Burgos-Debray. In 1983 Menchú returned briefly to Guatemala to campaign against the enforced resettlement of villagers by the governing junta, becoming a member of the Coordinating Commission of the Committee of Peasant Unity. Once her book was published, translated into eleven languages, and earned considerable profits, Menchú was in demand as a public speaker and traveled the world attending conferences and taking on high-profile international roles. She became a member of the UN Subcommission on the Prevention of Discrimination and Protection of Minorities and of the UN International Indian Treaty Council, joined the UN

Conference on the Decade of Women, and took on the role of observer of the UN Human Rights Committee and General Assembly.

And soon the prizes began flooding in: in 1988 the Nonino Prize; in 1990 the Monseñor Proaño Human Rights Prize and the United Nations Educational, Scientific, and Cultural Organization Education for Peace Prize; in 1991 the French Committee for Defense of Freedoms and Human Rights Prize; and an honorary doctorate from the Central American University of Nicaragua. Finally, in 1992, from among 130 candidates Menchú was selected for the Nobel Peace Prize, which in its citation lauded her as a "vivid symbol of peace and reconciliation across ethnic, cultural and social dividing lines." Much was made in the press of the fact that she was not only the youngest person (at thirty-three) to be awarded the peace prize but also the first indigenous person from the Americas to be so honored. In her acceptance of the award, she said she did so in recognition of the 500 years of genocide, repression, and discrimination suffered by the indigenous peoples of the Americas.

Menchú used her prize money to set up the Rigoberta Menchú Foundation in Mexico City, which later was able to move back to Guatemala City. It works for world peace based on the recognition of ethnic and cultural differences and the defense of human rights of indigenous peoples. In particular, it has campaigned against foreign investors' exploitation of oil reserves on indigenous lands and has also organized Guatemalan coffee pickers to obtain better wages from the U.S. coffee company Starbucks. The foundation also funds various aid programs to help destitute street children and the families of murdered political prisoners.

Menchú's detractors perceive her embroidered account of her early life as little more than simplistic propaganda that romanticizes her peasant homeland and paints an ingenuous portrait of innocent exploited peasants in opposition to evil government. Others, however, including the Nobel Committee, insist that despite its economy with the truth, Menchú's book is the work of a well-intentioned campaigner that has been exploited by the radical left in promotion of its own agenda.

In 1993 Menchú was appointed Goodwill Ambassador to the UN for the Year of the Indigenous Peoples and headed its summit conference in Chimaltenango, Guatemala. In 1996 Guatemala's thirty-six-year-long civil war finally came to an end, thanks in part to her campaigning. Menchú now heads the Indigenous Initiative for Peace. The Rigoberta Menchú Tum Foundation can be found on the Internet at www. rigobertamenchu.org.

References and Further Reading

Menchú, Rigoberta. 1984. *I, Rigoberta Menchú: An Indian Woman in Guatemala.* London: Verso.
——. 1998. *Crossing Borders.* London: Verso.
Stoll, David. 1999. *Rigoberta Menchú and the Story of All Poor Guatemalans.* Boulder: Westview Press.

Michel, Louise
(1830–1905)
France

The French revolutionary socialist and feminist Louise Michel was a born protester, who not only fought on the barricades of the 1871 Paris Commune but was a vigorous social campaigner, novelist, and accomplished poet. Unbowed by several periods of arduous imprisonment, she continued her political campaigning right up to her final days, dying at the age of seventy-five while on a lecture tour in the south of France.

Louise Michel was born illegitimate, the daughter of a servant girl and the son of a local chateau owner in France's Haut-Marne region. Her paternal grandparents, who were enlightened and educated people, brought her up and gave her a good education, inculcating in her a sense of social justice by encouraging her to read the works of Voltaire and Jean-Jacques Rousseau. Refusing all suitors, Louise decided to become a teacher, only to be dismissed in 1852 because of her outspoken views on the repressive regime of Napoleon III's Second Empire.

Michel traveled to Paris, which had become a hotbed of revolutionary activities, and for a while ran her own private school. In 1856 she joined various underground groups, including the First International (established by British and French socialists in 1864), as well as studying natural history and science at night school. She also began to write on social subjects, such as the position of women in the family and the need for working-class women to emancipate themselves both in the home and in the workplace. In 1869 Michel was a founding member of the Associa-

tion for the Rights of Women, which demanded their civil and employment rights and access to higher education. The Franco-Prussian War of 1870–1871 gave Michel an outlet for her Republican convictions. During this time she oversaw social and education policies as a member of the patriotic group the Club of the Nation in Danger, and also worked as a nurse. She became renowned as a fiery orator in the Women's Vigilance Committee of the eighteenth *arrondissement* during the four-month siege of Paris by the Prussians.

After the fall of the Second Empire in September 1871, Michel's fervent commitment to social progress drove her to take repeated risks with her own safety. In campaigning for a new democratic regime, she was at the head of a vanguard of women who enthusiastically joined the revolutionary commune that took over Paris. She attended to the wounded on the battlefield. Later, she led one of the men's battalions, brandishing a Remington rifle, and was one of the last to abandon the barricades at the Montmartre Cemetery in late May. Her exploits made Michel a legend, acquiring numerous romantic attributions inspired by her fearlessness, such as the "Red Virgin" of the commune, the "Grand Druidess of Anarchy," the "Inspirer," and the "Revolutionary Breath of the Commune."

When Michel discovered that her own mother had been taken hostage in the aftermath of the commune, she gave herself up in exchange and was incarcerated at Versailles. At her trial in December 1871 she was defiant, daring her judges to execute her with the words, "Since it seems that every heart that beats for freedom has no right to anything but a slug of lead, I demand my share" (Cole 1978, 39). Instead, sentenced to life imprisonment in August 1873, she was deported to the French colonies in the South Pacific at New Caledonia.

During the seven hard years of her imprisonment there, Louise refused to be cowed. She insisted on being given the same treatment as male prisoners but also made good use of her time by teaching and writing poetry and studying the botany of the islands and the life of the indigenous people, the Kanaks. Allowed to return to France after a political amnesty in 1880, Michel found that she had not been forgotten, when crowds greeted her at the station on her return. Her years in exile had not quelled her political voice, either, and she was soon back on the rostrum, campaigning loudly for women's emancipation. Her social concerns were powerfully laid out in several social novels she wrote at this time: *Poverty* (1881), *Women Despised* (1882), and *Daughter of the People* (1883).

Meanwhile, the French police closely monitored Michel's every move. She was arrested in March 1883 and a year later sentenced to six years of solitary confinement for conspiracy after inciting a break-in of a bakery during a food riot. After her release in 1889, yet again she became embroiled in political activities in the Vienne district. She remained utterly intractable: in 1890 she was still averring that intelligent women had a natural instinct for rebellion. But inevitably her continuing, unrepentant anarchist principles kept her permanently in the eye of the French authorities, who by now had resolved to be rid of her once and for all by committing her to a lunatic asylum.

Michel spent time in London in 1896 (the first of several stints in England during her remaining years). Here she adopted a more suburban version of revolutionary politics, living in East Dulwich and becoming a member of the British Fabian Society (founded by George Bernard Shaw and Beatrice and Sydney Webb) and taking an interest in the Russian revolutionary cause. When she died in Marseilles in 1905, she was accorded a huge funeral in Paris, attended by crowds as massive as those who had filled the streets for the great writer Victor Hugo in 1885.

References and Further Reading

Cole, G. D. H. 1978. "Louise Michel." *Observer Magazine* (26 November): 30–39.

Goldsmith, Margaret. 1935. *Seven Women against the World*. London: Methuen.

Lowry, Bullitt, and Elizabeth Ellington Gunter, eds. 1981. *The Red Virgin: Memoirs of Louise Michel*. Mobile: University of Alabama Press.

Moses, C. 1984. *French Feminism in the Nineteenth Century*. Albany: State University of New York Press.

Mullaney, Marie Marmo. 1990. "Sexual Politics in the Career and Legend of Louise Michel." *Signs* 15(2): 300–322.

Thomas, Edith. 1980. *Louise Michel*. Montreal: Black Rose.

Mink, Paule (Paulina Mekarska)
(1839–1900)
France

A member of the suffrage group Solidarity and pioneer of the rights of women workers during the Third Republic, the socialist feminist Paule Mink was a legendary figure during the Paris Commune of 1871. Born Paulina Mekarska in Clermont-Ferrand, her family members were Polish émigré nobles who had fled the 1830 revolution there. The family settled in Paris, where her father worked as clerk to a tax collector, and Mink gave language lessons and worked as a seamstress.

Mink's natural Republican sympathies were aroused as a young girl by the legacy of the 1848 revolution, and by the age of sixteen, she began joining various Republican and feminist societies. In 1866 she joined the first French feminist organization, the Society for the Demand of the Rights of Woman, established by Léon Richer and Marie Deraismes. Two years later Mink founded her own women's mutual aid society and began collaborating with Deraismes in giving public lectures on women's working and political rights. Her shortness of stature and unattractive looks notwithstanding (she had several teeth missing and was slightly deformed), Mink became a powerful public speaker noted for her sense of drama and wit. She provided for her children mostly single-handedly, combining earnings from her lecturing, sewing, and proofreading with handouts from friends.

As an opponent of the religious establishment and the monarchy, in 1869 Mink had no sooner published a single issue of the savagely satirical Republican journal, *The Flies and the Spider* (a reference to King Louis Napoleon's treatment of the masses), than her publishing activities were suppressed. She founded a cooperative society for workers and frequently gave lectures on her social theories to groups of workers, elaborating on women's emancipation and education, marriage, divorce, and motherhood. In all her arguments, she emphasized her belief that men's and women's natural abilities made their roles complementary and that mothers should be accorded greater respect for the roles they fulfilled. Above all, she urged that the working masses must be liberated economically from the misery of servitude and low wages. She emphasized this point with regard to working women in particular, who suffered the additional problems of sexual harassment and degradation that often led to prostitution and who should be relieved of the double burden of work and domestic duties.

Mink subsequently became a heroine of the Franco-Prussian War of 1870–1871, organizing the defense of Auxerre and visiting revolutionary clubs, both in Paris and in the provinces. She set up a club for workers and an ambulance service during the Paris Commune, as well as a school for poor children, and tried wherever she went to rally support for the revolutionaries in Paris. After the commune fell, she fled to Switzerland, was condemned in absentia, and was only able to return to France after a political amnesty in 1880. She returned from exile with three illegitimate children to support and lived in Montpellier, once again taking up activities for various socialist groups and becoming a leading figure in the socialist movement during the 1880s and 1890s. However, she disagreed with Hubertine Auclert, leader of Women's Suffrage, on her narrow political objective of women's suffrage only, Mink's concern being to emphasize not the separate issue of women's rights but their traditional role as strong helpmates who would support men in revolutionary activities. She was not convinced that women's suffrage alone would emancipate women, since she felt many were too much under the thumb of the church and would not vote independently. Nor would the vote liberate working women from the social miseries to which the capitalist system had abandoned them. Therefore, she contested whether suffrage was at all relevant to women's emancipation, which in her view could only come when a new socialist order had brought an end to the exploitation of all working people.

In the early 1880s Mink's views on suffrage were challenged by the liberal feminist Eugénie Potonié-Pierre. Mink gradually came to amend her views on women's participation in political activism and joined the suffrage organization Solidarity in 1893. Now living in Paris and convinced that women could act as moderators in political life and be a force for the elimination of corruption, Mink accepted the challenge of standing as a candidate for Solidarity in the municipal council elections. She drew ever closer to Potonié-Pierre within Solidarity and during 1891–1896 wrote a series of articles for Solidar-

ity's journal, *The Social Question,* eventually serving as editorial secretary from 1894 until it ceased publication in 1897.

After the death of Potonié-Pierre in 1898, Solidarity was taken over by Karoline Kauffman, and Mink, devastated by the loss of her old comrade and unable to work with the new leadership, became sidelined by the women's movement. She devoted herself to working for the unity of socialist women's organizations until her death in 1900, upon which a mass turnout of the public at her funeral celebrated her long-held reputation as a heroine of the commune.

See also Auclert, Hubertine; Deraismes, Marie; Potonié-Pierre, Eugénie.

References and Further Reading

Boxer, Marilyn J., and Jean H. Quaterat. 1978. *Socialist Women: European Socialist Feminism in the Nineteenth and Twentieth Centuries.* New York: Elsevier North-Holland.

Scott, Joan. 1974. *The Glassworkers of Carmaux.* Cambridge, MA: Harvard University Press.

Sowerwine, Charles. 1982. *Sisters or Citizens? Women and Socialism in France since 1876.* Cambridge: Cambridge University Press.

Mirovich, Zinaida
(1869–1913)
Russia

In the brief history of the Russian suffrage movement between 1905 and the onset of reaction in 1908, the All-Russian Union for Women's Equality, of which Zinaida Mirovich was a leader, for a few months was the largest women's organization. It succeeded in winning the support of a wide cross section of women in a network of eighty affiliated branches across Russia to make it the biggest organization of its kind. Mirovich also established closer links between Russian suffrage groups and the international women's movement.

Mirovich was a Moscow-based critic and translator and a specialist on the French Revolution. She wrote a biography of the French democratic leader Madame Roland and in 1892 published a study of Henrik Ibsen. She wrote on education in Russia and campaigned for women's suffrage as a leader of the All-Russian Union for Women's Equality (not to be confused with the All-Russian League for Women's Equality), which had been founded by a group of thirty women in Moscow in the winter of 1904 to 1905. It was one of several groups that emerged after the popular protest movement of that period had led to the establishment of the hoped-for democratic government of the First Duma. The union also succeeded in winning members away from the established and moderate Russian Women's Mutual Philanthropic Society, many of whose younger members had become dissatisfied with its lack of political objectives. Convinced that the struggle for women's suffrage was an inextricable part of the fight for political emancipation of all, the union under Mirovich and her associates Anna Kalmanovich, Mariya Chekhova, and Lyubov Gurevich demanded universal suffrage, irrespective of sex, nationality, religion, and marital status. It also demanded freedom of the press and of religious practice, freedom of association, an amnesty for political prisoners, and most important, the guaranteed civil rights of national groups within the empire. The union's primary objective upon its inception was to lobby the Duma under Prince Georgy Lvov for changes to the Constitution that would grant women voting rights in the local zemstvos (district assemblies) and in city councils. The union adopted the electioneering practices of English suffrage groups in its campaigns for the First and Second Dumas.

After holding its founding congress in May 1905, the union grew rapidly over the next year and a half to a membership that peaked between 8,000 and 10,000 (sources disagree), bolstered by support from Kadet members of the Duma. But its attempts at propagandizing, petitioning, and holding public meetings were constantly blocked by the police. It also had to face down antagonism from radical socialist groups who were opposed to the separatism of feminist groups. As a moderate suffragist, Mirovich defended the need for women's groups such as the union to remain nonpartisan, but doing so proved difficult at a time when the rivalry between Russian political factions was becoming increasingly intense. Mirovich admired the better-organized campaigning of the English suffragettes and gave frequent lectures on their activities, but she did not support their extreme, militant tactics. In 1906 she gave a lecture, "The Women's Movement in Contemporary Europe," in Moscow and Smolensk, but a year later when she announced a lecture on English feminists, the authorities banned it as potentially inflammatory. Hamstrung by tight police controls, the Russian suffrage movement never got as far as the smashed windows, hunger strikes, and other acts of civil disobedience so characteristic of the English movement. Sadly, by 1908 the All-Russian Union for Women's Equality had folded.

Meanwhile, Mirovich had become one of the few Russian suffragists familiar to the international women's movement. She had been one of six Russian delegates to the third International Woman Suffrage Alliance (IWSA) congress, held in Copenhagen in 1906 (the first Russian women's delegation to attend a congress outside Russia). At the congress, the union was affiliated with the IWSA, and Mirovich (as president of the Moscow branch) thereafter submitted occasional reports on the political situation for women in Russia, which were published in its journal *Jus Suffragii* until her death in 1913.

Despite the union's demise, in 1908 Mirovich and other Russian feminists finally succeeded, after several years of planning, in holding the first All-Russian Women's Congress, but it served only as a showpiece for the already moribund middle-class feminist movement in Russia. Mirovich and some colleagues in the union went on to join forces with the Moscow branch of the All-Russian League for Women's Equality in 1910, but there was a clash of personalities between Mirovich and one of its leaders, Mariya Raikh, and Mirovich and her supporters left the league in 1911. Little is known of Mirovich's final years. The journal of the IWSA reported in its obituary of her that she had spent much time in England, and Linda Edmondson confirms this period as being from the 1890s until her death in 1913. It is known that she maintained close links with English campaigners, in 1909 attending a suffrage congress in London and meeting hunger strikers shortly after their release from Holloway prison; she is also known to have spoken at a suffrage rally in Hyde Park. In 1911 she gave a paper at the Women's Education Congress in St. Petersburg on "The Necessity of Women's Enfranchisement for Their Rational Education." She was appointed an honorary vice president of the International Council of Women, and in 1911 she was a delegate to the IWSA congress in Stockholm. But illness prevented her from attending its next one, in Budapest in 1913, and she died soon after on 26 August.

See also Shishkina-Yavein, Poliksena.
References and Further Reading
Edmondson, Linda. 1984. *Feminism in Russia,
    1900–1917*. London: Heinemann.
Jus Suffragii (1 October 1913): 4. Obituary notice.
Stites, Richard. 1991 [1978]. *The Women's Liberation
    Movement in Russia: Feminism, Nihilism, and
    Bolshevism, 1860–1930*. Reprint, Princeton:
    Princeton University Press.

Mitchell, Hannah
(1871–1956)
United Kingdom

Best known for her powerful and vivid autobiography, *The Hard Way Up,* the working-class suffragette Hannah Mitchell was highly critical of woman's domestic role and gave voice to the dilemma facing married working women in Britain, eager to support the suffrage campaign but constrained by lives that were "one long round of cooking and sewing" (Crawford 1999, 416). In her gritty account of working-class life and politics, she exposed male prejudices in the socialist movement against women's campaigning, providing a sobering account of the difficult choices such women had to make and famously averring, "No cause can be won between dinner and tea and most of us who were married had to work with one hand tied behind us" (Liddington and Norris 2000, 16).

Born on a farm in the Derbyshire Peak District, Mitchell was denied schooling and was expected to stay at home and look after her father and three brothers. Loathing her domestic servitude and constantly running up against her mother's violent temper, she ran away when she was fourteen and took up work as a dressmaker in Bolton, Lancashire. She set about her self-education and became a socialist, attending the Sunday meetings of the Labour Church. She met fellow socialist Gibbon Mitchell, whom she married in 1895, insisting that he share all domestic duties equally with her. After undergoing an agonizing and protracted labor without medical help, she decided to have no more children rather than bring them up in poverty, seeing birth control as one of the few options open to her in her determination to have some kind of life of her own.

In 1900 the Mitchells moved to Ashton-under-Lyne, where Hannah again joined a local socialist group and through it the Independent Labour Party (ILP). In 1904 she was elected as a socialist candidate to the Ashton-under-Lyne Board of Guardians and joined the Bolton branch of the Women's Social and Political Union (WSPU). In 1905 she undertook a speaking tour in the Lancashire mill towns on behalf of the union and at the end of 1906 was offered a paid, part-time role as organizer in Oldham. But the strain of her suffrage commitments, which had also involved her in a speaking tour and by-election canvassing in the northeast, led to a nervous breakdown in 1907. By this time, she had also become disenchanted with the single-minded, dictatorial leadership of the WSPU by Emmeline and Christabel Pankhurst, neither of whom had commiserated with her during her illness. Feeling that the WSPU took no account of the strains and stresses of activism on individual women and saw the cause as being more important than those who worked for it, Mitchell left the WSPU and joined the Women's Freedom League in 1907. She also resumed her work for the Board of Guardians and was active in the Manchester branch of the ILP in the years leading up to World War I.

Mitchell's pacifism during World War I prompted her to become a member of the Women's Peace Crusade and the No-Conscription Fellowship, through which she supported her nineteen-year-old son's decision to be a conscientious objector. After the war, Mitchell joined the ILP and was elected its representative on the Manchester City Council (1924–1935), she was also a city magistrate (1926–1946); becoming a respected figure in local politics until her retirement. However, she continued to dislike the chauvinism of the male members of the ILP, who, she said, for all their support for women's rights, still expected the women members to lay on the tea and cakes at meetings. Her insightful autobiography, which clearly expresses her own sanguine views on the mixing of marriage and political activism, is now considered a primary text in the history of working women's activism in Britain. Like much of women's writing of her era, however, it languished unpublished for many years, finally becoming available in 1968.

See also Pankhurst, Christabel; Pankhurst, Emmeline.
References and Further Reading
Holton, Sandra. 1996. *Suffrage Days: Stories from the
    Women's Suffrage Movement*. London: Routledge.

Liddington, Jill, and Jill Norris. 2000 [1978]. *One Hand Tied behind Us.* Rev. ed. London: Virago.

Mitchell, Hannah. 1968. *The Hard Way Up: The Autobiography of Hannah Mitchell, Suffragette and Rebel.* London: Faber.

Oldfield, Sybil. 2001. *Women Humanitarians: A Biographical Dictionary of British Women Active between 1900 and 1950.* London: Continuum.

Crawford, Elizabeth. 1999. *The Women's Suffrage Movement, 1866–1928: A Reference Guide.* London: University College of London Press.

Montagu, Lily
(1873–1963)
United Kingdom

The distinguished religious reformer and intellectual Lily Montagu was a founder of the Jewish Religious Union (JRU) and as the first Jewish woman rabbi-without-title, a leader of Jewish Liberal Orthodoxy in Britain. Her accomplishments were considerable, yet she rates no entry in the *Encyclopedia Britannica,* despite being a cofounder, with Claude Montefiore (who *is* included), of British Liberal Judaism in the 1900s. Montagu's contribution to Jewish life and faith thus remains largely unknown outside Jewish scholarship, as do her considerable social concerns. A supporter of women's suffrage, she was very much the behind-the-scenes spiritual leader of the Jewish League for Woman Suffrage (JLWS), in which several of her female relatives were also active; more important, she worked hard to raise the social status of Jewish women and see them answer what she believed was God's call to extend their work in the home into active, public social service. Montagu was also a magistrate and community worker who was involved with Jewish youth through her West Central Girls' Club and was a founder of the National Organization of Girls' Clubs in Britain.

Lily Montagu's father, the banker and philanthropist Samuel Montagu, was a self-made millionaire who was raised to the barony as the first Baron Swaythling and enjoyed comfortable homes in Hampshire and Kensington. As one of ten children, Montagu was brought up in a devoutly Orthodox home and was educated at private schools. By the late 1880s, however, she had come increasingly to question her Orthodox faith, which kept her closely confined, and she sought ways of undertaking useful social service.

Her tutor, Simeon Singer, encouraged her to set up special children's services at the New West End Synagogue in 1890, and at around the same time, she began teaching evening classes for Jewish working girls with her sister Marian. In 1893, together with Marian and another sister, Netta, Montagu took over the running of Lady Rothschild's West Central Friday Night Club, the first club of its kind for Jewish working girls, which had been established in 1885. It would evolve into the West Central Jewish Day Settlement, which Montagu directed, despite some hostility from Orthodox Jewish groups, until almost the end of her life.

In her work, Montagu came into contact with the rapidly growing Jewish immigrant community and did what she could to help new arrivals settle in, urging working-class girls to join friendly societies in order to protect their own interests. In addition, Montagu worked for better conditions for Jewish workers in the sweatshops of the East End of London and lobbied for factory inspections. Her advice to Jewish women, to obtain the backing of the trade union movement by joining non-Jewish organizations such as the National Federation of Women Workers, raised eyebrows in the Jewish community, which discouraged any participation in groups outside their own close-knit religious ones. By the mid-1890s, the West Central Jewish Day Settlement was offering Jewish women vocational training in many trades, including dressmaking, cooking, sewing, wood- and metalworking, basket making, laundering, and shorthand, as well as ensuring their pastoral care with a constant emphasis on Jewish moral values and the provision of Hebrew lessons and Sabbath services.

In her midtwenties, under the influence of the ideas of the Jewish theologian Claude Montefiore, Montagu set about establishing a new form of Liberal Judaism that would adapt traditional Orthodox faith to the changes going on in society at large and the exigencies of modern-day life. In 1902, she and Montefiore founded the Jewish Religious Union for the Advancement of Liberal Judaism, which later developed into the Liberal Jewish Synagogue, in which she was an important lay preacher after giving her first sermon (as probably the first Jewish woman to preach in an Anglo-Jewish or even European synagogue) in 1918. Ellen Umansky (1983) argues that, in fact, Montagu was the real intellectual and guiding force behind Liberal Judaism and that Montefiore served as the necessary, acceptable male figurehead who had been invited by her to give credence to it. Within the movement, she would promote her own brand of equal rights Judaism, which called for an end to the double standard in sexual chastity and for Jewish women to be granted the same rights to divorce as men.

With time, the JRU and its work for Reform Judaism spread to the United States. Montagu also founded the Union of Liberal and Progressive Synagogues, which in 1926 was established internationally as the World Union for Progressive Judaism. In 1928 Montagu preached at its annual conference, held in Berlin. She served as secretary of this organization until her death. Although she preached regularly at her own West Central Jewish Congregation, constituted in 1928, she was not formally inducted as a lay minister until 1938.

Montagu had long been a supporter of the women's suffrage movement because of her sister Netta's involvement in the establishment of the Jewish League for Woman Suffrage (JLWS) in 1912. That year, Montagu protested the force-feeding of suffragettes in prison, taking her message to high places and appealing to her brother Edwin Montagu, then secretary for India. Not wishing to endanger her work for Liberal Judaism by appearing excessively militant, however, Montagu accepted the vice presidency of the JLWS in 1913 but otherwise offered mainly moral and spiritual support to it by regularly leading prayers at the beginning of meetings and suffrage events.

With the rise of fascism during the 1930s, Montagu helped hundreds of Jewish refugees fleeing from Europe by obtaining entry permits to Britain. She continued to help the needy and elderly and to oversee social work at the West Central Jewish Day Settlement, but this was destroyed by bombing in 1941. She published many pamphlets, speeches, and articles and fourteen books, mainly on theology, including *Prayers for Jewish Working Girls* (1895), *Religious and Social Service* (1918), *Religious Education in the Home* (1925), and *The Faith of a Jewish Woman* (1943). She was made a Commander of the Order of the British Empire in 1955.

Although Montagu's detractors might argue that she operated in an elite social milieu, coming as she did from a prominent and wealthy Anglo-Jewish family with considerable social connections, she was totally dedicated to her unstinting work in the Jewish community. In her own moderate and understated way, she cautiously forwarded the interests and emancipation of Jewish women while contributing greatly to the revitalization of the Jewish faith in Britain and the promotion of moral and religious standards. By the time of her death, she had become a revered figure who is now recognized as "the first official female religious leader in an organized Jewish movement" (Umansky 1983, 138–139). The importance of her contribution was underscored by the international violinist Yehudi Menuhin in a moving obituary of Montagu published in the *Times* in April 1964. For more information on Montagu, go to http://www.huc.edu/aja/Montagu.htm.

References and Further Reading

Crawford, Elizabeth. 1999. *The Women's Suffrage Movement, 1866–1928: A Reference Guide.* London: University College of London Press.

Kuzmack, Linda Gordon. 1990. *Woman's Cause: The Jewish Woman's Movement in Europe and the United States 1881–1933.* Columbus: Ohio State University Press.

Menuhin, Yehudi. 1964. "A Woman to Remember." *Times* (24 April).

Montagu, Eric. 1953. *Lily H. Montagu: Prophet of a Living Judaism.* New York: National Federation of Temple Sisterhoods.

Oldfield, Sybil. 2001. *Women Humanitarians: A Biographical Dictionary of British Women Active between 1900 and 1950.* London: Continuum.

Umansky, Ellen M. 1983. *Lily Montagu and the Advancement of Liberal Judaism: From Vision to Vocation.* New York: Edwin Mellen Press.

———. 1985. *Lily Montagu: Sermons, Addresses, Letters and Prayers.* New York: Edwin Mellen Press.

Montefiore, Dora
(1851–1927)
United Kingdom/Australia

The redoubtable suffragist Dora Montefiore was a founder of the women's suffrage movement in New South Wales before moving back to England to work first for the Women's Social and Political Union (WSPU) and later the Adult Suffrage Society. As a committed socialist who advocated civil disobedience rather than militancy, she found it difficult to adjust her principles to any particular organized suffrage group and remained a determined political maverick.

Montefiore was the daughter of a comfortably off surveyor and estate agent. Born into a large family in Tooting, in London, she grew up in Surrey, where she was educated privately at home and at Mrs. Creswell's School in Brighton. After leaving school, she assisted her father in his affairs before going to Australia in 1874, when she was twenty-three, to take over the management of her elder brother's household when his wife's health failed. She returned to England for her wedding in 1881 to a Jewish merchant, George Barrow Montefiore, whom she had met in Australia, and they settled in Sydney. But he died in 1889, after only eight years of marriage. For the first time, Montefiore confronted her own lack of legal rights as a woman, when she discovered that under existing law, she had no automatic rights of guardianship over her own two children. On her return to New South Wales, she began meeting with other women activists, convinced that the key to women's legal rights was their winning of the vote.

Montefiore set up a suffrage meeting in her own home in New South Wales in March 1891, at which the Womanhood Suffrage League was inaugurated and to which she was elected corresponding and later recording secretary, but a year later she left Australia, returning to England via Paris. She briefly involved herself in the moderate women's suffrage movement in 1896, as an executive member of the Central National Society for Women's Suffrage. However, she was soon disenchanted with its cautious policies and its willingness to accept a limited form of franchise (which had not been the case in Australia, where from the outset, women had campaigned for full adult suffrage). For a while, she was active in the Women's Liberal Federation and supported the Union of Practical Suffragists, a group of liberal women who sought to draw out the overt support of Liberal Party members of Parliament for women's suffrage. A developing friendship with Elizabeth Wolstenholme-Elmy, however, drew her into the Pankhursts' more militant Women's Social and Political Union in 1904.

During 1898 to 1905, Montefiore contributed regularly to the radical journal the *New Age*. She became an energetic activist in London, donating her own money to the WSPU and traveling and speaking across Britain, as well as representing it at the International Woman Suffrage Alliance congress in Berlin in 1904. She worked for a WSPU branch in the East End of London, liaising closely with Annie Kenney and Sylvia Pankhurst. As a socialist, she preferred activism among the working classes to the middle-class elite of the WSPU leadership, from which she rapidly became alienated.

In 1904 and 1905 Montefiore, having been active in the Union of Practical Suffragists, took a stand on "no taxation without representation"— refusing to pay her taxes until she was given the vote—and the bailiffs confiscated her possessions. She had previously withheld her taxes in protest at income tax being used to fund the Boer War in South Africa. In May 1906, things came to a head once again, when Montefiore barricaded herself in her home against the bailiffs, beginning a six-week "siege of Hammersmith," during which the press, giving much coverage to her protest, nicknamed her home "Fort Montefiore." Eventually she capitulated: her furniture was confiscated and sold. Montefiore bought it back herself, but she was obliged to live in more modest surroundings thereafter. Later that year, Montefiore's protests landed her in trouble: she was sent to Holloway Prison in October for causing a disturbance in the House of Commons.

Having established her own personal following in London and taken an active part in major rallies and demonstrations, Montefiore found Emmeline and Christabel Pankhurst difficult to work with after they assumed a virtual dictatorship of the WSPU. She left the union in 1907, resentful at having been marginalized by them. As an advocate of passive resistance—such as through her tax resistance—she disliked the militancy of WSPU campaigning and its sexual antagonism. Her desire, as a socialist, was to see all men and women have equal political rights, and this goal prompted her to work for full adult suffrage over the age of twenty-one, rather than the women's cause exclusively. In 1907 she joined Margaret Bondfield in the Adult Suffrage Society, and in 1909 she was made its honorary secretary. She also contributed articles to the society's journal, *Justice,* and in 1912 founded the *Adult Suffragist.*

During her years of activism, Montefiore was much traveled. Fluent in several languages, she became a popular speaker at suffrage conferences in the United States and Europe, although she was often too forthright in her socialist views for the middlebrow ladies of the International Woman Suffrage Alliance. In 1914 Montefiore became a member of the British Dominions Women's Suffrage Union, which united women working for suffrage in the former colonies.

During a return visit to Sydney in 1910, Montefiore edited her son Henry's newspaper, the *International Socialist Review of Australasia,* before going back to England again in 1912. The following year, during the Dublin lockout, she devised a plan to bring the dependents of strikers to England and lodge them with working-class families for the duration. But when she attempted to send the first fifty children over, she was accused of kidnapping and had to give up the idea.

In the 1900s Montefiore had been active in the Social Democratic Federation (SDF) in England, had served on its executive committee in 1903–1905, and had written for SDF publications. In 1907 she attended the Second International as an SDF representative and represented the Adult Suffrage Society at its women's subsidiary conference. In 1907 she became a member of the Socialist International Women's Bureau, remaining until 1918, when the women's franchise was achieved. She published pamphlets for the SDF, such as "Some Words to Socialist Women" (1908), "The Position of Women in the Socialist Movement" (1909), and "Prison Reform: From a Social Democratic Point of View" (1909), but eventually became an increasingly dissident voice. In 1920 she was a founding member of the British Communist Party, which caused problems when she sought to return to Australia in 1921 upon her son's death and had to sign an agreement not to disseminate communist propaganda if allowed reentry. During her six years back in Australia, she defied the order to serve as Australian delegate to an international congress of the Communist Party in Moscow in 1924. Montefiore published her autobiography, *From a Victorian to a Modern,* in 1927. She died at Hastings, on the south coast of England.

See also Bondfield, Margaret; Kenney, Annie; Pankhurst, Christabel; Pankhurst, Emmeline; Pankhurst, (Estelle) Sylvia; Wolstenholme-Elmy, Elizabeth.

References and Further Reading

Crawford, Elizabeth. 1999. *The Women's Suffrage Movement, 1866–1928: A Reference Guide.* London: University College of London Press.

Eustance, Claire, Joan Ryan, and Laura Ugolini, eds. 2000. *A Suffrage Reader: Charting Directions in British Suffrage History.* London: Leicester University Press.

Hunt, Karen. 1996. *Equivocal Feminists: The Social Democratic Federation and the Woman Question, 1884–1911,* chap. 9. Cambridge: Cambridge University Press.

Montefiore, Dora. 1927. *From a Victorian to a Modern.* London: E. Archer.

Oldfield, Audrey. 1992. *Woman Suffrage in Australia: A Gift or a Struggle?* Melbourne: Cambridge University Press.

Pankhurst, E. Sylvia. 1977 (1931). *The Suffrage Movement: An Intimate Account of Persons and Ideals.* Reprint, London: Virago.

Montessori, Maria
(1870–1952)
Italy

The steely determination of Italian educator Maria Montessori enabled her to overcome prejudice to become the first Italian woman to qualify as a doctor and afterwards single-handedly to revolutionize teaching methods for preschool and infant children. She changed ingrained perceptions of the ineducability of abnormal or deviant children by applying scientific principles to teaching methods, thus encouraging children to use their initiative and enabling those with learning or behavioral problems to fulfill their potential.

Born in the rural town of Chiaravalle, Acona, Montessori was an only child. Her army officer father, despite his liberal sympathies, opposed his daughter seeking further education. Her mother, although strict and authoritarian, fostered these ambitions. In 1875 the family moved to Rome, where Montessori completed her education in mathematics and engineering in 1890, graduating from the Leonardo da Vinci Technical Institute. By this time, she was determined to study medicine and entered Rome University, but she was obliged thereafter to overcome the barrage of disapproval that greeted all nineteenth-century women who attempted to enter the medical profession. (Montessori would later aver that her acceptance into medical school was thanks to the personal intercession of Pope Leo XIII.) Montessori's ambition and her keen

Maria Montessori (Popperfoto/Archive Photos)

feminism kept her going when she had to be escorted to her lectures and was obliged to do dissection alone, after the male students had left. She graduated in 1894 and then extended her training further with studies and fieldwork in psychology, pedagogy, and anthropology in Rome during 1898–1899 and 1901–1903. She also collaborated on various pedagogical articles with Dr. Giuseppe Montesano, which led to a brief relationship and the birth of a son in 1899, whom she left in the care of others until he grew up. In later life, Montessori's son would work in the wider dissemination of her educational theories.

Montessori's first appointment was as an assistant doctor in Rome University's psychiatric clinic, where, through her pediatric work, she first came into contact with children with mental disabilities and realized that their slow progress as learners was exacerbated by a lack of mental and creative stimulus. Believing that such children should not be consigned to oblivion by the state and that they could be provided with some kind of rewarding education, she accepted an appointment as director of a teacher-training establishment, the State Orthophrenic School of Rome (1899–1901). Here, the success of her innovative methods testified to the ability of eight-year-old children who had been deemed "slow learners" to pass state proficiency tests.

From the late 1890s, Montessori had also written and lectured on women's issues and pacifism, the two other topics that preoccupied her. In 1899 she toured Italy with a lecture entitled "The New Woman," in which she spoke on women's sexual conditioning and their right to equal pay in the workplace. From 1899 to 1906, Montessori continued conducting her own research into psychology and education while lecturing on hygiene at a women's college in Rome. From 1900 to 1907 she lectured in pedagogy at Rome University and from 1904 to 1908, she held the post of professor of anthropology there. In 1922 she was appointed government inspector of schools.

In 1906 Montessori finally began putting her pedagogical theories into practice when she took over the Casa dei Bambini ("children's house"), a children's nursery attached to an apartment building in the slum district of San Lorenzo. The facilities had been aimlessly vandalized by the children left unattended there while their parents were at work. Montessori gathered together toys and games and refurbished the building, and in 1907 the first sixty children were admitted. Thus was established the first Montessori school, where she evolved her revolutionary teaching methods for children aged three to six based on spontaneous learning that was uncompetitive and in an environment where children were given the freedom to discover things for themselves. It was a system of learning in which children were guided but not imposed upon by teachers and in which the traditional system of inducements and punishments was outlawed. Montessori discovered that the key was to allow children to engage in work voluntarily, at their own pace, and emphasized hands-on activities that used specially designed materials such as beads, puzzles, laces, frames, and wooden shapes in various textures and colors. Employed voluntarily by children in carefully graded, repetitive activities, such objects provided the mental and creative stimulation that encouraged dexterity and trained the senses. Such was the success of the system in enabling disadvantaged children to learn to read, write, and count by the age of six that she later developed new methods for the education of older children. A second Montessori school was opened in San Lorenzo in 1907 and another in Milan a year later. Others were established in Vienna and Geneva soon after; in 1912 the first Montessori school opened in the United States, and a research institute was established in Barcelona in 1917.

Montessori devoted much time to writing up her methods in groundbreaking books such as *Method of Scientific Pedagogy* (1909) and *The Montessori Method* (1912). During the course of her travels from 1914 onward, she constantly reappraised and perfected her techniques, which were passed on to other teachers through the establishment of Montessori teacher-training schools and were widely disseminated in Europe and the United States by Montessori herself. By 1923, such was the demand for Montessori's lectures that she gave up her academic and medical careers. She became renowned as an accomplished speaker over the next twenty years, traveling widely right up until her death at the age of eighty-one. In the last ten years of her life, she spent much time in India, where she was interned as an enemy alien during World War II.

During World War I, Montessori had become a leading pacifist, convinced that militarism was a social ill; that a harmonious society could only be built on peace, love, and justice; and that education had an important role to play in imparting such spiritual values. Her opposition to Benito Mussolini's fascist regime forced her to leave Italy in 1934, after which many of the Montessori schools were closed down. Thereafter, she lived in Spain and Sri Lanka before finally settling in the Netherlands, remaining active in the peace movement, giving lectures at the League of Nations, the International Bureau of Education, and the International Peace Congress in Brussels in 1936. She was honored by having two International Montessori Congresses on Peace and Education named after her in Copenhagen in 1937 and in San Remo, Italy, in 1949. Some of her peace lectures were collected as *Education and Peace* (1949).

After the war, Montessori reestablished the Montessori movement in Italy in 1947. Her later writings on education were also considerable, including *The Advanced Montessori Method* (1917–1918), *The Secret of Childhood* (1936), *Education for a New World* (1946), and *To Educate the Human Potential* (1948). Montessori was nominated for a Nobel Prize in 1949, 1950, and 1951. The Maria Montessori organization can be contacted at www.montessori.org.

References and Further Reading

Fynne, Robert John. 1924. *Montessori and Her Inspirers.* London: Longman's Green.

Josephson, Harold, Sandi Cooper, and Steven C. Hause et al., eds. 1985. *Biographical Dictionary of Modern Peace Leaders.* Westport, CT: Greenwood Press.

Kramer, Rita. 1989. *Maria Montessori: A Biography.* London: Montessori International.

Standing, E. M. 1957. *Maria Montessori: Her Life and Work.* London: Hollis and Carter.

More, Hannah
(1745–1833)
United Kingdom

The conservative moralist Hannah More was a prolific writer of religious tracts and homilies that were primary teaching aids in improving literacy levels of the poor. In her time, she was considered an oracle on many social and political issues. A contemporary of Mary Wollstonecraft, she offered a reactionary response to the arguments set out in favor of women's emancipation by her, arguing that women had no rights but many duties. Their education should be purely functional, she believed—to instruct them in their spiritual and domestic obligations in order that they might sustain the integrity and stability of the family. Similarly, More's own attempts to improve the elementary education of poor children were geared at promoting acceptance of their lot; she considered that the poor, like women, should learn the virtues of submission to their elders and betters. For all these obvious reasons she has come under considerable attack, and sometimes demonization, in the feminist writings of the second wave.

More was born at Fishponds in the parish of Stapleton, near Bristol. Her father was headmaster of a free school and intended his children to be educated in order to be self-supporting. After being taught Latin and mathematics at home, she attended the Misses More's boarding school in Bristol, run by her elder sisters, and proved to be an able linguist, mastering French, Italian, and Spanish. She went on to teach at the school herself and became engaged to William Turner in 1767. However, after a six-year wait, during which the bridegroom twice postponed the wedding and on a third occasion left the bride literally waiting at the church, he finally withdrew and compensated More with an allowance of £200 a year, which gave her financial independence.

As a result of this experience, by now determined never to marry, More took up a literary career. She began writing poetry and plays in 1773 and moved to London around this time. She was quickly accepted into social and literary circles, frequenting the famous Bluestocking salon of Elizabeth Montagu (which she later celebrated in a famous narrative poem of 1786, *The Bas Bleu, or Conversation*). There she regularly conversed with eminent figures, such as the actor-manager David Garrick, writer and critic Samuel Johnson, painter Joshua Reynolds, and historian Edmund Burke. Garrick produced two of her plays, *The Inflexible Captive* (1774) and *Percy* (1777), at the Covent Garden Theatre, but after he died in 1779, the year she wrote *The Fatal Falsehood,* More retreated from the theater to the bucolic environment of her cottage at Cowslip Green in Somerset to concentrate on more pious and philanthropic enterprises. In later life, as a guardian of public morals, she regretted her early connections with the worldliness of literary and thespian life.

In her new life, More became a supporter of abolition through her friendship with leading abolitionist William Wilberforce, which in turn drew her into the evangelical movement and a group of wealthy evangelicals and abolitionists known as the Clapham Sect. She was particularly aware of slavery through the slave trade still in existence via the port of Bristol, witnessing slaves in chains being unloaded from ships as they docked. In support of Wilberforce's abolition bill, she wrote exhortatory poems such as "The Slave Trade," in which she upheld the civil liberties of slaves and urged Britain to lead the world in abolishing the practice. She continued writing on the subject in the religious and moral tracts that she turned out beginning in 1778.

After her return to Somerset, much of More's time was taken up with relieving the widespread poverty of the mining villages of the Mendip Hills and Cheddar Gorge and setting up new schools for working-class children. Together with her sisters, she visited poor cottagers in their homes and workhouses, of which latter she asserted: "I believe I see more misery in a week than some people believe exists in the whole world" (Collingwood and Collingwood 1990, 74). She also launched what became known as the Mendip Scheme, a program to further elementary education, philanthropic work, and the establishment of industrial and domestic training schemes for the poor throughout the area. The More sisters proceeded to set up numerous institutions in these villages: Sunday schools offering lessons in reading and the scriptures; reading classes for young adults; and Women's Friendly Societies, which through their subscription schemes offered welfare benefits to the sick and nursing mothers and financial help with funerals. There were also austere day schools for illiterate poor children, where they were taught little more than to read the Bible and to understand their duty to their social superiors. More's schools did not teach the potentially inflammatory skill of writing, and she believed that the poor should not be educated beyond the requirements of a life in agriculture or domestic service. Once a year, large Mendip feasts were held, where the poor would be provided with as much food as they could eat. In Cheddar, More set up a school in a rented house at her own expense, offering Sunday school to 120 local children, evening classes in reading to young adults, and weekday school for thirty girls, where they were taught vocational skills such as sewing, spinning, and knitting. Similar schemes were run at the nearby villages Shipham, Nailsea, and Blagdon.

Yet even though More's day schools offered the most limited of daily curricula, she was often criticized and held under suspicion for seeking to educate the working classes above their station. Local farmers were often hostile to her work in the belief that the poor were incorrigibly wicked and ignorant and that by educating them, More was encouraging them to seek better jobs outside agriculture. This resentment finally boiled over at Blagdon in 1798, where the local curate, who also opposed her work, brought a trumped-up charge against a teacher at the school, accusing him of using his evening classes at the school as an unregistered base for fostering local dissenters (Calvinists and Methodists). After three years of quarrels and increasing acrimony, during which More was accused of fomenting both religious and political dissent in her schools, she was finally forced to close down the Blagdon school and threatened to close the others as well.

During the 1790s, More also produced a huge body of writing, turning out important tracts critical of public morality in "Thoughts on the Importance of the Manners of the Great to General Society" (1788) and "An Estimate of the Religion of the Fashionable World" (1790), both aimed primarily at the upper classes. But it was in her series of homilies for the poor, which preached clean living and piety, that she found her audience. In their rebuttal of Thomas Paine's *Rights of Man* (1791–1792) and its inflammatory remarks on individual liberty, which she saw as a worrying incitement to revolution, More emphasized that the poor were best kept firmly in their place, drilled into acceptance of their lot, and controlled by firm but benevolent landowners. The success of tracts such as "Village Politics," published under the pseudonym of Will Chip (1792), which was circulated in great numbers in Scotland and Ireland, sparked a series of 114 proselytizing *Cheap Repository Tracts*. During 1795–1798, More wrote fifty of them, and her sisters and supporters composed the rest, which were edited by More and marketed as reading texts for the poor.

In their day, the best known of these, such as "The Shepherd of Salisbury Plain" (1795), were welcomed as a novel means of accessing the social and religious consciences of the working classes. They were sold in the thousands at a halfpenny or penny each, often by itinerant hawkers, and proved to be the only "literature" found in the homes of many poor cottagers. More also used them as reading texts in her Sunday schools. Although More initially rued what she perceived as the artistic vulgarity of these tracts, which she felt were a poor substitute for her previous literary endeavors, as a pragmatist she believed that if she were to get her moral message across, she should write to suit the needs of her readers. The tracts, stories, and ballads, with their homiletic titles such as "The Story of Sinful Sally," "The Contented Cobbler and His Wife," and "The Riot, or Half a Loaf Is Better Than No Bread," tackled serious issues such as prostitution, popular superstition, and urban crime and promoted the virtues of religious observance and honest labor. The series achieved huge sales of reportedly 2 million, as a result of which the Religious Tract Society was founded.

Of particular interest to modern feminists have been More's evangelical arguments on the education of girls, outlined in her major 1799 work, *Strictures on the Modern System of Female Education,* a publication that quickly went through nine editions in two years and sold 19,000 copies. In it More, while stressing the importance of a good education for women, was dismissive of their being taught what she viewed as useless or frivolous accomplishments (such as singing and playing the piano) that could not be put to practical use in the home; as wives and mothers, their primary role was to provide a good moral example to their children. She emphasized the importance of history, logic, and religious instruction, subjects that would set examples and be formative of good habits and virtues such as humility and, above all, diligence. Young women from privileged backgrounds should, in her view, also allot a proportion of every day to charitable and philanthropic work. She also recommended firm parental controls being kept on young women's behavior, in order to eradicate the propensity to impetuosity and emotional outburst that More felt characterized the weak and foolish sides of the female nature. Because of such weaknesses, she argued that women should accept their role as subordinate to the loftier-minded male and confine themselves to the strictly domestic sphere. More's moralistic 1809 novel, *Coelebs in Search of a Wife,* would set the standard of the dutiful, domestic wife in her heroine Lucilla Stanley, a further denial of women's right to equality with men.

In 1801 More and her sisters settled in a house at Barley Wood near Wrington, where More set up a branch of the British and Foreign Bible Society and spent her remaining years engaged in religious and political writings, such as her *Moral Sketches* of 1819. By this time, her home had become a place of pilgrimage for evangelicals, the aristocracy, and fellow writers such as William Wordsworth and Samuel Coleridge. More continued to visit the poor and her schools at Cheddar, Shipham, and Nailsea, and gave large amounts of money to local charities. After all her younger sisters died, she moved to Bristol, where she died at the age of eighty-eight, leaving £30,000 in her will—a testament to her considerable earnings as a writer. An interesting reassessment of More's tracts by Julia Saunders, which views them as a valuable teaching aid drawn from accessible popular culture to which their readers could relate, can be found at http://www.users.ox.ac.uk~scat0385/more.html.

See also Wollstonecraft, Mary.

References and Further Reading

Collingwood, Jeremy, and Margaret Collingwood. 1990. *Hannah More.* Oxford: Lion Publishing.

Demers, Patricia. 1996. *The World of Hannah More.* Lexington: University Press of Kentucky.

Ford, Charles H. 1996. *Hannah More: A Critical Biography.* New York: P. Lang.

Hopkins, Mary Alden. 1947. *Hannah More and Her Circle.* New York: Longman's, Green.

Jones, M. G. 1952. *Hannah More.* Cambridge: Cambridge University Press.

Kowaleski-Wallace, Elizabeth. 1991. *Their Fathers' Daughters: Hannah More, Maria Edgeworth, and Patriarchal Complicity.* Oxford: Oxford University Press.

Krueger, Christine L. 1992. *The Reader's Repentance: Women Preachers, Women Writers, and Nineteenth-Century Social Discourse.* Chicago: University of Chicago Press.

More, Hannah. 1995 [1799]. *Strictures on the Modern System of Female Education.* Edited by Gina Luria. Oxford: Woodstock Books.

Prochaska, F. K. 1980. *Women and Philanthropy in Nineteenth-Century England.* Oxford: Clarendon Press.

Schofield, Mary Anne, and Celia Macheski. 1986. *Fetter'd or Free? British Women Novelists, 1670–1815.* Athens: Ohio University Press.

Moreau de Justo, Alicia
(1885–1986)
Argentina

One of Argentina's most distinguished and long-lived feminists and socialists, Alicia Moreau de Justo was a doctor, teacher, socialist activist, and journalist and was closely involved in the foundation of several human and women's rights organizations. She has come to be viewed not only as a seminal figure in the first wave of the Latin American women's movement but also as a reformer who was ahead of her time. She was closely associated with two Argentine women's associations: the Feminist Center and the National Feminist Union.

Moreau was born in London, where her French socialist parents had been exiled after the fall of the Paris Commune in 1871. The family emigrated to Argentina in 1890, where Moreau's father worked as a journalist and Socialist Party activist. In her teens, the young Alicia helped set up the Feminist Socialist Center with her socialist friends Fenia Chertkoff de Repetto and Gabriela Laperrière de Coni. The center ran child care and hygiene programs and campaigned against prostitution. In 1906 Moreau's embryonic social concerns found a forum in membership in the Argentine Association of Free Thought.

Along with three other Argentine feminist pioneers in the field of medicine and public health—Julieta Lanteri-Renshaw, Elvira Rawson de Dellepiane, and Cecilia Grierson—Moreau braved male opposition and studied medicine at the University of Buenos Aires. She graduated with distinction in 1914. During 1917–1919 she taught natural sciences, psychology, and anatomy at the University of La Plata, but by then she had already begun conducting health clinics for working-class women and collaborating with other feminists on educational projects. In all of her work, Moreau would emphasize the importance of the collective effort over and above the individual ego and would grow to dislike those feminists, such as Lanteri-Renshaw, whom she considered to be self-seeking and unwilling to subordinate themselves to collective work.

In 1911 Moreau published the first of many articles and pamphlets in publications such as the *International Socialist Review.* In her study *Feminism in Social Evolution,* she outlined the growing need for women to take their place in industrialized society, arguing that they had a crucial role to play both in the workplace and in the home. She was of the view that women's education should take precedence over other political demands. Once they had achieved better levels of education, they could argue for greater civil and political equality. In 1919 she published *The Civil Emancipation of Women,* in which she attacked the traditional cosseting of women and their lack of social and psychological freedom. Believing that women should not wait for political change but should organize themselves, in 1918 Moreau became president of the newly founded National Feminist Union, and a year later established its journal *Our Cause,* which became a forum for debate among all feminist groups.

In 1920 she founded the Women's Pro-Suffrage Committee, which aimed to involve working-class women in the drive for suffrage and reform of the civil code. Embarking on a long, tiring, and largely unrewarding campaign, she traveled South America on and off for the next twenty years attempting to raise social awareness among women. She also made frequent trips

Alicia Moreau de Justo (Karen Daniels)

abroad to attend and give papers at conferences, such as the International Congress of Women Workers in Washington, D.C. (of which she became honorary vice president), and the International Congress of Women Physicians in New York. At both of these, her mission was to help working mothers obtain access to better day care centers for their children, maternity rights, equal pay, and a maximum working week of forty-four hours. In 1924 legislation was introduced in Argentina that fulfilled some of Moreau's objectives, with women's workweek being limited to forty-eight hours maximum and a ban on night work for girls under eighteen.

In 1921 Moreau joined the Socialist Party. She would remain loyal to the socialist cause for the rest of her life. In 1922 she married another doctor, the Socialist Party's leader, Juan B. Justo, who had founded the party in 1896. The two of them became the party's leading light, although he died after they had been married only four years. In 1927 the Justos set up the famous socialist and cultural center the Casa del Pueblo (which was closed down by Juan Perón in 1953).

Since becoming a member of the Argentine League of Social Prophylaxis, which had been founded in 1919, Moreau had been a leading campaigner for sex education as the fundamental means of controlling the transmission of sexual disease. Like Paulina Luisi in Uruguay, she saw sexual behavior as a major social issue of the day and sought ways of educating people against the spread of venereal disease by teaching more responsible sexual behavior and a clearer understanding of biological functions. Her attitudes toward these issues were colored by her espousal of eugenics, although she opposed outright social control of human reproduction, favoring instead a systematic assault on ingrained attitudes about sexual behavior combined with emancipation of women in the civil and political spheres.

At the Congress of Women Physicians, Moreau had raised the subjects of prostitution and the white slave trade in Buenos Aires and the need for sex education in the schools and in the army. For her, women's suffrage was the primary means to obtain all objectives relating to social reform, and she enlisted the support of eminent American suffrage leaders such as Carrie Chapman Catt in lobbying the Argentine Chamber of Deputies for women's enfranchisement. In support of the Latin American women's campaign for suffrage, Catt was instrumental in setting up the groundbreaking first Pan-American Women's Congress held in Baltimore 1922, after which she toured South America.

In 1930, still fighting for the vote long after it had been granted to many women elsewhere in the world, Moreau founded the Socialist Women's Suffrage Committee, but by this time the socialists had fallen afoul of the new military regime in Argentina, led by General José Uriburu. The public failed to respond to the committee's campaign, and a public poll underlined the general belief among women in Buenos Aires in 1932 that suffrage should be extended to them only on a limited basis. In a 1931 pamphlet, "Socialism and the Woman," Moreau opposed the limited form of women's suffrage linked to property ownership that had been suggested. On this point, she refused to compromise and disagreed with her sister-in-law, Sara Justo (herself a leading socialist and founder of the Association of Argentine University Women), who supported a qualified form of suffrage and believed that illiterate women should be excluded from the vote. Indeed, Moreau considered such a compromise antipathetic to her late husband's (and Sara's brother's) socialist ideals.

Moreau remained at the forefront of socialist activities, in 1934 joining the board of the mainly male socialist organization Argentine Action. During the 1940s and 1950s, she remained fiercely anti-Peronist, despite Juan Perón's vote-winning promises for women's suffrage (granted in 1946), promoted on his behalf among working-class women by his wife Eva. Moreau remained cynical, as did many other middle-class feminists, about Perón's crude appeal to nationalism and his manipulation of his wife Eva's popularity with the working classes to his own political end. But she and other feminist critics of Juan Perón would be condemned for their failure to recognize the greatness of his leadership. Moreau remained highly critical of Argentine politics during this period and exposed the misuse of the vote by male politicians, joining with other opposition groups in denouncing political corruption. She unashamedly stood by her conviction that women, if given the chance, would occupy a higher moral ground in politics and be a civilizing force across all society: "Feminism is not an isolated issue. . . . Even though it signifies the emancipation of woman, it cannot refer to her alone; to elevate the woman is to elevate the child, the man, the family, and humanity" (Lavrin 1995, 35).

From the outset of her career until the 1970s, Moreau contributed to many Argentine journals, such as *Feminine Life,* a socialist magazine of the 1920s, and led the debate on suffrage during the 1940s in the national socialist daily, *The Vanguard,* and its women's supplement, *The Women's Vanguard* (becoming editor of *The Vanguard* in 1956–1962). She also contributed on a regular basis to the journal *New Humanity.*

In 1975 Moreau, by then a major figure in human rights campaigning in Argentina, joined with the radical politician Raúl Alfonsin in setting up a watchdog group to monitor the abuse of human rights under a succession of repressive military juntas. Between 1978 and her death in 1986, Moreau served as codirector of the Argentine Permanent Assembly for Human Rights (Alfonsin subsequently became president of Argentina from 1983 to 1989). In 1970 Moreau was awarded the Venus Dorada by the Feminist Circle of Buenos Aires for her long career in women's rights campaigning, and in 1984 she was named Woman of the Year and Physician of the Century in Argentina.

Moreau wrote several important books on socialism and women's rights: *The Civil Emancipation of Woman* (1919), *Feminism in Social Evolution* (1911), *Women in Democracy* (1945), *Socialism According to the Definition of Juan B. Justo* (1946), and *What Is Socialism in Argentina?* (1983). She also taught psychology for thirty years and was a respected academic in this field.

See also Catt, Carrie Chapman; Chertkoff de Repetto, Fenia; Grierson, Cecilia; Lanteri-Renshaw, Julieta; Laperrière de Coni, Gabriela; Luisi, Paulina; Perón, Eva; Rawson de Dellepiane, Elvira.

References and Further Reading

The Annual Obituary. 1986. New York: St. Martin's Press.

Carlson, Narifran. 1988. *Feminismo! The Woman's Movement in Argentina from Its Beginnings to Eva Perón.* Chicago: Academy Chicago Publications.

Lavrin, Asunción. 1995. *Women, Feminism, and Social Change in Argentina, Chile, and Uruguay 1890–1940.* Lincoln: University of Nebraska Press.

Tenenbaum, Barbara A., ed. 1996. *Encyclopedia of Latin American History and Culture.* Vol 4. New York: Charles Scribner's Sons.

Mother Teresa (Archive Photos)

Mother Teresa
(1910–1997)
Albania/India

An Albanian nun who devoted her life to working among the sick and poor of Calcutta, Mother Teresa built up a worldwide order of more than 3,000 Missionaries of Charity in eighty-seven countries and was revered as a living "saint of the gutters"; her elevation to official sainthood now awaits the approval of the Roman Catholic Church. Everything about Mother Teresa's outward frailty—the diminutive, stooped figure and the soft voice—belied a resilience and tenacity that enabled her to serve Indian people during a long life of rigorous self-denial in some of the world's worst slums.

Mother Teresa's deep and unshakeable sense of vocation was engendered at an early age. Born Agnes Gonxha Bojaxhiu, the daughter of an ethnic Albanian merchant who lived in Skopje, Macedonia, she was inspired by the work of Yugoslav Jesuits in India as a young girl and had already decided by the age of twelve that she wanted to serve the church. When she was eighteen, she traveled to Ireland to enter the novitiate and then left for Calcutta, where she joined the Sisters of Loreto—an Irish order established in India since the 1840s—and spent the next eighteen years teaching geography and history at a convent school for the daughters of the Bengali elite.

In 1946, divine revelation changed the course of Mother Teresa's life and work, when she heard the voice of God calling her to go and work with the underprivileged. She undertook some rudimentary medical training in Paris and, with modest financial backing from an Indian Catholic businessman, took up the nursing of the sick and dying in Calcutta's slums. By 1948 Mother Teresa had gathered around her a group of acolytes, and in 1950 she became an Indian citizen. She established her own order, the Missionaries of Charity, who soon became familiar for their adoption of an adapted form of the Indian sari. Two years later, she set up a hospice for the dying and in 1957 a leper colony known as the "Town of Peace." In 1965 the order finally opened its first branch, in Venezuela.

Mother Teresa always made a point of underlining the fact that she was but the instrument of divine will in all her philanthropic work: "By blood and origin I am all Albanian. My citizenship is Indian. I am a Catholic nun. As to my calling, I belong to the whole world. As to my heart, I belong entirely to the heart of Jesus" (obituary, *Independent,* 6 September 1997, 11). Her order, despite its humanitarian concerns, remained primarily a religious one. In 1965 the Pope promoted it to the status of a pontifical congregation.

Mother Teresa might have continued her life of good works in pious obscurity had it not been for her discovery by the media in 1970, after the British broadcaster Malcolm Muggeridge made a documentary about her work in Calcutta, entitled *Something Beautiful for God.* In 1973, the award to Mother Teresa of the first Templeton Prize for Religion enabled her to donate all £34,000 of the prize money to fund her work with the order and expand its operation. She began opening up missions in major cities and countries around the world and found herself looked upon as something of an international guru on the plight of the underprivileged.

In her lifetime, this modest, dedicated humanitarian was heaped with awards, including the Pope John XXIII Peace Prize in 1971, the Nobel Peace Prize in 1979, and the British Order of Merit in 1983. She extended her work to help the victims of the Bhopal chemical disaster of 1984 and those suffering from acquired immunodeficiency syndrome (AIDS). Yet despite such heartfelt dedication, Mother Teresa was not without her critics during, and even more so after, her lifetime. Many were suspicious that beneath the humility and self-denial there lurked the makings of a personality cult. Her detractors cited the contradictions between her own work and her opposition to other women working, as well as her fervent condemnation of divorce, abortion, and artificial contraception. In a radio interview in 1983, she stated: "I would not give a baby from one of my homes for adoption to a couple who use contraception. People who use contraceptives do not understand love." Her critics meanwhile argued that such remarks flew in the face of the abject misery brought on by overpopulation and overcrowding that she herself witnessed day in and day out in her work in the overrun slums of Calcutta.

Mother Teresa was forced to relinquish her leadership as superior general of the Missionaries of Charity in 1996 because of heart problems.

After her death, she was accorded a grand state funeral by the Indian authorities. Her loss came only days after the death of her admirer and fellow humanitarian, Diana, Princess of Wales, who had herself visited Mother Teresa at her mission a short time before her own death. Within weeks, the mythologizing of Mother Teresa's life and works had begun, with the release of a U.S. television movie entitled *Mother Teresa: In the Name of God's Poor.* In the meantime, her Missionaries of Charity in Calcutta have been criticized for placing limits on Mother's Teresa's own unqualified and unconditional charity by turning some people away from their doors. Without the firm, if not dictatorial, leadership of its charismatic founder, the Home for the Destitute and Dying is now coming under fire over its effective role in mitigating poverty and disease. And the revisionists have begun work on Mother Teresa's own reputation, suggesting that she accepted financial support from dubious figures such as Haitian dictator "Baby Doc" Duvalier and business tycoon Robert Maxwell. Meanwhile, claims of miracles associated with her name have already been submitted for Vatican approval, as a preliminary to what her admirers see as her inevitable elevation to the sainthood, which the Congregation for the Causes of Saints continues to deliberate in the Vatican. The official Mother Teresa website is www.tisv.be/mt/indmt.

References and Further Reading

Doig, Desmond. 1976. *Mother Teresa: Her People and Her Work.* London: Collins.

Mother Teresa. 1975. *A Gift for God.* London: Collins.

Sebba, Anna. 1997. *Mother Teresa: Beyond the Image.* London: Weidenfeld.

Spink, Kathryn. 1997. *Mother Teresa: An Authorised Biography.* London: HarperCollins.

Mott, Lucretia Coffin
(1793–1880)
United States

One of the much-loved and revered pioneers of the women's movement in the United States, the Quaker abolitionist and feminist Lucretia Mott was the guiding light, with Elizabeth Cady Stanton, of the landmark 1848 Seneca Falls Convention on Women's Rights. A woman of quiet good humor, Mott was earnest and dignified in her lifelong commitment to racial and women's equality. She could outface the rudest and most belligerent of critics, as well as the bigotry of members of her own Quaker community, in her defense of women's intellectual equality and their right to a place in active public life. She also became a respected international figure, through whom, as Margaret McFadden (1999) has shown, ongoing links between feminists in the United States and Europe were firmly established. Meeting her on a trip to the United States in 1857, the English feminist Barbara Bodichon remarked that she was "'full of grace' in every sense of the word. I do not wonder her preaching has stirred so many souls, her aspect is eloquent, her smile full of good things" (McFadden 1999, 26).

Born in Nantucket, Massachusetts, where her father worked on the whaling ships of the Atlantic Ocean, Mott spent her early years under the influence of her mother and female neighbors during her father's long absences at sea, thus instilling in her an unshakable conviction in women's equality with men. The family moved inland in 1804, and from the age of thirteen, Mott was educated at the Society of Friends' Nine Partners boarding school near Poughkeepsie, New York. She stayed on there as an unpaid teacher to pay the tuition of her younger sister. After discovering that female teachers at the school were paid only half the salary of male ones, Mott became an advocate of women teachers' right to equal pay.

In 1811 Lucretia married James Mott, a fellow teacher, and moved to Philadelphia, where the couple reared six children. As members of the more liberally minded Hicksite Quaker faction, the couple were mutually supportive in shared causes, and James eventually gave up his commission business because it made money from slave-produced cotton. Having natural gifts as an orator, Lucretia became a regular speaker at Quaker meetings from 1818 and in 1821 was ordained a minister. She began touring and lecturing on abolitionism, urging a boycott of slave-produced sugar and cotton and in 1829 speaking for the first time in black churches.

Mott attended the founding convention of the American Anti-Slavery Society (AASS), held by William Lloyd Garrison in 1833, but like all the other women present, she was not allowed to formally join. Later that year, the AASS changed its policy on women's exclusion, and Mott and several other women, seven of them free blacks, together founded a women's branch of the society

Lucretia Coffin Mott (Library of Congress)

in Philadelphia, with Mott as president. In May 1838 she and other women abolitionists had to run the gauntlet of mob violence, when they staged the first Anti-Slavery Convention of American Women, again held in Philadelphia. The baying crowds outside, accusing the convention's mixed audience of men and women, whites and blacks, of "promiscuity" for meeting together, only served to reinforce Mott's conviction that there were direct parallels between the slavery of blacks and the oppression of women. She would lay out her arguments on the subject in her 1840 pamphlet, "Slavery and 'The Woman Question.'"

When the American Anti-Slavery Society held its annual meeting in 1840, Mott was given a role in its administration by Garrison, along with Lydia Maria Child and Abby Kelly Foster. Several male members of the society walked out of the meeting in protest, and Mott would thereafter frequently be accused by conservatives in the Quaker movement of having "fanned the flames of dissension" (Spender 1982, 202) and of demoralizing the antislavery ranks by raising the issue of women's public participation. In London later that year for the World Anti-Slavery Convention, Mott, Stanton, and five other women who had traveled from the United States again found themselves banned from taking part in the proceedings. Refused the right to sit on the main convention floor as delegates, they were obliged to secrete themselves in the balcony at the back of the hall, screened behind a curtain.

During the convention, Stanton was deeply impressed by Mott, who introduced her to the English feminist Mary Wollstonecraft's *A Vindication of the Rights of Woman,* long sections of which Mott knew by heart. The two women struck up a lifelong friendship, and Stanton would later describe Mott as being "an entirely new revelation of womanhood" to her (Bacon 1980, 108). By the end of the convention, incensed by their segregation as women, Mott and Stanton returned to the United States determined to foster their own separate movement for women's rights and to set up a convention to discuss the subject.

Family and other commitments, however, prevented Mott and Stanton from bringing their plan to fruition until eight years later. In the intervening period, Mott was active in a range of causes: she spoke for abolition in the legislatures of Delaware, New Jersey, and Pennsylvania; inspired the establishment of the Northern Association for the Relief of Poor Women; and also defended the rights of striking handloom workers. She even had the courage to criticize her own Quaker community, protesting its attempts to impose changes on the traditional life of the local Seneca peoples.

In 1848 Lucretia Mott's name went down in the history books when she and Stanton finally organized the Seneca Falls Convention on Women's Rights—the first of its kind to be held in the United States. Mott also helped to draft the convention's manifesto, the now-famous *Declaration of Sentiments and Resolutions.* On the final day of its discussion, Mott also spoke on the right of women to take up the ministry and proposed "the overthrow of the monopoly of the pulpit" (Helsinger, Sheets, and Veeder 1983, 180). When the resolutions were finally voted on, Mott withheld her approval of resolution nine on women's suffrage for religious reasons. It was a fundamental Quaker principle at that time to boycott the vote until the U.S. government ended slavery. Like other Quaker women, Mott upheld this principle, although she would later modify her position on women's suffrage.

From Seneca Falls until her death, Mott re-mained a revered figure in the women's movement in the United States, as she traveled from one women's rights convention to another. In 1850 she published her "Discourse on Woman," in which she exposed the long-standing inequalities women had suffered legally and politically, most particularly in education and employment, and argued for their equality with husbands within marriage. During the 1850s, she traveled as a Quaker minister, and her advocacy of women's rights and equality in marriage was constantly reiterated in her sermons. Mott also made visits to prisons and mental asylums, throughout all of her campaigning being given unquestioning support by her husband, who joined her in her travels. Their harmonious life together became living confirmation of Mott's belief that "in the true relationship, the independence of the husband and wife is equal, their dependence mutual, and their obligations reciprocal" (Bacon 1980, 112).

The 1850s also marked Mott's increasing involvement with abolition in the lead-up to the Civil War. With the passing of the 1850 Fugitive Slave Act, the Motts' home was used as a staging post for the Underground Railroad, and during the war, as a pacifist, she continued to promote nonresistance and the rights of conscientious objectors, as well as organizing aid. Mott remained a powerful moral force during the war, in 1863 helping to found the Woman's National Loyal League, which had as its objective passage of a constitutional amendment outlawing slavery. In the wake of the subsequent passage of the Thirteenth Amendment, Mott became caught up in the debate on black suffrage. She supported the awarding of the vote to male blacks and their access to better education through the Friends Association of Philadelphia for the Aid and Elevation of the Freedman. She joined the American Equal Rights Association in 1866 to campaign not just against racial intolerance but also for suffrage and civil rights for *all* Americans, including the right of women to divorce if their marriage was oppressive. Mott often took on the role of mediator between opposing factions in both the abolitionist and women's movements. In 1869, after presiding at the first convention of the National Woman Suffrage Association (NWSA), she attempted to prevent the suffrage movement from splitting into the two factions of NWSA and the American Woman Suffrage Association. Similarly, she encouraged religious tolerance when, in 1867, she became a cofounder in Boston with other liberal Christians and Jews of the Free Religious Association.

As a Quaker, Mott supported the Society of Friends' "Testimony of Peace," which repudiated all violence and war, as well as all forms of coercive government. In 1839 she had become a member of the New England Non-Resistance Society and stayed true to her belief in nonresistance when faced with hostility and mob violence during abolitionist conventions. During the Civil War, despite giving moral support to John Brown's militant abolitionism, she had abhorred the violence of his actions at Harper's Ferry. After the war, she and Alfred Love cofounded the Universal Peace Union and Pennsylvania Peace Society, with Mott serving the former as vice president from 1870 and the latter as president until her death.

Such was her reputation that even during her lifetime Mott would be heralded as the grandmother of the women's movement. Elizabeth Cady Stanton defined her as "a woman emancipated from all faith in man-made creeds, from all fear of his denunciations" (Stanton, Anthony, and Gage 1881, I: 420). She continued to attend Quaker, women's rights, and suffrage conventions until her death, making her last public appearance at a Quaker convention in 1880 at the age of eighty-seven.

In 1923, Alice Paul of the National Woman's Party, who had led the campaign for a federal equal rights amendment, named it the Lucretia Mott Amendment in Mott's honor, when it finally reached Congress. Thereafter, with a determination true to Mott's example, she lobbied for it in Congress every year it was debated, until it was finally passed in 1972 (although it failed to be ratified by 1981).

See also Bodichon, Barbara; Child, Lydia Maria; Foster, Abby (Abigail) Kelley; Paul, Alice; Stanton, Elizabeth Cady; Wollstonecraft, Mary.

References and Further Reading
Bacon, Margaret Hope. 1980. *Valiant Friend: The Life of Lucretia Mott.* New York: Walker.
Cromwell, Otelia. 1971 [1958]. *Lucretia Mott.* Reprint, New York: Russell and Russell.
Flexner, Eleanor. 1975 [1959]. *A Century of Struggle: The Woman's Rights Movement in the United States.* Rev. ed. Cambridge, MA: Belknap Press of Harvard University.
Frost, Elizabeth, and Kathryn Cullen DuPont. 1992. *Women's Suffrage in America: An Eyewitness History.* New York: Facts on File.
Greene, Diana, ed. 1980. *Lucretia Mott: Her Complete Speeches and Sermons.* New York: Edwin Mellen Press.
Halbersleben, Karen I. 1993. *Women's Participation in the British Antislavery Movement 1824–1865.* Lewiston: Edwin Mellen Press.
Helsinger, Elizabeth K., Robin Lauterbach Sheets, and William Veeder. 1983. *The Woman Question: Social Issues, 1837–1883,* vol. 2, *Society and Literature in Britain and America, 1837–1883.* Manchester: Manchester University Press.
Hersch, Blanche G. 1978. *Slavery of Sex: Feminist Abolitionists in America.* Urbana: University of Illinois Press.
McFadden, Margaret. 1999. *Golden Cables of Sympathy: The Transatlantic Sources of Nineteenth-Century Feminism.* Lexington: University Press of Kentucky.
Melder, Keith E. 1977. *The Beginnings of Sisterhood: The American Woman's Rights Movement, 1800–1850.* New York: Schocken.
Spender, Dale. 1982. *Women of Ideas, and What Men Have Done to Them.* London: Routledge and Kegan Paul.
Stanton, Elizabeth Cady, Susan B. Anthony, and Matilda Joslyn Gage. 1881. *History of Woman Suffrage.* Vol. 1. New York: Fowler and Wells.
Sterling, Dorothy. 1964. *Lucretia Mott: Gentle Warrior.* Garden City, NY: Doubleday.
Taylor, Clare. 1974. *British and American Abolitionists: An Episode in Transatlantic Understanding.* Edinburgh: Edinburgh University Press.
Weatherford, Doris. 1998. *A History of the American Suffragist Movement.* Santa Barbara, CA: ABC-CLIO.

Mozzoni, Anna Maria
(1837–1920)
Italy

An inheritor of the Mazzinian spirit of democracy in *Risorgimento* Italy, Anna Mozzoni was a focal figure in emergent Italian feminism in the nineteenth century, producing many pamphlets and articles on women's issues during a period of forty years, yet never managing to draw the disparate strands of women's activism together into one consolidated movement. She was an outspoken critic of the stultifying life of the married woman, and considered women's rights to be an essential element of Italian nationhood, since it was their especial qualities that improved society. She sought reform of family law under the civil code of 1865 and joined Josephine Butler's international campaign against state-regulated prostitution.

Mozzoni was the daughter of a middle-class architect and grew up in Milan, educated from five to fourteen at a school for the daughters of the impoverished gentry. Her mother encouraged her interest in culture and literature, and Mozzoni read the novels of George Sand and the works of the French social theorist François Fourier.

The creation of a unified Italian state in 1861 finally brought with it a more favorable climate in which Italian women, encouraged by the support for women's emancipation of Giuseppe Garibaldi and Giuseppe Mazzini, placed great hopes in the acquisition of equal civil rights under a new civil code, introduced in 1865. Prompted by these developments, Mozzoni published the first critique of women's social position in Italy in 1864 with her groundbreaking work, *Woman and Her Social Relationships*. In it, she despaired at the lack of interest Italian women seemed to demonstrate in the social injustices they suffered and at their treatment as second-class citizens. She criticized her sex for its complacency, for meekly submitting to man-made laws without demanding a say in the making of them. Women, she argued, paid their taxes, and many worked to support their families—drudging in underpaid jobs to the point of ill health and exhaustion and often forced into prostitution as a last resort. She was appalled at the willingness with which middle-class women lived idle, useless lives, uncritically accepting the soft option of marriage, which in her view only perpetuated their low status and the atrophying of their intellects and sense of self-worth.

During the course of revisions of the civil code, Mozzoni engaged in detailed discussions with other women on its content, drawing inspiration from John Stuart Mills's 1869 work, *The Subjection of Women*, which she translated into Italian. In 1869 she began corresponding with Josephine Butler on state-regulated prostitution in Italy and at Butler's request provided her with a report on the situation in her country. When Josephine Butler toured the Continent in 1874–1875, she lent her support to the campaign being run by Mozzoni and other Italian feminists

for abolition of the Cavour Regulation of 1860, which obliged prostitutes to register with the police and have regular examinations. Mozzoni agreed to head the Milanese branch of the British, Continental, and General Federation for the Abolition of Government Regulation of Prostitution founded in 1875 by Butler, and endorsed her international campaign by publishing an article on the subject, "An Indispensable Duty," in *Woman* (a pioneering feminist journal run by Alaide Gualberta Beccari). But it would be an uphill struggle. Italian women, most of whom were illiterate, seemed reluctant to support the cause of women, seeing their own rights as a very poor second to the long struggle for nationhood that had just been won. Although activists tried to emulate the well-organized campaigning of reformers in other countries, activism in Italy remained limited. Mozzoni's hopes for working-class women to join the movement were frustrated by a lack of response, despite the fact that *Woman* claimed in 1876 to have collected 3,000 women's signatures on a petition calling for abolition of state-regulated prostitution. (In legislation passed in 1888, 1891, and 1905, the Cavour Regulation regarding prostitution was partially reformed, but the Italian campaign was not as successful as that in Britain and elsewhere. In 1931 and 1940, Mussolini's fascist government reintroduced the old regulations.

In the 1870s Mozzoni took a teaching post at the Agnesi High School for Girls, where she taught moral philosophy. She ventured into lecturing in public on women's education (one of the few women invited to do so by the Philological Society of Milan), advocating the establishment of secular schools in a move away from the heavily Roman Catholic–oriented curriculum of traditional convent education. At this time, she also gave birth to an illegitimate daughter, although she did not marry until she was forty-nine, in 1886. She continued to press for reform of the civil code, calling for more money to be used in the education of girls and for single women to be given greater civil rights. She had become increasingly alarmed at militarism during the time of the Franco-Prussian War (1870–1871) and became convinced that women's suffrage was the key to her sex having a greater say against the waging of wars. From the mid-1870s, she devoted time to working for women's suffrage at the municipal level, but the numerous petitions she raised (the last was in 1907) all failed. Time after time, her campaigning on a wide range of issues met with the full force of the church's opposition, which in the 1890s put pressure on the Italian government to close down women's liberal organizations such as the Federation of Women's Associations.

In 1877 Mozzoni traveled to Geneva to attend a congress on the abolition of state-regulated prostitution, acting as token representative of 200 Italian workers' societies. A year later, the government appointed her official representative of the Kingdom of Italy to the International Congress for Women's Rights, held in Paris at the time of the International Exposition. Mozzoni was in Rome three years later appealing for women's suffrage as a basic human right at the Universal Suffrage Convention. But she remained a lone, embattled voice, with her support coming mainly from male reformers who commended the report she had produced on the Geneva conference, in which she eloquently spoke of the all-too-easy descent into prostitution by many decent, honest women simply out of desperate economic necessity. She argued that it was not sufficient to abolish regulation of prostitution and that it was ludicrous that Italian law prohibited women from marrying without parental consent before the age of thirty yet obliged prostitutes as young as sixteen to register. She strongly argued that men should be made more culpable for their seduction of underage girls and for breach of promises to marry. They should also be made economically responsible for the wives and children they abandoned; it was precisely these issues, she believed, that reform of the civil code should address.

Not until 1881 did Mozzoni garner sufficient support to found the first autonomous Italian women's organization, the League to Promote the Interests of Women (LPIW), in Milan. Mozzoni's objective was to establish links with working women, and she became increasingly vocal on women's right to work, convinced that the workplace and paid employment were an honorable alternative to the restrictions of home and motherhood dictated by an intrusive papacy.

During the 1890s, additional branches of the LPIW were founded in other Italian cities, and in 1899 a Female Union and a journal of the same name were established in Milan. But by this time, cracks had appeared in the fragile Italian women's movement. Bourgeois moderates affiliated themselves with international organizations in the quest for suffrage (which remained a dormant issue in Italy until the next century), and many radical women, such as Anna Kuliscioff, embraced socialism (Kuliscioff founding the Socialist Party in 1892). Mozzoni herself became increasingly radical as she grew older, and by the time she died, she too was convinced that women would only gain their rights through socialism. It was not until 1908 that the first National Congress of Italian Feminists was held in Rome. In 1919, the year before her death, Mozzoni observed a session of the Italian government debating women's suffrage. She died in 1920, not knowing that it would be another twenty-five years before Italian women would win the vote.

See also Beccari, Alaide Gualberta; Butler, Josephine; Kuliscioff, Anna.

References and Further Reading

Gibson, Mary. 1986. *Prostitution and the State in Italy 1865–1915*. Columbus: Ohio State University Press.

Howard, Judith Jeffrey. 1977. "The Civil Code of 1865 and the Origins of the Feminist Movement in Italy." In Betty Caroli, Robert F. Harney, and Lydio Tomasi, eds., *The Italian Immigrant Woman in North America*. Toronto: The Multicultural History Society of Toronto.

———. 1990. "Visions of Reform, Visions of Revolution: Women's Activism in the New Italian Nation." In Frances Richardson Keller, ed., *Views of Women's Lives in Western Tradition*. Lewiston: Edwin Mellen Press.

Offen, Karen. 2000. *European Feminism 1700–1950: A Political History*. Stanford: Stanford University Press.

Robertson, Priscilla. 1982. *An Experience of Women: Pattern and Change in Nineteenth-Century Europe*. Philadelphia: Temple University Press.

M'rabet, Fadela
(1935–)
Algeria

The feminist and writer Fadela M'rabret, despite being born into a family with traditional links to the religious leadership of Islam, has openly criticized Arab society for its sexism and the prevalence of traditional laws favoring men. M'rabret studied at the University of Algiers and worked as a teacher. Her contact with a wide cross section of Algerian women via a radio show in which she discussed women's issues prompted her to write the novel *The Algerian Woman* (1964), a groundbreaking study of the repression of women in Algerian society. She followed it with *The Algerians* (1967), which again was bold in its confrontation of social and religious issues affecting women in Algeria. Her more recent feminist writings have, however, been criticized for describing women too often in the role of victim. M'rabret's attitude, as laid out in *The Algerian Woman,* was uncompromising: "The condition of the woman remains entirely the work of the man: it is the father, the brother, the cousin, the uncle, the husband who make the laws, and the behavior of the Arab woman is only the consequence or the reflection of masculine behavior toward her" (M'rabet 1969, 15).

After publishing *The Algeria of Illusions* in 1973, M'rabret was forced to leave Algeria, her critical stance placing her in jeopardy in light of the growth of fundamentalism in that country. When the Algerian family code was revised in 1984, she bravely came out in opposition to its continuing acceptance of polygamy and its favoring of the man in cases of divorce, child custody, and inheritance. M'rabret has since settled in Paris.

References and Further Reading

M'rabet, Fadela. 1969. *La Femme Algérienne suivi de les Algériennes.* Paris: F. Maspero.

Murphy, Emily Gowan
(1868–1933)
Canada

The Canadian journalist and feminist Emily Murphy was, according to fellow suffragist Nellie McClung, a woman who loved a fight. A founder of the Adult Suffrage Society, she was the first woman in the British Empire to achieve an appointment as a magistrate.

Murphy was the daughter of a wealthy landowner. Born in Cookstown, Ontario, she was educated at Bishop Strachan's School, an Anglican private school in Toronto, and grew up in a family environment that encouraged political discussion. Three of her brothers became lawyers, an interest that rubbed off on the young Emily. In 1887 she married Arthur Murphy, an Anglican minister and missionary who had a parish in Chatham, Ontario, where they lived for ten years. In 1898 they traveled to England, where Arthur took up missionary work, and also spent time in Germany. Upon her return to Canada, Murphy wrote lively travel sketches satirizing life in these two countries, *The Impressions of Janey Canuck Abroad* (1901), in which she parodied European manners and affectations and also exposed the downside of slum conditions. She also used "Janey Canuck" as a pen name for her 1910 book, *Janey Canuck in the West,* which depicted life in rural Manitoba. A novel of Alberta life, *Open Trails,* followed in 1912, and *Seeds of Pine* in 1914.

In 1904 the Murphys settled in Swan River, Manitoba, where Murphy took up journalism and struck up a close friendship with Nellie McClung, writing the literary pages of the *Winnipeg Telegram.* Three years later, they settled in Edmonton, Alberta, where Murphy wrote for the *Edmonton Journal* and became involved in social reform relating to the welfare of women and children. She was particularly sympathetic to the rights of rural women to a share of their marital property and joined the campaign for married women to be entitled to a one-third share, which came into force under the 1911 Dower Act. Murphy was also active in the suffrage movement in Alberta, in 1909 becoming honorary secretary of the Adult Suffrage Society, but she retained a special interest in women's legal rights and advocated the establishment of a special women and children's court for the trial of cases involving sexual abuse or divorce. Her interest in setting up such a court developed after members of the Council of Women of Edmonton had been disallowed from observing the trial of prostitutes on the grounds that the sexual nature of the case was not for the ears of mixed company.

Appalled by this discrimination, Murphy successfully lobbied the attorney general of Alberta in 1916 for a women's court to be established, to which she was appointed as police magistrate—the first woman to be elevated to such a post in the British Empire. But the legality of this appointment was challenged during her second case, when the lawyer for the defense said she was not a "person" under the law, and since she did not enjoy the concomitant legal rights or privileges, she therefore could not hold public office.

The interpretation of the word *persons* under

Canadian law continued to be challenged by Murphy and other feminists for more than a decade. In 1927 Murphy and four other women, including McClung—the "Famous Five," as they became known—used the legal right of any five people to come together to petition for a constitutional ruling to argue the wording of the British North America Act of 1867, in order to obtain a ruling on women's eligibility for the Canadian Senate. The campaign lasted two years (1927–1929); on 24 April 1928 the Supreme Court of Canada ruled that a woman was not a "person." It was only on appeal to the Judicial Committee of the British Privy Council on 18 October 1929 that the ruling was overturned and it was confirmed that the word *persons* in the 1867 British law implied women.

Murphy's work as a magistrate for fifteen years (1916–1931) reinforced her support for temperance and her concern with tackling rural poverty, prostitution, and drug and alcohol abuse. She made a particular study of the latter, producing a series of articles published in *McClean's* magazine, which were later collected as the *Black Candle* (1922) and prompted the introduction of new legislation on drug abuse that remained in operation until the 1960s. During her years of social service, Murphy acted as prison and asylum supervisor for Alberta's legislature, pioneered the establishment of the Victorian Order of Nurses in Edmonton, and was the first woman elected to the hospital board in Edmonton. She also promoted women's election as school trustees and was a founder of the Federated Women's Institute. Although her social concerns were deeply felt and hard fought, her critics have since argued that she was guided by a conservative perspective that rather too readily laid the blame for many of Canada's social ills at the door of ethnic minorities and newly arrived immigrants.

See also McClung, Nellie.

References and Further Reading
Benson, Eugene, and William Toye, eds. 1997. *Oxford Companion to Canadian Literature.* 2d ed. Oxford: Oxford University Press.
Cleverdon, Catherine Lyle. 1950. *The Woman Suffrage Movement in Canada.* Toronto: University of Toronto Press.
James, Donna. 2001. *Emily Murphy.* Toronto: Fitzhenry and Whiteside.
MacEwan, Grant. 1975. *And Mighty Women Too: Stories of Notable Western Canadian Women.* Saskatoon, SK: Western Producer Prairie Books.
Mander, Christine. 1985. *Emily Murphy, Rebel: First Female Magistrate in the British Empire.* Toronto: Simon and Schuster.
Munnings, Gladys. 1993. *Canadian Women of Distinction: Emily Ferguson Murphy, Agnes Campbell, Thérèse Casgrain, Molly (Mary) Brant, Frances Anne Hopkins.* Newmarket, ON: Quaker Press.
Pierson, Ruth Roach, ed. 1987. *Woman and Peace: Theoretical, Historical and Practical Perspectives.* London: Croom Helm.
Sanders, Byrne Hope. 1945. *Emily Murphy, Crusader: "Janey Canuck."* Toronto: Macmillan.

Musa, Nabawiyya
(1886–1951)
Egypt

A dogmatically defiant and determined woman, Musa was one of Egypt's leading female educators and feminists. She cofounded the Egyptian Feminist Union with Huda Sha'rawi in 1923, her driving conviction being that women could only attain true emancipation through the liberating effects of education. It would give them access to suitable employment, an argument that she outlined in her collected essays, published as *The Woman and Work* (1920). There were, however, limitations to what Musa considered suitable work for women. For her, women's primary role in the workplace was to improve the welfare of other women; as a nationalist, she also wanted to see Egyptians and women particularly trained for the jobs otherwise taken from them by better-educated and qualified foreigners and colonial administrators.

Born into the Egyptian middle classes at Zagazig in the province of Qalyubiyah in 1886, Musa came from a less privileged background than many Egyptian feminists of her generation. She was raised by her illiterate mother after her army captain father died when she was born. Educated at home, she taught herself Arabic from her brother's books and memorized the Qu'ran. She went on to study at the girls' section of the Abbas Primary School and took her exams in 1903, passing with a high score in Arabic. Determined to be a teacher, she defied her mother and social convention by entering teacher training at the Saniyah School. After graduating, along with her educationist contemporary Malak Hifni Nasif, in 1906, Musa went back to the Abbas Primary School to teach. In characteristic bullish style, she was quick to criticize the school's discriminatory rates of pay, with women teachers there being paid less than the men. The British authorities did not take kindly to her interference and her persistent calls for parity.

In 1907 Musa again made a nuisance of herself by petitioning the British Ministry of Education to become the first Egyptian woman to sit for the French baccalaureate examination, at that time available only to men. She got her way but was humiliated by having to take the exam in a separate room. As Margot Badran points out, taking the exam was no mean achievement: the next Egyptian woman would not take it until 1928. Much was made of this event in the press, especially when Musa came in thirty-fourth out of 300 candidates. As a result of newspaper reports about her academic success, she received several marriage proposals but turned them all down because married women were not allowed to teach. In any event, Musa appears to have had a particular aversion to the idea of marriage and more particularly sex, which she saw as animalistic and distasteful, averring: "I preferred to live as the master of men, not as their servant" (Badran 1995, 45).

Musa failed in her subsequent attempt to be admitted to the new Egyptian University in Cairo but did not accept such rejection meekly, protesting the university's narrow-mindedness in failing to promote women's further education. To compensate, she took part in a series of extracurricular lectures given at the university to women-only audiences in 1909–1910 and went on to give public lectures in al-Ahram in 1912.

Along with other first-wave Egyptian feminists, Musa made a symbolic gesture about her feminism by removing her veil, in her case as early as 1909, when she first headed a primary school for girls in Fayyum. In 1910 she transferred to the Women Teacher's Training School in Mansûra for four years, but once again her outspokenness and hostility toward officialdom brought trouble, and she was forced to leave in 1914. She became principal of the Wardiyan Women Teacher's Training School in Alexandria. There, however, she was forced to compromise her views in order to have any women to train and had to adhere to current modesty codes on dress and sexual segregation, although she still refused to wear the veil. In her estimation, the veil was misconstrued as a symbol of modesty; it was, as she saw it, a symbol of the continuing subjugation of women within the old harem system of seclusion, and all the time women continued to hide behind it, they would never progress.

In 1920 Musa collected several of her feminist and nationalist writings in *The Woman and Work,* an important milestone in Egyptian women's writing, which emphasized education as being essential to women's ability to take advantage of work opportunities alongside men. She saw work as an important way of empowering single mothers by releasing them from dependence on religious charity. And to her, women's crucial role as educators was a major contributor to the spread of a sense of national unity and service to the state. Many of the women teachers trained at her establishments acquitted themselves at the top of state exams.

In 1924 Musa became an inspector of girls' schools but two years later was dismissed for criticizing the Egyptian educational system. She returned to running two private schools for girls—the Tariqiyat al-Fatah primary school and the Banat al-Ashraf secondary school in Cairo, raising funds among upper-class Egyptian women (including Huda Sha'rawi) for money to keep them open. She was determined that the schools should retain their Egyptian cultural identity and resisted the appointment of foreigners as teachers. She also began publishing newspaper articles on women's issues under a pseudonym, calling for changes in the laws on divorce and polygamy. Later she edited the woman's page of a weekly and wrote poems and a novel. Musa went a long way toward galvanizing the Egyptian Feminist Union's widespread campaign for the establishment of girls' schools. She constantly ran the gauntlet of the Ministry of Education and helped found the Society for the Advancement of the Young Woman, together with, in 1937, the society's journal, *The Magazine of the Young Woman,* which championed the cause of reform and women's education.

In 1942 Musa attacked the prime minister for accommodating the wartime economic and strategic needs of the British, at a time when Egyptian nationalists were campaigning for British troops to leave their territory. As a result, her schools were closed, and she was imprisoned.

At her trial she was defended by a (male) feminist lawyer.

Notwithstanding Musa's obvious preeminence in the first wave of Egyptian feminism, a position viewed by Margot Badran as being on a par with that of Huda Sha'rawi, a somewhat unsympathetic portrait is painted of her by Nawal el-Saadawi. In her 1999 memoir, *A Daughter of Isis,* el-Saadawi describes how she attended the Nabawiyya Musa Secondary School in Abbassieh district in Cairo in 1943. Not long after arriving, she discovered that the pupils' nickname for Musa was "Bo'o Bo'o Effendi" (the big bad witch/wolf) and that the regime was draconian, with Musa coming across as a humorless, repressed spinster who actually hated women. She found Musa cold, unsmiling, and full of hatred: "School under her had become for me like a funeral where everything was the colour of mourning" (el-Saadawi 1999, 161). The effect was to make el-Saadawi hate school and education: "All I can see whenever I remember her is a face contracted in an ugly scowl, and big black eyes, big enough to absorb all the dark gloom in the world" (165).

See also Nasif, Malak Hifni; el-Saadawi, Nawal; Sha'rawi, Huda.

References and Further Reading

Badran, Margot. 1995. *Feminists, Islam and Nation: Gender and the Making of Modern Egypt.* Princeton: Princeton University Press.

el-Saadawi, Nawal. 1980. *The Hidden Face of Eve: Women in the Arab World.* London: Zed Books.

———. 1999. *Daughter of Isis: The Autobiography of Nawal El Saadawi.* London: Zed Books.

Muzzilli, Carolina
(1889–1917)
Argentina

The daughter of Italian immigrants and a seamstress by trade, Muzzilli's socialism was self-taught. She became a respected member of the Argentine movement, as well as a writer, labor organizer, and director of the *Women's Tribune,* an early feminist journal. She believed in direct action and took a strong stand against what she looked upon as the dilettante feminists of the upper classes, who she considered spent too much time talking and not enough doing. Muzzilli took her campaigning into the factories in an attack on the exploitation of women and child workers, in so doing becoming the first woman to be made an official of the National Department of Employment.

As a member of the working class, Muzzilli became incensed by what she saw as elitism in social welfare and reform. She suggested that the lukewarm activities of conservative feminists of the middle and upper classes be replaced with her own brand of "sportive" feminism, which would involve all women in her socialist vision of the class struggle. She elaborated on such ideas in her work for the *Women's Tribune,* took part in socialist-sponsored education programs (for the Beneficent Society), and wrote reports on factory conditions—particularly for women in the cigar and textile industries. Muzzilli was deeply concerned about the poor health of the working classes, a situation exacerbated by the unhealthy conditions in which they worked. In her view, a lack of due attention to the welfare of workers' physical well-being on the part of government provoked resentment and ultimately class conflict. For all the time that the workers were exploited by the richer classes and their children were malnourished as a result of poverty, class antagonisms would prevail. As a supporter of eugenics, Muzzilli was also concerned that in such situations its principles might be misapplied, with the declining mental and physical state of the working classes being used against them as a means of social control. She believed that the proper purpose of eugenics was to ensure the welfare of all, most particularly the underdefended worker.

In 1906 Muzzilli's industrial research, promoted by the Beneficent Society, was used as evidence in the campaign to enact legislation protecting workers. In 1913 she took part in the Congress for the Protection of Childhood, held in Buenos Aires. Muzzilli campaigned for the Socialist Party in 1916 and published a series of articles in *The Vanguard* in 1917, but her life was cut short by the onset of tuberculosis.

References and Further Reading

Lavrin, Asunción. 1995. *Women, Feminism, and Social Change in Argentina, Chile, and Uruguay 1890–1940.* Lincoln: University of Nebraska Press.

Myrdal, Alva
(1902–1986)
Sweden

Alva Myrdal enjoyed a preeminent position as a leading sociologist, human rights activist, expert on population growth, and later campaigner for nuclear disarmament. As a politician, she was able to promote her interest in social and child welfare through legislation in support of mothers and children to become one of the most influential Swedish women of her time. Convinced of the power of moral right over evil, Myrdal used her considerable intellectual gifts across a wide range of disciplines.

Born in Uppsala, Myrdal admired the social democratic principles of her father, a member of the Uppsala City Council, who encouraged her interests in social issues. After graduating from Stockholm University in 1924, she married the economist Gunnar Myrdal. Together they traveled to London, Leipzig, and Stockholm, where between 1925 and 1928 they studied population problems and economic conditions before accepting a one-year Rockefeller fellowship in the United States (1929–1930). Myrdal then studied at Geneva in 1930–1931 and took a master's degree in 1934 at the University of Uppsala. She also published the first of her many books, *Crisis in the Population Question,* a study of the falling Swedish birthrate written jointly with her husband. After a period working as a psychologist's assistant in Stockholm's Central Prison, Myrdal worked closely with the government on the establishment of a welfare state in Sweden and for women's equality, serving as an adviser to the Government Committee on Social Housing and the Royal Commission on Population.

In 1936 Myrdal founded the Social Pedagogical Institute in Stockholm, where as its director from 1936 to 1948, she developed the training of nursery and kindergarten teachers and expanded on her theories of progressive education and a program for reform of child care methods. In 1941 she and her husband published *Nation and Family: The Swedish Experiment in Democratic Family and Population Policy,* which argued that a healthy population could only be achieved through a program of public education and access to birth control combined with the introduction of state benefits, such as maternity relief (introduced in 1937) and child allowances (1947).

While Sweden remained neutral during World War II, Myrdal oversaw aid programs, headed a government commission on women's work, and served as chair of the Federation of Business and Professional Women. She helped other governments plan their postwar reconstruction programs, advising on housing, population, work for women, and educational reform.

In 1949 Myrdal entered the international civil service and was sent to New York, where she was the first woman to be appointed a department head at a United Nations Secretariat, as principal director of the Department of Social Affairs (1949–1950). From 1951 to 1955, she was director of the Department of Social Sciences in the UN Educational, Scientific, and Cultural Organization. Myrdal's attentions were increasingly drawn toward the problems of Third World development, and from 1955 to 1961 she served as either a minister or Swedish ambassador to India, Ceylon, Burma, and Nepal.

In 1956, during a fallow period in women's activism, described by Dale Spender as the "decade when nothing happened" (1983, 506), Myrdal collaborated with the English psychoanalyst Viola Klein on *Women's Two Roles.* In this landmark study of women in the home and the workplace, they described how middle-class women's entry into the workplace, fostered in part by a reaction to the lack of a sense of purpose within the home, should be encouraged by men. They urged fathers to make way for women's further integration by playing a greater role in the family and relieving mothers of some of the burden of domestic work, thus making it easier for married women to make the transition from part-time to full-time employment.

In 1961, upon her return to Sweden, Myrdal was nominated as special disarmament adviser to the foreign minister of Sweden. She entered parliament as a social democrat in 1962 and became a member of the Swedish cabinet, serving as minister of disarmament from 1966 to 1973 and minister of church affairs from 1969 to 1973. By this time, the Cold War had drawn her into work for world peace and disarmament, and she headed the Swedish delegation to the UN Disarmament Committee of the General Assembly from 1962 to 1973.

After Myrdal retired from parliament and the UN in 1973, she turned to writing and lecturing. Her writings on population, social welfare, and disarmament (some in collaboration with others) are extensive and include *Are We Too Many?* (1950), *America's Role in International Social Welfare* (1955), *Women's Two Roles: Home and Work* (1956), *The Game of Disarmament: How the United States and Russia Run the Arms Race* (1976), and *War, Weapons, and Everyday Violence* (1977).

Both Myrdal and her husband were awarded the West German Peace Prize in 1970. In addition, she received many awards and accolades for her exhaustive campaigning, including the first Albert Einstein Peace Award in 1980 and the Jawaharlal Nehru Award for International Understanding in 1981. She was nominated twice for the Nobel Peace Prize, resulting in an outcry in Sweden (the home of the Nobel Prizes), where public subscription raised $60,000 to provide her with their own People's Peace Prize. Finally, in 1982 she shared the Nobel Peace Prize with Alfonso García Robles of Mexico.

References and Further Reading

Annual Obituary. 1986. New York: St. Martin's Press.

Bok, Issela. 1991. *Alva Myrdal: A Daughter's Memoir.* Reading, MA: Addison-Wesley.

Lewis, Jane. 1990. "Myrdal, Klein, Women's Two Roles and Postwar Feminism 1945–1960." In Harold Smith, ed., *British Feminism in the Twentieth Century.* Aldershort, Hants: Edward Elgar.

Myrdal, Alva, and Viola Klein. 1956. *Women's Two Roles: Home and Work.* London: Routledge and Kegan Paul.

Spender, Dale. 1982. *Women of Ideas, and What Men Have Done to Them.* London: Routledge and Kegan Paul.

Wasson, Tyler, ed. 1987. *Nobel Prize Winners: An H. W. Wilson Biographical Dictionary.* New York: H. W. Wilson.

N

Nabarawi, Saiza
(1897–?)
Egypt

A liberal feminist and leader of the Egyptian peace movement, Nabarawi was a contemporary and associate of Huda Sha'rawi in the Egyptian Feminist Union (EFU) and a leader of feminist activities in Egypt during the 1920s and 1930s. She followed Sha'rawi's example and removed her veil at Cairo station after returning from an international women's conference in Rome in 1923. More notably, in terms of the history of feminism, she was probably the first woman to rediscover the 1880 French term *féministe* and to promote its use in its modern-day interpretation.

Nabarawi was born in the grand surroundings of the Minshawi Palace in Cairo. She was brought up by her stepmother and taken to Paris, where she was educated at lycées. At the age of fifteen, she returned to Egypt and continued her education as a boarder at the Nôtre Dame de Sion School, remaining in Alexandria until 1915.

Meanwhile, she had fallen under the influence of the Egyptian feminist Huda Sha'rawi, who had been a friend of her late stepmother. Under Sha'rawi's influence, she joined the EFU in 1923, when she was twenty-six. From 1925 to 1940, she was editor of the EFU's journal the *Egyptian Woman* (*L'Egyptienne,* the only feminist journal in Egypt to publish in French), which became a springboard for her contact with other international feminist organizations. In a 1931 article in the journal, she called for an end to polygamy and in others argued that economic independence and the control of its own resources were the key to Egypt's future national independence.

Nabarawi encouraged women's education by accompanying Sha'rawi to Shubra Secondary School for Girls in Cairo (established in 1925), where they spoke on the need for women to educate themselves. After Sha'rawi's death in 1947, Nabarawi became vice president of the EFU until 1949, when she was elected president. She also took over Sha'rawi's role in the International Woman Suffrage Alliance and set up a youth committee within the EFU to extend politicization among the young women of Cairo. As a leader of the EFU, she endorsed its preferred sphere of activity among poorer women in rural areas, emphasizing the pressing need for the provision of clean drinking water and the establishment of health and education facilities in these areas. She also worked for the provision of midwives and female doctors for poor women and their children.

Nabarawi's unqualified support for Egyptian independence led to her involvement in the popular disturbances of the early 1950s. Along with other leading Egyptian feminists, she set up the Women's Committee for Popular Resistance after trouble flared in the Canal Zone, leading to the military coup of 1952; she also led active resistance to British rule by Egyptian women and along with other activists crossed British lines to Ismailia, a city on the Suez Canal. But after the 1952 revolution, her activities were curtailed when President Gamal Abdel Nasser's new government suppressed all independent women's groups on the left.

During the ensuing government purge of feminist groups in the early 1950s, Nabarawi was forced to leave the EFU at a time when the women's movement in Egypt was at last developing a firm foothold, with Egyptian women finally winning the vote in 1956. Many in the organization, however, were not sorry to see her go. They had looked upon her as being too left-wing in her attitudes, and she was accused of being a communist. These opinions of her did not deter Nabarawi from pursuing her own political agenda, however. She kept up her commitment to reform through her writing on many topics, ranging from pacifism to the Palestine cause to philanthropic activities among Egypt's poor. Her Women's Committee for Popular Resistance restarted its activities in 1956. During the 1960s, Nabarawi was forced to keep a low political profile, but she retained her links with groups such as the International Democratic Federation of Women.

See also Sha'rawi, Huda.

References and Further Reading

Badran, Margot. 1995. *Feminists, Islam and Nation: Gender and the Making of Modern Egypt.* Princeton: Princeton University Press.

Naidu, Sarojini
(1879–1949)
India

After her early life as one of India's leading poets, Sarojini Naidu turned to vigorous campaigning against sectarianism, the caste system, and traditional practices that oppressed women, such as the enforced purdah of widows. She also took a key political role in the years leading up to Indian independence, as one of the first women to devote her life to a public career at a time when only a handful of Indian women were beginning to challenge long-held tradition and do so.

Naidu was born in Hyderabad, the daughter of a Muslim scientist, educator, and reformer. Her father recognized her considerable intellectual talents and ensured that she had a first-class education at Queen Mary's College in Lahore and the University of Madras. In 1895 she was granted a scholarship by the nizam of Hyderabad to study in England, where she attended King's College in London and Girton College at Cambridge. In England, she came under the influence of the writer Edmund Gosse, who encouraged her lyrical poetry writing while emphasizing the importance of her poetry's retaining its Indian cultural qualities rather than aping Western verse. She went on to publish several collections of verse in English, including *The Golden Thresh-*

old (1905), *The Bird of Time* (1912), and *The Broken Wing* (1917), eventually earning the sobriquet "the nightingale of India."

Forced to return to India because of ill health (she would be plagued all her life with heart trouble), Naidu married out of her caste in 1898 and began to take a serious interest in women's rights, in particular raising public awareness of the plight of Hindu widows. She had long been aware that until the status of Indian women was improved and their needs listened to, fundamental reform in India could never be achieved. She had already campaigned with British suffragists during her time in England and took up the cause of Indian home rule and women's suffrage, becoming a close associate of Mahatma Gandhi and a supporter of his *satyagraha* (civil disobedience) movement. The 1917 publication of *The Broken Wing* would prove to be her last poetry collection and bring an end to her time as a renowned literary hostess in Bombay. Naidu's involvement in the struggle for Indian independence began to take increasing precedence in her life, although her literary celebrity remained undiminished.

Her campaigning over subsequent years was exhausting and constantly undermined her precarious health. Because Naidu was a moderate, the essential component of all her vigorous speech making was an appeal to Indian religious unity, to the breaking down of ancient barriers of hatred. She felt that the nationalist campaign would never succeed if it did not accomplish this goal. She never let go of this idealistic vision, which she had remarked on as early as 1903 in a lecture to students: "I have no prejudice of race, creed, caste or color . . . and until you, students, have acquired and mastered that spirit of brotherhood, do not believe it possible that you will ever cease to be provincial, that you will cease to be sectarian—if I may use such a word—that you will ever be national" (Sen Gupta 1994, 135).

In 1917 Naidu kept her promise of representing Indian women across all castes and creeds, when she joined with Margaret Cousins and Annie Besant in founding the Women's Indian Association (WIA) and that same year led a deputation of fourteen representatives of the association to Lord Edwin Montagu, the secretary of state for India, calling for equal political and social status for women, including the vote, as part of British plans for political reform in In-

Sarojini Naidu (left; Archive Photos)

dia. The deputation also emphasized the need for primary and secondary education, especially for Indian girls, and for more training colleges and medical schools to be opened for women.

For the following two years, Naidu concentrated her energies on obtaining the franchise for women in India, appearing at many national conferences and branch meetings of the WIA. At a special session of the Bombay Provincial Council, she spoke in support of the resolution that all discussions of citizens' rights should refer clearly not just to men but also to women, a speech that helped achieve the passage of a resolution on women's franchise. In 1918 she was elected president of the provincial Indian National Congress in Bombay. A year later she joined a deputation of women from the All-India Home Rule League who traveled to England to give evidence in London before the joint parliamentary committee on women's suffrage in India. She also took the opportunity of canvassing Indian organizations in England on the issue. The efforts of the delegation were rewarded with only modest recommendations by the British government: for certain property qualifications, which effectively allowed only about 1 million Indian women the vote, and a commitment to improving women's literacy levels.

In 1919, as a committed pacifist, Naidu joined Gandhi's *satyagraha* movement without hesitation. As with any other cause she embraced, her commitment was wholehearted and passionate. On a brief visit to England in 1920 to consult doctors, she wrote to Gandhi: "The specialists think that my heart disease is in an advanced and dangerous state but I cannot rest till I stir the heart of the world to repentance over the tragedy of martyred India" (Kaur 1968, 172). Gandhi in turn put a huge amount of trust in Naidu's work. On her return to India and despite her continuing poor health, she personally tried to defuse tensions in areas where civil disobedience and unrest were most intense.

Naidu also extended her social and political concerns beyond India, when in 1924 she defended the rights of Indians living in South

Africa when she toured the country as Gandhi's emissary. She met with members of the British government and the South African parliament to present her views to them. By then recognized as a leading political figure, she was rewarded for her efforts on her return to India, when in 1925 she was elected the first woman president of the Indian National Congress. Taking this as official recognition of the legitimate place due to Indian women in the political life of the nation, Naidu set out an extensive domestic program of educational and rural reform and immediately began calling for a women's section to be set up, leading to the establishment by Naidu and Margaret Cousins of the All-India Women's Conference (AIWC) in 1926. This nonpolitical organization originated as a focus group for women's rights, concentrating on educational reform, and went on to become a leading voice in the women's pacifist cause that ultimately embraced the whole spectrum of political and social reform in India.

Naidu never seemed to stand still for one moment. In 1928–1929 she went on a lecture tour of the United States and also found time to attend the Pan-Pacific Women's Conference as the AIWC representative. On her return to India, she joined Gandhi's 1930 campaign against the salt law at his specific request, glad to be given the opportunity of showing that women could work alongside men in the popular protest movement. And indeed, Indian women proved to be an influential force in the campaign of passive resistance, supporting the marchers on the 241-mile salt march that year from Sabarmati to Dandi.

In May 1930 Naidu took over command of a raiding party of 2,000 that attacked the salt works at Dharasana. She went to prison for her participation and was released ten months later. Such was her courage and sense of humor that she made light of such experiences and once quipped that she "wouldn't mind being sent to jail, if I could be sure of getting a bath every day" (Bala 1986, 142). Shortly after her release in March 1931, she took part in the Second Round Table Conference on India, held in London, and in 1932, while serving as acting president of the Indian National Congress in defiance of a British ban on the congress, she was arrested and sent to jail for a year. Further run-ins with the British government occurred during World War II, when Naidu opposed the enlistment of Indian

servicemen in the British war effort and took part in the "Quit India" campaign. Naidu was arrested and found herself confined, along with other leaders including Gandhi, to the Khan Palace in Poona. But again she was released owing to her continuing ill health.

After Indian independence was achieved in 1947, Naidu became the first woman governor of an Indian state—Uttar Pradesh. By the time of her death in 1949, her natural linguistic gifts had helped her to become a fine if somewhat hyperbolic orator and an outstanding political and feminist leader. As a much-admired and revered patriot and national figure, she had used her wit, warmth, and compassion to mobilize women across Indian society to jointly campaign for improved social conditions and racial harmony.

See also Besant, Annie; Cousins, Margaret.

References and Further Reading

Bala, Usha, ed. 1986. *Indian Women Freedom Fighters.* New Delhi: Ramesh Jain.

Cousins, James, and Margaret Cousins. 1950. *We Two Together.* Madras: Ganesh.

Kaur, Manmohan. 1968. *Role of Women in the Freedom Movement.* Delhi: Sterling Publishers.

Naravan, V. S. 1980. *Sarojini Naidu: An Introduction to Her Life, Work and Poetry.* New Delhi: Orient Longmans.

Sen Gupta, Padmini. 1966. *Sarojini Naidu.* London: Asia Publishing House.

———, ed. 1994 [1944]. *Pioneer Women of India.* Reprint, Bombay: Thacker.

Nasif, Malak Hifni (pen name Bahithat al-Badiyah)
(1886–1918)
Egypt

Writing under her pen name, Bahithat al-Badiyah, which means "Searcher of the Desert," Nasif was one of the first Egyptian women to open up the discourse on women's education. Her involvement was prompted by the publication in 1899 of the (male) Egyptian judge Qasim Amin's landmark study, *Women's Emancipation.* Like many Islamic feminists of her time, Nasif saw women's education as the crucial liberating factor in any overall improvement in their economic and social status. During her short life, she became a formidable public speaker on the subject.

Nasif's father was a lawyer with cultural and literary interests who allowed his daughter to be educated outside the home. She attended the girls' section of the Abbas Primary School in Cairo and gained the distinction, along with Nabawiyya Musa, of being one of the first Egyptian girls to be allowed to go on to secondary education in a state school. Both women went from there to enroll in the teacher training program at the Saniyah school, and Nasif graduated in 1905 as one of the first women teachers in Egypt.

In 1907, however, Nasif was forced to abandon her teaching, submit to parental wishes, and get married. Her father's choice of husband was a Bedouin chief who already had one wife and child. Nasif found herself living a life of seclusion in a desert oasis, and her subjugation, as a second wife who was expected to educate her co-wife, caused her considerable anguish. But she would later draw on her own firsthand experiences of polygamy to write powerful discourses on the abuses suffered by women under this practice: "Divorce," she would later aver, "is less of a trial than polygamy. The first is misery plus freedom, while the latter is misery plus restriction" (Badran 1995, 129).

Despite the restrictions placed upon her, Nasif began writing articles on Egyptian society under her pen name while living in the oasis at Fayyum. These were published in the journal *al-Jarida* (the newspaper of the liberal secularist Umma Party), establishing Nasif as one of the first Egyptian feminist voices of the twentieth century and the first and most notable female contributor on a regular basis to Egyptian newspapers. Recognized for her incisive analytical essays on women's rights, she produced many articles and essays in her short lifetime. Some of these early pieces were published in 1909 under the title *Feminist Discourse* and became, according to Margot Badran, "a key text in Egyptian feminist history" (Badran 1995, 54).

Through her speeches and writings, Nasif raised the thorny issues of unveiling (which she thought lay women open to abuse), the early marriage of girls, and women's freedom to divorce unfaithful or violent husbands. Her determination to see an improvement in the status of Egyptian women was not an easy undertaking. As she admitted, it was "a vow that it is important to me to fulfill, even though its execution is arduous and the difficulties surrounding it are such that

despair almost blocks my path" (Ahmed 1992, 183). Despite her apprehension that education might expose Egyptian women, who till then had led sheltered lives, to morally corrupting influences, Nasif argued that if women had access to it then they would be better equipped to make their own decisions. In the course of opening up debate on this and other women's issues, she began corresponding with the Lebanese writer and feminist Mai Ziyadah in 1914, and their exchanges were published in *al-Jarida*.

In addition to her activities as a writer, Nasif took an active part in various charitable societies and women's associations, including the founding of an emergency medical service for women and a nursing school, using her own money to set up the latter in her own home. In Cairo in 1909 she spoke at a historic series of lectures for women, given by women from middle- and upper-class circles at the Egyptian University at Cairo. Despite the fact that to some extent those lecturing were preaching to audiences of the already converted, the spirit of the lectures gave a fillip to the call for women's education. More controversially, Nasif argued that women had a fundamental right to work outside the home and should be given greater opportunities to take on appropriate employment. For her, it was a matter of particular importance, now that manmade technological advances in the mechanization of sewing, spinning, weaving, and winnowing had deprived many women, particularly in poor and rural areas, of their traditional livelihood. For example, according to Nasif, women had once been the ones to winnow the wheat, but now "men run the bakeries" (Badran 1995, 166).

In 1911 Nasif took the ideas presented in her lectures a stage further, when she submitted a ten-point agenda on women's issues to the Egyptian Congress at Heliopolis (the speech was read out for her in deference to current social practice). As well as calling for basic domestic training for women in areas such as hygiene, child rearing, and first aid, Nasif called for elementary and higher education for women and for their right to train in professions such as teaching and nursing, in which they could provide a service to other women. Although the emphasis was on domestic skills, Nasif also wished to see women taught the Qu'ran and *shari'ah* (Islamic law) as well as other subjects. She challenged contemporary religious practice by arguing that women should once more be given access to mosques to pray as part of the congregation, as they had once done in the early days of Islam.

On a broader level, Nasif's agenda challenged the traditional male monopoly on work, for she passionately believed that women had the physical capability to take on many jobs that had for too long remained exclusively male. This restriction stemmed in part from the imposition of the rule of *hijab* regarding female modesty and the covering of the body, which also impeded women's ability to enter the workplace. But although she longed to see women escape the more oppressive aspects of the seclusion of the harem, she did not wish to see them aping Western cultural pursuits, such as dancing or acting, that would be deemed immodest under Islam. Nasif argued that women should find their own inherently Islamic ways of self-expression: "If we pursue anything western we shall destroy our own civilisation and a nation that has lost its civilisation grows weak and vanishes" (Badran and Cooke 1990, 231).

Although Nasif's demands were revolutionary for their time, feminist commentators have observed that by opting primarily for limited social roles for women and by underlining that the responsibility for implementing reform ultimately lay with men (who made the laws), she was merely endorsing the traditional role of women as perceived by men in Arab society. She has thus been criticized for expressing a tacit acceptance that women did not and perhaps never would have the political will or the muscle to implement these demands themselves. Yet she looked upon the particularly vexed question of veiling and unveiling as a strategic political weapon that women should use with care. It was her firm belief that women should control the decision with this regard: they should discard their veils not at the behest of other (mainly male reformers) but as and when the time was appropriate to *them.*

Tragically, Nasif died at the age of thirty-two in the influenza pandemic of 1918; she was given a major funeral attended by members of the Egyptian Ministry of Education and other dignitaries. An account of her life and work was serialized posthumously in a nine-part essay published from March 1919 to March 1920 in the journal *al-Mqtataf.* Nasif's guiding role in the development of the early feminist movement in Egypt was taken over by Huda Sha'rawi, who would later acknowledge Nasif's inspiration: "I used to talk to her inside myself. I heard her voice in my conscience" (Badran 1995, 73).

See also Musa, Nabawiyya; Sha'rawi, Huda; Ziyadah, Mai.

References and Further Reading

Ahmed, Leila. 1992. *Women and Gender in Islam: Historical Roots of a Modern Debate.* New Haven: Yale University Press.

Badran, Margot. 1995. *Feminists, Islam and Nation: Gender and the Making of Modern Egypt.* Princeton: Princeton University Press.

Badran, Margot, and Margaret Cooke, eds. 1990. *Opening the Gates: A Century of Arab Feminist Writing.* London: Virago.

Beck, L., and N. Keddie, eds. 1978. *Women in the Muslim World.* Cambridge, MA: Harvard University Press.

el-Saadawi, Nawal. 1980. *The Hidden Face of Eve: Women in the Arab World.* London: Zed Books.

Nation, Carry
(1846–1911)
United States

The image of U.S. temperance reformer Carry Nation has unwittingly become associated with that of the archetypal battleax—and this particular characterization could not be more apposite, for in real life she frequently resorted to wielding a hatchet in her crusade against liquor joints. She was the United States' flesh-and-blood answer to that great British mythical moral vigilante, Mrs. Grundy. Photographed in a sweeping black veil and clutching either her handbag or her hatchet, Nation was ever one to take resounding swipes with either instrument at those who refused to be persuaded to give up the demon drink. It was marriage to an alcoholic that turned her into such a fiery adversary, to become the unlikely head of a militant temperance campaign that, although rejected by the genteel mainstream of the Woman's Christian Temperance Union (WCTU), in which she remained an irritating maverick, nevertheless significantly contributed to the enactment of Prohibition in the United States nine years after Nation's death.

Born in Garrard County, Kentucky, Nation attended boarding school in Missouri and obtained a teaching certificate at Missouri State

Normal School, but her teaching career was interrupted when her father lost all his money in the Civil War and her mother became increasingly mentally unstable (there was a history of insanity on her side of the family). The family had to move to Belton, Missouri, where the evangelism of the Church of the Disciples of Christ had a profound impression on Nation. Her future work for temperance would be closely bound up with her sense of religious mission and her view of herself as a "bulldog running along at the feet of Jesus, barking at what He doesn't like" (Asbury 1929).

Nation made a disastrous marriage in 1867—to an alcoholic doctor, Charles Gloyd. The couple settled in Montana, where Nation tried to wean her husband from his drinking habit; after failing to do so, she left with their small daughter. He died of alcoholism within a year. Nation worked as a schoolteacher in Montana in order to support her daughter Charlien (who inherited her grandmother's insanity) and remarried in 1877. Her second husband, David Nation, was a lawyer and minister, and the family moved to Texas in 1879. Later, he accepted a post as pastor at Medicine Lodge, Kansas, where Nation took up philanthropic and evangelical work. Her work as a prison visitor intent on converting criminals to the ways of Christianity and abstinence further endorsed her abhorrence of the criminal effects of alcohol.

In 1890, when the state laws prohibiting alcohol in Kansas were weakened (the state had been technically "dry" since 1880) by the allowance of the sale of certain imported liquors in their original packaging, Nation launched herself into a head-on confrontation with those who made alcohol available. In 1892 she cofounded the Barber County, Kansas, branch of the WCTU and launched a crusade to close down illicit liquor joints in Kansas. An intermittently violent campaign was waged by Nation from 1899 to 1909, when she had no compunction about resorting to direct action. Accompanied by a group of female WCTU vigilantes, the terrifying, 6-foot-tall Nation marched into the bars of Medicine Lodge and after failing to convert drinkers by prayer and persuasion, began wielding bricks and her soon-to-be-recognized trademark—a hatchet. With no thought for her own safety, she proceeded to wreck the place, smashing glasses and bottles and hacking open barrels of drink, de-

Carrie Nation (Library of Congress)

stroying furniture and wall mirrors, while simultaneously breaking into impromptu bouts of hymn-singing, Bible oration, and prayers. Nation and her followers moved across the state with their message, becoming known as the "hatchetarians," engaged, as Nation herself eccentrically put it, in "the hatchetation of joints." Small hatchet-style brooches were made (bearing the inscription "Carry Nation, Joint Smasher") and were sold to raise money to fund Nation's campaign, as well as a succession of appropriately named temperance journals, such as *The Smasher's Mail* and *The Hatchet*. Nation also raised funds to run a refuge she had set up for the wives of alcoholics. The rest of her not inconsiderable earnings of $300 or so a week during her heyday went to pay off her endless fines.

By 1901, consumed by her cause (which she was convinced had been prompted by divine revelation), Nation found herself divorced for desertion by her husband, who disapproved of her avenging angel activities. She also extended her eccentric and inimitable style of censure to other subjects, lambasting smoking, fraternal orders and freemasonry (her first husband had frequently done his drinking at freemason meetings), tight corsets, short skirts, all kinds of "foreign" food, and even the modest barroom pinups of the day. In so doing, she made herself the object of frequent verbal and physical attack. She was shot at and arrested at least thirty times for causing a public nuisance or disturbing the peace. On one occasion in jail in 1901, she made her classic remark: "You have put me in here a cub, but I will come out roaring like a lion, and I will make all hell howl! (Beals 1962). That same year, the WCTU presented her with a medal inscribed "To the Bravest Woman in Kansas." Nation lectured across the United States to fund her campaign, which eventually extended from San Francisco to New York and south to Washington, D.C. She even took her message to the gallery of the U.S. Senate, where she interrupted proceedings. But in the end, the middle-class, straitlaced ladies of the WCTU got tired of her extremism, which was, it seemed, giving the movement a bad name. In 1904 Nation was expelled from the WCTU. Similarly, Nation's support for the women's suffrage movement was not welcomed either—and again she found herself disowned for her violent tactics.

Eventually, in 1904 Nation sat down and wrote her own apologia, *The Use and Need for the Life of Carry A. Nation,* a work so muddled in its argument and disorganized in its structure that despite selling 56,000 copies in five years, it served only to confirm that her eccentricity was now bordering on mental collapse. As late as 1908, Nation toured Great Britain, to be met largely by derision. In 1911, having finally given up her hatchet-wielding, she collapsed while lecturing in Eureka Springs, suffering the aftereffects of being beaten up by an enraged female bar owner in Montana. In her declining years, she had become an increasingly sad spectacle, exposing herself to open ridicule, such as by students she lectured to at Harvard and Yale Universities. With her mental state descending into paranoia, Nation moved to the seclusion of the Ozark mountains of Arkansas, where her health rapidly declined and she soon died. Eight years after her death, the passage of the Eighteenth Amendment in 1919 paved the way for the legal enactment in 1920 of the National Prohibition Act. Mean-

while, Carry Nation, one of the United States' most belligerent, most colorful, and definitely noisiest reformers had ensured she would never be forgotten—although perhaps not always for the right reasons.

References and Further Reading
Asbury, Herbert. 1929. *Carry Nation.* New York: Alfred A. Knopf.
Beals, Carleton. 1962. *Cyclone Carry: The Story of Carry Nation.* Philadelphia: Chilton.
Grace, Fran. 2001. *Carry A. Nation: Retelling the Life.* Bloomington: Indiana University Press.
Nation, Carry. 1908. *The Use and Need of the Life of Carry A. Nation, Written by Herself.* Topeka: F. M. Stevens & Sons.
Ross, Ishbel. 1965. *Charmers and Cranks: Twelve Famous American Women Who Defied the Conventions.* New York: Harper & Row.
Shea, Marion Axford. 1999. *Women Movers and Shakers.* Lincoln, NE: Media and Marketing Productions.
Taylor, Robert Lewis. 1966. *Vessel of Wrath: The Life and Times of Carry Nation.* New York: New American Library.

Nawaz, Begum Jahanarah Shah
(1896–?)
Pakistan

The Punjabi Muslim Jahanarah Shah Nawaz was a pioneer of women's emancipation in the region of India that later became Pakistan, renouncing purdah and becoming actively involved in the campaigning for women's rights through numerous women's organizations such as the All-India Muslim Women's Conference. Nawaz was brought up in a family that supported women's education and social work among the poor. She was educated at Queen Mary's College in Lahore and followed in her mother's footsteps by making a commitment to women's rights. As a supporter of the reform of religious marriage laws, she initiated a resolution against polygamy that was passed at the All-India Muslim Women's Conference in 1917. She was the first Muslim woman to be elected to the Lahore Municipal Council.

Nawaz's preeminent role in social reform came after she was elected the first female member of the All-India Muslim League. She was one of three women delegates to the Second and Third Round Table Conferences on India, held in

London during the early 1930s, who put forward the female perspective on home rule, arguing that Indian women had earned political recognition as a force for social improvement in the country. At the second conference, she was unequivocal in her support of the Indian National Congress's demand for universal adult franchise and lent her support to the compromise Poona Pact of 1932, which offered a limited franchise. Recognizing that women would not be given an unrestricted vote, Nawaz worked to achieve an improvement in the franchise ratio of 1:5 (men to women) as being better than no electoral change at all. In 1937 Nawaz was elected to the Punjab legislature; she later became a member of the Constituent Assembly.

References and Further Reading

Nawaz, J. A. Shah. 1971. *Father and Daughter: A Political Autobiography.* Lahore: Nigarishat.

Neilans, Alison
(1884–1942)
United Kingdom

The campaign of British social reformers against prostitution and vice might have seemed to have been won in 1885 with the repeal of the Contagious Diseases Acts. In fact, the social purity movement that had found its focus in the work of the Ladies' National Association (LNA) for the Abolition of State Regulation of Vice, under the leadership of Josephine Butler, continued long after her death and well into the twentieth century. In 1915 the LNA was renamed the Association for Moral and Social Hygiene (AMSH), and as yet unsung women such as the redoubtable Alison Neilans, general secretary of the AMSH, kept the issue alive at a time when feminist campaigning was on the wane.

Neilans was born at Coldstream-on-Tweed in Scotland and grew up in Camberwell, south London. She was educated at private school in Dulwich and learned her campaigning skills in the suffrage movement, as a member and organizer for the Women's Freedom League (WFL) after its establishment in 1907, during which time she was twice imprisoned, for one month in 1908 and again in 1909. The second period in jail came about as the result of an unfortunate act of militancy in October 1909 that went wrong. Together with another suffragist, Mrs. Chapin, Neilans had attempted to pour a chemical solution into a ballot box to destroy the votes inside, and in so doing the liquid splashed into the eye of an official, causing considerable pain and temporary blindness. She was sentenced to three months in Holloway Prison for causing grievous bodily harm and, in prison, went on a hunger strike and was force-fed. After her release, she was elevated to the WFL's executive committee in 1910 and was also a member of the Church League for Women's Suffrage in 1911. After leading a major campaign on behalf of the WFL in 1913 along the west coast of Scotland, Neilans increasingly concentrated on social and moral reform, finding Charlotte Despard's leadership of the WFL too autocratic. She worked with Sylvia Pankhurst in the East London Federation of Suffragettes in 1915 and was appointed general secretary of the AMSH in 1917. By this time, she was also editor of the AMSH journal, the *Shield* (later succeeded by the *British Review of Moral and Social Hygiene*), in which she published many articles on sexual issues and the protection of women and children.

The AMSH was one of many social purity and vigilance groups that came together in 1919 under a new umbrella organization, the British National Committee for the Suppression of the White Slave Traffic and the International Traffic in Women (1919–1938). As general secretary of the AMSH, Neilans led British debates on the legal rights of prostitutes, the brothel trade in women and young girls, and the sexual abuse of children; through the AMSH's association with the British National Committee, she was also a key figure in the international movement to monitor the white-slave traffic in women and children. In keeping women's issues such as these to the fore, she faced an uphill campaign; her close friend and collaborator Nina Boyle, after trying repeatedly to raise interest in the campaign among members of the International Woman Suffrage Alliance, finally gave up in disgust in 1928, accusing the women's movement of apathy.

During her years of campaigning in the 1920s and 1930s against the double standard in sexual morality, Neilans became well versed in issues relating to sexual relationships, child abuse, and prostitution. Together with Boyle, she also promoted the recruitment of women police, partly as a new profession for women but also in hopes of improving the treatment of prostitutes under arrest (Boyle had founded the Women Police Volunteers during World War I to patrol garrison towns and places where the sex trade operated). Neilans's lobbying with other reformers such as Nancy Astor helped secure the passage of the 1922 Criminal Law Amendment Act, which raised the age of consent to eighteen. She also supported Astor's drive in Parliament to obtain passage of a bill on prostitution and soliciting that would make the male clients of prostitutes also liable for prosecution. Much of Neilans's work for the AMSH was channeled into the International Abolitionist Federation, which conducted a similar campaign to end the double sexual standard elsewhere in the world by making the soliciting of prostitutes by men an offense. Within the federation, Neilans chaired two international committees on the white slave traffic in women and headed investigations of state-regulated prostitution in Syria and Turkey.

Neilans published Boyle's findings on sexual slavery in Britain's colonies during the 1930s and in 1935 published the text of a speech she had given on 27 February at Christ Church in Westminster, "Are Moral Standards Necessary?" In it, she argued for a clearer understanding that sexual morality was not a separate issue but an integral part of general Christian morality and that society should reject the double standard, which she labeled as "one of the ugliest and cruellest chapters in the history of morals and one which has had disastrous effects on society" (Neilans 1936, 3). In illustrating how prostitution, brothels, venereal disease, and pornography are all the "logical and inevitable results of society trying to evade the implications of the unity of the moral law," Neilans urged the promotion of equal standards of moral and sexual responsibility from both sexes. In an essay, "Changes in Sex Morality," that she contributed that year to *Our Freedom and Its Results,* edited by Ray Strachey, she developed her argument further, outlining in detail the history of women's activism for social purity through the LNA and the repeal of the Contagious Diseases Acts, the lobbying to raise the age of consent in 1922 under the Criminal Law Amendment Act, and further activism culminating in the 1933 International Convention against the Traffic in Women. In her wide-ranging discourse, which also covered the changing nature of marriage and family life, Neilans warned

against the advent of birth control, which she argued placed woman "if she chooses, in the same position of irresponsibility as the man" (Neilans 1936, 222).

Despite the fact that she is so little known today, Neilans was an important figure on the international feminist scene of her time, as an executive member of the International Council of Women (1929–1935) and of the International Alliance of Women for Suffrage and Equal Citizenship (the successor to the IWSA). In 1934 she was also on the executive of the Open Door Council, an organization opposed to protective legislation for women.

See also Astor, Nancy; Butler, Josephine; Despard, Charlotte; Pankhurst, (Estelle) Sylvia.

References and Further Reading

Crawford, Anne, et al., eds. 1983. *Europa Biographical Dictionary of British Women: Over 1000 Notable Women from Britain's Past.* London: Europa Publications.

Crawford, Elizabeth. 1999. *The Women's Suffrage Movement, 1866–1928: A Reference Guide.* London: University College of London Press.

Jeffreys, Sheila. 1985. *The Spinster and Her Enemies: Feminism and Sexuality 1880–1930.* London: Pandora.

Neilans, Allison. 1936. "Changes in Sex Morality." In Ray Strachey, ed., *Our Freedom and Its Results by Five Women.* London: Hogarth Press.

Nelken i Mausberger, Margarita
(1898–1968)
Spain

A little-known Spanish feminist and socialist, one of only three women elected to the republican government of 1931, Margarita Nelken died in the obscurity of exile in 1968. Of mixed Spanish, German, and Jewish parentage, she was born in Málaga. She had displayed a talent for art from an early age and when she was thirteen went to Paris to continue her education, living in bohemian circles on the Left Bank and later studying art history and museum curatorship. On her return to Spain, she lived in Madrid, where she was a cofounder of the Museum of Modern Art and worked as a curator both there and at the Prado Museum.

Her first forays into writing were studies on art and artists, after which she developed an interest in improving the education of poor children. She lived and worked in the working-class slums of Madrid, where she set up an orphanage for abandoned children, the House of the Children of Spain, only to have her philanthropic work blocked by the Roman Catholic Church because it did not come under its ecclesiastical control. Nelken was encouraged to continue her work by the Spanish socialists. She gave a series of lectures on social issues at the party's headquarters and took up propaganda work on women's rights and suffrage for the party, traveling throughout Spain during 1923–1931.

Nelken is best known for her 1919 study, *The Social Condition of Women in Spain: Current Status and Possible Development.* Inspired by John Stuart Mill's 1869 book, *The Subjection of Women,* Nelken described the misery of women's lives in a world where they remained the subordinates of men and under the social and moral control of the church. Their only hope of release from what Nelken described as a state of serfdom was to be emancipated through better education, greater economic independence, and the vote. But education would bring with it the threat of women taking jobs from men and a challenge to the traditional machismo of Spanish men, and Nelken was only too aware that such a dramatic change would require a difficult struggle. For her, the answer lay with socialism and the collective effort, and during her travels in Spain she tried to unite women's groups in the Socialist Party to campaign more efficiently for reform.

In 1931, after the Spanish monarchy collapsed, Nelken returned to Madrid and became chair of the Socialist Party's Committee on Women's Affairs. In the elections to the new national assembly that summer, she was one of three women elected, as a deputy for Badajoz, but she had to become a Spanish citizen first. In the national assembly, she opposed Clara Campoamor's calls for women's suffrage, arguing that Spanish levels of women's education lagged too far behind and that "to put a vote in the hands of a Spanish woman today is to fulfill the greatest desires of the reactionary" (Davies 1998, 105). Despite the cynicism of this remark, she nurtured the hope that conservative Catholicism in Spain might be eroded as women gained greater social and political rights. In the national assembly, therefore, she concentrated her arguments on women's education and sexual equality inside and outside

the family, in particular on the right to divorce, which she felt should be a woman's prerogative. She also proposed the creation of a system of social security to protect all workers.

At the end of 1931, Nelken devoted time to supporting the peasant protest movement in Badajoz in support of agrarian and constitutional reform and spoke at rallies and demonstrations. In the 1920s, she had developed a respect for the tough peasant women of southern Spain and was convinced that such women held the key to the emancipation of Spanish women at large. But like other feminists of her time, she despaired at the dismal lack of support accorded women's groups by the vast majority of Spanish women. Although she was reelected to the national assembly after the takeover of a new right-wing government in 1933, her attempts to introduce programs for women's education were stymied. In a wave of peasant strikes during 1934, and now active in the Workers' General Union, she returned to activism in the countryside in support of a general strike, but when it failed, she went into hiding, fleeing to France and then spending time in the Soviet Union. In 1935 she returned to Spain, where she cofounded the Committee of the Antifascist Auxiliary, a group dedicated to uniting women's groups against fascism, and was reelected to the Popular Front government of 1936. She continued working for the Socialist Party during the Civil War, as its assistant secretary, but in 1939, after General Franco came to power, she again had to flee. This time, she settled in Mexico, where she died in 1968.

Nelken's feminist writings, which remain untranslated, include "Feminism and Humanism" (1924) and "Woman, Man's Problem" and "The Problem of the Sexes" (both n.d.). She also published two novels in the 1920s, as well as *Spanish Women Writers* (1930) and *Woman before the Constituent Courts* (1931).

See also Campoamor, Clara.

References and Further Reading
Davies, Catherine. 1998. *Spanish Women's Writing 1849–1996.* London: Athlone Press.
Kern, Robert. 1981. "Margarita Nelken: Women and the Crisis of Spanish Politics." In Jane Slaughter and Robert Kern, eds., *European Women on the Left: Socialism, Feminism, and the Problems Faced by Political Women, 1880 to the Present.* Westport, CT: Greenwood Press.

Ngoyi, Lilian
(1911–1980)
South Africa

For the last sixteen years of her difficult life as a black activist and humanitarian in apartheid-riven South Africa, Lilian Ngoyi was under close surveillance. As president of the African National Congress (ANC) women's section and a powerful critic of the regime, she had earned the sobriquet "mother of the black resistance."

Ngoyi was born in the village of Gamatlala near Pretoria and was educated only to the primary level; her schooling at a Methodist school was curtailed when she had to help support her family after her miner-father became too ill to work. She trained for a while as a nurse at the Deep Mines Hospital in Pretoria and worked as a domestic servant and then as a machinist in a garment factory, in which latter employment (1945–1956) she became involved in the Garment Workers' Union (GWU), led by Solly Sachs and Johanna Cornelius. Married in 1934, Ngoyi was divorced shortly after having her three children and was left to support them by herself.

Ngoyi's campaigning for racial justice found its first outlet at the garment factory, where day after day she witnessed the exploitation of black women workers. She became a leader of the union's native branch and took part in a protest march against the exile of the GWU's communist leader, Sachs, in 1952.

In 1952 Ngoyi joined the ANC and took part in various acts of "defiance" against the color bar then in operation, such as entering a "whites only" post office. A year later, she became president of the ANC's women's section. She was arrested and briefly imprisoned in 1953 for being part of the ANC's campaign that protested against the extension of the pass laws to black women.

Ngoyi was a defiant and familiar public speaker on racial injustice during the 1950s. In 1954 she became one of four national vice presidents of the Federation of South African Women (FSAW), representing the Transvaal. After being an FSAW delegate to a conference in Lausanne of the International Democratic Federation of Women, she was invited to tour the communist East—the German Democratic Republic, the Soviet Union, and China—to raise awareness of and support for black civil rights.

Upon her return to South Africa, Ngoyi resumed her involvement in the anti–pass laws protest and addressed several rallies in the townships before heading a historic march with Helen Joseph by 20,000 women on 9 August 1956 that took the protest to the South African prime minister's offices in the Union Buildings in Pretoria. In December, as a result of the major role played by Ngoyi and other women in the ANC, she became the first woman to be elected to its national executive. But by this time, she and Joseph had been charged with high treason (she was one of thirty accused), and the trial dragged on for four years, until she was finally acquitted in March 1961.

Unrest in South Africa escalated in the late 1950s, and a state of emergency was declared in 1960 after the Sharpeville Massacre. Ngoyi's voice of protest was once again officially silenced. She was held without charge for seventy-one days in solitary confinement, and in October 1961, having continued to speak out in public, Ngoyi was placed under a banning order and confined to her home in Orlando township, with a brief period of respite between 1972 and 1975. There she struggled to earn a living by sewing.

Ngoyi's funeral in Soweto in 1980 provided a rallying point for 2,000 mourners and protestors, white as well as black, for whom she was an inspiring figure. Her friend from the Federation of South African Women, Helen Joseph, temporarily released from house arrest, was among the speakers.

See also Cornelius, Johanna; Joseph, Helen Beatrice.
References and Further Reading
The Annual Obituary. 1980–. New York: St. Martin's Press.
Karris, T., and G. M. Carter. 1977. *From Protest to Challenge: A Documentary History of Politics in South Africa 1882–1964*, vol. 4, *Political Profiles.* Stanford: Stanford University Press.
Stewart, Dianne. 1996. *Lillian Ngoyi, 1911–1980.* Cape Town: Maskew, Miller, Longman.
Uerwey, E. J. 1995. *New Dictionary of South African Biography.* Pretoria: HSRC Publishers.
Uweche, Raph, ed. 1996. *Makers of Modern Africa.* 3d ed. London: Africa Books.
Walker, Cheryl. 1991. *Women and Resistance in South Africa.* 2d ed. Cape Town: David Philip.

Niboyet, Eugénie
(1797–1883)
France

A St. Simonian and advocate of the moral reform of society who argued women's cause during the 1848 revolution at the French Constituent Assembly, Eugénie Niboyet was also one of the first professional women journalists in France. Through her writing, she promoted her ardent pacifism, her belief in women's suffrage, and her abhorrence of the death penalty.

Niboyet came from a Protestant middle-class family, originally from Geneva. Her father was a doctor in Montpellier; she was educated at home and married a Protestant lawyer at age twenty. Living in Lyons, she worked as a translator from English and published novels (*The Two Brothers* in 1839 and *Lucien* and *A Fortnight's Holiday* in 1841).

Moving to Paris, she took a post as secretary to the Society for Christian Morals in 1830, a society committed to the abolition of slavery, prison and social reform, world peace, and the education of the blind. Here she first heard lectures by the St. Simonians, a utopian group that supported sexual equality and women's emancipation, even though both its leaders and its theories were male-dominated. Niboyet welcomed St. Simonian ideas on morals and in particular their belief that women were not responsible for original sin. She became a dedicated supporter of the movement, winning over her husband as well, and progressed as far up the male hierarchy as possible, finally being appointed in 1832 as the head of the St. Simonian chapter of the fourth arrondissement of Paris.

Niboyet returned to Lyon in 1833 and took up journalism, founding and editing her own feminist newspaper there, the *Women's Adviser* (the first of its kind to be established outside Paris), to promote women's education and their higher moral values and to advocate the establishment of schools for poor children. She frequently contributed her own articles, including pioneering coverage of iniquitous court judgments against women in civil cases; supported women's rights to divorce; and in 1836 petitioned for the first time for women's suffrage. At this time, she was also writing for the middle-class feminist monthly, the *Women's Gazette* (1836–1838). This journal ran critiques of the French civil code in support of women's civil, educational, and professional rights and encouraged women to petition on issues such as divorce rights and the abolition of slavery and the death penalty. In 1836 Niboyet published a book on prison reform that advocated abolition of the death penalty, and in 1837 her educational treatise *The Blind and Their Education* appeared.

In the 1840s Niboyet was drawn to a new campaign—world peace. In 1843 she attended a peace congress in London and, inspired by the work of English pacifists, in 1844 helped establish a French peace society and the journal *Peace in the Two Worlds* (the journal ran February–October 1844). The peace society, although boasting only thirty-two members, attracted intellectuals to pacifism with its espousal of the Quaker ideal of peace as emanating from domestic harmony. Niboyet also contributed to another short-lived pacifist journal, the *Future* (October 1844 to April 1845); in both journals she argued for a reduction in spending on arms. In her view, the thirty years of peace enjoyed by France since the end of the Napoleonic Wars had promoted a great period of economic progress, and French national pride and prosperity could be better demonstrated in continuing this trend instead of increasing taxation to maintain the military. Economic growth could thus fund public works—build roads and railways—and relieve the misery of the working classes by bringing greater social justice.

In 1848, the year of revolution, with help from a St. Simonian woman banker, Niboyet brought out a daily socialist women's newspaper, the *Voice of Women*, which published forty-six issues from March to June in Paris and some provincial towns, another pioneering feminist publication that set out to provide women with "a library of practical information" (Rowbotham 1972, 120) and acted as a focus for the plethora of revolutionary clubs that sprang up that year, encouraging women to set up their own. The paper, which called for women to come together and work for their own emancipation from the slavery of both work and the domestic sphere and take part in politics as equal citizens with men, was also antiracist and abolitionist. In its first issue, it petitioned for women's political and social rights. Members of the editorial team soon formed a club of the same name—the Society of the Voice of Women—which brought together women of differing backgrounds to discuss politics, education, and the administration of cooperative workshops. The *Voice of Women* also propagated its editors' belief in equality for women within marriage and women's right to work.

Calling for women to be able to vote in the April 1848 elections, Niboyet and her colleagues urged the writer George Sand to stand for the National Assembly elections in June. Sand declined the suggestion, however, and soon after, Niboyet's journal was suppressed under new laws. Later, in 1863 when Niboyet published her memoir of 1848 (as *The True Book of Women*), she encapsulated within it her philosophy on the division of labor, in which men should work in commerce and politics and women should be responsible for morals and child care.

Niboyet's espousal of radicalism subsequently waned after Louis Napoleon's coup in 1851 and the suppression of women's organized political activities that came with the establishment of the Second Empire. Niboyet withdrew from political activism and moved back to Lyon. She concentrated on journalism, in particular defending the rights of women workers, but her writing became increasingly conservative in tone. She also translated works by Charles Dickens, the abolitionist Lydia Maria Child, and the Irish novelist Maria Edgeworth. She settled in Geneva after 1852, returning at the end of the Second Empire in 1871. She wrote articles for the new journal *Women's Rights* (founded in 1869), and continued to support the idea of separate peace organizations created by women. During the Paris Exposition of 1878 she attended the First International Congress on Women's Rights and the Congress of the Friends of Peace—both held in the city—at which latter event she urged women to establish their own peace organizations.

See also Child, Lydia Maria; Edgeworth, Maria; Sand, George.

References and Further Reading
Josephson, Harold, Sandi Cooper, and Steven C. Hause, et al., eds. 1985. *Biographical Dictionary of Modern Peace Leaders*. Westport, CT: Greenwood Press.
Moses, Claire Goldberg. 1984. *French Feminism in the Nineteenth Century*. Albany: State University of New York Press.
———. 1993. *Feminism, Socialism and French Romanticism*. Bloomington: Indiana University Press.
Offen, Karen. 2000. *European Feminisms 1700–1950: A Political History*. Stanford: Stanford University Press.
Rendall, J. 1987. *Equal or Different: Women's Politics 1800–1914*. Oxford: Blackwell.
Rowbotham, Sheila. 1972. *Women, Resistance, and Revolution*. Harmondsworth: Penguin.
Strumingher, Laura S. 1979. *Women and the Making of the Working Class: Lyon, 1830–1870*. St. Albans, VT: Eden Press.

Nightingale, Florence
(1820–1910)
United Kingdom

The life and reputation of the Victorian icon and originator of modern nursing, Florence Nightingale, have been subject to constant reevaluation and, latterly, even radical deconstruction. In the days when she was first sentimentalized in Victorian hagiographies written by her many admirers she was elevated, much against her own will, to the role of latter-day saint and "Lady with the Lamp." Her reputation was viewed as sacrosanct, and her work in the Crimea was seen as the pinnacle of dedicated self-sacrifice and humanitarian achievement to which all good Victorians should aspire. But the reality of Nightingale's sense of personal failure and despair is a far more compelling story, recently uncovered by Hugh Small (1998). After analyzing her own statistics, Nightingale came to the conclusion, a year after the Crimean War was over, that she had unwittingly contributed to the unnecessary deaths of thousands of the sick and wounded in her supposedly prestigious Barrack Hospital in Scutari. Although her posthumous, popular reputation was largely built on her work in women's nursing, in her determination to expose the official neglect of basic standards of hospital hygiene in the Crimea and with it her own culpability, Nightingale ultimately turned against the idea of the hospitalization of the sick and joined the movement for public health reform that sought to counter the high death rates from infectious diseases.

A fact less well known is that Nightingale was an exceptional statistician, who put her skills to good use in compiling vast dossiers on mortality rates that were significant aids in public health reform. She was also the first woman to be elected as a fellow of the Statistical Society. It was this work that, ultimately, she personally considered more important than her long-inflated reputation as the supposedly sole pioneer of women's nursing in Britain. This myth has now been demolished, with the British health workers' union, Unison, deciding in 1999 to abandon Nightingale as its mascot and founding mother of modern nursing. In the union's view, she was no longer an appropriate figure for the new millennium and was looked upon now as representing negative and backward-thinking elements in nursing.

Florence Nightingale was named after the Italian city where she was born during her parents' extended honeymoon in Europe. Returning to England, she spent her early life in two family homes, Lea Hurst in Derbyshire and Embley Park in Hampshire, interspersed with regular visits to London for the social season. She received an exceptional liberal education for her time. Her father, a Whig and a Unitarian, tutored her at home in Latin, Greek, French, German, and Italian. Together they also studied philosophy and history, as well as mathematics, a subject at that time considered unsuitable for young women. At the age of seventeen, the religiously devout Nightingale experienced a revelation that God had a particular mission for her—as yet unrevealed. It took years of escalating discontent, playing the role of the dutiful daughter and being slowly suffocated by the quiet domestic round, before she finally found her vocation. When she began breaking the monotony of her life with occasional charitable visits to the poor and the sick in workhouse hospitals and trips to nurse sick relatives, the idea of becoming a nurse took root.

In the meantime, Nightingale had determinedly put up barriers to any idea of marriage. In 1849 she finally rejected the prolonged courtship (since 1842) of Richard Monckton Milnes, unable to bear the prospect of a living death "nailed to a continuation, an exaggeration of my present life without hope of another" (Forster 1984, 104). She was by now utterly set on espousing useful, active work as an independent woman. Nightingale's loathing of the enforced idleness of women's lives would be unleashed in her later autobiographical piece, "Cassandra." Written in 1852 and originally included in her unpublished *Suggestions for Thought to Searchers after Religious Truth,* a "massive, disorganized and repetitive" work in the view of Janet Todd (1989, 500), "Cassandra" was not published until 1928. Nightingale was

thirty-two when she wrote this discourse on women's dependency and purposelessness, in which she raged about their lack of education and vocational outlets and the frittering away of their lives in shallow socializing. She had spent a third of her life imprisoned in this way, and "Cassandra" was a powerful indictment of her own gender. Nightingale denigrated women's adoption of the then-admired qualities of feminine weakness and inadequacy. She saw these traits as doing nothing but further empowering men while emphasizing the female sex's perceived physical feebleness and intellectual ineptitude. By rejecting marriage and the sublimation of her own vocation in that of a husband, she made clear the inadequacy of domestic life for women like herself of "passion, intellect, moral activity" (Nightingale 1978, 396). In its advocacy of women's work in their own separate sphere, "Cassandra" was a radical argument that had a direct influence later on *The Subjection of Women,* written by Nightingale's friend John Stuart Mill, who had not been able to persuade her to publish her own piece.

In 1844 Nightingale announced her desire to study nursing for three months at Salisbury Infirmary. Her parents' and sister's response to the request was extreme. They recoiled in horror at the thought of Florence moving among the Mrs. Gamps of Dickensian notoriety. Such a literary grotesque, who featured in Charles Dickens's recently serialized novel *Martin Chuzzlewhit* (1843–1844), was based on a real nurse who had been employed by his friend, the philanthropist Angela Burdett-Coutts. It had exaggerated the public notion of then-untrained nurses as filthy slatterns of dubious reputation, who liked their drink too much and neglected their patients. Nightingale despaired at her family's response and went into a deep depression. She resolved to continue visiting schools for poor children and hospitals whenever the family was in London and became engrossed in the private study of Blue Books on public health and social conditions, such as the 1840 report on the Health of Towns. Thanks to her mathematical skills, she was able to master the most complex of social statistics.

In 1850, Nightingale's parents, keen to dispel all ideas of nursing once and for all, sent her on a trip to Greece. On her way back to England, she made a detour to spend time observing the work of the nursing sisters at the Institution of Protestant Deaconesses, a hospital in Kaiserwerth, Germany. A year later, in July 1851, she finally persuaded her family to allow her to return there to train as a nurse. The regime was spartan and the hours long, but Nightingale was euphoric in her sense of personal liberation: "This is life. Now I know what it is to live and to love life. . . . I wish for no other earth, no other world than this" (Woodham-Smith 1950, 69). The reality of life at Kaiserwerth was grim, however: Nightingale observed operations and amputations performed without anesthetic, and the training, she admitted much later in 1897, had been "nil" and the standards of hygiene "horrible" (70). These deficiencies were compensated for by the institution's high moral tone and frequent calls to prayer, of which Nightingale heartily approved.

After three months at Kaiserwerth, she returned home, her mind irrevocably set on a nursing career. Soon after, she answered the call to nurse both her sick father and sister and then went to Paris in February 1853 to gain further nursing experience at the Convent of the Sisters of Charity. Within a couple of weeks, however, she was summoned back home, this time to nurse her sick grandmother. Only when she was offered the post of superintendent (without salary) of the Institute for the Care of Sick Gentlewomen in Harley Street, London, was Nightingale finally able to escape from what might otherwise have been the role of peripatetic nursemaid to her various relatives. Given a private allowance of £500 a year by her father, she took up her post in August 1853 and immediately invested much of her money in improvements at the institute to the plumbing and catering facilities. Nightingale also introduced an overhaul of its administration and nursing practices, but not without a battle with the hospital's governing body, which resented her interference. By this time, Nightingale was well versed in the workings of committees and reports, but for a woman of her vision and ambition, the institute was soon far too limited a sphere of activity, and she began looking for a new arena in which she could fulfill her sense of vocation.

It came when war broke out in the Crimea in March 1854 and British troops were sent there to fight in September. Reports of their sufferings by *Times* correspondent William Russell prompted Nightingale to offer to travel to the Crimea, chaperoned by two of her female friends, to nurse the wounded. In the event, she was asked by her friend Sidney Herbert, secretary of state for war, to head a party of thirty-eight nurses being sent to the military hospital established in old Turkish army barracks at Scutari, a suburb of the capital, Constantinople. Nightingale left on 21 October, arriving after an uncomfortable sea journey on 4 November. The situation that greeted her on her arrival was one of imminent catastrophe and the stink was overwhelming. "I have been well acquainted with the dwellings of the worst parts of most of the great cities in Europe," she wrote, "but have never been in any atmosphere which I could compare with that of the Barrack Hospital at night" (Nightingale 1978, 119).

The wounded, who were transported from the front lines 300 miles away across the Black Sea to the hospital at Scutari, were dying at an alarming rate. Mortality rates from postoperative trauma after the amputation of limbs without anesthetic were particularly high, but also many patients were picking up infections and fevers once they were hospitalized. A great many others suffered from malnutrition and scurvy and, during the winter months, from frostbite. The wards in which they were housed were filthy, without proper plumbing and infested with vermin. And soon they were overflowing with hundreds of additional wounded from the battle of Inkerman, which took place on 5 November, a day after Nightingale's arrival. Many of these new wounded did not even have straw pallets on which to lie. Medical supplies of the most basic kind were lacking: there were insufficient bandages, dressings, basins, towels, and soap; even operating tables were in short supply, as were food and water, clothing for the wounded—who often arrived half-naked—and clean linen. The nonexistent sanitation and lack of proper heating all contributed to the incidence of fevers and the spreading of diseases such as dysentery and cholera. The work of the nurses, who assisted male medical orderlies, was further hampered by the hostility of the army doctors, who had no desire to see their work undermined by women. In addition, Nightingale set rigorous standards, expecting her nurses to do the same work as men without claiming special dispensations or giving way to slackness or fatigue.

With ruthless efficiency, Nightingale set about cleaning up the hospital and purchasing supplies and clothing for the wounded with the use of £30,000 that had been raised for the purpose before her departure, thanks to publicity from *The Times*. Floors were scrubbed, walls repainted, corridors repaved, and the straw-strewn wards properly floored; laundries were set up where soldiers' wives took on the washing. Major improvements were made to the quality of the food provided when the famous chef, Alexis Soyer, who arrived at Scutari with Nightingale, established his bivouac kitchens to prepare nourishing soups and stews.

Despite their dedication, Nightingale held a low view of the nurses serving under her, many of whom she felt did not come up to her own high standards. Some, proving unsuitable, were sent home; others, such as Jane Shaw Stewart and the Reverend Mother Frances Bridgeman, who equaled Nightingale in their skill and dedication (although posterity chose to ignore them), tired of Nightingale's harsh and dictatorial manner and went elsewhere in the Crimea to nurse. The intrepid Mary Seacole, a Jamaican, had operated independently from the outset. Having banned her own nurses from the wards after 8.30 P.M. (fearful that they might succumb to improper advances from the soldiers), Nightingale patrolled the hospital corridors on her own. Thus was born the image of the "Lady with the Lamp," first publicized in the February 1855 edition of the *Illustrated London News* and later immortalized in an 1857 poem by Henry Wadsworth Longfellow, "Santa Filomena." Thanks to the publicity surrounding Nightingale's nursing achievements in the Crimea, the war became popular at home, led by that great enthusiast Queen Victoria. She sent a personal message to Nightingale in December 1855, accompanied by gifts for distribution among the wounded: "your goodness and self devotion in giving yourself up to the soothing attendance upon these wounded and sick soldiers has been observed by the Queen with sentiments of the highest approval and admiration" (Woodham-Smith 1950, 155).

There is no doubt that the injured revered Nightingale as a saint and miracle worker—in whose presence they would cease to cuss and swear—but Nightingale herself was never sentimental about her work, driven as she was by the ethics of efficiency and clinical detachment. After conducting her ward patrols, she would often sit up well into the night over her statistical tables,

preparing reports to be sent back to Sidney Herbert in England. Despite working herself to exhaustion and refusing to delegate, she overcame a bout of fever and demonstrated almost superhuman powers of resistance to the toll of her work. By the time the war was over, army statistics were proclaiming that thanks to Nightingale's work, the death rate among the wounded at the Barrack Hospital had dropped from 40 percent to 2 percent; but, as Small points out, Nightingale's work in the Crimea had been primarily "in disentangling hospital supplies from a mass of red tape" (1998, 43), not in furthering nursing techniques. There was also a huge discrepancy between the high death rate during the first winter of 1854–1855 when she first arrived at Scutari and that during the second, when the death rates dramatically dropped—but only after official sanitary inspection teams from England had instituted changes.

Nightingale did everything she could to avoid the huge publicity that greeted her return home, having remained at Scutari until the final evacuation of British troops in July 1856. The British nation now very rightly looked upon their Lady with the Lamp as public property, but Nightingale had no desire to promote her public image, refused interviews, and only grudgingly accepted the many gifts that were heaped upon her. She was duty-bound to acknowledge the grateful thanks and admiration of her queen, who presented her with a brooch in the style of a St. George's Cross and inscribed with the words "Blessed Are the Merciful." Although her popular, public career now effectively ended, her work as a reformer was only just beginning. But it was born of a period of intense introspection and despair. For within a year of her return from the Crimea, Nightingale collapsed and never fully recovered her health.

Opinions differ over the cause of Nightingale's mysterious physical incapacitation, which some see as psychosomatic and prompted by her own neuroses. It is probable that she succumbed to the long-term effects on her system of the bouts of dysentery, rheumatism, and fever that she had suffered in the Crimea. It has even been suggested that she suffered from brucellosis, a disease as yet unknown to Victorian doctors. The remaining years of her long life would be spent in determined isolation from the public gaze at a house in Mayfair, broken only occasionally by trips to the family homes in the country. Yet despite her physical infirmity, Nightingale's intellect was far from impaired, and she had a significant influence on social reform for many years thereafter, conducting her work while reclining on her sofa, where she also received government ministers, friends, and other visitors.

It is Hugh Small's contention that Nightingale's physical and mental collapse after returning from the Crimea was brought about by repressed guilt, after she recognized that during her tenure as superintendent of nursing at Scutari, "bad hygiene had killed thousands of patients in her hospital" (1998, 3). Soon after the war, she had been asked by Prime Minister Lord Palmerston to present a confidential report on the medical services there. She undertook the work convinced that the high death rate of 5,000 at the Barrack Hospital during the winter of 1854–1855 had arisen because the wounded sent to her were already in a mainly irretrievable state, which no amount of efficient nursing by her could have countered. But as she began analyzing her own statistics and notes, she realized that patients with relatively minor wounds had succumbed and died once evacuated to her hospital, whereas those who were treated in the open air, on the battlefield—often undergoing amputations in situ—usually survived. It was the spread of "miasmas" of infection (the term used in the days before Louis Pasteur articulated germ theory) that she concluded had killed her patients, not the wounds they had received on the battlefield. Her worst suspicions were confirmed when she evaluated the mortality statistics in consultation with Dr. William Farr, superintendent of the Statistical Department of the Registrar-General's Office. He was not, as his title suggests, a dry statistician but a pioneer in hygiene and public health and an early convert to the idea of airborne disease being spread in contaminated environments.

By May 1857, Nightingale had become convinced that the cause of many deaths at Scutari had been bad hygiene, caused by overcrowding in the poorly laid out and unventilated barracks and compounded by bad sanitation as the result of blocked sewers (which transmitted the lethal cholera germs). For all her assiduous reorganizing of supplies, her scrubbing, night patrols, and nourishing soups, her hospital had been, in her own view, little more than a death camp. She wrote up her conclusions in a report entitled "Notes on Matters Affecting the Health, Efficiency, and Hospital Administration of the British Army, Founded Chiefly on the Experience of the Late War," with the damning statistics contained in a new section, entitled "Causes of Disaster at Scutari," which she intended as an appendix. The Royal Commission into the Health of the Army sat during May–July 1857, but the government was reluctant to publish Farr and Nightingale's findings, which Small argues was probably in order to "protect the new public enthusiasm for nursing" and with it, no doubt, Nightingale's spotless reputation (1998, 114). These statistics were omitted as evidence from the final report. However, Nightingale circulated about 100 copies of the "Causes of Disaster at Scutari" privately to friends and public figures, thus ensuring it would one day come to light. In 1859 she enlisted the help of Harriet Martineau to leak some of these findings in a book, *England and Her Soldiers,* which was published under Martineau's name but at Nightingale's expense and reiterated Nightingale's conclusions.

The perception that hygiene was the essential factor in hospital care, over and above good administration and improved nursing training, shifted Nightingale's perspective on nursing thereafter. Her interest in the medical training of nurses was replaced by a mission to improve standards of public health, with Nightingale drawing parallels between her findings at Scutari and the high mortality rates from tuberculosis and whooping cough. These, she argued, moving ever closer to acceptance of new theories on the airborne transmission of disease, were the result of bad ventilation and overcrowding. Such conclusions also prompted Nightingale's consideration of the wider social aspects of deprivation— poor housing, lack of sanitation, unclean water supplies, and poor diet—and her support for legislation put to Parliament in 1867 by the eminent reformer Edwin Chadwick.

Not content with addressing the problems of the British army in the Crimea, Nightingale turned to investigating the high peacetime mortality rates among soldiers posted to India, writing endless letters and gathering evidence in support of what would become the 1859 Royal Commission on the Health of the British Army in India. Despite her continuing physical infirmity, her appetite for work was prodigious. Lytton Strachey has remarked on the paradox of

Nightingale's long life as a valetudinarian, observing that she was "an invalid of curious character . . . who was too weak to walk downstairs" but yet she "worked harder than most Cabinet Ministers" (1971, 151–152). In the preparation of her report, she interviewed members of royal commissions, ministers, and government officials and ploughed through two huge volumes of reports sent back from every military station in India. After sifting and assessing the information contained in them, she prepared a comprehensive account, the 800-page *Notes on Matters Affecting the Health, Efficiency and Hospital Administration of the British Army* (1858). A masterpiece of statistical analysis, it is crammed with exhaustive lists of facts and figures. It would become the Bible of public health reform work in Britain. As in her earlier, suppressed report, Nightingale demonstrated the alarming rate of mortality in army barracks in peacetime, which was double that of the population at large, and provided evidence of the unsanitary conditions in barracks and poor levels of health care. As part of her recommendations, Nightingale also devised an overhaul of the accounting system of the Army Medical Services in the early 1860s that would still be in use during World War II.

Although male officialdom never ceased to balk at being told what to do by an interfering woman, over the next thirty years Nightingale persisted in offering her unpaid advice on Indian reform. She wrote many papers on the subject, such as "How Some People Have Lived and Not Died in India." Although she was never able to visit the country, she had a considerable influence over colonial reform there, becoming an authority on village land tenure, education, public health, irrigation and sanitation, taxation, and municipal government. She also constantly drew attention to the ever-present threat of famine in India and later supported Indian nationalism and condemned the injustices of the salt tax.

For several years, Nightingale's work for army medical reform kept her away from the work she had been expected to embrace upon her return—the training of nurses. Many commentators have argued that an undue emphasis has been placed on this work to the detriment of Nightingale's other, much more important contributions to public health. And she would have been the first to agree that the promotion of herself as the sole arbiter of nursing standards in

Britain contributed to the neglect of other nursing pioneers from the Crimea, such as Bridgeman and Seacole. It also completely overlooked the pioneering work of Elizabeth Fry, now recognized by the British Medical Association as a founder of nursing practice. Fry had inspired the nursing methods of the German pastor Theodor Fliedner with her plans for improvements to nursing training and standards in Britain. In 1836 he had founded the Institution of Protestant Deaconesses at Kaiserwerth, which had put Nightingale on the path to her own nursing career.

Indeed, after realizing that hospital nursing could spread infectious disease, Nightingale turned violently against hospitals and was decidedly reluctant to become involved in hospital work again. She became convinced that the sick were better off being nursed at home. There was, however, the matter of the £45,000 proceeds from the Nightingale Fund established during the war, in 1855, to finance further nursing reforms by her. Nightingale therefore endorsed the money's use in the building of the Nightingale School for Nurses. She was disappointed in the decision to locate the school within the grounds of St. Thomas's Hospital in central London and not in the more healthy rural suburbs, and after taking a hand in the design of the school, ensuring its good ventilation, and setting out a yearlong training scheme geared to practical work on the wards, she took little active interest in it. Under its matron, Mrs. Wardroper, the Nightingale School trained new generations of midwives and nurses, who in turn promoted the "Nightingale Model" of nursing training in Britain and abroad, a method that in later years came under attack for its authoritarian attitudes, its close surveillance of trainees, and the undue emphasis on strict, military-style order. The regime imposed at St. Thomas's proved daunting to all but the most determined probationer nurses, and Nightingale as ever remained excessively critical of the caliber of most of the women who entered nursing training.

Nightingale laid down her methods in *Notes on Hospitals,* which covered the construction and administration of hospitals, and the landmark *Notes on Nursing: What It Is, and What It Is Not,* in 1859. The latter sold 15,000 copies in a month even at the price of five shillings (it remains in print today). The title, however, is misleading, for the emphasis in *Notes on Nursing* was placed by

Nightingale on simple, no-nonsense domestic hygiene and the care of the sick, not in hospitals but in their homes. This advice was taken note of by mothers and caretakers, and its wide circulation led to a drop in mortality rates from childhood diseases such as measles and scarlet fever. The application of Nightingale's nursing methods did, however, achieve greater long-term results in the reform of workhouse hospital administration and the pioneering of district nursing, which were undertaken at Liverpool Workhouse Infirmary by William Rathbone (father of Eleanor Rathbone). Beginning in 1864, he was assisted by the infirmary's matron, Agnes Jones, a woman of great dedication and compassion who died in a typhus epidemic there in 1868 (and whose work has yet to be properly credited). Nightingale pointed out the high death rate accompanying childbirth in public institutions, as opposed to childbirth taking place in the home, outlining her arguments in *Introductory Notes on Lying-In Institutions* (1871). She worked toward reform of the workhouse system in London, laying out a program involving the separate care of the sick and the insane among the workhouse population that contributed to the passage of the Metropolitan Poor Act in 1867.

Nightingale never lent her voice to the women's suffrage movement, privately doubting her sex's ability to use the franchise wisely and publicly arguing that there were far more pressing social evils that should be first addressed, such as women's economic position and their right to vocational work. She preferred, in any case, to work for women "off the stage than on it" (Woodham-Smith 1950, 367) and was indeed a powerful influence for social change who later claimed that by doing it her own way, she had had more administrative influence than if she had been "a borough returning two members to Parliament" (Woodham-Smith 1950, 367). She thus declined an invitation to join the London National Society for Women's Suffrage in 1867, although she had supported the 1850s campaign for a married women's property act led by her cousin Barbara Bodichon.

Nightingale's primary reformist work for women was confined to the repeal of the Contagious Diseases Acts, which was soon dominated by another determined and dedicated woman reformer who liked to lead from the front, Josephine Butler. Nightingale's knowledge of the effects of venereal disease had come through her medical experiences in Scutari and in London. Convinced that regulation of prostitutes was not the answer to what she viewed as an essentially moral problem, she had protested when the War Office had first begun talking of introducing Continental-style measures to control prostitutes operating near military bases in the early 1860s. She argued against the effectiveness of legislation in reducing the incidence of venereal disease, suggesting that troops should be provided with clubs and recreation facilities that discouraged their resorting to vice. Nevertheless, the first Contagious Diseases Act was passed in June 1864, although Lynn McDonald contends that Nightingale's lobbying prior to the bill's enactment had succeeded in obtaining "significant limiting of police powers" (1998, 202) in the final wording of the 1864 act.

Behind the door of her home in Mayfair, Nightingale remained an active voice in moral and social reform until the 1890s. She began going blind in 1895 and by 1901 had lost her sight altogether. Her mental powers, too, had begun to fail. She lived on for another nine years, in 1907 becoming the first woman to be awarded a new honor inaugurated by King Edward VII, the Order of Merit—a fact that reminded many of the British public that she was still alive. In 1908 she was only the second woman in British history to be granted the Freedom of the City of London. She left strict instructions to have no memorial and no state funeral and was buried, not in Westminster Abbey as the authorities wished, but in her family grave. The Florence Nightingale Museum in London is open to visitors; for information, go to http://www.florence-nightingale. co.uk. Hugh Small, author of a revealing 1998 study of Nightingale, has established a website with many useful links to other sites at http://www.florence-nightingale-avenging-angel.co.uk.

See also Bodichon, Barbara; Burdett-Coutts, Angela; Fry, Elizabeth; Martineau, Harriet; Rathbone, Eleanor; Seacole, Mary.

References and Further Reading

Boyd, Nancy. 1982. *Josephine Butler, Octavia Hill, Florence Nightingale: Three Victorian Women Who Changed Their World.* London: Macmillan.

Cook, Sir Edward. 1913. *The Life of Florence Nightingale* London: Macmillan.

Cope, Zachary. 1958. *Florence Nightingale and the Doctors.* London: Museum.

Forster, M. 1984. *Significant Sisters: The Grassroots of Active Feminism, 1839–1939*. London: Secker and Warburg.

Goldie, Sue M. 1987. *I Have Done My Duty: Florence Nightingale in the Crimean War, 1854–1856*. Manchester: Manchester University Press.

Huxley, Elspeth, and Josceline Grant. 1975. *Florence Nightingale*. London: Weidenfeld and Nicholson.

McDonald, Lynn, ed. 1998. *Women Theorists on Society and Politics*. Waterloo, ON: Wilfrid Laurier University Press.

Nightingale, Florence. 1978 [1928]. "Cassandra." In Ray Strachey, ed., *The Cause: A Brief History of the Women's Movement*. Reprint, London: Virago.

O'Malley, Ida. 1931. *Florence Nightingale 1820–1856*. London: Thornton Butterworth.

Small, Hugh. 1998. *Florence Nightingale: Avenging Angel*. London: Constable.

Smith, F. B. 1982. *Florence Nightingale: Reputation and Power*. London: Croom Helm.

Strachey, Lytton. 1971 [1918]. *Eminent Victorians*. Reprint, Harmondsworth: Penguin.

Todd, Janet. 1989. *Dictionary of British Women Writers*. London: Routledge.

Tuson, Penelope, ed. 1997. *The Queen's Daughters: An Anthology of Victorian Feminist Writings on India 1857–1900*. Reading, Berkshire, UK: Ithaca Press.

Vicinus, Martha. 1977. *A Widening Sphere: Changing Roles of Victorian Women*. Bloomington: Indiana University Press.

Vicinus, Martha, and Bea Nergaard, eds. 1989. *Ever Yours, Florence Nightingale*. London: Virago.

Woodham-Smith, Cecil. 1950. *Florence Nightingale, 1820–1910*. Edinburgh: Constable.

Noble, Christina
(1944–)
Ireland/Vietnam

Having suffered the deprivation of a tough Dublin childhood, followed by homelessness and abuse as a young wife, Christina Noble has exorcised her painful past through her dedication to the deprived street children of Saigon—offering them refuge, medical care, and an education under the auspices of the Christina Noble Children's Foundation. Her work has now stretched beyond Vietnam to fund-raising tours around the world and work in Mongolia for the rights of children in prison.

Noble was born 23 December 1944, one of a family of eight, and grew up in a grimly named Dublin slum—Marrowbone Lane. After her mother's early death, left hungry by their alco-holic father, Noble and her three younger siblings were split up and sent to institutions. She ran away from the first one and lived on the streets for a year until social services picked her up and sent her to St. Joseph's Industrial School, where under its draconian regime she was savagely beaten by the nuns. In the 1970s, now married, she became trapped in a terrifying round of domestic abuse, until she found the courage to leave in 1976. After several years of psychotherapy and a long rehabilitation from the trauma of her early life, Noble left her children behind in Surrey to go to Vietnam.

Noble arrived in Ho Chi Minh City in 1989, where she rapidly became aware of the terrible poverty and homelessness that were the legacy of the long, bitter Vietnam War. In particular, she was deeply moved by the plight of the many illegitimate and homeless Amerasian street children who had been fathered by American soldiers and abandoned after U.S. troops withdrew in 1975. She began to befriend the sickly and malnourished children living in the streets near her cheap hotel, bought them food, and tried to think of ways of helping them. Frequently rounded up by the police, the children were mostly street vendors who scavenged for enough to survive, not criminals. Many of them were literate and did not use drugs. Coming across the Center for the Rehabilitation of Malnourished Orphans in a seedy back street, Noble asked to be allowed to take over the use of a derelict building in its compound. She moved in here and lived amid the rats and leaking roof while waiting for permission from the Vietnamese government in Hanoi to convert the premises into a medical and social center for street children. Meanwhile, she solicited funds from local businesses, eventually raising enough to convert the ground floor into a special care center and clinic for the sickest children and the upstairs into recovery rooms and a daytime nursery where poor working people could leave their children. Despite receiving further funds from foreign businesspeople, the center's needs escalated, with Noble projecting that it would require $70,000 a year to stay open. At this point she returned to the United Kingdom to raise money and acquire medicine and equipment such as incubators and electrocardiogram machines. An article about the street children in the *Sunday People* prompted a generous response from the public and the offer of help from a volunteer nurse and a pediatrician. She returned to Vietnam having raised £100,000.

Once the Children's Medical and Social Center was up and running on 1 June 1991, Noble began extending the social aspects of her work. She talked to street children about their experiences. Many of them had been born to prostitutes and had been forced to beg by their pimps; some of the children were Burmese and had been kidnapped to work in Vietnamese brothels. Noble uncovered details of a horrifying trade in which children from Pakistan were either sold into prostitution or, in the case of boys, sold as camel jockeys in the affluent Middle East. There was also a conspicuous trade in virgins conducted by Taiwanese men, who sold girls as young as twelve into Vietnamese brothels, and more recently children had become prey to Western pedophiles arriving in Vietnam for the express purpose of abusing vulnerable children. Many children, out of desperate poverty and hunger, had been caught up in crime and drug abuse. There were also many disabled children who, in Vietnam, were frequently abandoned by their parents. Many of Noble's children suffered from the long-term effects of disease and injury that had not been treated or the psychological damage of neglect and abuse.

Soon after the center opened, it was besieged by anxious parents who had traveled in from rural areas with their sick and frequently highly infectious children. The center administered vaccinations for polio, diphtheria, and other diseases, but its major task was to tackle the medical problems related to malnutrition, giving instruction also to street children and their families in better hygiene and health care. The center's Sunshine School set up an education program, which began with eighty pupils and required an additional $20,000 a year to run. Filmmakers from several countries and a steady flow of journalists and photographers helped keep the center in the public eye and attracted eminent visitors, such as Mother Teresa. Noble published a book about her life and her work entitled *Bridge across My Sorrows* and undertook book tours in Germany and Australia in 1992–1993 to promote the book (it was published in the United Kingdom in 1994). In the latter country, she underwent an operation to remove a malignant tumor, which was caught just in time. Back in Vietnam, she took over a build-ing in District 10 of Saigon and opened up another center. Her foundation was rapidly expanding to take on various philanthropic projects suggested by Vietnamese organizations.

In 1997 Noble traveled to the former Soviet republic of Mongolia to visit a colleague who was working in the capital, Ulan Bator. In a country in the throes of economic collapse, the decay of its infrastructure, and an alarming rise in alcoholism, she visited children being held on charges, mainly of petty theft, in the police detention center. She discovered sixty or so children, inadequately dressed and huddled together in cold cells, infested with lice, covered in ulcers and cuts, and many of them suffering from gonorrhea and syphilis for which there were no medicines to treat them. Determined to improve their miserable lives, Noble enlisted official support to build a small village of traditional *gers* (movable tent dwellings). She also took time to visit other children's prisons and studied the conditions of poor children in Mongolia, many of them orphans who lived on the streets and, like the children of Vietnam, supported themselves mainly by stealing and prostitution. She discovered children living in underground tunnels near the hot water pipes that served the city. Returning to Ireland, she went on a round of fund-raising to attract attention to her new project and returned to Mongolia with a volunteer, Wendy Evans. In 1998 they supervised the construction of a *ger* village to house about thirty-six children under the supervision of adults and set up literacy classes for boys in prison.

In 1998 the Christina Noble Children's Foundation (CNCF) was launched in Ireland with Mary McAleese as its Irish president. Noble then embarked once more on an exhausting tour to promote the work of her foundation, which now has branches in fourteen countries and runs sponsorship schemes for its deprived children. Her work in Vietnam alone has transformed the lives of 80,000 children, with the Sunshine School having a staff of fifty and an intake of around seventy-five children at any given time; its choir, orchestra, and soccer team are all flourishing. She has plans to expand the Sunshine School and its medical center further to accommodate 400 children and cope with the growing number of outpatients being treated at the rate of 1,000 or so every month. Other ambitious plans include introducing kindergarten teachers, specialists in physiology and psychology, and special facilities for deaf and blind children and those who have been sexually abused. For more information on the foundation, see its website: http://www.cncf.org. Noble has been accorded many awards for her work, including the (British) People of the Year Award (1997) and the Reader's Digest Heroes Award (1996), and was nominated one of the Women of the Year (UK, 1995). In 1997 the work of the CNCF in Vietnam was honored by the Red Cross.

References and Further Reading

Noble, Christina. 1994. *Bridge across My Sorrows: The Christina Noble Story.* London: John Murray.

———. 1998. *Mama Tina.* London: John Murray.

Noble, Christina, and Robert Coram. 1994. *Nobody's Child: A Woman's Abusive Past and the Inspiring Dream That Led Her to Rescue the Street Children of Saigon.* New York: Grove Press.

Noonuccal, Oodgeroo Moongalba (Kath Walker)
(1920–1993)
Australia

The Aboriginal poet and civil rights activist Oodgeroo Noonuccal became her nation's first published writer in 1964 with her poetry collection *We Are Going,* and later set up a center for the promotion of Aboriginal culture and history. She was born Kathleen Ruska on North Stradbroke Island, off the coast of Brisbane in Queensland, a member of the Noonuccal tribe. After a primary education, she pursued her own studies and began writing poetry. From the age of thirteen, she worked in domestic service in Brisbane. During World War II, Noonuccal joined the Australian Women's Army Service, working at a telephone switchboard.

Disillusioned with the established political parties' failure to address Aboriginal issues, she joined the Australian Communist Party. In 1960 she became secretary of the Federal Council for the Advancement of Aborigines and Torres Strait Islanders and worked toward the integration rather than the assimilation of Aboriginals and improvements to their civil and political status. She traveled across Australia speaking in support of Aboriginal suffrage, which was finally achieved in 1967 under amendments to the Australian Constitution.

In 1964, by that time in her forties, Noonuccal

was encouraged by other women writers to publish her poetry. Redolent with pride in her Aboriginal heritage and warning of the threat of its loss through assimilation and the dispossession of Aboriginals from their traditional homelands, *We Are Going* was followed in 1966 by *The Dawn Is at Hand.* These two collections were later reissued as *My People, A Kath Walker Collection* (1970; Walker was her married name). A collection of aboriginal legends for children, *Stradbroke Dreamtime,* was published in 1972, which together with *Father Sky and Mother Earth* (1981) strove to preserve ancient Aboriginal culture among younger generations.

Noonuccal was awarded a Fulbright scholarship to study in the United States, where she lectured on Aboriginal rights during 1978–1979. She received the Mary Gilmore Medal in 1970 and was made a Member of the Order of the British Empire (MBE). She also received the Jessie Litchfield Award in 1975, but in 1988 handed back the MBE she had received in 1970, in protest of the racial abuse of Aboriginals under former British colonial rule. Now becoming increasingly radicalized, she adopted the Aboriginal tribal name of Oodgeroo Noonuccal. She served on the Aboriginal Arts Board and established a Centre for Aboriginal Culture on North Stradbroke Island, in which both Aboriginal and white children were invited to participate. In 1989 the Australian composer Malcolm Williamson set some of her poems to music as *The Dawn Is at Hand.* Her other published works include *The Rainbow Serpent* (1988), *The Spirit of Australia* (1989), *Towards a Global Village in the Southern Hemisphere* (1989), and *Australian Legends and Landscapes* (1990).

References and Further Reading

Beier, Ulli. 1985. *Quandamooka: The Art of Kath Walker.* Bathurst, NSW: Robert Brown and Associates in Association with the Aboriginal Artists Agency.

Buck, Claire, ed. 1992. *Bloomsbury Guide to Women's Literature.* London: Bloomsbury.

Cochrane, Kathie. 1994. *Oodgeroo.* St. Lucia: University of Queensland Press.

Grassby, A. J. 1991. *Oodgeroo Noonuccal: Poet, Painter, and Elder of Her People.* South Melbourne: Macmillan.

Noonuccal, Oodgeroo. 1994. *Stradbroke Dreamtime.* New York: Lothrop, Lee, and Shepard Books.

Penguin Biographical Dictionary of Women. 1998. Harmondsworth: Penguin.

Shoemaker, Adam, ed. 1994. *Oodgeroo: A Tribute.* St. Lucia: University of Queensland Press.

Taylor, Gail. 1999. *Oodgeroo Noonuccal.* Sydney: Hodder Education.

Wilde, William H., Joy Hooton, and Barry Andrews. 1994. *Oxford Companion to Australian Literature.* 2d ed. Melbourne: Oxford University Press.

Norton, Caroline
(1808–1877)
United Kingdom

Caroline Norton (Library of Congress)

One of the great scandals of the Victorian era, involving Prime Minister Lord Melbourne and prominent literary figure Caroline Norton, brought to the fore the injustices of the existing marriage laws in Britain, which gave married women no right to their property or the custody of their children. Norton had the advantage of her literary skills with which to argue forcefully not just her own case but for changes in women's legal rights; she did not, however, employ these gifts in extending her arguments to wider calls for women's emancipation. Although setting great store by women being treated equally with men under the law, she had initially been dismissive of all ideas of women's equality with men. Only her bitter experiences of how the double standard applied in cases of divorce and custody led her to modify that view.

Norton was the granddaughter of the playwright Richard Brinsley Sheridan and the daughter of a famous society beauty, Caroline Henrietta Callander. One of seven children, she was bright, articulate, and witty and wrote poetry in her teens. After her father's early death in 1816, Caroline's penurious mother began scouting around for suitable husbands for her three beautiful daughters. The barrister and member of Parliament (MP) George Chapple Norton had become infatuated with Caroline when she was sixteen, and in 1827 they married. The marriage was an unmitigated disaster. George Norton proved to be a coarse, indolent, and jealous drunk who relied on his wife's good connections for his own political advancement. Caroline became the frequent physical butt, even when pregnant, of his fits of violent anger. When the couple encountered financial difficulties, she began publishing her poetry. *The Sorrows of Rosalie: A Tale with Other Poems* came out in 1829 and *The Undying One* in 1830. She also explored social conditions, attacking child labor in her narrative poems, *A Voice from the Factories* (1836) and *A Child of the Islands* (1845). Other poetry collections—*The Dream, and Other Poems* (1840) and *The Lady of Garaye* (1862)—established her reputation as a leading poet of her day, who was admired by Samuel Coleridge. In 1831 Caroline became editor of the popular monthly journal *La Belle Assemblée.*

The Norton marriage encountered further difficulties after George lost his seat in Parliament in 1830. Caroline bore three sons in quick succession, but the marriage was punctuated with frequent and often violent arguments, leading to her miscarrying a fourth child in 1835 after being beaten by George. After another such incident in 1836, she fled to her sister's home. Upon her return, her husband refused her access to the children. By this time a well-known social and literary figure, Caroline had conducted a literary salon at which prominent people, including Lord Melbourne, were regular visitors. Men found her attractive and fascinating; women, however, found her self-regarding and false. She certainly had a reputation as a lover of the limelight and of risqué conversation and had a tendency to be impulsive, if not at times indiscreet, such as by holding private tête-à-têtes with Melbourne. In declining middle age, the prime minister had become a lonely figure of whom she was genuinely fond; opinions differ as to whether the relationship was ever a sexual one. George Norton became jealous and, seeing an opportunity to extract money, in June 1836 took Caroline and Melbourne to court, accusing them of "criminal conversation" (a legal euphemism for adultery) and suing Melbourne for £10,000 in damages. Caroline was granted no legal representation, for as a married woman, she had no individual status under the ancient legal term of "coverture" that still governed married women's lives. Their identities were deemed, on marriage, as being absorbed by their husband's; in addition, upon marriage, under the law of coverture, women in early nineteenth-century England lost all right to their own property.

Despite the case against her not being proved because of lack of evidence (it may well have been brought by Norton as much to destroy Melbourne's political reputation as his wife's), Caroline's social position was ruined, and her husband compounded matters by using the law to get his revenge on her. Unable to divorce (he could not divorce her because the adultery case had been thrown out by the court), the couple separated, but George denied Caroline custody and even access to her children. Caring nothing for her financial difficulties or her sullied reputation, Caroline was distraught at being kept from her children and embarked on a long fight to obtain access to them. She approached a sympathetic MP and barrister, Thomas Talfourd, who introduced the Infant Custody Act, the first piece of legislation to be introduced in England directly affecting the position of women. Caroline laid out her case in two pamphlets, "The Natural Claim of a Mother to the Custody of Her Child as Affected by the Common Law Right of the Father" and "Separation of the Mother and Child by the Law of Custody of Infants Considered" (1837), in both of which she described the sufferings of children denied access to their mothers in such cases, and with great eloquence gave voice to the depths of maternal love. Women, she asserted, could transcend almost any pain or injustice except the loss of their children.

The bill was debated in the House of Lords,

but the outcome seemed gloomy. Norton was castigated as a "she-devil" who sought to overturn the very foundation of society. Her response was to write yet another pamphlet, "A Plain Letter to the Lord Chancellor on the Infant Custody Bill," published in 1839 under the pseudonym Peace Stevenson (she felt that it would not be taken seriously if seen to be written by a woman). The pamphlet was circulated among MPs and supporters, and the bill became law in 1839. Further acts in 1873 and 1886 extended the custody rights of mothers, but it would not be until 1925 that women in Britain would be granted equal rights with men over their children. Under the 1839 legislation, mothers could be allowed custody of their children under the age of seven, provided they had not committed adultery; they were also allowed regulated access to children above that age. Meanwhile, Norton's husband had sent their three sons away to school in Scotland, which did not recognize English law. He refused at first even to tell Caroline where the boys were, but in 1842, after a riding accident, eight-year-old William contracted blood poisoning and died, upon which Norton finally relented and allowed Caroline to visit the others.

The strains took their toll on Caroline, who lived alone from 1843, cold-shouldered by polite society, although her literary successes continued. David Cecil argues that she allowed the wrongs against her to become an "obsession" in later life and "set [herself] up as a sort of professional injured person, theatrically lamenting the unexampled cruelty, with which she had been treated, to every individual she met," a fact that alienated some supporters (1954, 305). Even Melbourne tired of her often unpredictable, impetuous behavior, and her continued propensity for indiscretion worried him, although in 1841 he had been ousted as Prime Minister.

Besides continuing to write novels and poetry, Caroline began writing in support of divorce reform. In 1854 she published an essay, "English Laws for Women in the Nineteenth Century," and soon found her arguments supported by Barbara Bodichon in her own pamphlet, "A Brief Summary in Plain Language of the Most Important Laws Concerning Women," published that same year. In Norton's passionate plea for an end to what she described as the "feudal barbarity" of English laws regarding women's status, she explained her determination to fight for changes:

"Even now my friends say to me, 'Why write? Why struggle? It is the Law! You will do no good!' But if everyone slacked courage with that doubt, nothing would ever be achieved in this world. This much I will do, woman though I be. I will put on record what the law for women was in England in the years of civilisation and Christianity, 1855, and the eighteenth year of the reign of a female sovereign!" (Strachey 1978, 75).

Although the couple was officially separated, George Norton had been able to keep all Caroline's furniture and property and could legally control her copyrights and the income from her literary endeavors. He continued to make financial demands on her, in the early 1850s trying to get his hands on Caroline's recent legacies from her parents and refusing to pay her allowance. She could do nothing but run up debts and leave it to the creditors to sue George for payment. She also responded, as always, by appealing to high places—this time the queen herself—with "A Letter to the Queen on Lord Chancellor Cranworth's Marriage and Divorce Bill," in which she forcefully argued for an end to the double standard in the treatment of men and women in divorce cases and made the classic observation: "I exist and I suffer; but the law denies my existence" (1855, 96). She worked for the provisions of a new Marriage and Divorce Act, passed in 1857, which abolished some of the inequalities. It gave separated and divorced women control over their own property and earnings, although married women were excluded, and laid down requirements for maintenance payments to former wives. But a divorce remained prohibitively difficult for a woman to obtain; she could only divorce her husband if she could prove extreme acts such as rape, incestuous adultery, sodomy, or bestiality. A husband, meanwhile, had every right to cast out his wife for adultery alone. The Married Women's Property Committee, organized by Barbara Bodichon in 1856, would continue to fight for reforms, which eventually came in 1870, 1878, and 1882.

After her husband's death in 1875, Caroline Norton gave up writing. She married Sir William Stirling-Maxwell, an old friend, in 1877 but died only three months later. She wrote four novels that were extremely popular in their time: *The Wife and Woman's Reward* (1838), *Stuart of Dunleath* (1851), *Lost and Saved* (1863), and *Old Sir Douglas* (1867). Based on her own experiences, they paint a bleak portrait of marriage. Although her literary works soon became obscure, Caroline Norton's bold and often lonely defense of her rights as a mother and a wage earner would be a landmark in women's social history in nineteenth-century Britain and an inspiration to the later feminist and suffrage movements that gained momentum after the passage of the 1857 Marriage and Divorce Act. Useful accounts of Norton's life and work can be found on http://www.digital.library.upenn.edu/women/norton and http://.writepage.com/others/nortonc.htm.

See also Bodichon, Barbara.

References and Further Reading

Acland, Alice. 1948. *Caroline Norton*. London: Constable.

Cecil, David. 1954. *Lord M.* London: Constable.

Chedzoy, Alan. 1992. *A Scandalous Woman: The Story of Caroline Norton*. London: Allison and Busby.

Forster, Margaret. 1986. *Significant Sisters: The Grassroots of Active Feminism, 1839–1939*. Harmondsworth: Penguin.

Helsinger, Elizabeth K., Robin Lauterbach Sheets, and William Veeder. 1983. *The Woman Question: Social Issues, 1837–1883*, vol. 2, *Society and Literature in Britain and America, 1837–1883*. Manchester: Manchester University Press.

Hoge, James O., and Jane Marcus. 1978. *Selected Writings of Caroline Norton*. Delmar, NY: Scholars' Facsimiles and Reprints.

Holcombe, Lee. 1983. *Wives and Property: Reform of the Married Women's Property Law in Nineteenth-Century England*. Toronto: University of Toronto Press.

Norton, Caroline. 1855. "A Letter to the Queen on Lord Chancellor Cranworth's Marriage and Divorce Bill." London: Lonman, Brown, Green, and Longmans.

Perkins, Jane Grey. 1909. *The Life of Mrs. Norton*. London: John Murray.

Poovey, Mary. 1989. *Uneven Developments: The Ideological Work of Gender in Mid-Victorian Britain*. London: Virago.

Strachey, Ray. 1978 [1928]. *The Cause: A Brief History of the Women's Movement*. Reprint, London: Virago.

O

O'Brien, Charlotte Grace
(1845–1909)
Ireland/United States

For many years, Charlotte O'Brien sustained a solo crusade to control the widespread exploitation of poor immigrants in the United States by setting up a women's mission in New York and campaigning for greater controls to be made over the overcrowding of emigrants traveling steerage.

O'Brien's father, William, who came from an ancient Protestant landowning family that had 5,000 acres in County Limerick, had been a leader of the nationalist rebellion in Tipperary in 1848 and was condemned for treason and transported to Tasmania when she was a small child. She grew up at Cahirmoyle in County Limerick and was educated by a governess at home. Father and daughter were reunited on his return to Ireland in 1854, and they moved to Wales. On her father's death in 1856 (he was pardoned in 1854), O'Brien went to live with her brother Edward in Cahirmoyle and looked after his three children when his first wife died. O'Brien, who was almost totally deaf, turned to writing at this time and also pursued her interests in botany, which resulted in the 1881 publication of *Wild Flowers of the Undercliffe,* a study of the flowers on the Isle of Wight. In 1878 she produced a novel, *Light and Shade,* about the 1867 Fenian Uprising in Ireland and a volume of poetry, *Drama and Lyrics,* in 1880. Moving to her own home in County Limerick, she continued to write verse of an increasingly nationalistic and political content.

In 1880 O'Brien published a poem entitled "The Irish Poor Man," in which she mourned the "draining away of the life-blood of a nation" (Cullen and Luddy 1995, 240–241) through mass emigration to the United States. Her mounting concern for the plight of Irish emigrants led her to begin an intensive social campaign and set up a support network for emigrants in Ireland and the United States. These activities would take up the next two years of her life until lack of support, combined with her deafness and ill health, forced her to abandon them. After her attention was drawn to the appalling conditions on board the coffin ships that plied the emigrant trade between Ireland and the United States, O'Brien began touring the dockside of Queenstown (now Cobh). This, the major port serving the emigrant shipping trade, was situated in Cork harbor in southwestern Ireland. O'Brien began inspecting steerage conditions and wrote on the subject in local newspapers, including the *Munster News,* highlighting the deliberate overcrowding of these ships through the sale of tickets to more people than the ships had room to accommodate. She soon produced a major exposé of this and other abuses of poor emigrants—in particular, the sexual abuse of single females—in an article entitled "Horrors of an Emigrant Ship." Its publication in the influential *Pall Mall Gazette* in 1881 prompted a public outcry and a government investigation into the practices of the White Star shipping line, which operated out of the Irish seaports. The British Board of Trade, after due deliberation, denied that there was a problem.

However, O'Brien was not content to sit and wait for government to make lukewarm initiatives, despite the fact that she had the support of several Irish members of Parliament. At Queenstown, she went on board emigrant ships with a medical inspector to see for herself what improvements in conditions had been made. By this time, her articles in the press had prompted numerous emigrants to write to her about their own experiences on board the ships, and because most of them were Roman Catholics, O'Brien felt it was incumbent upon the Roman Catholic Church in Ireland and in New York to help monitor conditions by providing chaplains at the major ports and lending their support to improving conditions. Realizing that she had to see for herself the kind of accommodation offered to emigrants, O'Brien traveled steerage to New York, afterward calling for further improvements. She also offered practical advice to would-be female emigrants about what food and clothing to take, stressing that they should not travel alone.

After taking a closer look at the depots where immigrants were received in New York and at the dirty and overcrowded lodging houses in which so many of them found temporary accommodation before leaving Irish ports, in November 1881 O'Brien resolved to offer her own practical help by setting up a lodging house, the O'Brien Emigrants' Home, in Queenstown. Here, she offered bed, breakfast, and an evening meal to 105 emigrants, mainly women and children, for two shillings a day. She later set up a hot drinks and refreshments stall on Admiralty Pier nearby. On a broader level, she attempted to set standards of cleanliness in all dockside lodging houses by calling for the government to ensure that they abided by the measures of the Public Health (Ireland) Act of 1878. Such vigorous campaigning inevitably aroused hostility among local traders, who saw O'Brien's facilities as a threat to their own businesses and closed ranks, refusing to supply her. She was therefore obliged to send for food and clothing for the Emigrants' Home to Cork City, 15 miles away. By now O'Brien had become a voice that the shipping companies could ill afford to ignore, and by the autumn of 1882 most of them had complied with her demand that single women be provided with separate accommodations and that washing facilities and lavatories be improved.

Sadly, O'Brien's efforts received little encouragement from the institution most able to initiate widespread support for her work—the Roman Catholic Church. And so O'Brien took her message to the people through a series of public lectures, covering 4,000 miles across the United States from 1882–1883 and speaking mainly to Irish Americans to galvanize support for a more widespread network of help for Irish immigrants on both sides of the Atlantic. In New York she saw the miserable conditions in the seedy tenement blocks in which newly arrived immigrants lived and noted with concern the high mortality rates among infants. Nor were the facilities greeting emigrants in Castle Garden (the precursor to Ellis Island) any better, where little attempt was made to provide food and drink or accommodation and where illiterate female immigrants fell easy victim to unscrupulous offers of employment that often led them into prostitution and vice. Once again, O'Brien urged the Roman Catholic Church to appoint a chaplain at Castle Garden, and on 1 January 1884 the mission of Our Lady of the Rosary was set up; between 1884 and 1890 it gave assistance to 25,000 Irish immigrant women.

For all her selfless work, O'Brien's campaigning for better conditions on board emigrant ships and for improved lodgings on arrival was frequently misinterpreted as indicating her personal approval (as a Protestant) of the mass emigration from Ireland of Catholics. In fact, when the British government offered £5 assisted passages to Irish emigrants under the Arrears of Rent (Ireland) Act of 1882, she had criticized the government for encouraging emigration as a form of social cleansing. Eventually, O'Brien's profound deafness and the onset of ill health in 1883 forced her to abandon her work in the United States. Her lodging house in Queenstown was closed down a year later because of financial difficulties. She went to live in Foynes in County Limerick, where she resumed writing poetry as well as articles on women's rights. She also took up gardening and rekindled her love of botany, completing a major study, "The Flora of the Barony of Shanid," published in the *Irish Naturalist* in 1907. In the 1890s O'Brien converted to Catholicism and became increasingly reclusive in her final years, although as a supporter of the Gaelic League from its foundation in 1893, she continued to foster the Gaelic language and indigenous handicrafts. She lived in Clonskeagh, County Dublin, where her home became a venue for Irish writers and artists.

References and Further Reading

Cullen, Mary, and Maria Luddy. 1995. *Women, Power and Consciousness in Nineteenth-Century Ireland. Eight Biographical Studies.* Dublin: Attic Press.

Diner, Hasia R. 1983. *Erin's Daughters in America: Irish Immigrant Women in the Nineteenth Century.* Baltimore: Johns Hopkins University Press.

Gwynn, Stephen. 1909. *Charlotte Grace O'Brien: Selections from her Writings and Correspondence*, with a Memoir by S. Gwynn. Dublin: n.p.

Ó Céirín, Kit, and Cyril Ó Céirín, eds. 1996. *Women of Ireland: A Biographic Dictionary*. Kinvara, County Galway: Tír Eolas.

Orzeszkowa, Eliza
(1841–1910)
Poland

The rise of a women's movement in Poland was for long made impossible by the fragmented nature of the country, which over so many centuries was subject to constant invasion and partition among Russia, Austria, and Prussia. Eliza Orzeszkowa's was a rare humanist and feminist voice, trapped in the Polish provinces, from where she produced powerful fiction inspired by the ideals of social justice and equality that had sparked the ill-fated Polish uprising of 1863.

Born Elzbieta Pawlowski on the family estate near Grodno, which was then part of Lithuania, Orzeszkowa was educated at home by governesses and spent five years at a girls' boarding school in Warsaw before being married at the age of sixteen to a wealthy Polish nobleman, Piotr Orzeszko. The couple settled on his estate in the Pripet Marshes of Polesie, a remote area of outstanding natural beauty.

During the period from her marriage until 1863, despite the disapproval of her conservative husband, Eliza was drawn into the struggle for Polish independence and the emancipation of the peasants in the Kobryn district. When her husband finally joined the revolutionary movement, he was arrested and sent to Siberia, but the marriage was already a failure, and Orzeszkowa did not follow him. The estate was confiscated by the czarist authorities, and Orzeszkowa turned to writing as a way of earning a living, at a time when this was a very difficult profession for women in Poland to follow.

Shut away in the town of Grodno under police surveillance, she read widely in French, Russian, and Polish and wrote at length on the position of women and the "little people" of the rural environs—the Jews and shopkeepers, farmers, peasants, and traders. She concerned herself in particular with the need of the individual, whether woman or Jew, to overcome social prejudices and conventions in order to find self-fulfillment.

Women in particular, she believed, needed to escape the confines of "church, kitchen and children" (Kridl 1956, 373). Many of her works were translated into Russian, German, Swedish, and Czech and used as propaganda in the struggle for women's emancipation and against the racial discrimination meted out to the Jews that was so widespread in czarist Russia. Her first forays, in the essay "A Few Words about Women" (1871) and novels such as *Waclawa's Journal* (1870) and *Marta* (1872), portrayed women who, as the victims of arranged marriages, became oppressed wives who were prevented from obtaining an education or following a profession. The emancipationist content of *Marta* made it popular among German feminists when it was translated soon after. In her stories about Jews, Orzeszkowa attempted a rare thing—as a non-Jew, to write humanely and with compassion about a large element of czarist society who were treated as outcasts and looked upon as both mysterious and threatening. Although she offered no radical solution, favoring the easier option of assimilation, a story such as "Mighty Samson" (1877) was one of the first to illustrate, in the words of the Russian novelist Mikhail Saltykov-Shchedrin, "how much goodness lies concealed in tormented Jewry and what an inexpressible tragedy hovers over its existence" (Lvov-Rogachevsky 1979, 17).

Orzeszkowa was not a great intellectual, but her writing is suffused with love, humanity, and compassion for the sufferings of the underprivileged and driven by a strong sense of patriotism and national identity. She criticized the writer Joseph Conrad as being one of Poland's many intellectuals who had chosen to flee rather than stay and fight for independence and for having given up writing in his native tongue of Polish.

After a long battle to have her marriage annulled and in the wake of the confiscation and sale of her marital estate, Orzeszkowa had to find creative ways to support herself. She opened a bookshop where she ran her own publishing imprint and founded schools in Grodno. But the czarist authorities, suspicious of what they perceived as a potentially subversive venture, closed down the bookshop and publishing enterprise in 1882 and she was kept under police surveillance for a further five years. In 1894 she married again, to a doctor, but he died in 1896.

Orzeszkowa's most famous novel was so popular that it was twice adapted for the silent cinema in 1911 and 1916 versions (with Yiddish intertitles for the Jewish audiences of the shtetl and the diaspora). A sentimental melodrama with dark and gloomy overtones, *Meir Ezofowicz* (1878) vividly describes the narrowness of life for the Jewish population confined to the shtetl, raising the subject of the integration of the Jews into Polish society and also confronting the conflict between traditional Orthodoxy and progressive Judaism. The novel's eponymous Jewish hero rebels against his strict upbringing and religious fanaticism, only to be cursed and driven out from his home.

Orzeszkowa also wrote vividly on the lives of the Polish peasantry in *Dziudziowie* (1885, its title being the name of a peasant family), highlighting the persistence of peasant superstition and ignorance; *The Boor* tackles the controversial subject of the rescue of a fallen woman by a kind-hearted peasant, but she later leaves him to return to prostitution. Orzeszkowa's best-known and most admired work, *On the Banks of the Niemen* (1888), was a critique of Polish society and the landed gentry in Lithuania (then part of a Polish-Lithuanian state under Russian rule) and contained richly evocative descriptions of the countryside that attracted such widespread public admiration that it was reprinted many times.

References and Further Reading

Kridl, Manfred. 1956. *A Survey of Polish Literature and Culture.* Gravenhage: Slavistic Reprintings.

Lvov-Rogachevsky, V. 1979. *A History of Russian Jewish Literature.* Ann Arbor: Ardis. (There is no biography of Orzeszkowa in English, and only rare, passing references appear in English-language sources. This book provides an overview of the context in which she wrote.)

Orzeszkowa, Eliza. 1980. *The Forsaken, or Meir Ezofowich* [sic]. Bournemouth, UK: Delamare.

Osório, Ana da Castro
(1872–1935)
Portugal

The essayist, educator, and children's author Ana da Castro Osório was a founding mother of feminist activities in Portugal. In 1905, Osório published the seminal text in the emergent Portuguese women's movement, the *Address to Portuguese Women*, in which she emphasized that "to educate the woman—that is the main prob-

lem to develop and implement. This is what we call feminism" (Flanz 1983, 42). Osório led calls for revision of the civil code of 1867 that gained ground after the foundation of the Republican League of Portuguese Women in 1909. The league brought women together to fight for changes to the divorce laws and for women to be allowed equal parental rights with men, to be admitted to jury service, and to be granted the vote. It also urged better access to education for women that would allow them entry to the professions and took the lead in tackling social problems such as prostitution. Success was rapidly achieved in 1910 with the passage of new family and divorce laws and the admission of women into the Portuguese civil service.

Osório's first published works were books for children; she also wrote numerous pamphlets on education, later collected as *The Good of the Nation*. In 1911 she founded the Association for Feminist Propaganda and edited its short-lived journal, the *Portuguese Woman*.

In her feminist activities and work in women's welfare and for legal reform, Osório worked closely with Adelaide Cabete (1867–1935), a doctor and writer on health issues relating to women and children, with whom she had founded the Republican League of Portuguese Women. In 1914 Adelaide Cabete founded the National Council of Portuguese Women as a national umbrella organization for women's groups, which affiliated itself with the International Council of Women, but Osório and Cabete's international feminist activities were soon sidelined by the outbreak of World War I.

In 1917 Osório initiated a National Crusade of Portuguese Women to provide relief to the families of Portuguese soldiers fighting in the war. Feminist activity took time to recover lost ground after the war; in 1924 Cabete set up the first feminist congress in Portugal, held in Lisbon. Osório lost the support of Cabete in 1929 when the latter went to work in Angola. Women's suffrage was finally won in Portugal in 1931, but significant coverage of this country's feminist and suffrage movements in English has yet to appear.

References and Further Reading

Flanz, Gisbert H. 1983. *Comparative Women's Rights and Political Participation in Europe.* Epping, Essex: Bowker.

Sadlier, Darlene J. 1991. "The Struggle for Women's Rights in Portugal." *Camões Center Quarterly* 3(1–2): 32–36.

Otto-Peters, Luise
(1819–1895)
Germany

As a leading Christian moderate and pioneer of German feminism during the German revolution of 1848, Otto-Peters exposed social prejudice and explored women's emancipation through her social novels and her political journalism. She was particularly committed to the rights of working women and their representation by trade unions.

One of four daughters of a high court judge, she grew up in Leipzig in an enlightened home where she was encouraged to read the newspapers. Orphaned at sixteen, she was largely self-educated, reading widely and developing a passion for social issues. Partially self-supporting thanks to a small inheritance, Otto was able to fund her writing for periodicals such as *Our Planet,* the *Cornet,* and the *Lighthouse.* Encouraged by the social novels of early German woman writer Bettina von Arnim, in 1843 Otto-Peters published her first novel, *Ludwig the Waiter,* which tackled prejudice toward the working classes. *Kathinka,* a book about the emancipation of women, followed in 1844, the year in which Otto-Peters began publishing the *Women's Journal for Higher Feminine Interests.* Her social concerns were also reflected in her poetry, *Songs of a German Girl* (1847).

During the 1848 revolutionary upheavals, Otto-Peters was a leading advocate of women's rights. Believing that women had a duty to take part in government as much as men, she demanded the vote for women and equality with men. She published her articles and novels under the pseudonym Otto Stern and produced the *Women's Newspaper* (1849–1852). Her objective, emblazoned on its masthead, was to "enlist women for the kingdom of freedom" and to lead campaigns such as that calling for the creation of a women's college in Hamburg (Smith 1989, 245). In its pages, Otto-Peters rejected radical changes to traditional gender roles, a fact that caused her to criticize more radical feminists. She did not want women to throw over their ma-

Luise Otto-Peters (Corbis/Bettmann)

ternal roles but emphasized the need for them to make themselves useful in the public sphere in ways that were "womanly"—an argument developed in her three-volume novel *Castle and Factory* (1859–1861), which she was forced to amend in order to get past the censor. Otto-Peters saw the main avenues of women's activity as religious and ethical, thus relegating them to the realms of social welfare—improving bad housing, countering poverty, and supporting the oppressed working classes.

As the events of 1848 unraveled, Otto-Peters advocated direct political action, appealing to male workers to assist women workers in organizing and editing the radical newspaper *Equality.* She had met and fallen in love with a revolutionary hero and poet, August Peters, who was arrested and condemned to death. After his sentence was commuted, Luise waited seven years for his release. She was allowed to visit him only once a year. They eventually married after his release in 1858, and he died in 1864.

In 1849 she published a long essay on women in the workforce and a poem, "The Lacemakers," on how so many succumbed to blindness from hours of close work. She also drew attention to the exploitation of women in the spinning mills, describing the brutalizing effects of mechanization. She exposed the persecution of seamstresses by the tailors' guild, which had the right to search their homes and confiscate forbidden additional work that they may have taken to supplement their meager incomes. The *Women's Newspaper,* which also encouraged contributions from working women, was banned by the Monarchist group, and Otto-Peters, who had all this time been under surveillance by the police, was persecuted and ostracized in the aftermath.

In 1865 Otto-Peters resumed her activities after the death of her husband and was instrumental in reviving the German women's movement. She established the Association for Women's Education in Leipzig, with the objective of improving women's intellectual qualifications and raising the quality and pay of the work they did. She was elected president and worked in an administrative capacity, setting up branches in other cities that offered evening entertainment and health and child care advice to working women. She also opened Sunday schools and schools for women's continuing education, where she introduced science and gymnastics.

With Leipzig rapidly becoming a center for the labor movement, she urged the convening of the first German women's congress there in 1865. Attendees discussed the problems middle-class women encountered in employment and set up an educational program to train poor girls for paid employment and offer cultural enlightenment to factory girls and domestic servants by reading Immanuel Kant, G. W. F. Hegel, and other edifying writers to them as they sat in knitting circles. Her Association for Women's Education was one of thirty-four women's groups that merged in 1865 with the larger middle-class General German Women's Association (GGWA), cofounded by Otto-Peters in Leipzig in 1865 and of which she was elected president. Hampered by government bans on women's participation in political organizations, the association was obliged to remain modest in its objectives, concentrating on philanthropic work, women's education and employment, and their training in certain professions. The GGWA organized numerous lobbies and petitions to the Reichstag on women's employment, in 1867 calling for women to be allowed to work in the postal service and in 1872 for more women to be trained and employed as teachers in lower schools. In

1877 under Otto-Peters, the GGWA petitioned for reform of the marriage laws.

In 1875 Otto-Peters and Auguste Schmidt founded a new feminist periodical, *New Highways,* which emphasized women's education and character building. That same year she wrote a polemical essay, "The Right of Women to Gainful Employment: A Book of Women's Lives Today."

References and Further Reading

Frevert, Ute. 1990. *Women in German History: From Bourgeois Emancipation to Sexual Liberation.* Oxford: Berg Publishers.

Joeres, Ruth-Ellen B., and Mary Jo Maynes, eds. 1986. *German Women in the Eighteenth and Nineteenth Centuries: A Social and Literary History.* Bloomington: Indiana University Press.

Offen, Karen. 2000. *European Feminisms 1700–1950: A Political History.* Stanford: Stanford University Press.

Prelinger, Catherine M. 1980. "The *Frauen-Zeitung* (1849–1852): Harmony and Dissonance in Mid-Century German Feminism." *History of European Ideas* 11: 245–251.

Smith, Bonnie G. 1989. *Changing Lives: Women in European History since 1700.* Lexington, MA: D. C. Heath.

Ovington, Mary White
(1865–1951)
United States

The white civil rights activist Mary White Ovington moved from an early career in social work to become a founding member of the first major civil rights organization in the United States, the National Association for the Advancement of Colored People (NAACP). The daughter of Unitarian parents who were teachers and advocates of women's emancipation and the abolition of slavery, she was born and grew up in Brooklyn. After being educated at a private school, the Packer Collegiate Institute (1888–1891), Ovington attended the Harvard Annex (1891–1893), which later became Radcliffe College. But after only two and a half years, the failure of her father's business forced her to abandon her studies.

Ovington's sense of social justice had first been aroused by the sermons of her local preacher, John White Chadwick, at the Second Unitarian Church in Brooklyn Heights. She was much inspired too by the work of settlement pioneer Jane Addams at Hull House in Chicago and in 1895 took an appointment as registrar at the Pratt Institute in Brooklyn. She became head worker (1895–1903) at the institute's newly established Greenpoint Settlement in Brooklyn. There, in a depressed, working-class milieu, for the first time in her hitherto sheltered and comfortable life, Ovington came into contact with deprived black families, later admitting her extreme ignorance until then of the injustices of housing segregation and economic deprivation that such families suffered.

As a result of her interest in social welfare, Ovington became assistant secretary of New York's Social Reform Club. It was at a gathering of this group of intellectuals and socialists in 1903 that she heard the black activist Booker T. Washington speak on racial injustice and set her sights on working for black civil rights. A subsequent correspondence with black scholar W. E. B. Du Bois, leader of the Niagara movement, served to further radicalize Ovington, who also found outlets for her social concerns in membership in the National League for the Protection of Colored Women and the Committee for Improving the Industrial Condition of Negroes in New York.

In 1904 Ovington left Greenpoint but was laid low by typhoid and took a year to recover. She nevertheless remained intent on working for the underprivileged black community. Through her association with Mary Simkhovitch, who ran the Greenwich House Settlement, Ovington secured a fellowship in 1904 to make a study of inner-city housing and urban employment problems in the deprived black community of New York, published in 1911 as *Half a Man: The Status of the Negro in New York.* Another landmark work, "The Status of the Negro in the United States," followed in 1913 in the *New Review.*

In 1905 Ovington finally joined the Socialist Party, where she associated with other radical women such as Crystal Eastman. During the early 1900s, she was also active in the National Consumers' League, which set out to raise consumer awareness about the labor of underpaid and exploited women and children employed to produce the goods they bought and to obtain protective legislation against their abuse.

In February 1909 Ovington was one of several women, including Mary Church Terrell, Ida B. Wells-Barnett, and Jane Addams, who joined with white and black civil rights leaders in New York to found the NAACP. Its objective was to defend black people against discrimination in employment, education, and housing and to fight segregation and escalating race hatred in the South. Ovington served the NAACP with dedication for thirty-eight years, first as executive secretary beginning in 1910, then as chair (1919–1932), and finally as treasurer from 1932 until her retirement in 1947. Her activism invited much criticism from the white American right wing, which accused her of promoting miscegenation; equally, some blacks resented the presence of a middle-class white woman in a predominantly black civil rights organization. Ovington was clear in her own mind, however, that no white woman should set herself up as representing the interests of black women in the United States. This they should be allowed to do themselves, and in 1921 she lobbied Alice Paul's National Woman's Party to undertake an investigation of the status of black women in the South and to include a black woman speaker in its party conference in Washington, D.C.

Ovington was also active in the women's suffrage and peace movements and opposed U.S. entry into World War I. She continued her civil rights campaigning during the war years, writing for the socialist journal *The Messenger,* which had been established by civil rights and labor leader Asa Randolph in 1917. Her other journalistic achievements included articles for radical publications such as the NAACP's *Crisis, The Call,* and Max Eastman's influential left-wing pacifist magazine, *The Masses.* During the Harlem Renaissance of the 1920s, Ovington welcomed black literary and cultural achievements, and in 1927 she published cameos of black leaders in *Portraits in Color.* Ovington serialized her memoirs of her work for black civil rights in the *Baltimore Afro-American* during 1932–1933; these were later republished as *Black and White Sat Down Together* (1995). In 1947 she contributed one of the first popular histories of the NAACP, *The Walls Came Tumbling Down.*

See also Addams, Jane; Eastman, Crystal; Paul, Alice; Terrell, Mary Church; Wells-Barnett, Ida B.

References and Further Reading

Adickes, Sandra. 1997. *To Be Young Was Very Heaven: Women in New York before the Great War.* Basingstoke: Macmillan.

Berson, Robin Kadison. 1994. *Marching to a Different Drummer: Unrecognized Heroes of American History.* Westport, CT: Greenwood Press.

Kellogg, Charles Flint. 1967. *NAACP: A History of the National Association for the Advancement of Colored People, 1909–1920*. Baltimore: Johns Hopkins University Press.

Lewis, David L. 1994. *The Portable Harlem Renaissance Reader*. New York: Viking.

Ovington, Mary White. 1995. *Black and White Sat Down Together: The Reminiscences of an NAACP Founder, Mary White Ovington*. New York: Feminist Press.

Wedin, Carolyn. 1997. *Inheritors of the Spirit: Mary White Ovington and the Founding of the NAACP*. New York: John Wiley.

P

Pandit, Vijaya Lakshmi
(1900–1990)
India

The distinguished Indian feminist and supporter of the Indian independence movement—her adopted names "Vijaya" and "Lakshmi" mean "victory" and "prosperity," respectively—was the most eminent Indian female leader of her generation. Although her high international profile enabled her to draw attention to social and political issues in India, she was not without critics of her own lavish, privileged lifestyle.

Born Swarup Kumari Nehru into a cultured, wealthy family of lawyers in the state of Uttar Pradesh, Pandit was the sister of the future Indian prime minister Jawaharlal Nehru and the daughter of a leading politician and associate of Mahatma Gandhi, Motilal Nehru. She grew up in a mansion in the European quarter of Allahabad, where she was privately educated by an English governess. Although she did not go on to study at university, Pandit inevitably came under the influence of the intellectual and political Indian elite through the associations of her father and brother with the Indian National Congress movement.

In 1920 Pandit began gathering the support of Indian women for the nationalist cause and often found herself in jail for her activities after her marriage in 1921 to Ranjit Pandit, a lawyer and follower of Mahatma Gandhi. Pandit joined her husband as a leading activist in the civil disobedience movement of the 1930s that demanded Indian independence, supported the Swadeshi movement's boycott of British goods, and was jailed three times: in 1931–1933 (for eighteen months), 1940 (for six months), and 1942 (for seven months).

Pandit's work for Indian independence was always carried out in tandem with her broader commitment to human rights and the feminist cause. She shared the belief with her friend and colleague Sarojini Naidu that India would only become strong politically when its men and women enjoyed equal political and human rights: "If we would be nation builders in the real sense, we must free our minds from superstition and bias. We must go forward together with our men, and by friendship and cooperation and faith, build up Indian history together on equal terms in every department of life. Only then shall we achieve the unity and progress of the Indian nation and be entitled to call ourselves nation-builders" (Sen Gupta 1994, 153–154). Pandit herself led the vanguard by being the first Indian woman, along with Muthulakshmi Reddi, to take on leading roles in government and in the international diplomatic arena.

During the first half of the 1930s, Pandit worked in local government and served as chair of an education committee that worked to promote adult literacy on the Soviet model. She stood in the general election in 1936 and became a member of Parliament in 1937 for the rural constituency of Cawnpore Bilhaur. Soon after, she was appointed Uttar Pradesh's first female minister (of local self-government and public health), in which capacity she worked hard to promote health and education services and personally toured villages afflicted by a cholera epidemic, organizing health care and famine relief. She prided herself on always proving that in politics, women did not shrink from doing men's work, and also made a point of stressing the ability of poor women in rural areas to grasp the fundamental importance to them of the vote.

Arrested in 1942 for her involvement in

Vijaya Lakshmi Pandit (Archive Photos)

Gandhi's "Quit India" civil disobedience movement, Pandit was released early due to health problems. Immediately upon her release in 1943, she helped famine victims in Bengal and became president of the Save the Children Fund Committee started by the All-India Women's Conference (AIWC), which rescued destitute children from the streets.

Upon the death of her husband in 1944, Pandit discovered at first hand the outmoded Indian inheritance laws, when as a Hindu widow she was not allowed to inherit her husband's property and was denied access to his bank accounts, since under Hindu law he had no legal heirs (i.e., sons—the couple had had three daughters). She called for changes in these laws and lent weight to a campaign mounted by the AIWC for the reform of Hindu widows' rights.

In Pandit's case, widowhood did not prompt a traditional retreat from public life; indeed, financial necessity prompted her to take on a lecture tour of the United States. In 1945 she took on two important roles, the first at Gandhi's request,

as the head of an Indian delegation to the Pacific Relations Conference, held in Virginia, and the other at the San Francisco Conference on the Charter of the United Nations. At the latter, she represented the American India League as the spokesperson for the 600 million people of India and Southeast Asia. Pandit made full use of her time in the United States to speak on Indian issues, such as literacy levels and health care, citing the situation in the country as presenting a "moral challenge" and condemning the long years of imperialism and colonization that had bred racial disharmony. She lived up to her principles in 1946, when she spoke in support of a UN motion condemning the infringement of the human rights of South Africa's many Indian subjects, a cause she would continue to pursue over the next few decades, when she called for a trade boycott of South Africa in 1963.

During 1946–1947 Pandit again took up the post of minister of local self-government and health, this time in Uttar Pradesh, but by the time Indian independence was granted in 1947, she had embarked on a new fifteen-year career as a diplomat. She was serving as Indian ambassador in Moscow at the time, the first of a succession of highly distinguished posts (ambassador to the Soviet Union, United States, Ireland, Great Britain, and Spain). In addition, in 1953, Pandit made history by becoming the first female and first Asian president of the UN General Assembly. Here she took a strong position on human rights, opposing the introduction of apartheid in South Africa. Upon her return to India, despite support for her becoming vice president, Indian president Sarvepalli Radhakrishnan turned down the idea, and Pandit became governor of Maharashtra (1962–1964), returning as a member of Parliament (1964–1968) after the death of her brother, when she contested his seat at Phalpur and won by a huge majority of 58,000 votes.

During the 1970s, Pandit joined an opposition group, taking a stand against the rigid rule of Indira Gandhi—her niece—(whom she had already called to account during Indira Gandhi's authoritarian governorship of Bombay in 1961). When Gandhi's rule became increasingly totalitarian in the mid-1970s and she declared a state of emergency in 1975, Pandit again came out in opposition to the suspension of civil liberties. She subsequently retired from politics, although even at the end of her life she was ready to criticize the policies of her great-nephew, Gandhi's son, Rajiv.

Despite her glamorous, privileged lifestyle, beautiful clothes, and cultured, Westernized manners, Pandit's undoubted social concerns were both profound and passionate. Her political skills earned her considerable international respect among world leaders. She was heaped with honorary doctorates and awards and feted as a distinguished elder stateswoman to the end of her long and fulfilled ninety years.

See also Naidu, Sarojini.
References and Further Reading
Andrews, Robert Hardy. 1967. *A Lamp for India: The Story of Madame Pandit*. London: Barker.
Brittain, Vera. 1965. *Envoy Extraordinary*. London: George Allen and Unwin.
Pandit, Vijay. 1979. *The Scope of Happiness: A Personal Memoir*. London: Weidenfeld and Nicolson.
Sen Gupta, Padmini, ed. 1994 [1944]. *Pioneer Women of India*. Reprint, Bombay: Thacker.

Pankhurst, Christabel
(1880–1958)
United Kingdom

Christabel Pankhurst is a problematic figure in the history of the women's militant suffrage movement in Britain. Her posthumous reputation, filtered through the often considerably biased memoirs of both her admirers and detractors, has been further overlaid by some hostile and misogynist accounts of the Pankhursts that appeared in the 1970s and 1980s. She was undoubtedly a controversial and compelling figure, in her lifetime accused of excessive ego, arrogance—even megalomania—and frequently remarked upon as being autocratic, cold, and undemonstrative. In her classic 1982 work, *Women of Ideas and What Men Have Done to Them*, Dale Spender argued that mostly male commentators had indiscriminately demonized Pankhurst; more recent feminist writing has sought to uncover other sides to her complex personality. For many of her otherwise sympathetic critics, Christabel has been hoisted with the petard of her own unrepentant hostility toward men in her espousal of the postsuffrage social purity crusade as a born-again Christian, a dramatic U-turn for a woman who was, during the period 1903–1914, one of the most radical voices in British feminism.

Christabel's personality was beset by contradictions: luminously beautiful and always stylishly dressed, in contrast to her often dowdy sister Sylvia, she was unable to give love to the many who adored her; gifted with a remarkable intellect, she was intolerant of lesser mortals; a brilliant tactician and noted for her wit and flair as a public speaker, she abandoned these gifts for the dogma of evangelizing in the 1920s. Apologists argue that it was her overriding dedication to the cause that impelled Christabel to ride roughshod over the feelings of those at her beck and call and save herself, as the brains behind the Women's Social and Political Union (WSPU), from the enervating effects of prison and hunger strike by fleeing to Paris at the height of the militant campaign.

A bright child, Christabel was educated at home by governesses until she was thirteen and then at Southport and Manchester High Schools. From 1885 to 1893, the Pankhurst family lived in London. Christabel originally entertained hopes of becoming a dancer, but financial difficulties brought about by the untimely death of her father in 1898 obliged her to help her mother run a shop near their home when they returned to Manchester.

In the autumn of 1900, an encounter at Owen's College Women's Debating Society with suffragists Esther Roper and Eva Gore-Booth, members of the North of England Society for Women's Suffrage and local trade union organizers, led to Pankhurst's recruitment to their committee and her participation in political work among northern working-class mill girls. Jill Liddington and Jill Norris note, however, that even at this early stage in her career, Christabel had "scant patience with the foot-slogging drudgery of grass roots politics" (2000, 171). And although she joined Roper and Gore-Booth in the Manchester branch of the Women's Trade Union Council and they became close friends, unlike her sister Sylvia, Christabel's heart was never in activism among the working classes.

Emmeline Pankhurst had always entertained high ambitions for her clever and beautiful eldest daughter and hoped she would follow in her father's footsteps and study law. Roper encouraged Christabel in this career choice, but it was impossible for her to train in the male bastion of the British legal profession—Lincoln's Inn in London. She studied instead at Owen's College,

Christabel Pankhurst (right front; Museum of London)

part of Manchester's Victoria University (1903–1906); her mother, whom Christabel joined in the newly founded WSPU, would defer thereafter to Christabel's greater political genius. For the following two years, Christabel campaigned uncontroversially in and around Lancashire, with support from socialist leaders such as Keir Hardie, but both she and Emmeline were becoming impatient with the lack of overt commitment to women's suffrage by the Independent Labour Party. As early as 1904, as Elizabeth Crawford (1999, 488) points out, Christabel was already deeply skeptical of the likelihood of working-class men, any more than those in the middle and upper classes, ever conceding political power to women, a view she discussed in a pamphlet, "Parliamentary Vote for Women." She soon became convinced that women could not and should not rely on any of the established male-led political parties to effect their political emancipation, an argument she was soon presenting in her regular speeches to large audiences in Manchester.

On 13 October 1905, WSPU activities took a new turn; in a return to the kind of combative campaigning not seen since the Chartist movement of the 1830s and 1840s, it embraced direct action. Attending a Liberal Party election meeting chaired by Sir Edward Grey at the Free Trade Hall in Manchester, Christabel and her loyal acolyte, Annie Kenney, heckled candidate Winston Churchill over whether his government, if elected, would introduce a bill on women's suffrage. Shouting "Votes for Women," Kenney and Pankhurst unfurled suffrage banners and disrupted the meeting. Jostled outside, Pankhurst then made a defiant gesture that would set the suffrage campaign on a new path: she deliberately provoked her own arrest by spitting at a policeman. Refusing to pay her fine, she served seven days' imprisonment in Manchester's grim Strangeways jail and with it garnered unprecedented press coverage for the WSPU. Two hundred triumphant suffragettes greeted Pankhurst after her release from jail, by which date even that sober daily, *The Times,* had given coverage to her imprisonment. The rise of WSPU militancy in London, led by Christabel's sister Sylvia and Dora Montefiore, was inexorable thereafter.

Christabel, however, remained in Manchester with her mother to complete her law degree in 1906. She then moved to London as a salaried employee of the WSPU and wrested the leadership from Sylvia, who in any event was reluctant to abandon the working-class base of support she had built up in the East End. Christabel resumed her regular speech making, this time at Speaker's Corner in London's Hyde Park, and, supremely confident in her own physical and intellectual charisma, set out to make the WSPU cause attractive to women from what she considered the more influential middle and upper classes. In February 1907 Christabel was arrested for leading a deputation to the House of Commons and served fourteen days in prison. But she was reluctant to lose her grip on the leadership and in September, after she and her mother cancelled the WSPU annual conference and withdrew its constitution, there was a mass defection from the union in protest at the increasingly elitist nature of the union's inner sanctum. Christabel's undisguised opposition to democratic leadership provoked Charlotte Despard, Teresa Billington-Greig, and others to break away and form the Women's Freedom League. Others left because they disagreed with Christabel's and Emmeline's willingness to accept only a limited form of women's suffrage that would enfranchise middle-class and upper-class women only and largely exclude the working classes.

The tenor of the new high-profile movement, which turned into a military-style crusade under the control of Christabel and Emmeline Pankhurst, was marked by a huge suffrage march of around 250,000 WSPU members through Hyde Park in June 1908 and rallies at London's Albert and Caxton Halls in October. But the WSPU's militancy came up against the obduracy of new Liberal prime minister Herbert Asquith, an avowed opponent of women's suffrage. Christabel was arrested in October for calling for a mass deputation to march on the House of Commons. During her trial, she called the home secretary as a witness and cross-examined him herself, proving a veritable "Suffragette Portia" in court, according to the newspapers. She was found guilty and sentenced to ten weeks in prison. Eight months later, in July 1909, the first hunger strike was undertaken by an imprisoned WSPU member, Marion Wallace-Dunlop, and was soon followed by many others. But the Road to Calvary of imprisonment, hunger strikes, and episodes of force-feeding would not be Christabel's. Such were her crucial talents as a campaign organizer that she would not risk incarceration, or so her apologists have argued. Meanwhile, her sister Sylvia and mother would endure numerous debilitating periods in prison.

After the failure of the Conciliation Bill (drafted by fifty-four pro–women's suffrage Liberal members of Parliament) on 10 November 1910, Christabel's commitment to militancy hardened, and she openly advocated an all-or-nothing policy of civil disobedience. From early in 1911, the favored mode of protest became window smashing; but it would be Christabel's loyal troops and the WSPU's leaders, her mother and the Pethick-Lawrences, who risked arrest. Christabel fled to Paris, from where she refused to delegate the leadership to her minions in London and orchestrated what was effectively a guerrilla war. It is hard to resist the obvious parallels with that other notable political exile, Vladimir Ilyich Lenin, the brains of the Russian Social Democratic Party, who from his various bolt holes in Europe (albeit modest compared to the comfort in which Christabel lived) controlled the exploits of his hive of activists back in Russia. Thus Christabel became another of history's famous leaders in exile over the course of the next two and a half years.

Back in Britain, WSPU members set fire to mailboxes; burned unused churches, racecourse stands, and cricket pavilions; poured acid on golf courses; cut telegraph lines; and smashed windows galore in a last-ditch attempt to win the vote for women in Britain. In 1912 the Pethick-Lawrences, increasingly uneasy that the militant campaign was getting out of hand, were unceremoniously ousted from the WSPU by Christabel, who from her base in Paris turned to producing a stream of WSPU propaganda. With her mother and sister in and out of prison, she directed the English campaign via regular visits from Kenney and other WSPU couriers and edited and wrote articles for the WSPU journal, the *Suffragette* (1912 to 1920). In it, she established a virulently antimale rhetoric through a major serious of articles on the double sexual standard, prostitution, and the white slave trade, insisting on a rate of infection of innocent married women with venereal disease by promiscuous husbands as high as three in five. WSPU members selling copies of the *Suffragette* on the streets containing these articles wore placards that proclaimed Christabel's new mantra, "Votes for Women and Chastity for Men," and called on women to "wear the white flower of a blameless life."

Published in book form as *The Great Scourge and How to End It*, in her articles Christabel laid the blame for the "the great cause of physical, mental and moral degeneracy, and of race suicide" firmly at men's door (1913, vi). Claiming that 75–80 percent of men were already infected with gonorrhea when they married, she warned of the high risk women faced of contracting the disease from their husbands. Her response was radical in its simplicity: it was the lack of a vote that kept women economically, sexually, and politically subordinate to men and thus prone to sexual abuse and exploitation by them, both as wives and as prostitutes. Seeing the plague of venereal disease as auguring the destruction of society itself, she argued that the only recourse was for women to reject sexual slavery, fight for suffrage, and through it go on to redeem humanity.

When World War I broke out in 1914, Christabel and her mother agreed in August to call a truce in the WSPU campaign and to support the war effort. Christabel turned her back on the loyal following of her sister Sylvia's East London Federation of Suffragettes and cold-shouldered Sylvia for her socialist pacifism. The object of Christabel's vitriol was now turned on the German military aggressor. With all jailed suffragettes released on amnesty, she returned to the United Kingdom to lead women's parades and propaganda rallies, calling men to arms and women to the munitions industry. The *Suffragette* became a repository of British jingoism under its new title *Britannia*, with its exhortations to British womanhood to join the fight against the "Hun." Christabel was unforgiving of those suffragists, such as her sister, who proclaimed their pacifism and joined the international peace movement; in her eyes, their action was as traitorous as that of members of religious and socialist groups who also refused to beat the drum of militarism. With her mother, she began lobbying for the United States to enter the war in support of the Allies, in October 1914 going on a six-month speaking tour there and then returning to Paris, where she remained until 1917. In November 1917, shortly after the revolution in

Russia, she and Emmeline reformed the WSPU as the Women's Party, with a reactionary message warning of the dangers of bolshevism and outlining a plan for national "Industrial Salvation" (Crawford 1999, 725). The party was short-lived and folded in the summer of 1919.

By the end of the war, the political fire in Christabel had gone out, and reaction had set in; she remained a passionate feminist but rejected the idea that political campaigning would ever effect social change and became estranged from the British women's movement. After women over thirty were given the vote in the United Kingdom in 1918 under the Representation of the People Act, Christabel stood for the northern seat of Smethwick in the general election on a far-right ticket based on her opposition to home rule in Ireland, support for control of trade unions, and her advocacy of draconian war reparations against Germany that threatened nothing less than its postwar economic annihilation. Her electoral campaign was a failure, and after 1920 Christabel turned to social purity campaigning, often dressing in white to emphasize her message and her own sexual inviolability.

In 1921 Christabel left the United Kingdom to join her mother, who was living in Canada. From there she went to the United States, where she joined the Second Adventists and turned to writing and lecturing on Christian topics and preaching the second coming, inspired by her reading of the Apocalypse of St. John of Patmos. She produced numerous books and tracts on the subject during 1921–1932, such as "The Lord Cometh" (1923), "Pressing Problems of the Closing Age" (1924), and "The World's Unrest" (1926). Christabel was back in England for most of the 1930s, during which time she was honored as a Dame Commander of the Order of the British Empire (DBE) in 1936; but sources say little on her other activities. By 1940 she was back in the United States, settling in California, where her later life was lived in obscurity; she died alone at her home in Santa Monica. Her *New York Times* obituary referred to the erstwhile suffrage leader, in her day a central figure in British political life, as latterly being a "militant campaigner for Christ."

Christabel's total rejection of men and her solidarity with her own sex inevitably have aroused debate over her sexuality. Whether she was an active lesbian is not known, but she certainly moved in lesbian groups during her years in

Paris. Evidence in support of the rumors has yet to be presented. Her account of the suffrage campaign in Britain, *Unshackled: The Story of How We Won the Vote,* which it is thought Christabel wrote in the 1930s, was published posthumously in 1959, but it does not discuss the conflicts within the WSPU. The suffragist Elizabeth Robins, who became disenchanted with Christabel's leadership of the WSPU, is said to have based the character of Miss Ernestine Blunt on Christabel in her play *Votes for Women* (1906); her novel *The Convert* (1907) also drew on much of Christabel's writings and speeches.

In tandem with her mother, Christabel Pankhurst dedicated her ruthless political will and organizing skills to a high-profile political campaign that would make its mark on the twentieth century and that, in the nature of its emphasis on an exclusive sisterhood of women working together for their own empowerment, without doubt laid the foundations of the women's liberation movement of the 1970s.

See also Billington-Greig, Teresa; Despard, Charlotte; Gore-Booth, Eva; Kenney, Annie; Montefiore, Dora; Pethick-Lawrence, Emmeline; Robins, Elizabeth.

References and Further Reading

Billington-Greig, Teresa. 1911. *The Militant Suffrage Movement: Emancipation in a Hurry.* London: F. Palmer.

Castle, Barbara. 1987. *Sylvia and Christabel Pankhurst.* Harmondsworth: Penguin Books.

Crawford, Elizabeth. 1999. *The Women's Suffrage Movement, 1866–1928: A Reference Guide.* London: University College of London Press.

Kenney, Annie. 1924. *Memoirs of a Militant.* London: Edward Arnold.

Liddington, Jill, and Jill Norris. 2000 [1978]. *One Hand Tied behind Us.* Rev. ed. London: Virago.

Mackenzie, Midge. 1975. *Shoulder to Shoulder.* London: Penguin.

Mitchell, David. 1967. *The Fighting Pankhursts: A Study in Tenacity.* London: Jonathan Cape.

———. 1977. *Queen Christabel: A Biography of Christabel Pankhurst.* London: Macdonald and Jane's.

Pankhurst, Christabel. 1913. *The Great Scourge and How to End It.* London: Woman's Press.

———. 1987 [1959]. *Unshackled: The Story of How We Won the Vote.* Reprint, London: Cresset Women's Voices.

Pankhurst, E. Sylvia. 1977 [1931]. *The Suffrage Movement: An Intimate Account of Persons and Ideals.* Reprint, London: Virago.

Pethick-Lawrence, Emmeline. 1938. *My Part in a Changing World.* London: Victor Gollancz.

Purvis, June. 1996. "A 'Pair of . . . Infernal Queens'"? A Reassessment of Emmeline and Christabel Pankhurst, First Wave Feminists in Edwardian Britain." *Women's History Review* 5, no. 2: 259–280.

———. 1998. "Christabel Pankhurst and the Women's Social and Political Union." In Maroula Joannu and June Purvis, eds., *The Women's Suffrage Movement: New Feminist Perspectives.* Manchester: Manchester University Press.

Rosen, Andrew. 1993 [1974]. *Rise Up, Women! Militant Campaign of the WSPU 1903–1904.* Reprint, London: Routledge.

Sarah, Elizabeth. 1983. "Christabel Pankhurst: Reclaiming Her Power." In Dale Spender, ed., *Feminist Theorists: Three Centuries of Women's Intellectual Traditions.* London: Women's Press.

Smith, Harold L., ed. 1990. *British Feminism in the Twentieth Century.* Aldershot: Edward Elgar.

Spender, Dale. 1982. *Women of Ideas, and What Men Have Done to Them.* London: Routledge and Kegan Paul.

Pankhurst, Emmeline
(1858–1928)
United Kingdom

The name of Emmeline Pankhurst is synonymous with the British suffrage movement. In her leadership of its militant wing, she seemed born to a predestined purpose. If her daughter Christabel was the militant movement's stage manager and mastermind, then Emmeline was its self-dramatizing epicenter, a woman of reckless courage who turned suffering for the cause into high art. She was born into radicalism, learned women's rights from her feminist mother, and early acquired a sense of theater, which, when coupled with her austere beauty, gracious demeanor, and eloquent rhetoric, commanded attention and often received hero worship. She could also be ruthless, dictatorial, impetuous, and impatient. She was always a woman in a hurry, restless to get things done, and when things did not happen quickly enough, she turned to direct action and militancy. Enduring the agonies of repeated hunger strikes and force-feedings, she pushed her own increasingly frail body to the edge of total collapse on several occasions and no doubt shortened her life in so doing. The reward for such sacrifice was immortal-

Emmeline Pankhurst (Courtesy of Helen Rappaport)

completing her studies, she married in 1879. Her husband, Richard Pankhurst, who was forty-four years old to her twenty, was a radical barrister active in many social causes. He had been on the Manchester Committee for the Enfranchisement of Women, had supported the women defendants in the 1868 test case in Manchester on municipal suffrage, and had drafted the Married Women's Property Bill, introduced in 1868. From 1880 to 1889, Emmeline gave birth to five children, which for some time precluded her involvement in political activities.

In 1885 the Pankhursts moved to London, but Richard's radicalism proved a stumbling block in his ability to establish a large enough clientele as a barrister, and he suffered increasing ill health. The couple mixed in bohemian and artistic circles in London and joined the Fabian Society after William Gladstone's Liberal Party failed to introduce women's suffrage in its 1884 Reform Bill. They became friendly with other socialists such as Annie Besant, Keir Hardie, and William Morris. In 1889 Emmeline and Richard were founding members with Elizabeth Wolstenholme-Elmy of the Women's Franchise League, set up in response to the limited suffrage demands of existing groups (which favored the vote for unmarried women and widows only) and that worked to further the rights of married women. By 1893 Richard's infirmity and the failure of Emmeline's fancy goods shop in Tottentham Court Road forced the family to return to Manchester, where they joined the Independent Labour Party (ILP) and resumed their local political work, with Richard again standing unsuccessfully for election to Parliament.

Emmeline's appointment at the end of 1894 as a Poor Law Guardian, under new legislation allowing women to be elected to such bodies (she later also served on the Manchester School Board), brought her face-to-face with the realities of poverty during her workhouse visits. Her husband's death in 1898 made the need for her to find a source of income even more pressing. Left with considerable debts and four children (Henry had died in 1888 at the age of four) to support, she opened another shop and moved to a more modest house. She gave up her post on the Board of Guardians to take a paid job as registrar of births and deaths in the working-class district of Rusholme, in Manchester (which she held until 1907). This work brought her into fur-

ity as the leading figure of what became a latter-day religious crusade in which she played the role of Joan of Arc.

In a speech at Carnegie Hall in October 1909, during a fund-raising trip to the United States, Emmeline remarked: "I am what you call a hooligan" (Mackenzie 1975, 142), but her background, although radical, was far from revolutionary. She was one of ten children of a well-off middle-class calico printer in Manchester; her parents were cast in the Victorian philanthropic tradition as advocates of human progress, abolition, and women's emancipation. As a child, Emmeline's reading material was often abolitionist tracts and novels such as *Uncle Tom's Cabin* by Harriet Beecher Stowe. She was by nature rebellious and, even in her teenage years, had a somewhat regal manner and a stylish dress sense to match that would be noted by many.

After being educated at school in Manchester, Emmeline was sent to board at the Ecole Normale, a finishing school in Paris; two years after ther contact with poor working-class women, with Pankhurst encountering many widows living in penury, teenage girls with illegitimate babies, and women deserted by husbands. Such experiences further convinced her that women's position in society could only be improved if they were given the vote. In 1902 Pankhurst was a founding member of the Manchester Central branch of the ILP, but she was becoming disillusioned with the male domination of labor politics. When in 1903, her daughter Sylvia was asked to paint a mural in an ILP meeting hall from which, Emmeline discovered, women would be excluded, she became furious and resigned from the ILP. For her, it was the final proof that if women wanted to achieve suffrage, they had to go it alone.

Not wishing to join Millicent Garrett Fawcett's moderate National Union of Women's Suffrage Societies, which was affiliated with the Liberal Party, on 10 October 1903 Pankhurst cofounded the Women's Social and Political Union (WSPU) with other members of the Manchester branch of the ILP at her home in Nelson Street, with the slogan "Deeds Not Words." In the early stages of its peaceful local campaigning, the WSPU, which was for some time a relatively small organization, drew many members from the ILP. It lobbied for support among working women, including many in the Lancashire cotton mills, and won women such as Annie Kenney and Hannah Mitchell to the cause.

The nature of WSPU campaigning changed in 1905 after Christabel Pankhurst and Kenney were arrested and imprisoned for interrupting a Liberal Party election meeting (deliberately contrived by Christabel to provoke arrest). Emmeline realized the full value of publicity to be gained for the cause from high-profile acts of civil disobedience and militancy. As the campaign cranked up and WSPU members became more vocal and confrontational, the *Daily Mail* coined the term *suffragette* to describe this new breed of feminist campaigner. The years 1906 to 1914 would mark a high point in women's political campaigning in Britain, not repeated until the second wave of the feminist movement in the 1970s.

In 1907 Pankhurst, in continuous financial difficulty, moved from Manchester to London, having transferred the WSPU's political base there in 1906. Over the following years, she had

no permanent home, living sometimes at WSPU treasurer Emmeline Pethick-Lawrence's flat or in cheap hotels and rented flats and scraping a living from speaking tours around the country and in the United States from 1908 to 1912. She had a memorable speaking voice and relished the combat of public debate, as one eyewitness remarked: "I never heard a political speaker... who was more completely master of his subject, or who seemed to welcome noisy interruptions with such zest" (Crawford 1999, 505). Throughout her WSPU campaigning, Emmeline marshaled and led her suffrage troops from the front, like a general. In September 1907, with the ruthless pragmatism of military campaigners, she and Christabel made the decision to abolish the WSPU constitution and take control of the movement. WSPU members were expected to accept Emmeline's decisions without challenge for the sake of the cause; her critics would see this as dictatorial, an act whereby she cut herself off from the grass roots of the membership.

In 1908 after the Liberal government under new Prime Minister Herbert Asquith failed to carry a bill on women's enfranchisement, Emmeline endorsed an increase in WSPU militancy. She suffered the first of many periods of imprisonment, in February 1908 beginning a sentence of six weeks in Holloway jail; a further term followed in October. Meanwhile, window smashing by WSPU members had become a potent symbol not only of WSPU defiance but of the power of popular protest, with Emmeline later averring: "The argument of the broken window pane is the most valuable argument in modern politics" (Dangerfield 1936, 145). Ever-larger WSPU rallies, costume parades, and torchlight processions raised suffrage activism to public entertainment, reaching a high point in June when at least 250,000 people joined a mass rally in Hyde Park. Such events would also be staged in the United States by suffrage leader Alice Paul, who had spent time working with the suffrage campaign in England. At the end of 1909, Emmeline left for a fund-raising lecture tour of the United States organized by U.S. suffragists, including Harriot Stanton Blatch; a second tour came in October 1911. Nothing would deter her from her single-minded campaign, even though in 1910 she suffered the loss of her son Harry (who died of polio) and her sister Mary (who had been imprisoned for suffrage campaigning). When she was once more arrested and imprisoned in 1912, for throwing a stone at the prime minister's home in Downing Street, Emmeline demanded to be treated as a political prisoner; for her the suffrage campaign was nothing less than a war, particularly after the Liberal government had blocked the passage of Conciliation Bills on women's suffrage in 1910 and 1911. Sentenced to nine months' imprisonment, Pankhurst went on a hunger strike in June but was released three days later.

The years 1912–1914 marked the final stage of WSPU militancy, with Christabel masterminding the organization of the WSPU from Paris. Emmeline Pethick-Lawrence and her husband were ousted as treasurers, and Emmeline Pankhurst took control of a pared-down leadership in London. The Pethick-Lawrences, who had been loyal and unquestioning servants of the organization, accepted their ejection with good grace. Emmeline Pethick-Lawrence graciously recorded in her memoirs that although both Christabel and Emmeline were "quite ruthless" in their dealings with other people but that "men and women of destiny are like that" (1938, 69).

In April 1913 Emmeline was once again arrested, for incitement to break the law, and this time sentenced to three years in prison. As soon as she was jailed, she went on a hunger strike, and so a pattern was established. The Prisoners' Temporary Discharge for Ill Health Act—popularly known as the Cat and Mouse Act—was brought hastily into operation, under which hunger-striking suffragettes were released long enough to recover and then rearrested. Released under the act and back into the arms of adoring supporters, nurses, and well-wishers, Pankhurst was rearrested after six weeks but was back out again within days, having resumed her hunger strike. She endured nine periods of hunger, thirst, and even sleep strikes over a period of sixteen months; her total number of imprisonments eventually reached fourteen.

In October 1913, during a period of freedom, Emmeline attempted to go on another fund-raising tour of the United States but was detained at Ellis Island. This caused a public uproar, and the ensuing publicity garnered a further much-needed £4,000 in donations from supporters. But upon her return to the United Kingdom, she was once again arrested and once more in and out of prison on hunger and thirst strikes, often carried out of jail on a stretcher, such was her extreme state. By this time, a desperate government was resorting to overkill in its enlistment of huge numbers of police to fight off protests by suffragettes on every—often very public—occasion of Emmeline Pankhurst's rearrest. In the midst of such scenes, the tiny and increasingly fragile figure of Pankhurst often became completely lost. Her exhausting and stubborn pattern of protest had ensured that by the end of July 1914, when she managed to get across to France after her latest release, she had served only about twenty-three days of her three-year sentence.

In August 1914 WSPU militancy, and with it Emmeline's imprisonments, came to a sudden halt when Emmeline and Christabel embraced the war effort and agreed to temporarily shelve the suffrage campaign, exhorting British women to join shoulder to shoulder with men to defeat the Germans. Emmeline lobbied the trade unions to accept women workers in the munitions industry and also volunteered for propaganda missions to the United States and Russia. In Petrograd, she personally inspected the famous Women's Battalion of Death organized by Maria Bochkareva, a woman after Emmeline's own heart who had lobbied the tsar in 1914 to be allowed to enlist in the army. With the WSPU journal the *Suffragette* jingoistically renamed *Britannia,* Emmeline set about arousing the patriotic spirit of British women and recruiting them to war industries with the same fervor with which she had sought recruits to the WSPU. She set up a home for illegitimate and unwanted war babies in Kensington and went back to the United States to fund-raise on its behalf. But her war work was colored by a frighteningly blinkered demonization of the entire German people and, for that matter, of pacifists and conscientious objectors. Her attitude fueled the fires of xenophobia in Britain and divided the opposing forces in the conflict along naively simplistic lines, with the French portrayed as innocent victims of the rapacious "Huns." These prejudices carried over into support by both Emmeline and her daughter Christabel for the imposition of draconian postwar reparations on Germany.

At the end of the war, Emmeline's long fight for women's suffrage ended when the British government finally awarded women the vote in 1918. But it was a limited reward for the 1,000 or so women who had suffered imprisonment, force-feeding, and police brutality during suffrage campaigning. For the limited franchise was applicable only to women over thirty who were property holders in their own right or married to property holders and also those over thirty holding university degrees. Thus it excluded the majority of working-class women. Although it emancipated Emmeline Pankhurst and many of her class, most British women would have to wait another ten years to be fully enfranchised under universal suffrage measures in 1928. (The decision to set an age limit of thirty in 1918 had consciously been made in order to exclude women of a younger age from enfranchisement and thus prevent an imbalance in the male-female vote after so many younger men had been killed during World War I.)

In 1918 and 1919, Emmeline again visited the United States and also Canada, promoting her own and Christabel's social purity campaign and lecturing on the dangers of venereal disease for the National Council for Combating Venereal Diseases. She also spoke in support of temperance and warned against the dangers of the new communist state in Bolshevik Russia. She remained in Canada until 1924, living in Toronto. Ill health forced a period of rest in Bermuda, after which, in perennial financial difficulty, she went to France in 1925, for a while running a genteel tea shop on the Riviera. Emmeline returned to the United Kingdom in 1926, once more living a hand-to-mouth existence in cheap accommodations. She joined the Conservative Party and prepared to stand as a candidate in the Labour Party constituency of Whitechapel at the next election, an act seen as a deliberate slap in the face to her socialist daughter Sylvia, who worked for many years in the East End. But Emmeline's health finally failed, and she died on 14 June 1928. Estranged from all three of her daughters (the youngest, Adela, had emigrated to Australia) and practically penniless, she left only £86 in her will. Her death came just three weeks after the Equal Enfranchisement Act finally gave the vote to all women over the age of twenty-one.

The writer Rebecca West (1992) has talked of Pankhurst living and campaigning in the spirit of the principles of the French Revolution: liberty, equality, and fraternity. Certainly, she developed a brand of "romantic feminism" (as Holton 1990 describes it) that was all her own. Although many would challenge West's view, arguing that her elitist and dictatorial leadership of the WSPU was far from democratic, Emmeline Pankhurst was a woman of enormous courage who appeared to have no fear for her own safety or of the physical tolls of hunger striking on her body. Her friend the suffragette and composer Ethel Smyth saw in her an "otherworldliness," a quality that while perhaps defying comprehension, compels respect: "There was in her a deep sense of what in my Carlyle-ridden youth people used to call the Immensities; the things that lie beyond life and death, effort and fruition, success and failure, love and the dying away of love" (Smyth 1987, 295).

In March 1930, a bronze statue was erected in Emmeline Pankhurst's memory at Victoria Tower Gardens in sight of the Houses of Parliament. In October 1999, she was voted Woman of the Century by the Women of the Year Assembly in London for "acting as "the catalyst . . . that enabled women to leave their household chores and establish their own place in modern society" (*The Times,* 12 October 1999). The Pankhurst family home at 62 Nelson Street in Manchester was saved from developers and is now a Pankhurst museum and women's center. For further information on the Pankhurst Centre, go to www.manchester2002-ukCentre.com/museums/museums6.html. For archival information, go to the Fawcett Library's web site: http://www.lgu.ac.uk/fawcett.

See also Becker, Lydia; Besant, Annie; Blatch, Harriot Stanton; Kenney, Annie; Mitchell, Hannah; Paul, Alice; Pethick-Lawrence, Emmeline; Stowe, Harriet Beecher; Wolstenholme-Elmy, Elizabeth.

References and Further Reading

Crawford, Elizabeth. 1999. *The Women's Suffrage Movement, 1866–1928: A Reference Guide.* London: University College of London Press.

Dangerfield, George. 1936. *The Strange Death of Liberal England.* London: Constable.

Harrison, Brian. 1987. *Prudent Revolutionaries: Portraits of British Feminists between the Wars.* Oxford: Clarendon Press.

Holton, Sandra Stanley. 1986. *Feminism and Democracy: Women's Suffrage and Reform Politics in Britain, 1900–1918.* Cambridge: Cambridge University Press.

———. 1990. "In Sorrowful Wrath: Suffrage Militancy and the Romantic Feminism of Emmeline Pankhurst." In H. L. Smith, ed., *British Feminism in the Twentieth Century.* Aldershot: Edward Elgar.

———. 1996. *Suffrage Days: Stories from the Women's Suffrage Movement.* London: Routledge.

Joannu, Maroula, and June Purvis, eds. 1998. *The Women's Suffrage Movement: New Feminist Perspectives.* Manchester: Manchester University Press.

Mackenzie, Midge. 1975. *Shoulder to Shoulder.* London: Penguin.

Marcus, Jane, ed. 1987. *Suffrage and the Pankhursts.* London: Routledge and Kegan Paul.

Mitchell, David. 1967. *The Fighting Pankhursts: A Study in Tenacity.* London: Jonathan Cape.

Pankhurst, Christabel. 1987 [1959]. *Unshackled: The Story of How We Won the Vote.* Reprint, London: Cresset Women's Voices.

Pankhurst, E. Sylvia. 1935. *Life of Emmeline Pankhurst.* London: Laurie.

———. 1977 [1931]. *The Suffragette Movement: An Intimate Account of Persons and Ideals.* Reprint, London: Virago.

Pankhurst, Emmeline. 1914. *My Own Story.* London: Eveleigh Nash. (This book was ghostwritten by Rheta Childe Dorr.)

Pethick-Lawrence, Emmeline. 1938. *My Part in a Changing World.* London: Victor Gollancz.

Purvis, June. 1996. "A 'Pair of . . . Infernal Queens'"? A Reassessment of Emmeline and Christabel Pankhurst, First Wave Feminists in Edwardian Britain." *Women's History Review.* 5, no. 2: 259–280.

Purvis, June, and Sandra Stanley Holton, eds. 2000. *Votes for Women.* London and New York: Routledge.

Smyth, Ethel. 1987. *Memoirs of Ethel Smyth.* Abridged and introduced by Ronald Crichton. London: Viking.

Spender, Dale. 1982. *Women of Ideas, and What Men Have Done to Them.* London: Routledge and Kegan Paul.

Vicinus, Martha. 1985. *Independent Women, Work and Community for Single Women, 1850–1920.* London: Virago.

West, Rebecca. 1992. "A Reed of Steel." In Jane Marcus, ed., *The Young Rebecca.* London: Macmillan.

Pankhurst, (Estelle) Sylvia
(1882–1960)
United Kingdom

The British suffragette Sylvia Pankhurst, generally perceived as the sensitive, artistic sister of the more ruthless and determined Christabel, has in the past been viewed as the most high-profile casualty (along with Emmeline Pethick-Lawrence) of her mother's and sister's single-mindedness and exclusivity in their leadership of the Women's Social and Political Union (WSPU). She gave up her artistic career to join them in the militant suffrage campaign, but as a long-standing socialist-feminist and pacifist, there were always broader humanitarian interests that pulled her in other directions. Whereas Christabel would always be ruled by her head and would make pragmatic decisions in the light of political expediency, Sylvia's "passion of pity" (as Pethick-Lawrence so brilliantly encapsulated it) would lead her into broader, more diffuse, and deeply felt social aspirations. Her pacifism in the end made her ill-suited to the military machine that the WSPU became. In her attempt to reconcile her socialist sympathies with WSPU diktat, she came into conflict with mother and sister and was ultimately estranged from them at the outbreak of World War I. Although her mother changed political camps and became a Tory in later life and her sister embraced the social purity movement, Sylvia Pankhurst remained a grassroots socialist and channeled her political idealism into the cause of Ethiopian independence.

Born in Manchester, Sylvia Pankhurst was the second of her parents' five children. The family moved to London when she was three but were forced by financial difficulties to return north in 1893, where Sylvia finished her education at Manchester High School and won a scholarship to the Municipal School of Art. She suffered greatly by the early death of her father, Richard Pankhurst, in 1898. From him she had acquired her radical socialist beliefs, and to them she remained true. He had been her rock and her inspiration; without him she felt alienated, with all her mother Emmeline's affections being lavished on her favorite and eldest child, Christabel.

A gifted artist, Sylvia won several medals for her work, a traveling scholarship to Venice, and finally a National Scholarship in 1904 to complete her training at the Royal College of Art in Kensington. Despite the prospects before her of a successful art career, after completing her studies in 1906, she joined her mother's and sister's suffrage organization, the Women's Social and Political Union (founded in 1903), rather than pursue a full-time artistic career, and supported herself with occasional freelance work. For a while, before her mother and sister had moved from Manchester back to London, she was in charge of WSPU activities in the capital as honorary secretary. She applied her creative talents to designing the organization's soon-to-be-familiar trappings: its logo, various banners and posters, the winged angel on the cover of its journal *Votes for Women,* its membership card, and later on the famous "Holloway brooch" worn by all suffragettes who had been jailed. She even produced an elegant ceramic "Suffragette Tea Service." In 1903 she painted a mural at an Independent Labour Party (ILP) meeting hall in Salford to commemorate her father's work.

In about 1905, Sylvia developed a close friendship with the socialist leader and founder of the ILP, Keir Hardie (with whom she had an affair) and absorbed the socialist writings of William Morris and Edward Carpenter. In October 1906, Sylvia suffered her first imprisonment. A further three weeks in Holloway Prison followed in 1907, after which she returned north to make art studies of working women. Back in London in the summer of 1908, she organized WSPU activities in the west of London while writing for *Votes for Women.* In 1910 she produced one of the first histories of the WSPU, published in 1911 as *The Suffragette: The History of the Women's Militant Suffrage Movement 1905–10.*

When Sylvia was away on an exhausting fundraising tour in the United States and Canada in the first months of 1911 and again in 1912, WSPU militancy escalated, and her sister Christabel decamped to France. Sylvia was dismayed by this and by what she saw as her sister's manipulative control of the WSPU, but in Christabel's absence she was in the forefront of WSPU work in the north of England and then increasingly in the East End of London, where she sought to galvanize a mass working-class movement in support of women's suffrage. She began founding WSPU branches there, which grouped together under her leadership as the East London Federation (ELF) of Suffragettes. By this time, Sylvia's fierce loyalty to working-class objectives—at a time when the WSPU had deserted its erstwhile ally, the ILP, and the cause of suffrage for all in favor of a limited franchise for women—was in marked contrast to the objectives of her sister Christabel. With social concerns uppermost in her mind, Sylvia argued that women's suffrage could only be won as a part of social and economic reform of society at large through the work of the labor movement. These ideals increasingly preoccupied her over and above the issues of women's suffrage. Concerned, too, that the WSPU leadership of her mother and sister was elitist, she continued to try to bridge the gap between its inner sanctum and her own grassroots suffrage groups.

Sylvia's first two attempts to earn her prison stripes along with other suffragettes were defused when her fines were paid by anonymous donors. On her third arrest, in February 1913, for breaking windows, she was sent to Holloway Prison, immediately went on a hunger and thirst strike, and soon refused to sleep as well. In this, she was as determinedly militant as her mother and endured ten hunger and thirst (as well as sleep) strikes in the months until June 1914, becoming in that brief period one of the WSPU's most imprisoned suffragettes. Meanwhile, her sister Christabel kept out of harm's way in Paris. And although Sylvia's suffering was appalling, it was her mother, as the figurehead of the movement, who garnered most of the publicity.

In the meantime, in 1912 Sylvia had established her own East End publication, the *Women's Dreadnought.* As war loomed, its pacifist tone became more pronounced and after war broke out in 1914, she took advantage of the suspension of suffrage activities to publicize other socialist issues and condemn militarism. With the WSPU giving its wholehearted support to the war effort, Sylvia's family loyalties evaporated. She saw the material objectives of war as no justification for the sacrifice of so many lives, and with another WSPU defector, Charlotte Despard, she established the Women's Peace Army to lobby for a negotiated peace settlement. She had already been instructed to remove the ELF from the WSPU at Christabel's behest, and now she renamed her women's journal the *Workers' Dreadnought,* broadening its coverage of socialist issues and including in it her own, somewhat nebulous theories on revolution and social philosophy.

During World War I, the ELF would be one of the few women's suffrage groups to remain active and lobby for adult suffrage, with Sylvia turning her artistic flair to the staging of colorful suffrage parades as part of her ongoing war against capitalism. The *Dreadnought* would often be fined for its antiwar propaganda. During the war, the ELF undertook valuable social work inspired by the settlement work of Jane Addams in Chicago:

it set up welfare and maternity clinics and appealed for essential supplies of milk, eggs, and medicine for destitute mothers and their children. A Montessori day nursery was also opened, as well as cost-price restaurants, a cooperative toy factory, and recreational centers. Sylvia constantly lobbied for financial assistance to be given to working wives and mothers who had got into financial difficulty while their men were away fighting, establishing a League of Rights for Soldiers' and Sailors' Wives and Relatives.

As a socialist, Sylvia welcomed the Russian Revolution in 1917; she joined the Hands Off Russia Campaign during the Allied war of intervention that attempted to secure the victory of anti-Bolshevik White forces (meanwhile, her mother and sister were already warning of the menace of Bolshevism). In 1920, determined to visit Russia, she stowed away on a Finnish ship, and in Petrograd met Vladimir Ilyich Lenin (who remained unimpressed, branding her as an amateur). She returned enamored with Bolshevik Russia and, convinced that the socialist experiment there was working, founded the People's Russian Information Bureau. She published *Soviet Russia as I Saw It* in 1921, began proclaiming the virtues of workers' soviets as a form of democratic government that should be adopted in Britain, and changed the name of the East London Federation to the overtly Soviet-sounding Workers' Socialist Federation.

In 1921, soon after her visit to Russia, Sylvia published a contentious article entitled "Discontent on the Lower Deck" in the *Workers' Dreadnought* (which now proclaimed itself the "Organ of the Communist Party") and was sent to prison for sedition. Disillusionment with communism also soon followed. Just as she had come to dislike her sister's and mother's autocratic rule of the WSPU, so she became disillusioned with Lenin's stranglehold over the Bolshevik government. The Communist Party in Britain expelled her after she refused to allow it to take over ideological control of the *Workers' Dreadnought*. Final bitter disenchantment came with the onset of the Stalinist purges in the 1930s and the arrest and show trial of the political economist Nikolay Bukharin, whom she had greatly admired.

The interwar years were a restless and rootless time for Sylvia, who found herself out on a political limb and for a while without a cause. She continued to be a prolific writer, producing arti-

cles; a collection of poems about her prison experiences, *Writ on Cold Slate* (1921); *India and the Earthly Paradise* (1926); and *Save the Mothers* (1930), which highlighted mortality rates in childbirth and argued for state maternity benefits. As she began to lose contact with mainstream Labour Party politics, she gave herself over to utopian socialist ideals. In an April 1928 interview in the *News of the World,* she stated unequivocally: "Socialism is the greatest thing in life for me. You will never crush it out of me or kill it." She sought to establish a way of life based on communal living and work and closed down the *Workers' Dreadnought* in 1924. She ran a low-cost café in Woodford Green and ate and dressed simply. A relationship with an Italian socialist exile, Silvio Corio, resulted in the birth of her son Richard in 1927, when she was forty-four, but Sylvia refused to marry Corio or take his name.

This event horrified her mother, who had in later life embraced a deeply conservative position; the two women did not reconcile before Emmeline's death a year later. In 1931 Sylvia published her memoirs, *The Suffragette Movement: An Intimate Account of Persons and Ideals,* which became a major source on suffrage history (eventually republished during the second wave of feminism in 1977). Impressive in its recall of a vast canvas of people and events, the book is nevertheless flawed because it fails to cover the mainstream nonmilitant movement, and Sylvia's biography of her mother, *Life of Emmeline Pankhurst* (1935), was also disappointingly unrevealing. She did, however, prove to be fiercely defensive of her mother's reputation and in later life sued author Roger Fulford over what she saw as crude distortions of the truth about the WSPU campaign in his 1957 book, *Votes for Women.*

In the mid-1930s, largely due to Corio's influence, Sylvia found a new and all-consuming crusade—the establishment of an independent Ethiopia, free of fascist Italian rule—that would absorb her till her death. After Italian fascist forces were ordered by Benito Mussolini to invade the Ethiopian (then Abyssinian) kingdom of Emperor Haile Selassie in 1935, she founded the Abyssinian Association with other left-wing activists and established and edited *New Times and Ethiopia News* (1936–1956), which called on the League of Nations to defend Ethiopia's right to self-determination and its people against racism and colonialism. In her work, she collaborated with black activists such as the British-based Una Marson and left-wing British women, including Nancy Cunard and Winifred Holtby. Anti-imperialist as well as antifascist in tone, the newspaper sold widely in West Africa and the West Indies where Haile Selassie was greatly revered, with a circulation approaching 40,000; copies were also smuggled to rebel forces in Ethiopia. In addition, Sylvia produced many pamphlets and letters in support of the country's independence from Italian rule and against racism. Her antifascist activities led her to support the Republicans during the Spanish Civil War and to help Jewish refugees fleeing Nazi Germany. During World War II, she continued to defend Ethiopian independence from Italy despite numerous threats made against her and visited Ethiopia in 1944 after it had been occupied by the Allies, vehemently opposing calls for it to be made a British protectorate.

Much of the remainder of Sylvia's life was taken up by a new and passionate interest in Ethiopian culture, art, and history. She oversaw fund-raising efforts to build the new Princess Tsahai Memorial Hospital after visiting the country again during 1951–1952 and wrote a major study, *Ethiopia: A Cultural History* (1955). The following year Sylvia settled permanently in Addis Ababa, where she founded a voluntary welfare organization, the Social Service Society, and wrote for the *Ethiopian Observer,* as well as continuing to publish the *New Times* until 1956. Emperor Haile Selassie honored her work with the award of Ethiopia's highest honor, the Queen of Sheba, first class. Pankhurst died in Addis Ababa; she was given a state funeral and buried in the grounds of the city's Holy Trinity Cathedral.

See also Addams, Jane; Cunard, Nancy; Despard, Charlotte; Holtby, Winifred; Marson, Una; Pankhurst, Christabel; Pankhurst, Emmeline; Pethick-Lawrence, Emmeline.

References and Further Reading

Bullock, Ian, and Richard Pankhurst, eds. 1992. *Sylvia Pankhurst: From Artist to Anti-Fascist.* Basingstoke: Macmillan.

Castle, Barbara. 1987. *Sylvia and Christabel Pankhurst.* Harmondsworth: Penguin.

Crawford, Elizabeth. 1999. *The Women's Suffrage Movement, 1866–1928: A Reference Guide.* London: University College of London Press.

Davis, Mary. 1999. *Sylvia Pankhurst: A Life in Radical Politics.* London: Pluto.

Harrison, Brian. 1987. *Prudent Revolutionaries: Portraits of British Feminists between the Wars.* Oxford: Clarendon Press.

Mackenzie, Midge. 1975. *Shoulder to Shoulder.* London: Penguin.

Mitchell, David. 1967. *The Fighting Pankhursts: A Study in Tenacity.* London: Jonathan Cape.

Oldfield, Sybil. 2001. *Women Humanitarians: A Biographical Dictionary of British Women Active between 1900 and 1950.* London: Continuum.

Pankhurst, E. Sylvia. 1935. *Life of Emmeline Pankhurst.* London: Laurie.

———. 1977 [1931]. *The Suffrage Movement: An Intimate Account of Persons and Ideals.* Reprint, London: Virago.

Pankhurst, Richard. 1979. *Sylvia Pankhurst: Artist and Crusader.* London: Paddington Press.

Purvis, June, and Sandra Stanley Holton, eds. 2000. *Votes for Women.* London and New York: Routledge.

Romero, Patricia E. 1987. *Sylvia Pankhurst: Portrait of a Radical.* New Haven, CT: Yale University Press.

Rosen, Andrew. 1993 [1974]. *Rise Up, Women! Militant Campaign of the WSPU 1903–1904.* Reprint, London: Routledge.

Slaughter, Jane, and Robert Kern. 1981. *European Women on the Left: Socialism, Feminism, and the Problems Faced by Political Women, 1880 to the Present.* Westport, CT: Greenwood Press.

Winslow, Barbara. 1996. *Sylvia Pankhurst: Sexual Politics and Political Activism.* London: UCL Press.

Pappenheim, Bertha
(1859–1936)
Austria

Bertha Pappenheim has two very distinct identities: she is probably most famous as the patient known as "Anna O"—whose "talking cure" under hypnosis was the basis for the development of Sigmund Freud's pioneering therapies of psychoanalysis in the treatment of pathological behaviors. In later life, Pappenheim, a volatile and passionate Jewish woman who was affected deeply by her studies of social deprivation, became a significant but now forgotten social worker and campaigner against prostitution and white slavery, as leader of the Jewish Women's League.

Pappenheim was born into a wealthy Orthodox Jewish family in Vienna. She was educated at a private Catholic school, where she studied the opening of the professions to women. During the 1890s, Pappenheim began writing on social issues, such as child poverty, in the 1890 short story collection *In the Second Hand Shop* and the play *Women's Rights* (1899), about the sexual and economic exploitation of women. She also wrote articles about women's emancipation, as well as translating Mary Wollstonecraft's *A Vindication of the Rights of Woman*. After running a soup kitchen for Jewish immigrants and a Jewish nursery school in 1895, Pappenheim became head of an orphanage for Jewish girls in Frankfurt.

Pappenheim's work took her to the Middle East and eastern Europe. After visiting the towns of the Jewish Pale of Settlement in Galicia, Romania, and Russia, she became particularly concerned at the high numbers of Jewish girls caught up in prostitution and in 1900 published a pamphlet, "The Jewish Problem in Galicia." Determined to work for the welfare of such oppressed Jewish women, who she believed were driven into prostitution by poverty and anti-Semitism, in 1902 she founded the Care for Women Society, which arranged foster care for orphans and offered assistance and counseling to women seeking training for employment. Pappenheim also developed methods of social work through this society and passed on her research and casework techniques to other women volunteers. In 1924 her account of her study of prostitution and white slavery, *Sisyphus Work,* was published in Leipzig.

In 1904, at a congress of the International Council of Women held in Berlin, Pappenheim came together with other Jewish women to found the Jewish Women's League and for the next twenty years served as its president. Grounding itself in Jewish ethical codes and a respect for Jewish tradition, the league modeled its work on that of similar voluntary Jewish women's organizations such as the Jewish Association for the Protection of Girls, Women, and Children in London. It set up case work on various women's issues, especially prostitution and white slavery, concentrating its activities on the trafficking in poor Jewish girls from the Pale and liaising with other activists in the International Abolitionist Federation. Pappenheim mounted an energetic propaganda campaign, traveling widely, lecturing and opening advice centers, and founding subsidiary branches in eastern Europe. In 1910 she published pamphlets on the social

Bertha Pappenheim (German Heritage Foundation)

French, Italian, and English, but as with many middle-class Jewish daughters, her intellectual talents were suppressed, and she led a dull domestic routine of reading and embroidery, punctuated only by occasional excursions to carry out charity work. When she was twenty-one, Pappenheim suffered the onset of nervous illness after nursing her dying father. She was treated by psychoanalyst Josef Breuer twice daily during 1880–1882 for a variety of hysterical symptoms. He induced a form of autohypnosis that released her pent-up emotions and that was referred to by Pappenheim as a "talking cure." In November 1882 she recounted her story to Breuer's collaborator, Freud, who adopted Breuer's method.

Over the next few years, Pappenheim suffered mental relapses but learned to deal with her illness. She moved to Frankfurt in 1889, where she lived with relatives and joined them in their work for Jewish charities. Pappenheim increasingly devoted herself to social causes, became interested in the work of the educator Helene Lange, and supported her appeal for women's education and conditions of the Jews in Galicia, and the league helped poor working girls avoid the trap of prostitution by setting up educational institutes, clubs, and dormitories. Volunteers also worked at stations and ports where immigrant girls arrived and assisted them in finding employment. Rehabilitation was also offered to prostitutes and delinquent girls through vocational retraining in needlework, typing, and home economics. But as Marion Kaplan (1979) points out, training in domestic service placed many of these girls in situations in which they would once more be vulnerable to sexual exploitation by male employers.

In her work, Pappenheim had constantly to contend with the blinkered attitudes of the male Orthodox Jewish establishment, the religious values of which accentuated women's role as wives and mothers without granting them the right to any kind of autonomy or financial independence. She sought rabbinical reforms that would give Jewish women greater rights in divorce and property inheritance. In particular, she argued the case for civil as well as religious marriage ceremonies, so that Jewish women could obtain civil divorces when marriages broke down rather than be left at the mercy of husbands who refused to grant them the *get*—a religious divorce.

In 1907 Pappenheim founded a Home for Endangered Girls at Neu Isenberg specifically for Jewish unmarried mothers, their children, and delinquent girls and served as one of its housemothers until her death. She also worked as a health campaigner, visiting hospitals that treated venereal disease, brothels, schools, and orphanages, and led study groups on the ethics of social work at the Frankfurt Lehrhaus. In 1916 Pappenheim published an article titled "Woe to Him Whose Conscience Sleeps," in which she advocated the establishment of a national Jewish welfare association. The Central Welfare Office of German Jews was established a year later, and she became its deputy vice president. After World War I, much of Pappenheim's work against the white slave trade was taken over by the League of Nations, but during the 1920s and 1930s, the League of Jewish Women continued to gain members, reaching fifty. It continued to work for social welfare until it was suppressed by the Nazis in 1938. Despite the ominous rise of anti-Semitism in Adolf Hitler's Germany, Pappenheim remained a patriotic German Jew who opposed Zionism and Jewish emigration, which she felt destroyed families. She suffered as a consequence; by 1935, with the passing of the anti-Semitic racial laws in Germany, she realized her error, but by then she was already ill with terminal cancer. In the spring of 1936 she was interrogated by the Gestapo after one of the girls at the Isenberg home criticized Hitler.

Pappenheim died soon after at Isenberg. The home for which she had worked so tirelessly was attacked on *Kristallnacht* (10 November 1938) and finally closed down by the Nazis in 1942. Its remaining inmates were sent to the concentration camp at Theresienstadt, and the building was transferred to the Hitler Youth organization.

See also Lange, Helene.

References and Further Reading

Bristow, Edward. 1982. *Prostitution and Prejudice: The Jewish Campaign against White Slavery, 1870–1939.* Oxford: Clarendon Press.

Dresner, Ruth Rapp. 1981. "The Work of Bertha Pappenheim." *Judaism* 30: 204–211.

Edinger, Dora. 1968. *Bertha Pappenheim: Freud's Anna O.* Highland Park, IL: Congregation Solel.

Kaplan, Marion. 1979. *The Jewish Feminist Movement in Germany: The Campaigns of the Judischen Frauenbund 1904–1938.* Westport, CT: Greenwood Press.

———. 1984. "Sisterhood under Siege: Feminism and Anti-Semitism in Germany, 1904–1938." In Renate Bridenthal, Atina Grossman, and Marion Kaplan, eds. *When Biology Became Destiny: Women in Weimar and Nazi Germany.* New York: Monthly Review Press.

Pardo Bazán, Emilia
(1852–1921)
Spain

The foremost woman novelist of nineteenth-century Spain, Emilia Pardo Bazán exploited her exceptional literary gifts and talent for social commentary to develop the tradition of naturalistic writing in her country as well as to champion the education and emancipation of women. Elevated as a countess in 1908, she became somewhat grand in manner in her later years as a member of the Catholic oligarchy.

Pardo Bazán was an only child, born into an old aristocratic family in La Coruña in Galicia, which would be the rural setting for many of her novels. After the 1868 revolution in Spain, her father entered parliament, and the family moved to

Madrid. At the age of seventeen, Pardo Bazán married a law student. Having been an avid reader since childhood, she took up writing and developed an interest in progressive ideas on science (including Darwinism), philosophy, and women's rights.

In 1880 she began editing the *Galician Review* and was soon well known in literary circles. She first attracted attention with her 1883 essay, "The Critical Issue," a discussion of the naturalistic novels of the French writer Emile Zola, whose work inspired her to begin writing in the same vein. In her outstanding social novel, *The Manors of Ulloa* (1886), she produced a powerful exposé of the physical and moral degeneracy of the Spanish upper classes, their neglect of their wives and children (legitimate and illegitimate), and their disregard for their estates and workers. Its sequel, *Mother Nature* (1887), explored the topic of incest and its destructive effect on an ancient family line. The scope of Pardo Bazán's intellect and descriptive powers also prompted a novel, *The Female Orator* (1883), the first of its kind in Spain, about the plight of women tobacco workers.

Pardo Bazán's husband was unable to countenance his wife's discussion of these and other controversial social issues in her writings, however, and separated from her in the 1880s. By this time, she had openly come to share many of the same sensibilities toward women's position as her compatriot, the penal reformer Concepción Arenal. Pardo Bazán shared Arenal's acute awareness of the social difficulties for young middle-class women who wished to take up employment and be liberated from lives of idleness, and in her 1889 article "The Spanish Woman," described the chilling alternative they faced as being to "stay in their father's house and get mouldy, like nuns without a vocation in a convent" (Davies 1998, 24). In 1890 Pardo Bazán published a series of articles, also entitled "The Spanish Woman," in the *Fortnightly Review*, as well as two feminist novels, *The Test* and *A Christian Woman*. She also used the journal she founded in 1890, *New Critical Theater*, as a forum for her feminist ideas. In the following years, in essays such as "An Opinion on Women" (1892), she argued in support of women's aspirations beyond the realms of marriage and motherhood and endorsed their need for nonsexual supportive relationships with both sexes. Her 1896 novel, *Memories of a Bachelor*, would

advocate women's paid employment as being an important contributor to social well-being and national prosperity.

In 1891 Pardo Bazán nominated Concepción Arenal for the chair of the Royal Academy and later repeatedly and unsuccessfully nominated herself. After her father's death, she succeeded in having his hereditary title transferred to her rather than becoming extinct and thereafter insisted always on being addressed as "countess." Confident in her elevated social and literary status, Pardo Bazán boldly accepted the chair in romance languages and literatures at the Central University of Madrid in 1916, the first woman to hold such a position in Spain. In 1906 she had also become the first woman president of the Madrid Athenaeum and in 1907 the first woman to be appointed to the Council of Public Instruction. But her own successes did not diminish her sense of disappointment at the failure of feminism to ignite in Spain. In 1913 she sadly recorded the fact that the suffrage movement in her own country showed "no signs of life," compared to the movements in countries such as the United States and Britain. But at the end of a forty-year career, as one of Spain's most consistent and prolific writers and author of nineteen novels and 500 short stories, she had made a significant contribution to public awareness of women's and other social issues.

See also Arenal, Concepción.
References and Further Reading
Davies, Catherine. 1998. *Spanish Women's Writing 1849–1996*. London: Athlone Press.
Gonzalez-Arias, Francisca. 1992. *Portrait of a Woman as Artist: Emilia Pardo Bazán and the Modern Novel in France and Spain*. New York: Garland.
Hemingway, Maurice. 1983. *Emilia Pardo Bazán: The Making of a Novelist*. New York: Cambridge University Press.
Pattison, Walter Thomas. 1971. *Emilia Pardo Bazán*. New York: Twayne.

Parks, Rosa
(1913–)
United States

Since that auspicious day in December 1955 when she refused to give up her bus seat to a white man, Rosa Parks has been the first lady of the civil rights movement in the United States.

Rosa Parks (Library of Congress)

Although she was never a gifted orator, such as Fanny Lou Hamer or Ella Baker, her quiet, unassuming dignity has spoken volumes about the oppression endured by American blacks during the long years of segregation in the South and has inspired many others in the fight for justice and racial equality in the United States.

Born in Tuskegee, Alabama, Parks grew up in Montgomery's rigidly segregated environment. She attended Montgomery Industrial School and Alabama State High School and worked as a seamstress and housekeeper before marrying a civil rights activist, Raymond Parks, in 1932. After joining the National Association for the Advancement of Colored People (NAACP) during World War II, Parks served as secretary of its Montgomery branch from 1943 to 1956. With her husband, she took an interest in the problems of racial inequality in the South and joined voter registration drives for the Montgomery Voters League.

On 1 December 1955 Parks sparked what is now seen as the birth of the civil rights movement in the United States and with it the beginning of the dismantling of the draconian Jim Crow laws in the South. On her way home after work as a tailor's assistant at a local department store, she made a simple but symbolic protest by refusing to give up her bus seat to a white man. According to the municipal laws then in operation in Montgomery, whites had seating precedence over blacks when the bus was full. Parks said later in her autobiography, *Rosa Parks: My Story* (1992), that something in her had finally snapped. She simply "was tired of giving in to white people." The bus driver called the police, and Parks was arrested. Immediately, the Women's Political Council in Montgomery distributed thousands of handbills calling for a boycott of the buses on the day of Parks's trial. While she was out on bail awaiting trial, a groundswell of black support for Parks's action snowballed, leading to the establishment, on the day of Parks's conviction, of the Montgomery Improvement Association under the leadership of local Baptist minister Martin Luther King, Jr.

Parks's subsequent fine of $10 plus $4 costs, which she immediately appealed, ensured that her case became a national cause célèbre. The Montgomery Improvement Association organized a citywide boycott of the bus company, initially scheduled for one day—Monday, 5 December—but it lasted for 381 days, ending on 21 December 1956, and involving 50,000 blacks in the city. Because 70 percent of those using the buses in Montgomery were black, the boycott cost the bus company dearly, and the protest marked the beginning of a national nonviolent civil resistance program under King's charismatic leadership. This movement was modeled on the passive resistance methods used by Mahatma Gandhi in the campaign for India's independence. Its participants were subjected to considerable harassment and physical attack. Meanwhile, Parks, who helped organize the boycott, was dismissed from her job, as was her husband. Her appeal had become a federal suit that was taken up as a test case by the NAACP to challenge segregation on the buses in the South as being a violation of the constitutional rights of blacks.

In fact, Parks was preceded by three women who were arrested for similar protests, beginning with that of fifteen-year-old Claudette Colvin nine months previously. But Colvin was single and pregnant, and the male moral majority of the NAACP decided that Parks, as a married woman with a spotless record, was a better candidate for a test case. They felt she had the necessary gravitas to endure the close scrutiny of both the media and the courts; and indeed Parks was rapidly elevated to secular sainthood as a political innocent, when even at that time she was known for her civil rights activism and feminism. For as many as twelve years earlier, she had been thrown off a bus under local segregation laws for refusing to get off and reboard through the blacks-only entrance at the back after paying for her ticket at the front of the bus. In the event, Parks proved the perfect defendant in court; as an esteemed member of the local church, demurely dressed, calm, and self-contained, she garnered enormous public attention and respect. On 20 December 1956, the Supreme Court declared segregated seating on southern buses unconstitutional.

Although her case was over, Parks and her husband continued to suffer harassment, and both fell victim to stress and illness when they could not find work. They moved to Detroit, where despite considerable personal and financial hardship, they remained active in the civil rights movement, with Parks once more earning her living as a dressmaker. She joined King's Southern Christian Leadership Conference in Detroit and became active in numerous youth and cultural projects, as well as serving as a deaconess for St. Matthews' African Methodist Episcopal Church. In 1965 she took up what would be a twenty-three-year post as secretary to Congressman John Conyers, Jr., during which time she also lectured to youth groups on the history of the civil rights movement.

Shortly before her retirement in 1988, Parks founded the Rosa and Raymond Parks Institute for Self-Development, a program teaching racial equality and offering career training for young blacks. Revered as the "mother of the civil rights movement," Parks has been the recipient of numerous honorary degrees and awards, including the NAACP's Spingarn Medal (1979), the Martin Luther King Nonviolent Peace Prize (1980), the Eleanor Roosevelt Women of Courage Award (1984), the Presidential Medal of Freedom (1996), and, in 1999, the Congressional Medal of Honor. In November 2000, a Rosa Parks Library and Museum was opened in Montgomery under the auspices of Troy State University to document the history of the civil rights movement in the United States. For further information on the Rosa Parks Library and Museum, contact http://www.tsum.edu/.

See also Baker, Ella; Hamer, Fanny Lou.

References and Further Reading
Brinkley, Douglas. 2001. *Mine Eyes Have Seen the Glory: The Life of Rosa Parks*. London: Weidenfeld.
Friese, Kay. 1990. *Rosa Parks*. Englewood Cliffs, NJ: Silver-Burdette.
Giddings, Paula. 1984. *When and Where I Enter: The Impact of Black Women on Race and Sex in America*. New York: W. W. Norton.
King, Martin Luther, Jr. 1958. *Stride toward Freedom: The Montgomery Story*. New York: Harper.
Parks, Rosa, with Gregory J. Reed. 1994. *Quiet Strength: The Faith, the Hope, and the Heart of a Woman Who Changed a Nation*. Grand Rapids, MI: Zondervan.
Parks, Rosa, with Jim Haskins. 1992. *Rosa Parks: My Story*. New York: Dial Books.
Robinson, Jo Ann. 1987. *The Montgomery Bus Boycott and the Women Who Started It*. Knoxville: University of Tennessee Press.

Parnell, Anna
(1852–1911)
Ireland

Anna Parnell and her sister Fanny (1849–1882), siblings of the charismatic Irish politician Charles Parnell, founded the Ladies' Land League in Dublin in 1881, to continue protesting the eviction of Irish tenant farmers resisting rent increases, after the male leaders of the Irish Land League had been arrested and imprisoned. As the first Irish women's organization dedicated to nationalist interests, it served as a precursor to Maud Gonne's Daughters of Ireland (not founded till 1900), and offered Irish women their first, albeit brief, opportunity of becoming involved in political activism.

Born at Avondale, County Wicklow, into the Anglo-Irish Protestant gentry, as a young woman Anna Parnell became interested in the work of American feminists, partly due to the influence of her American mother. Her parents separated when she was small and for a while Anna lived with her mother and some of her siblings in Paris, where she was educated at home by governesses, absorbing literature, political science, and philosophy. After her father's death in 1859, the resulting debts forced the family to move back to Dublin. In 1864 she published some poems in support of the Fenian cause. She became increasingly alienated from traditional landowning society and abhorred its exploitation of the Irish agricultural worker. She saw a parallel in the sexual exploitation of women; throughout her life she would pride herself on preserving her own independence of mind and spirit.

After studying art in Paris and London until the mid-1870s, when her brother Charles was elected to parliament and assumed leadership of the Irish agrarian movement, Anna was drawn into the Irish cause. She joined her mother and sister Fanny, who in 1873 had left for the USA and were now living in Bordenstown, New Jersey. The Parnell women began meeting with Fenians and Irish nationalists in the USA and fund-raising among American sympathizers for famine relief in Ireland. Fanny, like Anna, wrote patriotic poetry, which was published in Irish newspapers in the United States, and later toured Canada for the Irish cause (she died young at the age of thirty-three). By 1880 the Land War in Ireland (as the agrarian protest movement became known) had escalated and the embattled Irish Land League that had been leading the protest campaign was badly in need of funds. With the encouragement of the leader of the league, Michael Davitt, the three Parnell women launched an appeal "to the Irish women of America" in New York in October 1880 at which the Ladies' Land League was inaugurated and of which Mrs. Parnell was elected president. Anna and her sister worked exhaustively setting up branches of the league across the USA and in January 1881 Anna returned to Dublin, at Davitt's request, to formally establish the Ladies' Land League in Ireland. She began holding public meetings and rallies, from the outset encouraging women to play a prominent role in defending evicted tenants and campaigning for them to be loaned money by the government so that they could buy their own land. She arranged shelter for dispossessed families and helped the wives and children of those in prison by setting up the Political Prisoners' Aid Society in 1882.

But soon she found herself in conflict with her brother Charles, who wanted to see Ladies' Land League funds diverted straight to the political campaign, and who had become increasingly dictatorial about how it should run its affairs. Brother and sister fell out and became estranged. Anna's brief period at the head of the Ladies' Land League, during her brother's imprisonment from October 1881 to May 1882, was soon eclipsed. She and her female co-campaigners now found themselves marginalized in the agrarian movement—an ironic outcome, considering that some of them had been far more militant than the men. The movement had run up debts, and Anna herself was almost destitute. Parnell paid these off on condition that the Ladies' Land League would be disbanded. This, combined with the debacle of Parnell's sellout over the Second Land Act, agreeing with Prime Minister William Glastone's terms under the Kilmainham treaty of 1882, led Anna to look upon her brother as a traitor to the cause. She never spoke to him again. For her, the treaty was a rejection of all the principles for which the Ladies' Land League had worked so hard and a denial of the effectiveness of women in political campaigning. In 1907 she wrote a history of the Irish agrarian movement, the title of which reflected her anger and bitterness: "The Land League: Tale of a Great Sham," which remained unpublished until long after her death. In it, she made clear that women's role in the Ladies' Land League had been far more than simply one of handing out soup to the dispossessed. She also argued strongly for women's enfranchisement and for their right to inherit property, which in Ireland was all too often denied them (as in her own case and that of her sister). Deeply pessimistic about the future for Ireland, she observed somewhat presciently that "in spite of its poor prospects, armed rebellion seems likely to be the next thing either tried or played at, here" (Cullen and Luddy 1995, 285).

In 1908 Parnell campaigned for the Sinn Féin candidate in the North Leitrim election, but by then she was deeply disillusioned with the world of male-driven politics. Feeling betrayed, she became a recluse and, after coming into a small inheritance, left Ireland to live in and around the English West Country, spending time at Ilfracombe in Devon and an artists' colony in Cornwall. She drowned in a public swimming bath during one of her daily swims in Ilfracombe in 1911; some suggest it was suicide.

See also Gonne, Maud.

References and Further Reading

Coté, Jane. 1991. *Fanny and Anna Parnell: Ireland's Patriot Sisters.* Basingstoke: Macmillan.
Cullen, Mary, and Maria Luddy. 1995. *Women, Power and Consciousness in Nineteenth-Century Ireland. Eight Biographical Studies.* Dublin: Attic Press.
Luddy, Maria. 1995. *Women in Ireland, 1800–1918.* Cork: Cork University Press.
Ó Céirín, Kit, and Cyril Ó Céirín, eds. 1996. *Women of Ireland: A Biographic Dictionary.* Kinvara, County Galway: Tír Eolas.
Ward, Margaret. 1983. *Unmanageable Revolutionaries: Women and Irish Nationalism.* London: Pluto Press.

Parren, Callirhoé Siganou
(1861–1940)
Greece

Born in Crete, the Greek educator and journalist Callirhoé Parren was one of a small group of women who fought to improve literacy standards for women in nineteenth-century Greece and encourage their long-overdue liberation into the public sphere through improved access to higher education. She trained as a teacher at the pioneering educational establishment in Athens, the Arsakeion, which sent out teachers into Rus-

Callirhoé Siganou Parren (Lydia Sinclair)

sia, the Balkans, Egypt, and Asia Minor. Parren taught at a girls' school in Andrianoupolis and for ten years in a succession of girls' schools in Russia and the Balkans, becoming conversant in English, French, Italian, and Russian. After marrying a French journalist, Jean Parren, she gave up teaching and settled in Athens, where she became a journalist in the mid-1880s.

In 1887 she began publishing the first Greek weekly publication run by and for women, the *Ladies' Journal,* which for the next thirty years would be "the voice of female consciousness in a male world" (Buck 1992, 897). The following year she was a delegate to the International Congress on Women's Rights held in Paris, and in 1893 she addressed the World's Congress of Representatives in Chicago, as an official representative of Queen Olga of Greece.

Over the years, the *Ladies' Journal* became an important mouthpiece for articles that embraced both cultural and social issues and argued against the inequality between the sexes and the social injustices that operated against women under the law and in prison, social customs, family life, and education. Aware of the low social status of Greek women, which was perpetuated by their lack of education, Karren sent a memorandum to the Greek prime minister, Hailaos Trikoupis, calling for girls to be admitted to the university and the polytechnic school. Her campaign was the culmination of a growing movement among Greek women for education in the years after the country's liberation from Turkish rule. It was the first sphere outside the home into which women's rights campaigners ventured from the 1840s onward, with foremother Evanthia Kairi (1797–1866) having laid the groundwork with her writings on education, based on her work at a girls' school in Kyonides, Asia Minor. Sappho Leontias (1832–1900) followed her with her books on education for women, and Kalliopi Kehajia (1839–1905) founded the Society for Promoting Women's Education in 1872.

By the end of the nineteenth century Parren had created forums for Greek women to campaign for their rights (although she deliberately chose not to demand suffrage, considering that this might alienate conservative opinion), with the foundation in 1894 of the Union for the Emancipation of Women and in 1896 of the Union of Greek Women. Thanks to the raised voice of women, legal reform followed to protect children and working women, and the University of Athens was opened to them. In 1911 Callirhoé's Lyceum of Greek Women was established, offering not just instruction in traditional domestic tasks such as cooking and child care but also training for employment. That same year, Athens hosted the first Panhellenic Women's Congress.

Parren's philanthropic activities were many: she set up and ran a school where widows and orphan girls were offered literacy classes and founded a hospital for the incurably sick. Although she voiced her tacit support for women's suffrage, it was not until 1920, when Anna Theodoropoulos founded the Greek League for Women's Rights, that the movement for women's suffrage and civil and political rights in Greece really began to make headway.

Parren wrote two feminist novels in which she described heroines seeking to liberate themselves from male domination, as well as *A History of Greek Women from 1650–1860*. In 1936, the year Greece celebrated the fiftieth anniversary of her entry into public life, she was awarded the Golden Cross of the Savior of the Greek Academy for her advocacy of women's education, which had resulted in the opening of the Greek universities to women.

References and Further Reading

Buck, Claire. 1992. *Bloomsbury Guide to Women's Literature*. London: Bloomsbury.

Offen, Karen. 2000. *European Feminisms, 1700–1950*. Stanford: Stanford University Press.

Sewall, May Wright, ed. 1894. *The World's Congress of Representative Women*. Chicago: Rand, McNally (contains two addresses given by Parren).

Varikas, Eleni. 1993. "Gender and National Identity in *Fin de Siècle* Greece." *Gender and History* 5(2): 269–283.

Paterson, Emma
(1848–1886)
United Kingdom

The founder of the women's trade union movement in England, Emma Paterson graduated from establishing friendly societies for women's trades to lobbying exhaustively over many years for the acceptance of women within the male-dominated Trade Union Congress. She was born into a middle-class family in London and was educated at home. Her father, who was a head teacher at a parish school in central London, encouraged her studies and her desire to take up useful employment, and she was apprenticed to a bookbinder. But when he died when she was sixteen, she had to give up her apprenticeship and teach at a school run by her mother for two years. She took a job as a clerk and later assistant secretary of the Working Men's Club and Institute Union (WMCII, 1866–1872), through which she began associating with trade unionists and socialists and through which she was asked in 1873 to also take up the post of secretary of the Central Committee of the National Society for Women's Suffrage.

Unfortunately, Paterson's career in the society was short-lived; she was dismissed because she apparently lacked the stamina for campaigning or a talent for public speaking. Although she retained an interest in the suffrage campaign, she had become convinced that unionization was as important to working women as suffrage and turned to the labor movement. In 1873 she married a cabinetmaker, Thomas Paterson, whom she had met at the WMCII. They traveled to the

United States together on an extended honeymoon, where they investigated women's friendly societies and trade union organization. Paterson was particularly impressed with the Parasol and Umbrella Makers' Union and the Women's Typographical Union in New York. After her return in April 1874, she advertised for support for a friendly society for women workers, publishing an appeal, "The Position of Working Women and How to Improve It," in the *Labour News*. In this article, she outlined her ideas for a Women's Protective and Provident League (WPPL), which held its inaugural meeting in July, with support from Emilia Dilke.

With its objective to help women fight for better wages through peaceful negotiation rather than strike action, the WPPL first set about organizing women bookbinders, then dressmakers and workers in associated garment trades, such as collar making and shirt making, and later those in the millinery and artificial flower-making trades. It branched into regional industries: the hosiery trade in Leicester, cigar making and pickle and jam making, upholstering, and later typing. The WPPL relied on a bedrock of mainly middle-class supporters who raised funds to launch subsidiary trade societies, but such was the lack of sustained membership and sufficient funds, with many unskilled women only sporadically employed, that many of the thirty or so societies that were established were short-lived.

Paterson was opposed to the idea of protective legislation for women workers only and the shortening of their working day, arguing that these measures would limit the spheres in which they could be employed. She was also convinced that by treating women as a separate case—in the same category as child workers—protective legislation would inevitably bring with it lower wages. Instead, she relied on the somewhat unrealistic hope that responsible employers could be persuaded, through moral argument and their own sense of fair play, to negotiate remunerative rates of employment with their women workers.

In 1875 Paterson became the first woman delegate to the annual conference of the Trades Union Congress and attended regularly until her death. She encountered considerable opposition among the male membership toward the idea of women's work, many of them clinging to the chauvinistic conviction that men should be better paid in order that their wives could remain at home. Paterson also discovered that many trade unionists were skeptical that women could ever successfully organize themselves into unions and her advocacy of mixed-sex trade unions was greeted with little enthusiasm. Nevertheless, Paterson became a persistent, if not irritating, presence at conferences, where she constantly called for the greater involvement of women in trade unionism and came up against ongoing fierce resistance to the idea, born of male fears, that women would usurp men's jobs because they would undersell themselves.

In 1876, in order to establish and run the WPPL's *Women's Union Journal,* Paterson learned printing techniques at the Victoria Press, an all-women publishing house established by her friend, the feminist Emily Faithfull. She founded the Women's Printing Society to produce the journal, which featured articles on suffrage, education, exercise such as swimming, women's legal rights, and her own hobbyhorse—rational dress. The central office of the WPPL in London in time became an important meeting place for women workers and trade unionists and operated its own cooperative store. It also offered a traveling library, an employment agency, leisure facilities such as a swimming pool, a rest house by the sea, saving schemes, and day excursions.

As Sally Alexander argues (1994), the WPPL, for all its inadequacies and limited successes, "inaugurated the only sustained phase of women's independent trade unions in Britain between 1874 and 1920" (57). Yet, as she also points out, Paterson's organization of the WPPL and her editing of its *Women's Union Journal* were largely overlooked in histories of the labor movement, such as the 1894 *History of Trade Unionism* by Beatrice and Sidney Webb.

After 1878, with the Factory and Workshops Acts enforcing special provisions for women, including the large population of female outworkers, Paterson was forced to change her position on protective legislation and shifted her emphasis to the promotion of women factory inspectors to ensure that working women's interests were best served. With the support of the Trades Union Congress, years of concerted lobbying finally brought parliamentary approval in 1893. But in 1886, Paterson had died, prematurely, of diabetes. Her friend and colleague Emilia Dilke took over the leadership of the WPPL, which adopted the new name of the Women's Trade Union League in 1890. During her short and active life, Paterson also served as secretary of the Vigilance Association for the Defence of Personal Rights, and was involved in the cooperative movement and school board elections.

See also Dilke, Emilia; Webb, Beatrice.

References and Further Reading
Alexander, Sally. 1994. *Becoming a Woman and Other Essays in Nineteenth and Twentieth Century Feminist History.* London: Virago.
Baylen, J. O., and N. J. Gossman, eds. 1979–1984. *Biographical Dictionary of Modern British Radicals.* 3 vols. Hassocks, Sussex: Harvester Press.
Bellamy, Joyce M., and John Saville, eds. 1982. *Dictionary of Labour Biography.* London: Macmillan.
Boone, Gladys. 1942. *The Women's Trade Union Leagues in Great Britain and the United States of America.* New York: Columbia University Press.
Goldman, Harold. 1974. *Emma Paterson: She Led Woman into a Man's World.* London: Lawrence and Wishart.
Levine, Philippa. 1990. *Feminist Lives in Victorian England: Private Roles and Public Commitment.* Oxford: Blackwell.
Lewenhak, Sheila. 1977. *Women and Trade Unions: An Outline History of Women in the British Trade Union Movement.* London: Ernest Benn.
Rowbotham, Sheila. 1992. *Women in Movement: Feminism and Social Action.* New York: Routledge.
Soldon, Norbert C. 1978. *Women in British Trade Unions 1874–1976.* Dublin: Gill and Macmillan.

Patkar, Medha
(1954–)
India

The courage of Medha Patkar in facing down government and the World Bank in her attempts to protect her environment from being flooded by the Sardar Sarovar Dam development in the Indian state of Gujarat is a testament to the will of the individual against the power of the developers. After studying social sciences at the university, Patkar went to live among tribal groups in the Narmada Valley, where from the 1980s she began alerting the local peoples to the threat of a large-scale industrial development project planned for the region that would disrupt their traditional way of life. Patkar and her colleague Baba Amte led mounting opposition to what became the Narmada Valley Project—a government plan to develop about thirty large dams and numerous small ones along the banks of the Narmada River, which included the construction of two major dams at Sardar Sarovar and Narmada Sagar, and which was supported by a $450 million loan from the World Bank. The effect of such a project would be to flood 37,000 hectares of forest and agricultural land and with it displace 320,000 poor peasants, quite apart from the damage that would be done to the natural environment and indigenous species of animals and birds. Warning against the vastness of such a human and ecological tragedy, Patkar and Amte founded the Narmada Bachao Andolan (NBA), which has been fighting this and other encroachments on the natural environment since the 1980s. The NBA argues that small-scale rural projects that do not disrupt the local ecology or way of life and that are backed by government strategies to supply energy and water will improve local farming in an environmentally friendly way. The protest movement against the Narmada development gathered support over the years, culminating in a major confrontation between demonstrators and developers in 1991, during which Patkar went on a twenty-one-day fast. Further hunger strikes by Patkar in protest at the development followed in 1993 and 1994, by which time the World Bank had withdrawn its support, condemning the project as ill-conceived. In 1993 the Indian government was forced to agree to review the project and two years later put a temporary stay on further construction. But this was renewed in 2000 after six years of fighting in the courts had failed to quash the project altogether and a supreme court ruling allowed the work to be resumed. The NBA immediately appealed this decision.

Since she began campaigning for the NBA, Patkar has become the leader of the National Alliance of People's Movements and a member of the World Commission on Dams. As a member of the latter, she was involved in a wider survey of dam projects both in India and on other continents, leading to a study of the impact on the local economy and environment of 150 dams. In 1998, appalled at the insistence of the Indian government on going ahead with nuclear testing, Patkar called for an official investigation into the environmental effects of tests carried out at Pokharan in May of that year.

In their campaigning, Patkar and her supporters have adopted the traditional civil disobedience tactics pioneered by Mahatma Gandhi's *satyagraha* movement of the 1930s and 1940s, with groups of protesters gathering in the towns of Sikka, Bharad, Pipalchip, and Jalsindi. In 1999 Patkar was once again arrested along with 275 members of the NBA for protesting the potential loss of many Indian villages to the floodplain created by the Sardar Sarovar Dam project. Villagers too have joined her in threatening to drown themselves in the floodwaters if the project goes ahead. The campaign has attracted worldwide attention and support from Booker Prize–winning Indian novelist Arundhati Roy. Despite the hunger strikes, arrests, and beatings that she has endured, Patkar remains scathing in her criticism of India's big dam projects, arguing that they will do nothing to resolve India's growing water shortages. Much of the water from the Sardar Sarovar project, she argues, will reach not those impoverished rural districts prone to drought that most need it, but the cities and big industry.

Patkar has been awarded the Goldman Environmental Prize and the Right Livelihood Award for her work. A website set up by the Friends of River Narmada—an international coalition of supporters of the protest—contains a discussion of the project and also highlights other environmental issues in India. Contact www.narmada.org.

References and Further Reading

Aubrey, Wallace, and David Gancher. 1993. *Eco-Heroes: Twelve Tales of Environmental Victory.* San Francisco: Mercury House.

Fisher, William F., ed. 1997. *Toward Sustainable Development? Struggling over India's Narmada River.* Jaipur: Rawat Publications.

Hacker, Carlotta. 1999. *Humanitarians.* New York: Crabtree.

Paul, Alice
(1885–1977)
United States

One of the most forceful U.S. suffragists and feminist leaders to emerge in the years prior to World War I, Alice Paul was a qualified lawyer, an able publicist, and an organizer of large-scale suffrage rallies who endured prison sentences for her militancy both in the United States and the United Kingdom. In 1923 Paul helped draft the Equal Rights Amendment to the U.S. Constitution. After being introduced every year in Congress for nearly fifty years, it was finally passed in 1972 but failed to achieve ratification by a sufficient number of U.S. states.

A member of the Hicksite Quaker community, Paul was born into an eminent Quaker family in Moorestown, New Jersey. After being educated in Quaker schools, she attended Swarthmore College until 1905, where she majored in biology, after which she studied at the New York School of Philanthropy for a year. Her postgraduate studies at the University of Pennsylvania brought her a master's degree in economics and sociology in 1907.

In 1907 Paul took up work on a College Settlement Association Scholarship at a settlement house in New York, where she helped establish women's trade unions and became a visitor for the New York Charity Organization Society. After obtaining a diploma at the New York School of Social Work, she decided to study methods in Germany. From there, she traveled to England on a fellowship to the Woodbrooke Settlement for Religious and Social Studies in Birmingham, where she also attended courses in economics at the university. She later transferred to the London School of Economics and worked for a settlement house in the district of Canning Town, taking employment in a car works to witness firsthand the problems encountered by workers.

Paul's experience in settlement work had already impressed upon her the urgent need for political change in addition to social reform. Captivated by the combative spirit of Christabel and Emmeline Pankhurst in promoting women's rights, as Harriot Stanton Blatch had been before her, in 1908 Paul wholeheartedly joined their militant suffrage organization, the Women's Social and Political Union (WSPU). A year later, while studying at the London School of Economics, she was asked to join a deputation to lobby the British prime minister, Herbert Asquith, at the House of Commons in June, an event that ended in scuffles and the arrest of Paul and others. By the time she returned home in 1910, Paul had been imprisoned in England twice (at Holloway Prison) and Scotland once (in Dundee) for taking part in demonstrations. Despite her Quaker pacifist convictions, Paul

Alice Paul (Library of Congress)

had joined in throwing bricks and smashing windows, exploits that were publicized in the U.S. as well as the British press. Soon after returning home early in 1910, Paul addressed a Quaker meeting in Moorestown, where she proudly admitted that, like Emmeline Pankhurst, she saw window smashing as a legitimate tactic in the cause of women's suffrage and that "she attached no particular sanctity to a twenty-five-cent window-pane" since she herself "had broken forty-eight" (Bacon 1986, 193). But Paul's militancy inevitably proved problematic for her religious community, and she rapidly became distanced from it. It would also prove impossible for a feisty individualist such as Paul to settle in the mainstream of the U.S. suffrage movement to which, in the summer of 1911, she offered her support.

After enrolling at the University of Pennsylvania to complete her doctorate on the legal position of women in Pennsylvania (awarded in 1912; she earned a doctorate in civil law in 1928), Paul joined the Pennsylvania Suffrage Associa-

tion. Together with a friend and associate in the English suffrage movement, Lucy Burns, she began staging outdoor suffrage meetings. She offered to take on the mission of reviving the Congressional Committee of the National American Woman Suffrage Association (NAWSA) in 1912, at a time when the suffrage movement in the United States was at a particularly low ebb. Having moved to Washington, D.C., Paul joined with more radical suffragists on the Congressional Committee, such as Crystal Eastman and Mary Ritter Beard, in restoring a higher public profile to women's suffrage campaigning, throwing herself into the organization of petitions all over the United States and with tremendous vigor taking on essential fund-raising.

On 3 March 1913 Paul, echoing the activities of Blatch in New York, organized a spectacular march of 5,000 women suffragists down Pennsylvania Avenue in Washington to demand the federal vote for women. Paul's adoption of increasingly radical tactics, however, soon invited controversy and obliged the more moderate leader of the NAWSA, Anna Howard Shaw, to distance the conservative mainstream from her activities despite the effectiveness of some of her campaigning. With many women in NAWSA content to fight for the vote on a state-by-state basis, Paul had become frustrated by the pace of NAWSA's campaign. She also disagreed increasingly with Shaw over the control and funding of the Congressional Committee. Shaw insisted that the committee remain subordinate to NAWSA's national committee, and Paul, equally insistently, demanded autonomy and set up her own separate weekly publication, *The Suffragist*. Soon after, Paul established the Congressional Union within NAWSA, to fund-raise specifically for the work of the Congressional Committee. But, unable to reconcile her differences with Shaw, Paul left NAWSA early in 1914, taking with her the Congressional Union, which took the full name of the Congressional Union for Woman Suffrage. In March 1917 the union officially amalgamated with a group of women from states that had already awarded women the vote to form the National Woman's Party (NWP), with Paul as chair.

As leader of the Congressional Union, from 1914 Paul led an increasingly forceful campaign for the introduction of a federal amendment on women's suffrage, employing an ambitious program of press and even cinema campaigning.

She also staged publicity motorcades—including a 1915 "auto pilgrimage" across the United States in which participants gathered signatures for a petition—as well as a series of conventions, marches, and pageants. After 1916, she even resorted to civil disobedience tactics—hunger strikes, and pickets reminiscent of the WSPU in the United Kingdom—in an attempt to prevent the reelection of the Democratic president, Woodrow Wilson, who Paul felt was unsympathetic toward women's suffrage. The Congressional Union lost the battle for suffrage in ten out of eleven state elections that it subsequently fought, but when the United States entered the war in Europe in April 1917, Paul felt that the suffrage cause had gained new leverage. She openly criticized the government for fighting to preserve democracy in Europe, when it was not practicing what it preached at home—that is, giving women the vote. Becoming highly critical of Wilson's government, members of the National Woman's Party began picketing the White House early in 1917. Paul and other women regularly chained themselves to the iron fence, paraded with banners referring to "Kaiser Wilson," and on one occasion burned an effigy of Wilson, in what Richard Evans has described as "a personal vendetta against the President" (Evans 1977, 195).

Paul was arrested and sentenced with sixty-six other suffragists, most of whom were held at the Occuquan Workhouse for sixty days. Paul was kept in solitary confinement, and when her demands to be treated as a political prisoner were refused, went on a three-week hunger strike, during which she was force-fed through her nose and then removed to a psychiatric hospital. Paul and her colleagues had to contend with much public hostility at this time; they were accused of being traitors to the country, and their militancy was seen as being counterproductive during a time of national emergency. When Paul was released in January 1918, Wilson had changed his position on women's suffrage at the federal level, in view of the pressing need for women's support of the war effort. But Paul did not let up on militant campaigning until the Nineteenth Amendment was introduced in Congress in 1919 and finally ratified in August 1920.

It was not, by any means, the end of Paul's campaigning. She took up further studies and won a string of law degrees (from Washington College in 1922 and the American University in 1927 and 1928) in order to be better equipped in the fight to end discrimination against women in the workplace. During 1919–1920, she found the NWP caught up in the "red scare" when her continuing militancy led to accusations of links to Russian communists, but as the 1920s went on, the ranks of the NWP were joined by increasing numbers of professional women working with Paul toward the passage of the Equal Rights Amendment (named by Paul the "Lucretia Mott Amendment"). For Paul, it was an extremely long campaign, with many women's groups and especially trade unionists continuing to prefer separate, protective legislation for women, which Paul saw as excluding women from many professions.

During the 1920s, Paul spent much time in Europe, extending her work on women's equal rights to the international arena. From 1927 to 1937, she was chair of the Woman's Research Foundation and in 1928 founded the World Party for Equal Rights for Women (which became the World Women's Party in 1938), based in Geneva, Switzerland. She also lobbied the League of Nations for women's equal rights worldwide and for an Equal Nationality Treaty (which was adopted in 1933). At home, she supported the Equal Nationality Act, passed in the United States in 1934. During 1930–1933, she headed the nationality committee of the Inter-American Commission of Women Working Toward Women's Rights in Latin America, and in 1936 she joined the Laws Committee of the International Council of Women. Paul also campaigned for specific references to sexual equality to be added to the preamble of the United Nations Charter in 1945 and Title VII of the 1964 U.S. Civil Rights Act.

When the United States entered World War II in 1941, Paul returned home, all the more convinced that wars could be averted if women had more political muscle. She continued to push for an Equal Rights Amendment, which was passed by the Senate in 1950 but then went into limbo until the second wave of the women's movement revived it. It was finally passed by both houses of Congress in March 1972. However, when Paul died five years later, only thirty-five states had voted for the amendment, and by its deadline in 1982 it had still not been approved by the three more states needed for ratification.

As one of the most charismatic speakers and committed U.S. activists of the twentieth century, Paul's long years of fanatical campaigning were characterized by her high sense of drama. After she died, the women's movement found itself dealing with an onslaught from the right wing, with new attempts to defuse the cause of women's equal rights, such as that led by Phyllis Schlafly (who had been an equally outspoken opponent of the ERA), threatening the principles for which Paul had fought so hard.

See also Beard, Mary Ritter; Blatch, Harriot Stanton; Catt, Carrie Chapman; Eastman, Crystal; Mott, Lucretia Coffin; Pankhurst, Christabel; Pankhurst, Emmeline; Schlafly, Phyllis.

References and Further Reading
Bacon, Margaret Hope. 1986. *Mothers of Feminism: The Story of Quaker Women in America*. San Francisco: Harper and Row.
Blatch, Harriot Stanton, and Alma Lutz. 1940. *Challenging Years: The Memoirs of Harriot Stanton Blatch*. New York: G. P. Putnam and Sons.
Crawford, Elizabeth. 1999. *The Women's Suffrage Movement, 1866–1928: A Reference Guide*. London: University College of London Press.
Evans, Richard. 1977. *The Feminists: Women's Emancipation Movements in Europe, America and Australasia 1840–1920*. London: Croom Helm.
Frost, Elizabeth, and Kathryn Cullen DuPont. 1992. *Women's Suffrage in America: An Eyewitness History*. New York: Facts on File.
Fry, A. R. 1976. *Conversations with Alice Paul: Woman Suffrage and the Equal Rights Amendment*. Berkeley: University of California Press.
Irwin, Inez Haynes. 1964. *Up Hill with Banners Flying*. Penobscot, ME: Traversity Press. (Originally published as *The Story of the Woman's Party*. 1921. New York: Harcourt, Brace.)
Kraditor, Aileen. 1981 [1965]. *The Ideas of the Woman Suffrage Movement 1890–1920*. Reprint, New York: W. W. Norton.
Lunardini, Christine A. 1986. *From Equal Suffrage to Equal Rights: Alice Paul and the National Woman's Party, 1910–1928*. New York: New York University Press.
Stevens, Doris. 1976 [1920]. *Jailed for Freedom*. Reprint, New York: Schocken Books.
Weatherford, Doris. 1998. *A History of the American Suffragist Movement*. Santa Barbara, CA: ABC-CLIO.
Willis, Jean L. 1983. "Alice Paul: The Quintessential Feminist." In Dale Spender, ed., *Feminist Theorists: Three Centuries of Women's Intellectual Traditions*. London: Women's Press.

Peabody, Elizabeth
(1804–1894)
United States

The Transcendentalist educator Elizabeth Peabody, a warm and eccentric woman, contributed in no small way to the intellectual life of Boston during the 1840s and 1850s and was later a pioneer of kindergarten education in the United States. Born in Billerica, Massachusetts, Peabody was educated with her sisters Sophia and Mary at the private school run by her mother in Salem, where she later worked as a teacher herself. When she was only sixteen, Peabody attempted to set up her own school at Lancaster in 1820, but when this venture failed, she worked as a governess in Maine for two years. In Boston, she came into contact with other intellectuals and, after setting up another school at Brookline in 1825, was invited to take the post of secretary and copyist to Unitarian theologian William Ellery Channing, who had enrolled his daughter at the school. As a religious leader involved in the New England Transcendentalist movement, Channing introduced Peabody to his liberal theological beliefs and wide knowledge of literature and philosophy during their close association until 1834. In 1837, largely through Channing's recommendation, Peabody became, along with Margaret Fuller, one of the few female members of the elite Transcendentalist Club.

In 1827, as a reflection of her frustration that higher education was still not open to women, Peabody began giving a series of readings and discussions in private homes that became known as her "Historical School," drawing on her own interests in theology, philosophy, and history. (She urged that the latter subject be included in the school curriculum, in 1856 providing her own text *A Chronological History of the United States*.) By 1832, Peabody's school had closed, and in need of a means of financial support, she gave up private tutoring and published a textbook, *First Steps to the Study of History* (1832). Giving up her post with Channing, she became an assistant to the educator Bronson Alcott (father of the novelist Louisa May Alcott) who had set up his new, progressive Temple School in Boston in September 1834, in particular becoming a devotee of Alcott's penchant for Socratic debate. Elizabeth admired Alcott's intellect and his pioneering methods and in 1835 published

Elizabeth Peabody (Dover Pictorial Archives)

an account of her experiences, *Records of a School,* taken from her journal. Alcott became an increasingly controversial figure, however, and Peabody's involvement with the Temple School brought her renewed difficulties in finding other employment.

For all her love of intellectual discussion, Peabody feared being labeled as a bluestocking, yet she continued to yearn for a "serious pursuit" within the limitations of what was then socially acceptable for women. And so, in 1839, she moved with her family to a house at 13 West Street in a residential area of Boston, where she opened a modest bookshop. In itself, the move underlined Peabody's belief that women could go into business as the equals of men, and from the outset, she intended the bookshop to function as a venue for the interchange of ideas by providing access to foreign books and giving the shop the appearance of a comfortable family library. Soon Peabody's shop on West Street had become an unofficial club for literary gatherings, Transcendentalist meetings, and, most notably, Margaret Fuller's famous Wednesday afternoon series of "conversations." Members of Brook Farm, an experimental utopian community of Transcendentalists, also met here. Peabody also

became one of the first woman publishers in the United States, when she began publishing translations from German by Fuller as well as the early works of her brother-in-law, the writer Nathaniel Hawthorne (who married Sophia Peabody in 1842).

For a year, Peabody coedited the Transcendentalist literary monthly the *Dial* with Fuller (1842–1843) and wrote articles for it and the journal *Aesthetic Papers,* her most notable being "A Glimpse of Christ's Idea of Society," an article that emphasized the importance of the education of young children and also promoted the work of the Brook Farm community in creating "the kingdom of God on earth." With the demise of the Transcendentalist movement by 1845, however, Peabody's bookshop went into decline, and after closing it in 1850 she returned to teaching, at the Eagleswood School in New Jersey. During the late 1850s, she was drawn into the abolitionist campaign while continuing to write and lecture on education.

In 1859 Peabody's life changed when she learned of the new kindergarten movement being introduced in Germany by Friedrich Froebel. She resolved to establish her own school based on its methods, which encouraged children to think and explore things for themselves rather than be taught everything by rote. With its emphasis too on nurture and the encouragement of the child's moral and intellectual capabilities, it appealed to Peabody as the perfect medium for her own strongly held beliefs about the spiritual aspects of education. She saw it as the conduit for inculcating Christian values and making a better society and believed that the presence of kindergartens would raise the moral tone of the environments around them, particularly in deprived and slum areas. In 1861 Peabody founded the first English-speaking kindergarten in the United States in Boston to provide a showcase for Froebel's pioneering methods, which she explained in her 1863 book, *Moral Culture of Infancy, and Kindergarten Guide.*

At home in the years of the Civil War (1861–1865), Peabody realized that at fifty-seven she was too old to join Dorothea Dix's nurses in the Sanitary Commission and traveled to Washington to take up philanthropic work among lost and abandoned black children, who were living rough and begging on the streets of the capital. She set up an orphanage and engaged teachers for these children, organized fund-raising fairs, and with the help of her nieces Ellen and Mary, raised enough money to build a school.

During 1867–1868, Peabody spent time in Germany studying kindergarten methods in greater detail and returned to the United States with several experienced German kindergarten teachers in order to spread the word and train others. Also in 1868, Peabody took up lecturing on education and inspired the creation of more private kindergartens, in St. Louis and San Francisco, and in 1870 the first public one, in Boston, which was supported by donations, until in 1877 a single benefactor took over its funding. She also fostered training schools for kindergarten teachers, such as that at New York City's Normal College, and edited a journal, the *Kindergarten Messenger* (1873–1876), in which she promoted Froebel's ideas. In 1877 Peabody was elected president of the American Froebel Union. She also succeeded in persuading the publishers Ernst Steiger and Milton Bradley to publish several of her education materials for children, such as *Kindergarten Culture* (1870), *The Kindergarten in Italy* (1872), and *Letters to Kindergarteners* (1886).

In the summer of 1882, Peabody was invited to lecture at Bronson Alcott's Concord Summer School of Philosophy, returning in subsequent years until the school closed in 1888. In her eighties, she became passionate about the women's suffrage movement and held meetings at her home. She also advocated improved access to education for Native Americans and made considerable donations from her own funds to Sarah Winnemucca's school for Paiute Indians. Shortly before her death, she took up yet another cause, the international peace movement. The Elizabeth Peabody House was opened in Boston in her memory in 1896, for use as a settlement house and kindergarten for the then-large immigrant community. In 1979 the house relocated to Somerville, Massachusetts. For information on the continuing work of the Elizabeth Peabody house, go to http://www.volunteersolutions.org/volunteer.

See also Dix, Dorothea Lynde; Fuller, (Sarah) Margaret.

References and Further Reading

Baylor, Ruth M. 1965. *Elizabeth Palmer Peabody: Kindergarten Pioneer.* Philadelphia: University of Philadelphia Press.

Brooks, Gladys. 1957. *Three Wise Virgins.* New York: Dutton.

Ronda, Bruce A. 1991. *Elizabeth Peabody: A Reformer on Her Own Terms.* Cambridge, MA: Harvard University Press.

Sayder, A. 1972. *Dauntless Women in Childhood Education, 1856–1931.* Washington, DC: Association for Childhood Education International.

Tharp, Louise Hall. 1950. *The Peabody Sisters of Salem.* Boston: Little, Brown.

Pechey-Phipson, Edith
(1846–1908)
United Kingdom/India

The medical pioneer Edith Pechey-Phipson was one of the first five women to study medicine at a university in Britain. Born near Colchester, Essex, she was one of seven children of a Baptist minister. Before joining Sophia Jex-Blake and three others in applying for admission to medical training at Edinburgh Medical School in 1869, she had worked as a governess.

Pechey-Phipson distinguished herself in the medical school examinations, winning the chemistry prize and the Hope Scholarship, neither of which, as a woman, she was actually allowed to accept. This injustice propelled the quiet, unassuming Pechey-Phipson into the center of considerable local debate over the issue, which set the tone for the levels of antipathy from male students to the unwanted academic rivalry of the group of five women. Pechey-Phipson and her colleagues persisted in their studies, forever coming up against unfair treatment by the university authorities and its male lecturers. When the university eventually reneged on its policy and refused to grant the five women their degrees, she was forced to find another way of qualifying. After spending a year gaining some clinical experience as resident house surgeon and secretary at the Birmingham and Midlands Hospital for Women and Children, she went with Jex-Blake to Switzerland to complete her required quota of hospital hours and take examinations for her degree, being awarded a medical degree at Bern in 1877.

After being given a license to practice soon after by the Royal College of Physicians in Dublin, Ireland—the first university in the United Kingdom to recognize women doctors—Pechey-Phipson set herself up in private practice in Leeds. A year later, in 1879, she was a founding member of the Medical Women's Federation in England, becoming president in 1882. During the years 1877–1883, she gave numerous public lectures on physiology at the Ladies' Education Association in Leeds and other northern cities.

In 1883, after studying surgical procedures in Vienna, Pechey-Phipson went to India under the auspices of the Medical Women for India Fund (MWIF), which she had been instrumental in setting up. There she encountered new hostilities and prejudices in her efforts to further both medicine as a career for Indian women and the gynecological and natal care of Hindu and Muslim women, which was circumscribed by strict religious beliefs and practices. Together with other European and American women doctors, Pechey-Phipson pioneered the provision of modern medical treatment in India. She encouraged a new generation of Indian women, including Rukhmabai, to take up medical studies and trained many of them at her own hospital. Through the MWIF, Pechey-Phipson also lobbied for the admission of Indian women to medical studies at Bombay University.

Soon after arriving in India, Pechey-Phipson was appointed medical superintendent of the new Cama Hospital for Women and Children in Bombay, which had been funded by an Indian businessman. She learned Hindustani and in July 1884, with funding from another patron, set up the Jaffer Sulleman Dispensary for Women and Children while awaiting completion of building work at the Cama Hospital. The dispensary was quickly besieged with patients, with Pechey-Phipson sometimes seeing as many as 100 a day in addition to running her own private practice. The Cama Hospital finally opened in 1886, and almost immediately Pechey-Phipson began campaigning, in the face of considerable public disapproval, to establish a training school for nurses there. Much of her time at the hospital would be taken up with endless bureaucracy, delays, and disputes over funding, staffing, and salaries; meanwhile, the dispensary, which was still averaging sixty patients a day in 1886, was suffering from a desperate shortage of women doctors. By 1888, such was the demand for women's medical care by women doctors and nurses at the Cama Hospital that Pechey-Phipson was applying for funds to expand the hospital.

In 1889, Edith married Herbert Phipson, secretary of the MWIF, and together they were ex-tremely active in Indian social and cultural life, taking every opportunity to lobby for financial support for the Cama Hospital. Sharing an interest in Asian history and culture, they were members of the Royal Asiatic Society, which Pechey-Phipson served as vice president (1892–1893). Sensitive to Indian traditions, she spoke out tactfully against the practice of child marriage, in an 1890 lecture arguing against it on medical grounds. She had seen the results of pregnancy and childbirth in sexually and physically immature girls, many of whom died; those who lived were often left sterile and produced sickly babies. The speech, "To the Hindus of Bombay on the Subject of Child Marriage," was reproduced as a pamphlet and circulated in thousands of copies, provoking widespread debate in India. By the end of the 1880s, Pechey-Phipson had become a notable public speaker in Bombay and a leading advocate of the extension of women's education in India, supporting the opening of schools for child widows.

In 1891 Edith established the Pechey-Phipson Sanatorium for Women and Children in the hills of the Deccan, north of Bombay. Funded by private subscription, it offered family accommodation for convalescents and their dependents in a group of ten cottages, which was expanded during 1922–1938. Pechey-Phipson retired from the Cama Hospital in 1894 but remained in private practice in Bombay. By this time, the first trained Indian women doctors were entering practice and taking over posts held by white Europeans at Indian hospitals. Pechey-Phipson came out of retirement in 1896 to help combat an outbreak of bubonic plague and cholera in Bombay, during which she was critical of the failure of the authorities to provide adequate medical facilities quickly enough and instituted house-to-house medical inspection teams.

In 1905 Pechey-Phipson returned home via Australia and Canada. In her final years, she was an active supporter of women's suffrage, giving speeches to the Leeds Women's Suffrage Society and attending the third congress of the Women's Suffrage Alliance in Copenhagen in 1906 on its behalf. She died of breast cancer at Folkestone in 1908.

See also Jex-Blake, Sophia; Rukhmabai.
References and Further Reading
Balfour, Margaret I., and Ruth Young. 1929. *The Work*

of Medical Women in India. London: Oxford University Press.

Bell, Enid Moberley. 1953. *Storming the Citadel: The Rise of the Woman Doctor.* London: Constable.

Jayawardena, Kumari. 1995. *The White Woman's Other Burden: Western Women and South Asia during British Rule.* London: Routledge.

Lovejoy, Esther Pohl. 1957. *Women Doctors of the World.* New York: Macmillan.

Lutzker, Edythe. 1973. *Edith Pechey-Phipson M.D.: The Story of England's Foremost Pioneering Woman Doctor.* New York: Exposition Press.

Todd, Margaret. 1918. *The Life of Sophia Jex Blake.* London: Macmillan.

Peckover, Priscilla
(1833–1931)
United Kingdom

The name of Quaker pacifist Priscilla Peckover, who established a considerable network of women peace campaigners in Britain in the 1880s, is known only within accounts of the women's peace movement. Yet she was one of the first women in England to become involved in such activism, beginning as early as 1879, and spent her long life in furthering the cause of peace mediation and disarmament through her many European connections.

Peckover was born in Wisbech, Cambridgeshire, into an eminent Quaker banking family known for its philanthropy and pacifism (her brother Alexander was a leader of the Peace Society). After being educated at home by governesses, Peckover spent the greater portion of her early life looking after Alexander's children when he was widowed, and became a respected member of her local Quaker community, which accepted her as a preacher in November 1877. Through the Society of Friends' support for pacifism, she joined the Women's Peace and Arbitration Auxiliary of the Peace Society. Discovering how few women were active in the movement, by 1879 Peckover had become consumed by a personal mission, prompted by her religious devoutness, to further the cause of peace in her local Christian community. She published a declaration calling on women to uphold peace (at a time when Britain was fighting colonial wars against the Afghans and Zulus) and rapidly enlisted the support of 150 local women to found a Women's Local Peace Association (WLPA). Under Peckover's devoted leadership, it rapidly grew, and Wisbech became an unlikely but major regional center for pacifist campaigning in England at that time. The WLPA eventually established thirty branches with 15,000 members in the United Kingdom, and membership further increased when it joined forces with other pacifist groups in Europe, such as the Baptists in France and Germany.

The WLPA amalgamated with the men's peace committee in Wisbech in 1881 to found the Wisbech Local Peace Association, which aimed to forward international conciliation and peace arbitration and lobby against militarization. Peckover worked tirelessly, establishing links with pacifist groups in Scandinavia, Switzerland, Spain, Russia, and Italy, whom she was able to reach thanks to her skills as a linguist. She further consolidated international links between pacifists from 1882 through her quarterly journal, *Peace and Goodwill, A Sequel to the Olive Leaf,* which she edited for almost fifty years and which championed the work of other women pacifists. From her home in Wisbech, Peckover also played a major role in disseminating pacifist literature in the United Kingdom and abroad, translating many of the tracts and pamphlets herself for foreign consumption. She greatly applauded the appointment of fellow pacifist Bertha von Suttner, as secretary of the International Council of the Women's Standing Committee on Peace and International Arbitration in 1899.

Peckover never ceased her efforts to reach out to non-Christian groups, constantly arguing the importance of cooperation between all races and creeds in the cause of peace—a typical example being her "Earnest Appeal to All Women Everywhere" during General Charles Gordon's campaign against insurrection in the Sudan in the mid-1880s. Peckover was equally vociferous in her opposition to the Boer War (1899–1902); she later opposed calls for the introduction of compulsory national service, expressing her apprehension at the growth of militaristic organizations for the young, such as the Boys' Brigade. During World War I, she was one of many women pacifists in England who in 1915 signed an "Open Christmas Letter" to women in Germany and Austria, calling on them to join forces to try to end the war. But sadly, the mounting climate of jingoism in Britain during the war years decimated the membership of the WLPA. In

1914 it had boasted 8,000 members, but by war's end it had lost half of them. Although Peckover never let up on her work for pacifism until the day she died, just short of her ninety-eighth birthday, her journal died with her. A woman of tremendous modesty and quiet dignity who outside of her peace campaigning led a most retiring life, she was nominated for a Nobel Peace Prize after World War I. The work of Peckover and the WLPA survives in an archive housed at the Swarthmore College Peace Collection. See http://www.swarthmore.edu/Library/peace.

See also Suttner, Bertha Félice Sophie von.

References and Further Reading

Josephson, Harold, Sandi Cooper, and Steven C. Hause et al., eds. 1985. *Biographical Dictionary of Modern Peace Leaders.* Westport, CT: Greenwood Press.

Liddington, Jill. 1989. *The Long Road to Greenham: Feminism and Anti-Militarism in Britain since 1820.* London: Virago.

Oldfield, Sybil. 2001. *Women Humanitarians: A Biographical Dictionary of British Women Active between 1900 and 1950.* London: Continuum.

Pierson, Ruth Roach, ed. 1987. *Woman and Peace: Theoretical, Historical and Practical Perspectives.* London: Croom Helm.

Wiltsher, Anne. 1985. *Most Dangerous Women: Feminist Peace Campaigners of the Great War.* London: Pandora, and Westport, CT: Greenwood Press.

Pelletier, Madeleine
(1874–1939)
France

Madeleine Pelletier was probably the most individualistic personality in the militant French suffrage organization, Women's Solidarity, in the years leading up to World War I. A leading writer on gender and sexual politics who published forty books and pamphlets, she was in addition a pioneer woman psychiatrist, doctor, and supporter of abortion. As a radical and a pacifist with anarchist sympathies, she spent much of her life isolated by her extremism. Her public image of overt androgyny—she favored dressing in men's clothing and cutting her hair short in support of women's right "not to be a woman in the way society expects"—further alienated her from the conservative majority in the women's movement and led to her own vilification and persecution.

Pelletier endured a repressed, deeply conservative upbringing in a lower-middle-class family in Les Halles, Paris's fruit and vegetable market (also a notorious red-light district), where her parents worked. She had a brief period of convent education (1881–1886), but after suffering the neuroses of her religious fanatic mother and sexual abuse by her father, she left home at the age of twelve. She embarked on her own self-education, overcoming male hostility and family objections to become one of the first French women to be admitted to Paris's medical school in 1898. By the time she qualified as a doctor in 1902, Pelletier was in contact with feminists through the work of the newspaper *The Sling (La Fronde)*. She enlisted its support in her application to take the examination for an internship in psychiatry (1902–1903), and against the odds, subsequently obtained a post in a mental asylum as one of the first women in France to be hired by the French Welfare Board. In 1906 she became a medical officer in the postal and telegraph service and ran a small private practice at which she would perform illegal abortions.

From the end of the 1890s, Pelletier also worked increasingly for women's equality. She lobbied for Freemasonry to be opened to women, having herself been initiated into a mixed-sex lodge in 1904. In 1906 she assumed leadership of a small suffragist group, Women's Solidarity, which under her impetus from 1907 increasingly espoused the kind of direct action adopted in England by the Pankhursts' Women's Social and Political Union. In 1907 Pelletier founded and edited the monthly journal the *Suffragist,* which ran until 1914 and was revived in 1919, and on its pages laid out her own set of demands for the complete emancipation of women. She had three basic requirements: the repeal of all laws subjugating one sex to another, the admission of women to the professions and public posts, and the acceptance of women in political roles. Pelletier's articles in support of women's rights and reflecting her increasingly left-wing views were also published in *The Social War* and *Women's Voice*.

Pelletier occupied a unique position in the French women's movement of the time for her uncompromising views on female sexuality. Her overwhelming desire was to remove the element of sexual difference that underpinned so many social attitudes and perpetuated women's secondary role, which, she felt, was the result of centuries of brainwashing of women and the creation of superficial "feminine" traits. "The mentality of slaves revolts me. I do not like women as they are" (Scott 1996, 135), she claimed. Convinced that femininity was women's misfortune, Pelletier insisted that there should be no differentiation between the sexes based on mere physiology and made the radical suggestion that male and female categories should be done away with altogether, so that women could be looked upon first and foremost as *individuals*. Sexuality was a superficial difference that could be eliminated if women eschewed conventional "female" behavior and the kind of dress that emphasized their flirtatiousness and attractiveness to men—veils, feathers, flowers, corsets, and so on. With this in mind, Pelletier argued that women had every right to adopt masculine modes of dress as a means of eliminating their sexual difference and being treated as equals with men. She herself adopted short hair, a collar and tie, and men's jackets (although she wore trousers only occasionally), asserting: "I wear these exterior signs of liberty in order that they may say, that they may proclaim, that I desire freedom" (Scott 1996, 140). For Pelletier, the final affirmation of her own elimination of sexual difference was to walk through the red-light district of Les Halles at night and be solicited by prostitutes thinking her to be a man.

In her medical work, Pelletier was an equally forthright supporter of women's sexual emancipation and understood the plight of working women who struggled to maintain both jobs and homes in the face of numerous unwanted pregnancies. As a neo-Malthusian, she advocated social progress based on the elimination of disease and deprivation. Although the penalties for performing abortions were considerably increased in France in 1920, Pelletier boldly supported birth control in the first trimester of pregnancy. She defied the ban on the dissemination of birth control literature, giving lectures and producing informative leaflets for women on birth control and arguing that women should be released from the "biological bondage" of motherhood. Since motherhood was being encouraged at the time in light of dropping birthrates, she argued that the state must assume some responsibility for the economic well-being of mothers and the upbringing of healthy children if it wished to halt this decline.

Inevitably, Pelletier was denounced as an enemy of the family and for being unpatriotic for taking such an uncompromising stand. When she stood in 1910 as a candidate for Women's Solidarity in elections to the National Assembly, her militant socialism garnered little support. As the threat of war gathered in Europe, Pelletier condemned militarism as antifeminist and warmongering as a manifestation of how capitalism profited at the expense of the working classes by diverting workers' concerns about their rights into support for the war machine. As a result, she found herself marginalized as one of a small group of women pacifists during World War I. In a vain effort to win women's suffrage, she suggested that if women were conscripted to fight, then they could be given the vote. In 1915 she tried and failed to join the male medical corps and volunteered instead for the Red Cross, nursing wounded from both sides at the front.

For many years, Pelletier was involved in the socialist movement as a member of the French section of the Socialist International. In 1915 she had called for an international conference of socialist women in Bern, Switzerland. She welcomed the Russian Revolution of 1917 and supported the Third International, making her own pilgrimage to the socialist utopia in July 1921— a sobering experience when she discovered that Russian women had been enslaved rather than emancipated by the revolution. But dedicated as she was to gender issues, Pelletier became disillusioned when the French Communist Party would not endorse women's suffrage as part of its program, and left the party in 1925, turning to anarchism. In the last years of her life, dismayed by the failure of collective political action to effect change in France, Pelletier concentrated on her medical practice and her campaign for birth control. From 1933 she had been under surveillance by the authorities for performing illegal abortions, and in 1939 she was arrested. However, Pelletier had been partially paralyzed by a stroke two years earlier, and the judge deemed that she was unfit to be sent to prison, committing her instead to a mental hospital. Pelletier's health collapsed, and she died six months later.

Pelletier produced numerous works on women's issues, including *Woman's Struggle for Her Rights* (1908), *The Sexual Emancipation of Woman* (1911; its chapter on abortion was republished separately as a pamphlet in 1913); *The Feminist Education of Girls* (1914); and her 1919 work on the theory of individualism (*Individualism*). In her final years she turned to fiction and published an autobiographical novel, *The Virgin Woman* (1933), in which she expressed support for celibacy, having chosen to remain celibate out of her own distaste for the unjust way in which women were treated sexually by men.

See also Pankhurst, Christabel; Pankhurst, Emmeline; Pankhurst, (Estelle) Sylvia.

References and Further Reading
Boxer, Marilyn J., and Jean H. Quaterat. 1978. *Socialist Women: European Socialist Feminism in the Nineteenth and Early Twentieth Centuries.* New York: Elsevier North-Holland.
Gordon, Felicia. 1990. *The Integral Feminist: Madeleine Pelletier 1874–1939.* Cambridge: Polity.
Gordon, Felicia, and Máire Cross. 1996. *Early French Feminism, 1830–1940: A Passion for Liberty.* Cheltenham: Edward Elgar.
Hause, Steven C., with Anne R. Kenny. 1984. *Women's Suffrage and Social Politics in the French Third Republic.* Princeton, NJ: Princeton University Press.
Josephson, Harold, Sandi Cooper, and Steven C. Hause et al., eds. 1985. *Biographical Dictionary of Modern Peace Leaders.* Westport, CT: Greenwood Press.
Orr, Clarissa Campbell. 1996. *Wollstonecraft's Daughters: Womanhood in England and France 1780–1920.* Manchester: Manchester University Press.
Scott, Joan Wallach. 1996. *Only Paradoxes to Offer: French Feminists and the Rights of Man.* Cambridge, MA: Harvard University Press.
Sowerwine, Charles. 1982. *Sisters or Citizens? Women and Socialism in France since 1876.* Cambridge: Cambridge University Press.

Perkins, Frances Coralie
(1882–1965)
United States

Frances Perkins was the first woman in the United States to be appointed to a cabinet post, as secretary of labor, and one of the longest-serving members (twelve years) of Franklin Delano Roosevelt's New Deal government. She made full use of her position to fulfill her self-appointed mission of pioneering the issues of industrial health and safety in which she believed so fervently. During the economic hardships of the Great Depression, she did all in her power to create training schemes and work for the unemployed. She was also instrumental in the introduction of important legislation on Social Security, the minimum wage, and child labor.

Perkins was born into a wealthy Republican family in Boston and grew up in Worcester, Massachusetts. She was educated at Worcester Classical High School and then attended Mount Holyoke College in Massachusetts (1898–1902), majoring in physics and chemistry. As part of her coursework, she investigated local employment problems and poverty and came under the influence of social reformer Florence Kelley after hearing her lecture. Through Kelley she joined the National Consumers' League, a pressure group that lobbied manufacturers to improve working conditions.

After she graduated from Mount Holyoke in 1902, Perkins took a teaching post at the Ferry Hall School in Chicago and became a part-time volunteer settlement house worker at Jane Addams's Hull House. For the first time, she became aware of the exploitation of immigrant labor by unscrupulous employers and took on the task of confronting them when they had shortchanged workers. Having decided on a career in social work, she moved to Philadelphia to work as secretary to the Philadelphia Research and Protective Association, which brought her into close contact with immigrant girls and black migrant female workers from the South during 1907–1909.

In 1909 Perkins won a fellowship from the Russell Sage Foundation to study at the New York School of Philanthropy and earned her master's degree in social economics the following year at Columbia University. The next twenty years of Perkins's life were spent in public service in the city, first as executive secretary of the city's Consumers' League (1910–1912). Here, in collaboration with Kelley, she lobbied for better working conditions and pay for women and child workers, particularly those in New York's garment trade. The 1911 Triangle Shirtwaist Company Fire, in which 146 people tragically lost their lives because of an absence of fire exits in the overcrowded building in which they worked, was a watershed for Perkins. Having seen some of its victims jump to their deaths to escape the fire, she dedicated herself thereafter to fight for better working conditions in the city's sweatshops. She became an investigator for the State Factory Committee and helped secure a statutory fifty-four-hour week for working women (later reduced to forty-eight). For five years (1912–1917), she performed similar work for the New York City Committee on Safety, becoming an authority on health and safety in the workplace.

During World War I, Perkins served as director of the New York Council of Organization for War Service. In 1919 she accepted an important new post as the first woman on New York's State Industrial Commission, in which capacity she initiated numerous progressive policies and served on numerous labor committees during 1923–1933. She mediated during strikes as head of the commission's Bureau of Mediation and Arbitration and worked toward the passing of the Workmen's Compensation Act. She served the New York Industrial Board as chair from 1926 to 1929.

Perkins had by this time shifted position in her political loyalties from staunch Republican to Democrat, as an admirer of the policies of New York state governor Franklin D. Roosevelt. In 1929 he promoted her to Industrial Commissioner for New York state; Perkins was one of the preeminent women in industrial relations and labor reform in the city, and she took the opportunity to promote her ideas on unemployment insurance and financial assistance for the elderly. Roosevelt, recognizing Perkins's dedication and efficiency, invited her to become secretary of labor when he was elected president in 1932.

Perkins hesitated to assume such a challenging role in a government dominated by men and with economic depression still raging. She felt the job should have gone to a trade unionist but bravely committed herself to furthering her visionary reform policies during the New Deal era. For Perkins, the New Deal represented an opportunity for government to show its compassionate, humanitarian side by addressing the social issues that really mattered and contributing to the greater good. In the twelve years of her office, she was instrumental in strengthening the role of the Department of Labor and building up an efficient Bureau of Labor Statistics, which provided valuable statistical studies to back the important labor legislation that she introduced. She fought tooth and nail to further the unionization of exploited and low-paid workers, particularly immigrants.

It was not an easy ride for Perkins, however, with some male trade unionists hostile to taking the lead from a woman, men in big business suspicious of her reformist policies and her labor sympathies, and the right wing in Congress unwilling to take her seriously. There were accusations of communist sympathies and allegations that she was either a Jewish subversive or a Soviet agent. Nevertheless, Perkins pushed ahead with measures to help the unemployed (through the Federal Emergency Relief Administration); to provide jobs and training (under a new Civilian Conservation Corps); and to introduce better working conditions, insurance schemes, and unemployment benefits (as chair of the Committee on Economic Security). She expounded on her ideas in her 1934 book, *People at Work,* and played a key role in drafting and passing the Social Security Act (1935) and the National Labor Relations Act (1935) as well as closely supervising the Fair Labor Standards Act and the Wages and Hours Act of 1938, which set minimum wages and the maximum working week and prohibited child labor under the age of sixteen.

The strains of political office prompted Perkins to try to resign in 1940, but Roosevelt would have none of it. In the event, Perkins's contribution to women's employment in war industries during World War II was both practical and inspirational. During the Depression years, she had argued that working women should relinquish their jobs to unemployed men with families, but as secretary of labor, she now became responsible for the promotion of women's wartime work through that famous American icon—Rosie the Riveter. This propaganda figure, seen everywhere on official posters, contributed so greatly to the wartime liberation of women in the U.S. workplace that men returning home from the armed forces after the war ended found women reluctant to go quietly back to the kitchen. This in itself was a great irony, since Perkins, as a believer in family life, was equivocal in her support for women's work if it took them away from their families. She opposed an Equal Rights Amendment; based on her own observation of the poor conditions in which many women worked, she believed protective legislation was essential for women. Because Perkins felt that mothers' primary duty was to their children, she eventually became estranged from Eleanor Roosevelt, with whom she disagreed over the establishment of day care centers for the children of working mothers during World War II.

Perkins remained in office until the death of Franklin D. Roosevelt in 1945, publishing her reminiscences of him, *The Roosevelt I Knew,* in 1946 and continuing in public service thereafter as a civil service commissioner (1946–1952) under President Harry Truman's government. In 1957 she accepted a professorship at Cornell School of Industrial Relations, where she lectured on labor and industry.

During her years in the spotlight, Perkins kept her private life private. She had married in 1913, choosing to retain her maiden name, but her husband, Paul Wilson, had been plagued by mental illness and became manic-depressive. Perkins remained fiercely loyal to him, however, and credited his intellectual stimulus in her own career. A devout Episcopalian, Perkins was an admirably modest woman who had to fight her own shyness in fulfilling her public duties. She was later recognized as "the best man in the Cabinet" by General Hugh Johnson (Evans 1998, 258). A profile of Perkins can be found on the Social Security Administration website at http:// www.ssa.gov/history.fpbiossa.html. Links to other websites on Perkins can also be found at http://www.educate. si.edu/spotlight/labour.html.

See also Addams, Jane; Kelley, Florence; Roosevelt, (Anna) Eleanor.

References and Further Reading

Biddle, Marcia McKenna. 1979. *Contributions of Women: Labor.* Minneapolis: Dillon Press.
Evans, Harold. 1998. *The American Century.* London: Jonathan Cape.
Kramer, Barbara. 2000. *Trailblazing Women: First in Their Fields.* Berkeley Heights, NJ: Enslow Publishers.
Leighninger, L. 2001. "Frances Perkins: Champion of the New Deal." *Affilia* 16(3), 398–399.
Martin, George W. 1976. *Madam Secretary: Frances Perkins.* Boston: Houghton Mifflin.
Roosevelt, Eleanor, and Lorena A. Hickok. 1954. *Ladies of Courage.* New York: Putnam.
Severn, Bill. 1976. *Frances Perkins: A Member of the Cabinet.* New York: Hawthorn Books.
Shea, Marian Axford. 1999. *Women Movers and Shakers.* Lincoln, NE: Media Productions and Marketing.
Wandersee, Winifred D. 1993. "'I'd Rather Pass a Law Than Organize a Union': Frances Perkins and the Reformist Approach to Organized Labor." *Labor History* 34(1): 5.

Perón, Eva
(1919–1952)
Argentina

Eva Perón—heroine of the *descamisados* (Argentina's underprivileged working classes) and for many Argentines an enduring secular saint— might seem an unlikely social reformer. Yet she was the first woman to make the campaign for social justice and popular democracy a glamorous, high-profile one for a woman. This accomplishment was but one facet of the Cinderella syndrome surrounding her effortless rise to public adulation and to a unique position of influence in the until-then male-dominated world of Latin American politics.

Perón's own roots had been poor and working-class, and she rose from obscurity and a decidedly dubious early career to marry the future president of Argentina. Once in the public eye, Eva Perón lent her status as political superstar to her own program of good works and encouraged other women to join her, convinced that social action was second nature to their sex. Naturally enough, her critics have questioned the real extent of her commitment to reform, arguing that the driving force behind her welfare activities was primarily her desire to keep her husband in power and curry public favor. But whatever her motives, Eva Perón's influence, as an unofficial minister of health and labor, brought with it undeniable social benefits. Indeed, some might argue that if Juan Perón had not met and married María Eva Duarte in 1945 (as she then was called), women's suffrage would not have been achieved in 1947 in Argentina.

Details of Eva Perón's early life are scant. In the 1930s and early 1940s, she began her professional life working the dance halls of Buenos Aires. She graduated to an acting career in radio and later films, achieving a degree of celebrity in historical radio serials, enough to become known as "señorita Radio." As a member of the trade union of radio workers, she began to get involved in politics at the time of the 1943 military coup and started hobnobbing with politicians. She met the then-minister of labor and welfare, Juan Perón, when she responded to his call for help with disaster relief after an earthquake at San Juan in January 1944. She became his mistress, and they married in 1945. When Perón became president the following year, Eva began to pursue her interests in labor relations and social welfare by involving herself in running the ministry of health and labor and overseeing the allocation of its funds. Once in a position of power, however, she had no qualms about suppressing trade union and media opposition to Perón by seeing that dissidents were removed from positions of influence.

In appealing for grassroots support for women's rights and her various social programs, with unwitting irony the beautiful Eva, herself immaculately groomed and impeccably dressed, made the cause of Argentina's impoverished *descamisados* her own. In Spanish meaning literally the "shirtless ones" and metaphorically "poor, wretched," this name for the Argentine urban working classes later became a nickname for Peronist supporters. Evita—the illegitimate girl from the back streets of Los Toldos in provincial Buenos Aires—had garnered the adoration of the notoriously mistrustful working classes, something that no other political leader had ever managed to achieve.

Evita made a particular point of galvanizing the support of women for Perón and organized a Women's Peronist Party in 1949. In so doing she managed to get the party to admit a fixed quota of women members, which eventually resulted in women being allowed to take a place in the Argentine Congress in the early 1950s, ahead of women in other Latin American states. In the meantime, Evita had run up against the snobbery of the upper-class philanthropists, who were less than charitably disposed to her aspirations to rise above her own humble station. The Charitable Welfare Society thus declined to make Evita its patron. She had her revenge by closing it down and at a stroke defusing its work in Argentina. Instead, she set up her own spectacularly successful and glitzy Maria Eva Duarte de Perón Social Aid Foundation. This was a large-scale state charity, funded by a national lottery, that dwarfed independent charitable groups in its scope and in its huge injection of funds, many of them coming from sycophantic admirers and the rest coerced from businesspeople. The foundation's money, which was never audited (Evita claimed that she never stopped to count it because she was too busy giving it away), was channeled into funding aid programs in education, hospitals, and the welfare of the elderly; building children's playgrounds; and doling out clothes

Eva Perón (Archive Photos)

and toys to poor families. Evita also initiated a network of day care centers in poor districts that offered legal advice, free medical care, and literacy and sewing classes and encouraged women to meet, exchange ideas, and promote their work. Ultimately, such centers would become useful focus groups for female support for Evita's Peronist Women's Party. To promote the foundation, Evita was constantly on the move among her adoring public, giving speeches and ministering to the sick and diseased like a latter-day miracleworker. She put her hands on suppurating wounds and kissed syphilitics—if the eyewitness accounts are true—in an uncanny parallel with another twentieth-century icon, Diana, Princess of Wales.

An inborn hatred of the old Argentine oligarchy prompted Evita to make the upper classes a particular target (she once remarked that they made her "want to bite them just as one crunches into a carrot or a radish"). Having herself been born illegitimate, she made a point of snubbing those elite philanthropists who sneered at her, drawing a clear distinction between the amateurism of their do-gooding charity and her own far-reaching brand of social aid. As she herself encapsulated it: "Charity tends to perpetuate poverty; social aid does away with it once and for all. Charity leaves a man just where he was before. Social aid restores him to society as an individual worthy of all respect and not as a man with a grievance. Charity is the generosity of the fortunate; aid levels up social inequalities. Charity separates the rich from the poor; social aid raises the needy person and sets him on the same level with the rich" (speech at the American Congress of Industrial Medicine, 5 December 1949).

Such was her popularity that in 1951 Evita decided to take an official post and was nominated for the vice presidency for forthcoming elections in 1952. But growing resentment of her in the military forced her to withdraw. In any case, she was already terminally ill with the cancer that would kill her in July 1952 at the age of thirty-three. Prayer vigils by the nation failed to save her from her acknowledged greatest enemy, time. Evita died not long after seeing her husband sworn in for a second term of office.

Evita's corpse was preserved for posterity, and she was given an official lying-in-state where the distraught masses by the thousands could come and pay their last respects—the kind of obsequies until then accorded only the likes of Vladimir Ilyich Lenin in the Soviet Union. Eva Perón became an immortal; Juan Perón, meanwhile, was ousted from power in 1955 and died a year after returning in short-lived political triumph in 1973. The ineffectual presidency of his third wife Isabel, who tried to ride on the back of Evita's hallowed memory as "Isabelita" Perón, ended in house arrest after two years. During this time, Evita's mummified body had suffered the indignity of displacement, disfigurement, removal to Spain and back, and reburial—all brought about by the changing climate of Argentine politics—until it was finally laid to rest in the Duarte family crypt in Buenos Aires in 1976.

Charismatic and vivacious, "the spiritual chief of the Argentine nation" as Congress dubbed her, Evita played the part of an exemplary Catholic in her public life. And like a sacred text, the book in which she elaborated on her social mission, *The Purpose of My Life*, became prescribed reading in schools. A hugely successful musical, *Evita*, was written about her life by Tim Rice and Andrew Lloyd Webber. In 1996 it became a film starring Madonna, and although it made clear allusions to a slightly tarnished early career (there are suggestions of prostitution), it also did much to reignite the Evita cult in Argentina, which shows no sign of dimming. An official website, maintained by her family, can be found at www.evita-peron.org. Another website has useful information and links: www.users.drak.net/Kyril/eva011/.

References and Further Reading
Barnes, John. 1978. *Evita, First Lady: A Biography of Eva Perón*. New York: Grove Press.
Fraser, Nicholas. 1996. *Evita: The Real Lives of Eva Perón*. London: André Deutsch.
Fraser, Nicholas, and Marysa Navarro. 1980. *Eva Perón*. London: André Deutsch.
Harbison, A. W. 1981. *Evita: A Legend for the Seventies*. London: Star Books.
———. 1997. *Evita: Saint or Sinner?* London: Boxtree.
Henderson, James, and Linda Roddy Henderson. 1978. *Ten Notable Women of Latin America*. Chicago: Nelson Hall.
Main, Mary. 1980. *Evita: The Woman with the Whip*. New York: Dodd and Mead & Co.
Navarro, Marysa. 1977. "The Case of Eva Perón." *Signs* 3(1): 229–240.
Perón, Eva. 1953. *My Mission in Life*. New York: Vantage Press.
Taylor, Julie M. 1979. *Evita Perón: The Myths of a Woman*. Oxford: Blackwell.

Pethick-Lawrence, Emmeline
(1867–1954)
United Kingdom

Prior to her career in women's suffrage, Emmeline Pethick-Lawrence spent many years in settlement work in London, pioneering a working girls' club to provide a crucial respite from East End slum life. She was later invited to join the inner sanctum of Christabel and Emmeline Pankhurst's Women's Social and Political Union (WSPU), with her husband providing funds and a single-minded dedication that ultimately went unrewarded. A tolerant and hardworking activist who was generous even when cast out by the Pankhursts, she unquestioningly accepted the greater importance of the cause.

Pethick-Lawrence was one of thirteen children. Her father was a Bristol businessman from whom she learned the qualities of tolerance and a hatred of injustice that would characterize her later activism. Brought up in a nonconformist home environment, she was educated at boarding school in England and finishing schools in

France and Germany. After returning home, she balked at the idea of spending her best years helping to look after her younger siblings. Through a relative, she obtained voluntary social work at the West London Methodist Mission in 1891, staying for five years as a "sister of the people" and leading a club for working girls mainly employed in the clothing industry (1890–1895). However, she wanted to live and work more closely with the girls, and she and her colleague Mary Neal left to set up their own settlement in 1895, the focal point of which was their Espérance Social Guild for Girls. It provided a recreational outlet for working girls for two hours at the end of the working day and a welcome escape from their often overcrowded homes. Pethick-Lawrence described this work in 1898 in a chapter contributed to Will Reason's book, *University and Social Settlements.*

The Espérance offered classes in drama, folk songs, and dance (it was later instrumental in the preservation of Morris dancing and English folk music). In 1897 Pethick-Lawrence collaborated with Lily Montagu and her sister Marian, doing similar work for Jewish working girls through their West Central Synagogue. Together they established the Green Lady Hostel, which offered a holiday scheme for working girls by the sea at Littlehampton. As a result of her close contact with working girls, Pethick-Lawrence began to study the problems they encountered—low wages, long hours, poor working conditions—and encouraged them to challenge management on unfair practice and treatment. Living in a cheap flat in a working-class community was an exhilarating experience for Pethick-Lawrence that fostered much intellectual discussion: "We read, discussed, debated and experimented and felt that all life lay before us to be changed and moulded by our vision and desire" (Pethick-Lawrence 1938, 88). In 1897, after becoming aware of the particular problems dressmakers encountered in their work, Pethick-Lawrence set up a dressmaking cooperative with the gloriously pretentious name of Maison Espérance, where twenty-five women worked eight-hour days in return for a decent wage and annual holidays.

Although she had decided against marrying, in 1899 Emmeline met newspaper proprietor and editor Frederick Lawrence, himself a socialist involved in settlement work in Canning Town. They married in 1901, when Emmeline

was thirty-four, and combined their surnames. They were active in work for the Independent Labour Party and, as dedicated pacifists, heavily involved in protests against the Boer War (1899–1902). While they were visiting South Africa during 1905–1906, Emmeline first read about the activities of the Women's Social and Political Union and the first arrest of suffragettes—Christabel Pankhurst and Annie Kenney (to whom Emmeline later became greatly attached). Upon her return to England, Pethick-Lawrence was introduced to the WSPU leadership by the socialist Keir Hardie and joined the union in February 1906. Soon after, she was appointed treasurer and proved to be adept in both raising and holding onto funds, as "a wizard money-raiser" (Stocks 1970, 68) augmenting WSPU funds by £134,000 in six years.

Pethick-Lawrence had her first run-in with the authorities in 1906, when she was arrested during WSPU lobbying at the House of Commons. Although she was released within days after suffering a nervous collapse, she would be imprisoned five times in six years (1906–1912) for her activism, on which occasions her husband Frederick began deputizing for her at the WSPU. His financial skills (and his own money) proved too crucial for him to be excluded under the WSPU's women-only policy. The Pethick-Lawrences were extremely enterprising in raising the money to keep the organization afloat; in 1907 they founded and coedited the newspaper *Votes for Women,* frequently contributing their own money to cover costs and for many years using their home as the WSPU's headquarters. With Emmeline Pankhurst often in prison or weakened by bouts of hunger striking, they became crucial to the day-to-day running of the organization alongside Christabel Pankhurst. They helped organize major WSPU rallies; chose the WSPU's familiar colors of purple, white, and green; and staged some of its most colorful publicity-grabbing parades.

In 1912 the tenor of WSPU activities changed as acts of militancy escalated. Both Pethick-Lawrences, as leading lights of the WSPU, were arrested for conspiracy to damage property after a spate of window smashing by members but served only a small part of their nine-month sentences. As treasurers, they were later held liable for the damage and taken to court. They refused to pay, and their property was confiscated and sold. Christabel Pankhurst tried to persuade them to leave the WSPU, planning to escalate militancy still further and aware of the risk of further financial losses that the Pethick-Lawrences might incur as a result. The Pethick-Lawrences, uneasy about alienating public opinion by maintaining the new violent turn in WSPU campaigning, protested its continuation to Pankhurst. Her response was to unceremoniously expel them from the WSPU.

The Pethick-Lawrences went graciously, according to Mary Stocks, "without any attempt to precipitate a sympathetic breakaway movement, without a word of protest or self-justification," knowing that "any sign of internecine strife in the suffrage ranks would harm the cause" (1970, 69). In her later account of her suffrage activities, Pethick-Lawrence with touching charity recalled that such was the irrevocability with which the Pankhursts broke with her that Christabel, whom she had frequently welcomed into her own home, became a stranger. But aware that the cause was more important than individual personalities, she attributed the peremptory dismissal she had received as being symptomatic of the peculiar brand of ruthlessness required by women "of destiny" such as the Pankhursts, whom she described as "like some irresistible force in nature—a tidal wave, or a river in full flood" (Pethick-Lawrence 1938, 285).

For a while, the Pethick-Lawrences continued to published *Votes for Women*, although not as the WSPU journal, broadening its coverage to other issues related to women's political and social disadvantages, with Emmeline contributing numerous articles. In 1914 they joined the United Suffragists, a mixed-sex group supporting women's suffrage. In 1912 Emmeline went to the United States to attend a women's peace conference and thereafter found a new vocation in peace work. She became a close associate of leading U.S. pacifists Jane Addams and Rosika Schwimmer, with them building up the women's peace movement in the United States. During World War I, Emmeline was active in attempts at peace mediation, in 1915 attending the international congress of women at The Hague, traveling there from the United States with Addams and forty-seven U.S. delegates. In the event, she was one of only three British women able to attend when the British government refused to allow delegates to travel to Europe. At the congress, Pethick-Lawrence was elected treasurer

of what would become known after 1919 as the Women's International League for Peace and Freedom. After World War I, she continued to work for peace arbitration and disarmament, while retaining many other interests, such as her work for the Council for Adult Suffrage, which continued to lobby for women to be given equal voting rights with men (achieved in 1928).

After unsuccessfully standing as a Labour candidate in the 1918 general election, Pethick-Lawrence pursued her socialist and reformist interests in other ways, as vice president of the Six Point Group, a women's legal pressure group, and a member of the executive committee of the Open Door Council, which opposed protective legislation for women workers. She gave her support to the dissemination of birth-control literature in Britain by Marie Stopes and was president of the Women's Freedom League (1926–1933) and a member of the Suffragette Fellowship. In 1938 she published her engaging memoirs, *My Part in a Changing World,* but increasing ill health put an end to her activism by the time World War II broke out in 1939.

Noted as a fine, if florid, orator, during her association with the WSPU Emmeline Pethick-Lawrence added passion and flair to its rhetoric and a dignity and grace to its campaigning. In 1908, in one of eleven pamphlets she contributed to the WSPU campaign, entitled "The Faith That Is in Us: The New Crusade," she wrote that the vote's true significance lay in "the spiritual enfranchisement of Womanhood; the release of women, the repairing, the rebuilding of that great temple of womanhood, which has been so ruined and defaced" (Vicinus 1985, 249). She became Lady Pethick-Lawrence when her husband was knighted in 1945.

See also Addams, Jane; Kenney, Annie; Montagu, Lily; Pankhurst, Christabel; Pankhurst, Emmeline; Schwimmer, Rosika; Stopes, Marie.

References and Further Reading

Alberti, Johanna. 1989. *Beyond Suffrage: Feminists in War and Peace, 1914–1928.* London: Macmillan.

Bagwell, P. 1987. *Outcast London, a Christian Response: The West London Mission of the Methodist Church 1887–1989.* London: Epworth Press.

Brittain, Vera. 1963. *Pethick-Lawrence: A Portrait.* London: Allen and Unwin.

Crawford, Elizabeth. 1999. *The Women's Suffrage Movement, 1866–1928: A Reference Guide.* London: University College of London Press.

Harrison, Brian. 1987. *Prudent Revolutionaries: Portraits of British Feminists between the Wars.* Oxford: Clarendon Press.

Kenney, Annie. 1924. *Memories of a Militant.* London: Arnold.

Liddington, Jill. 1989. *The Long Road to Greenham: Feminism and Anti-Militarism in Britain since 1820.* London: Virago.

Oldfield, Sybil. 2001. *Women Humanitarians: A Biographical Dictionary of British Women Active between 1900 and 1950.* London: Continuum.

Pankhurst, Christabel. 1987 [1959]. *Unshackled: The Story of How We Won the Vote.* Reprint, London: Cresset Women's Voices.

Pethick-Lawrence, Emmeline. 1938. *My Part in a Changing World.* London: Victor Gollancz.

Pethick-Lawrence, Frederick. 1942. *Fate Has Been Kind.* London: Hutchinson.

Rosen, Andrew. 1993 [1974]. *Rise Up, Women! Militant Campaign of the WSPU 1903–1904.* Reprint, London: Routledge.

Stocks, Mary. 1970. *My Commonplace Book.* London: Peter Davies.

Vicinus, Martha. 1985. *Independent Women, Work and Community for Single Women, 1850–1920.* London: Virago.

Wiltsher, Anne. 1985. *Most Dangerous Women: Feminist Peace Campaigners of the Great War.* London: Pandora, and Westport, CT: Greenwood Press.

Pizzey, Erin
(1939–)
United Kingdom

One of the first feminist campaigners of the second wave to bring public attention to the problems of domestic violence, Erin Pizzey initiated the British movement to combat the physical abuse of women by their husbands and partners, establishing a refuge for battered wives in London in 1971. The success of her Chiswick Women's Aid would mark the beginning of many years of on-off confrontation with the authorities over problems of overcrowding. Her published works on domestic violence brought with them confrontations of a different kind—with other feminists—when Pizzey argued that the problem of violence was inherent in both men and women and that men, for too long in her view demonized by the women's movement, could also be the victims of domestic violence at the hands of women.

Pizzey's father was a diplomat; after her birth in China, she grew up in homes in South Africa, Beirut, the United States, and Iran before being sent to board at St. Antony's convent school in Dorset, England. She left home at the age of seventeen and in 1961 married broadcaster Jack Pizzey. During the 1960s, feeling isolated at home with two children on her husband's frequent absences, she began working in a community center in Chiswick as a welfare benefit adviser. Here she met women victims of domestic abuse, unable to leave their violent husbands because they had no means of support for themselves and their children. In 1971, with a group of friends, she set up a small women's center in a terraced house in Hounslow, which became an unofficial refuge for these women and their children. In 1974 she secured larger premises in Chiswick, where she founded Chiswick Women's Aid. Her initial intake of thirty-six rapidly grew to over 100; because of its avowed "open door" policy, Chiswick Women's Aid never turned anyone away. In 1972 the center was visited by U.S. feminists who set up similar ventures in the United States, and in 1976 Pizzey went there on a lecture tour, speaking and fund-raising in sixteen cities.

Pizzey's refusal to turn needy women away from the refuge soon led to overcrowding problems and the first of numerous court appearances over the health and fire hazards that these precipitated. The subsequent award of a grant through the Urban Aid Scheme, coupled with the financial and moral support of anonymous donors and influential patrons such as Lord Goodman, enabled the center to extend its work, take on more staff, and house 150 women and children on average. Other centers rapidly sprang up, often as illegal squats in empty houses, bringing the total in Britain by 1976 to ninety. Feminist campaigning on the issue of domestic violence led directly to new legislation, with the passage in 1976 of the Domestic Violence and Matrimonial Proceedings Act. The refuge, which again came under threat of closure for overcrowding in 1977, was eventually saved.

In 1974, Pizzey provoked considerable public debate with her book, *Scream Quietly or the Neighbours Will Hear*, the first of its kind to tackle the subject of modern-day wife beating. Her work for battered wives resulted in lecture tours across the world, where she helped set up other refuges. In 1979 she further extended her work to cover violence in the family, as director of Chiswick Family Rescue. Divorced from her first husband, she married Jeffrey Shapiro in 1980 and with him collaborated on a book on their work with problem families, *Prone to Violence* (1982). In it Pizzey described the deep psychological wounds inflicted on children by violence within the family and her ten years' work in rehabilitating its victims and recording their case histories. She argued that domestic violence often created what she termed "an addiction to pain" in young children exposed to it, which in adulthood could in turn unleash violence in them. In daring to suggest, however, that men could be the victims of domestic violence, meted out by women who as children had been the victims of physical or sexual abuse, she brought down on herself the wrath of many feminists. The book was largely boycotted by the women's movement, who felt its arguments were counterproductive to all the many gains in women's rights since the early 1970s.

In the 1990s, unable to tolerate the continuing hostility to her ideas in the United Kingdom, Pizzey went abroad and turned to writing popular fiction. She lived for some years in Italy and in 1994 was awarded the San Valentino d'Oro Prize for Literature. After her second marriage failed in 1997, she returned to the United Kingdom. By this time, she was in considerable financial difficulty and was forced to live for a while on welfare. She had not lost her fighting spirit, however, and in 1999 relaunched her campaign against *all* violence in the family—by women as well as men—arguing for the rights of fathers to create a closer bond with their children. She regretted that her women's refuge had been, as she felt, "hijacked" by the women's movement in the 1970s and turned into a vehicle for man-hating and the demolition of traditional family structures. The ensuing "gender war" launched by feminists against men in Britain, she argued, had led to punitive legislation against divorced and separated fathers. In challenging the feminist movement's creation of men as the enemy, she reiterated her belief that "until women stop attacking all men, branding them as rapists and batterers, we will never have a women's movement which truly represents all women" (Pugh 2000, 332). The feminist response was to accuse Pizzey of oversimplifying the arguments of the feminist movement and of

diverting attention from the issues that really mattered. By choosing to ignore the positive side to what had been a complex and diverse women's movement over the last thirty years, they felt, she had overlooked its great strengths by emphasizing its weaknesses.

Pizzey has been the recipient of several awards, including the 1981 Diploma of Honor by the International Order of Volunteers for Peace, the 1983 Nancy Astor Award for journalism, and the 1987 Distinguished Leadership Award from the World Congress of Victimology. Her most recent works are *Kisses* (1995) and *The Wicked World of Women* (1996); she has also contributed articles to the *New Statesman, Sunday Times,* and *Cosmopolitan* magazine. For further information on Pizzey, linked to her various writings now posted on other websites, see http://www.forever.freeshell.org/pizzey.htm.

References and Further Reading

Goodchild, Sophie. 1999. "Pizzey Makes a Stand for the Battered Man." *Independent* (28 March): 6.

Laurance, Jeremy. 1991. "Sex Talks: Jeremy Laurance Talks to Erin Pizzey, the Battered Women's Campaigner Turned Steamy Novelist." *New Statesman Society,* (8 February): 23.

Pizzey, Erin. 1978. *Infernal Child: A Memoir.* London: Gollancz.

———. 1996. "Influences: Erin Pizzey, Campaigner for Women." *New Statesman Society,* 24 May, 21.

Pugh, Martin. 2000. *Women and the Women's Movement in Britain 1914–1999.* 2d ed. Basingstoke: Macmillan.

Plamínková, Františka
(1875–1942)
Czechoslovakia

The Czech branch of the Women's International League for Peace and Freedom (WILPF) paid a high price during World War II. Educator, feminist, and patriot Františka Plamínková was one of six Czech feminists executed by the Nazis. After the nation was established at the Treaty of Versailles at the end of World War I, she had been the founding mother of the Czech movement for women's suffrage and leader of the broader movement within the Austro-Hungarian Empire. She also headed a campaign calling for the representation of women in the Bohemian Diet.

Plamínková was born in Prague and studied

at the School of Arts and Crafts of the University of Prague. She worked as a teacher and later a schools inspector until 1918, at the end of the war suggesting the creation of a School of Experimental Psychology of the Child. In 1903 she cofounded the Women's Club of Prague and in 1905 the Committee for Women's Suffrage, both of which had a strong national orientation to the rights of women in Bohemia, who, she claimed, "are classed by the Austrian Government with criminals and other undesirable citizens" (Evans 1977, 96). Plamínková was particularly determined to fight for women's equal status in the professions, such as her own—teaching—and the law.

The kingdom of Bohemia (which later formed part of Czechoslovakia) was, from 1618 until 1918, part of the Austro-Hungarian Empire, and Czech feminists there were particularly combative in asserting their political rights. Their strong sense of nationalism compelled them to make sometimes unreasonable demands, prompted by the particularly virulent antagonism between Czech and German speakers in the Austro-Hungarian Empire. Czech feminists frequently called for the greater use of the Czech language, such as in 1909, when Czech members demanded that their language be made the fourth official language of the International Woman Suffrage Alliance (IWSA). Similarly, in 1912 Plamínková and other Czech suffragists refused to be represented at a feminist conference in Vienna because the proceedings were to be held in German, the official language of the empire. In 1911 and 1912, Czech suffragists under Plamínková mounted a vigorous campaign to gather a petition to present to the Bohemian Diet on women's suffrage, which resulted in Czech women being the first in central Europe to be allowed to nominate and elect women candidates in by-elections to the Diet. But the whole enterprise proved to be a token exercise when the Habsburg governor of Bohemia refused to ratify the women's election. After the proclamation of the Republic of Czechoslovakia, uniting the peoples of Bohemia, Moravia, and Slovakia in October 1918, Plamínková became a proud defender of her newfound nationhood. IWSA leader Carrie Chapman Catt, who had visited Prague in 1906 and 1909 to encourage women's suffrage campaigning there, visited Czechoslovakia in 1922, when she was personally introduced by Plamínková to the country's new leader, Tomáš Masaryk.

In 1918 Plamínková had been elected to the municipal council of Prague, where she served for six years. In 1925 she was elevated to the Senate, where she held a post in the Commission for the Budget and Foreign Affairs. During her years in the Czech government, she maintained a special interest in the economic situation of women, acting as vice president of the Society for the Protection of Feminine Interests and founding a refuge for mothers and children and a workshop for old and sickly women. She represented children's rights, working for blind children and for special children's tribunals, as well as for the protection of illegitimate children and the recognition of their paternity. In 1925 Plamínková was elected vice president of the International Council of Women (ICW), having brought together fifty Czech women's organizations in 1923 to found a Czech National Council of Women affiliated with the ICW, through which she established links with many international organizations. One such link brought her an invitation in 1927 to undertake a lecture tour in Spain, the first extended to a woman official by its dictator, Miguel Primo de Rivera. She visited Madrid, Seville, and Salamanca, where she toured with three lectures: "Woman: Her Importance to the State, the Community and the Family"; "Women's Suffrage in Czechoslovakia"; and "The Women's Movement in the World."

During the 1930s, Plamínková served as a Czech delegate to the League of Nations, where she spoke out on conditions in Czech prisons. She was also active in the Open Door International and the International Federation of Business and Professional Women and was chair of the IWSA Committee on Like Conditions of Work for Men and Women.

Plamínková was naturally drawn into the pacifist movement, attending a major peace conference in Brussels in 1936 and serving on the Disarmament Committee of the Women's International League for Peace and Freedom. In 1939 she bravely—and unwisely—returned to Czechoslovakia after attending an IWSA conference in Copenhagen, at which fellow delegates had begged her to take refuge in England. But she felt compelled to help the women of her country "face their dreadful fate," as she put it (Peck 1944, 463), and returned home. As a woman and a Jew who had been active in many civil rights organizations as well as an influential member of the Senate, she was one of the first political leaders to be arrested by the Gestapo. Her detainment came in retaliation for the assassination of the German Nazi governor Reinhard Heydrich by Czech patriots in May 1942. After her arrest, Plamínková was held in terrible conditions in prison for many months. And then, after the German army suffered terrible reverses on the Russian front, she was released temporarily and ordered to oversee the Czech National Council of Women in collecting furs and warm clothing from the Czech population to be taken to the German soldiers in the snows of Russia and Ukraine. News of Plamínková on the IWSA circuit then dried up, and it was only several months later, in March 1943, that word filtered back via Germany and then Sweden that Plamínková had been tortured in prison and then hanged in a concentration camp. Before her death, she was decorated by both the French president and the king of Yugoslavia (for her relief work there during the Balkan Wars of 1912–1913). A detailed tribute to Plamínková, on the occasion of her sixtieth birthday, published in French as "Un Flambeau de Féminisme" in the *International Woman Suffrage News,* April 1935, testified to the love and respect in which she was held by the international women's movement. The journal also contains regular reports by Plamínková on the Czech suffrage movement.

See also Catt, Carrie Chapman.

References and Further Reading
Bosch, Mineke. 1990. *Politics and Friendship: Letters from the International Woman Alliance, 1902–42.* Columbus: Ohio State University Press.
David, Katherine. 1991. "Czech Feminists and Nationalism in the Late Habsburg Monarchy: The First in Austria." *Journal of Women's History* 3(2): 26–45.
Evans, Richard. 1977. *The Feminists: Women's Emancipation Movements in Europe, America and Australasia 1840–1920.* London: Croom Helm.
Peck, Mary Gray. 1944. *Carrie Chapman Catt.* New York: H. W. Wilson.

Pokrovskaya, Mariya
(1852–after 1917)
Russia

During the period 1905–1917 in Russia, three major groups of women activists came to the fore to campaign for democratic change, social reform, and women's suffrage. The Russian Women's Mutual Philanthropic Society (RWMPS), which had been in existence since 1895, had been joined by the All-Russian Union for Women's Equality in 1905. But many women found these two societies polarized between militancy (the union) and conservatism (the RWMPS). In December 1905 a third option was presented: feminist doctor and pioneer of public health Mariya Pokrovskaya founded the more overtly political Women's Progressive Party.

The facts of Pokrovskaya's early life are obscure: she was born in Nizhniy-Lomov in Penza province. After being educated at home, she became a private tutor. In 1876 she enrolled in the women's medical courses in St. Petersburg and after graduation worked as a doctor for a zemstvo (district assembly) at Glubukov in Pskov province. Over the next six years spent in rural practice, Pokrovskaya made an exhaustive study of the living conditions of local peasants, attempting to correlate links between the incidence of particular diseases and bad housing and unsafe drinking water. She became particularly concerned about the high numbers of peasants suffering with respiratory problems and trachoma, caused, she felt, by the dirt and lack of ventilation in their dark, smoky dwellings.

In 1888 Pokrovskaya gave up zemstvo work and moved to St. Petersburg, where she established a medical practice, making a study of the health and living conditions of workers in the slums and factories of the Vyborg side—the notoriously unhealthy and overcrowded industrial region northeast of the city (and in 1917 a hotbed of revolutionary activity). She published her findings in a series of articles in the *Messenger of Social Hygiene* in 1895–1896, recommending the construction of better and more sanitary housing and the dissemination of literature on public health and hygiene. Pokrovskaya further bolstered her arguments with a detailed survey of standards in other countries—France, Prussia, England, and Switzerland—which appeared in 1897 as *Sanitary Inspection of Dwellings and San-*

itary Organization. In 1900 she turned her attention to the health issues associated with prostitution in *Struggle with Prostitution,* in which she described her case studies of 103 Russian prostitutes and compared her findings with a similar survey in Paris. Her conclusion endorsed what other feminist pioneers had also been arguing: long working hours and low wages for women—in factories, dressmaking, and domestic service—pushed women into the relatively "easier" life of prostitution. Only a radical overhaul of society, in particular of arrogant male attitudes toward women and control of men's unbridled sexuality, would effect any change. Meanwhile, Pokrovskaya recommended the sanitary supervision of brothels and became involved in the international campaign against state-regulated prostitution. But this social issue was never addressed by the government in Russia and devolved in the main to the good works of women charity workers, who could do little more than offer basic nursing care to sick prostitutes. Pokrovskaya's own arguments were published in 1902 in the moralistic tome *The Medical-Police Supervision of Prostitution Contributes to the Degeneration of the Nation.* She would later complain that even the women organizers of the first All-Russian Women's Congress, held in 1908, had not devoted sufficient time to discussion of this pressing social issue.

As time went on and her obsession with the social issues affecting women deepened, Pokrovskaya became increasingly antimale in outlook. Richard Stites (1991) argues that this antipathy, which oriented her feminism toward sexual rather than political issues, was born of her years of working against prostitution. She certainly took the opportunity at every turn to blame many social injustices on the moral shortcomings and inertia of the opposite sex, insisting that if women played a role in the Duma, such social ills would be properly and promptly addressed. In September 1904 she finally created her own vehicle for the discussion of women's issues—the first of its kind in Russia, and the only one until 1907—when she set up the journal *Woman's Messenger.* Regular extracts of articles from this journal became a valuable source on the progress of the women's movement in Russia, and filtered out to the West via the pages of the International Woman Suffrage Alliance journal, *Jus Suffragii.*

For a while, Pokrovskaya had been active in the RWMPS, at the turn of century led by Anna Shabanova, but became dissatisfied with its lack of political focus. In 1905 she founded the Women's Progressive Party, aimed at offering women a political voice through discussions held at its Women's Club. The party, which sought democratic government under a constitutional monarchy, offered a clear-cut program of social demands, not just for women's suffrage but also for the legal and economic equality of women. It also advocated civil rights; labor, factory, and family reforms; and the abolition of state-regulated prostitution. But despite its broad-based, socializing principles, in its rigid exclusion of men the party alienated potential support. Pokrovskaya's hopes for peaceful change and women's suffrage were dashed by the successive failure of the first, second, and third Dumas.

After the outbreak of war in 1914, Pokrovskaya urged women to grasp the opportunity of emphasizing their moral ascendancy by undertaking humanitarian work for the peaceful renewal of society. In her view the war was, if any more proof were needed, the ultimate manifestation of male domination and aggression. In St. Petersburg in 1915, she initiated a Women's Economic Union to help combat the terrible food shortages in the capital during the war by setting up a shop and a canteen to provide cheap meals for its members. But her hopes of following the example of Sylvia Pankhurst in East London, by establishing a network of cheap restaurants, clinics, nurseries, and workshops for the poor and unemployed, were never realized. Pokrovksaya's story was, like that of many other Russian women activists of her time, cut short by the onset of revolution and the chaos of civil war. Little is known of her final years. She continued her campaigning through the Women's Progressive Party, which survived the 1917 Revolution, although it increasingly narrowed its objectives to women's issues. It is not known when or where she died. Pokrovskaya also published several homiletic short stories based on her medical work among the working classes of the slums of St. Petersburg, including a fictionalized autobiography in 1903: *How I Was a City Doctor for the Poor.*

See also Shabanova, Anna; Stasova, Nadezhda; Trubnikova, Mariya.

References and Further Reading

Edmondson, Linda. 1984. *Feminism in Russia, 1900–1917.* London: Heinemann.

Stites, Richard. 1991 [1978]. *The Women's Liberation Movement in Russia: Feminism, Nihilism, and Bolshevism, 1860–1930.* Reprint, Princeton: Princeton University Press.

Tuve, Jeanette E. 1984. *The First Russian Women Physicians.* Newtonville, MA: Oriental Research Partners.

Popelin, Marie
(1846–1913)
Belgium

A leading campaigner for women's equality and an international pacifist, the lawyer Marie Popelin fought a long and fruitless campaign to be admitted to the bar as Belgium's first female lawyer, but her story has yet to figure in English-language sources on women's history, and the available facts about her life in English remain few. Popelin graduated as a doctor of law in 1888 but was refused admittance to the bar by the Brussels court of appeals because arguing cases was a public office deemed unsuitable for women. At that time, women were not admitted as lawyers and Popelin worked as a legal consultant. In 1889 she chaired the legislation sessions of the second French international congress on women's rights, held in Paris.

Popelin was founder and president in 1892 of the first feminist group in French-speaking Belgium, the League for Women's Rights, and in 1897 she organized an international feminist congress in Brussels. She became first president of the Council of Belgian Women in 1905, which acted as a mediating body for women's groups in Belgium and was affiliated with the International Woman Suffrage Alliance. She acted as a regular delegate to international conferences. In 1910, thanks to Popelin's campaigning, the first women's club, the Lyceum, opened in Belgium. It would not be until 1922, a year after Belgian women won the vote, that they were finally allowed to practice as lawyers, when Marcelle Renson was appointed to the court of appeals and later went on to serve in the International Court of Justice in The Hague.

Marie Popelin (North Wind Picture Archives)

Popp, Adelheid
(1869–1939)
Austria

Adelheid Popp, trade union leader, radical socialist, and feminist, was the woman whose energetic organizing and vivid public speaking almost single-handedly aroused Austrian women to fight for their rights. For many years, she pioneered the socialist *Working Woman's Newspaper,* long before women were allowed to become members of trade unions, and led the first strike by Austrian women workers in 1893. Eventually, she was one of the first women to be elected to the Austrian parliament.

Born Adelheid Dworak at Inzersdorf, near Vienna, she was the fifteenth daughter of a poor weaver. She had little education and suffered a brutalized childhood in which she witnessed her mother's frequent beatings by her father and "only knew the great room in which we worked, slept, ate and quarreled" (Fout 1984, 200). Her childhood was spent helping her mother work cripplingly long hours in various home industries to earn a few shillings to feed them all. Her education was cut short at the age of ten, when she was forced to leave school to help support her family, earning 5 pence for a twelve-hour factory day. Popp spent years of drudgery in factories—including a metal plant, where she had to carry burning material from an underground room—and in domestic service, her paltry earnings boosted by extra sewing, all of which damaged her health. At the age of fourteen, she suffered a nervous illness and, after spending time in a psychiatric ward, was abandoned at a workhouse by her mother. Despite her lack of education, Popp was an avid reader of workers' newspapers and socialist writings in what little spare time she had and became interested in the ideas of the influential socialist writer August Bebel.

Encouraged by Bebel's work *Woman and Socialism* (1883), in which he argued for the emancipation of women as an essential part of the liberation of all society from exploitation, Popp overcame her naturally timid, self-conscious nature and asked her brother to take her to a Social Democratic Labor Party meeting. At one such gathering, she eventually gave an impromptu speech on women's need for mental enlightenment and to find a useful outlet in social welfare. On subsequent occasions, Popp spoke on the exploitation of women workers, entering socialist politics "with the wish of encouraging those numerous working women who possess hearts full of a longing to do something, but who always draw back again, because they do not trust their own capabilities" (Popp 1912, 133). Popp became a leader of the Austrian Socialist Women's Association (ASWA), in 1892 assuming the editorship of its pioneering publication, the *Working Woman's Newspaper,* at the age of twenty-three.

In 1893 Popp attended the International Socialist Congress in Zurich, where she took part in debates on protective legislation for women, including an eight-hour day, maternity leave, and prohibition of night work for women. That same year she also set up a women's discussion group called Libertas to provide an opportunity for women to gain experience in public speaking and debate as a preliminary to taking a role in political life. She took an active role in organizing women, first by embracing the cause of female domestic workers. Without any backing from the male-dominated Austrian trade union movement, she led one of the first women's strikes, of 600 garment workers near Vienna who were calling for better wages and improvements in working conditions, but suffered both family disapproval and the contempt of male trade unionists as a consequence. Her advocacy of women's trade unions led in 1896 to a failed attempt (by one vote) to get the Austrian trade union bodies to back an official women's organization. She also

Adelheid Popp (German Heritage Foundation)

spent two weeks in prison that year for writing against the materialistic basis of many marriages, which, she argued, were too often founded on "money and speculation" rather than on love.

In the twentieth century, Popp turned her attention within the ASWA to women's suffrage and their equality with men in pay, legal rights, and divorces, as well as continuing to call for protective legislation for women workers and nursery care for their children. She now worked closely with the Social Democratic Party in supporting its calls for universal male franchise ahead of that for women, in the belief that the election of sympathetic socialist deputies would sooner bring about the enfranchisement of women. With this in mind she worked hard to recruit more women to the SDP; after the Russian Revolution in 1917, when the leading feminist in the Socialist International, Clara Zetkin, became a communist, Popp took on a more high-profile role. When Austrian women were given the vote in 1918 she was in the first group of women elected to the legislature. During the 1920s Popp and other women in the Austrian Social Democratic Party were effective in forwarding women's issues as well as calling for radical revisions of the Austrian penal code, which outlawed abortion and the dissemination of literature on contraception.

But it was in her writings that Popp left a lasting legacy. In 1909 she published anonymously *Story of the Youth of a Working Woman as Told by Herself,* a work that would be internationally recognized as a leading work in the history of women's autobiographical writing, running to six editions by 1930. It is a coruscating account of the misery and deprivation endured by urban industrial workers and recounts in graphic detail the humiliation experienced by women, both in the home at the hands of drunken husbands and in the workplace through sexual harassment from male workers and employers.

In a 1911 essay, "Women Are Awakening," Popp had arrived at the conclusion that socialism offered the only way forward for the awakening of women from their "spiritual sleep," in that it alone would provide them with the sense of self-worth needed to fight for their own rights as well as those of all the poorest and most oppressed in society. In all her work, she remained loyal to the fight for socialism, which she placed before her feminist concerns, and defended party unity by frequently seeking to conciliate between differing factions.

References and Further Reading

Bader-Zaar, Birgitta. 1996. "Women in Austrian Politics, 1890–1934: Goals and Vision." In David F. Good, Margarete Grander, and Mary Jo Maynes, eds. *Austrian Women in the Nineteenth and Twentieth Centuries: Cross Disciplinary Perspectives.* Providence: Berghahn Books.

Boxer, Marilyn J., and Jean H. Quaterat. 1978. *Socialist Women: European Socialist Feminism in the Nineteenth and Early Twentieth Centuries.* New York: Elsevier North-Holland.

Crawford, Elizabeth. 1999. *The Women's Suffrage Movement, 1866–1928: A Reference Guide.* London: University College of London Press.

Fout, John C. 1984. *German Women in the Nineteenth Century: A Social History.* New York: Holmes and Meier.

Hannam, June, Mitzi Aucheterlonie, and Katherine Holden, eds. 2000. *International Encyclopedia of Women's Suffrage.* Santa Barbara: ABC-CLIO.

Joeres, Ruth-Ellen B., and Mary Jo Maynes, eds. 1986. *German Women in the Eighteenth and Nineteenth Centuries: A Social and Literary History.* Bloomington: Indiana University Press.

Popp, Adelheid. 1912. *Autobiography of a Working Woman.* London: T. F. Unwin.

Smith, Bonnie G. 1989. *Changing Lives: Women in European History since 1700.* Lexington, MA: D. C. Heath.

Potonié-Pierre, Eugénie
(1844–1898)
France

A pioneer of socialist feminism in France, Potonié-Pierre was a founder of the Women's Solidarity Group. A respected teacher and labor organizer, she mellowed into a leading moderate of the 1890s and, with the writer Séverine, became an important link between the women's rights and pacifist movements in France. In 1878 she settled in Paris, where she spent her life organizing and speaking for social justice and equal pay for workers. A year later she met the pacifist Eduard Potonié and cohabited with him, sharing their names and calling for gender equality. Together the couple worked for workers' cooperatives and discussed with government officials the working conditions of women in public services such as the post office. They also devoted their energies to international peace and campaigned for free and secular education.

In 1880 Potonié-Pierre joined with Léonie Rouzade and Marguerite Tinayre to found the short-lived socialist group, the Women's Union, which named itself after a women's group that had been active during the time of the Paris Commune of 1871, reiterating that group's emphasis on women's equality with men. She was involved in another group, the Women's Socialist League, in 1889, and took part in a campaign by feminists that shadowed the elections of the National Assembly on the occasion of the centennial of the French Revolution. But with the league soon fraught by internal dissent, during the 1890s Potonié-Pierre dedicated herself to the establishment of an international network of feminists and peace activists who would take up humanitarian causes. Together with her husband, she called for disarmament, arguing, as many pacifists did at the time, that the arms race was causing poverty and that poverty in the home was, in turn, a major source of women's oppression.

In 1891, Potonié-Pierre was involved with Maria Martin and others in founding one of the most influential groups of the French women's movement, the Women's Solidarity Group, an organization that offered a middle way between socialist feminism and the conservative, bourgeois majority in the women's movement. Informally known as Solidarity, the group retained links with the socialist movement but concerned itself mainly with philanthropic work among working women and campaigning for suffrage. Potonié-Pierre, now a prominent figure with the retirement of Marie Deraismes and Hubertine Auclert's absence in Algeria, still hoped for a greater coming-together of women's groups in their mutual causes, and in 1892 she was instrumental in bringing eight Parisian women's groups into a French Federation of Feminist Societies (FFFS)—occasioning the popularization of the French term *féministe*, begun by Hubertine Auclert in the 1880s. The FFFS staged the first General Congress of Feminist Institutions that May, after which, as Karen Offen points out (2000, 183), the term became widely used in the French-language press. But within two months, Potonié-Pierre resigned from the federation after a dispute over her leadership and it disintegrated shortly thereafter.

Potonié-Pierre resumed her international work; in 1893 she and her husband cowrote a utopian novel, *A Little Later,* which envisioned international peace and social justice. In 1893, along with Paule Mink and three others, Potonié-Pierre unsuccessfully stood for Women's Solidarity as a candidate in National Assembly elections. Potonié's dream of an international network of feminists and peace activists came into being in 1895 when, with the English Quaker pacifist Ellen Robinson, she cofounded the mainly Anglo-French organization, the International Union of Women, to link groups in the United States, United Kingdom, France, Italy, and Germany. In 1896, Potonié spoke on feminist issues at the first international women's congress held in Germany, in Berlin, and later that year organized another feminist congress, sponsored by Solidarity, Maria Vérone's French League for the Rights of Women, still searching for peaceful social change. Two years later, while leading a French deputation to a feminist congress in Brussels, she died suddenly of a cerebral hemorrhage.

See also Mink, Paule; Séverine; Veróne, Maria.

References and Further Reading

Josephson, Harold, Sandi Cooper, and Steven C. Hause et al., eds. 1985. *Biographical Dictionary of Modern Peace Leaders.* Westport, CT: Greenwood Press.

Moses, Claire Goldberg. 1984. *French Feminism in the Nineteenth Century.* Albany: State University of New York Press.

Offen, Karen. 2000. *European Feminisms 1700–1950: A Political History.* Palo Alto: Stanford University Press.

Sowerwine, Charles. 1982. *Sisters or Citizens? Women and Socialism in France since 1876.* Cambridge: Cambridge University Press.

Uglow, Jennifer, ed. 1998. *Macmillan Dictionary of Women's Biography.* 3d ed. Basingstoke: Macmillan.

Prejean, Sister Helen
(1939–)
United States

In 1995 the release of the powerful death-row film, *Dead Man Walking,* brought the work of the U.S. campaigner against the death penalty, Sister Helen Prejean, to an international audience. Based on her own book of the same name, the film was both a harrowing and a moving account of Prejean's experiences as a death-row counselor within the walls of the Louisiana State Penitentiary.

Prejean was born and grew up in Louisiana. She joined a Roman Catholic order, the Sisters of St. Joseph of Medaille, at the age of eighteen in 1957, studied for a degree in English and education at St. Mary's Dominican College in New Orleans, and earned an M.A. in religious education at St. Paul's University in Ottawa, Canada. She taught in junior and senior high schools and served as religious education director of a Roman Catholic parish. In 1981 she took up work among the inner-city poor and homeless as a member of the St. Thomas Housing Project in Louisiana. Her involvement with convicted murderers began when she was asked to be a pen pal of Patrick Sonnier, an inmate on death row. She began visiting him in prison two and a half years later, at Sonnier's request, Prejean accompanied him to his execution—the first in Louisiana since the 1960s. The experience had an indelible effect on her, convincing Prejean that as a witness to judicial murder, she must now tell the American public what the death penalty was *really* like.

Prejean commenced her campaigning against the death penalty by talking to small local groups and sociology classes at Loyola University. Her work was prompted by her conviction that God is not vengeful and that the condemned, when all hope is lost of a reprieve, should go to their deaths at least having acknowledged responsibility for what they have done. She also has an implicit belief in the articles of the United Nations Universal Declaration of Human Rights, which protects the individual from torture and legalized killing, arguing that the enforcement of the death penalty is inherently and morally wrong because it is a form of judicial torture that also inflicts suffering upon the family of the perpetrator of a crime. Like many other abolitionists in the United States, Prejean constantly emphasizes the high proportion of disadvantaged black and Hispanic people who suffer the death penalty in a system that provides those from the American underclasses with only the minimum of legal aid. Responsive to the feelings of the families of victims as well as their killers and to their natural desire for some form of retribution, in 1989 Prejean helped found Survive, an organization in New Orleans to assist the families of victims of crime in coming to terms with their loss.

In 1994 Prejean published *Dead Man Walking: An Eyewitness Account of the Death Penalty in the United States,* which had its film rights quickly snapped up and was nominated for a Pulitzer Prize. It has since been translated into ten languages. Respected as an expert on the uses and abuses of capital punishment in the United States, she is much in demand as a public speaker on the subject. She also trains other death-row counselors and spiritual advisers. Talking and writing about witnessing numerous executions is in itself a draining experience for Prejean, who has said: "It doesn't matter how many times you accompany someone to their death, each time is different and awful and takes time to get over. Writing about it helps me to heal" (*Independent,* 8 April 2000). The release of the movie *Dead Man Walking* in 1995 and the subsequent Academy Award won by Susan Sarandon for her role as Prejean prompted mass media coverage in the United States and abroad and fueled the widening public debate on the vexed subject of the death penalty.

Through various international human rights groups, Prejean continues to fight for the exploration of alternatives to the death penalty, knowing that currently 75 percent of the U.S. public support its use for first-degree murder. She feels that the time is long overdue for prisons to cease being looked upon merely as places of punishment and the death penalty as a symbol of how tough the United States is on crime. Support for the death penalty, Prejean argues, is symptomatic of the deeply entrenched racism in American society; and in her opinion it will continue to prevail all the time that people feel let down and insufficiently protected by the police and the criminal justice system.

Now based in New Orleans, Prejean is heading an international campaign, supported by Amnesty International, that is calling for a worldwide moratorium on the death penalty. This moratorium, which is sponsored by the United Nations, has yet to receive the endorsement of the United States, China, Iran, or Iraq. Prejean also collaborates with the American Friends Service Committee in promoting cooperation between religious groups on prison reform. In 2000 she gave the keynote address at the First National Meeting on Care of the Dying in Prisons and Jails, as part of the Project on Death in America. Under this program, she also seeks to address the growing problem of acquired immunodeficiency syndrome (AIDS), tuberculosis, and suicide in prison as well as health care there in general.

Prejean is engaged in writing a book about women's struggle for equality in the Roman Catholic Church and another on her own spiritual journey, *Hand on the Tiller, Face in the Wind—Travel Notes of a Believer.* Despite her now considerable public profile, she continues to insist, as she asserted in *Dead Man Walking,* that she is merely "an ordinary person" who has become "involved in extraordinary events." For further information on Prejean's work, see http:// www.soros.org/death/sisterhelen/.

References and Further Reading

Collopy, Michael, and Jason Gardner. 2000. *Architects of Peace: Visions of Hope in Words and Images.* Novato, CA: New World Library.

Prejean, Sister Helen. 1994. *Dead Man Walking: An Eyewitness Acoount of the Death Penalty in the United States.* New York: Vintage.

Q

Qiu Jin (Ch'iu Chin, Jiu Jin)
(1875–1907)
China

One of the first Chinese women to openly call for women's equal rights with men, Qiu Jin became not only the first female martyr in the revolutionary movement against the Ch'ing dynasty but also an enduring feminist icon. Little is known of the few educated women who became caught up in the embryonic women's movement in China at the beginning of the twentieth century. Such had been the subordination of women until that time that Qiu had to look for inspiration in mythical Chinese heroines such as the sixth-century Mulan and Western female role models such as Joan of Arc and French and Russian female revolutionaries (Madame de Staël, Madame Roland, and Sofya Perovskaya). She longed to see her own fellow Chinese women liberated from centuries of servitude, to see them "rise as birds in flight" and "serve as lamps in dark chambers" (Croll 1978, 68). In order to promote her own radical ideas, she frequently dressed as a man, obliged to accede that in patrilineal Chinese society, it was the male who was independent and strong.

Qiu was the eldest daughter of a middle-class government lawyer and an intellectually enlightened mother. She was brought up in a relatively liberal, scholarly family and given a classical education, developing considerable skill in writing elegant poetry. But Chinese society at this time was still firmly entrenched in the traditional Confucian values that placed the family before the state and woman's role totally subservient to that of men. At the age of eighteen, Qiu was obliged to accept an arranged marriage. She and her husband moved to Beijing in 1900 at the time of the Boxer Rebellion, where she witnessed the violence firsthand and joined the growing opposition movement to the Ch'ing dynasty that had ruled China since 1664.

By the turn of the twentieth century, Qiu had become a dedicated feminist and had become deeply antipathetic to her own life of privilege in Beijing. She sought equality for women after centuries of being obliged to "live lower than cattle" and be "mated like cows and horses." She abhorred the Chinese traditional practice of footbinding. It had been adopted during the T'ang dynasty (618–907 C.E.) as an aesthetic ideal that involved the distortion of a woman's foot into the 3-inch "Golden Lily" and had, over time, become a sexual fetish symbolizing the physical "hobbling" of women. Equally, Qiu loathed the tradition of concubinage, which obliged women to dress and look like painted dolls. In her opinion "concubinage is truly a hell on earth which competes with the hell of the dead" (Fox 1978, 32). Inspired by the Russian female revolutionaries and anarchists she admired, Qiu absorbed radical and reformist literature and began to make contact with other women activists. She soon became so determined to pursue a revolutionary path toward the liberation of China that she took the unprecedented step of abandoning her husband and children in order to go to Japan, where she joined the ranks of exiled Chinese in Tokyo who were campaigning for the overthrow of the Ch'ing dynasty.

Arriving in early 1904, Qiu became one of 100 or so Chinese women involved in various revolutionary clubs in Tokyo. She studied Japanese at a language school and then enrolled at the Girls' Practical School run by pioneering (male) educator Shimoda Utako. She was soon involved in running the Humanitarian Society, a women's association founded in 1902 and dedicated to promoting women's right to education. She also joined a fledgling Chinese women's organization based in Tokyo—the Mututal Love Association—and in 1905 was the first woman to be admitted into Sun Yat-sen's revolutionary group, the Restoration Alliance. Qiu became a notable and passionate public speaker, wrote revolutionary articles, and helped to organize anti-Ch'ing propaganda. She founded *Colloquial Magazine,* which encouraged writing in colloquial, spoken Chinese in preference to high literary style. In it she elaborated on the subjection and sufferings of Chinese women in her own "Respectful Proclamation to China's 200 Million Women Comrades" and urged illiterate women to educate and thus liberate themselves. Upon her arrival in Japan, Qiu had unbound her feet and had developed her physical capabilities, learning martial arts, gymnastics, and archery. She proved herself the equal of her male corevolutionaries, drank wine with them, and often wore men's clothes. She was an accomplished horsewoman (riding astride); was skillful at boxing, in the use of a sword (which she always carried), and in the making of bombs; and passed on her many skills to other women fighters.

In 1906 Qiu returned to China and began teaching physical education, history, and language at the Minde and Xunyang Girls' Schools. She also began trying to galvanize women's support for revolutionary change and social reform. In Shanghai in 1907, she founded the first, short-lived Chinese feminist publication, the *Chinese Women's Journal,* in which she propagated her beliefs that a strong nation could only be created on the basis of the liberation of Chinese women within the family. She lambasted traditional Chinese practice that kept women in a subordinate role and denied them an education but also railed at Chinese women themselves for having given tacit support to the old ways for so long through their inbred passivity. She urged them to leave their homes, seek an education, and earn a living.

In 1907 Qiu went back to her home at Shaoxing, in the province of Zhejiang, and took up the post of principal of the Datong College of Physical Culture. With its motto of "Restore our native rule and our national rights," this institution became the hotbed for her plans for insurrection. From there she ran a branch of the Rev-

olutionary League, established the Sports Society of the North District (effectively a military training group), and came into close contact with other activists, including her cousin, Xu Xilin, who was plotting an uprising in Hangchow for 8 July that year. But the plot was ill-timed; fighting broke out early, and Xu was killed. Refusing to flee for her life, Qiu held out till her last bullets had gone and she was arrested.

Despite being tortured, Qiu refused to confess to having plotted revolution. Her only defense, in a heroic gesture of self-sacrifice in court, was a single line of poetry that she composed from the characters that made up her own name: "Autumn rain and autumn wind will make me die of sorrow." At the age of only thirty-two, she was beheaded on 15 July 1907. She left behind a final poem ending with the words: "My great aim has not yet been realized, but my ambition has still not been submerged. My heart breaks when I think of China!" (Fox 1978, 34). After the 1911 revolution in China, Qiu was reinterred by the Western Lake in Hangchow, the burial site she had originally chosen for herself near the grave of a Sung dynasty hero, Yo Fei. A pavilion dedicated to the wind and rain was eventually erected over her grave in recognition of her status as a national heroine.

References and Further Reading

Croll, Elizabeth. 1978. *Feminism and Socialism in China.* New York: Schocken Books.

Fan Hong. 1997. *Footbinding, Feminism and Freedom.* Portland, OR: Frank Cass.

Fox, James. 1978. "Feminists in the Firing Line." *Observer Magazine* (26 November): 33–34.

Gilmartin, Christina Kelly, G. Hershatter, L. Rofel, and T. White, eds. 1994. *Engendering China: Women, Culture and the State.* Cambridge, MA: Harvard University Press.

Jayawardena, K. 1986. *Feminism and Nationalism in the Third World.* London: Zed Books.

Ono Kazuko. 1978. *Chinese Women in a Century of Revolution.* Stanford: Stanford University Press.

Snow, Helen Foster. 1967. *Women in Modern China.* The Hague: Mouton.

Spence, Jonathan D. 1982. *The Gate of Heavenly Peace: The Chinese and Their Revolution, 1895–1980.* London: Faber and Faber.

Qurratul-Ayn (Tahira; born Fatemeh Baraghani)
(1817–1852)
Iran

The extraordinary and now legendary Qurratul-Ayn—poet, individualist, and intellectual—became a leading preacher of the nineteenth-century Babist movement and drew around herself admirers and enemies alike in her short life. She unveiled in 1848 at a time when such an act by a woman was a dangerous contravention of strict Islamic law and when, as Farzaneh Milani observes (1992), there had been no previously documented history of women's protest against veiling in Iran.

A notable beauty as well as a brilliant, independent thinker, Qurratul-Ayn was "arguably the most interesting woman in Iran's history" (Afkhami and Friedl 1994, 191). Her rejection of the veil was a facet of her rejection of *shar'iah*, traditional Islamic law that restricted the lives of women. Although much of the detail of her life has become bound up in the apocrypha of feminist sainthood, her short life as a fiercely nationalist poet who supposedly fought in battles alongside male Babists gained Qurratul-Ayn the respect of political commentators such as Lord George Curzon, who in his 1892 history of Persia described her life as being "one of the most affecting episodes in modern history" (Mahmoudi 1985, 84).

Born Fatemeh Baraghani into a family of devout Shi'i mullahs in Qazvin, Mazenderan province, Qurratul-Ayn was allowed access to an education that was exceptional for women at that time. She was instructed by her father, a lawyer, and by private tutors in Persian, Arabic, jurisprudence, and theology. She quickly developed a great hunger for knowledge and a skill for debating religious issues with her father and his pupils (albeit from behind a curtain segregating her from them). But, as Milani eloquently notes, "In the society of mid-nineteenth-century Iran, knowledge, like a child, was only legitimized if properly fathered by a man"; it was looked upon as a dangerous weapon in the hands of women (1992, 77). As a result, limitations were placed on Qurratul-Ayn's quest for knowledge outside the home, and although she had the intellectual ability to succeed her father as a religious scholar, she would never have been allowed to study in a the-

ological college. Instead, as convention decreed, she was married to her cousin, Mulla Muhammad, the son of a prayer leader, when she was fourteen years old.

For the next thirteen years Qurratul-Ayn lived in Iraq, while her husband pursued his religious studies there, and during this time she continued her own, private religious studies. On her return to Iran, she began openly discussing religious issues and challenging the traditional male interpretation of dogma. She increasingly found herself drawn to the ideas of the Islamic scholar Shaykh Ahmadi Ahsai, the theologian behind the growing Babist movement in Iran. Because this new interpretation of Islam offered a more liberal attitude toward the religious customs that for centuries had so confined women, she embraced this opportunity of gaining greater personal and intellectual liberty. Her refusal to give up this interest and accept a life of seclusion and subservience led to frequent conflict with her husband. Eventually, she abandoned him and their three children in order to preach the Babist faith and to challenge religious scholars of her time through the medium of formal debate.

Qurratul-Ayn subsequently traveled back to Iraq, to the Shi'i center at Karbala, to study the Sheykhi texts that constituted the foundation of the theories of Babism with followers of Ahsai (who had since died). Here she met the self-proclaimed Babist leader, Mirza Ali Muhammad, who had nominated himself the *bab* (gateway) to the true Islamic faith, thus founding the Babist (later called Baha'ist) movement. Qurratul-Ayn began actively teaching the theology of Ahsai from behind a curtain, as the sole woman among eighteen disciples of the Bab. She also actively proselytized for Babism as a faith that held out the hope of spiritual and moral renewal and social reform favoring women. Qurratul-Ayn began preaching for the right of women to be liberated from their lives of seclusion and for their protection from the abuses of polygamy and physical violence at the hands of men. Everywhere she went her public appearances caused an uproar—not just because of the sheer fact that she was a woman preaching in public but also because of her charisma, the undisputed depths of her learning, and the eloquence of her argument. She went even further, it is said, by eventually taking up the sword and dressing as a man to take part in acts of insurrection alongside

Babist fighters who recited her poems as the mantra of the faith. Her growing following in the Babist movement (with her acolytes known as the Qurratiyeh) accelerated the simultaneous demonization and idealization of Qurratul-Ayn on both sides of the popular consciousness.

Throughout her time in Iraq, Qurratul-Ayn was kept under surveillance by the authorities and eventually was deported for her activities, leaving for Iran in about 1847 with about thirty followers and preaching and recruiting new acolytes en route. Back at Qazvin, both her father and father-in-law tried to put a stop to Qurratul-Ayn's activities and make her return to her domestic duties, but she refused. Her husband, Mulla Muhammad, divorced her. Later that same year, Qurratul-Ayn's former father-in-law, Mulla Taqi, was attacked and stabbed in his mosque, and Qurratul-Ayn was accused of complicity in the murder and placed under house arrest. She went into hiding for a year in Tehran and later traveled to Badasht in northern Iran in 1848 to attend a twenty-one-day Babist convention of eighty male delegates, where she preached in public, famously without a veil, and proclaimed Babism an independent faith. The inevitable uproar at such a brazen appearance in public by an unveiled woman led to accusations of sin, madness, and heresy and resulted in Qurratul-Ayn spending the remainder of her life on the run from her enemies.

Qurratul-Ayn was later arrested and charged with collaboration in the murder of Mulla Taqi, but after she received an audience with the shah, he ordered that she be left alone. She was placed under house arrest at the home of the Tehran chief of police. But after an assassination attempt was made on the shah by three Babists, her execution was ordered. According to legend, she was strangled with one of her own silk scarves and her body thrown into a well. As Farzaneh Milani has pointed out, the Persian words for strangulation, *khafeh kardan,* refer to "suppressing, stifling, silencing"; the strangling of Qurratul-Ayn thus silenced the unique intellectual voice of a woman born way ahead of her time.

One hundred years after her death, a collection of Qurratul-Ayn's poetry was published, but the provenance of some of the verses is disputed. Although her arguments, both in her public preaching and in her poetry, were confined to theology, her questioning of the traditional relegation of women in Iran to anonymity and seclusion remains an early expression of the spirit of feminism before the movement itself came into being. Rejecting women's role as being simply that of the submissive and predominantly *silent* servants of men, she unknowingly gave voice to what would later become a worldwide desire on the part of women to have an equal role in society alongside them.

Inevitably, much of the scant detail of Qurratul-Ayn's life has become lost in the legend surrounding her; a reflection of this hagiography was initiated in her own lifetime, when the Bab accorded her the name "Qurratul-Ayn," which means "Solace of the Eyes"; she also acquired another popular attribution, "Tahira" (the pure one). Some commentators looked upon her appearance in Iran at this time as little short of a miracle. Her detractors, meanwhile, condemned her as a madwoman, a crazed heretic, "caught in her own self-destructive messianic ethos," as Milani interprets it (1992, 79). In addition, the inevitable accusations of loose morals and sexual promiscuity were also laid at her door. Predictably, many men, her husband and father-in-law included, put it all down to her infringement of the male preserve of study and her obsession with learning. It was quite simple, really—Qurratul-Ayn had been "ruined by reading."

References and Further Reading

Afkhami, M., and E. Friedl, eds. 1994. *In the Eye of the Storm: Women in Post-Revolutionary Iran.* New York: Tavris.

Bayat-Philipp, Mangol. 1978. "Women and Revolution in Iran, 1905–1911." In Lois Beck and Nicki Keddie, eds., *Women in the Muslim World.* Cambridge, MA: Harvard University Press.

Mahmoudi, Hoda. 1985. "Tahira: An Early Iranian "Feminist." In A. Fathi, ed., *Women and the Family in Iran.* Leiden: E. J. Brill.

Milani, Farzaneh. 1992. *Veils and Words: The Emerging Voices of Iranian Women.* London and New York: I. B. Tauris.

R

Rahnavard, Zahra
(active since 1979)
Iran

The wife of Iran's fifth prime minister Mir Hussein Musavi since the 1979 Revolution, Rahnavard has sought to reinterpret the emancipation of Iranian women within the strictures of "true Islam." Since the 1979 Revolution, she has become a leading newspaper columnist, social activist, and author, writing on Islam and women's affairs. Although she has written in support of reveiling and the traditional Islamic values that place women back on what she calls the "right path," she has underlined the need for men also to respect the laws of *hijab* (modesty in dress) in the same way as women. As the head of the Women's Social and Cultural Council, established in 1989 as one of seven government committees exploring various social issues, Rahnavard has called for these committees to be more equally represented by women members and has been an outspoken critic of the government's failure to accord women what, in her opinion, are their legitimate social and civil rights under the Qu'ran.

Rahnavard is one of a new wave of feminists in Iran who have rejected what they see as the "imperialist culture" that under the shahs encouraged Iranian women to become Westernized. In her view, unveiling was imposed by state legislation and enslaved women to makeup, Westernized dress, and so on. To retain the veil and re-adopt the *hijab* is therefore a clear act of defiance and rejection of the old imperial rule. Rahnavard also reaffirms women's traditional roles as wives and mothers, averring that the inculcation of Western values under the shahs served only to divorce them from their traditional duties and to raise them up once again as sex objects. Thus, she sees the reintroduction of the veil and the *chador* (traditional full-length dress) as an empowering rather than a retrograde act. In a fine study of Islamic women, *Price of Honour*, Jan Goodwin cites Rahnavard as stating that "the Veil enables [women] to become human beings in their own right. Once people cease to be distracted by women's physical appearance, they can begin to hear their views and recognize the inner person" (Goodwin 1995, 112–113).

Rahnavard concludes that Western values, by encouraging women to arouse male lust through their modes of dress and social behavior, have thus "failed women totally and left them bereft of honour and dignity" (Afshar 1994, 3). She has argued that the natural division of labor between men as providers and women as nurturers has been undervalued. Although she is convinced that women's primary role remains to set the moral example through the bringing up of their children, a fact that prevents many from being able to enter the workplace, she nevertheless supports the right of those who are able to work. Since the 1979 Revolution, women have been forced to leave the workplace and go back into the home. Their economic needs have been marginalized despite the fact that many women lost sons and husbands in the eight-year Iran-Iraq War (1980–1988). After such terrible depredations, in a country that had lost thousands of its men, Rahnavard insists that women should have been allowed into the workplace to make up the losses in manpower. She has argued forcefully that women can just as well serve God in the labor market and in politics as in the home. If there were a more equal balance between men and women in government, there would be a greater flow of ideas, and women would give impetus to the defeat of those elements that are conservative and antirevolutionary.

As the wife of a high-profile politician, Rahnavard tried to make use of her position to call for women to be represented in government and given the opportunity to take up public appointments. Her activities were ultimately prejudicial to her husband's political ambitions, however; his nomination as prime minister was opposed because of his wife's radical position on women's rights. Nevertheless, Rahnavard continued to express her views as a member of the Women's Social and Cultural Council. She has also been critical of Iranian divorce laws and has fought discrimination against women in the religious, social, and political spheres of Iranian life. In the 1990s she pointed out that women "remained invisible" (Afshar 1998, 84) and were not mentioned in five-year economic plans. Rahnavard is now chancellor of the all-women Al-Zahra University as well as a lecturer at the University of Tehran.

References and Further Reading

Afshar, Haleh. 1994. *Why Fundamentalism?* York: University of York.

———. 1998. *Islam and Feminisms.* Basingstoke: Macmillan.

Goodwin, Jan. 1995. *Price of Honour: Muslim Women Lift the Veil of Silence in the Islamic World.* London: Warner Books.

Paidar, Parvin. 1995. *Women and the Political Process in Twentieth-Century Iran.* Cambridge: Cambridge University Press.

Ramabai, Pandita Saraswati
(1858–1922)
India

The legendary educationist, reformer, and Sanskrit scholar Pandita Ramabai was one of the first Indian women to tackle the problems of caste and child marriage. She sparked widespread controversy in India when she became a Christian and published a book titled *The High-Caste Hindu Woman,* in which she condemned the traditional treatment of child widows and described the abject misery of many poor women's lives.

Ramabai enjoyed the rare privilege of being taught the sacred Hindu scriptures in Sanskrit and Vedic by her mother, who as a child bride had learned them from her Brahmin scholar-husband, Anant Padmanabha Dongre. Dongre, a supporter of women's education, became something of a guru in the remote, forested area of the Western Ghats, where the family lived and farmed rice fields and coconut plantations. He took over the education of his daughter, Ramabai, who by the age of twelve had apparently memorized 20,000 sacred verses at her mother's knee. But the family suffered much hostility as a result of allowing its women to study sacred works, and they were ostracized by local villagers. Nevertheless, many students and pilgrims made their way to Ramabai's home to study at her father's ashram. Eventually, the family's generosity toward such people left them in debt, and they were dispossessed. Forced to wander, living from hand to mouth, Ramabai's family went on a pilgrimage to holy places where her father would teach and beg a living.

Finding herself orphaned at sixteen after the death of most of her family in a famine, Ramabai suffered another three years of destitution, traveling some 4,000 miles on foot around India with her brother. It was during this time that her social conscience was roused when she witnessed firsthand the sufferings of poor Hindu women. She began addressing rural meetings throughout Bengal on educational reform and women's emancipation. She finally settled in Calcutta in 1878, where aside from lecturing on her social concerns, she taught the Sanskrit texts she had learned. She had also acquired skills in Marathi, Kanarese, Hindustani, and Bengali and would later compile textbooks in Marathi specifically for the use of Indian schoolgirls. As her fame as a Sanskrit scholar in her own right spread among influential, high-caste Reform Hindu pundits (the Brahmo Samaj), she was honored by them with the titles "pandita" (eminent teacher) and "saraswati" (goddess of learning). As a confirmed feminist, she also began proselytizing on women's emancipation among enlightened Bengali women, meeting the educator Francina Sorabji (mother of the reformers Cornelia and Susie Sorabji), who encouraged her to take up practical service. Ramabai also inevitably attracted the attention of Christian missionaries based in Bombay through the auspices of Frances Willard's Woman's Christian Temperance Union.

After her brother's death in 1880, Pandita was

Pandita Saraswati Ramabai (Courtesy of UCSB Davidson Library, Special Collections)

refused to be treated by men. Her plea reached even the ears of Queen Victoria, and an outpouring of support from British philanthropists led to the establishment of the National Association to Supply Female Medical Aid to the Women of India by Lady Harriot Dufferin, wife of the British viceroy of India. At the queen's specific request Lady Dufferin had organized fundraising efforts that would result in the training of some of the first Indian female doctors.

Having been impressed by the work of Christian missionaries in India and finding it difficult to earn a living as a widow, Ramabai determined to undertake medical training herself. She raised funds through the publication of a pamphlet entitled "Morals for Women" and traveled to England in 1883, despite disapproval of such an act by a Hindu woman. There she was embraced by her English supporters, learned English, and converted to Christianity in September 1883 after spending time with the Anglican Sisters of St. Mary the Virgin at Wantage, in Oxfordshire. There has been some debate over the true motives behind Ramabai's conversion; Antoinette Burton (1998) sees it as a necessary way of protecting her own "respectability" as an Indian woman in England. Certainly, Ramabai did not adopt the Christian faith without expressing some intellectual doubts about Christian tenets and Anglican orthodoxy more particularly. By the end of her long friendship with Sister Geraldine of Wantage, conducted mainly by letter, she had come into doctrinal conflict with her over numerous issues.

In 1884 Ramabai took a post at the elite Cheltenham Ladies' College, where she taught Sanskrit and continued, under the guidance of the college principal and feminist Dorothea Beale, to study English literature, mathematics, and science. Less overtly, Beale tried to steer Ramabai's religious faith into a more appropriate, noncritical direction. In 1886, with the encouragement of her cousin Anandibai Joshi (who was about to receive her degree as the first Indian woman to qualify as a doctor after training in Philadelphia) and having resisted pressure to return immediately to India on an evangelizing mission, Ramabai went on to the United States, originally with the idea of studying medicine herself. However, her interests in education drew her toward the work of the educator Friedrich Froebel. Because his system encouraged children to think independently, she

left alone and unprotected, for her enlightened parents had not married her off as a young girl. Six months after his death, she defied convention by marrying out of her high, Brahmin caste into a lower one, to a friend of her brother's, Bipin Behari Das. She found herself shunned by friends and relatives. Within two years, her husband died of cholera, and once again alone and friendless, Ramabai and her small daughter moved to Poona. Painfully aware of the suffering of young widows condemned to live their lives in purdah in a state known as "cold suttee" (i.e., a state that fell short of immolating themselves on their husbands' funeral pyres), Ramabai decided to help them acquire the education denied them by early marriage and to learn ways of supporting themselves financially. She founded Arya Mahila Samaj (the Aryan Women's Society) in June 1882 for the promotion of women's education, and its members lent their support that year to a special agenda on women that was part of the British government's Hunter Commission on Education in India. Ramabai herself gave evidence to the commission, during which she highlighted the desperate need for female doctors and teachers to be trained to work with women—especially doctors, since native women saw in it a radical means of changing the old concepts of religious and secular education. In 1886 Ramabai enrolled as a student at a kindergarten teacher–training school. Impressed by the quality of schoolbooks in the United States, she also devised a series of primers in Marathi and translated other educational textbooks to use when back in India. During a lecture tour, she concentrated her energies on raising consciousness not just about the lot of Indian women but about Native American women as well.

While in the United States, Ramabai had published her book *The High-Caste Hindu Woman,* which included an introduction by Dr. Rachel Bodley, the principal of the Women's Medical College in Philadelphia, where Ramabai's cousin had studied. Bodley was unequivocal in her opinion of Ramabai's work as breaking "the silence of a thousand years" in its passionate exposition of the sufferings of Indian women. As Kumari Jayawardena has observed, Ramabai's breadth of knowledge and social understanding were exceptional for her time. She had "an understanding of social reality gained through her nomadic travels and a command of Hindu ideology gained through her knowledge of the scriptures" (Jayawardena 1995, 91). Although discussion of the subject was not new, Ramabai's book described a catalogue of abuses against women in great detail and drew painful attention to the lives of servitude they endured and the reluctance of Hindu families to have or provide for girl children. She described high levels of infanticide, observing: "The census of 1870 revealed the curious fact that three hundred children were stolen in one year by wolves from the city of Umritzur, *all the children being girls,* and this under the very nose of the English Government" (Chapman 1891, 44–45). The book, which rapidly sold 10,000 copies before she left the United States, helped Ramabai raise money for her projected refuge for high-caste Indian child-widows, as did the establishment of the American Ramabai Association in Boston in December 1887. Ramabai's staunch American feminist supporters, such as Cornell University's Ramabai Circle for the Elevation of Women in India, formally undertook to fund her home for widows in India for the next ten years.

On her return to India in February 1889, Ramabai made it clear that she did not want to be made use of as the token Indian woman working for white, philanthropic causes. Nor did she wish to undertake missionary activities; she wanted to set up her own reform program, based on the belief that first and foremost Indian men should be educated into the wisdom of improving the lot of the average Indian woman. She began promoting Froebel's educational methods and opened the Sharada Sadan (house of the goddess of learning) for high-caste and destitute widows in Bombay, where the women were given an education and taught handicrafts. Here, many frequently also chose to convert to Christianity—the latter causing considerable local opposition to Ramabai's activities. The same year, she also opened a day school in Bombay, which attracted the daughters of Reform Hindus willing to see them better educated. After an attack by the Indian nationalist politician Bal Gangadhar Tilak, who accused her of deliberately seeking to convert women to Christianity, there was considerable public outcry, and several of Ramabai's Indian supporters turned their backs on her. Meanwhile, the Sharada Sadan was transferred to newly built premises in Poona in 1890. By 1892, it housed forty women.

As a result of continuing accusations that she was supposedly proselytizing for Christian converts, and despite the fact that Ramabai made a particular point of allowing freedom of religious practice in her home, she transferred her activities in 1891 to a women's and children's refuge located on a farm known as the Ramabai Mukti Sadan (house of salvation) at Kedgaon, 35 miles from Poona. Ramabai herself also retreated somewhat from public life. But her natural compassion drew her out again, when in 1896–1897 a terrible famine broke out in the provinces of central India, and the Ramabai Mukti Sadan saw its numbers swell to 300. She taught these refugee women handicrafts, such as weaving saris and making baskets, and set up a school for their children and facilities for the care of the physically and mentally handicapped.

In 1898 Ramabai's appeal for further funding brought a flood of financial assistance from U.S. supporters and the construction of a new house of salvation in Mukti. When the local government in Poona placed restrictions on her intake of women, Ramabai transferred to her premises in Kedgaon. After another famine in 1900, the institution set up various additional shelters when its numbers swelled to 1,900. Ramabai and her workers set up fifty classes to deal with this increased intake, and 400 children were looked after in the establishment's kindergarten. She also set up a training school for teachers, instituted remedial teaching methods with the emphasis on morality and social responsibility, and established an industrial school that taught practical skills and handicrafts.

Despite her adoption of Christianity, Ramabai's everyday life was a hybrid of Christian observance and Reform Hinduism. She supported the Woman's Christian Temperance Union but rejected the more stultifying aspects of Victorian Anglicanism and retained a respect for independence of religious worship. She observed a degree of Hindu ritual practice in matters pertaining to diet, dress, and hours of prayer. She always wore the white sari of a Hindu widow, cut her hair short rather than shaving her head completely as Hindu widows did, and prepared her vegetarian meals according to strict Hindu practice. Nevertheless, she also ensured that the door to her room was left open for the benefit of the curious, whenever she, her daughter, or other converts conducted Christian worship. The ambivalence of her position as a Christianized Hindu was a constant source of worry among her supporters, who thought her commitment to doctrine was suspect. As Burton concludes, Ramabai refused to be the epitome of a "colonial Christian" or to turn her back on her cultural inheritance, a fact later reflected in Sarojini Naidu's words to a gathering of 320 people at Ramabai's memorial service, when she declared her to be "the greatest Christian saint among the Hindus."

See also Beale, Dorothea; Joshi, Anandibai; Sorabji, Cornelia; Sorabji, Susie; Willard, Frances.

References and Further Reading

Burton, Antoinette. 1998. *At the Heart of Empire: Indians and the Colonial Encounter in Late-Victorian Britain.* Berkeley: University of California Press.

Chapman, Mrs. E. F. 1891. *Sketches of Some Distinguished Indian Women.* London: W. H. Allen.

Dongre, R. K., and J. F. Patterson. 1963. *Pandita Ramabai: A Life of Faith and Prayer.* Madras: Christian Literature Society.

Dyer, Helen. 1900. *Pandita Ramabai: The Story of Her Life.* New York: Fleming H. Revell Company.

Fuller, M. L. B. 1928. *The Triumph of an Indian Widow.* New York: Christian Alliance Publishing Company.

Jayawardena, Kumari. 1995. *The White Woman's Other Burden: Western Women and South Asia during British Rule.* London: Routledge.

Kosambi, Meera. 1998. "Multiple Contestations: Pandita Ramabai's Educational and Missionary Activities in Late Nineteenth-Century India and Abroad." *Women's History Review* 7(2): 193–208.

———, ed. 2000. *Pandita Ramabai through Her Own Words: Selected Works.* New York: Oxford University Press.

Macnicol, Nicol. 1996 [1926]. *Pandita Ramabai.* Reprint, New Delhi: Good Books.

Ramabai, Pandita. 1981 [1887]. *The High-Caste Hindu Woman.* Reprint, Bombay: Maharashtra State Board for Literature and Culture.

Sen Gupta, Padmini. 1944. *Pioneer Indian Women.* Bombay: Thacker and Co.

———. 1970. *Pandita Ramabai Saraswati: Her Life and Work.* Bombay: Asia Publishing House.

Tuson, Penelope, ed. 1997. *The Queen's Daughters: An Anthology of Victorian Feminist Writings on India, 1857–1900.* Reading, Berkshire: Ithaca Press.

Ramphele, Mamphela
(1948–)
South Africa

A leading figure in the African National Congress (ANC), Ramphele was banished to the Northern Transvaal for her activities as a founding member, with Steve Biko, of the black consciousness movement in the late 1960s. She worked as a doctor and community health worker, becoming a respected university administrator and a leading voice in South Africa on social welfare and community development.

Ramphele was born near Pietersburg in the Northern Transvaal, the daughter of two schoolteachers. She was educated at the Bethesda Normal College, a Dutch Reformed Church school in Pietersburg, and at Setotolwane High School and went on to study medicine at the University of Natal, graduating in 1972. During her time as a student, when she was working at the Mount Coke Mission Hospital in the Eastern Cape, she had joined the black consciousness movement and worked with Steve Biko and other students in the South African Students' Organization in setting up community programs. In 1975 she established the Zanempilo Health Clinic at King William's Town and worked as its medical officer.

In 1976, in the wake of the mass protest move-

Mamphela Ramphele (AP Photo/Martial Trezzini)

ment in Soweto, Ramphele was arrested and held in detention under the Internal Security Act for four and a half months. Shortly after returning to her work at the clinic, in April 1977 she was placed under a banning order, removed from her clinic, and exiled to Lenyenye, a remote rural township near Tzaneen in Northern Transvaal. In 1978 she had a son by Steve Biko. At Lenyenye, she kept up her commitment to community health, over the next six years working as a roving doctor for the Ithesung Community Health Programme based in Trichardsdal.

In the 1980s, Ramphele resumed her studies, gaining a diploma in tropical health and hygiene at the University of Witwatersrand in 1982. In 1983 she took a degree in commerce and that year was nominated as Woman of the Year by the *Johannesburg Star* for her work in self-help projects. In 1984, when the ban against her was lifted, Ramphele went to Cape Town to take on a research fellowship, working on the Second Carnegie Foundation Inquiry into Poverty and Development in Southern Africa. The project's subsequent report was published by Ramphele in 1989 in collaboration with Francis Wilson as *Uprooting Poverty: The South African Challenge*. It won the 1990 Noma Award for African scholars.

In 1991 Ramphele produced a book about Steve Biko and the black consciousness movement titled *Bounds of Possibility: The Legacy of Steve Biko and Black Consciousness* and spent the next two years studying the lives of black migrant workers, detailing the squalid conditions in which they lived in the hostels of Langa in Cape Town. Her powerful indictment of the exploitation of these workers was published as *A Bed Called Home: Life in the Migrant Labour Hostels of Cape Town* (1993), and she was awarded her Ph.D. in social anthropology.

In 1995, as director of the Institute for Democracy in South Africa's Public Information Centre, Ramphele took on the challenge of monitoring the new democratic regime in South Africa. In 1996 she turned to academic administration, becoming the first black woman to be vice chancellor of a historically white institution, the University of Cape Town. She has received numerous awards, including three honorary doctorates, and serves on the boards of nongovernmental organizations and major corporations. Despite South Africa's move to majority black rule, Ramphele does not consider her fight to be over. She still has to counter the double prejudice in her professional life against both her sex and her color and continues to speak out on a wide range of issues: the hardships endured by South Africa's underprivileged black migrant population, the education of black children, civil rights, ecological issues, and the eradication of poverty in Africa.

References and Further Reading
Harlen, Judith. 2000. *Mamphela Ramphele: Ending Apartheid in South Africa.* New York: Feminist Press.
Ramphele, Mamphela. 1991. *Bounds of Possibility: The Legacy of Steve Biko and Black Consciousness.* London: Zed Books.
———. 1993. *A Bed Called Home: Life in the Migrant Labour Hostels of Cape Town.* Cape Town: David Philip.
———. 1996. *Mamphela Ramphele: A Life.* Cape Town: David Philip.
———. 1997. *Across Boundaries: The Journey of a South African Woman Leader.* New York: Feminist Press.
Wilson, Francis. 1989. *Uprooting Poverty: The South African Challenge.* Report for the Second Carnegie Foundation Inquiry into Poverty and Development in Southern Africa. New York: W. W. Norton.

Ranade, Ramabai
(1862–1922)
India

An educator and reformer who called for the introduction of compulsory primary education for girls in India, Ramabai Ranade nevertheless remained a devout woman who lived an orthodox Hindu life. She was married at the age of ten to judge and social reformer Mahadev Govind Ranade, who was inspired by the work of Pandita Ramabai and had helped her set up her women's organization, Arya Mahila Samaj (the Aryan Women's Society). Ranade was educated by her husband at home and later met Pandita Ramabai through her husband in 1882. She became active in the Arya Mahila Samaj and ran meetings in her own home, where the society's members fostered the acquisition of domestic skills such as first aid and needlecraft and provided lessons in reading and writing for poor, illiterate women. In 1884 Ranade gave a speech in Poona attended by Sir James Ferguson, governor of Bombay, on the need for a girls' high school in the city. She also planned philanthropic work, organizing a women's relief committee to provide aid during times of famine or epidemic. In 1887 her reformer-husband founded the Indian National Social Conference to coordinate local social and relief work among the poor and underprivileged.

On the inauguration of the Bharata Mahila Parishad (Ladies' Social Conference) in 1905, Ranade, by that time a widow, gave a speech calling on women to join in volunteer work, such as educating orphans, inspecting schools for girls, and helping widows in financial distress find respectable employment. She founded the Seva Sadan (House of Service) in Bombay for the education of women, also offering training in domestic tasks. She set up a Seva Sadan Nursing and Medical Association, where she enlisted the help of high-caste widows and encouraged potential nurses to train at the Sasoon Hospital in Poona. Other good works in Poona encouraged by her included the care of women and child pilgrims at the annual pilgrimage to the temple at Alandi.

Throughout her widowhood, Ranade remained highly active: she founded an Industrial House of Service in Poona, helped with famine relief in 1919, and in 1917 was one of a group of Indian delegates to Secretary of State Lord Edwin Montagu who pressed for the introduction of primary and secondary education for girls. Ranade became one of the first Indian women to enter prisons to help female inmates, offering her services at the Yerowda prison as a female "chaplain," which included reading sacred scriptures to them. As a result of her efforts, other women in Bengal began undertaking prison visiting in 1911.

See also Ramabai, Pandita Saraswati.
References and Further Reading
Ranade, Ramabai. 1938 *The Autobiography of a Hindu Lady.* New York: Longmans.

Rankin, Jeanette
(1880–1973)
United States

Jeanette Rankin is famous for being the first woman elected to the U.S. Congress. She represented the state of Montana during two terms of office in 1917–1919 and 1941–1943, being elected to her first term before U.S. women won the vote at the federal level. Although her refusal to compromise on her pacifist beliefs cost her dearly in her political career, during her time in Congress, Rankin promoted labor reform affecting women and children and worked for improved health care. As an opponent of militarism, she lobbied on pacifist issues through two world wars and the Vietnam War.

Rankin was born on a ranch in Missoula, in the frontier state of Montana. She studied biology at the University of Montana until 1902 and, after spending several years helping to care for her six siblings after her father's death, eventually went to New York to study at the School of Philanthropy (1908–1909). She took up social work for the Children's Home Society in Spokane, Washington, but returned to her studies in 1910 at the University of Washington. Here she joined the campaign for women's suffrage before traveling back to Montana to lobby for state-level women's suffrage there through the Montana Equal Franchise Society. More suffrage work in New York, California, and Ohio followed, and in 1913 Rankin was appointed field secretary of the National American Woman Suffrage Association. She embarked on a two-year suffrage drive across fifteen U.S. states, finally opting to stand for election as a Republican candidate in Montana, when it gave women the state vote in November 1914. During her electoral campaign, which was geared to the female vote with its program of child welfare reform, pacifism, and Prohibition, Rankin rode on horseback across the state gathering support and in 1916 became the first woman in the United States to be elected to the House of Representatives.

Four days after Rankin took her seat on 2 April 1917, she was faced with a difficult personal decision, when Congress held a vote on U.S. entry into World War I. Many suffragists urged Rankin to do the patriotic thing and support the motion, but unable to go against her pacifist conscience, she joined a minority of forty-nine male con-

Jeanette Rankin (Library of Congress)

gressmen in voting against going to war. Her decision cost her all chances of being reelected in 1918, but during the short time she was in office Rankin worked for a federal amendment on women's suffrage and was instrumental in getting the first bill granting independent citizenship to married women through Congress. In addition, she sponsored government schemes on instruction in hygiene and health care for pregnant and nursing mothers under the proposed Robertson-Rankin bill, which became law as the Sheppard-Towner Maternity and Infancy Protection Act in 1921—the first piece of women's protective legislation to be passed by Congress after women won the vote.

After losing her seat in Congress, Rankin found a role for herself in the pacifist movement. In 1919 she joined leading feminist-pacifists Jane Addams and Florence Kelley in attending the second international congress of women in Zurich, which saw the foundation of the Women's International League for Peace and Freedom, of which Rankin later briefly became field secretary and a member of the board. Upon her return to the United States, Rankin spent the interwar period as a lobbyist and social reformer, for four years (1920–1924) serving as field secretary of Kelley's National Consumers' League, which urged those who bought manufactured goods to develop a greater sense of responsibility toward the labor—often that of underpaid women—that was exploited to produce them.

In 1928 Rankin moved to a farm she had bought in Georgia. There, having found it difficult to work within the international pacifist movement, she founded the Georgia Peace Society in 1928. From 1929 to 1939, she worked as a field organizer for the National Council for the Prevention of War before finding herself unable to continue because of differences with other members over her role and the council's policies. With another war breaking out in Europe, Rankin returned to Montana to campaign once again for election as an isolationist Republican on a pacifist ticket. She returned to Congress in 1941 but in December again found herself having to vote on U.S. entry into another world war, hot on the heels of the destruction of the U.S. fleet at Pearl Harbor. Despite widespread public support for what was seen, even by many self-proclaimed pacifists, as a "just" war, Rankin refused to support the vote. She was adamant that since she could not, as a woman, fight a war, she was not prepared to vote to send anyone else to do so either. This time, hers would be the sole vote cast in Congress against the declaration of war. In 1943 when she stood for reelection, Rankin again lost her seat. Realizing that a political career was impossible because of her pacifism, she returned to ranching in Montana and pursuing other social issues.

In the years after World War II, Rankin continued to support pacifism and nonviolence, having famously commented in 1947: "Small use it will be to save democracy for the race if we cannot save the race for democracy" (Josephson 1974). She studied the civil disobedience methods used by Mahatma Gandhi in India, visiting that country seven times during 1946–1971. During the 1950s, she lectured and gave interviews on women's rights, militarism, and disarmament (speaking out against the war in Korea) and criticized the U.S. government for its encroachments in the underdeveloped Third World.

The rise of a new women's movement in the late 1960s revived Rankin's militancy and feminism. She tried to set up a women's cooperative

homestead on a farm in Georgia, and in 1968, at the age of eighty-seven, she led a specially formed "Jeanette Rankin Brigade" of 5,000 radical women on a march on Capitol Hill against the war in Vietnam. Thus, Rankin lived to see a new generation of women take up her own lifelong fight for peace and women's equality. With the political climate in the United States changing, Rankin once again considered standing for Congress, but her hopes for a third term of office were destroyed by the onset of illness. The Jeanette Rankin Foundation commemorates the work of Rankin with its annual scholarships to women over the age of thirty-five seeking vocational training or further education to better facilitate their work in the community. Its website contains links to several sites about Rankin's life and work at http://www.wmst.unt.edu/jrf/.

See also Addams, Jane; Kelley, Florence.

References and Further Reading

Anderson, Kathryn. 1997. "Steps to Political Equality: Woman Suffrage and Electoral Politics in the Lives of Emily Newell Blair, Anne Henrietta Martin, and Jeanette Rankin." *Frontiers* 18(1): 107–121.

Giles, Kevin S. 1980. *Flight of the Dove: The Story of Jeanette Rankin.* Beaverton, OR: Touchstone Press.

Josephson, Hanna. 1974. *First Lady in Congress: Jeanette Rankin.* Indianapolis: Bobbs-Merrill.

Kaptur, Marcy. 1996. *Women of Congress: A Twentieth-Century Odyssey.* Washington, DC: Congressional Quarterly.

Kramer, Barbara. 2000. *Trailblazing Women: First in Their Fields.* Berkeley Heights, NJ: Enslow.

Schott, Linda K. 1997. *Reconstructing Women's Thoughts: The Women's International League for Peace and Freedom before World War II.* Stanford: Stanford University Press.

Ransome-Kuti, Fumilayo
(1900–1978)
Nigeria

Educator, nationalist, and founder of the Nigerian Women's Union, which opposed the abuses of British indirect rule, Ransome-Kuti was a keen supporter of the Yoruba language and culture and a pioneer in literacy projects among the market women of Egbaland. Born in Abeokuta, she attended an Anglican primary school and was one of the first girls to study at Abeokuta Grammar School. She taught at the school before obtaining a scholarship to study music and domestic science at Wincham Hall College in Manchester, England (1919–1922). She returned to serve as principal of the Abeokuta Girls' School (1923–1924) before marrying a leading educator and Anglican vicar, Israel Ransome-Kuti, in 1925.

From 1925 to 1932, Ransome-Kuti lived at Ijebu-Ode, where her husband ran the grammar school and she founded a nursery school. Returning to Abeokuta in 1932, Ransome-Kuti resumed teaching at the grammar school there. During the 1940s she became involved in numerous Christian and philanthropic activities, founding the Abeokuta Ladies' Club (ALC) in 1942 to enlist educated women to administer welfare and health care and help illiterate market women in Egbaland learn to read. In her literacy classes from 1944, she learned of the way in which market women were heavily and indiscriminately taxed by the local ruler (the *alake*) who administered the Sole Native Authority System. He was profiteering by commandeering these women's produce—mainly rice—without payment in order to fulfill supplies to the British colonial authorities during World War II.

Ransome-Kuti transformed the ALC into the Nigerian Women's Union (NWU) in 1946 to fight this abuse and petition for the *alake*'s business practices to be brought under control. A vigil by a large group of women led to demonstrations, and as a result the taxation was abolished in 1949 and the *alake* was deported. With an influx of native women into the union, it now became a major force for women's welfare, with branches of the NWU in 1948 offering maternity and children's clinics and running weaving cooperatives. The NWU also took on a broader range of campaigning for women's rights, sanitation, and the provision of clean water and adult education.

Ransome-Kuti's fame as a prominent leader of the anticolonial movement in Nigeria grew during the 1940s as she extended her role from local community leadership to advocacy of Nigerian political emancipation. She joined the National Council of Nigerian Citizens (NCNC) and in 1947 was the only female delegate advocating Nigerian independence who met with the British government in London. Ransome-Kuti also served as a member of the NCNC's National Executive, from which position she fought against chauvinism in Nigerian politics and for the extension of suffrage to women. Ransome-Kuti developed many international contacts with groups such as the Fabian Colonial Bureau and the Women's International Democratic Federation (WIDF), for which she wrote a report on the conditions of women in Nigeria in 1948. As a convinced pacifist, she also admired Mahatma Gandhi's nonviolent resistance to colonial rule in India. In 1952 she attended the Conference in Defense of Children and the World Congress of Women, both sponsored by the WIDF, of which she was elected vice president that year. In 1953 Ransome-Kuti set up a conference of women's organizations, which resulted in the establishment of the Federation of Nigerian Women's Societies with her as president.

Under the auspices of the WIDF, in 1956 Ransome-Kuti visited China, but because of her links with communists, the British authorities refused to allow her a passport to visit Eastern Europe. Although she was never a member of the Communist Party, Ransome-Kuti's admiration for communist achievements and her links with the Eastern bloc at times deterred other women's organizations from giving her their full support, and she was not able to visit the Eastern bloc until after Nigerian independence in 1960.

During her years of activism, Ransome-Kuti traveled in Nigeria and Ghana, raising women's consciousness and working for female suffrage and political representation. Her many humanitarian projects brought international awards, such as the Lenin Peace Prize in 1970, an honorary degree in law from Nigeria's University of Ibadan, and an honorary chieftaincy.

Ransome-Kuti's death came as the tragic culmination of years of unrest beginning in 1966, when Nigeria went through a series of military coups. In 1977, during a raid on her politically active son Fela's house by the military junta, Ransome-Kuti was thrown from an upstairs window. She lingered on for a year but eventually died of her injuries. During her life, she had worked for the human rights of all oppressed and exploited ethnic groups and in particular for the restoration of traditional economic power to Nigerian market women.

References and Further Reading
Johnson-Odim, Cheryl. 1997. *From Women and the Nation: Fumilayo Ransome-Kuti of Nigeria.* Urbana: University of Illinois Press.

Johnson-Odim, Cheryl, and Margaret Strobel. 1992. *Expanding the Boundaries of Women's History.* Bloomington: Indiana University Press.

Mba, Nina Emma. 1982. *Nigerian Women Mobilized: Women's Political Activity in Southern Nigeria, 1900–1965.* Berkeley: University of California Press.

Rathbone, Eleanor
(1872–1946)
United Kingdom

At a time when the United Kingdom was in economic depression and the women's movement in decline, the independent member of Parliament (MP) Eleanor Rathbone was one of a handful of interwar "new" feminists who sought innovative ways of addressing the particular economic needs of women and enhancing their self-determination. Her emphasis on protective measures favoring women as mothers brought her into conflict with egalitarian feminists who opposed all form of sexual discrimination, particularly legislation that defined women's sphere of activity as being within the home. Having started out as a social investigator in Liverpool's docklands, Rathbone began suggesting alternatives to the workhouse system twenty years or more before a Labour government introduced measures under the welfare state. A recognized expert in economic affairs and the family, she pioneered the concept of family allowances, arguing that women should be able, economically, to stay at home with their children. She also supported greater availability of methods of birth control and from the late 1920s committed herself to social reform in India and the campaign against child marriage.

One of ten children from two marriages, Rathbone was born into a family of Liverpool Quaker merchants with a long tradition of reform and philanthropy through several generations. Her father, the Liberal MP and social reformer William Rathbone, instilled in her from an early age a strong sense of social responsibility. A wealthy and influential figure in Liverpool, he had pioneered reform of nursing care in its workhouses in close collaboration with Florence Nightingale and Agnes Weston and was a supporter of women's suffrage.

Growing up in homes in Liverpool and London, Rathbone was mainly taught by governesses. After briefly attending Kensington High School, she resisted attempts by her domineering mother to advance her in society and propel her toward a good marriage and persuaded her parents to allow her to go to university. In 1893 she entered Somerville College, Oxford, to study classics (1893–1896), during her studies demonstrating a fine intellect that led fellow students to nickname her "the Philosopher."

Upon her return to Liverpool, her father provided Rathbone with the moral example and the financial security to take up social reform. Although he had eight sons, they all succeeded in disappointing William; it was Eleanor in whom he invested his philanthropic and political ambitions. She quickly followed her father's example, in 1897 taking up voluntary work for the Liverpool Central Relief Society (and remaining a member for fifteen years). Through the society and as secretary of the Liverpool Women's Industrial Council, she earned respect locally for her specialist knowledge of municipal services and inner-city social problems.

In 1900 Rathbone temporarily gave up her social work to spend eighteen months nursing her sick father. After his death in 1902, she spent two years preparing *William Rathbone: A Memoir* (1905), during which time she joined the Victoria Women's Settlement run by Elizabeth Macadam, where she became lifelong friends with the feminist preacher Maude Royden. In 1903 Rathbone conducted an inquiry into the cavalier treatment of casual laborers at the Liverpool docks and the economic plight of their families, and in 1909, she was the first woman elected to Liverpool City Council, serving it for twenty-five years, until 1934. In the years leading up to World War I, she continued investigating local social and economic conditions, including housing. Her study of unemployment among Liverpool dockers was published in 1909 as *How the Casual Labourer Lives,* and in 1913 she brought out her *Report on the Liverpool Women's Industrial Council Survey of Widows under the Poor Law.* Even during her later career in Parliament, Rathbone would retain close links with Liverpool, assisting in the establishment of the School of Social Service at Liverpool University, where she occasionally lectured on economics.

For many years, Rathbone had also been a constitutional suffragist. In 1898 she was appointed secretary of the Liverpool branch of the

National Society for Women's Suffrage, and in 1900 she became a member of the executive committee of its umbrella organization, the National Union of Women's Suffrage Societies (NUWSS). But in 1912 she opposed NUWSS leader Millicent Garrett Fawcett's decision to ally the party with the Independent Labour Party and establish an Election Fighting Fund in support of Labour candidates sympathetic to women's suffrage. Rathbone resigned but rejoined on the outbreak of World War I in 1914.

In 1913 Rathbone demonstrated considerable foresight in establishing the first Women's Citizen's Association in Liverpool, a move made in anticipation of women soon winning the vote. She envisaged the association as arousing the political interests of women and preparing them for civic responsibility; in particular, she hoped to enlighten working-class and other women from the younger generation who had not been involved in the suffrage campaign (which was put on hold as soon as war broke out).

During World War I, Rathbone initiated an important welfare scheme in Liverpool, the Soldiers' and Sailors' Families Association. The first tentative experiment in her later campaign for family allowances, it distributed service separation allowances, quantified according to the size of the family and paid to the wives of men at the front. The work also heightened Rathbone's awareness of the plight of families living on the poverty line. In the autumn of 1917, Rathbone set up the Family Endowment Committee, an informal group including Royden, Mary Stocks, and Kate Courtney, to work out a scheme for family endowment (as family allowances were then described). The results of their planning appeared in pamphlet form as "Equal Pay and the Family: A Proposal for the National Endowment of Motherhood."

Rathbone's position on family allowances would open up the gathering debate between equal rights feminists and those like herself who supported some form of state remuneration to mothers for the valuable role they played. "Equal Pay and the Family" was written in the belief that the majority of working women accepted the inevitability of receiving less pay than men and that family allowances would give women greater economic independence. Rathbone considered that the equal rights feminists were misguided in their continuing demand for unachievable levels of wage equality and that welfare benefits like those

she advocated would ease the pressure on married men to demand higher wages in order to support their families. Convinced of the benefits of small and regular payments made directly to wives and mothers rather than into their husbands' pay packets, which would put greater spending power in the hands of women, Rathbone believed that her plan would lead to a diminution in male wage demands and with it greater wage parity for both men and women in the workplace.

Rathbone's ultimate goal, and one that she single-mindedly pursued for thirty years, was that family allowances would not only enhance women's individual economic status but also improve the nutrition and health of their families. Soon, however, she came up against the vehement opposition of NUWSS leader and equal rights advocate Fawcett, when Rathbone started arguing her case in earnest after the war ended in 1918. Fawcett's opposition was born of her Victorian belief that welfare measures such as these took away parents' responsibility for their own children, and other feminists would object to Rathbone's proposals on family allowances as being antifeminist, designed to keep women in the home and uphold traditional patriarchal structures. Liberal economists saw potential dangers in such welfare provisions eroding the incentive to work by creating a catch-22, whereby the lower-paid would be better off if they did not work and lived on government benefits. Trade unionists also voiced their opposition, worrying that the basic wage would drop as a result.

In 1919, when Fawcett retired, Rathbone took over the presidency of the NUWSS, now reconstituted as the National Union of Societies for Equal Citizenship (NUSEC), and dedicated to the ongoing fight to achieve full suffrage for all adults over twenty-one. In 1922 she ran unsuccessfully for the Toxteth seat in Liverpool, eventually securing election to Parliament in 1929 as the (only) independent member of Parliament for the Combined English Universities and remaining in office until her death in 1946. Rathbone continued to pioneer welfare legislation, reiterating her theories in her highly influential 1924 work, *The Disinherited Family,* which she backed up with sound social research and statistics.

In 1925 Rathbone's annual presidential address to NUSEC provoked considerable debate between equal rights feminists and the "new feminists" such as herself, who were supporters of family allowances as a precondition to the equalization of pay. In 1926 NUSEC scored its first success when legislation was passed on widows' pensions, but splits in the union developed in 1927 over the introduction of policies on birth control and family allowances. When NUSEC officially endorsed Rathbone's welfare proposals in recognition of motherhood as a service to society, eleven members of the executive council left to join other single-issue organizations and pressure groups such as the Six Point Group and Open Door Council, both of which were opposed to protective legislation, and the Association for Moral and Social Hygiene, which campaigned against the white slave trade and for the protection of children. With others branching off into activism for the Labour Party and the trade union movement, the British women's movement in the 1920s and 1930s became increasingly polarized between socialist and middle-class old-school reformers.

In 1927 Rathbone's attention turned to reform in India, after she read with horror the exposés of child marriage practices there by U.S. journalist Katherine Mayo in her controversial—many said muckraking—book *Mother India.* Such was Rathbone's concern for the physical well-being of sexually immature girls forced into early motherhood and suffering inadequate health care in pregnancy and childbirth, that through NUSEC she circulated a questionnaire on the subject to women's groups in India. She later confirmed that this issue prompted her to once again stand for Parliament. She called a conference in London on Indian Social Evils that September, but Indian activists such as Dhanvanthi Rama Rau (who, living in London at the time, was able to attend) accused her of being intrusive in Indian affairs from a distance of 15,000 miles and thought she should leave this responsibility to Indian campaigners. This and other charges of patronizing, imperialist interference would dog Rathbone's well-intentioned preoccupation with Indian affairs. She continued to argue in Parliament and through the India Office for the age at marriage in India to be raised to fourteen, contributing to the passing of the Child Marriage Restraint Act (popularly known as the Sarda Act of 1929). In 1929 Rathbone raised the issue of women's suffrage in India and was again criticized for her unwanted patronage, with Indian campaigners once more understandably resentful of her desire to domi-

nate their own political campaigns. After visiting India in 1932 to investigate the effectiveness of the Sarda Act in preventing child marriage, Rathbone also met with Indian women activists in major cities in order to promote women's suffrage there. In 1933 she founded the British Committee for Indian Women's Franchise to lobby for an improvement in the ratio of male to female voters from the government-recommended 1:20 to 1:5.

Rathbone's 1934 book, *Child Marriage, the Indian Minotaur: An Object Lesson from the Past to the Future,* attempted a more balanced account than Mayo's hysterical condemnation of Hindu traditions by also describing similar cases of child marriage among Muslims and blaming the British colonial authorities for failing to confront the issue for so long. She suggested the foundation of an All-India Society for the Abolition of Child Marriage, appointed by that year's All-India Women's Conference. As an advocate of constitutional government in India (but not independence), Rathbone served on several committees during 1927–1935 that contributed to the passing of the Government of India Act of 1935. But by this time, other colonial issues were also preoccupying her: female genital mutilation in Africa caused her grave concern, and in 1929 she joined the Committee for the Protection of Coloured Women in the Colonies, which set out to combat the practice. During the 1930s she would speak out also on the white slave trade in Africa and forced marriage in Arab communities in Palestine, as well as advocating better education and vocational training facilities for women in Britain's African colonies.

Throughout the 1930s, Rathbone spread her sympathies and her activism widely: as an antifascist she denounced Benito Mussolini's invasion of Ethiopia (then Abyssinia), publishing *The Tragedy of Abyssinia: What Britain Feels and Thinks and Wants* (1936). She supported the Republicans in Spain and called for intervention during the Spanish Civil War, visiting the country with Royden in 1936, founding the Basque Children's Committee, and acting as chair of the National Joint Committee for Spanish Relief. She naturally opposed appeasement with Adolf Hitler and, as a member of the executive committee of the League of Nations Union, advocated collective security and a cultural and economic boycott of Germany, in 1937 arguing her case in *War Can Be Averted: The Achievability of Collective Security*. That same year, she toured eastern Europe, drawing attention to the dangers of German incursions and, despite the widespread mistrust of communism, calling for a military alliance with the Soviet Union.

After World War II broke out in 1939, Rathbone came to the defense of noncitizens (mainly German Jewish refugees) in Britain interned on the Isle of Man; throughout 1939–1945, she worked tirelessly for refugees as a founder of the Parliamentary Committee on Refugees and the National Committee for Rescue from Nazi Terror. When disgruntled rumblings were heard in Britain against the numbers of Jewish refugees entering the country, she challenged anti-Semitism in her 1944 book, *Falsehoods and Facts about the Jews*. After the war, she protested British controls over Jewish immigration to Palestine and became a passionate supporter of the Zionist cause.

Having become involved in the postwar refugee problem, Rathbone continued to draw attention to the crisis of Europe's displaced and starving peoples, especially in Germany and Poland, through her work for Save Europe Now and the United Nations Relief and Rehabilitation Agency. She lobbied hard for the British in Palestine to increase the quotas of Jewish refugees allowed to immigrate. At the end of the war, she accurately predicted further refugee problems with the creation of the Soviet bloc. But her work was cut short when she died suddenly of a heart attack.

In 1940 Rathbone had published *The Case for Family Allowances*. It had a direct influence on Ernest Beveridge's 1942 report on welfare legislation, which would be the cornerstone of the welfare state finally inaugurated by a Labour government in 1946. She lived just long enough to witness the passage of the 1945 Family Allowances Act, when she was precipitated into a successful, last-minute protest when the wording of the legislation proposed paying the money to fathers.

From charity work through the pursuit of the many and wide-ranging causes she embraced, Rathbone epitomized the best in welfare feminism during the interwar years, whatever the merits or demerits of her principles, based as they were on a traditional view of motherhood. Oblivious to her considerable wealth, she lived and dressed modestly; although forceful, if not domineering, in her public life, she was reticent on sexual matters and her own private life, which she spent for more than forty years in the companionship of Elizabeth Macadam at her house in London (until they were bombed out in 1940 during the Blitz). In her career in Parliament, she remained fiercely independent of party affiliations; in her perseverance, compassion, and overwhelming Christian sense of social duty, she was one of the last to be cast in the mold of the Victorian tradition of reform.

See also Courtney, Kathleen D'Olier; Fawcett, Millicent Garrett; Nightingale, Florence; Rau, Dhanvanthi Rama; Royden, Maude.

References and Further Reading
Alberti, Johanna. 1989. *Beyond Suffrage: Feminists in War and Peace, 1914–1928*. London: Macmillan.
———. 1996. *Eleanor Rathbone*. London: Sage Publications.
Brookes, Pamela. 1967. *Women at Westminster: An Account of Women in the British Parliament 1918–1966*. London: Peter Davies.
Chaudhuri, Nupur, and Margaret Strobel, eds. 1992. *Western Women and Imperialism: Complicity and Resistance*. Bloomington: Indiana University Press.
Field, Frank. 1996. "Portrait of a Great MP." *Financial Times*, 21 September.
Fleming, Susie, ed. 1986. *Eleanor Rathbone: Spokeswoman for a Movement*. Bristol: Falling Wall Press.
Hollis, Patricia, ed. 1987. *Ladies Elect: Women in English Local Government 1865–1914*. Oxford: Clarendon Press.
Holton, Sandra Stanley. 1986. *Feminism and Democracy: Women's Suffrage and Reform Politics in Britain, 1900–1918*. Cambridge: Cambridge University Press.
Jayawardena, Kumari. 1995. *The White Woman's Other Burden: Western Women and South Asia during British Rule*. London: Routledge.
Macnicol, John. 1980. *The Movement for Family Allowances 1918–1945*. London: Heinemann.
Oldfield, Sybil. 1997. "Eleanor Rathbone and India: Cultural Imperialist or Friend to Women?" *Asian Journal of Women's Studies* 3(3): 157–168.
———. 2001. *Women Humanitarians: A Biographical Dictionary of British Women Active between 1900 and 1950*. London: Continuum.
Pedersen, Susan. 1993. *Family, Dependence, and the Origins of the Welfare State: Britain and France, 1914–1945*. Cambridge: Cambridge University Press.
———. 1996. "Rathbone and Daughter: Feminism and the Father in the Fin-de-Siècle." *Journal of*

Victorian Culture 1(1): 98–117. (Pedersen is currently preparing a biography of Rathbone.)

Pujol, M. A. 1992. *Feminism and Anti-Feminism in Early Economic Thought*. Aldershot: Edward Elgar.

Purvis, June, and Sandra Stanley Holton, eds. 2000. *Votes for Women*. London and New York: Routledge.

Ramusack, Barbara N. 1981. "Catalysts or Helpers? British Feminists, Indian Women's Rights, and Indian Independence." In Gail Minault, ed., *The Extended Family: Women and Political Participation in India and Pakistan*. Delhi: Chanakya Publications.

Rathbone, Eleanor. 1924. *The Disinherited Family*. London: Edward Arnold.

———. 1949. *Family Allowances* (with an epilogue and new chapter on the family allowances movement of 1924–1947 by Eva Hubback). London: Allen and Unwin.

Smith, Harold L., ed. 1990. *British Feminism in the Twentieth Century*. Aldershot: Edward Elgar.

Stocks, Mary. 1949. *Eleanor Rathbone: A Biography*. London: Gollancz.

Rau, Dhanvanthi Rama
(1893–1987)
India

The Indian family planning campaigner Dhanvanthi Rama Rau was one of the prime movers for reform of the Hindu laws on marriage, divorce, and inheritance affecting women. Inspired by the American birth control campaigner Margaret Sanger, Rau's work made available to women for the first time a whole network of family planning and health clinics across India.

Rau was born in a village in southwestern India where her father worked as a civil servant on the railways. Both her parents were supporters of women's rights and allowed her to be educated at school and college in Madras, where she studied English as one of only eleven female students out of 700. There she found herself treated as a social outcast and came under considerable criticism for daring to insult her caste by studying outside the home, but she faced out her critics, taking an interest in the feminist campaigning of Margaret Cousins and Sarojini Naidu. In 1917, after graduating from Queen Mary's College in Madras with an M.A., she accepted a post as assistant professor of English at that institution, again with parental support (although her father had taken a great deal of persuading). Over the next couple of years, Rau developed a reputation as a leading female academic.

In 1919 Rau got married in a civil ceremony and out of her caste, raising much criticism among her Kashmiri community at home. Her husband, Benegal Narsing Rau, was later knighted as one of the outstanding Indian jurists of his generation. After the birth of her daughters, she devoted herself to social work and to raising people's consciousness about the need for reform—both legal and social—and in particular the development of higher standards of women's education that would prepare them for more responsible roles in society. As a member of the All-India Women's Conference (AIWC), she was particularly involved in the All-India Anti–Child Marriage Abolition League, which came together in 1927 to support the passage of the Sarda Act in 1929. For long a major objective of Indian reformers, the act raised the legal age of marriage for girls to fourteen. It became law in 1930 as the Child Marriage Restraint Act.

In 1927 Rau was in England when a furor broke out over U.S. journalist Katherine Mayo's controversial book *Mother India*, which outlined in gruesome detail the sufferings of child brides during pregnancy and childbirth. It also catalogued their treatment by brutal and untrained dais (Indian midwives) and castigated Hinduism for its backward attitude toward women's welfare and other issues. The English reformer Eleanor Rathbone called a Conference on Indian Social Evils, which was attended by leading suffragists such as Sylvia Pankhurst and Emmeline Pethick-Lawrence. Rau was deeply disturbed by this attack on her native culture and protested Mayo's slander of India and Indian tradition. She was particularly incensed by the condemnation that poured forth from the mouths of critics such as Rathbone, who at that time had never even visited India, and argued that British reformers should offer moral support but leave the work of Indian reform to the Indians. She disseminated her views in a series of talks on India and Indian life in which she attempted to dispel some of the exaggerations of Mayo's book and temper them with enlightened discussion on Indian life and tradition—all of which enlisted many sympathizers and redressed some of the balance.

Her husband's diplomatic post brought Rau to England in 1929, providing her with easy access to feminists, suffragists, and other campaigners. She represented India when the annual congress of the AIWC was held in London in 1936. After meeting Margaret Sanger, Rau was won over to the importance of the growing birth control campaign in the Third World and also became a member of the International Alliance of Women for Suffrage and Equal Citizenship (1932–1938). After nine years in Britain, Rau returned to India and, with the help of two British supporters, Dr. Helena Wright and Mrs. Seligman, took up a major campaign to spread the word on birth control, offering free advice and contraceptives to women in rural areas.

When famine broke out in Bijapur in 1943, Rau diverted her work to famine relief in her capacity as president of the Bombay Women's Committee. By then she was also heavily committed to the work of the AIWC, first as its vice president (1939–1946) and then as president (1946–1947). As president, she traveled all over India, inspecting schools, maternity centers, and child care and literacy projects. This most influential pressure group on women's issues and social reform in India served as a forum for the campaigning skills of many influential Indian women reformers. After the partition of India in 1947, Rau turned to work for the National Council of Child Welfare (NCCW), which dealt with the problems of child refugees from Pakistan as well as inspecting slums and treating sick children.

By the end of World War II, Rau again left India to follow her diplomat husband to Washington, D.C., where he was Indian ambassador. Her study of the work of the United Nations on the issue of overpopulation, combined with her own observations while working for the NCCW in India, convinced her of the international importance of birth control. As a member of the Advisory Panel on Health to the National Planning Commission after the war, Rau enlisted many volunteers and raised funds to hire medical experts and social workers in the war against overpopulation. As a result, in 1949 she founded the All-India Family Planning Association (AIFPA), which opened its first Family Welfare Centre in Bombay.

During her long presidency of the AIFPA, Rau fought a protracted campaign to raise the standards of child welfare and nutrition. In 1951 she organized its first conference, attended by 110 delegates, where she asserted that the low levels of Indian life expectancy would not improve without birth control. Margaret Sanger, who was deeply impressed with Rau's work, asked her in 1952 to organize an international conference on family planning in India, which welcomed many delegates from Asian countries. At the end of the conference, Sanger and Rau were nominated as copresidents of the International Planned Parenthood Federation, which came into being in 1953.

By this time, such was Rau's influential position that the Indian government accepted family planning as an integral part of its first five-year plan. Rau was appointed to the Family Planning and Research Committee of the Ministry of Health, from where she established family planning clinics, advocated the proper training of personnel, and traveled all over India spreading the word. As president of the AIFPA, she organized further high-profile conferences in India. She invited representatives from other welfare agencies to view the organization's work, took the activities of the AIFPA into the regions, and set up educational programs on birth control—all of which led to the formation of many local branches of the AIFPA. She also served on the Moral and Social Hygiene Committee, which was looking into prostitution and the running of brothels, and spent time talking to the women who worked in them and studying their living conditions. She discovered many were forced into prostitution in the cities to help support their families in rural areas, and she wrote to the government about their plight, highlighting also the frequent abuse of prostitutes in local refuges.

During her campaigning years, Rau served on numerous welfare, family planning, and social reform committees and received many awards in recognition of her services to family planning, including the Padma Bhushan Award (1959), the Watumal Foundation Distinguished Service Award (1967), and the Society of Man's Award for Peace. One of her last undertakings in 1963 was to take on the presidency of the International Planned Parenthood Federation, which she held until her retirement in 1967.

In 1977 Rama Rau published her memoirs, titled *An Inheritance,* in which she gave a fascinating account of the home life and social customs experienced by girls of her caste and the suffering caused by early marriage. Her observation of these things had led to her confirmed belief in the need for reform of women's traditional role in Indian society and brought about her own crucial role in the transformation of the lives of so many ordinary Indian women.

See also Cousins, Margaret; Naidu, Sarojini; Pankhurst, (Estelle) Sylvia; Pethick-Lawrence, Emmeline; Rathbone, Eleanor; Sanger, Margaret.

References and Further Reading

Evans, Barbara. 1984. *Freedom to Choose: The Life and Work of Dr. Helena Wright, Pioneer of Contraception.* London: Bodley Head.
Harish, Ranjana. 1993. *Indian Women's Autobiographies.* New Delhi: Arnold.
Rau, Dhanvanthi Rama. 1977. *An Inheritance: The Memoirs of Dhanvanthi Rama Rau.* London: Heinemann.

Rawson de Dellepiane, Elvira
(1867–1954)
Argentina

Doctor, suffragist, educationist, and cofounder of the Manuela Gorritti Center and the Argentine Association for the Rights of Woman, Elvira Rawson de Dellepiane campaigned for a radical overhaul of the patriarchal system that for centuries had denied Argentine women a stake in political life and social welfare. She sought an improvement in conditions for all workers, for women's health care and hygiene, and for the rights and physical well-being of children.

Rawson was the granddaughter of an immigrant from North America. She grew up in Junín and was educated at the normal school in Mendoza until 1884. She went on to study at the University of Buenos Aires, but after being barred from taking up the law, she studied medicine, becoming one of the first Argentine women to qualify, in 1892. During her studies, in 1890 she had been involved in a popular protest led by the Civic Radical Union against government involvement in electoral fraud. She married a radical lawyer and politician, Manuel Dellepiane, who was sympathetic to women's rights. Despite having seven children, during the 1890s she found time to develop her interests in women's health issues.

Early in her career, Rawson began making a close study of female sexuality and the various health problems women faced: during puberty, as the result of early marriage, during pregnancy,

and after childbirth. In 1892 she published her doctoral thesis, entitled "Notes on Woman's Hygiene," in which she emphasized the importance of personal hygiene in marriage and motherhood and outlined her belief that tight corsets and restrictive dress were detrimental to women's health, as was lack of exercise. Although her attempt to raise such issues was daring at the time, Rawson tended to simplify the solutions to such problems, seeing them as being dependent to a great extent on changes in individual behavior and the voluntary adoption of strict moral codes and sexual restraint. She did, however, defend women's right to choose to work as prostitutes rather than endure the arduous working conditions of factories and sweatshops.

In 1902 Rawson helped found the Argentine Association of University Women; in 1905 she became a member of the Argentine National Council of Women and organized a women's group for the discussion of social and political reform—the Feminist Center. The center lent its support to the Argentine Association of Free Thought, founded in 1905, an intellectual society that debated social issues and was a pressure group for women's civil and political equality with men. The center also adopted an ambitious program of its own for the emancipation of women from their subordinate role in society, by calling for reform of the civil code to give women a role in government, education, and the judiciary. It claimed maternity rights for women, supported their right to equal pay in the workplace, and demanded that women have equal political rights with men. It was, however, hampered in its enlistment of widespread support because its title, "Feminist," discouraged more moderate women from joining. A name change three months later to the Manuela Gorritti Center (named after a popular Argentine feminist writer) transformed the situation, and over the next thirteen years the center became a much-valued meeting place and forum for women. In 1910 Rawson, who was concerned for the welfare of single mothers, also gave Gorritti's name to a refuge for unmarried mothers that she established.

In 1910 Rawson helped plan the First International Feminist Congress in Argentina, held in Buenos Aires, at which she urged a major revision of Argentina's civil code to improve the status of women, not only in political terms but also within the family. She proposed that women should have full adult status and that married women should have the same control over their property and earnings as their husbands. In cases of divorce, women should be allowed custody of their children (unless there was good, moral reason for this not being granted). The congress also discussed improvements in the standards of working conditions and hours for both men and women and called for government legislation to protect child workers. Rawson's campaigning in this respect eventually led to a 1924 change in the law that restricted working hours and laid down a minimum age and basic safety requirements.

Although a member of her husband's Radical Party (which had no official program in support of women's rights despite her husband's support), Rawson managed to retain an evenhanded approach to the various women's groups that proliferated in Argentina in the 1900s. She often acted as a conciliator between the conservative and generally upper-class wing of the women's movement and those on the more liberal left, particularly in terms of avoiding conflict between feminists who were Catholics and those who sought to challenge the established church.

Over the next few years, Rawson was instrumental in setting up several organizations: in 1913 she took part in the Argentine National Congress of the Child and set up health care for children at a kindergarten in the neighborhood of La Boca, where she showed the mothers better standards of hygiene in child care; in 1919 she founded the Association for the Rights of Woman to fight for the legal enactment of political and civil rights; and in 1920 she was behind the founding of a Women's Committee on Social Hygiene and organized a series of lectures on morality. She was in Santiago in 1924 to represent Argentina at the fourth Pan-American Congress on the Child. In 1928 at the Third International Feminist Congress in Buenos Aires, Rawson, as president, gave a keynote address on women's suffrage and supported the campaign that monitored the debate on suffrage in the Argentine Senate, only to see the bill shelved in 1932.

Although Rawson supported changes in divorce laws, she had reservations about how such changes might affect the welfare of children of divorced parents and the rights of women, who, although allowed legally to divorce, were not provided with protection of their economic rights under the law. She also reserved her judgment on the militant element in the women's suffrage movement. Although she admired the work of women such as the Pankhursts and the American Carrie Chapman Catt, she felt that extremism in women's political activism was divisive. For Rawson, it was also more important that women should achieve civil rights before being granted suffrage.

Throughout her life, Rawson maintained her commitment to health care. From 1907 to 1918, she served as a school medical inspector for the National Department of Hygiene; she also served in this capacity from 1919 to 1934 for the National Council of Education. In 1916 she set up and administered at Upsallata near her home in Mendoza the first rest home for women teachers and students who were chronically sick, and in 1920–1922 she was a specialist in hygiene and child care at the National Home for Military Orphans, which was attached to one of the national girls' high schools.

See also Abella de Ramírez, María; Grierson, Cecilia; Lanteri-Renshaw, Julia; Laperrière de Coni, Gabriela.

References and Further Reading

Carlson, Narifran. 1988. *Feminismo! The Woman's Movement in Argentina from Its Beginnings to Eva Perón.* Chicago: Academy Chicago Publications.
Lavrin, Asunción. 1995. *Women, Feminism, and Social Change in Argentina, Chile, and Uruguay 1890–1940.* Lincoln: University of Nebraska Press.
Tenenbaum, Barbara A., ed. 1996. *Encyclopedia of Latin American History and Culture.* Vol 2. New York: Charles Scribner's Sons.

Reddi, Muthulakshmi
(1886–1968)
India

Muthulakshmi Reddi scored two notable landmarks in the history of the women's movement in India: she was the first Indian woman to earn a medical degree in India, from Madras University in 1912, and she was also the first Indian woman to serve on a government body, as a member of the Madras State Legislative Council in 1927. A friend and close associate of the respected feminist and reformer Sarojini Naidu, Reddi was in the vanguard of campaigning that brought an improvement in women's rights in

India when she, Naidu, and Annie Besant founded the Women's Indian Association (WIA) in 1917.

Reddi came from a middle-class Brahman family in the state of Pudukottah. Her mother was from the Isai Velala caste, which traditionally served the fine arts by providing music and dance at temples, a fact that led to Reddi's later campaign on behalf of *devadasis* (temple girls) and, more generally, the immoral traffic in women and children.

As a small girl, Reddi attended a boys' school in the face of considerable opposition from the parents of many of its pupils, eventually being one of the ten students who was graduated in 1902 out of a total of 100. Because education for most Indian girls ceased at the age of ten, Reddi continued her education at home. Her father then had to petition the maharajah for her to be allowed to study at the all-boy Maharaja's College at Pudukottah. When she decided to go on to medical school in Madras in 1907, she faced an unrelenting wall of prejudice, first from her mother who wished her to marry. She obtained her medical degree in 1912, the first woman in India to do so, taking up a post at the Government Hospital for Women and Children in Madras. Reddi also agreed, finally and reluctantly (because she felt it would interfere with her medical career), to get married at the age of twenty-eight in a civil ceremony.

At first Reddi limited her campaigning to women's and social issues, feeling that women could be most effective in those areas rather than in party politics. But in 1926 she was persuaded by the WIA to accept nomination as the first female member of the Madras State Legislative Council (1927–1930), later becoming its deputy speaker. Having taken her seat, she promptly called for legislation on health care, such as the construction of children's hospitals, the recruitment of women doctors and nurses, and the institution of compulsory health checks for girls in schools. Her interest in medicine and the welfare of women and children in particular would lead her to set up the first children's hospital in India (1927); the Avvai Home for Orphans in Madras (1930) and the Avvai Rural Medical Service (1943), which offered medical care to poor women and children; and the first cancer research hospital (1952), with its own laboratory and clinic, in Adyar in Madras. She also served as

secretary of the Madras Children's Aid Society in 1924–1926.

At the All-India Women's Conference (AIWC) in 1926, Reddi promoted the Sarda Act (which eventually became law as the Child Marriage Restraint Act in 1930). Reddi and her campaigners had tried to get the Madras state legislature to accept a minimum marriage age of sixteen for girls and twenty-four for boys. In 1928 she was a member of the Joshi Committee (along with other leading campaigners such as Pandita Ramabai and Rukhmabai), which reported to the Madras State Legislative Council on raising the age of consent. In support of her argument, she revealed that almost one-quarter of all married women were widows, many of them child-widows who had been married off to much older men. In the event, the 1930 act forbade child marriages of girls under fourteen and of boys under sixteen, and despite its being inadequate in the eyes of many feminists, it was a groundbreaking piece of legislation, the first act of law passed as a direct result of the work of Indian women's pressure groups such as the AIWC. The 1931 census would later reveal that 3 million girls and 2 million boys had been rushed into premature marriage in the six months before the new age restrictions of the law came into force. The census also concluded that 100 out of every 1,000 of these girl brides would die in childbirth.

Child marriage was but one of many issues the AIWC raised at this time regarding the rights of children, women's education, and suffrage. With AIWC support, Reddi also tried to push through the *devadasi* bill to prohibit the practice of underage girls being dedicated to temples as prostitutes. This latter campaign took a year to be introduced into the legislature because of the enormous opposition from traditionalists. They argued that the *devadasi* caste must be preserved to maintain the Indian fine arts. Although there was partial enactment of the bill in 1929, the bulk of it would not become law until 1947, resulting in a total of eighteen years of campaigning on Reddi's part at a time when she was no longer a member of government. Reddi would always take a strong moral line both on the issue of prostitution and on the introduction of birth control methods, which she saw as encouraging promiscuity. She also set up refuges for women rescued from brothels or who had suffered mistreatment at the hands of the police.

Reddi also raised the subject of women's education in the legislature. In 1928 Reddi agreed to become a member of the Hartog Committee, which was set up to look into the current state of education in India. A year later, she asked the government to urgently address the backwardness of the current educational system for women, particularly at the primary and secondary levels. She called for the creation of local committees of women to monitor girls' education in rural areas and for the government to provide funding to develop educational facilities for girls. She urged the training of women teachers for the most crucial kindergarten level and advocated the establishment of an Indian university for women.

Reddi resigned from the legislative council in 1930 in protest at the arrest of Mahatma Gandhi and joined her friend Sarojini Naidu in the nationalist movement, realizing that further social change would not come without a commitment to the broader issue of Indian independence. She took on the editorship of the journal *Stri Dharma* (1931–1940) as a forum for the grievances against British governance of India and supported temperance and movements to promote greater tolerance of untouchables. She campaigned against the seclusion of women in purdah, considering it a slight on female integrity that women could not be trusted to be responsible for their own chastity and loyalty. In 1931 she was elected president of the AIWC and in 1933 served as president of an All-Asia Women's Conference in Lahore.

In 1932 Reddi accompanied Sarojini Naidu to London to give evidence before the Joint Parliamentary Committee on Indian women's rights (which was part of the Second Roundtable Conference on Indian constitutional reform), calling for full citizenship and the franchise for all women. But she later came to realize that obtaining the vote for all Indian women would not necessarily serve the cause of women best. Realizing that such legislation would not happen in India in a hurry, and if it did, it would extend the vote to many women in the thrall of more conservative, reactionary husbands, she accepted that a few enlightened and well-chosen women in government could be more effective.

Like many of her contemporaries in the reform movement in India, Reddi suffered much antagonism in her fight against traditional cultural and religious prejudices, which looked upon her kind of reformers as being "home-breakers who were trying to bring woman unnecessarily out of her beautiful cocoon" (Lakshmi 1984, 14).

See also Besant, Annie; Cousins, Margaret; Naidu, Sarojini; Ramabai, Pandita Saraswati; Rukhmabai.

References and Further Reading
Basu, Aparna. 1986. *The Pathfinder: Dr. Muthulakshmi Reddi.* Pune: All-India Women's Conference.
Lakshmi, C. S. 1984. *The Face behind the Mask: Women in Tamil Literature.* New Delhi: Vikas Publishing House.
Reddi, Muthulakshmi. 1964. *Autobiography of Mrs. S. Muthulakshmi.* Madras: n.p.

Richard, Marthe
(1889–1982)
France

Marthe Richard's early life seemed an unlikely background for a social reformer: she was a secret agent during World War I and a heroine of the French Resistance during World War II. But in the postwar years, as a member of the Paris Municipal Council, she led an important campaign to close down the licensed brothels of Paris.

Born in a village in Alsace-Lorraine (then German-occupied eastern France), Richard had a troubled early life. She ran away from reform school at the age of seventeen and was one of the first Frenchwomen to learn to parachute. She obtained a pilot's license in 1912. Her first husband, Henri Richer, was killed during World War I at the battle of Verdun in 1916. Afterward, being a good driver and a good shot, as well as speaking several languages, Richard was recruited as a secret agent and sent undercover to San Sebastián in Spain. There she worked as a double agent, luring the German naval attaché, Baron von Krohn, into a sexual relationship, extracting information on the movements of German submarines, and spying on the German military presence in Spain. After the war Richard was awarded the Legion of Honor; she also published an account of her adventures in *I Spied for France,* which was later turned into a film.

Richard married for the second time to an Englishman (Thomas Crompton), but on his death just before World War II, she returned to France to work for the Resistance, helping to run an underground railroad for allied airmen who had crashed in France. At war's end Richard, now married for a third time, was elected a city councilor in Paris. She straightaway launched a vigorous cleanup campaign of Paris's 178 licensed brothels, in particular raising the issue of the exploitation of young girls by brothel keepers, who encouraged them to enter the trade on promises of far more money than they could earn by legitimate means. Richard saw much of the problem as stemming from the unequal pay offered to women in industry and set out proposals for vocational training for reformed prostitutes.

Richard succeeded in closing down Paris's licensed brothels in 1945 and elsewhere in France a year later. In 1946 the "Richard Law" was passed, making all prostitution illegal. Unfortunately, as other similar campaigns have proved, this measure did not solve the problem but only forced prostitutes to ply their trade in the back streets. In an attempt to counter this result, Richard suggested in 1952 that the government sponsor designated apartments for the use of prostitutes, so that they would not fall back under the control of brothel keepers. But by 1970, with around 35,000 prostitutes operating in Paris, she was forced to reluctantly agree that strictly controlled legal prostitution was a better option, after it had become clear that the problem persisted. In 1973 at the age of eighty-four, Richard supported a plan for the establishment of "Eros centers" for licensed prostitutes along the lines of those introduced in Germany.

References and Further Reading
Annual Obituary 1982. New York: St. Martin's Press.
Ladoux, Georges. 1932. *Marthe Richard, the Skylark: The Foremost Woman Spy of France.* London: Cassell.
Richard, Marthe. 1935. *I Spied for France: My Last Secret Missions 1936–9.* Translated by Gerald Griffin. London: J. Long.

Robins, Elizabeth
(1862–1952)
United States/United Kingdom

The American-born novelist and suffragist Elizabeth Robins was one of the great beauties of her day. She became an eloquent and dignified voice in the women's suffrage movement in the United Kingdom after having pursued a successful career on the stage as a pioneer interpreter of the strong-minded women of Henrik Ibsen's innovative plays.

Born in Louisville, Kentucky, Robins was the daughter of a banker from an old slave-owning family from the South. She spent her childhood in Staten Island, New York; after her mother was hospitalized with mental illness, she lived with her grandmother at Zanesville, Ohio, where she completed her schooling at the Putnam Female Seminary. Her father would have liked her to study medicine, but after entering Vassar College to do so at the age of eighteen, Robins quickly abandoned the idea to become an actress. After touring with several theatrical companies, she joined the Boston Museum Stock Company in 1883. In 1885 she married the actor George Parks, but plagued by financial problems and his own lack of artistic success, he committed suicide by drowning two years later. Robins rejected all subsequent marriage proposals, choosing to spend the rest of her life in the company of her network of loyal female friends, notably Dr. Octavia Wilberforce. But in her lifetime she would have many notable admirers, including Henry James, John Masefield, George Bernard Shaw, and Oscar Wilde.

After visiting Norway, Robins settled in London in 1889. A meeting that Oscar Wilde arranged for her with the actor-manager Herbert Beerbohm Tree ensured her acceptance in the British theatrical world. She became consumed by the work of Ibsen after seeing Janet Achurch in *The Doll's House,* and Robins performed her first Ibsen role in *Pillars of Society* (1889). Eschewing the stereotypical roles then available to actresses, Robins embraced the challenges of Ibsen, spending the best part of the years 1891–1897 acting in and producing his plays. As Mrs. Linde in *The Doll's House* (1891), she was a considerable success, and the play ran for five weeks. Further acclaim came with Robins's portrayal of the eponymous heroine of *Hedda Gabler* (also 1891). Robins learned Norwegian and persuaded Ibsen to give her the rights to translate *The Master Builder,* with Robins playing the lead, Hilda Wangel, in her own production in 1893, during an Ibsen Repertory Series in which she also played other Ibsen heroines, Rebecca West and Agnes Brand.

Robins's feminism was reflected in her willingness to fund and set up many of her own productions, as an actress-manager at the New Century Theatre, founded in 1898. There she attempted to provide better roles for women than the usual fodder, as well as making a clear statement against the monopoly of male theatrical management in London's theater community, but she lost much of her own money in the process. Eventually, Robins found she could earn more by turning her hand to writing, which she did increasingly from the 1890s, when she began publishing novels with a feminist content under the pseudonym C. E. Raimond. Her first, and one of the most notable of her fifteen novels, was *George Mandeville's Husband* (1894), which satirized bluestockings and contained a veiled portrait of writer George Eliot.

In 1898 Robins took a production of *Hedda Gabler* to the United States. In 1900 she made a perilous trip to the Klondike during Alaska's gold rush. While searching for her brother Raymond, who had disappeared there, she contracted typhoid and nearly died, but she gained experiences used later in journal articles, her best-selling 1904 novel, *The Magnetic North,* and *Come and Find Me* (1908). Robins's Alaskan diary was finally published in 1999.

The year 1902 marked Robins's last stage appearance. After playing in an adaptation of Mrs. Humphry Ward's *Eleanor,* she gave up acting to write and pursue journalism. Although she had always been fervent in her feminism, she had not joined any women's suffrage groups. In November 1905 she finally became a convert to the suffrage cause and began writing vignettes about women's enfranchisement that were staged at suffrage rallies and meetings in the United Kingdom and the United States. For a while, she remained sympathetic to both the constitutional and the militant wings of the suffrage movement but by 1906 finally rejected the constitutional National Union of Women's Suffrage Societies and joined the militants of the Women's Social and Political Union (WSPU), which, given her public profile, welcomed her with enthusiasm as an important catch. Robins joined the WSPU's Central Committee, but despite being an actress was reticent about public speaking on behalf of the cause. Eventually she did relent and became one of its most sought-after speakers, admired for her beauty and charisma and responsible for persuading many other women to join the cause. But although she was unqualified in her defense

of militancy, as an American, she was scrupulous never to involve herself in acts of WSPU violence that might result in arrest and imprisonment and with it, her deportation.

Robins's 1906 suffrage play *Votes for Women!* was successfully staged at the (now Royal) Court Theatre in London in April 1907 and became the basis for one of the first and best-remembered "suffrage novels," *The Convert* (1907). The novel was a serious attempt by Robins to counter the hostile press representation of suffragettes in Britain until that time and explain the true nature of women's commitment to the cause, born of their long exploitation by men. Written in documentary style, it was based on her own observations of WSPU figures such as Christabel Pankhurst and Teresa Billington-Greig and drew also on accounts of activism by mill girl Hannah Mitchell in order to present a sympathetic portrayal of working-class women in the suffrage movement, which Robins hoped would demolish the popular perception of the cause as being dominated by middle- and upper-class women. Originally published in a limited print run, the work was unavailable for seventy years until it was rediscovered and reprinted by the Woman's Press in 1980 during the second wave of the women's movement. In 1908 Robins was a founding member of the Women Writer's Suffrage League and served as president (1908–1912). She was also active in the Actresses Franchise League founded that same year.

Robins remained with the WSPU after a major split in the membership over its tight central control by the Pankhursts in 1907. Although still technically on its committee, she took little part in the union's day-to-day management but did join discreetly and gracefully in its public rallies, electioneering, and deputations to Parliament. In addition, she contributed numerous letters to *The Times* and articles on suffrage to journals such as *Votes for Women,* the *Pall Mall Gazette, Westminster Gazette, Fortnightly Review,* and the U.S. journals *Collier's Weekly* and *McClure's Magazine.* A notable article by her defending WSPU window smashing, "Sermons in Stones," appeared in the *Contemporary Review* in April 1912, and in *The Times* that year Robins published a powerful riposte to antisuffragist Mrs. Humphry Ward, "In Defense of the Militants," which was republished as a pamphlet by the WSPU. In it, Robins revealed the level of commitment and passion for the cause of WSPU members. For many of them, the suffrage campaign had become a religious crusade for which they were willing to suffer and which she challenged its critics to dismiss at their peril. Privately, however, Robins was becoming disturbed by the escalating and random acts of WSPU violence, especially arson, that endangered life and that she felt would alienate public support. The summary removal from office of Emmeline Pethick-Lawrence, with whom Robins shared similar views, precipitated her resignation in the late summer of 1912, but not without presenting a powerful critique of Christabel Pankhurst's stranglehold on the leadership. Although her activism for suffrage dropped off, Robins retained her moral support for the campaign through her publication in 1913 of *Way Stations,* a collection of her suffrage speeches and essays in which she also gave an account of the British campaign.

Robins thereafter confined her activism to her writing, which often discussed the uncomfortable topics of prostitution, divorce, and abortion, particularly in the 1913 novel *My Little Sister* (U.S. title, *Where Are You Going To?*), which portrayed the white slave trade. During World War I, she volunteered as a nurse and was a member of the International Committee of Women for Permanent Peace (1915–1925), which after 1919 became the Women's International League for Peace and Freedom. From 1920 Robins was a director and contributor to Lady Rhondda's feminist journal *Time and Tide,* publishing articles that reflected her pacifism and her support for peace mediation through the League of Nations. In 1921 she joined the Six Point Group, an equal-rights pressure group, in January 1923 publishing "The Six Point Group Supplement" in *Time and Tide,* which outlined the group's advocacy of support for widows and unmarried mothers, the protection of children, and equal pay and employment opportunities for women.

In 1924 Robins made her final and probably most penetrating contribution to the feminist polemic on sexuality in her anonymously published *Ancilla's Share: An Indictment of Sex-Antagonism,* a work strongly pacifist in tone in which she encapsulated her feminist beliefs. Much admired by Virginia Woolf and seen by some commentators as the inspiration for Woolf's own essay on women's right to economic and creative independence, *A Room of One's Own, Ancilla's Share* is now the subject of feminist rediscovery and discussion.

In 1908 Robins had developed a close friendship with Octavia Wilberforce, whom she supported in her determination to become a doctor. The two women shared a farmhouse near Henfield in Sussex, where Wilberforce set up her own medical practice and where they offered accommodation to suffragettes who had gone on hunger strike and had been temporarily released from jail under the Cat and Mouse Act. With the encouragement of Wilberforce, Robins undertook voluntary work in 1922 as vice president of the South London Hospital for Women and also served on the board of the New Sussex Hospital for Women and Children in Brighton. In 1927, at Wilberforce's suggestion, she made over her home in Sussex as a convalescent home for women professionals that is still in use today. In 1940 Robins published her memoirs, *Both Sides of the Curtain.*

In 1905 Robins's brother Raymond, himself a noted social reformer (and for whose education Robins had paid out of her earnings as an actress), had married U.S. feminist and leader of the Women's Trade Union League Margaret Dreier. Through her, Elizabeth developed and maintained links with women activists in the United States, including Margaret's trade-unionist sister, Mary. An Elizabeth Robins homepage with links to other sites has been established by Robins's biographer, Joanne E. Gates, at http://www.jsu.edu/depart/english/robins.

See also Billington-Greig, Teresa; Dreier, Mary Elisabeth; Mitchell, Hannah; Pankhurst, Christabel; Pethick-Lawrence, Emmeline; Robins, Margaret Dreier; Ward, Mary.

References and Further Reading

Alberti, Johanna. 1989. *Beyond Suffrage: Feminists in War and Peace, 1914–1928.* London: Macmillan.

Crawford, Elizabeth. 1999. *The Women's Suffrage Movement, 1866–1928: A Reference Guide.* London: University College of London Press.

Gates, Joanna E. 1994. *Elizabeth Robins, 1862–1952: Actress, Novelist, Feminist.* Tuscaloosa: University of Alabama Press.

Hannam, June, Mitzi Auchterlonie, and Katherine Holden. 2001. *International Encyclopedia of Women's Suffrage.* Santa Barbara: ABC-CLIO.

Holledge, Julie. 1981. *Innocent Flowers: Women in the Edwardian Theatre.* London: Virago.

Joannu, Maroula, and June Purvis, eds. 1998. *The Women's Suffrage Movement: New Feminist*

Perspectives. Manchester: Manchester University Press.

John, Angela V. 1995. *Elizabeth Robins: Staging a Life, 1862–1952*. London: Routledge.

Marcus, Jane. 1985. *Art and Anger: Reading Like a Woman*. Columbus: Miami University of Ohio Press.

Nicholls, C. S., ed. 1993. *Dictionary of National Biography: Missing Persons*. Oxford: Oxford University Press.

Robins, Elizabeth. 1940. *Both Sides of the Curtain*. London: Heinemann.

———. 1980 [1907]. *The Convert*. Introduction by Jane Marcus. Reprint, London: Women's Press.

Sage, Lorna, ed. 1999. *The Cambridge Guide to Women's Writing*. Cambridge: Cambridge University Press.

Showalter, Elaine. 1999 [1977]. *A Literature of Their Own: British Women Novelists from Brontë to Lessing*. Reprint, London: Virago.

Spender, Dale. 1982. *Women of Ideas, and What Men Have Done to Them*. London: Routledge and Kegan Paul.

Stowell, Sheila. 1992. *A Stage of Their Own: Feminist Playwrights of the Suffrage Era*. Manchester: Manchester University Press.

Margaret Dreier Robins (Library of Congress)

Robins, Margaret Dreier
(1868–1945)
United States

The trade union leader and social reformer Margaret Robins channeled much of her considerable wealth into promoting the working rights of women and children. She came from a wealthy German immigrant family with an evangelical background that inculcated an awareness of social responsibility and an espousal of humanitarian good works in both Robins and her sister, Mary Elisabeth Dreier.

Robins was born in Brooklyn, New York, and was educated at a private school in Brooklyn Heights. She traveled to Germany to visit relatives, studied philosophy and history privately with a local pastor, and at the age of nineteen took up philanthropic work as a volunteer of the women's auxiliary at the Brooklyn Hospital. There she was appalled to discover the high number of children afflicted by work-related illnesses, such as those suffering prematurely with rheumatism as a direct result of standing for long hours in water during the manufacturing process in the rubber-making industry.

In 1902 Robins became a member of the State Charities Aid Association, in which capacity she visited mental asylums. She became ever more convinced that acts of private charity were insufficient to meet the widespread deprivation and suffering that she encountered. In 1897, Robins's father, who had made his fortune in the iron smelting business, died, leaving his wealth to be divided among his five children. Her inheritance provided Robins with a private income that enabled her to pursue her social concerns. In 1903 she joined the Woman's Municipal League and, as chair of its legislative committee, sought a wide range of social reform. After conducting research on organized prostitution in the city, she initiated a shakeup of the malpractices of New York's employment agencies, which were notorious for their exploitation of women in domestic service (often luring newly arrived young women from Europe and the South into prostitution). In 1904, with her sister Mary, Robins was asked to join the emergent Women's Trade Union League

(WTUL), and in 1905 she became president of its New York branch. She served as national president from 1907–1921, during which time she also edited the journal *Life and Labor* and pumped a great deal of her own money into the WTUL and its programs, a fact that would sometimes prompt accusations that her domination of the organization was excessive.

In 1905 Margaret married Raymond Robins, the brother of U.S. actress and feminist Elizabeth Robins, who was himself active in settlement work and the reform movement. Despite their comfortable incomes (Raymond had made money in the Klondike gold rush) the couple moved to a tenement in Chicago's slum district, where Margaret collaborated with settlement workers such as Jane Addams and Mary McDowell, joined the Chicago branch of the WTUL, and from 1906 to 1917 served on the board of the Chicago Fellowship of Labor. There she devoted her considerable physical energy to the stresses and strains of the fight for the unionization of women glove makers, boot and shoe workers, and waitresses and for better pay and working conditions. In her leadership of the WTUL, Robins constantly emphasized the importance of fellowship among members and their training in organizational skills. She saw the WTUL as offering a training ground in social leadership to working women and encouraged them to fulfill their own potential as lobbyists, rather than merely relying on others to achieve protective legislation for them. To further this end, she set up a training school for young women trade unionists (1914–1926) and also raised support for the establishment of libraries and social and recreational groups for women workers.

In much of her work, Robins collaborated closely with the outstanding Jewish labor organizer Rose Schneiderman, particularly during the strikes by mainly immigrant women in the garment industry that took place during 1909–1911 in New York, Philadelphia, and Chicago. During the 1909–1910 strike in the New York garment industry, which involved 20,000 workers, Robins initiated boycotts of readymade garments in sympathy with the plight of the sweatshop workers who made them. By 1911, thanks to Robins's hard work, the WTUL had attracted many new women to its ranks and increased its number of branches from three to eleven.

During World War I, Robins took up the cause of international labor, in 1919 overseeing the first International Congress of Working Women, which was held in Washington, D.C. She had supported the Republican Party during World War I, but her Republicanism precipitated conflicts of interest in her social causes; in 1922 she resigned from the WTUL to serve as president of her own brainchild, the International Federation of Working Women (1921–1923), and joined the education committee of the American Federation of Labor. Having given her considerable support to the suffragist, pacifist, and trade union movement during her years of activism, in 1925 Robins retired to her estate in Florida and contented herself with local charitable work for the Young Women's Christian Association, the Red Cross, and the League of Women Voters. Eventually, she shifted her political position to give her enthusiastic support to the Democrats and reform programs introduced under President Franklin D. Roosevelt's New Deal in 1933. She rejoined the executive board of the WTUL in 1934 and accepted the chair of its committee on southern work in 1937.

See also Addams, Jane; Dreier, Mary Elisabeth; McDowell, Mary; Robins, Elizabeth; Schneiderman, Rose.

References and Further Reading

Boone, Gladys. 1942. *The Women's Trade Union Leagues in Great Britain and the United States of America.* New York: Columbia University Press.

Chambers, Clarke A. 1963. *Seedtime of Reform: American Social Service and Social Action, 1918–1933.* Minneapolis: University of Minnesota Press.

Davis, Allen F. 1967. *Spearheads for Reform: The Social Settlements and the Progressive Movement 1890–1914.* New York: Oxford University Press.

Dell, Floyd. 1913. *Woman as World Builders: Studies in Modern Feminism.* Chicago: Forbes and Company.

Dreier, Mary E. 1950. *Margaret Dreier Robins: Her Life, Letters, and Work.* New York: Island Press Cooperative.

Dye, Nancy Schrom. 1980. *As Equals and as Sisters: Feminism, the Labor Movement and the Women's Trade Union League of New York.* Columbia: University of Missouri Press.

Flexner, Eleanor. 1975 [1959]. *A Century of Struggle: The Woman's Rights Movement in the United States.* Rev. ed., Cambridge, MA: Belknap Press of Harvard University.

Foner, Philip. 1979. *Women and the American Labor Movement, vol. 1: From Colonial Times to the Eve of World War I.* New York: Free Press.

Payne, Elizabeth Anne. 1988. *Reform, Labor, and Feminism: Margaret Dreier Robins and the Women's Trade Union League.* Urbana: University of Illinois Press.

Tax, Meredith. 1980. *The Rising of the Women: Feminist Solidarity and Class Conflict 1880–1917.* New York: Monthly Review Press.

Wertheimer, Barbara M. 1977. *We Were There: The Story of Working Women in America.* New York: Pantheon Books.

Rodríguez Acosta, Ofelia
(1902–1975)
Cuba

One of the most influential women in Cuba in the first half of the twentieth century, the feminist novelist and journalist Ofelia Rodríguez Acosta shared many of the views on the exploitation of women held by her compatriot, Mariblanca Sabas Alomá. Born in Pinar del Río, the daughter of a writer and intellectual, Rodríguez showed great intellectual promise at a young age, writing her first book when she was twelve. She studied at the Institute of Havana and, after graduating in 1925, obtained a government grant to study in Europe and Mexico. From 1923 to 1928, she was a member of the Women's Club of Cuba and later joined the Women's Labor Union.

In 1927 Rodríguez founded the journal *The Female Spartan.* From 1929 to 1932, she wrote for numerous journals, including *Bohemia, The World,* and *Social,* and worked on novels emphasizing social themes. She attempted to gain wider notice of her views by giving a series of public lectures in 1932 at the Lyceum Lawn and Tennis Club in Havana, with themes such as "The Social Tragedy of Woman," in which she developed her views on their exploitation. These lectures were in part an extension of a debate on the philosophical aspects of women's position upon which she had embarked with the Russian philosopher Anton Nemilov after reading his book, *The Biological Tragedy of Women,* in 1929. In her 1932 speeches, Rodríguez argued that women's biological makeup was at the root of men's social perceptions and abuse of them and that women were rejected by men when they suffered the physical changes that affected their sexuality: menstruation, menopause, old age, and so on.

As an admirer of the work of Bertrand Russell, Rodríguez felt that women could only really liberate themselves through free love and a rejection of religious, social, and sexual strictures. They should be bolder in their choice of fathers for their children and retain their independence within relationships without becoming enslaved to domestic servitude. Rodríguez's ideas on male and female social and sexual behavior were at the heart of her controversial 1927 novel, *The Life Offering* (*La Vida Manda*), which portrayed through her heroine Gertrudis a woman's need for and right to sexual fulfillment. The novel was, needless to say, condemned as erotic and pornographic.

In 1933 Rodríguez traveled to Spain and France and in 1940 settled in Mexico. Throughout her career, she was unable to shake off a fundamentally pessimistic attitude toward reform. Ultimately, she felt that real social change depended on the will of the individual and could not be effected even by revolutionary upheaval. Women would inevitably remain economically dependent on men, unless they took a personal hand in their own liberation. She saw man-woman relationships as flawed and transient, and her disillusionment and cynicism about human relationships eventually led to mental breakdown and her death in a lunatic asylum.

See also Sabas Alomá, Mariblanca.

References and Further Reading

Stoner, K. Lynn. 1991. *From the House to the Streets: The Cuban Woman's Movement for Legal Reform 1898–1940.* Durham, NC: Duke University Press.

Roland, Pauline
(1805–1852)
France

The St. Simonian utopian socialist and sexual radical of the 1830s Pauline Roland criticized the inferior position of women in marriage and advocated free love and female autonomy. It was her fundamental belief that "woman alone is the family" (Moses 1984, 231), and she adhered to this belief in her own dogged insistence on a woman's right to be the sole provider for her children, irrespective of the support of men.

Having struggled for many years to provide for her own children in this way, in maturity Roland rejected free love, admitting that the life of a lone parent had been hard, and advocated marriage based on fidelity as the only true basis of family life.

Roland grew up in Normandy, where her widowed mother ran a post office in Falaise and made sacrifices so that her two daughters could have a good education. At a girls' boarding school in Falaise, Roland fell in love with a married teacher, Desprez (who had a tendency to attract his impressionable young pupils). He introduced her to the socialist writings of Henri de St. Simon, which called for social regeneration through a new harmonious network of workers' cooperatives. Leaving the school, Roland went to Paris alone to seek work and entered into free-love relationships with two successive partners within the St. Simonian community—Adolphe Guéroult and Jean-François Aicard—acknowledging her own responsibility to provide both for herself and her children (she had four during the 1830s) and insisting they take her name. When Flora Tristan died of typhoid in 1844, she also took care of her daughter Aline.

Roland turned to journalism to support her family, writing for the feminist newspapers the *Free Woman* and *Women's Tribune* in 1834 and submitting entries for the *New Encyclopedia,* the *Independent Review,* and the *Serial Review.* She also produced educational materials and wrote history books for male and female readers, completing a history of France in 1835; of England in 1838; and of England, Scotland, and Ireland in 1844.

Eventually, the relationship with Aicard foundered over financial difficulties and his infidelity, by which time even the broad-minded members of the St. Simonian community had come to look on Roland's behavior as scandalous. She withdrew from St. Simonian circles in Paris and in 1847 joined a community in the country, at Boussac, where she also helped run and teach at the school. In 1848, with the outbreak of revolutionary activities in France, she returned to Paris in December to become one of the most active women campaigning for equal rights during the short-lived Second Republic, publishing regular articles in Pierre-Joseph Proudhon's *The Representative of the People,* as well as working with Jeanne Deroin and other feminists on *Women's Opinion* from January to August 1849.

With Jeanne Deroin, Roland founded the Fraternal Association of Socialist Male and Female Teachers and Professors in 1849, advocating women's education until age eighteen and their entry into the professions alongside men. That October, Roland was also one of the key conveners with Deroin of the Union of Workers' Associations, an attempt to reinvigorate the cooperative movement of 1848 through "fraternal organizations," and was elected to its central committee. But the union was closed down in May 1850, and on 29 May Roland was one of thirty activists arrested for working for the cooperative movement with Deroin and holding political meetings. At her trial for conspiracy, where she was arraigned also for "socialism, feminism and debauchery," Roland was tried as much for her free-love relationships as her socialist concerns. Sentenced to six months in prison, she used her time to proselytize among women prison inmates, many of them prostitutes, and continued to support her family by writing. She and Deroin, who had also been imprisoned, addressed a "Letter to the Convention of the Women of America" from their prison cells, which they sent to the U.S. women's rights convention of 1851, applauding their work and appealing for support for women in France. On her release in July 1851, Roland returned to Paris, where she took part in resistance to Louis Napoleon's coup. Arrested again in December 1851, Roland was sent to a penal colony in Algeria. Leading figures such as the writer George Sand interceded to obtain her release, but she died in Lyon on 15 December 1852, on her way back to Paris.

See also Deroin, Jeanne; Sand, George; Tristan, Flora.

References and Further Reading

Gordon, Felicia, and Máire Cross. 1996. *Early French Feminism, 1830–1940: A Passion for Liberty.* Cheltenham: Edward Elgar.

Moses, C. 1984. *French Feminism in the Nineteenth Century.* Albany: State University of New York Press.

Rendall, J. 1985. *The Origins of Modern Feminism: Women in Britain, France, and the United States 1780–1860.* Chicago: University of Chicago Press.

Rowbotham, Sheila. 1999. *Threads through Time: Writings on History and Autobiography.* London: Penguin.

Roosevelt, (Anna) Eleanor
(1884–1962)
United States

As the wife of Franklin D. Roosevelt, the president of the United States, the humanitarian Eleanor Roosevelt could not have been better placed to arouse public interest in the many social causes to which she dedicated her life. Indeed, such was the success with which she overcame her natural shyness to carve out her own independent career in public service, as a champion of minority groups, the dispossessed, and the underprivileged, that she became one of the most prestigious and powerful women in the United States, not only during her husband's four successive terms of office (1933–1945), but right up until her death.

Born into the same influential and wealthy Roosevelt family of New York as her future husband (he was a fifth cousin), Eleanor suffered a miserable childhood despite her background of privilege. Losing her parents by the age of ten, she grew up under the tight rein of her maternal grandmother with little sense of her own self-worth. After attending Allenswood finishing school in England, she entered New York society in 1902, but finding the life of a debutante shallow and unrewarding, Roosevelt joined the New York settlement movement, teaching calisthenics and dance in its house on Rivington Street and volunteering her services, at the age of seventeen, to Florence Kelley's National Consumers' League.

American society was somewhat taken aback in 1905 when the plain, tall, and gawky-looking Eleanor married New York's most desirable bachelor, the handsome up-and-coming politician Franklin D. Roosevelt, a man known for his gregariousness and attractiveness to women. When her husband's political career gathered pace after he entered the New York Senate in 1910, Eleanor successfully juggled the care of her five children with the demands of a domineering mother-in-law and her duties as a political hostess. In later years, Franklin would commend his wife's dignity and intellect, although he never credited her in public for her long years of social activism. And although Eleanor never cured Roosevelt's womanizing, she exerted a strong moral influence over him and acted as a perpetual and sometimes irksome spur to his social conscience. During World War I, she was glad to relinquish some of her more tiresome social duties in favor of relief work for the Red Cross, visiting the wounded in hospitals and organizing women's volunteer work in support of the war effort.

The Roosevelts faced a crisis in their marriage when, in 1918, Eleanor discovered her husband's adultery with her social secretary, Lucy Mercer. Although they did not divorce (to do so would have been the kiss of death to his political career), the couple's relationship was platonic thereafter, with Eleanor later exacting a more subtle form of revenge, aimed at her husband's stomach, by hiring a housekeeper at the White House who was legendary for her terrible cooking. Indeed, Eleanor Roosevelt succeeded in salvaging from the wreckage of her failed marriage a newborn self-assertiveness that enabled her to take a public role alongside her husband that was no longer merely functional but increasingly proactive. When Roosevelt was disabled by polio between 1922 and 1928, Eleanor came into her own as a member of the women's division of the State Democratic Committee and acted as Roosevelt's proxy at many official functions. She also learned to overcome her reticence about public speaking and was increasingly drawn into her own separate spheres of interest, supporting organizations such as the League of Women Voters (from 1920) and the Women's Trade Union League (from 1922). From 1926 onward, Roosevelt spent much of her time with her close circle of female friends and liberal activists, sharing a home with Nancy Cook and Marian Dickerman, with whom she set up the nonprofit Val-Kill furniture factory in New York, which gave work to unemployed and disabled men.

During the 1920s, Roosevelt was also honored by being invited to join what was perceived as the "holy of holies," the board of the Leslie Suffrage Commission. This body had been set up to oversee the spending of a legacy of $1 million made to the National American Woman Suffrage Association by Mrs. Frank Leslie. By the time Roosevelt won his first term as president in 1933, Eleanor had established a considerable reputation for herself among leading women social reformers. She toured, promoting reforms under Roosevelt's New Deal of 1933, a program that her most recent biographer, Blanche Wiesen Cook, contends embodied many of Eleanor's own social and feminist ideals. For the next twelve years, as First Lady she garnered a massive national audi-

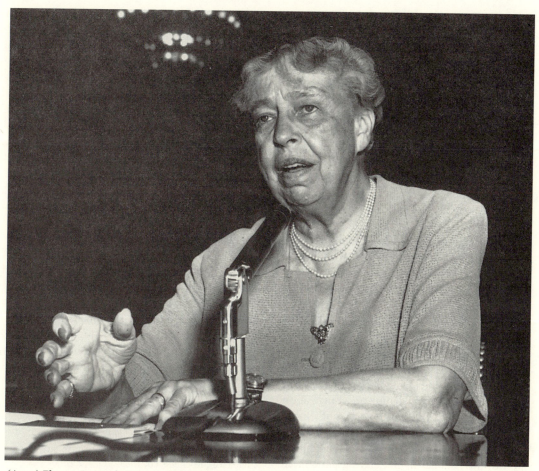

(Anna) Eleanor Roosevelt (Library of Congress)

ence for her social concerns by writing a syndi-cated newspaper column, *My Day* (beginning in 1936), staging her own radio show, and wherever possible drawing attention to her own special causes on the many occasions on which she was invited to address public functions. She traveled extensively in the United States, in what amounted to the role of an unofficial cabinet minister, and regularly reported back to her hus-band on the social issues that most concerned her: health care, housing, unemployment, civil rights, youth projects through the American Stu-dent Union and the American Youth Congress (1936–1940), child welfare, and slum clearance. She also persistently lobbied for women to be given more roles in government and at every pos-sible opportunity facilitated an interchange be-tween women reformers and Roosevelt's admin-istration. She did so by inviting representatives of oppressed and minority groups to the White

House to meet the president, such as cotton mill workers from the South or workers from the gar-ment industry. Discovering that the measures of the New Deal were insufficiently addressing the needs of the growing numbers of unemployed, Eleanor Roosevelt constantly suggested new projects aimed at providing employment.

In 1933 she inaugurated her own press confer-ences at the White House, to which she invited only women reporters. Throughout this decade, taking advantage of her unique position, she made bold attempts to publicly fight racial preju-dice. In 1936 she invited sixty mainly black girls from the National Industrial School in Washing-ton to a garden party at the White House, an event that enraged southern newspapers. She also invited the black opera singer Marian Anderson, whom she greatly admired, to sing at the White House. When in 1939 the Daughters of the Amer-ican Revolution (DAR) banned Anderson from appearing at a concert at Constitution Hall, Roosevelt resigned from the DAR in protest, as did other leading U.S. women. She also made public her hatred of racial violence by lobbying for the unsuccessful Costigan-Wagner antilynching bill and worked for the civil rights movement, serving as a mediator between her husband and the National Association for the Advancement of Colored People. It was largely due to Eleanor Roosevelt's influence that the black educationist Mary McCleod Bethune, whom she greatly admired, was appointed to the National Advisory Committee of the National Youth Administration, from where she launched a widespread campaign against racial discrimination.

When the United States entered World War II in 1941, Roosevelt took the role of codirector of the Office of Civilian Defense and urged the involvement of women in the war effort, as well as calling for an end to racial discrimination in the armed forces and among black workers in wartime industries. She went on morale-boosting trips to U.S. troops in the South Pacific, the United Kingdom, and elsewhere, but by war's end her single-minded campaigning on a range of often thorny issues was causing regular conflict with her husband. After his death in 1945, Eleanor Roosevelt finally came into her own as a highly respected international figure. Having announced her withdrawal from public life, within a year she had accepted President Harry S Truman's call to become one of five U.S. delegates to the newly established United Nations. In the remaining years of her life, Roosevelt embraced such causes as international peace mediation, control of the arms race, and human rights. From 1947 to 1951, she was chair of the commission, which in 1948 drew up the landmark Declaration of Human Rights. Roosevelt stayed on at the UN until 1952 and the election of President Dwight D. Eisenhower, thereafter maintaining her link with it through the American Association for the United Nations. She vigorously opposed the communist witch hunts of the McCarthy era and, after the establishment of the new state of Israel, was a passionate supporter of Zionism.

In her seventies, Roosevelt toured India, Japan, and the Soviet Union and during 1961–1962 was persuaded back into an official role as chair of President John F. Kennedy's Commission on the Status of Women. She published numerous books about her life and work, including *This Is My Story* (1937), *The Lady of the White House* (1938), *The Moral Basis of Democracy* (1940), *This I Remember* (1949), *On My Own* (1958), and *The Autobiography of Eleanor Roosevelt* (1961). During her time as "First Lady of the Western World" (in President Truman's words), she met all the world leaders of her day and has often been given the accolade of being the single most influential woman of the twentieth century. Yet Eleanor Roosevelt herself always modestly averred that she simply embraced good causes as they presented themselves to her: "As for accomplishments, I just did what I had to do as things came along" (*New York Times,* 8 October 1954). As a woman of high principles and fair-mindedness, she was never afraid of the challenges of political opponents and detractors. A site devoted to the life and work of Roosevelt and with links to others can be found at http://personalweb.smcvt.edu/smahady. There is also a somewhat anodyne official White House biography at http://www.whitehouse.gov/WH/glimpsefirstladies.

See also Bethune, Mary McCleod; Kelley, Florence.

References and Further Reading
Black, Allida M. 1996. *Casting Her Own Shadow: Eleanor Roosevelt and the Shaping of Postwar Liberalism.* New York: Columbia University Press.
Chadakoff, Rochelle, ed. 1989. Vol. 1, *Eleanor Roosevelt's My Day;* David Emblidge, ed. 1990; 1991, vols. 2 and 3. New York: Pharaos Books.
Cook, Blanche Wiesen. 1993, 2000. *Eleanor Roosevelt.* Vol. 1, 1884–1932; vol. 2, 1933–1938. New York: Viking.
Freedman, Russell. 1993. *Eleanor Roosevelt: A Life of Discovery.* New York: Clarion.
Hareven, Tamara. 1968. *Eleanor Roosevelt: An American Conscience.* Chicago: Quadrangle.
Kearney, James. 1968. *Anna Eleanor Roosevelt: The Evolution of a Reformer.* Boston: Houghton Mifflin.
Kerber, Linda K., and Jane DeHart-Mathews. 2000. *Women's America: Refocusing the Past.* New York: Oxford University Press.
Lash, Joseph P. 1971. *Eleanor and Franklin.* New York: Norton.
———. 1972. *Eleanor: The Years Alone.* New York: Norton.
MacLeish, Archibald. 1965. *The Eleanor Roosevelt Story.* Boston: Houghton Mifflin.
Orleck, Annelise. 1995. *Common Sense and a Little Fire: Women and Working-Class Politics in the United States, 1900–1965.* Chapel Hill: University of North Carolina Press.

Rose, Ernestine
(1810–1892)
Poland/United States

The Polish-born freethinker, secularist, and feminist Ernestine Rose was an outstanding intellectual. Her contribution to the early women's movement in the United States, for many years as its first and only Jewish woman activist, has yet to be properly acknowledged. Yet it is she, along with another immigrant, the Scottish-born Frances Wright, whom women such as Elizabeth Cady Stanton and Susan B. Anthony acknowledged as being one of the pioneer advocates of women's suffrage in the United States. Biographical material on Rose's life is limited; she herself admitted that she had kept no personal papers or records, and in assessing her achievements, modestly stated: "I used my humble powers to the uttermost, and raised my voice in behalf of Human Rights in general, and the elevation and Rights of Woman in particular, nearly all my life" (Spender 1982, 272).

A rabbi's daughter, Rose was born in Piotrków Trybunalski, Poland, in what was then part of the Jewish Pale of Settlement of the Russian Empire. A natural-born rebel who had been taught the Torah and Talmud and brought up in a strict Orthodox home, she rejected the constraints of her religion at the age of fourteen, in particular its subordination of women. At sixteen she went to the secular courts to fight for her dead mother's inheritance, when her father was about to make it over as a dowry on her marriage to an older man. Soon after, giving up her inheritance to her father of her own free will, she left for Germany, where she lived alone in Berlin for two years and supported herself by selling her own invention, a deodorizing perfumed paper. After that, Rose spent time in the Netherlands and France before arriving in England in 1831, having survived a shipwreck where she had lost all her possessions. There she mixed with reformers such as Elizabeth Fry and the radical leader Robert Owen, with him cofounding a utopian-socialist group, the Association of All Classes of All Nations, in 1835.

In 1836 Rose married the jeweler and silversmith William Rose, also a follower of Robert Owen, and at age twenty-six emigrated with him to the United States, where they opened their own shop selling silver goods and a brand of toilet water concocted by Ernestine. As an admirer of another rebel and individualist, Frances Wright, who had been an early advocate of women's rights in the United States, Rose joined other émigré intellectuals in the Society for Moral Philanthropists. She demonstrated a flair for public speaking (becoming known as the "Queen of the Platform") and began lecturing at the society, speaking out on "the evils of the social system, the formation of human character, slavery, the rights of woman, and other reform questions" (Stanton et al. 1881, 97). Rose was supported financially by her husband in her endless touring—she traveled west to Ohio and south to Kentucky, often journeying long distances alone and in considerable discomfort. She also regularly attended conventions staged by freethinkers. During her first winter in the United States, she began petitioning the New York state legislature in support of a bill for reform of women's property rights introduced by Thomas Herttell. Rose toured almost every major city in the state and over the course of the next eleven years assaulted the state legislature with regular petitions, addressing it on five occasions. In April 1848, the New York legislature passed the Married Women's Property Act, which allowed divorced women to retain some of their possessions. It was expanded in 1860. As Dale Spender so rightly points out (1982, 272–273), Rose's achievement is all the more commendable when one bears in mind that as a Polish immigrant and stranger to U.S. shores, she bravely took to the road, lecturing for women's rights for all of twelve years before the first women's rights convention was staged at Seneca Falls (1848).

Rose was supported in her campaigning on marriage reform by Anthony, Stanton, and Lucretia Mott, but she was unusual for her time in that she unequivocally argued that woman had the same intellectual capacity as man and that "where her mind has been called out at all, [woman's] . . . intellect is as bright, as capacious, and as powerful as man's" (Bolt 1993, 92). In 1843, together with other utopian socialists of both sexes, she founded an Owenite colony in Skaneateles, New York, a venture that lasted until 1846.

During the 1850s, in addition to working for women's rights, Rose supported the causes of temperance and abolitionism. She spoke at the first national convention for women's rights, held in Worcester, Massachusetts, in 1850, where she called for a resolution on women's political, social, and legal equality with men, and regularly attended national and state conventions thereafter. Indeed, the third national women's rights convention, held in Syracuse in 1852, was marked by a forceful debate over the Bible's position on women's rights. The traditional Christian view, voiced by the preacher Antoinette Brown Blackwell, was hotly contested by freethinker Rose, who challenged the need for any "written authority," biblical or otherwise, to pontificate on the basic human rights to which she believed women were entitled.

At the tenth national women's rights convention in New York in 1860, Rose paid tribute to the pioneering work of Frances Wright and joined in another intensive debate, this time on marriage reform. Here she challenged her detractors, who had accused her of supporting "free love," asserting that "to me, in its truest significance, love must be free, or it ceases to be love" (Helsinger, Sheets, and Veeder 1983, 35). Furthermore, Rose argued that it was immoral for society to oppose divorce and expect two people to remain together in what amounted to a relationship of legalized prostitution, where "there are only discord and misery to themselves, and vice and crime to society" (36). Instead, Rose advocated a woman's right to divorce on the grounds of cruelty and willful desertion and for habitual drinking and other vices.

During the Civil War, Rose joined Stanton and Anthony in working for abolition through the Woman's National Loyal League. In 1867 she spoke at the first annual meeting of the American Equal Rights Association, held in New York, to resume the fight for women's suffrage, which had been sidelined by the war. Like many other suffragists, Rose was dismayed at the award of suffrage to male blacks ahead of women under the Fourteenth and Fifteenth Amendments and joined Anthony and Stanton in founding the National Woman Suffrage Association. But by this time, Rose was suffering from ill health as a result of her long years of campaigning, and she went to Europe in 1869 for a rest cure, only days after finally taking U.S. citizenship. She settled in England in 1870, where she took an interest in the suffrage movement as well as the work of the Universal Peace Union, and returned to the United States to sell her possessions there and attend the 1873 convention of the National Woman Suffrage Association. In December 1882,

Elizabeth Cady Stanton visited a sad and dispirited Rose in her lodgings in London, finding her still "as bright, witty, and sarcastic as ever" but remarking with compassion on Rose's isolation, "with not one soul with a drop of her blood in their veins living, not one life-long friend at hand on whom to call" (Stanton and Blatch 1922, 201). Stanton urged Rose to return to the United States, but Rose felt that she no longer had the physical strength for the voyage.

During her years of activism, Rose contributed regular articles to the *Boston Investigator,* a journal of free thought, and published a pamphlet, "A Defence of Atheism." She did not produce an account of her life or her achievements, except for a brief summary provided to Stanton, Anthony, and Mathilda Joslyn Gage for the *History of Woman Suffrage.*

Admired for the sharpness and logic of her argument, Rose was also an accomplished linguist, able to converse in Polish, English, German, French, Dutch, and Hebrew. She is now one of many lost voices from the early days of the U.S. women's movement who is being restored to her proper place in history, through recent studies such as those by Sherry Ceniza (1998) and Carol Kolmerton (1999). She is buried at that famous resting place of many pioneering freethinkers, writers, and socialists, Highgate Cemetery in London, not far from the grave of Karl Marx. A long and informative article on Rose can be found on the American Atheists site at http://www.atheists.org/Atheism/ roots/rose.

See also Anthony, Susan B.; Blackwell, Antoinette Brown; Fry, Elizabeth; Mott, Lucretia Coffin; Stanton, Elizabeth Cady; Wright, Frances.

References and Further Reading

Bolt, Christine. 1993. *The Women's Movements in the United States and Britain from the 1790s to the 1920s.* London: Harvester Wheatsheaf.

Ceniza, Sherry. 1998. *Walt Whitman and Nineteenth-Century Women Reformers.* Tuscaloosa: University of Alabama Press, chap. 4.

Flexner, Eleanor. 1975 [1959]. *A Century of Struggle: The Woman's Rights Movement in the United States.* Rev. ed., Cambridge, MA: Belknap Press of Harvard University.

Frost, Elizabeth, and Kathryn Cullen DuPont. 1992. *Women's Suffrage in America: An Eyewitness History.* New York: Facts on File.

Helsinger, Elizabeth K., Robin Lauterbach Sheets, and William Veeder. 1983. *The Woman Question: Social Issues, 1837–1883,* vol. 2, *Society and*

Literature in Britain and America, 1837–1883. Manchester: Manchester University Press.

Kolmerton, Carol A. 1999. *The American Life of Ernestine L. Rose.* Syracuse: Syracuse University Press.

O'Connor, Lillian. 1954. *Pioneer Women Orators: Rhetoric in the Ante-Bellum Reform Movement.* New York: Columbia University Press.

Spender, Dale. 1982. *Women of Ideas, and What Men Have Done to Them.* London: Routledge and Kegan Paul.

Stanton, Elizabeth Cady, Susan B. Anthony, Matilda Joslyn Gage, and Ida Husted Harper. 1881. *History of Woman Suffrage.* Vol 1. New York: Fowler and Wells.

Stanton, Theodore, and Harriot Stanton Blatch, eds. 1922. *Elizabeth Cady Stanton as Revealed in Her Letters, Diaries, and Reminiscences.* New York: Arno Press.

Suhl, Yuri. 1959. *Ernestine Rose and the Battle for Human Rights.* New York: Reynal.

———. 1970. *Eloquent Crusader: Ernestine L. Rose.* New York: J. Messner.

Wiseman, Alberta. 1976. *Rebels and Reformers, Biographies of Four Jewish Americans.* Garden City, NY: Zenith Books.

Roussel, Nelly
(1878–1922)
France

The militant orator Nelly Roussel was considered by many French feminists to be their most powerful and idiosyncratic speaker. As a neo-Malthusian and supporter of birth control, in 1904 Roussel took a leaf out of Aristophanes' classic play *Lysistrata,* calling on women to enlist their sexuality in the fight against their own oppression. In the Greek play, women had refused their husbands conjugal rights in order to put a stop to war; in a similar vein, Roussel boldly advocated "birth strikes" and sexual abstinence in support of women receiving financial remuneration for maternity.

A middle-class Parisian who grew up in a liberal household, Roussel left home to marry sculptor Henri Godit when she was twenty. She remained an outspoken rebel for the rest of her life, which was cut short by tuberculosis when she was only forty-four. She developed her talent as a public speaker from her years as an elocution teacher. From 1903 to 1913, Roussel went on the annual lecture circuit, talking to a wide range of mixed groups, from freemasons to trade unions to pacifists, on women's sexual rights and birth control, which she particularly wanted to be made available to working-class women. In one year alone she traveled across fifteen *départements,* giving thirty-four speeches, including her most often requested one, "Let Us Create the Citizenness."

Roussel's outspoken views invited much hostility and ridicule, for her central argument was that mothers should be viewed as workers. Their role in producing new generations was central to society, and yet they were the poorest paid and most neglected by the state. She argued that those women who wished to dedicate themselves to childbearing should receive a "maternity salary" in recompense for childbearing; "the first, the most sacred, and nevertheless—what an inconceivable aberration—the least discussed and the least respected of liberties" (Offen 2000, 241). Roussel believed that if society did not recognize mothers' right to a wage, then they, like any other workers, had every right to strike in order to protect their own interests. From 1904, when she made a landmark speech calling for radical reform of the French Civil Code, she began calling for a "strike of the womb." In 1913 she loudly protested when family allowances granted by the state to families with more than four children were paid to the fathers rather than the mothers. And again in 1919, after the French government, worried by the falling birthrate, began actively encouraging women to have more children to make up for those lost during World War I, she urged women to withdraw from their undervalued reproductive roles.

References and Further Reading

Hause, Steven C., with Anne R. Kenny. 1984. *Women's Suffrage and Social Politics in the French Third Republic.* Princeton: Princeton University Press.

Offen, Karen. 2000. *European Feminisms 1700–1950: A Political History.* Stanford: Stanford University Press.

Royden, Maude
(1876–1956)
United Kingdom

The lay preacher, suffragist, and international pacifist Maude Royden was a leading Christian feminist who, having helped win the vote in 1918, devoted herself thereafter to women's spiritual and economic welfare and lobbied for their ordination into the priesthood of the Church of England. As a gifted and charismatic speaker, Royden lent her oratorical skills to propagating moral and ethical issues of the interwar years in the belief that since men and women are equal in the sight of God, they should adhere to the same moral standard.

Royden grew up in Liverpool, where her father was a shipowner and sometime mayor. She was educated at Dorothea Beale's progressive Cheltenham Ladies' College and studied history at St. Margaret Hall, Oxford, graduating in 1899. In Liverpool, she worked at the Victoria Women's Settlement (1899–1902), where she struck up a friendship with Eleanor Rathbone. As a frustrated cleric, she took up parish work in South Luffenham, Rutland, where she came under the lifelong influence of the Reverend Hudson Shaw; their deep love for each other would remain platonic through the years of his wife's prolonged mental illness. Royden lived on and off with the Shaws from 1909, until she and Hudson were finally able to marry after his wife's death in 1944. She would describe this aspect of her life in her later memoir, *A Three-Fold Chord* (1947).

In 1905 Royden moved to Oxford, where she took up a lectureship for the Oxford University extension classes. In 1908 she joined the National Union of Women's Suffrage Societies (NUWSS), beginning a long affiliation with the women's movement, during which she would become one of its outstanding public speakers. She found her work for suffrage uplifting, opening up as it did lines of sympathy with other disenfranchised social groups. Relating her work for suffrage closely to her life as a Christian, in 1910 she became chair of the Church League for Women's Suffrage. From 1909 she was a regular contributor to the NUWSS journal, *Common Cause,* acting as its editor from April 1913 to February 1915.

In 1911, as a friend of suffragist Isabella Ford and influenced by her activism with working women, Royden wrote an NUWSS pamphlet, "Votes and Wages: How Women's Suffrage Will Improve the Economic Position of Women," in an attempt to defuse male hostility toward women's work and prove that enfranchisement would end women's economic exploitation. In answer to worried trade unionists who saw their jobs as under threat from women, Royden argued that the vote would give women the political power to eradicate low wages and their exclusion from trades that had been closed to them. In turn, they would no longer need to undercut men in those trades in which they did work. In 1911 Royden was elected to the NUWSS's executive committee and that autumn took up a speaking tour of the United States, followed by an equally intensive campaign across the United Kingdom in 1912. She produced other important suffrage pamphlets before World War I, including "How Women Use the Vote" (1912) and "Chance: The Predominance of Men in Anti-Suffrage Finance and Organization" (1913), and took up further responsibilities as president, in 1913, of the Chester Women's Suffrage Society and vice president of the Oxford Women's Suffrage Society. She also found time to travel to Budapest in 1913 for a conference of the International Woman Suffrage Alliance.

Back in London on the outbreak of war, Royden wanted suffragists to work for peace rather than in support of militarism. But she quickly had to concede that the majority of women were behind the war effort. She concentrated therefore on emphasizing ways in which their practical support could be put to good use in promoting a better postwar world by accentuating their particular antimilitaristic, maternal qualities. In her strong advocacy of women's special contribution to society as mothers, she concurred with her friend Rathbone on the payment of family allowances directly to mothers.

In December 1914, Royden was one of several British women pacifists who signed an "open Christmas letter" to the women of Germany and Austria, calling on them to support peace mediation. She served as secretary of the Fellowship of Reconciliation and continued to argue against NUWSS support for the war. In April 1915, she was one of eleven leaders, along with her friends Catherine Marshall and Kate Courtney, who resigned from the NUWSS when it formally endorsed the war effort. Prevented from traveling to The Hague to attend an international women's peace conference, she was nevertheless instrumental in the establishment of the British section of the International Committee of Women for Permanent Peace that grew out of it, and she was appointed one of the committee's three vice presidents.

In 1917 Royden published an important essay, "Modern Love," in *The Making of Woman: Oxford Essays in Feminism.* In it she applauded her sex's achievements, condemned the sexual double standard, and (despite her own enforced celibacy) affirmed women's right to physical love and its enjoyments, provided that the human body was accorded the same respect as the human spirit. A gifted preacher, Royden was not able to practice her skills in the Anglican church (women were barred from becoming priests); although she did not renounce her membership, she accepted the post as assistant preacher in the Congregational Church at the City Temple, London (1917–1920). One of many feminists impressed with her charismatic speaking powers was actress and writer Elizabeth Robins, who heard Royden preach on several occasions in 1918 and spoke of her as a guiding influence in the postwar women's international campaign for peace. Royden became increasingly vocal in her criticism of the entrenched position of the established church against progressive reform and the ordination of women, observing in a now notable quotation made in a speech at the Queen's Hall, London: "The Church should go forward along the path of progress and be no longer satisfied only to represent the Conservative Party at prayer" (*The Times,* 17 July 1917).

In her Queen's Hall speech, Royden was also one of the first to start claiming the vote for women before hostilities had ceased. When World War I ended, she spoke out on sexual morality and birth control and was an early patron of Marie Stopes's Holloway clinic and of Rathbone's scheme for family allowances. Royden believed that greater respect and remuneration should be accorded to women who chose to be mothers, in hopes that if they received such financial benefits, they would remove themselves as competition in an already overcrowded and underpaid workplace.

During the interwar years, Royden continued her campaign for women's admission into the priesthood; in 1920 she was a cofounder of the Interdenominational Fellowship Services, based in Kensington, and later moved with it to the Guildhouse in Eccleston Square, where her services attracted huge audiences. In 1927, while attending the international suffrage congress in Paris, she preached at the American Church, and during the mid-1930s she undertook preaching tours of the United States, Australia, New Zealand, and the Far East. She was increasingly preoccupied with the rise of fascism and militarism, however, and in 1932 called for a Peace Army of volunteers to go to Manchuria and mediate when the Japanese invaded and set up a puppet state (the mission never took place). In 1936 she gave up her pulpit at the Guildhouse, but although she had been a supporter of the Peace Pledge Union, Royden renounced her pacifism on the outbreak of World War II, in the belief that this was a just war against fascism.

During World War II, Royden published *Women's Partnership in the New World,* describing with pride and enthusiasm the opportunities for women to enter new spheres of activity. Commenting on Marie Curie's discovery of radium, she remarked, "Because such women exist I shall resent and denounce every attempt to dogmatize about 'woman's sphere' or to deny women complete freedom to decide for themselves what they shall attempt and what is within their powers" (1941, 26). In the spirit of Royden, the Catholic campaigner Lavinia Byrne is now campaigning for women's ordination in the Roman Catholic Church.

See also Beale, Dorothea; Byrne, Lavinia; Courtney, Kathleen D'Olier; Ford, Isabella; Marshall, Catherine; Rathbone, Eleanor; Robins, Elizabeth; Stopes, Marie.

References and Further Reading
Alberti, Johanna. 1989. *Beyond Suffrage: Feminists in War and Peace, 1914–1928.* London: Macmillan.
Byrne, Lavinia. 1995. *The Hidden Voice: Christian Women and Social Change.* London: SPCK.
Crawford, Elizabeth. 1999. *The Women's Suffrage Movement, 1866–1928: A Reference Guide.* London: University College of London Press.
Fletcher, Sheila. 1989. *Maude Royden: A Life.* Oxford: Blackwell.
Oldfield, Sybil. 1989. *Women against the Iron Fist: Alternatives to Militarism 1900–1989.* Oxford: Basil Blackwell.
———. 2001. *Women Humanitarians: A Biographical Dictionary of British Women Active between 1900 and 1950.* London: Continuum.
Royden, Maude. 1941. *Women's Partnership in the New World.* London: Allen and Unwin.
———. 1947. *A Three-Fold Cord.* London: Victor Gollancz.
Thompson, Dorothy. 1983. *Over Our Dead Bodies: Women against the Bomb.* London: Virago.
Wiltsher, Anne. 1985. *Most Dangerous Women: Feminist Peace Campaigners of the Great War.* London: Pandora, and Westport, CT: Greenwood Press.

Rukhmabai
(1864–1955)
India

The story of Rukhmabai, a moving account of rebellion against the traditional Indian practice of child marriage, has for long been overlooked in the broader history of women's rights. Yet in its day, her celebrated legal test case, which dragged on through the courts for four years (from 1884 to 1888) and inspired considerable debate on child marriage, became a *cause célèbre*, much discussed by feminists and detractors alike.

The story began in 1876 when the eleven-year-old Rukhmabai was given in marriage to a man of nineteen, Dadaji Bhikaji, a poor relative of her stepfather. After the religious marriage ceremony had taken place, Rukhmabai, a girl of some intellectual talents and cultured interests, remained at home with her own family. She continued to educate herself, using books provided by a local Free Church Mission school, since education over the age of ten was not available to Indian girls at that time. Meanwhile, she and her family hoped her illiterate husband would adopt a similar course of action.

When Rukhmabai reached puberty, the time when the marriage should traditionally have been consummated, her stepfather, Sakharam Arjun, a medical doctor with interests in social and religious reform, refused to allow her to live with her husband on account of her young age. For the next eleven years, Rukhamabai continued to resist consummating the marriage, and her husband was fobbed off with various excuses. A naturally indolent man who had no inclination to educate himself, he indulged in a life of some sexual dissipation and eventually found himself in considerable debt. In March 1884, when he was thirty and Rukhmabai twenty-two, he filed suit for his full conjugal rights and, more important to him, access to the 25,000 rupees' worth of property that she owned.

Horrified at the thought that she might at last be compelled to live with Bhikaji and be trapped for life with an intellectual inferior whom she neither loved nor respected, Rukhmabai averred that she would rather go to prison than enter married life with him. She argued that her husband's penury and the fact that he was sick with tuberculosis meant that he was in no fit state to properly provide for her. However, her reason for resisting the marriage was a more fundamental, personal one, as she herself stated in one of two letters she sent anonymously to *The Times of India* in June 1885: "It comes between me and the thing which I prize above all others—study and mental cultivation. Without the least fault of mine I am doomed to seclusion" (Chandra 1998, 17). Signing the letter "A Hindoo Lady," Rukhmabai expanded on her own experience, developing a wider discourse on the miserable lives of Indian child brides. She talked of how their enjoyment of childhood and education was cut short, usually at the age of ten, by the onerous duties of married life; how they were often subjected to mental and physical abuse at the hands of their husbands' families; and how early widowhood in many cases then condemned them to long lives in seclusion, with no access to education or further opportunities for self-improvement. Marriage for Indian girls, she argued, should come no earlier than the age of fifteen. But, more perceptively, in her spirited and intelligent argument, she underlined the terrible psychological damage that so many repressed young brides suffered. They became "timid, languid, melancholy, sickly, devoid of cheerfulness and therefore incapable of communicating to others" (Chandra 1998, 30). She passionately believed that many Indian women wanted more out of life than this servitude: "Do not think that we are satisfied with the life of drudgery that we live, and that we have no taste for and aspiration after a higher life" (30).

Having had the temerity to challenge the weight of long-held Hindu tradition, Rukhmabai lent renewed impetus to the humanitarian debate over the abuse of underage girls, which had been gathering pace in India since the late 1870s. Undaunted, she continued to educate herself and developed an unshakeable crusading spirit while the case dragged through the Indian courts. As Sudhir Chandra argues, the legal case became a personal crusade, for it presented her with a golden opportunity: that of offering herself as a martyr to the cause of reform. As part of her own defense, Rukhmabai also offered an intelligent and radical challenge to the marriage laws. Her argument was that she had been married at an age when she was too immature to understand the full implications of married life and that therefore she should not be legally bound by the marriage agreement.

In September 1885, the case was heard in the Bombay High Court under British law, even though the law on restitution of conjugal rights was obsolete in Britain itself. Rukhmabai was defended by three eminent lawyers sympathetic to the wider legal ramifications of her case. The judge, hampered by having to apply English laws to Hindu religious practice, rejected Bhikaji's petition on basic moral grounds, concluding that Rukhmabai could not be compelled to consummate the marriage against her will. But on appeal in March–April 1886, the Bombay High Court reversed this decision and remanded the case for retrial.

Meanwhile, a group of outraged supporters, including the Indian reformer Behramji Malabari (who had written on child marriage and enforced widowhood); the educators and reformers Pandita Ramabai and Ramabai Ranade; the editor of *The Times of India,* Henry Curwen; as well as missionaries in India and feminists in the United States and United Kingdom, together mounted a campaign in support of Rukhmabai's appeal. Her case was even discussed in the House of Lords, with her supporters petitioning the British government on the iniquity of the judgment against her. Led by Millicent Garrett Fawcett, feminists in the UK set up a Ruhkmabai Committee to support her through her appeal, although for as long as she could, Rukhmabai proudly refused all offers of financial assistance. Much mileage would obviously be made out of this case in the West, albeit in often hysterical and exaggerated accounts in print, which made a self-righteous tale out of the plight of "the courageous girl who refused to live with her brutal and worthless husband" (Burton 1998, 108).

The case was retried in March 1887, and Rukhmabai was ordered by the judge to go to her husband's home within one month and allow him his conjugal rights; if she refused, she would be sent to prison for six months. Rukhmabai remained defiant, and the issue was not finally resolved until Queen Victoria intervened and Rukhmabai's marriage was dissolved by royal decree. In July 1888, Rukhmabai agreed to buy Bhikaji off with a payment of 2,000 rupees "in satisfaction of all costs," so that he could then remarry, which he did immediately. Rukhmabai also paid her own legal costs, as well as another personal price—that of being forbidden under Hindu law to remarry. In this instance, such a ban was probably irrelevant, for Rukhmabai, with her burning sense of social purpose, had determined to train as a doctor. For some time, she had been receiving support from British doctors in India, such as Edith Pechey Phipson, the director of the Cama Hospital in Bombay. With her encouragement, Rukhmabai improved her English and went to England in 1889 to study at the London School of Medicine for Women (which had been established in 1874 by Elizabeth Garrett Anderson, Sophia Jex-Blake, and others). Her studies were funded by feminist sympathizers Walter McLaren and his wife Eva, a suffragist, and the Countess of Dufferin's Fund for Supplying Medical Aid to the Women of India. Unable to qualify in England, like other English medical students, Rukhmabai had to go to Edinburgh to sit for her final professional examination with the stolid support of Jex-Blake, who had become a close friend.

Rukhmabai returned to India in 1895, where Pechey-Phipson obtained a post for her as chief medical officer at the women's hospital at Surat, which marked the commencement of a distinguished thirty-five-year career in medicine. In 1904 Bhikaji died. It is interesting to note that despite her fierce resistance to Hindu tradition and the fact that she had never even lived with him as his wife, Rukhmabai felt compelled to adopt the traditional widow's sari on her former husband's demise in order to avoid adding further fuel to local prejudice against her work as a doctor in Surat. As Chandra (1998) suggests, no doubt she considered this conformist act a necessary compromise if it meant that local women—reluctant at the best of times to visit doctors—would continue to attend her hospital. In 1918 Rukhmabai was offered a role in the Women's Medical Service but opted for the post of chief medical officer at the Zenana (women's) State Hospital in Rajkot. Until her retirement in 1929, she devoted herself to treating women at that hospital, as well as continuing to support the wider movement for women's emancipation and her own personal campaign against child marriage. In 1929 she published a pamphlet, "Purdah—the Need for Its Abolition," arguing that young widows were being denied the chance to contribute actively to Indian society.

Rukhmabai was, for her time, one of the most important figures in the cause of women's rights in colonial India. The courage with which she endured years of vilification and humiliation for defying convention and for challenging both the British legal system and Hindu religious practice was extraordinary. During the course of her long life, she inspired many other Indian women to take up medicine and social service.

See also Jex-Blake, Sophia; Pechey-Phipson, Edith; Ramabai, Pandita Saraswati; Ranade, Ramabai.

References and Further Reading

Burton, Antoinette. 1998a. *At the Heart of Empire: Indians and the Colonial Encounter in Late-Victorian Britain.* Berkeley: University of California Press.

———. 1998b. "From 'Child-Bride' to 'Hindoo Lady': Rukhmabai and the Debate about Sexual Respectability in Imperial Britain." *American Historical Review* 104(4): 1119–1146.

Chandra, Sudhir. 1998. *Enslaved Daughters: Colonialism, Law and Women's Rights.* Delhi: Oxford University Press.

Lutzker, Edythe. 1973. *Edith Pechey-Phipson MD.* New York: Exposition Press.

Rutnam, Mary
(1873–1962)
Canada/Sri Lanka

The Canadian doctor and gynecologist Mary Rutnam, who made medicine her life's work in Sri Lanka over a fifty-year career, rose to national prominence and veneration as a leading figure in women's health, birth control, health education, child care, and other social issues. Along with her many commitments to women's and children's health care, Rutnam also worked for the rights of prisoners, supported the temperance movement, and wrote standard texts on health and hygiene for schoolchildren.

Born Mary Irwin in Elora, Ontario, into a Presbyterian family, Rutnam studied medicine at the Women's Medical College of Trinity College in Toronto. Upon her graduation, she answered an advertisement by the American Board of Commissioners for Foreign Missions to take up missionary work in Asia and did preparatory training in New York in 1896. There she met and married a Christian Tamil, Samuel Christmas Rutnam, who had come to the United States to give lectures against opium smoking and had stayed to study at Princeton University.

Arriving in Sri Lanka (then the British colony of Ceylon) to take up her appointment at the McCleod Hospital for Women in Inuvil, Putnam was immediately ostracized from missionary work for making a mixed marriage. She moved to Colombo with her husband and worked temporarily in a government hospital, where she taught female medical students. But she was refused a position at the hospital on the grounds that her medical degree was from Canada and not Britain. Instead, she opened her own practice as a gynecologist and attracted many Muslim female patients who would not have consulted male doctors.

In 1904 Putnam began collaborating with another Canadian doctor in improving medical and social facilities for Ceylonese women. They set up the Girls' Friendly Society and the Ceylon Women's Union that year, offering advice on child care and maternal health, organizing discussion groups on women's rights, and exchanging books.

In 1909, speaking at the fifth annual meeting of the Ceylon Women's Union, Rutnam decried government for spending too much money on housing criminals instead of funding grassroots work in raising moral standards in the home. The subject of women's rights and suffrage was also raised at this meeting. On a return visit to Canada in 1907–1908, Rutnam caught up on the development of women's organizations there and gave lectures on life for women in Ceylon. On her return to Colombo, she encouraged a group of Tamil women to set up the Tamil Women's Union, a nondenominational organization to promote Tamil culture and education projects, such as a school for poor Tamil children. Throughout her many activities, Rutnam gravitated toward Ceylonese women and away from white, European Christian groups.

Rutnam's work for women's health in Ceylon was extensive: in 1909 she ran a six-week lecture course in nursing and disseminated her message on important health issues through frequent lectures, exhibitions, and newspaper articles. She published a textbook on hygiene titled *A Health Manual for Schools* in 1923 and the *Homecraft Manual for Ceylon Schools* in 1933. The latter, far from being a manual on homemaking, as its title might suggest, tackled issues such as the exploitation of children as servants, denounced their maltreatment by employers, and encouraged young women to take up social work.

Sex education was also a major element of Rutnam's social work, as was her championing of the moral principles of the Girl Guide movement, which she inaugurated in Ceylon in 1922. She ran her own nursing home for women, where she offered birth control, and criticized poor standards of hygiene in state-run maternity hospitals. Aware of the high incidence of rickets among children, she launched a campaign to get the Ceylonese to drink more milk and eat more nutritious foods while simultaneously condemning alcohol abuse through her work for the Woman's Christian Temperance Union of Ceylon. In 1934–1935 Rutnam's medical skills were called upon during a major malaria epidemic, and she and her son joined relief teams working in the Kegalle district.

In the 1930s public work began to take up a huge part of Rutnam's time with the organization of conferences on women's issues and, from 1932, a prominent role in the family planning movement. She helped set up the first family planning clinic in Ceylon in 1937, but her plans were thwarted by war, and it was 1953 before she could take this campaign further.

From 1927 Rutnam took an increasingly high-profile role in the suffrage campaign in Ceylon, with the foundation of the Women's Franchise Union (WFU), which supported a limited franchise for women. When women won the vote in 1931, the WFU became the Women's Political Union and worked for democratic rights for women everywhere, with Rutnam becoming its first president. In 1937 she was the first woman to successfully contest a seat on a municipal council, that of Bambalapitiya in Colombo, defying native critics who looked upon her as a foreign interloper and white Catholics who opposed her support for birth control. During her time in office, Rutnam supervised sanitation projects, urban renewal, and local poor relief, but birth control critics had her removed a year later, when she started trying to establish more family planning clinics.

Inspired by the work of women's institutes in Canada, Rutnam inaugurated similar organizations in Ceylon from 1931, which set out to work among the rural poor and encourage their participation in society. The network of institutes that grew up under Rutnam's presidency over the next thirteen years was named the Ceylon Women's Society (Lanka Mahila Samiti)—a name used by similar women's groups in Bengal, India. These groups went out to the villages and taught women health care, first aid, nursing, and cookery, as well as offering literacy and handicraft classes. The society opened its first nursery school in 1947; by 1981 it had become the largest women's organization in the country. Its work was taken over in 1944 by the formation of the All-Ceylon Women's Conference, of which Rutnam was a cofounder. Under its auspices, she broadened her concerns to tackle the traditional dowry system, the rights of female prisoners and factory workers, adoption, adult education, and crèche facilities for working mothers.

In 1949, by that time retired from her medical practice, Rutnam was lauded on the occasion of her seventy-sixth birthday for her devotion to social causes. She turned down offers of awards from Great Britain, preferring instead in 1958 to accept the Public Service Award from the Ramón Magsaysay Foundation for her services to the Sri Lankan people. After her death in 1962, funds were raised to establish a lasting memorial to her—a women's and children's waiting room at the Lady Ridgeway Hospital for Children in Colombo.

References and Further Reading
Jayawardena, Kumari. 1993. *Dr. Mary Rutnam: A Canadian Pioneer of Women's Rights in Sri Lanka.* Colombo: Social Scientists' Association.

Rye, Maria
(1829–1903)
United Kingdom

In nineteenth-century Britain, there were very few options open to a middle-class woman in reduced circumstances who sought respectable, gainful employment. She could either hope to fall back on the mercy of relatives or become a governess, a profession already very oversubscribed. In midcentury a third option—emigration—was opened up for such women by organizations such as the Female Middle-Class Emigration Society (1862–1886), founded by Maria Rye. With the British Empire rapidly establishing new colonies around the world, emigration seemed to offer new prospects. Only a limited number of women were able to find work as governess under the scheme, but many found other sources of employment in domestic service. Rye later extended her work to assist destitute children and working-class families in emigrating.

Rye was one of nine children of a London solicitor. Educated at home by governesses, she followed the traditional middle-class path into local charitable work and supported a proposed Married Women's Property Act, initiated in 1855 by members of the Langham Place Circle, which involved her in the gathering of signatures for a petition presented in Parliament in 1856. She was also active from 1859 in the group's Society for Promoting the Employment of Women, which under Jessie Boucherett's guidance developed numerous spheres of work—in printing, telegraphy, bookkeeping, and office work—that were not too physically taxing and offered respectable employment to middle-class women. Some members of the group, such as Barbara Bodichon and Bessie Rayner Parkes, had rapidly come to the conclusion that office work provided the least controversial opportunity of employment for middle-class women in financial need. Rye concurred and in 1859 set up a law stationer's business, to offer employment to women in the copying of legal documents, in a house obtained for the purpose at Lincoln's Inn Fields by the Langham Place Circle. Rye was soon deluged with applications for work: "on one occasion 810 women applied for a single position paying only £15 a year" (Hammerton 1977, 55). To accommodate this glut of "redundant" or "superfluous" women (as they were then termed) desperate to find employment, Rye privately assisted some twenty-two of the applicants in obtaining loans to emigrate. She also helped establish a school to train women telegraphers, run by Isa Craig, and became one of the founding shareholders in Emily Faithfull's Victoria Press, which was run entirely by women.

In June 1860 Rye published an article entitled "On Assisted Emigration" in the *English Woman's Journal.* She quickly found, however, through her correspondence with supporters of the scheme in Australia, New Zealand, and Natal (in South Africa), that the primary need in the British colonies was for women willing to take up more physical, domestic work. After describing her emigration scheme at the Social Science Congress in 1861, Rye called for donations to help establish a proper society. Rye's pamphlet, "Emigration of Educated Women," published that year by the Victoria Press, provoked considerable discussion of the issue in *The Times.*

With the assistance of Bodichon, who lobbied her network of influential friends and philanthropists, enough financial sponsorship was raised by July 1862 for Rye and Jane Lewin to found the Female Middle-Class Emigration Society, which would serve as the prototype for several other similar organizations. Rye and her colleagues' work involved them in writing letters of introduction and securing a decent place for emigrants to stay when they arrived at their destination. Jane Rendall has described Rye's emigration scheme as a "defeatist remedy" (1985, 185), and, indeed, word began to filter back to England that many women arriving in remote colonies found few job opportunities as governesses and that these were badly paid, although some of Rye's own protégées appear to have had more success. As a woman of evangelical background, she was anxious that the women she sent should contribute to the raising of the moral tone in the shantytowns of developing countries, such as Australia. But in essence, female emigration became an extension of the marriage market and worked to the advantage of male colonizers, which is why the society had many male backers. Mindful of the greater demand for servants and domestic workers, Rye began to develop a two-tier system (offering different travel rates), with one track for middle-class women who were prepared to take governess posts and one for lower-middle-class women who would accept domestic roles.

Over the next few years, Rye traveled widely to see firsthand how women were faring, not just in their new lives but also on board emigrant ships. Aware of the hard life such women would have to face, whatever their social status, she emphasized prior preparation and a modicum of skill in cooking, sewing, doing housework, and laundering. She sailed to British Columbia, working there in tandem with the Columbian Emigration Society to promote immigration of working-class women—some from the northern cotton mills of Lancashire—before herself traveling, at the end of 1862, to Australia and New Zealand in the company of 100 emigrant women (only eight of whom were actually governesses). She spent much of the period until 1865 developing a reception network for female emigrants in those countries and appointing the society's representatives there, but more and more, after her return from her travels in 1865, her work was geared toward promoting working-class emigration and, eventually, in order to alleviate economic misery, the emigration of whole families.

Meanwhile, because the Langham Place Circle was committed to the campaign for women's suffrage, whereas Rye believed firmly in women's separate spheres of nonpolitical activism, she withdrew from the group and the emigration society to concentrate on her own emigration work. Her successor, Jane Lewin, adopted new policies narrowing the society's emigration work to the placement primarily of governesses, thus reducing the numbers of women it was able to assist and limiting the society's operation. In 1892 the society became part of the United British Women's Emigration Association.

Rye's own experiences of the high rates of sickness and death on emigrant ships, which left numerous children orphaned, prompted her to turn to their welfare and the possibilities of child emigration. In 1869, with the support of eminent reformer Lord Shaftesbury, she established a home for poor children (mainly girls from workhouse schools in Liverpool) aged five to twelve in Peckham, in south London. In the hope of saving them from falling into crime and prostitution, she arranged the emigration from 1869 of many such "waifs and strays" to Canada, where she had established "Our Western Home" for them at Niagara. She often accompanied them on the voyage herself. In 1891 Rye was influential in the founding of the Church of England Waifs and Strays Society, which by the end of the century had provided assisted passages to 8,000 poor children. Much of her work in child emigration was emulated by Dr. Thomas Barnardo.

In 1895 Rye was forced by illness to retire to Hemel Hempstead on an annual civil list pension of £70, awarded by Queen Victoria in gratitude for her work for emigrant women. The emigration scheme she had initiated continued until 1915, when the Peckham home, known as the Emigration Home for Destitute Little Girls, was closed down. Although some critics have accused Rye of inhumanity in the indiscriminate separation of poor children from their families (a criticism leveled also at Barnardo), it has been pointed out that many of the intrepid British women who first emigrated to Australia, New Zealand, and Canada under her scheme also took with them to the colonies a feminist fighting spirit and sowed the seeds of the women's suffrage movements there. Websites giving useful information on archival sources on Rye's work can be found at http://sca.lib.liv.ac.uk/collections/socialwork/rye.htm and http://www.nram.org.nz/e/38/w6.html.

See also Bodichon, Barbara; Boucherett, Jessie.
References and Further Reading
Diamond, Marion. 1999. *Emigration and Empire: The Life of Maria S. Rye.* New York: Garland Publishing.

Hammerton, James A. 1977. "Feminism and Female Emigration 1861–1886." In Martha Vicinus, ed., *A Widening Sphere: Changing Roles of Victorian Women.* Bloomington: Indiana University Press.

———. 1979. *Emigrant Gentlewomen: Genteel Poverty and Female Emigration 1830–1914.* London: Croom Helm.

Holcombe, Lee. 1983. *Wives and Property: Reform of the Married Women's Property Law in Nineteenth-Century England.* Toronto: University of Toronto Press.

Orr, Clarissa Campbell, ed. 1996. *Wollstonecraft's Daughters: Womanhood in England and France, 1780–1920.* Manchester: Manchester University Press.

Rendall, Jane. 1985. *The Origins of Modern Feminism: Women in Britain, France, and the United States 1780–1860.* Chicago: University of Chicago Press.

Rye, Maria. 1987 [1859]. "The Rise and Progress of Telegraphs." In Candida Ann Lacey, ed., *Barbara Leigh Smith Bodichon and the Langham Place Group.* London: Routledge and Kegan Paul.

———. 1987 [1860]. "On Assisted Emigration." In Candida Ann Lacey, ed., *Barbara Leigh Smith Bodichon and the Langham Place Group.* London: Routledge and Kegan Paul.

Wagner, Gillian. 1979. *Children of the Empire.* London: Weidenfeld and Nicolson (for a discussion of the fate of Rye's child emigrants).

S

el-Saadawi, Nawal
(1931–)
Egypt

The controversial Egyptian doctor, sociologist, and feminist Nawal el-Saadawi, looked upon by many as the Simone de Beauvoir of the Arab world, led a new wave of reformist activity among Arab feminists in the early 1950s in Egypt. From the outset, el-Saadawi courted controversy throughout the Muslim world by being the first Arab woman to tackle the taboo subject of female sexuality, elaborating her ideas in her groundbreaking book *Women and Sex* (1971; 1972 in English). As a fierce critic of both the Egyptian government and, for many years, traditional Islam, she has suffered imprisonment, censorship, and death threats during a career that has produced more than thirty books.

El-Saadawi has been a powerful commentator on the physical abuse of Arab women and their exposure to prostitution, sexual exploitation, and venereal disease. Most notably, she was for many years the foremost campaigner in the Arab world against the practice of clitoridectomy, describing in horrifying and graphic detail the sexual mutilation of Egyptian girls and giving a disturbing account of her own experience of the practice at the age of six.

El-Saadawi was born in Kafr Tahla, a village in the Nile delta. Her father, a cultured man who became general controller of education for the province of Menufia, allowed her to refuse early marriage at the age of ten, continue her education at secondary school, and study psychiatry at Cairo University. El-Saadawi received her doctorate in 1955 and in 1966 took a further degree in public health at Columbia University in the United States. During this period, she worked as a doctor in rural areas and later as a psychiatrist for the al-Quasser al-Aini Hospital in Cairo. In 1966 she was appointed director of health education by the Egyptian government and later edited the government publication *Health Magazine* (1970–1973).

Her leading role in matters of public health alerted el-Saadawi to many pressing social issues, particularly with regard to the treatment of women and children and the continuing prevalence of traditional misogynistic attitudes toward women as initiators of sin. She had begun publishing short stories in 1957, and through her writing, both fictional and nonfictional, she began challenging Egyptian society to confront many prevailing moral and sexual issues and double standards. In particular, she emphasized the sexual exploitation of women behind closed doors and the symbolic imposition of the veil, which she saw as reinforcing male control over women and their supposedly dangerous sexuality. Like her male precursor, Qasim Amin, who had argued similarly as far back as 1899 in his book *Women's Emancipation*, el-Saadawi contended that veiling was a social convention, not an Islamic tradition. So, too, was the practice of clitoridectomy, which its proponents supported through what she also saw as a misinterpretation of Islamic law.

El-Saadawi once observed, "My troubles started the day I held a pen in my hand" (Goodwin 1995, 331), and indeed her first and most important literary landmark, *Women and Sex,* marked the beginning of a lifelong moral discourse with both the Egyptian state and Islam. The book caused a furor with its open discussion of female sexuality, the right of Arab women to sexual fulfillment, and the Muslim obsession with the virginity of young girls. She illustrated

Nawal el-Saadawi (Robert Maas/Corbis)

how the imposition of the strict moral code of virginity in Arab society has led to many cases of abuse and ill-treatment of young women and the frequent infliction of deep psychological harm. In conjunction with her argument on the sexual liberation of Arab women, she also called for their economic emancipation and their right to train for and enter the workplace alongside men. The book was quickly censored and her writing banned, and el-Saadawi lost her job as director of health education, as well as her editorship of *Health Magazine* and her membership in the medical association of Egypt.

Undeterred, el-Saadawi set up the Solidarity of Arab Women's Association in Cairo in the 1970s. After lobbying for support from liberal male politicians, this pan-Arab association brought out a magazine for the discussion of women's issues that was circulated privately and debated the interpretation of Islamic law with regard to women. The government kept a close watch on this and all el-Saadawi's activities. From 1973 to 1976, she returned to medical research on women and neurosis at Aín Shams University. She continued to write, but her outspokenness meant she had to publish in Beirut, Lebanon, because her work would have been censored in Egypt.

Nevertheless, el-Saadawi's commitment to women's issues continued: in 1976 she attended an international tribunal on crimes against women in Brussels, and from 1979 to 1980 she joined the United Nations in Addis Ababa as an adviser on women's programs. Back in Egypt in 1980, she fell afoul of Anwar Sadat's government when she began writing again. Influenced by the tumultuous changes taking place in Iran after the revolution of 1979, el-Saadawi sought to redress criticism of her work in the Muslim world and revised her position on traditional Islam. She argued in *The Hidden Face of Eve* (1980) that Islam's traditional values did not denigrate women and that both Judaism and Christianity had in the past been equally chauvinistic in their treatment of women. Thus she underlined the fact that Muslim women had not always been the victims of an oppressive male patriarchal system. When the Qu'ran was composed in the seventh century, "women at the time of the Prophet obtained rights of which today they are deprived in most Arab countries" (el-Saadawi 1980, 211). This shift in position and her argument in support of the original equality that women enjoyed alongside men under Islam has, however, lost her some support among the new generation of feminists. Many women saw this as an about-face, after years of being one of Islam's fiercest critics, and as being damaging to the cause of women, particularly when the vast majority of Arab women live truly repressed lives.

Despite these criticisms, el-Saadawi's courageous ongoing support for the Solidarity of Arab Women's Association, through her journalism, and public speaking led, in 1980, to accusations of her having committed "crimes against the state." President Anwar Sadat ordered the arrest of el-Saadawi and 1,535 others in a roundup of dissident elements. She and other women involved in publishing the feminist magazine *Confrontation* were accused of having printed articles critical of Sadat's government, and once again her books were banned. Her apartment in Cairo was raided, and she was held in prison for eighty days, to be released after Sadat's assassination in October. She published *Memoirs from the Women's Prison* about her experiences in the Qanatir prison (in English, 1986) and founded the Pan-Arab Women's Organization in 1982. With the resurgence of feminism in Egypt, el-Saadawi once more stepped into frontline feminist politics, as president of the organization calling for the democratic integration of women into all aspects of Arab life and society.

However, el-Saadawi's continuing high international profile (built on the success of the English translations of her books in the West), coupled with her radical views on the position of women in Arab society, has made her forever open to attack from both government and religious authorities. When she criticized the reimposition of veiling in Egypt, Iran, and Saudi Arabia in the wake of the Islamic Revolution of 1979 in Iran, attacks on her were renewed. In 1992 her name went on a death list compiled by fundamentalist groups, despite the attempt she had made in *The Hidden Face of Eve* to take a more conciliatory line toward Islam and rediscover what she saw as the positive aspects of "true Islam." El-Saadawi was forced to leave Egypt for her own safety. In 1993 she reluctantly left her home in Giza and settled in North Carolina, where she lectured at Duke University. Six years later she was able to return to Egypt, in 2000 settling back in Cairo. But not long after her return she was once more at the center of a controversy over her refusal to kowtow to Islamic laws that she considers unfeminist. With the resurgence of Islam in Egypt, el-Saadawi brought the wrath of the fundamentalists on her when in June 2001 a lawsuit was filed against her, under the Islamic law of *Hisba* (the right of a citizen to bring a civil prosecution against another for breaches of Islamic code). El-Saadawi was accused by lawyer Nabih Wahsh of discouraging the wearing of the veil and, in a newspaper interview that March, of alleging that the kissing by religious pilgrims of the sacred stone of Muhammad in Mecca was akin to idolatry. If el-Saadawi is found guilty of being an apostate, under Islamic law her husband of thirty-seven years will be compelled to divorce her, a threat that does not intimidate a woman of her unshakeable convictions.

In addition to her political and social works, el-Saadawi has written seven successful novels, the most notable being *Two Women in One* (1975) and *Woman at Point Zero* (1983), short stories, and plays, many of which tackle issues relating to women's status in the Arab world. They describe the debilitating psychological effects of sexual oppression and women's constant struggle to be treated as equals. Like her nonfiction essays, they do not shrink from discussing sexual issues such as prostitution, incest, and illegitimacy as well as sexual and psychological abuse—instances of which she came across all too often in her work as a doctor. In so doing, el-Saadawi has laid herself open to public vilification and persecution. But nothing, it seems, will make her abandon her campaigning against the limitations imposed on Arab women's social and sexual freedom and the need for political and legal changes that will ensure that Arab society as a whole becomes more democratic.

References and Further Reading

Goodwin, Jan. 1995. *Price of Honor: Muslim Women Lift the Veil of Silence in the Islamic World.* London: Warner Books.

Prasad, Raekha. 2000. "Lone Star of the Nile." The Guardian Profile. *Guardian*, 17 June, 6–7.

el-Saadawi, Nawal. 1980. *The Hidden Face of Eve: Women in the Arab World.* London: Zed Books.

———. 1991. *Searching.* Translated by Shirley Eber. London: Zed Books.

———. 1994. *Memoirs from the Women's Prison.* Translated by Marilyn Booth. Berkeley: University of California Press.

———. 1999. *A Daughter of Isis: The Autobiography of Nawal El Saadawi.* London: Zed Books.

Sabas Alomá, Mariblanca
(1901–)
Cuba

The leading Cuban feminist and journalist, Mariblanca Sabas Alomá, is best remembered among her compatriots in the women's movement for her "maternal feminism," reflected in a lifelong support for the rights of illegitimate children and unmarried mothers.

Born in Santiago de Cuba in 1901, Sabas began working as a journalist in around 1918, writing for newspapers and journals such as *Free Cuba* (1918), *Cuban News* (1919–1923), and *Rising* (1918–1923). She won gold medals for her poetry in a Santiago competition in 1923. She moved to Havana that year, where she attended the first national women's congress held in Cuba and became one of only two female founding members of the Marxist-dominated Minority Group, a cultural association dedicated also to social change that was active from 1923 to 1927.

Between 1923 and 1927 Sabas spent much time abroad, studying art and literature in Mexico, art appreciation at New York's Columbia University, and Spanish literature at the University of Río Piedras in Puerto Rico. After traveling extensively in Latin America, where she attended various women's conferences, she returned to Havana in 1927, where she wrote a weekly column for the journal *Cartels* (1928–1933), which provoked criticism for its often sarcastic and belligerent tone. She also alienated herself from feminists from the upper classes by berating them for their elitism. Convinced that acts of charity were not enough to affect social change, she saw the philanthropy of the upper-class elite as a form of exhibitionism. Such women betrayed their sex, she felt, by being too concerned with their own social status.

Sabas was radical in her views on how women could and should change their lives. She saw their economic independence as being crucial to their liberation and felt they should take more extreme steps to free themselves from their traditional subordination to men and domestic duties. Even as she sought the liberation of women from the traditional roles in which they were abused and exploited, however, she made much of what she saw as the mystique of motherhood. She appreciated the fundamental power mothers had, not only in changing entrenched social attitudes but also in molding the generations of the future: "Women create men and make them as women wish them to be. The mother in the home is the one who forges the character and spiritual models for her children. . . . If men are bad, then a great part of the responsibility belongs to women" (Stoner 1991, 92). Like other feminists of her time, Sabas was convinced of the moral superiority of women. But although she located herself on the political left and endorsed revolutionary change, she did not want to see women abandon their primary nurturing roles in society. What she did wish for, most passionately, was to see the transforming effect of women's natural dignity and their moral example—what she termed their sense of outrage—have a positive and ameliorative effect on men's social and sexual behavior. As for the problem of prostitution, in her view it needed a government solution. Better employment opportunities should be provided for women, she argued, so that they did not need to have recourse to the vice trade.

Sabas's advocacy of women's sexual freedom, her support for illegitimate children, and her condemnation of the double standards condoned in the sexual behavior of adulterous men inevitably invoked heavy criticism from all sides. The Catholic Church saw her as a heretic; polite society condemned her for being perverted or even "homosexual." She was one of several leading Cuban feminists who believed that illegitimate children should enjoy the same civil status as children born in wedlock. But she recognized that such children were stigmatized, as were those from divorced homes, and opposed the placing of illegitimate children in foundling institutions. Such was Sabas's strength of feeling on this issue that in 1925 she walked out of the second national women's congress, along with several other women on the left, in protest at the failure of the majority of delegates to support a resolution on equal rights for illegitimate children.

Sabas was equally vociferous in her support for women's right to divorce and against the perpetuation of unhappy marriages, for which she blamed women as much as men. To her it was far better to escape the deadening and dehumanizing prison of an unhappy marriage: "Enlightened solitude," she wrote, "is preferable to relationships that are darkened by lies" (Stoner 1991, 96).

Sabas did not restrict her activism to women's issues—she also wrote in support of the rights of workers' pay and conditions, in particular pointing up the anomaly of the longer working day demanded of Cuban employees of foreign firms than any foreign workers employed there. She supported a strike by Woolworth's shop assistants, who were protesting their economic exploitation by the U.S.-based company. During her long career in journalism, Sabas contributed to and edited a diverse range of journals and newspapers, in Latin America and Spain. She is also noted for her avant-garde poetry.

See also Collado, María; Domínguez Navarro, Ofelia; Gómez de Avellaneda y Arteaga, Gertrudis; Rodríguez Acosta, Ofelia.

References and Further Reading

Stoner, K. Lynn. 1991. *From the House to the Streets: The Cuban Woman's Movement for Legal Reform, 1898–1940.* Durham: Duke University Press.

Saghal, Manmohini Zutshi
(1909–)
India

A humanitarian who worked in organized labor and on a wide cross section of social welfare projects, Saghal was born in Allahabad in northern India and grew up in Lahore, a member of the influential, progressive Nehru family. Her father, Ladli Prasad Zutshi, was the nephew of the eminent Indian politician Motilal Nehru. Her feminist mother had been involved in philanthropic work and running ladies' clubs and had had the temerity to attend Young Women's Christian Association (YWCA) evening classes by bicycle at a time when "no other Indian lady of her status in Lahore had the courage to do this" (Saghal 1994, 33). She encouraged Saghal and her sisters to follow her example and not only ride bicycles but also horses. She also urged her four daughters to pursue a higher education, and Saghal completed her M.A. degree in history at college in Lahore in 1929.

During Mahatma Gandhi's civil disobedience movement of the 1920s and 1930s, Saghal joined in public protests and spoke out against colonial rule; she was sent to prison for her activities (on one occasion with her mother and two of her sisters) in 1930, 1931, and 1932. But these protests never spilled over into revolutionary violence, for she was a committed pacifist. In 1935 she became principal of a Congress Party school (the Bihar Mahila Vidyapith) in Bihar province, where she attempted to introduce changes, such as offering physical fitness classes for the older female students, but met with much opposition from their families.

Saghal married in 1935 and settled in Bombay, where she took on social work. During food shortages in the early period after Indian independence in 1947, she became a member of the All-India Women's Central Food Council, which ran a canteen in Delhi and provided meals that used commodities other than the wheat and rice that were in short supply. After the partition of India caused a massive displacement of people, she began to work with refugees, on a token salary of one rupee per month, in the women's section of the Ministry of Rehabilitation. She also helped to run its home for displaced women and their children. Saghal organized loans and financial assistance so that those who had lost their property could set themselves up in business again. She later became president of the Indian Women's Craft Society and resigned from the ministry in 1954 to take on more welfare work.

In 1952 Saghal stood as a candidate in the first Indian general election, but having failed to get elected, she turned her energies to organized labor. She became chair of the Northern Railway Employees Union and president of the Fishermen's Union and the Union of the Lower Division of Clerks in the Ministry of Defence. She took an active interest in the living conditions at workers' camps, organizing better sanitation, the installation of water systems, and eventually relocating such workers to new sites. She helped a group of municipal workers who were heavily in debt by arranging loans for them and was made honorary director of the social and welfare rehabilitation directorate.

In 1973 Saghal joined the National Federation of Indian Women and took up the cause of abused wives, especially those who had been the victims of fire attacks. She also helped wives who had been abandoned obtain financial support for themselves and their children. Saghal worked for the Indian Council for Child Welfare, encouraging further education and adoption, and was a patron of the Aryta Anathalaya orphanage, established in 1950 to offer a home to 600 children.

Saghal's forty years of work for the Delhi Commonwealth Women's Association involved her in various welfare activities. For nine years she acted as president of the Family Planning Association in Delhi. As president of the Indian Council of Social Welfare, she was still active in the 1990s, supervising the building of a hostel for working men in New Delhi.

References and Further Reading
Saghal, Manmohini Zutshi. 1994. *An Indian Freedom Fighter Recalls Her Life.* Armonk, NY: M. E. Sharpe.

al-Said, Aminah
(1914–1995)
Egypt

As a journalist, translator, and women's rights campaigner, Aminah al-Said was the first high-profile woman professional in Egyptian publishing and the only leading feminist voice not to be suppressed by President Gamal Abdel Nasser during the 1950s because she "used her pen to promote women's causes within the framework of the Arab socialist revolution" (Kandiyoti 1991, 217). Along with her elder sister Karimah (who in 1965 became the first Egyptian woman to hold the post of minister of education), Aminah al-Said kept the issue of women's civil and social rights alive during the fallow years between the death of Huda Sha'rawi in 1947 and the outspoken campaigning of Nawal el-Saadawi that began in the 1970s.

Born in Asyût, al-Said benefited from having parents with liberal-progressive attitudes, who believed in women's education and did not marry her off at a young age. Instead, they moved to the capital, Cairo, so that their daughters would be better able to pursue an education. Al-Said did so at the Shubra Secondary School for Girls, one of the first Egyptian state schools to offer girls the same education provided to boys. While still a young girl, she developed an interest in women's rights, inspired in part by a meeting with Huda Sha'rawi when she visited the school.

During the Egyptian nationalist disturbances of the late 1920s, al-Said became politically active and at age fourteen joined the youth group of Sha'rawi's Egyptian Feminist Union (EFU). In 1931 al-Said became one of the first small groups of women who attended the Egyptian University at Cairo, studying in the faculty of arts. After graduating in 1935, she took up a career in journalism at the journal *al-Musawwar* (eventually becoming its editor in 1973). During the 1940s, al-Said proceeded to carve out a career for herself in journalism and became a leading member of the publishing establishment. She also wrote novels, children's stories, and travel pieces. During this period she traveled in the Middle East—Syria, Lebanon, Transjordan, and Palestine—gauging women's support for an all-embracing union of Arab feminists, and by 1945 was editing the EFU's journal, *The Arab Woman*. She also served as an EFU delegate to the All-India Women's Conference held in 1946.

In 1954 al-Said founded *Eve,* the first mass-circulation women's weekly magazine in Egypt. In her editorials over the next twenty-seven years (until her retirement in 1981), she contributed many discussions of women's issues at a time when other Egyptian feminists had been forced into silence by the Nasser regime. She provided an impetus to Egyptian women's suffrage in January 1956, when she gave an important lecture on women's right to the vote after hearing that the new Constitution being drafted would not grant them this right. Nasser's government responded to this and other pressure by granting women the vote in 1956, but it was linked to a prerequisite level of literacy on the part of those women petitioning to be registered as voters.

Although seen by some critics as an establishment figure whose writings were condoned because she supported the broader government policy on improved education and work opportunities for all Egyptians—not just women—al-Said was no toady. She used her preeminent position in Egyptian publishing to promote her own beliefs in social justice. As a member of the board of the Press Syndicate from 1956 (and its vice president from 1958), which set the standards for reporting in the Egyptian media; vice president of the Egyptian Union of Journalists (1959–1970); and secretary-general of the Pan-Arab League Women's Union (1958–1969), she was uniquely placed to call for reform of the Egyptian personal status code. For too long, it had given men the freedom to divorce their wives and to practice polygamy while controlling the lives of their wives and daughters in social, economic, and political terms. The debate about personal status laws dissipated upon the outbreak of the Six-Day War with Israel in 1967, but in an article in *Eve* in November 1972, al-Said attacked moves among Arab women to readopt the wearing of the veil. Seeing this as a retrograde step and describing the veil as being "the enemy of civilization and progress," she looked upon veils as "these white garments, resembling the shrouds of the dead" (Talhami 1996, 54). Nevertheless, in other respects al-Said's position was very much one in support of the traditional role of women within Islam—as wives and mothers.

In 1975 al-Said became president of the administrative council of the established and respected publishing firm Dar al-Hilal, which produced *al-Musawwar.* As a friend of President Anwar Sadat, she was influential, along with Sadat's wife Jehan, in exerting pressure on the government finally to rescind the 1929 personal status code and with it relax traditional patriarchal practice, although the rise of Islamic fundamentalism in Egypt has, since her death, prompted a return to such practices.

See also el-Saadawi, Nawal; Sha'rawi, Huda.

References and Further Reading

Ahmed, Leila. 1992. *Women and Gender in Islam: Historical Roots of a Modern Debate.* New Haven: Yale University Press.

Badran, Margot. 1995. *Feminists, Islam and Nation: Gender and the Making of Modern Egypt.* Princeton: Princeton University Press.

Encyclopedia Britannica Book of the Year: Events of 1995. 1996. Chicago: Encyclopedia Britannica.

Kandiyoti, Deniz. 1991. *Women, Islam and the State.* Basingstoke: Macmillan.

Talhami, Ghada Hashem. 1996. *The Mobilization of Muslim Women in Egypt.* Gainesville: University Press of Florida.

Salomon, Alice
(1872–1948)
Germany/United States

Alice Salomon, sometimes referred to as "the German Jane Addams," was the outstanding pioneer of social work in Germany. As well as being active in the women's and peace movements, in 1899 she set up the first German training establishment for social workers and was inspirational in the development of the discipline, in 1929 founding the International Association of Schools of Social Work (IASSW) and serving as its president and secretary.

Born in Berlin into a wealthy Jewish family, Salomon defied the narrowness of her conventional upbringing by educating herself. After an unhappy love affair, she never married but devoted herself instead to social issues, in 1893 joining the Girls' and Women's Groups for Social Assistance Work and setting up the first tentative training course for women social workers. Such was her single-mindedness that in 1899, with no funding and no staff, Salomon set up a one-year course to train charity workers. This, the first training of its kind in Germany, made a modest beginning by offering lectures on welfare, public health, and the poor laws.

Intent on her own acquisition of further skills, Salomon lobbied for admission to the University of Berlin and matriculated in 1902. At the age of thirty-four, she completed her Ph.D. in economics, presenting a thesis on the inequality of pay between men and women in the same professions.

In 1908 Salomon formally established the Women's School for Social Work. Under her directorship from 1908 to 1928, it became a pioneering institution that offered training and fieldwork to social workers. Its volunteer teaching staff was enlisted by Salomon from women in public life who had experience in doing charity work and understood the poor laws. Salomon composed its training manuals, and the school became the prototype for the education of social workers throughout Germany.

Salomon was active in the Federation of German Women's Associations (FGWA) founded in 1894, in 1900 becoming the youngest member of its executive board and later rising to secretary and then vice president. In 1904 she helped organize the International Congress of Women held in Berlin by the International Council of Women (ICW) and chaired committees on women's employment, labor legislation, and the professions. In 1909 she was elected corresponding secretary of the ICW and traveled to Canada to give a report to its annual congress. There she met Jane Addams and, impressed by her work, made the first of several visits to the United States, where she studied the Hull House settlements and American social work methods and also gave lectures on the new republican government in Germany. During World War I, she supported the women's movement's contribution to the war effort, acting as local head of the women's department of the War Office. She established a women's volunteer corps and enlisted women to serve behind the lines on the eastern front. At war's end, she was decorated with the Red Cross Medal and the Cross of Merit. In 1919, however, Salomon resigned from the FGWA when it refused to elect her as its president because of her Jewish origins (even though she had renounced Judaism and been baptized as a Protestant in 1914). Thereafter she devoted herself to the international women's movement. In 1923 the American reformer Julia Lathrop visited Salomon in Berlin and asked her to be one of five honorary delegates to the National Convention of Social Work held that year in Washington, D.C., where Salomon gave a paper entitled "The Relation of the Church to Social Workers."

Salomon was greatly taken with the freedoms enjoyed by women in the United States, which allowed them to play an active, respected role in welfare. Impressed by these standards of professionalism, she returned to Germany convinced that the New World offered "a paradise for women." For the rest of her life, Salomon would retain close contact with Jane Addams and progressive women reformers there (in 1911 she had arranged the German translation of Addams's autobiography, *Twenty Years at Hull House,* which Salomon used as a text in her social work school). She also wrote numerous pamphlets on social reform in the United States and a collection of travel writings, *Culture in the Making,* which touched on race relations issues there.

In 1925 Salomon changed the name of the Women's School for Social Work to the German Academy for Women's Social and Pedagogic Work in order to train graduate social workers in research and the administration of social welfare projects. By the early 1930s, she had become an influential figure, serving as president of the Federation of German Schools of Social Work, whose concepts became influential outside Germany. In 1928 she chaired the Committee on Social Work Training at the first international conference on social work, held in Paris, which prompted the establishment of the IASSW a year later. In 1932 the German Academy was renamed the Salomon Academy in honor of her pioneering work. By this, the year of her sixtieth birthday, she had been elected to the executives of all the leading social and philanthropic organizations in her native land and was presented with the Silver Medal for Service to the State.

A year later when the Nazis came to power, Salomon's name was removed from the academy's title because she was a Jew. Shortly afterward, the school was closed down, and its records were destroyed. She was forced to resign from the vice presidency of the ICW but bravely stayed on in Germany, joining the Christian resistance to Nazism led by the theologian Martin Niemöller. In 1937 she was brought before the Gestapo and interrogated. Informed that Jews or Christians of Jewish ancestry who had frequently traveled abroad for considerable periods had to leave the country or be sent to a concentration camp, Salomon was given three weeks to organize her affairs, after which she was stripped of her property and left the country. Knowing that she had friends and supporters in the United States, she went to New York, only to find the country in the grips of the Great Depression. Many of her old contacts had died, and Salomon struggled to find employ-

ment, occasionally lecturing on social work. She became a U.S. citizen, wrote her autobiography, *Character Is Destiny,* and tried for many years to find a publisher, but it remained unpublished until rediscovered by the feminist movement in the 1980s. Salomon, who had won such respect among American reformers, died alone and largely forgotten in New York City in 1948.

See also Addams, Jane; Lathrop, Julia.

References and Further Reading
Allen, Ann Taylor. 1991. *Feminism and Motherhood in Germany, 1800–1914.* New Brunswick: Rutgers University Press.
Josephson, Harold, Sandi Cooper, and Steven C. Hause et al., eds. 1985. *Biographical Dictionary of Modern Peace Leaders.* Westport, CT: Greenwood Press.
Kendall, Katherine A. 1989. "Women at the Helm: Three Extraordinary Leaders." *Affilia: A Journal of Women and Social Work* 4, no. 1: 23–32.
Salomon, Alice. 1937. *Education for Social Work.* Zurich: Verlag für Recht und Gesellschaft AG.
Sklar, Kathryn Kish. 1998. *Social Justice Feminists in the United States and Germany: A Dialogue in Documents 1885–1933.* Ithaca: Cornell University Press.

Sand, George (Amandine-Aurore-Lucile Dudevant née Dupin)
(1804–1876)
France

The French romantic novelist George Sand, famous now for her unconventional lifestyle and her numerous love affairs, including those with the composers Frédéric Chopin and Franz Liszt, was in her lifetime a literary lioness and one of the most influential women of her generation. Her output was prodigious; she was admired around the world and translated into many languages. Although her novels have not endured and now are largely unread, as a pioneer of the feminist novel in the 1830s, Sand developed a powerful critique of marriage and sexuality that gave impetus to the cause of women's emancipation and their right to passion and sexual liberty.

The illegitimate daughter of an aristocrat, Sand was brought up by her grandmother at the family château at Nohant and was educated at a Paris convent. Sand's mother was ostracized by her lover's family after his early death because she was of a lower class, but her daughter, the beautiful and cultured Amandine-Aurore-Lucile (as she then was), married well in 1822. Sand's husband, Baron Casimir Dudevant, provided her with a comfortable lifestyle, but she was unable to tolerate the narrow confines of marriage and with it the burdensome narrowness of provincial life. Taking their two children, she left him and settled in Paris, where she entered into a liaison with writer Jules Sandeau in 1831. She began submitting articles cowritten with Sandeau to the newspaper *Figaro* under the name Jules Sand. It was at this time that Sand first adopted men's clothing—donning trousers and boots in order to enjoy the freedom and anonymity of walking the streets of Paris late at night unmolested.

In Paris, Sand moved in bohemian circles, and became notorious in the literary salons for wearing trousers, sitting cross-legged like a man, smoking cigars, and rolling her own cigarettes. During the 1830s she entered into a series of affairs with artistic figures, such as the writers Prosper Mérimée and Alfred de Musset. Feeling that she lacked the talent to take up polemical journalism, she began producing a torrent of feminist novels that built up a huge reading audience and the admiration of many other writers worldwide. Titles such as *Indiana* (1832), *Valentine* (1832), *Lélia* (1833), and *Jacques* (1834) all elaborate with considerable compassion on the trap of marriage, the sexual slavery and domestic tyranny perpetuated by it, and the oppression of bright and vivacious wives by their boorish husbands. As a woman who had boldly engineered her own sexual liberation, Sand criticized the stereotypical male view of woman's role and the man-made marriage laws that kept women prisoners. She offered an idealistic, romantic alternative of relationships based on free self-expression and love in stories that were considered risqué for their erotic elements. Sand's message was embraced by radical Unitarians, who undertook the first translations of her novels into English as ammunition in the cause of women's emancipation. They believed that Sand, by ennobling women in fiction, had got to the crux of what was rotten in society. In her own life, she obtained a legal separation in 1838 in order to regain her lost property, forfeited when she left her husband.

During the 1840s, Sand expressed her growing sympathies with working people and artisans in

George Sand (Archive Photos)

socialist novels such as *The Journeyman Joiner* and *The Miller of Angibault* (1845). Works such as *Horace* (1841) were even accused of being communist in tone. Sand then produced a series of idealized pastoral novels, including *The Haunted Marsh* (1846), *Francis the Waif* (1847–1848), and *Little Fadette* (1849), in which she tackled social, humanitarian, and religious issues and sought social change based in religious belief and virtue. Her works had a considerable influence on English writers such as the Brontës, Elizabeth Barrett Browning, and George Eliot (herself later named "the English George Sand"), but an even more profound impact in Russia, where Fyodor Dostoyevsky, Ivan Turgenev, Vissarion Belinsky, Alexander Herzen, and Mikhail Bakunin were all admirers. In an 1847 letter to Sand, Turgenev's mistress, the French singer Pauline Viardot, remarked that in Russia "all your works are translated from the moment they appear.... Everyone reads them, from top to bottom of the social ladder.... Men adore you. . . . Women idolise you. . . . All in all you reign, in Russia, more sovereign than the Tsar" (Jack 1999, 283).

Despite her unequivocal support for the equality and liberty of the working classes, Sand never joined an official group. She played an intellectual, not an active, role in the 1848 revolution in France, acting as a propagandist for the Republican movement. She called for a moral regeneration of society based on Christian values of male-female equality, which she expressed in her work of that year, *Letters to the People.* During the upheavals, she published articles in the *Bulletin of the Republic,* calling for democracy and emphasizing in particular the lot of the poor peasantry and of French women, neither of whom had the vote. Seen by many St. Simonian feminists of the time, such as Jeanne Deroin and Eugénie Niboyet, as a political icon, Sand was nominated by them as a candidate for election to a new national assembly. But she refused the nomination, not wishing to be elected by male voters on behalf of women who had no franchise.

During the last third of her life, Sand retired to the family château at Nohant, which became a mecca for artists and writers. She continued writing novels (throughout her life producing on average two books every year) to support her entourage of family and friends. She also published her twenty-volume autobiography, *History of My Life* (1855, published in English as *My Life*). The phenomenon of Sand's huge international success during her lifetime is equaled by the abrupt falling away of interest in her work, collected and now largely unread in an exhausting 105 volumes. Although her crowded personal and literary life may have prevented her from any sustained public involvement in social causes, the humanitarian tone of Sand's novels testifies to a lifetime's commitment to challenging conventional ideology and seeking reform based on Christian socialist principles. As she herself once remarked, "Me, I have no theories. I live my life asking questions" (Jack 1999, 370).

See also Deroin, Jeanne; Niboyet, Eugénie.

References and Further Reading
Barry, Joseph. 1975. *Infamous Woman: The Life of George Sand.* Garden City, NY: Doubleday.
Cate, Curtis. 1975. *George Sand: A Biography.* Boston: Houghton Mifflin.
Datlot, N., J. Fuchs, and D. A. Powell. 1991. *The World of George Sand.* New York: Greenwood.
Dickson, D. 1988. *George Sand: A Brave Man, the Most Womanly Woman.* Oxford: Berg.
Edwards, Samuel. 1972. *George Sand: A Biography of the First Modern Liberated Woman.* New York: McKay.
Jack, Belinda. 1999. *George Sand: A Woman's Life Writ Large.* London: Chatto.

Sanger, Margaret
(1879–1966)
United States

Margaret Sanger's passionate advocacy of voluntary motherhood and birth control, the latter a catchphrase she herself coined in 1914, was pursued with determined single-mindedness for many years in the face of vilification, censorship, and legal harassment from church, state, and the moral guardians of society. Her convictions had their roots in her own difficult childhood as the sixth of eleven children of poor Irish immigrants and in her belief that no woman should have to endure successive and unwanted pregnancies.

Sanger was born into a working-class family in Corning, New York. Her Irish-born father, Michael Higgins, a freethinker and socialist, never made much of a living, and Sanger was only able to attend private coeducational school at Claverack College and then at Hudson River Institute (1897–1899), thanks to the financial support of her two older sisters. She took a job as a student teacher in a public school in New Jersey, but when her mother became terminally ill with tuberculosis, she had to give up work to help look after her younger siblings. When she was eighteen, Sanger embarked on a three-year training as a nurse at White Plains Hospital in New York, where she also gained firsthand experience in obstetrics. She continued her training at the Manhattan Eye and Ear Hospital, where she met the architect William Sanger at a dance and soon got married.

After conceiving her first child, Sanger became ill with tuberculosis but recovered to have two more children. She became bored and restless with domestic life, however, and when the family moved to Manhattan from Westchester in 1912, Sanger joined Labour Five, a branch of the Socialist Party, and began mixing with other radicals, intellectuals, and feminists, such as Emma Goldman in Greenwich Village. Goldman was an early and equally vocal campaigner for birth control, but Sanger, although admiring Goldman's radicalism and advocacy of women's sexual freedom, did not take to her hectoring manner. At this time, Sanger also supported the campaign for trade union rights being waged by the Industrial Workers of the World (Wobblies) and joined Elizabeth Gurley Flynn on the picket lines of major strikes by textile workers in Lawrence, Massachusetts, in 1912 and Paterson, New Jersey, in 1913.

In the early 1900s, working as an obstetrical nurse in and around New York's Lower East Side, Sanger regularly encountered women enduring or seeking to terminate unwanted pregnancies and saw the horrifying results of botched abortions. She realized the desperate need of women to escape the endless spiral of poverty and pregnancy and obtain reliable contraceptive advice. In 1912, after witnessing the death of one woman, Sadie Sachs, from septicemia following an abortion, Sanger was galvanized into action, later writing that she had vowed never to "go back again to nurse women's ailing bodies while their miseries were as vast as the stars." Her course was set: "I was now finished with superficial cures, with doctors and nurses and social workers who were brought face to face with this overwhelming truth of women's needs and yet turned to pass on the other side" (Sanger 1931, 56).

She began giving health talks for the Socialist Party's Women's Commission and freely discussed problems such as venereal disease in a series of radical articles on health care for the socialist newspaper the *New York Call*. Under a regular column entitled "What Every Mother Should Know" (with the word *Mother* changed to *Girl* for the second series), Sanger discussed not just pregnancy and menstruation but also the taboo topic of masturbation. The response was unprecedented; on all sides Sanger was besieged with pleas from working-class women asking her to do more. Unfortunately, the U.S. post office, which controlled the distribution by mail of pamphlets such as Sanger's, invoked the 1873 Comstock Law outlawing sending "obscene" publications through the mail and banned an issue of the *Call* containing an article by Sanger on venereal disease. The magazine challenged this ban and later had it overturned.

Undeterred by the threat of prosecution, Sanger began researching contraceptive methods while continuing her volunteer work for Lillian

Margaret Sanger (Library of Congress)

Wald's Visiting Nurses Association on the Lower East Side. In 1913 she went on a three-month trip to Europe to study work on contraception being done there. She met Malthusian thinkers and French socialists in Paris and acquired various samples, returning to the United States in 1914 to begin a campaign to disseminate contraceptive advice and looking for loopholes in the Comstock Law. Her socialist friends in New York encouraged her to publish on the subject, and in March 1914 Sanger managed to raise enough funds to produce the first issue of a monthly radical journal, the *Woman Rebel*, which discussed sexual freedom and health issues and was sent out to 2,000 subscribers. But by that time, the postal service was clamping down hard on the dissemination of this and other "seditious" literature through the mail. Sanger was charged with breaking the law in August 1914 (not, however, for advocating birth control but for publishing an article on political assassination in *Woman Rebel*). Although she relished a test case in court on birth control issues, she did not wish to be tried on this particular charge and decided to jump bail and leave the country. Leaving her children in the care of sympathizers, she set sail for Liverpool in November 1914 under the name Bertha Watson.

In her absence, Sanger asked her supporters to release 100,000 copies of a pioneering pamphlet she had written, entitled "Family Limitation," in which she gave detailed instructions on birth control methods. This work reached a mass audience, selling 10 million copies over the next twenty years. In its sixteen pages, Sanger argued that working families should have no more than two children, since in her view, this number was all that an average working wage could sustain, and also described various contraceptive methods. In Sanger's absence, her husband was prosecuted for possession of the pamphlet and sentenced to thirty days in prison.

In London in 1914, Sanger studied the history of birth control methods at the British Museum. She met and had an affair with the British sexologist Havelock Ellis, under whose influence she developed her ideas on female sexuality and her advocacy of women's right to sexual pleasure. She also met the British birth control campaigner Marie Stopes, who suggested she investigate the contraceptive methods being pioneered in the Netherlands. In 1915 Sanger went to The Hague to examine the newly developed Mensinga diaphragm, known as the Dutch cap. She was disappointed not to be granted a meeting with the Dutch birth control pioneer Aletta Jacobs while there (as a qualified doctor, Jacobs did not take the lay practitioner Sanger seriously at first; they eventually met in 1925) but came back convinced of the effectiveness of this new contraceptive device.

In Sanger's absence, the birth control movement in the United States had found a new advocate in Mary Ware Dennett. Disliking Sanger's confrontational tactics and publicity-seeking manner (as she perceived it), Dennett eschewed Sanger's advocacy of direct action and began a legal challenge for repeal of the Comstock Law in New York state. She did so through a new organization set up in 1915, the National Birth Control League. The flamboyant Sanger, who liked to lead from the front, would have an uneasy relationship with the more retiring Dennett, just as she had with Goldman, after she managed to get a safe passage back to the United States in 1915 during World War I. She was ready to face prosecution for the article in the *Woman Rebel,* but after an outpouring of public sympathy when her daughter died of pneumonia (a fact for which she would always blame herself), the au-

thorities decided to drop the charges against her in February 1916.

Sanger was eager to begin opening clinics offering free advice on birth control and in 1916 embarked on a nationwide lecture tour, for three months giving the same well-practiced speech on 119 occasions and raising support from rich patrons. She finally found a loophole in the Comstock Law, which stipulated that doctors could legally give advice on birth control if it related to the cure or prevention of sexual or life-threatening diseases. Sanger expanded her interpretation of this ruling to include excessive childbearing as in itself being life-threatening.

In 1916 Sanger opened her first birth control clinic, in the Brownsville neighborhood of Brooklyn, prior to which she had leafleted the immigrant communities of the area with pamphlets written in Yiddish and Italian, exhorting them: "Mothers! Can you afford to have a large family? Do you want any more children? If not, why do you have them?" (Forster 1984, 264). One hundred and forty women queued up for a consultation on the clinic's first day, 16 October 1916, where Sanger, with no qualified doctors, was assisted by her sister Ethel and friend Fania Mindell. Police raided the clinic after nine days, and Sanger was convicted of being a "public nuisance" and sentenced to thirty days in the Queens Penitentiary for Women.

After World War I, birth control became a national issue, and Sanger emphasized its importance on medical grounds through a new journal, the *Birth Control Review,* set up in 1917. She sought to give her movement gravitas and political clout by moving away from her associates on the left and toward the patronage of wealthy and influential supporters in business, the professions, and academia. She divorced William Sanger in 1920 and married for a second time in 1922, her new husband being a rich oil man, Noah Slee. With his support and funding, Sanger widened her birth control projects and imported Dutch caps from Europe, smuggled in oil drums via an oil refinery in Canada owned by Slee, who also had contraceptive jelly manufactured at his own plant in New Jersey.

In 1920, Sanger published *Women and the New Race,* a work pacifist in tone, in which she advocated "free motherhood," arguing that women should be responsible for their own protection against unwanted pregnancies, and also urged them to refuse to go on producing children as fodder for war machines. The book reflected Sanger's increasing espousal of social Darwinism and eugenics (her *Birth Control Review* had as its motto "To Breed a Race of Thoroughbreds"). Although she never embraced the unsavory policies of social and racial control linked to this movement, Sanger's interest in the creation of a healthier nation by eradicating genetically transmitted diseases and mental illness through controlled breeding inevitably led to accusations of racism.

In 1921 Sanger founded a lobbying group, the American Birth Control League, serving as its president until opposition from its conservative mainstream to her continuing radicalism led her to resign in 1928. She also organized the first national birth control conference that year, held in New York City. In 1923, with funding from her husband, Sanger opened the Birth Control Clinical Research Bureau on Fifth Avenue, which was staffed by doctors and social workers and became a prototype for more than 300 similar clinics set up across the United States over the next fifteen years. From 1929, her newly formed National Committee on Federal Legislation for Birth Control lent a higher profile to campaigning for legal changes. Finally, in 1936, Sanger achieved her major objective of winning the legal right for doctors to advise on methods of birth control, when *United States* v. *One Package of Japanese Pessaries* was argued before the Supreme Court. The high court's ruling legalized the importation of contraceptive devices for prescription by doctors. A year later, the American Medical Association endorsed the role of doctors as providers of contraceptive advice. Sanger took the cause a stage further by campaigning for government-supported public health policies on birth control, both at home and abroad. In 1942 the legitimacy of her work was finally recognized, when the American Birth Control League and other organizations combined to form the Planned Parenthood Federation of America, with Sanger as honorary chair. Her role in the mainstream U.S. movement effectively over, Sanger turned her attention to the dissemination of birth control methods in the rest of the world through the Birth Control International Information Centre in London, which she cofounded with Edith How-Martyn in 1929.

In 1925 Sanger had helped to plan the Sixth International Birth Control Conference in New York, and in 1927 she organized the World Population Conference in Geneva. In the postwar years, Sanger's growing concern about the explosion of populations in the Third World led her to become first president (1953–1959) of the International Planned Parenthood Federation, established in Bombay, and to promote its work in India and others parts of Asia. She continued to raise funds for research on an even better female contraceptive, using money left by her husband on his death in 1943 and from the philanthropist Katharine Dexter McCormick to pay for development of intrauterine devices and the contraceptive pill.

Sanger published numerous books and articles on birth control, contraception, and women's sexuality, including *What Every Mother Should Know* (1917), *Woman and the New Race* (1920), *Motherhood in Bondage* (1928), and *My Fight for Birth Control* (1931). An excellent website on the life and work of Margaret Sanger can be found at http://www.nyu.edu/projects/sanger/. A useful discussion of the work and conflicting interests of Sanger and Dennett in the U.S. birth control movement can also be found at http://www.womhist.binghamton.edu/birth/.

See also Dennett, Mary Ware; Flynn, Elizabeth Gurley; Goldman, Emma; How-Martyn, Edith; Jacobs, Aletta; Stopes, Marie; Wald, Lillian D.

References and Further Reading

Adickes, Sandra. 1997. *To Be Young Was Very Heaven: Women in New York before the Great War.* Basingstoke: Macmillan.

Bolt, Christine. 1993. *The Women's Movements in the United States and Britain from the 1790s to the 1920s.* London: Harvester Wheatsheaf.

Buhle, Mari Jo. 1981. *Women and American Socialism, 1870–1920.* Urbana: University of Illinois Press.

Chesler, Ellen. 1992. *Woman of Valor: Margaret Sanger and the Birth Control Movement in America.* New York: Simon and Schuster.

Forster, M. 1984. *Significant Sisters: The Grassroots of Active Feminism, 1839–1939.* London: Secker and Warburg.

Gordon, Linda. 1990. *Woman's Body, Woman's Right: Birth Control in America.* New York: Penguin.

Kennedy, David. 1970. *Birth Control in America: The Career of Margaret Sanger.* New Haven: Yale University Press.

Kerber, Linda K., and Jane DeHart-Mathews. 2000. *Women's America: Refocusing the Past.* New York: Oxford University Press.

McCann, Carole R. 1994. *Birth Control Politics in the United States, 1916–1945.* Ithaca, NY: Cornell University Press.

Reed, James. 1978. *From Public Vice to Private Virtue: The Birth Control Movement and American Society since 1830.* Princeton: Princeton University Press.

Reynolds, Moira Davison. 1994. *Women Advocates of Reproductive Rights: 11 Who Led the Struggle in the United States and Great Britain.* Jefferson, NC: McFarland.

Sanger, Margaret. 1931. *My Fight for Birth Control.* New York: Farrar & Rhinehart.

———. 1938. *Margaret Sanger: An Autobiography.* New York: Norton.

Spender, Dale. 1982. *Women of Ideas, and What Men Have Done to Them.* London: Routledge and Kegan Paul.

Santoso, Maria Ullfah (later Soebadio)
(1911–1988)
Indonesia

Santoso was a pioneer for women's equality in Asia from the 1930s, who founded the Indonesian Women's Society and fought for the drafting of a reformist marriage law of 1952 that was rejected by the Muslim government. A more progressive draft in 1958 was also rejected.

Born in Serang, West Java, Santoso studied law in the Netherlands at the University of Leiden. Throughout the 1930s she played a key role in promoting women's rights. At the second congress of the National Indonesia Party in Bandung in 1931, Santoso described a program she had devised to initiate a national education program for women (which would make it compulsory at the primary level), which she believed would improve their working lives and encourage them to take a greater interest in politics. In 1937 she headed a commission set up to study polygamy and draft new legislation about the practice.

In 1938 Santoso became president of a board created to improve literacy standards among women, which had been envisioned as being fundamental in raising women's political consciousness and with it the suffrage campaign in Indonesia. To help get women elected to local governments, Santoso was sponsored by the Federation of Indonesian Women (established in 1929) as a potential candidate for the People's Council established by the Dutch colonial gov-

ernment. Unfortunately, she lost out to a Eurasian woman resident in Indonesia. In 1938 she served as president of the committee of investigation into Muslim matrimonial legislation and wrote a working paper entitled "The Position of Indonesian Woman in Matrimonial Law," which was well researched and submitted practical advice on ways in which family life for Indonesian women could be improved. Santoso spoke on the subject of marriage reform at the Third Congress of Indonesian Women held in 1938, calling for greater consideration on the part of polygamous Muslim men in the equal treatment of their wives.

Santoso presided over the first women's congress in Indonesia, held in 1945. The next year she became Indonesia's first woman to hold an elective office (as minister of social affairs), an important step in her campaign to see Indonesian women achieve a greater involvement in government. In addition, she oversaw a body set up to study matrimonial law. When her government appointment ended in 1947, she served as a delegate to the Inter-Asian Relations Conference, held in New Delhi. From 1947 to 1956, Santoso worked as secretary to the prime minister. In 1952 she was assigned the role of vice president of the Indonesian Mission for Child Welfare in Burma. Throughout the 1950s, she worked toward increased participation of Asian women in public life, heading an Indonesian delegation at a seminar on the subject in Bangkok and taking a leading role in the organization of the Federation of Indonesian Women's Associations, an umbrella organization for women's groups that by 1955 coordinated the work of forty-five member associations. At the group's fourth congress in 1957, Santoso was nominated head of its new secretariat.

She continued to write articles on suffrage and women's right to hold government office and remained closely involved in the redrafting of the marriage law. She spoke out against polygamy and child marriage and suggested changes in the ritual Islamic divorce procedure, arguing that a divorced wife should receive alimony and financial support for her children. Although she aimed to reform traditional Muslim practices, Santoso maintained a neutral, apolitical position on the subject. In her campaigning against polygamy, she was careful to respect the wishes of practicing Muslims and ensure that the new legislation was in accordance with the precepts of the Qu'ran. The new draft marriage law was passed in 1954. Women finally achieved full suffrage in Indonesia in 1955.

References and Further Reading

Kahin, George. 1989. "In Memoriam: Maria Ullfah Soebadio, 1911–1988." *Indonesia* 49 (April): 119–120.

Vreede-de Stuers, Cora. 1960. *The Indonesian Woman: Struggles and Achievements.* The Hague: Mouton.

Schlafly, Phyllis
(1924–)
United States

For many years, the right-wing opposition to the passing of an Equal Rights Amendment (ERA) in the United States was led by Roman Catholic antifeminist campaigner Phyllis Schlafly, who has since become one of the most influential self-appointed moral guardians of American society. She is a staunch supporter of the preservation of traditional family values through her lobbying group and national volunteer organization, Eagle Forum.

Born in St. Louis, Missouri, Schlafly was educated at the Academy of the Sacred Heart. She studied at Washington University in St. Louis (1941–1944), working in a munitions factory during the war to pay for her studies. Awarded a scholarship to Radcliffe College in Massachusetts, Schlafly obtained her M.A. in political science in 1945. During 1945–1949, Schlafly worked as a congressional researcher and then as a librarian and researcher for the St. Louis First National Bank. Afterward, she married the conservative lawyer Philip Schlafly and devoted herself to rearing her six children and taking up community work and broadcasting. For many years, she was closely involved in Republican Party politics, standing for election to Congress three times and in 1964 serving as first vice president of the National Federation of Republican Women (NFRW). In 1958 she and her husband cofounded the Cardinal Mindszenty Foundation to raise public awareness of the threat of communism.

In 1964 Schlafly published a contentious book, *A Choice, Not an Echo,* in support of the presidential nomination of Republican Barry Gold-

water. It sold 3 million copies and attracted much attention with its accusations that the Republican Party was controlled by an inner elite, an argument that helped Goldwater win his nomination. Schlafly subsequently wrote five books (1964–1978) on U.S. strategic defense policy with Rear Admiral Chester Ward, in which she continued to argue for an increased U.S. nuclear missile defense system against the Soviet threat.

When she failed to be reelected to the NFRW in 1967, Schlafly set up her own organization, the Eagle Trust Fund, to lobby for conservative congressional candidates. She began publishing her own newspaper, the *Phyllis Schlafly Report,* as a forum for attacks on the emergent feminist movement. In 1972 Schlafly assumed the leadership of an antifeminist crusade, when she launched the "Stop ERA" campaign and spoke in thirty U.S. states to defeat feminists lobbying for the long-overdue ratification of the Equal Rights Amendment, originally conceived of by Alice Paul in 1923. In defense of her actions, Schlafly argued that the ERA would threaten family stability by making women eligible for military service and forcing them into the workplace as equal breadwinners with men. Insisting that her motive was to protect women's rights to remain wives and mothers, she wrote on the subject in a 1974 issue of *Ms.* magazine, arguing that feminist claims about women's subordination were erroneous. Schlafly was joined in her lobbying of senators by the united forces of the Moral Majority, the American Conservative Union, and various religious groups, going so far as to present them with home-produced goodies made by happy housewives that defined those timeless and much valued talents, such as bread and jam making, to which she felt women were vocationally suited. As a result of Schlafly's vigorous campaigning, the ERA failed to be ratified by a sufficient number of U.S. states before its deadline (already extended from 1979) had passed in 1982.

Since 1973, the highly articulate and well-groomed Schlafly has represented Middle America, her conventional appearance belying a toughness in debating the issues she supports on her own radio show (*Phyllis Schlafly Live*) and cable TV programs, as well as on the lecture circuit. In the 1970s, she began writing a syndicated column for Copley News Service, and in 1975 she founded the Eagle Forum to defend traditional family values in the face of the growing women's liberation movement. This organization later absorbed Schlafly's arguments on U.S. defense and foreign policy while continuing to address social issues such as homosexuality, pornography, abortion, divorce, extramarital sex, and adultery. Schlafly outlined her antifeminist ideas in *The Power of the Positive Woman* (1977), which attacked feminists' demands for sexual equality by underlining women's differences from men and their need to operate in separate and noncompetitive spheres. She based much of her argument on the claim that the ERA was redundant for women in the United States, since they already had the means to control their own destinies. In what would seem a contradiction of this point, she has taken a stand against sex education, which might enable young women better to protect themselves, and is equally adamantly opposed to promotion of a better understanding of acquired immunodeficiency syndrome (AIDS).

In recent years, Schlafly has moved on to work for parental rights in the public school system and for revisions of the class curriculum, suggesting that classic works such as William Golding's *Lord of the Flies* and John Steinbeck's *Of Mice and Men* are inappropriate reading matter. She has conducted a campaign for tighter controls over TV and radio advertising and to protect individual privacy (opposing new government policy on encryption) and is also a vociferous campaigner in support of the continuation of nuclear defense strategies. Her sixteen published works include *Equal Pay for Unequal Work* (1984), *Child Abuse in the Classroom* (1984), and *Who Will Rock the Cradle* (1989). During 1985–1991, Schlafly was a member of the Commission on the Bicentennial of the U.S. Constitution. She supported the Republican 1992 election campaign in its antihomosexual and antiabortion positions.

Schlafly promotes her many causes through her lobbying group, Eagle Forum, which is based in St. Louis, Missouri. Her regular columns are syndicated in many newspapers, and monthly editions of the *Phyllis Schlafly Report* can be read on Eagle Forum's website at http://www.eagle forum.org/.

Schlafly has received awards such as the 1963 Woman of Achievement in Public Affairs award, from the St. Louis newspaper the *Globe-Democrat*. In 1977 *Good Housekeeping* magazine nominated her as one of the "ten most admired women in the world," and in 1992 she was nominated as Illinois Mother of the Year.

See also Paul, Alice.

References and Further Reading

Blee, Kathleen M., ed. 1998. *No Middle Ground: Women and Radical Protest.* New York: New York University Press.

Faludi, Susan. 1991. *Backlash: The Undeclared War against American Women.* New York: Crown.

Felsenthal, Carol. 1981. *The Sweetheart of the Silent Majority: The Biography of Phyllis Schlafly.* Garden City: Doubleday.

Kerber, Linda K., and Jane DeHart-Mathews. 2000. *Women's America: Refocusing the Past.* New York: Oxford University Press.

Mansbridge, Jane J. 1986. *Why We Lost the ERA.* Chicago: University of Chicago Press.

Schlafly, Phyllis. 1964. *A Choice, Not an Echo.* Alton, IL: Pere Marquette Press.

Schoenbaum, Eleanora, ed. 1979. *Political Profiles: The Nixon Ford Years.* New York: Facts on File.

Schneiderman, Rose
(1882–1972)
Poland/United States

The Jewish trade union organizer Rose Schneiderman led the first major strikes by women garment workers from New York's sweatshops in the 1900s. Although only 4 feet, 9 inches tall, she was a powerhouse of energy and an outstanding public speaker on trade union rights and the plight of women workers. Her vigorous campaigning and tough negotiating achieved improvements in rates of pay and a reduction in the working day for women to eight hours. As a supporter of women's suffrage, Schneiderman also encouraged women workers to join the campaign for the vote, seeing their enhanced political power as an effective means of gaining labor legislation and giving new depth to a revitalized suffrage movement.

Schneiderman came from an Orthodox Jewish family and grew up in Saven, a ghetto in Poland, then part of the Russian Empire. Her family emigrated to New York in 1890, where her father, a tailor, died two years later, leaving the family poverty-stricken. Schneiderman and her siblings spent much of their young lives in orphanages, until she was old enough to leave school to look after her younger siblings while her mother worked. She returned to school to study until ninth grade and then took a job in a department store. The wages were only $2 for a sixty-four-hour week, so she moved to a cap-making factory in 1898 for a wage of $6 a week.

On a prolonged stay with family friends in Montreal during 1902, Schneiderman was first introduced to socialist ideas. On her return to New York in 1903, she became active in radical politics on the Lower East Side, joining the Socialist Party and encouraging fellow women workers to set up a local women's branch of the male-run United Cloth Hat and Cap-Makers Union, which was dominated by Jewish socialists. In 1903 Schneiderman was elected to the union's executive board, becoming the first woman to hold such a high office in a male trade union, in so doing disproving her mother's advice that "men don't want a woman with a big mouth" (Trager 1994, 368). She led a strike in the cap-making industry in 1905, the year in which she was elected to the executive board of the Women's Trade Union League (WTUL), an umbrella organization set up in 1903 to encourage women to unionize.

As a leading light of the WTUL, Schneiderman set about organizing women in those trades where they were most exploited, targeting paper-box makers, laundry workers, and waitresses and, most famously, the garment industry. She achieved her most important work as a full-time labor organizer for the WTUL from 1908, thanks to a scholarship from a rich patron to attend the Rand School of Social Science. During 1909–1910, she led a major strike by around 20,000 mainly female members of the Ladies' Waist Makers' Union for better wages and working conditions. The resulting settlement led to the establishment of the International Ladies' Garment Workers' Union (ILGWU), and Schneiderman encouraged the growth of its membership, traveling widely during 1909–1914 and lobbying for support and funds from wealthy patrons. In 1910 she led a strike of ILGWU women in the cloak-making industry, and in 1913 she organized one by lingerie makers. After the terrible Triangle Shirtwaist Factory fire in March 1911 in which 146 people died, Schneiderman gave a famous speech at the Metropolitan Opera House, in which she emphasized the urgency of direct action: "I would be a traitor to these poor burned bodies, if I came here to talk good fellowship. We have tried you good people of the public and found you wanting" (Biddle 1979, 123). By 1913, of the 72,500 members of the WTUL, 63,000 were garment workers.

Schneiderman briefly took on the role of a national organizer for the WTUL in 1915–1916 but gave up, feeling too isolated in her work when she was not given enough backing by male trade unionists. She returned to her work for the WTUL in New York and also set about educating herself by reading widely. Through her work for the WTUL, Schneiderman came into contact with many women sympathizers in the suffrage movement and in 1912 gave over time to fight for women's suffrage, working for the National American Woman Suffrage Association's campaign for the state vote in Cleveland, Ohio. She also worked closely with the Equality League of Self-Supporting Women, established in New York by Harriot Stanton Blatch, and served as chair of the industrial section of New York state's Woman Suffrage Party from 1917. During this period of activism until 1917, Schneiderman spoke regularly on women's suffrage at trade union meetings and lectured for the vote before and during World War I. In 1917 women in New York state were given the vote, and with this improved political muscle, Schneiderman increased lobbying at the state level for a forty-eight-hour workweek for women and a minimum wage.

After the vote was won for women at the national level in 1920, Schneiderman, who opposed the campaign for an Equal Rights Amendment in favor of protective legislation for women, went back to trade union work and cofounded the New York Farmer-Labor Party. She ran unsuccessfully for the Senate in 1920 on the party's ticket. In 1919 she helped organize the International Congress of Working Women and in 1920 attended the Paris peace conference on behalf of U.S. women workers. As president of the New York branch of the WTUL from 1918 to 1955 and of the national WTUL from 1926 until it was disbanded in 1950, she became an influential figure in U.S. trade unionism and cooperated closely with Eleanor Roosevelt, who joined the WTUL in 1922. Schneiderman shifted politically toward the Democrats and through Roosevelt indoctrinated her husband, the future president, Franklin D. Roosevelt, on labor relations and legislation, later becoming one of several experts he called on as his unofficial "brain trust." In 1933, when Roosevelt introduced the New Deal, Schneiderman was the sole woman appointed to the National Labor Relations Board, an advisory body set up under the National Industry Recovery Act, where she introduced industrial codes of practice to protect working women before the board was declared unconstitutional in 1936. From 1937 to 1943, Schneiderman was secretary of the New York State Department of Labor.

Schneiderman resigned at sixty from her public offices, although she acted as director of a summer school for working women held at Bryn Mawr College (where she insisted on blacks being allowed to take part). In 1967 she published her autobiography, *All for One.*

See also Blatch, Harriot Stanton; Roosevelt, (Anna) Eleanor.

References and Further Reading
Adickes, Sandra. 1997. *To Be Young Was Very Heaven: Women in New York before the Great War.* Basingstoke: Macmillan.
Biddle, Marcia McKenna. 1979. *Contributions of Women: Labor.* Minneapolis: Dillon Press.
Boone, Gladys. 1942. *The Women's Trade Union Leagues in Great Britain and the United States of America.* New York: Columbia University Press.
Buhle, Mari Jo. 1981. *Women and American Socialism, 1870–1920.* Urbana: University of Illinois Press.
Chambers, Clarke A. 1963. *Seedtime of Reform: American Social Service and Social Action, 1918–1933.* Minneapolis: University of Minnesota Press.
Dye, Nancy Schrom. 1980. *As Equals and as Sisters: Feminism, the Labor Movement and the Women's Trade Union League of New York.* Columbia: University of Missouri Press.
Foner, Philip. 1979. *Women and the American Labor Movement,* vol. 1: *From Colonial Times to the Eve of World War I.* New York: Free Press.
Orleck, Annelise. 1995. *Common Sense and a Little Fire: Women and Working-Class Politics in the United States, 1900–1965.* Chapel Hill: University of North Carolina Press.
Schneiderman, Rose, with Lucy Goldthwaite. 1967. *All for One.* New York: Eriksson.
Trager, James. 1994. *The Women's Chronology: A Year-by-Year Record, from Prehistory to the Present.* London: Aurum Press.
Wertheimer, Barbara M. 1977. *We Were There: The Story of Working Women in America.* New York: Pantheon Books.

Schreiber, Adele
(1872–1957)
Austria

Adele Schreiber was one of the Austrian women's movement's most persuasive speakers and became well known internationally as a long-standing member of the International Woman Suffrage Alliance (IWSA). She managed to hold on to her prominent role in the German suffrage movement despite her support for free love and for the radical League for the Protection of Motherhood and Sexual Reform (LPMSR).

Born in Vienna of a Jewish family, Schreiber settled in Berlin, where she took up work as a journalist for the *Frankfurt Times.* She also visited England to observe work there in the settlement house movement. As a member of Helene Stöcker's League for the Protection of Motherhood and Sexual Reform, she was a guiding influence in her practical approach to the subject, whereas Stöcker was very much the movement's theoretician. Schreiber became a powerful defender of the rights of unmarried mothers and illegitimate children, being of the opinion that the contribution of mothers to society was grossly undervalued. She also argued that divorce was a better option for couples whose marriages had broken down and was in the better interests of any children involved, and that the traditional exertion of parental authority through corporal punishment should be prohibited by law. Schreiber supported the LPMSR's fight to repeal Section 218 of the criminal code, which criminalized abortion, but rather than approaching the issue of sexuality through still illegal channels of contraception and abortion, as did other birth control reformers, she emphasized the need for reform of sexual behavior. In 1906 the league petitioned the Reichstag on the need for public sex education. But when Schreiber tried to lecture in Hamburg on the subject in 1908, she was prevented by the police. Schreiber's observation of the neglect of women's and children's welfare by the state only made her more convinced in turn that women's suffrage was essential if they were to be better able to defend their social and political rights.

A believer in practical action, Schreiber requested funds from the LPMSR to build maternity homes. She founded a model maternity home in Berlin in 1904 and encouraged women to breastfeed their children. But in 1910 she came into conflict with Stöcker over this use of funds and other personal issues and resigned from the league to set up the German Society for the Rights of Mothers and Children, a body devoted to practical action and counseling.

In 1919 when German women finally gained the vote, Schreiber, a Social Democrat, was elected as one of the first thirty-four women admitted to the first Reichstag of the new Weimar Republic. She continued to be active in women's rights, sitting on a committee that drafted a bill on the abolition of state-regulated prostitution. She also served as president of the German Red Cross. In 1933, with the rise of Adolf Hitler to power, Schreiber was forced into exile, and her money and possessions were confiscated by the Nazis. Her Aryan husband also divorced her.

In 1904 Schreiber had been a founding member of the International Woman Suffrage Alliance and remained in the organization until 1942; in 1945 she was elected vice president of the International Council of Women and collaborated in the writing of its history, published in 1956 as *Journey towards Freedom*. She lived the remainder of her life in exile—in England during the war and from 1947 in Zurich—making lecture tours of Europe and the United States.

Olive Schreiner (Library of Congress)

See also Stöcker, Helene.
References and Further Reading

Allen, Ann Taylor. 1985. "Mothers of the New Generation: Adele Schreiber, Helene Stöcker, and the Evolution of a German Idea of Motherhood, 1900–1914." *Signs* 10(3): 418–438.

O'Barr, Jean F., Deborah Pope, and Mary Wyer. 1990. *Ties That Bind: Essays on Mothering and Patriarchy*. Chicago: University of Chicago Press.

Schreiber, Adele, and Margaret Mathieson. 1955. *Journey towards Freedom: Written for the Golden Jubilee of the International Alliance of Women*. Copenhagen: International Alliance of Women.

Schreiner, Olive
(1855–1920)
South Africa

Olive Schreiner dedicated her life to women's emancipation and equality between the sexes. At the expense of her persistently poor health and in the face of her disappointment at her own childlessness, she never stopped defending the rights of women while remaining outside the mainstream of the women's movement. Through her many articles, letters, and pamphlets she also spoke out on the oppression of South Africa's minority groups—blacks, Jews, and Afrikaners.

One of twelve children of a Lutheran missionary of German descent and his English wife, Schreiner had a harsh upbringing on a Wesleyan mission station in Wittebergen Reserve in the Karoo region of Cape Colony (later Basutoland, now Lesotho in southern Africa). Her authoritarian mother, who forbade the speaking of Afrikaans and favored corporal punishment, taught her to read and write, but Schreiner was mostly self-educated and remained a solitary, determinedly individualistic child. She was an avid reader, feasting on a diet of Charles Darwin, Herbert Spencer, Edward Gibbon, Johann Wolfgang von Goethe, and John Stuart Mill, and soon rejected the narrowness of her religious upbringing, pronouncing herself a freethinker at the age of sixteen, after having read Herbert Spencer's 1862 work, *First Principles*.

The family was broken up in 1865 when Schreiner's impractical father, forever trying to find ways of relieving the family's grinding poverty, was removed from his post by the London Missionary Society for having tried to set up a business venture. Schreiner, left to fend for herself, worked at the Girqualand goldfields, where in the 1870s she became engaged to and was jilted by a Swiss businessman, Julius Gau. In 1873 she joined her sister Ettie in housekeeping for their brother Theo, who was working the diamond mines at the New Rush camp at Kimberley, and went on to take a succession of governess jobs over the next seven years for Afrikaner families in the Karoo. This place of remote semidesert, with its stark and arid beauty, would remain the great and enduring love of Schreiner's life and provided much of the background for her writing, most notably her classic novel, *The Story of an African Farm,* which she began writing in 1874. Unable to publish the book in South Africa because of its controversial feminist content, Schreiner scraped together the money for a ticket to England in 1881 with help from her siblings.

At this time, Schreiner, who had read many medical works as a young woman, wanted to train as a doctor. She worked for a while at the Royal Infirmary in Edinburgh and attended lectures at the London School of Medicine for Women. But the onset of asthma put an end to her ambitions, even of training as a nurse. She finally found a publisher for *The Story of an African Farm* in 1883, bringing it out under the pseudonym of Ralph Iron. With its determined and independent young heroine seeking to carve out her own destiny and break away from a narrow and remote colonial life, it was embraced by the burgeoning women's movement and has ever since been looked upon as one of the classic works of that era. The book was a huge success, but Schreiner disliked the celebrity and indeed the unwanted notoriety (for its unconventional views on marriage and religion) thrust upon her by the novel's publication and went to live in London's East End.

During her time in England, Schreiner developed friendships with progressive intellectuals and Fabian socialists such as Edward Carpenter, Eleanor Marx, and the sex psychologist Havelock Ellis, with whom she had a very close but not sexual relationship. She studied the social conditions of women's lives by meeting with women workers and prostitutes. She also became active in the Men and Women's Club, a group founded by Karl Pearson (later a leading eugenicist) and others that promoted intellectual association between the sexes and debated issues of male-female equality.

Schreiner returned to Cape Town in 1889 after having lived a peripatetic and restless life in England and Europe, where she had sought respite from her chronic asthma (which some suggest was in part a psychosomatic response to her difficult childhood). After meeting Cecil Rhodes in 1890 through her brother William, who was attorney general in Rhodes's government, she had at first invested great hope in the political future of colonial Africa. This hope had evaporated after the Jameson Raid of 1896, when the British had attempted to overthrow the Boer government in the Transvaal. Schreiner's own bitter disappointment in Rhodes's government is reflected in her novelized polemical tract, *Trooper Halket of Mashonaland* (1897), which is critical of imperialist ambitions in Rhodesia (present-day Zimbabwe) as embodied in Rhodes's British South Africa Charter Company. It is also an indictment of the indifference of British settlers to the sufferings of the indigenous Bantu people.

In 1894, when she was nearly forty, Schreiner married. Her husband—farmer, lawyer, and former member of Parliament Samuel Cronwright—acceded to her feminist wishes and took her name (becoming Cronwright-Schreiner). Together the couple became leading figures in the intellectual and political life of South Africa and supported the Afrikaner settlers in the period leading to the Boer War (1899–1902). At this time, Schreiner produced many polemical tracts and newspaper articles on racism and imperialism (collected in 1923 as *Thoughts on South Africa*). In her 1899 political tract entitled "An English South African Woman's View of the Situation," she pointed out the British lack of understanding of the Afrikaner cause and the lengths to which pioneer settlers would go to defend their independence.

As a pacifist, Schreiner was appalled at the outbreak of the Boer War, during which her home was looted and her papers were destroyed; she herself was constrained under martial law. Meanwhile, the first few years of her married life had been marred by the loss of a child only eighteen hours after birth and several miscarriages. Schreiner had thrown herself into her writing, spending many years working on a long, difficult, and posthumously published novel about women's fight for social justice and personal fulfillment, *From Man to Man* (1926). She also worked on *Woman and Labor,* publishing a revised version in 1911 after a much longer draft was destroyed during the Boer War. This groundbreaking feminist text, described by Vera Brittain as "the Bible of the Women's Movement," is a study of the economic position of women and an impassioned plea for them to be trained for productive work. Schreiner described the stunted, unfulfilled lives of married women condemned to "parasitism" as the slaves of their husbands. She had seen otherwise in the Karoo, where the hardworking Afrikaner women settlers had earned her respect for sharing the labor with their menfolk. In her view, the economic dependence of women not only demeaned them but also the men who continued to exploit them, and the social controls imposed on women through such enslavement would continue to prevail until society itself evolved into a more democratic and humane one in which labor was divided equitably between the sexes. The most emotive aspect of Schreiner's argument also highlighted her pacifist views, that women are the true bearers—"the primal munition," as she puts it—of the cost of war. Having carried, given birth to, and nurtured the men who fight and die in wars, their agony is greatest: "We pay the first cost on all human life," she said (Schreiner 1978, 169). She was convinced that if women had political power, wars would not happen because women are natural conciliators.

In 1913 Schreiner abandoned her marriage (the couple never divorced) to spend the final seven years of her life mainly in England. There, during World War I, where her German-sounding name aroused suspicion and prejudice as she moved from one boardinghouse to another, she worked for pacifism and supported conscientious objectors through the Union of Democratic Control and the No-Conscription Fellowship. But these final years were lonely, full of a sense of loss (she never got over the death of her child), and dogged by ill health and depression.

Schreiner finally returned to her African roots in 1920 and died within months, in Wynburg, Cape Colony. A year after her death, her husband had her body reburied under a cairn, together with that of her baby and her favorite dog, on the summit of Buffels Kop amid the African landscape that she so loved. This lonely monument and Schreiner's pioneering writing on women's emancipation and on the rights of Afrikaners and blacks in South Africa would become a beacon for those who would fight racism on that continent in the long hard years to come.

See also Hobhouse, Emily.

References and Further Reading

Banks, O. 1985/1990. *The Biographical Dictionary of British Feminists*, vol. 1, *1800–1930*. London: Harvester Wheatsheaf.

Brandon, Ruth. 1990. *The New Women and the Old Men*. London: Martin Secker and Warburg.

Clayton, Cherry. 1983. *Olive Schreiner*. Johannesburg: McGraw Hill.

Cronwright-Schreiner, Samuel C. 1924. *The Life of Olive Schreiner*. London: F. T. Unwin.

First, Ruth, and Ann Scott. 1980. *Olive Schreiner*. London: Deutsch.

Josephson, Harold, Sandi Cooper, and Steven C. Hause et al., eds. 1985. *Biographical Dictionary of Modern Peace Leaders*. Westport, CT: Greenwood Press.

McDonald, Lynn, ed. 1998. *Women Theorists on Society and Politics*. Waterloo, ON: Wilfrid Laurier University Press.

Schreiner, Olive. 1978 [1911]. *Woman and Labor*. Reprint, London: Virago.

Stanley, Liz. 1983. "Olive Schreiner: New Women, Free Women, All Women." In Dale Spender, ed., *Feminist Theorists: Three Centuries of Women's Intellectual Traditions*. London: Women's Press.

Schwimmer, Rosika
(1877–1948)
Hungary/United States

Few women in the international pacifist movement were as courageous and outspoken as the Hungarian Jew Rosika Schwimmer. She once proudly proclaimed, "I am an uncompromising pacifist. I have no sense of nationalism, only a consciousness of belonging to the human family" (Bussey and Tims 1980, 80). In this belief she was a dominating—some said domineering—influence and an outstanding speaker, not only in the international pacifist movement, where she advocated the concept of continuous mediation to try to bring World War I to an end, but also in the vigorous movement for women's suffrage in Hungary.

Rosika Schwimmer (Bettmann/Corbis)

Born in Budapest, the daughter of a farmer and horse dealer, Schwimmer attended convent school for eight years, receiving private tuition in music and languages. Coming from a liberal, reformist background, she took up journalism and joined the women's movement, which in Hungary was dominated by Jewish activists linked to the Liberal Democratic Party. Her initiation into a lifetime's activism came after she attended the 1904 congress held by the International Council of Women (ICW) in Berlin, at which the International Woman Suffrage Alliance was founded. Upon her return to Budapest, Schwimmer founded a National Council of Women and the Hungarian Feminist Association (HFA). Thanks to her energies and those of her cofounder of the HFA, Vilma Glücklich, a strong and vocal movement rapidly sprang up in Hungary, committed to land reform, women's suffrage, and trade unionism. As a close associate of the German

feminist leaders Anita Augspurg and Lida Gustava Heymann and inspired by them and radical feminists in the British suffrage organization the Women's Social and Political Union, Schwimmer inaugurated a militant campaign of leafleting and lobbying deputies in the Hungarian Diet for women's suffrage. As an advocate of birth control, she also joined the International Neo-Malthusian League. A fluent English-speaker, in 1904 Schwimmer translated Charlotte Perkins Gilman's 1898 work, *Women and Economics,* into Hungarian.

In 1912 Schwimmer was at the center of an onslaught on government by women activists after it reneged on its promise of a limited form of women's franchise linked to property ownership. Schwimmer organized a demonstration at the Hungarian Diet, and the movement reached its high point in 1913, when she and other Hungarian suffragists mounted the seventh congress of the International Woman Suffrage Alliance in Budapest, with great success.

As a member of the Hungarian Peace Society and editor of the pacifist journal *Woman and Society* (1907–1928, later known as the *Woman*), Schwimmer sought by all means possible to stem the tide of war in 1914. She moved to London early in 1914 and worked as a newspaper correspondent. In August, shortly after war broke out, she went to the United States on a personal mission to ask President Woodrow Wilson to endorse her plan to establish a mediation conference of neutral nations. She toured the United States with English pacifist Emmeline Pethick-Lawrence, lecturing to pacifist and suffrage groups. Impressed with Schwimmer's magnetism and energy and inspired by her mission, in January 1915 American pacifists gathered to found a Women's Peace Party in the United States, led by Jane Addams. Schwimmer remained in the United States until February to attend an emergency peace conference in Chicago.

By April 1915, Schwimmer and others who were still persisting in their attempts to mediate in the war set up an International Congress of Women at The Hague. Between May and June 1915 after the conference ended, at Schwimmer's suggestion, two groups of delegates visited fourteen countries, with Schwimmer joining the group that visited Scandinavia (she was refused entry into Russia). The findings of the mission were published in October, after which Schwimmer and the Dutch feminist leader Aletta Jacobs were elected vice presidents of the new International Committee of Women for Permanent Peace under the presidency of Jane Addams and affiliated with the International Woman Suffrage Alliance. In November 1915, in her quest for support for neutral mediation by the United States and nonbelligerent European states to end the war, Schwimmer joined the "peace ship" funded by Henry Ford. It attempted to breach the widespread censorship of reports on pacifist activities and set out to visit belligerent nations on a mission to mediate for peace. Met with derision and also held in suspicion as a Hungarian Jew by xenophobic elements in the United States and Europe, Schwimmer left the ship when it docked in Christiana (now Oslo) in Norway. She refused to abandon her cause, initiating the International Committee for Immediate Mediation in June 1916, which sent envoys to England, Germany, and Russia, again without success.

Meanwhile, Schwimmer's dictatorial manner had alienated many members of the International Committee of Women for Permanent Peace. She resigned from its board, feeling that it had betrayed its precepts by not doing enough to try to stop the war. All of Schwimmer's tireless lobbying did little to raise support for peace among the majority of patriotically minded members of the international women's movement, whose thoughts had turned to the defense of their own nationhood. However, the disjointed wartime peace movement would pave the way for the postwar activities of the committee under its new name—the Women's International League for Peace and Freedom (WILPF).

After the end of the war, Schwimmer returned to her homeland in October 1918 and was appointed to the National Council of Fifteen of the new republic, under the pro-suffrage prime minister Mihály Károlyi. She was the first Hungarian woman to be appointed an ambassador. But she never formally took up her post in Switzerland, her career being cut short by revolution and the overthrow of Károlyi, who was replaced by the communist dictatorship of Béla Kun, upon which Schwimmer resigned her post in protest.

Another political upheaval a year later, which brought with it in 1921 limited suffrage for certain Hungarian women over thirty, led to the establishment of a conservative and pro-monarchy government led by the deeply anti-Semitic Admiral Miklós Horthy de Nagybánya, whose dictatorship forced Schwimmer, as a Jew, to abandon the movement she had led for sixteen years and go into exile. She was smuggled out of Hungary on a boat down the Danube and taken to safety in Vienna. In a new spirit of optimism, Schwimmer settled in the United States in 1921. But she did not find the refuge she had hoped for, meeting instead with hostility for her socialist and pacifist connections and constant accusations of being a Soviet sympathizer and a German spy. Blacklisted and unable to work, she depended for financial support on her friends and her sister Franciska, with whom she lived. Many of the following years were consumed by lawsuits against those who slandered her, before Schwimmer found herself embroiled in what became notorious as the "Schwimmer case." She fought a long battle in the courts for U.S. citizenship, beginning in October 1927 when the Chicago district court rejected her application because as a pacifist she would not take the oath promising to bear arms in defense of her country. The Court of Appeals reversed the decision as a hypothetical one (as a woman, she would not be asked to bear arms anyway), but the case dragged on until 1929, when the Supreme Court upheld the original ruling. This decision came despite an impassioned appeal in support of her right to freedom of thought by Schwimmer's famous counsel, Oliver Wendell Holmes, and the united support of the American branch of the WILPF. No doubt prompted by these experiences, in 1933 Schwimmer called for stateless people to be granted world citizenship. She herself would die stateless.

In the late 1930s, appalled by the rise of fascism in Italy and Germany, Schwimmer advocated the concept of a world federal government, an idea that she developed with her friend Lola Maverick Lloyd and that led to the foundation in 1937 of the Campaign for World Government. In that year, on her sixtieth birthday, she was awarded the World Peace Prize. Schwimmer and Lloyd expounded their theories in pamphlets such as "Chaos, War, or a New World Order?" (1937) and "Union Now for Peace or War?" (1939). Schwimmer also alerted Carrie Chapman Catt to Nazi intentions toward the Jews of Europe in 1933, which prompted Catt to establish a Protest Committee of Non-Jewish Women Against the Persecution of Jews in Germany. In the final three years of her life, Schwimmer's pacifism remained undiminished. She was repeatedly nominated for the Nobel Peace Prize, but the years of exhausting campaigning had worn her out, and she developed diabetes, which further exacerbated her ill health. She died in 1948 before the Nobel Peace Prize for that year was announced. In the event, no award was made in that category, signaling the likelihood that death had denied Schwimmer the long-overdue recognition of a lifetime's self-sacrifice to pacifism.

See also Addams, Jane; Augspurg, Anita; Gilman, Charlotte Perkins; Glücklich, Vilma; Heymann, Lida Gustava; Jacobs, Aletta; Pethick-Lawrence, Emmeline.

References and Further Reading

Bussey, Gertrude, and Margaret Tims. 1980 [1960]. *Pioneers for Peace: Women's International League for Peace and Freedom 1915–1965*. Reprint, London: George Allen and Unwin.

Josephson, Harold, Sandi Cooper, and Steven C. Hause et al., eds. 1985. *Biographical Dictionary of Modern Peace Leaders*. Westport, CT: Greenwood Press.

Liddington, Jill. 1989. *The Long Road to Greenham: Feminism and Anti-Militarism in Britain since 1820*. London: Virago.

Sicherman, Barbara, and Carol Hurd Green, eds. 1980. *Notable American Women 1607–1950: A Biographical Dictionary*, vol. 4, *The Modern Period*. Cambridge, MA: Belknap Press of Harvard University.

Wiltsher, Anne. 1985. *Most Dangerous Women: Feminist Peace Campaigners of the Great War*. London: Pandora, and Westport, CT: Greenwood Press.

Wynner, Edith. 1947 [1939]. *Rosika Schwimmer, World Patriot*. Reprint, New York: Degen.

Scott, Rose
(1847–1925)
Australia

The international suffragist and social purity and peace campaigner Rose Scott was a firm believer in the Victorian advocacy of women's dedication to duty, the care of others, and the moral rehabilitation of society. Exuding old-world gentility and charm and often described as "the Rose without the thorn," she established close and enduring links with many suffragists around the world. She believed that women's enfranchisement would empower them in the erosion of selfish and intemperate masculine behavior, replacing it with the feminine spirit of cooperation and social service.

Rose Scott was born into a pioneering family of colonial landed gentry on a ranch near Singleton in the Hunter Valley of New South Wales. Although her early life was spent in rural isolation, it was a happy one. She was educated at home by her mother and became an avid reader of books on literature and history. After her father died in 1879, her modest inheritance allowed her to move to a pleasant suburb of Sydney. A notable beauty, Scott turned down numerous offers of marriage and devoted herself to the care of her mother and, after 1880, her baby nephew, when her sister Augusta died. In Sydney she established Friday night and Saturday afternoon political and literary salons in her home. Frequented as they were by politicians, philanthropists, the clergy, academics, artists, and members of the business world and legal professions, the salons became a focus for her many social and political contacts.

In 1889 Scott's first social campaign involved her in the movement to raise the age of consent from fourteen to sixteen under a new Vice Suppression Bill. That year she was a founder of the Women's Literary Society, which developed into the Womanhood Suffrage League (WSL) of New South Wales, established by Scott and Dora Montefiore in 1891, with Scott elected as secretary and remaining its leading light and public speaker until 1902. Through the WSL, she built up a strong network of contacts and worked with suffragists such as Montefiore, Louisa Lawson, and Vida Goldstein. With the latter, who led the suffrage movement in Melbourne, Scott conducted a detailed exchange by letter on tactics and the progress of suffrage campaigning.

In 1891 the leadership of the WSL was challenged from within, and a breakaway group left to found the more radical Women's Progressive Association. Scott, a firm believer in concerted persuasion rather than militancy and direct action, lobbied vigorously for women's suffrage, petitioning government, trade unions, and socialist members of Parliament, whom she felt would be more readily disposed to it. She wrote endless letters to the press, politicians, and influential public figures and organized regular deputations to the New South Wales legislature. Scott's belief in women's civilizing influence and their role as moral guardians colored much of her suffrage campaigning. "I can imagine no more effectual way of raising the tone of Public Opinion, of purifying its moral sentiments," she averred, "than by imparting into Public life the woman's influence and something of that tenderness, refinement and Purity for which women are especially noted" (Lake 1999, 28).

In 1902 the New South Wales legislature gave women the state vote. Disliking party politics and believing that women should act independently, Scott chose not to stand for election to Parliament. She preferred pursuing a variety of social concerns, such as the raising of the age of consent and other issues relating to social purity, temperance, the movement for earlier closing hours for shops and factories (which became law in 1899), seating for shop girls, and control of the sweatshop system. Scott was particularly concerned to combat the sexual degradation of women, both within marriage and in the sex trade, through a denunciation of the double sexual standard and the male predilection for other intemperate activities such as drinking and gambling.

With the demise of the Womanhood Suffrage League of New South Wales in 1902 after the achievement of the state and federal votes for women, Scott founded a new organization, the Women's Political Educational League, serving as president until 1910 and encouraging women to use their vote wisely. In the twentieth century, she took the lead in establishing a women's pacifist movement in New South Wales, in 1907 cofounding the Peace Society, which she served as president from 1908 to 1917. As Malcolm Saunders points out (Josephson et al. 1985, 865), Scott's work in this area was almost totally ignored in Australia, because it was considered— during World War I, especially—to be a betrayal both of her own family's strong connections with the military and of Australia's staunch support for the British war effort.

Since the 1890s Scott had made an open profession of her pacifist concerns and her support for international peace mediation. She opposed the Boer War (1899–1902), channeling her concern into the plight of women and children from Afrikaner families interned in camps by the British authorities. This concern had prompted her establishment of the Peace Soci-

ety as a sister branch of that in London, dedicated to promoting international peace mediation and the abandonment of militarism, particularly in Australian schools. The Peace Society also opposed federal plans for compulsory military training for young men. In 1913 the London Peace Society made Scott an honorary vice president. When war broke out in Europe in 1914, she accepted its necessity as a just one against German imperialism, although she protested the internment of German immigrants in New South Wales. But as a moderate, she was against the militancy of the anticonscription campaign and, in failing health, resigned in 1917.

Scott retired from public life in 1922. Throughout her thirty years of activism, she was a popular public speaker, touring the United States and United Kingdom, and became a pundit on many women's issues. At all times she was revered as a gracious and restrained elder stateswoman. She gave her support to a great variety of organizations: the International Woman Suffrage Alliance (maintaining a close correspondence with Carrie Chapman Catt), the League of Women, Sydney University Women's College, the women's committee of the Prisoners' Aid Society, the Tailoresses' Union (established in 1901), and the National Council of Women of New South Wales, which she served as international secretary from 1904 to 1921. She took an interest in legal reform, advocating that special courts be set up to try juvenile offenders, and also was influential in the establishment of a special women's prison at Long Bay in 1908, after presenting a report on the appalling conditions at Darlinghurst Prison.

See also Catt, Carrie Chapman; Goldstein, Vida; Lawson, Louisa; Montefiore, Dora.

References and Further Reading

Allen, Judith A. 1994. *Rose Scott: A Vision and Revision in Feminism.* Melbourne: Oxford University Press.

Eldershaw, F., ed. 1938. *The Peaceful Army: A Memorial to the Pioneer Women of Australia: 1788–1938.* Sydney: A. W. Baker.

Josephson, Harold, Sandi Cooper, and Steven C. Hause et al., eds. 1985. *Biographical Dictionary of Modern Peace Leaders.* Westport, CT: Greenwood Press.

Lake, Marilyn. 1999. *Getting Equal: The History of Australian Feminism.* London: Allen and Unwin.

Oldfield, Audrey. 1992. *Woman Suffrage in Australia: A Gift or a Struggle?* Melbourne: Cambridge University Press.

Pike, Douglas Henry, ed. *Australian Dictionary of Biography.* 1966–. Melbourne: Melbourne University Press.

Scudder, Vida
(1861–1954)
United States

Born in India as the only child of a Congregationalist missionary, Vida Scudder eschewed marriage and motherhood to live a sheltered life devoted to the care of her widowed mother until 1920. As a member of a privileged class, she felt that she had a duty to undertake public service to improve the lot of others, and true to the principles of Christian socialism and social justice, she became a pioneer of the U.S. settlement movement.

Scudder's family returned to Massachusetts when her father was drowned in 1862, and for some time thereafter she and her mother traveled in Europe. After being educated in private schools abroad and at the Girls' Latin School in Boston (until 1880), Scudder entered Smith College. She did postgraduate studies at Oxford University in 1884, where she was influenced by social radicalism and the writings of John Ruskin, Charles Kingsley, and Leo Tolstoy.

After her return to Boston in 1885, Scudder did little for two years, finally taking a post at Wellesley College teaching English in 1887, and gaining her M.A. from Smith College in 1889. Despite Scudder's uncompromising socialist beliefs, which regularly caused problems for the academic establishment at Wellesley College, she was given a professorship in 1910 and remained there until her retirement in 1928. She published numerous scholarly works on literature, including *The Life of the Spirit in Modern English Poets* (1895), *Social Ideals in English Letters* (1898), and *Introduction to the Study of English Literature* (1901).

Increasingly conscience-stricken about her life of privilege and convinced of the need to find ways of countering worker exploitation, from 1887 Scudder became involved in the foundation of the College Settlements Association (CSA), which opened a house on Rivington Street in New York in 1889. She also promoted the work of the CSA as secretary of its electoral board. In 1892 Scudder obtained leave from Wellesley College to spend a year helping to set up the Denison House settlement in Boston and remained a leading light of its management for twenty years.

Scudder's social activism was at all times closely tied to her devout Episcopalian beliefs. In 1889 she joined the Christian socialists and the Christian Social Union. A staunch supporter of labor rights and the theories on class of Karl Marx, she joined the Boston Central Labor Union to further the creation of a classless society based on equal opportunity.

In 1901 continuing conflicts with Wellesley College over her socialism led to a nervous breakdown, and Scudder spent two years traveling in Europe. She founded an Italian Circle at Denison House to offer a social and cultural outlet for local immigrant workers. In 1903 she took on a new role as a labor organizer for the Women's Trade Union League. Becoming increasingly radical in her activism, in 1911 she was a founding member of the Episcopal Church's Socialist League and joined the Socialist Party. After joining the pickets during a 1912 textile strike in Lawrence, Massachusetts, Scudder again found her academic career in jeopardy—a situation exacerbated by her publication in 1911 of an article titled "Class-Consciousness" in *Atlantic Monthly.* She decided regretfully to give up her work for Denison House and withdrew from activism to teach and write, living on campus at Wellesley College.

Scudder supported U.S. entry into World War I in 1917, a fact that caused a breach with some of her pacifist friends. After the war she was an organizer, in 1919, of the Church League for Industrial Democracy and became increasingly pacifist in her views. In 1923 she joined the Fellowship of Reconciliation and supported international pacifism during the 1930s through her work for the Women's International League for Peace and Freedom.

After retiring from Wellesley College in 1928, Scudder continued with her research and writing and taught Christian ethics in summer school. She produced a considerable body of work on religious and social topics as well as English literature, most notably her scholarly history of the Franciscans, *The Franciscan Adventure: A Study in the First Hundred Years of the Order of St. Frances of Assisi* (1931), and her autobiography, *On Journey,* in 1937. As a lifelong member of the Society of the Companions of the Holy Cross, a contemplative group of Episcopalian women

that promoted racial harmony and social reconciliation, Scudder lived a quiet but exemplary life
characteristic of a generation of now-forgotten
social reformers who resolved to make some
small contribution to the betterment of society.

References and Further Reading
Chambers, Clarke A. 1963. *Seedtime of Reform:
American Social Service and Social Action,
1918–1933.* Minneapolis: University of Minnesota
Press.
Corcoran, Teresa S. 1982. *Vida Dutton Scudder.*
Boston: G. K. Hall.
Darling, Pam. 1994. *New Wine: The Story of Women
Transforming Leadership and Power in the
Episcopal Church.* Boston: Cowley.
Davis, Allen F. 1967. *Spearheads for Reform: The
Social Settlements and the Progressive Movement
1890–1914.* New York: Oxford University Press.
Donovan, Mary S. 1994. *A Different Call: Women's
Ministries in the Episcopal Church.* Ridgefield, CT:
Morehouse.
Scudder, Vida. 1937. *On Journey.* Boston: E. P.
Dutton.

Seacole, Mary
(1805–1881)
Jamaica

The achievements of the Jamaican Creole
woman Mary Seacole, who ignored the indifference of British War Office bureaucracy to travel
to the Crimea to pioneer the nursing of the sick
and wounded during the war of 1854–1856 at
her own expense, have been all too often eclipsed
by the work of her more eminent and influential
contemporary, Florence Nightingale. For many
years, Seacole's unique contribution to the development of nursing and the treatment of tropical
diseases lay buried, until her work was rediscovered in the 1970s. Since then, she has become a
role model for black nurses and civil rights campaigners.

Mary Jane Grant was born in Kingston, Jamaica, of mixed parentage. Her father was a
Scottish soldier at the army base there, and her
mother was a free black and herbalist who ran a
boardinghouse. As a young girl, Seacole developed a fascination for medicine and nursing after being taught herbal medicine by her mother.
She resolved to become a "doctress" and helped
nurse the sick during epidemics of cholera and
yellow fever, in the latter instance looking after

sick British soldiers at the military camp at Up-
Park Town, near Kingston. Sometime around
1836 she met Edwin Horatio Seacole, a British
serviceman (and godson of Horatio Nelson)
whom her mother had been nursing. They married in November, but he died within a few
months. For a while, Seacole ran the boardinghouse her mother had left her, rebuilding it after
a fire in 1843. Word about her nursing skills had
spread among the British officers based in
Kingston, and she frequently nursed them as well
as their wives when they were sick, learning new
skills from British naval and military surgeons
when they were posted to Kingston.

In her determination to remain self-supporting, Seacole traveled into territory where any
conventional woman would never venture. At
the age of forty-five, she left Jamaica to join her
brother, Edward, in the Central American frontier gold-mining town of Cruces, where she ran a
store and hotel and also nursed people during
outbreaks of cholera, gaining further experience
in the treatment of tropical diseases.

After three years in Colombia and Panama,
Seacole returned to Jamaica in 1853 but was
soon restless and in need of a purpose. When the
Crimean War broke out in 1854, she realized her
moment had come and immediately sailed for
England, where she offered her services to the
War Office. When the might of officialdom con-
spired to block her (as it had done one or two
other West Indian women who had offered to go
and nurse the wounded), and Florence Nightingale (no doubt for the same reasons of racial
prejudice) also declined her offer to join her
band of nurses, Seacole did it her own way—
making the three-week, 3,000-mile journey by
boat to Balaclava via Constantinople and the
Bosporus.

Arriving in early 1855, Seacole used her Jamaican experience in running boardinghouses
to construct and provision her own "British hotel" for sick and convalescent officers at a place
she named "Spring Hill," near Balaclava. Above
the ground-floor store and canteen was a sick
bay where she nursed the wounded, dispensed
her own herbal medicines, and introduced methods of nursing that emphasized cleanliness,
plenty of ventilation, and an abundance of her
own home-cooked food. She funded her work by
selling general supplies to the soldiers and found
the work greatly fulfilling, despite its horrors and

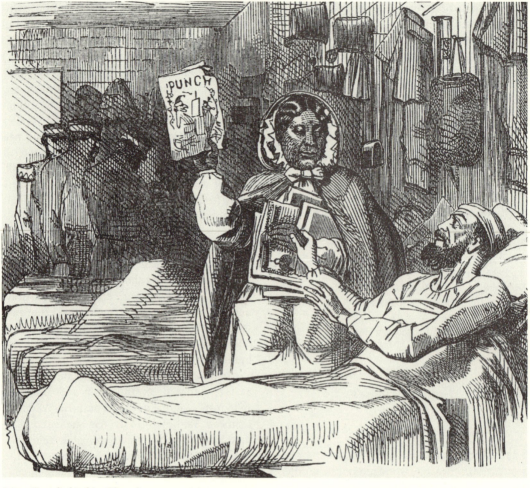

Mary Seacole (Archive Photos)

the risks she ran in attending the wounded on the battlefield. Seacole soon became a familiar figure, known to the soldiers as "Mother Seacole"; she had no fear of riding out alone on her mule with supplies of food and drink and medicine for the wounded. And those she helped in turn accorded her a gratitude and respect that transcended the barriers of color and prejudice. Seacole had the skill of a natural healer, and the native methods taught her by her mother, combined with her own long experience treating tropical disease, were often more successful than conventional medicine in nursing the many battlefield sicknesses—diarrhea, dysentery, jaundice—that took a far greater toll on the troops than did death in battle (of 20,000 war dead, 17,000 died of sickness or frostbite during the terrible Russian winter of 1855–1856).

At the sudden end of the war, Seacole was left high and dry with a lot of unsold supplies and found herself in the London Bankruptcy Court. Officers who had known of her endeavors in the Crimea collaborated with her admirers in England, such as the prince and princess of Wales, to raise funds for her. The public had come to know of Seacole's good works through publications such as *The Times, Punch,* and *The Illustrated London News* and the 1857 publication of her autobiography, *The Wonderful Adventures of Mrs. Seacole in Many Lands.* It is said that Seacole's healing skills found new employment in her capacity as masseuse to the princess of Wales (who suffered from lameness). When she died in London in 1881, Seacole was buried in St. Mary's Catholic Cemetery at Kensal Green. And then, for nearly a century, her humanitarian work was forgotten.

Seacole greatly enjoyed her brief period of public fame but at heart always looked upon her accomplishments as no more than the fulfillment of her own innate sense of duty: "I do not pray to God that I may never see its [war] like again, for I wish to be useful all my life and it is in scenes of horror and distress that a woman can do so much" (Seacole 1988, xxxii). She had proved her usefulness to the British army and to nursing practice as an "unknown Creole woman" (75), as she modestly described herself, in so doing underlining that although Florence Nightingale might have had the intellectual and administrative skills to run a hospital in the Crimea, practical skills such as Seacole's were equally important.

See also Nightingale, Florence.

References and Further Reading

Seacole, Mary. 1988 [1857]. *The Wonderful Adventures of Mrs. Seacole in Many Lands.* Introduction by William L. Andrews. Reprint, Oxford: Oxford University Press.

Seaton, Helen J. "Another Florence Nightingale: The Rediscovery of Mary Seacole." Accessed at www.icml.org/Monday/hlg3/seaton.

Séverine (Caroline Rémy)
(1855–1929)
France

Séverine, a woman of great compassion, beauty, and humanitarian concerns, was one of the most outspoken women journalists in France of the 1890s, pioneering radical journalism as a profession for women. An eminent philanthropist and international peace campaigner in the Association of Women for Peace and Disarmament, she also devoted herself to recruiting working-class women from the poorer districts of Paris to the struggle for social reform and defense of the underprivileged. She remained an independent figure, never afraid to speak out against social and sexual injustice, who practiced what she preached in her private life while remaining outside the suffrage movement until 1913.

Born in Paris, the daughter of a civil servant, Séverine escaped her unhappy home life by marrying young at the age of sixteen. Both her first and second marriages were short-lived, leaving Séverine with two children to support. Her unsatisfactory marriages would later contribute to her involvement in 1905 on an extraparliamentary committee for the reform of the Napoleonic Code relating to marriage.

In the early 1880s in Paris, she met the former Communard and socialist Jules Vallès and worked with him on the journal *The Awakening* under the pseudonym Arthur Vintgras, carrying on the editorship after his death in 1885. Quickly developing a skill for journalism, she also submitted articles to *Gil Blas, France,* and *Morning* and edited Vallès's other journal, *The Cry of the People* (1886–1888), during which time she wrote in defense of women's rights and striking miners. She questioned women's readiness for suffrage during her early career, however, believing that they were not sufficiently educated to understand the full political implications of the vote.

From the late 1880s through the 1890s, Séverine entered a period of inconsistency, coming out against the wrongfully imprisoned Jewish army officer Alfred Dreyfus and then changing tack to support the conservative Boulangists who attempted to overturn the French republic during the 1880s. For long a notable advocate of pacifism, she cofounded the Association of Journalist Friends of Peace in 1897. She also joined the League for the Rights of Man and the Socialist Party and became a regular delegate at international peace congresses, criticizing male optimism over peace initiatives at a time when an arms buildup was gathering pace in Europe.

Séverine found her true voice in investigative journalism, which was driven by her concern for the rights of the underprivileged. She raised funds through her journalism for good causes, also donating generously from her own earnings. In the pages of her own journal, *Towards the Light,* and Durand's *La Fronde* (The Sling), she wrote on women's suffrage, and she was a regular contributor to the journal *Humanity.* Although she came to support women's suffrage, she was disappointed in the inability of the various French women's suffrage groups to unify in a concerted campaign. In 1914 Séverine initiated a meeting of seventeen organizations to mount a public and pacific demonstration in support of women's suffrage, reminding activists: "One can claim one's rights without gnashing one's teeth; one can desire justice without preaching hate" (Hause 1984). Séverine herself negotiated with the government for permission to hold a mass meeting in the Tuileries Gardens in Paris, followed by a parade, in support of women's suffrage. On the day of the gathering, 5,000–6,000 participants turned out for what would be the apogee of the French suffrage campaign before the outbreak of war stopped the movement dead in its tracks.

Just prior to World War I, Séverine was elected to the Permanent Delegation of French Peace Societies. She continued her militant antiwar writing in the journal of the Society for the Critical and Documentary Studies of the War, in which she took the French to task for their rosy view of their own supposed "innocence" as instigators of the war that broke out in 1914. By 1917 she had moved further left to welcome the Russian Revolution and communism.

After World War I, Séverine remained an active peace campaigner in the Association for Peace and Disarmament, the International Peace Bureau, and the International Pacifist Association of Journalists. She argued against national conscription and appealed to the League of Nations to call for an end to it, cofounding the League for the Recognition of Conscientious Objection. She was one of the first continental members of the new English pacifist group War Resisters International.

Before the war, Séverine had raised feminist issues even within the literary world: in 1903 she criticized the Prix Goncourt for its all-male jury and with other feminist writers founded the Prix Fémina the following year. But her individualistic approach frequently led to her vilification on all sides, despite her undoubted humanitarian concerns. The women's movement often criticized her for not joining any established women's group; equally, she was castigated by the mainstream press for tackling controversial subjects such as abortion and sexual violence in her journalism. She wrote on a wide range of issues, from conditions in the mines to French neglect of poor workers in colonial Algeria; in 1927 she joined the international protest at the execution in the United States of the Italian immigrant socialists Nicola Sacco and Bartolomeo Vanzetti. Many of her articles were collected in *Red Pages* (1893), *Mystical Pages* (1895), and *Towards the Light* (1900).

References and Further Reading

Hause, Steven C., with Anne R. Kenny. 1984. *Women's Suffrage and Social Politics in the French Third Republic*. Princeton, NJ: Princeton University Press.

Josephson, Harold, Sandi Cooper, and Steven C. Hause et al., eds. 1985. *Biographical Dictionary of Modern Peace Leaders*. Westport, CT: Greenwood Press.

Shabanova, Anna
(1848–1932)
Russia

One of the first women doctors in Russia, Anna Shabanova had a successful career as a specialist in Leningrad's leading hospital for children's diseases, pioneering the treatment of rickets in particular. She also spent a lifetime passing on her skills to other doctors, vigorously promoting women's medical education and remaining a lifelong champion of women's rights. A pacifist during the last years of the Russian Empire, she survived into the Stalinist period to be honored as a "Hero of Labor."

Born in Smolensk, Shabanova was the daughter of an army lieutenant. She was educated at a girls' boarding school, but when her parents suffered financial losses she was forced to abandon her education at the age of fifteen and become self-supporting. Moving to Moscow, she took various jobs as a private tutor, governess, and translator. She joined radical women's groups and helped to create a women's sewing cooperative modeled on a utopian ideal, cherished by so many young radicals, that had been immortalized in Nikolay Chernyshevsky's 1863 novel *What Is to Be Done?* In April 1866 the cooperative was broken up by the authorities, and Shabanova was arrested and kept in solitary confinement for six months.

In the late 1860s Shabanova was once more active in the campaigns for women's higher education, in particular supporting their access to medical training. In 1868 she went to St. Petersburg to enroll at the Medical Surgical Academy but was refused. Unable to raise the money to join other Russian women who had gone to Zurich to study medicine, she went to Helsinki, Finland, to study medicine—in Swedish—remaining there for the next two and a half years. When medical courses in Russia were finally opened to women, Shabanova returned in 1873 to continue clinical studies under the pediatrician K. A. Raukhfus. In 1877, after years of self-sacrifice and hard work, Shabanova sat for her exams but was only given a certificate to treat women and children in the local zemstvos (district assemblies). Raukhfus flouted this ruling by employing her as his assistant in a children's clinic at the Nikolaevsky Army Hospital, where in her turn Shabanova trained other women medical students between 1878 and 1884. She also simultaneously took up what would become a lifetime's work as a pediatrician at Prince Oldenburg Children's Hospital.

In 1878 Shabanova published the first of a considerable opus of scholarly medical works, which would range across pediatrics, preventive medicine, children's diet, and the results of her research into the treatment of the diseases of her day that killed so many children: diphtheria, whooping cough, tuberculosis, typhus, and rickets. She also taught first aid courses at women's gymnasiums and wrote a textbook on first aid. With Mariya Pokrovskaya, Shabanova led the Russian women's campaign against state-regulated prostitution.

In St. Petersburg Shabanova and Raukhfus cofounded the Society for the Treatment of Chronically Ill Children, which established a hospital at Gatchina in 1883. Such uncontroversial, worthy philanthropic work attracted the patronage of the Russian nobility, including the empress, who made annual visits, but Shabanova took her concern for such children beyond the confines of their treatment in her determination to see that they were placed into decent homes, not merely sent back into the same conditions that had exacerbated their original illnesses. After publication of her pamphlet "The Struggle with Chronically Ill Children" in 1897, donations flooded in, enabling her to establish a children's rest home by the sea at Vindava.

Shabanova became eminent in numerous societies and was a regular speaker at medical congresses, both in Russia—notably the Priogov Congresses of the Society of Russian Doctors—and abroad. She was one of the first women to be admitted into the St. Petersburg Medical Society for Pediatricians. In 1895, with Anna Filosova, she took over the Russian Women's Mutual Philanthropic Society (RWMPS) after the death of Nadezhda Stasova, exhibiting a rather highhanded style of leadership until 1917. The society found itself confined to marking time in its activism because Shabanova insisted it pursue only legal activities. Members primarily raised funds to help women students pay for university studies and ran hostels and canteens for working women. Attempts at running reading circles and seminars were quashed by 1901. After the inauguration of the First Duma in 1905, Shabanova urged the RWMPS to step up its calls for women's suffrage and other rights. But in all her activism, as a pacifist she remained nonmilitant in the face of the constant setbacks with which the Russian women's movement had to contend. In 1902 she proposed the idea of a national women's congress to be held in June 1905. But the 1905 revolution intervened, and it was not until 1908 that Shabanova's project became reality. The First All-Russian Women's Congress, a showcase for the moderate majority in the Russian women's movement, was heckled by a group of socialist women led by Alexandra Kollontai and drew the attention of the international women's movement to Shabanova's campaigning. She was invited to attend women's congresses abroad—in 1910 in Buenos Aires and in 1912 at Stockholm—where she was elected an honorary member of the International Woman Suffrage Alliance (IWSA). Shabanova served as an envoy of Czar Nicholas II to pacifist peace conferences in Europe, which attempted to prevent the outbreak of war in 1914. She also served as chair of the Russian women's section of the Women's International League founded in 1915.

In 1917, after the February Revolution, Shabanova briefly realized the ambition of the late Anna Filosova of establishing a Russian affiliate of the International Council of Women (ICW). But the October Revolution put an end to all bourgeois women's groups in Russia, although Shabanova remained an honorary vice president of the ICW. She made no overt commitment to socialist politics, continuing to work as a consultant at the Prince Oldenburg Hospital until she was in her eighties, passing on her skills to a new generation of women doctors and nurses, and becoming president of the Society of Women Physicians. As the author of forty books and pamphlets, she was also elected president of the Society of Women Authors. The final years of her life were punctuated by a string of accolades: in 1923 she was elected to the Court of Honor of the Union of Doctors of Petrograd (formerly St. Petersburg; renamed Leningrad in 1924), and in 1925 she was made a judge of tribunal of the Medical Union of Leningrad. Her contribution to pediatrics was also acknowledged in the United States, when in 1929 she was elected a member of the American Academy of Science in Philadelphia.

In 1928, on the occasion of her eightieth birthday, the Soviet government made Shabanova a

Hero of Labor, and her work as a pioneer of women's medical education was lauded in *Pravda*. She was also sufficiently well known in the international women's movement for her death in 1932 to be recorded with regret on the pages of the *International Woman Suffrage News*.

See also Filosova, Anna; Kollontai, Alexandra; Pokrovskaya, Mariya.

References and Further Reading

Edmondson, Linda. 1984. *Feminism in Russia, 1900–1917*. London: Heinemann.

Stites, Richard. 1991 [1978]. *The Women's Liberation Movement in Russia: Feminism, Nihilism, and Bolshevism, 1860–1930*. Reprint, Princeton, NJ: Princeton University Press.

Tuve, Jeanette E. 1984. *The First Russian Women Physicians*. Newtonville, MA: Oriental Research Partners.

Shafiq, Durriyah
(1908–1975)
Egypt

A writer of poetry and prose in French, Shafiq was the charismatic leader of the women's organization she founded, the Daughter of the Nile Union. Sadly, her life was blighted by bouts of mental instability and depression, culminating in her probable suicide at the age of sixty-seven.

Shafiq was born in Tanta, Egypt, to an upper-class family and grew up in Mansura. Her father was an engineer; her mother died when Shafiq was eleven years old. She was educated at a pre-school run by Italian nuns and then the French mission school of St. Vincent de Paul in Alexandria, before studying for her baccalaureate in Cairo, which she passed in second place. Having nursed a burning desire to study at the Sorbonne in Paris and already interested in women's issues, she approached the leading Egyptian feminist, Huda Sha'rawi, who helped her obtain a scholarship from the Ministry of Education.

Shafiq left Egypt to study in Paris in 1928. While there, she wrote for the Egyptian Feminist Union (EFU) magazine, *Egyptian Woman,* and got married twice. Her first marriage lasted barely a year, and her second, to her cousin Nour al-Din Ragai, an Egyptian lawyer, took place in 1937. Having obtained her degree in 1933, she presented two theses, her second being on women and religious law in contemporary Egypt. She returned to Cairo in the late 1930s, going back to Paris to defend her doctoral theses in 1940. On her return to Egypt, Shafiq taught at the Alexandria College for Girls and the Saniyah School and acted for some time as a French-language inspector for the Ministry of Education. But her heart was not in teaching, and she turned more and more to writing, taking up journalism and the promotion of women's issues on a full-time basis.

During the 1930s, Shafiq distanced herself from the EFU because she felt it was not radical enough in its objectives, but she never ceased to respect her mentor and gave a moving eulogy at Sha'rawi's funeral in 1947. She now established her own distinct political voice, founding several journals, including the women's magazine *The New Woman* in 1945 and the feminist Arabic-language journal *Daughter of the Nile,* from which sprang in 1948 a new, broad-reaching feminist organization, the Daughter of the Nile Union. At first, Shafiq had been apprehensive about demanding equal rights with men because of the long-established traditions of Islamic religious law that placed women firmly in the home. But she became increasingly convinced that women had much to contribute, and like other international feminists, she believed they were a force for good in a world riven with conflict. The union affiliated itself with the International Council of Women (ICW), and Shafiq was elected to the ICW's executive committee.

The Daughter of the Nile Union became the focus for Shafiq's personal crusade for women's political and working rights. Unlike the predominantly upper-class EFU, the union enlisted a broad-based following among Egyptian middle-class women. In 1948, in an editorial in *Daughter of the Nile,* Shafiq called for equal voting rights for men and women, commenting: "Is it not a shame that one's male cook is given the right to vote, while his mistress is denied that right?" (Talhami 1996, 17). The union worked toward social and economic reform and a return to the promises of the 1923 Egyptian constitution, which had supported equal rights for women. It set up literacy and health care projects in poor communities, gave vocational training to young people, and helped find jobs for poor women who came to the cities from rural areas.

During the struggle for Egyptian independence, the union trained its members in guerrilla

Durriyah Shafiq (AP/Wide World Photos)

tactics. Shafiq's espousal of the nationalist cause evolved into a wider campaign for women's franchise and their social liberation through reform of the personal status laws. In 1951 she staged a legendary and dramatic challenge when she led 1,500 members of the union on a demonstration. Together they stormed the Egyptian parliament and disrupted the proceedings, demanding political and other rights. Having brought the parliamentary process to a standstill, Shafiq inaugurated a sit-in and hunger strike, which lasted for a week. During 1952, Shafiq enlisted a 200-strong women's military unit in a series of strikes and demonstrations against both King Farouk I's government and the British protectorate.

Under the regime of President Gamal Abdel Nasser, Shafiq continued to campaign for a return to democracy and tried to stand in the general election of 1952 in a final drive to achieve wider electoral rights for women. In 1953 she published a "White Paper on the Rights of the Egyptian Woman," and a year later publicly deplored the exclusion of women from the 1954

Constituent Assembly. Such was her fervent, if not obsessive, commitment to achieving her political goals that she once again went on a hunger strike in protest. She was joined by eight other members of the Daughter of the Nile Union in an eight-day protest held at the Press Syndicate, which was supported by other women around Egypt, who joined in sympathy hunger strikes. Shafiq gave up the hunger strike only when she received a written assurance that the government would guarantee women's political rights. In 1956 the vote was eventually given to Egyptian women—but only those literate enough to read a ballot paper.

By the end of 1956, the Egyptian feminist movement had been badly affected by the upheavals of the independence struggle and the Suez Crisis, and all women's groups in Egypt were suppressed by Nasser's government. Shafiq's emotional style of campaigning was belittled in the press; she had also brought the wrath of conservative religious belief on her head for criticizing the Islamic personal status laws that allowed polygamy and favored men in cases of divorce and child custody. In 1957 she announced yet another hunger strike, this time staged outside the Indian embassy, calling for the withdrawal of Israel from Egyptian land in Sinai and protesting the dictatorship of Nasser's government. The membership of the Daughter of the Nile Union now found it difficult to come to terms with Shafiq's position, for many of them idolized her, as did some of her erstwhile supporters in the public at large, for having contributed to Egypt's liberation from British rule. Eventually, the movement turned against her, and she was forced out of the union. Soon after, the government placed Shafiq under house arrest as part of a concerted roundup of political activists and dissidents. The Daughter of the Nile Union and its journal were closed down by Nasser in 1957. As Ahmed has observed, Shafiq miscalculated by opposing Nasser politically: "In protesting his dictatorship she was playing to the wrong—Western—gallery" (1992, 206).

Incarcerated in her flat at Zamalek, Shafiq refused to be silent and protested to the United Nations about the abuse of human rights in Egypt. She also set about writing her memoirs and wrote poetry (five volumes of which were published in Paris). There followed a series of mental breakdowns. Shafiq constantly shifted her position, launching into bouts of defiance followed by retreat into silence. After President Anwar Sadat came to power in 1970, her house arrest was lifted, but twelve years of close surveillance had taken their toll on her mental health, and the outbreak of the Arab-Israeli War in 1973 further affected her mental stability. On 20 September 1975, she threw herself from the balcony of her sixth-floor flat.

References and Further Reading

Ahmed, Leila. 1992. *Women and Gender in Islam: Historical Roots of a Modern Debate.* New Haven: Yale University Press.

Badran, Margot. 1995. *Feminists, Islam and Nation: Gender and the Making of Modern Egypt.* Princeton: Princeton University Press.

Nelson, Cynthia. 1996. *Doria Shafiq, Egyptian Feminist: A Woman Apart.* Gainesville: University of Florida Press.

Roberts, Frank C., ed. 1971–1979. *Obituaries from The Times,* vol. 3, 1971–1979. Reading: Newspaper Archive Developments.

Talhami, Ghada Hashem. 1996. *The Mobilization of Muslim Women in Egypt.* Gainesville: University of Florida Press.

Sha'rawi, Huda
(1879–1947)
Egypt

Huda Sha'rawi was the organizing spirit behind the most active women's group in Egypt, the Egyptian Feminist Union, during the period of its liberal political experiment (1923–1952). Her legacy and influence have been considerable, despite the fact that present-day feminist interpretations of her work tend to look upon her origins as bourgeois and the EFU as essentially elitist in its membership, composed as it was of upper-class women mainly from the Egyptian land-owning class.

Yet ironically, Sha'rawi was only able to achieve the things she did and fund her numerous feminist causes as a direct result of this privileged background. She was born Nur al-Huda Sultan into a very wealthy upper-class family in Minia in upper Egypt. Her father, who owned a large estate, held several official posts, including governor of Asyût and inspector-general of upper Egypt. At home, Sha'rawi learned calligraphy and the piano and spoke Turkish, French, and Arabic, absorbing the intellectual and cultural influences of all these languages. She also undertook her own course of self-study, reading her brother's books on philosophy and literature. Sha'rawi's father died when she was five, and the family moved to Cairo, where at the age of thirteen and in order to keep her father's estates in the family, she was married to her guardian, Ali Sha'rawi. Her husband was in his late forties at the time and already had another wife. When the fourteen-year-old Huda became pregnant (and unavailable to satisfy his sexual demands), Ali Sha'rawi broke his promise of monogamy and went back to his first wife. Huda resisted resuming relations with her husband for the next seven years but was finally pressured into returning to him at the age of twenty-one because her brother refused to marry until she did so (because of the dishonor he felt this brought on the family).

By the time she reassumed her social position with her husband, Sha'rawi had begun taking an interest in women's concerns and philanthropy. She also became friendly with the society hostess Eugénie Le Brun (a Frenchwoman who had converted to Islam after marrying a Turko-Circassian landowner from the elite ruling class). Despite the tone of privilege surrounding her salon,

Le Brun contributed two books on women in Islam, in which she criticized their social and civil oppression. Together with other women of her class who had educated themselves within the confines of the harem, Sha'rawi began venturing out to attend Le Brun's Saturday salon in Cairo. Here women held polite debates on social issues such as veiling. Like her contemporary and feminist alter ego, Malak Hifni Nasif, Sha'rawi believed that women should not abandon the veil until such time as men began to be more responsible in their own sexual behavior. Meanwhile, women should make use of its symbolic significance as a weapon rather than as a social inhibitor.

Sha'rawi's first women's venture was modest: together with Princess Ain al-Hayat, in 1908 she set up a society named the Muhammad Ali the Great, a philanthropic organization that gave literacy classes and taught poor women sewing. Sha'rawi later became its executive head. In 1909 she set up a dispensary offering health care to poor women and enlisted the help of her rich society friends in both funding and running it. She became involved in organizing lectures for women on women's issues and in 1910 opened one of the first girls' schools in Cairo, which emphasized a well-rounded education for girls, not just domestic and vocational training.

As one of the founders of two new societies in 1914, the Women's Refinement Union and the Ladies' Literary Improvement Society, Sha'rawi sought to extend consciousness-raising activities among a wider cross section of Egyptian women. But soon political upheaval in Egypt diverted her attention away from women's concerns to the broader issue of Egyptian independence. Her husband had become a founder of the Wafdist movement of Egyptian nationalists, and Sha'rawi became president of its militant Wafdist Women's Central Committee (WWCC), established in 1920. She rose to national prominence after being drawn into the 1919–1920 Egyptian nationalist movement, along with other wives of leading activists calling for an end to the British protectorate and a boycott of foreign goods. Her home became a rallying point for protesters after the arrest and deportation of the nationalist leader Sa'd Zaghlul. She persuaded women to participate in nationalist demonstrations and organized a march of 350 women to the High Commission to protest the killing of Egyptians

Huda Sha'rawi (right, with Saiza Nabarawi)(Library of Congress)

by British forces. After her husband's death in 1922, Sha'rawi kept up her commitment to Egyptian independence, granted nominally that same year but with no franchise for women.

Sha'rawi's activities as president of the WWCC and leader of a 1921 petition for Egyptian independence were the grounding for her own campaign for social reform. When she was forty-four, together with ten other women she founded the Egyptian Feminist Union (EFU) on 16 March 1923, with the particular aim of achieving women's education and social welfare and the vote—the latter not being a prominent issue on the political agenda of the Wafd. The EFU had a broad spectrum of objectives. One of Sha'rawi's first acts as head of this new society came a couple of months later when she boldly led the first delegation of Egyptian women to the annual congress of the International Woman

Suffrage Alliance (IWSA) held in Rome in May 1923, where they publicized the program of the EFU. On her return by train from Alexandria, Sha'rawi and her close friend Saiza Nabarawi both unveiled at Cairo railway station as they got off the train. This single, well-publicized act became something of an apocryphal landmark in the history of women in Egypt, with some sources talking of Sha'rawi romantically casting her veil into the sea. Later commentators have pointed out that, as such, it held little significance for Egyptian women, except those of the middle and upper classes. The vast majority of ordinary women in rural areas did not wear the veil anyway because it impeded their work in the fields. As Leila Ahmed (1992) has pointed out: "It is the *idea* of the veil much more than the veil's material presence that is the powerful signifier": the veil was a metaphor for women's seclusion and passivity in Egyptian society at the time.

In 1924 the EFU, in conjunction with the WWCC, published a wide-ranging and ambitious joint program of thirty-two social and political "Demands of the Egyptian Woman." This document called for compulsory primary school education and better access to higher education, particularly for women. Further demands included women's suffrage, their equality with men under Islam, the wider dissemination of Arabic texts (in preference to the then-dominant French translations), prison reform, the prohibition of state-licensed prostitution, and the reform of the personal status codes relating to polygamy and divorce.

Sha'rawi also founded the EFU's own journal, *The Egyptian Woman,* in 1925, and Nabarawi became its editor. It published Arabic as well as French editions to counter accusations from some feminists (such as Durriyah Shafiq) that the union was too Westernized and elitist in its cultural orientation. When she could, Sha'rawi herself gave speeches in Arabic. The journal—and Sha'rawi's message—thus began to reach a wider audience and promoted the discussion of many issues, including in particular reform of the laws on divorce and polygamy.

The EFU had 220 members by the late 1920s, most of them middle-class women, and transferred its operation to Cairo. It widened its scope, providing scholarships for Egyptian women to study in Europe, giving financial aid to widows and training to poor girls, and opening a dispensary for poor women and children—all activities run on money raised by members. Sha'rawi was keen to encourage other talented Egyptian women to fulfill their intellectual potential, including Shafiq, whom she sponsored through her university course at the Sorbonne in Paris. The organization also became increasingly regional in its operation, extending into rural areas in upper Egypt, where Sha'rawi set up several dispensaries (a particular interest of hers) in her home province, as well as schools, orphanages, workshops, and clubs offering help and support to unemployed and poor women. The EFU also guided women toward self-help by establishing a model farm in Giza and assisting women workers in the textile and handicraft industries.

From 1929, Sha'rawi was helped in her work by Aminah al-Said, who read speeches for her at IWSA conferences, such as at Istanbul in 1935 and Copenhagen in 1939. In 1935 Sha'rawi lectured at the American University of Cairo on feminist issues, including antipolygamy law. In 1944 she became president of the newly created All-Arab Federation of Women. As late as 1945 she took a stand against nuclear weapons and attended a conference on the subject; that same year, she received her country's highest honor, the Nishan al-Kamal.

Throughout her career, Sha'rawi hedged her calls for social reform by keeping her demands within Islamic teaching—an act of political balancing that was mindful of not alienating conservative religious opinion. Recent feminist criticism tends to apply contemporary values retrospectively to Sha'rawi's work, often unfairly claiming that her views were too much molded by Western perceptions of the position of the Arab woman. The criticism seems to be that the reforms she called for were based on Western institutions and ways rather than on a revival of true Islamic practice. Sha'rawi is even castigated for not writing her memoirs, *Harem Years* (written shortly before her death), in Arabic. Such criticism fails to acknowledge, however, that imperfect though she was, Sha'rawi was a huge inspiration to many other women, as well as other Arab feminists such as Aminah al-Said, Saiza Nabarawi, and Nabawiyya Musa. And as Margot Badran argues, although much has been made of the role of the male reformer Qasim Amin in promoting women's rights in the Islamic world at the turn of the twentieth century, Sha'rawi and other women of her generation have yet to achieve full recognition for their contributions to Egyptian social history.

See also Barakat, Hidiya Hanim; Nabarawi, Saiza; Nasif, Malak Hifni; al-Said, Aminah; Shafiq, Durriyah.

References and Further Reading

Ahmed, Leila. 1992. *Women and Gender in Islam: Historical Roots of a Modern Debate.* New Haven: Yale University Press.

Badran, Margot. 1995. *Feminists, Islam and Nation: Gender and the Making of Modern Egypt.* Princeton: Princeton University Press.

Golden, Kristen, and Barbara Findlen, eds. 1998. *Remarkable Women of the Twentieth Century.* New York: Friedman/Fairfax Publishers in Association with Corbis.

Hacker, Carlotta. 1999. *Rebels.* New York: Crabtree.

Jayawardena, Kumari. 1986. *Feminism and Nationalism in the Third World.* London: Zed Books.

Sha'rawi, Huda. 1987. *Harem Years: The Memoirs of an Egyptian Feminist.* London: Virago.

Anna Howard Shaw (Dover Pictorial Archives)

Shaw, Anna Howard
(1847–1919)
United States

Temperance and suffrage leader Anna Howard Shaw became one of the first women, along with Olympia Brown and Antoinette Brown Blackwell, to break into the male-dominated sphere of religious ministry. She was ordained as a Methodist minister in 1880 and then took up medical studies at the age of thirty-five.

Shaw was born in Newcastle-upon-Tyne, England, and her family emigrated to the United States when she was four. She lived in Lawrence, Massachusetts, where her Unitarian father was active in the abolitionist movement, and then moved to a pioneer colony on the frontier in Mecosta County, Michigan, growing up in a log cabin near Big Rapids. Precocious at school and an avid reader, Shaw demonstrated a gift for oratory at an early age. She taught in a local frontier school from the age of fifteen and, after the Civil War, moved into Big Rapids to live with her sister. It was here that she first heard the Universalist preacher Marianna Thompson and decided to follow her vocation for the ministry. Shaw went back to high school and studied elocution and debating. After converting to Methodism,

she gave her first sermon in 1870 and a year later was licensed as a Methodist Episcopal preacher.

With the encouragement of Mary Livermore, Shaw entered Albion College in Michigan in 1873, where she studied for two years, paying her way by preaching and lecturing on temperance. In 1876 she became the first woman to study for a degree in theology at the Divinity School of Boston University, enduring considerable personal hardship until the Woman's Foreign Missionary Society provided her with much-needed funding. After graduating in 1878, she supported herself as a locum preacher in Cape Cod and was appointed to a congregation in East Dennis. Shaw joined the independent Methodist Protestant Church in 1880, when the New England Methodist Conference refused to allow her to be ordained and revoked her right to preach. She gave lectures on temperance and suffrage during the next three years but in 1883 decided to return to school to train as a doctor. She entered medical school in Boston and earned her degree in medicine in 1886.

But again Shaw changed direction, having come to the conclusion that the only effective way in which she could further the rights of women was through fighting for political change—that is, for women's suffrage. This, she felt, must come first if women were to be able to fight for equality with men in other spheres. In 1885 she had already decided to give up preaching to lecture in support of women's suffrage for the Massachusetts Woman Suffrage Association and, at the request of Frances Willard, to lecture on temperance for the Woman's Christian Temperance Union (WCTU).

It is as an outstanding orator rather than as a theorist or organizer that Shaw became an extremely influential figure in the temperance and suffrage campaigns, lecturing across the United States and working with both branches of the women's suffrage movement—Susan B. Anthony's National Woman Suffrage Association and Lucy Stone's American Woman Suffrage Association—until they amalgamated in 1890 as the National American Woman Suffrage Association (NAWSA). During 1886–1892, Shaw was national superintendent of franchise for the WCTU, but after Anthony ended her term as president of NAWSA from 1892 to 1900, she invited not Shaw but the more politically astute Carrie Chapman Catt to succeed her in 1900. Shaw continued as vice president until 1904, when Catt was obliged to give up the presidency because of her husband's illness. She succeeded Catt as president of NAWSA in 1904 but proved to be a less able business manager and administrator than Catt, who had excelled at both, and she made matters worse by trying to decentralize NAWSA. Shaw developed a reputation for being overcritical of her colleagues in the association, clashed with other members, particularly Alice Paul and her Congressional Committee, and as a result, NAWSA suffered several high-profile defections, including those of Paul and Florence Kelley. Although Shaw was reelected president in 1912, it was with a reduced majority, and NAWSA went into decline until her resignation in 1915 and the triumphant return of the ever-popular Catt. In retirement, Shaw wrote her autobiography, *The Story of a Pioneer* (1915).

Shaw's own short and stout physical appearance, her individualism, and her savage put-downs of male opponents, which William O'Neill argues unfortunately fit "the stereotype promoted by antisuffragists of the sharp-tongued, man-hating feminist" (1989, 121), alienated many male advocates of women's suffrage, a loss of support that the movement could ill afford. Male politicians again had to contend with Shaw's combative character when she was appointed to the Woman's Committee of the Council of National Defense during World War I. The council, established to placate suffragists during the war years, was a token organization that was never properly exploited, as Shaw constantly pointed out. Indeed, Shaw's appointment backfired on the government in that she demanded a far greater level of involvement for women in the war effort and refused to go away quietly. At war's end, Shaw supported President Woodrow Wilson's version of the peace treaty to end World War I and his work to establish the League of Nations. In her final years, she remained an energetic figure, appearing at many women's conferences, suffrage demonstrations, and congressional hearings. She was awarded the Distinguished Service Medal for her wartime service and a month before she died saw the Nineteenth Amendment on women's suffrage passed in Congress. Shaw's work was later commemorated with the establishment of the Anna Howard Shaw Women's Studies Center at Albion College. The Mecosta County Women's Historical Council has created a website in commemoration of Shaw's work, which includes the text of her autobiography and has links to many other sites. Go to http://www.sharewords.com/AHShaw/.

See also Anthony, Susan B.; Blackwell, Antoinette Brown; Brown, Olympia; Catt, Carrie Chapman; Kelley, Florence; Livermore, Mary; Paul, Alice; Stone, Lucy; Willard, Frances.

References and Further Reading

Anthony, Susan B., and Ida Husted Harper. 1902, 1922. *History of Woman Suffrage.* Vols. 4–6. Indianapolis, IN: Hollenbeck Press (vol. 4); New York: NAWSA (vol. 5–6).

Flexner, Eleanor. 1975 [1959]. *A Century of Struggle: The Woman's Rights Movement in the United States.* Rev. ed., Cambridge, MA: Belknap Press of Harvard University.

Kraditor, Aileen. 1981 [1965]. *The Ideas of the Woman Suffrage Movement 1890–1920.* Reprint, New York: W. W. Norton.

Linkugel, Wil A., and Martha Solomon. 1990. *Anna Howard Shaw: Suffrage Orator and Social Reformer.* Westport, CT: Greenwood Press.

O'Neill, William L. 1989. *Feminism in America: A History.* 2d ed. New Brunswick, NJ: Transaction.

Shaw, Anna Howard. 1994 [1915]. *The Story of a Pioneer.* Reprint, Cleveland: Pilgrim Press.

Weatherford, Doris. 1998. *A History of the American Suffragist Movement.* Santa Barbara, CA: ABC-CLIO.

Sheehy-Skeffington, Hannah
(1877–1946)
Ireland

The Irish feminist, suffragist, and campaigner for home rule Hannah Sheehy-Skeffington was one of the movement's most articulate and ardent idealists. She was also the founder of the largest and most militant of all the Irish suffrage societies, the Irish Women's Franchise League (IWFL). Her life, however, was lived out in the shadow cast by her husband's murder by a British officer in 1916.

Born Hannah Sheehy in County Cork, the daughter of an Irish Land League activist and member of Parliament, Sheehy-Skeffington was educated by Dominican nuns before becoming one of the first of her generation to benefit from the opening of higher education in Ireland to women. She studied modern languages at St. Mary's University College in Dublin and graduated in 1899. She would remain a leading voice in the Irish Association of Women Graduates, which she joined in 1901 and which promoted the employment of university-educated women. After graduating, she took up a post teaching French and German at the Rathmines Vocational School.

In 1903 Sheehy married the Irish radical and journalist Frank Skeffington, a frail figure who was nevertheless an energetic campaigner for Irish independence, vegetarianism, and pacifism and who supported his wife in her commitment to women's suffrage. In 1902 she joined the Irish Women's Suffrage and Local Government Association, but by 1908 she found the organization to be insufficiently radical in its approach. Instead, with Margaret Cousins and Constance de Markievicz, she founded the Irish Women's Franchise League along the more militant lines of Emmeline and Christabel Pankhurst's Women's Social and Political Union (WSPU), with the demand that the Irish nationalist movement include women's suffrage in its political agenda. She soon became a seasoned campaigner, inured to the constant physical and verbal abuse hurled at suffragists in their public activities and averring that she and her contemporaries proved that "suffs were good sports" (Sheehy-Skeffington and Owens 1975, 14). In 1910 Sheehy-Skeffington traveled to London to lead an Irish contingent in major suffrage marches. By then she had overcome her natural shyness to become a fine public speaker and one of the most compelling voices in the Irish movement. She also wrote regular articles on suffrage in the *Irish Nation* and in 1912 founded the IWFL's own journal, the *Irish Citizen,* with her husband Frank.

In 1912 Sheehy-Skeffington was imprisoned for breaking windows in government buildings in a surge of protest made by Irish suffragists against the exclusion of women from the vote in the projected Irish Home Rule Bill. She was sent to Mountjoy prison for thirty days, where she went on the first of several hunger strikes during her political career.

After her release from prison, Sheehy-Skeffington concentrated her energies on her work for the IWFL and became its chair. During the 1913 lockout of striking Irish trade unionists, she and many other Irish suffragists in Dublin helped run food kitchens for the strikers and their families. She was subjected to a second period in jail for supposedly assaulting a police officer, but a hunger strike again precipitated her early release. However, her continuing militancy had by now cost her the job at Rathmines, which had been in jeopardy ever since she had begun openly campaigning for equal pay for women schoolteachers in Irish convents.

As a result of losing her job, Sheehy-Skeffington was able to commit more time to her political activities, but during World War I she took an increasing dislike to the Pankhursts' jingoistic leadership of the women's movement and of its support for the war effort. The Pankhursts' attempt to take over control of the IWFL was the last straw, with Hannah seeing this as a blatant attempt to exploit the Irish suffrage cause for British political ends. The majority of suffragists involved in the Irish campaign had made clear their opposition to the war and, more important, the conscription of Irish soldiers. Both Sheehy-Skeffington and her husband campaigned vigorously against it through various socialist, pacifist, and suffrage groups.

The turning point in Sheehy-Skeffington's political career was the senseless summary execution of her pacifist husband Frank by a rogue British officer during the Easter Rising in 1916. Frank had been organizing a Citizens' Defence Force to combat looting during the fighting and had happened simply to be in the wrong place at the wrong time. This event galvanized Sheehy-Skeffington into even more militant activity and the abandonment of her religious beliefs. She fought for a royal commission to investigate the circumstances of Frank's death but considered the result a whitewash, orchestrated to protect British interests.

Determined to finish the work toward Irish independence that she and her husband had begun together, she embarked on a two-year lecture tour in the United States, mainly to Irish societies and suffrage groups, where she highlighted the brutal methods used by British troops in suppressing the opposition to British rule in Ireland. She also continued to oppose conscription in the face of attempts by the American authorities to censor those of her speeches considered detrimental to the Allied war effort. She also personally presented a petition to the White House in an attempt to enlist President Woodrow Wilson's support for Irish independence.

On her return to Ireland in 1918, Sheehy-Skeffington was once more imprisoned for her activities, this time in Holloway prison, where she went on a hunger strike and was released under the terms of the Cat and Mouse Act, which allowed hunger strikers to be released until they had sufficiently recovered their strength to be reimprisoned. Later that year, during the first general election in the United Kingdom in which women candidates were allowed to stand, she gave numerous lectures as well as becoming involved in the City of Dublin Municipal Teachers' Association in its fight for better pay. In 1919 she took up local politics, becoming a county councilor in Dublin.

During the Irish civil war of 1922–1923, Sheehy-Skeffington continued to track the brutal methods of British troops—in this case the infamous Black and Tans—and joined with Irish women across the whole spectrum of political parties in attempting to bring an end to the violence. In 1922–1923 she once again undertook a trip to the United States, raising funds for the families of Republicans taken prisoner during the fighting as part of her commitment to the Women's Prisoners' Defence League (WPDL), founded by Maud Gonne and Charlotte Despard.

In 1921 Sheehy-Skeffington had led a deputation to Michael Collins and Arthur Griffith who were negotiating the Anglo-Irish Treaty with Britain, insisting that women's views on the terms of any agreement on Irish independence should be consulted and lobbying for the release of political prisoners. With Eamonn De Valera, she opposed the terms of the treaty, but found herself unable to work with De Valera and his Fianna Fáil party, founded in 1926. She had a particular aversion to what she considered to be De Valera's paternalistic policies, which to her were retrograde in their view of women as primarily homemakers. Her impatience with and condemnation of De Valera were outspoken and highlighted the impossibility of her being able to reconcile her support for Fianna Fáil and feminist issues. She soon broke with De Valera and the party, despite being appointed to its executive body, in disagreement over the wording of the Irish oath of allegiance.

Her time was now taken up increasingly with pacifist causes; she became a delegate at conferences of the Women's International League for Peace and Freedom in 1926 and 1929. As one of the Friends of Soviet Russia, along with Charlotte Despard she went on a six-week tour of the Soviet Union in 1930 to study the communist system. She was particularly impressed with the equality given to women in the workplace, but like Despard and many others who were overeager to affirm the success of the Soviet experiment, she failed to perceive the abuses of human rights lurking so close to the surface of a seemingly model socialist system. On her return Sheehy-Skeffington wrote numerous newspaper articles on her opposition to the antifeminist aspects of De Valera's draft constitution of 1937, on censorship, sex education, and women's issues and undertook more lecture tours in Canada and the United States. In 1943, at the age of sixty-six, she and three other women stood as candidates for the Dáil but failed to be elected. Disillusion set in, but it was only ill health that put a stop to her campaigning. Her will never deserted her, and, to the end, Hannah Sheehy-Skeffington refused to compromise her fiercely held views. As a woman who had never ceased to rebuke male politicians for their persistently chauvinistic policies, Sheehy-Skeffington had proved herself a worthy adversary and one who was fearless in taking on the Irish political establishment over its lack of support for women's rights.

See also Cousins, Margaret; Despard, Charlotte;

Gonne, Maud; Markievicz, Constance de; Pankhurst, Christabel; Pankhurst, Emmeline.

References and Further Reading

Levenson, Leah, and Jerry H. Natterstad. 1988. *Hanna Sheehy Skeffington: A Pioneering Irish Feminist.* Syracuse: Syracuse University Press.

Luddy, Maria. 1995. *Hannah Sheehy Skeffington.* Dublin: Historical Association of Ireland.

Owens, Rosemary Cullen. 1984. *Smashing Times: A History of the Irish Women's Suffrage Movement 1889–1922.* Dublin: Attic Press.

Sheehy-Skeffington, Andrée, and Rosemary Owens, eds. 1975. *Votes for Women: Irish Women's Struggle for the Vote.* Dublin: Skeffington and Owens.

Sheppard, Kate
(1847–1934)
United Kingdom/New Zealand

The power of one of the world's most influential women's organizations, the Woman's Christian Temperance Union (WCTU), was manifested most particularly in New Zealand, where campaigning for women's suffrage was organized among its ranks from the late 1880s. Much of the smooth running of the WCTU campaign can be credited to the exemplary efficiency of its outstanding propagandist on suffrage, Kate Sheppard, who headed its Franchise and Legislative Department, which organized the suffrage campaign across branches of the WCTU throughout New Zealand. As a pivotal figure in one of the shortest and most effective suffrage campaigns fought anywhere in the world, Sheppard became one of the first women in the world to win the vote—in 1893—twenty years or more before most other women.

Sheppard was born in Liverpool of Scottish parents. She grew up on Islay in Scotland. Her father, a lawyer, died in 1862, leaving her mother with five children to support. After Sheppard's elder sister emigrated to Australia, the rest of the family followed in 1868. She married a Christchurch shopkeeper and city councilor who was a member of her local Trinity Congregational Church in 1871. She had a reasonably comfortable domestic life, teaching Sunday school and Bible classes and becoming active in the local Ladies' Association. She embraced the temperance movement when it was established in New Zealand by American Mary Clement Leavitt in 1885.

The temperance crusade prompted Sheppard's first feminist stirrings; initially they were reflected in an advocacy of the physical emancipation of women through exercise. She was a dress reformer and cycling enthusiast and one of the first women seen on a bicycle in Christchurch. She began to question the lack of political and civil status of women, who, she argued, were classified along with juveniles, criminals, and lunatics. Without women being given a political voice, she felt that social reform could not be effected.

The first appeal in New Zealand on women's rights had come from Mary Müller, under the alias of "Femina," in her 1869 work, *An Appeal to the Men of New Zealand.* It had initiated the campaign for reform of the property laws affecting married women, but it was the temperance crusade that had brought with it the mass mobilization of women in defense of family values and social purity, with many working to raise the age of consent, to reform divorce laws, and to foster social work among the poor and destitute.

After 1887, when Sheppard was appointed National Franchise Superintendent of the WCTU, her work for temperance drew her into the suffrage campaign and helped her forge important links with suffrage and temperance workers in Britain and the United States. In 1888 she published a pamphlet, "Ten Reasons Why the Women of New Zealand Should Vote," which was regularly quoted in debates on the subject and in which she drew on the arguments of John Stuart Mill's 1869 work, *The Subjection of Women.* A petition on women's suffrage in 1888 called into question the definition of the word *elector* in existing legislation. Sheppard began touring New Zealand, speaking on suffrage and organizing four further petitions. Several years of debate and campaigning followed in the House of Representatives, with the WCTU keeping up the pressure thanks to Sheppard's skills as a propagandist. She orchestrated press coverage of the campaign; printed suffrage articles and pamphlets; and efficiently coordinated meetings, the distribution of literature, and the lobbying of members of Parliament (MPs), as well as writing countless letters. In 1888 she won the important support for the suffrage cause of Liberal MP Sir John Hall and cooperated closely with him thereafter. In 1890 and 1891, the WCTU organized two more petitions on women's suffrage, which were presented to Parliament by Sir John. In 1892, a fourth petition contained 20,274 signatures—but all to no avail.

In order to galvanize the maximum support for yet another assault on Parliament, Sheppard took up a regular women's page in the fortnightly temperance journal, the *Prohibitionist,* in 1891, publicizing the suffrage campaign under the pen name of "Penelope." At the head of a team of 600 volunteers, she organized a final, mammoth petition, sending WCTU members out into remote rural areas to gather signatures for a document that would be 766 feet long and contain 31,872 signatures, representing nearly one-third of the entire female population. It was presented to the New Zealand legislature in 1893 by Sir John Hall and passed by the lower house despite huge pressure from the antisuffrage lobby, which had garnered considerable support from the liquor trade, with opponents setting up counterpetitions for signature in public houses and offering payment to those who went out and collected them. The lower house was in favor of women's suffrage, however, and the governor of New Zealand gave his assent to an Electoral Act on women's suffrage on 19 September 1893, making women in New Zealand the first in the British colonies to be awarded suffrage and the first in the world to be given the vote in national elections. Only ten weeks later, they exercised that right in a general election, at which an estimated 65 percent of newly enfranchised women cast their votes.

Sheppard followed up the suffrage triumph in New Zealand with a visit to the United Kingdom and the Continent in 1894, during which she spoke on the New Zealand suffrage campaign and met with British suffragists. She was asked to establish a New Zealand branch of the International Council of Women (ICW) and was elected its first president (1896–1899). With the help of Lady Anna Stout, Sheppard established the National Council of Women, New Zealand (NCW) and turned it into a powerful lobby for social reform, through which she advocated equal status for marriage partners, mothers' and fathers' equal rights in the control and care of children, improvements to divorce legislation, and various health and educational reforms. Through the NCW's official monthly journal, the *White Ribbon,* which she edited from 1895 to 1903, she also furthered the cause of women's election to Parliament (achieved in 1919, although the first

woman was not elected until 1933) and women's rights to a share of their husband's income; she also continued to advocate dress reform and favored birth control.

In the 1900s Sheppard began suffering ill health and was forced to reduce her activities and turn down the chance of becoming franchise superintendent for the World's Woman's Christian Temperance Union. She continued to write, publishing *Women's Suffrage in New Zealand* in 1907, and maintained a considerable correspondence with international feminists and suffragists such as Millicent Garrett Fawcett and Carrie Chapman Catt. She became increasingly close to her old friends William and Jennie Lovell Smith and, after her husband decided to live in England, in 1905 began sharing a home with them, which prompted much speculation about the true nature of their relationship. In 1925, by which time both she and William had lost their respective spouses, they married.

Noted for her warmth, charm, and tolerance, Sheppard was also a talented and persuasive speaker who favored women's greater access to education and vocational training, to economic independence and a career, and to a role in all aspects of public life, including the legislature, police, and judiciary. Her contribution to New Zealand women's history is commemorated in the Kate Sheppard Memorial on the banks of the Avon River at Christchurch. Her face can also be seen on the New Zealand $10 note. A useful account of Kate Sheppard's life and suffrage campaign can be found at http://www.nzedge.com/heroes/sheppard.html.

See also Catt, Carrie Chapman; Fawcett, Millicent Garrett; Stout, Lady Anna.

References and Further Reading

Daley, Caroline, and Melanie Nolan. 1994. *Suffrage and Beyond: International Feminist Perspectives.* New York: New York University Press.

Devaliant, Judith. 1992. *Kate Sheppard, a Biography: The Fight for Women's Votes in New Zealand.* Auckland: Penguin Books.

Grimshaw, Patricia. 1987. *Women's Suffrage in New Zealand.* Auckland: Oxford University Press.

Lovell-Smith, Margaret, ed. 1992. *The Woman Question: Writings by the Women Who Won the Vote.* Auckland: New Women's Press.

Malcolm, Tessa. 1993. "Katherine Sheppard." In *The Dictionary of New Zealand Biography,* vol. 2. Wellington, NZ: Allen and Unwin and the Department of Internal Affairs.

Shirreff, Emily Anne
(1814–1897)
United Kingdom

An early pioneer of women's education who lived a quiet life in modest Christian piety, Emily Shirreff collaborated closely with her sister Maria Georgina Shirreff Grey (1816–1906) in extending secondary education for girls in Britain and furthering the training of women teachers. As the daughter of a naval officer, Shirreff spent her early years abroad in France and Gibraltar, where her father had official appointments. When she was twenty, the family finally returned home to England. By this time, having been taught by governesses but largely self-educated in several languages, she took up writing. Her first publication, *Letters from Spain and Barbary* (1835), cowritten with her younger sister Maria, was an account of their time in Gibraltar. Together, the sisters established a wide circle of scientific and intellectual acquaintants, but in 1841 Maria married into the politically influential Grey family. Six years later, the Greys moved in with Emily and her mother on her father's death, and the sisters again collaborated on *Thoughts on Self-Culture, Addressed to Women* (1850), written in support of women's education, and in 1853 on a novel, *Passion and Principle*.

Emily's meeting with the historian Henry Buckle in 1853 brought with it shared interests in history, and she succeeded in winning Buckle over to the cause of women's education. He in turn lent her valuable assistance in the writing of *Intellectual Education and Its Influence on the Character and Happiness of Women* (1857). The possibility of marriage to Buckle briefly came and went; after his death in 1861, Shirreff, who herself did not enjoy the best of health, gave up her life to spinsterhood and the care of her various sick and elderly relatives. She kept in touch with the debate on women's emancipation, signing the 1866 petition on women's suffrage gathered by members of the Langham Place Circle; her sister Maria, however, would be more openly supportive of the movement.

It was not until she reached her fifties that Shirreff took on a more public life. Convinced of women's crucial role as guardians of the spiritual and moral development of future generations, she became increasingly active in education reform. In 1869 she was a cofounder and, for a short time, an honorary mistress of Girton College, at its first home in Hitchin, near Cambridge. But like many other women who worked with the difficult and demanding Emily Davies, the college's principal, she found Davies's dictatorial manner intimidating. Although Shirreff retained her post on the college's executive committee until her death in 1897, she found other outlets for her educational interests.

In 1871 she took on the role of organizing secretary of the National Union for Improving the Education of Women of All Classes (popularly known as the Women's Education Union), founded by her sister Maria. This organization, set up in response to a government commission that had exposed the woeful inadequacies of girls' education, lobbied the charity commissioners to provide better secondary education for girls and improve the standards for teacher training. Shirreff coedited the *Journal of the Women's Educational Union* until it ceased publication in 1882 and organized fund-raising to provide scholarships and study loans.

The work of the WEU spawned the Girls' Public Day School Company (GPDS) in 1872, which offered shares to investors to raise money to set up nondenominational schools, seventeen of which were established in the company's first ten years. (The GPDS became a trust in 1905.) A program of evening classes for teachers was inaugurated by the company, offering a range of academic subjects, including science and physical education, that were considered progressive for girls' schools at that time. In 1877 the GPDS incorporated a Teachers' Training and Registration Society to set up the Maria Grey Training College for teachers a year later.

From the mid-1870s, Shirreff developed a keen interest in the educational theories of Friedrich Froebel. From 1875 until her death, she was a founding member and president of the Froebel Society and wrote pamphlets on his work. These included "Principles of the Kindergarten System" (1876) and "Friedrich Froebel: A Sketch of His Life" (1877), as well as articles for the *Journal of Kindergarten Schools*. She gave numerous papers at society meetings and Social Science Congresses on the Froebel system of kindergarten education, emphasizing always the crucial importance of mothers as role models. A training scheme for kindergarten teachers was instituted at the Maria Grey Training College in

1878. After the union was disbanded in 1882, Shirreff gave her time over completely to work for the Froebel Society, publishing a major text, *Kindergarten at Home,* in 1884. She spent much time in Italy during the 1870s and 1880s, where she had many friends among its expatriate American community, and became a great lover of Italian history and culture. In old age, with Maria widowed, the two sisters lived in quiet retirement.

See also Davies, (Sarah) Emily.
References and Further Reading
Banks, Olive, ed. 1985, 1990. *The Biographical Dictionary of British Feminists,* vol. 1, *1800–1930;* vol. 2, *1900–1945.* Brighton: Harvester Wheatsheaf.
Baylen, J. O., and N. J. Gossman, eds. 1979–1984. *Biographical Dictionary of Modern British Radicals.* 3 vols. Hassocks, Sussex: Harvester Press.
Dictionary of National Biography. First published 1888–1900 in 64 vols. Supplements published every ten years, 1901–1985. London and Oxford: Oxford University Press.
Ellsworth, Edward D. 1979. *Liberators of the Female Mind: The Shirreff Sisters: Education as Reform and the Women's Movement.* London: Greenwood Press.
Hays, Frances. 1885. *Women of the Day: A Biographical Dictionary of Notable Contemporaries.* London: Chatto and Windus.

Shishkina-Yavein, Poliksena
(c. 1874–1950s)
Russia

The story of Poliksena Shishkina-Yavein serves as a reminder of the many gaps that remain in the history of women's activism at the turn of the twentieth century. She was a prominent figure in the Russian women's suffrage movement that gained ground after the 1905 revolution. Reports of Russian campaigning were regularly featured on the pages of *Jus Suffragii,* the organ of the International Woman Suffrage Alliance (IWSA), culminating in a special issue featuring the successful winning of the vote in 1917, during Shishkina-Yavein's presidency of the All-Russian League for Women's Equality. And then—silence. The occasional few inches of column space on women's activism in Bolshevik Russia dwindled away to nothing until, in June 1921, the pacifist Chrystal MacMillan appealed on the pages of the journal for aid for Shishkina-Yavein,

now a widow with two children and a displaced person.

Although little is known of her later life in Soviet Russia, little enough is known of her life before about 1907 either, except that she was a doctor in St. Petersburg and was married to another practitioner. Like other Russian women who became active after 1905 (in part inspired by the vigorous suffrage movement in nearby Finland), Shishkina-Yavein had placed great hopes for improvements to women's political and civil rights on the new Duma, an attempt at a constitutional government that the czar had been obliged to institute after the revolution of 1905. But four successive Dumas—in 1906, 1907, 1907–1912, and 1912–1917—were soon dissolved by the ultra-reactionary czar when their demands became too radical for his liking. The All-Russian League for Women's Equality, founded in 1907 as a successor to the upper-class and ineffectual Union of Russian Women (but for some time relatively inactive), was one of several women's national organizations in existence during this period that were sanctioned by the government. After the First All-Russian Women's Congress was held in St. Petersburg in 1908, the moribund bourgeois women's movement, discouraged by a lack of progress since 1905, revived. The All-Russian League for Women's Equality, now with a membership of around 1,000, had began organizing in earnest to lobby the Duma for women's suffrage, garnering along the way the support of other moderate women's groups, such as the Russian Women's Mutual Philanthropic Society (RWMPS).

After Shishkina-Yavein was elected president of the All-Russian League for Women's Equality in 1910, she embarked on a drive to recruit women from a wider area. Membership grew to around 1,500–2,000 at its height, but the great majority were inhabitants of St. Petersburg. As a doctor, Shishkina-Yavein also became active in the campaign for the abolition of state-regulated prostitution and legal brothels. In 1913 at the Pirogov Medical Congress, she spoke on her campaign for abolition. She subsequently collaborated with a doctor and Duma deputy, Andrei Shingarev, on the drafting of a bill to abolish inspection of prostitutes and to close down brothels that was linked to a broader medical drive to control the spread of venereal disease. The legislation was not passed, and in 1917, after women's suffrage had been won, Shishkina-Yavein renewed her campaigning on the issue.

During World War I, Shishkina-Yavein and her colleagues in the league temporarily abandoned the cause of suffrage and diverted their activities into war work. In 1915, when a delegation from the 1915 women's peace congress in The Hague that had established an International Committee of Women for Permanent Peace arrived in Petrograd (as St. Petersburg had been renamed when the war broke out), Shishkina-Yavein welcomed its members into her home. But she was reticent about committing herself to pacifism, for like many other Russian women activists, including members of the RWMPS, her first loyalties were to patriotic duty and humanitarian aid to the sick and wounded. As a doctor, Shishkina-Yavein volunteered her medical services to the army. A major article featuring photographs of Shishkina-Yavein and colleagues working in their own lazaretto for wounded soldiers appeared in *Jus Suffragii* in January 1917. The lazaretto was funded and run by branches of the league in Petrograd. The league also initiated a training course for 2,000 Sisters of Charity to go to the front, opened a home for refugee girls, and ran canteens providing cheap, hot meals for 1,500 people daily. In June 1917 Shishkina-Yavein would proudly watch a Russian women's army battalion—nicknamed the "Battalion of Death"—march off to the front lines.

During the February Revolution in 1917, there was a wave of food strikes and demonstrations, many of them dominated by women. The program of Prince Georgiy Lvov's new provisional government had failed to make any mention of women's enfranchisement and prompted the league into vigorous campaigning once more for women's suffrage and a voice in the promised constituent assembly. Its members were extremely active leafleting and lobbying in women's schools, factories, and mills and on the streets during an intensive period of endless meetings and rallies in the capital. During this period, Shishkina-Yavein's league gathered support from ninety other women's organizations from around the provinces. In May Shishkina-Yavein, in a nod to the Social Democrats in the provisional government, reorganized the league under a new name that reflected its broad base of support and the changing times. As the Republican Union of Democratic Women's Organizations, it attempted to extend its appeal to workers and trade unionists but had little impact in this direction.

The league's crowning moment came on a cold wet day—9 March 1917—when a large procession of up to 40,000 women, headed by Shishkina-Yavein and the revolutionary heroine Vera Figner and accompanied by brass bands and banners, marched from the Petrograd Duma to the Tauride Palace, intent on lobbying the provisional government for an explicit commitment to women's suffrage. En route, outside the premises of the Council of Workingmen's and Soldiers Deputies, the women called for the council's official endorsement of their demands. As they waited in the cold, Shishkina-Yavein gave a rousing speech calling for equal civil and political rights for women but received a noncommittal response. The marchers then headed to the offices of Prince Lvov to present their resolution to the provisional government, demanding that the phrase referring to a "universal, equal, direct and secret" ballot should be added to the Constitution "without distinction of sex" (*Jus Suffragii,* June 1921, 134). The promise that the Duma would extend electoral rights to women was finally fulfilled on 20 July 1917, and further legislation followed in August granting women in the civil service equality of job opportunity, status, and pay.

The year 1917 marked both the apogee of the bourgeois Russian women's movement and its equally meteoric descent into obscurity. After the October Revolution, feminist organizations and journals were rapidly closed down by the Bolsheviks, who at the end of 1918 centralized control of women's issues under a new women's section—known as the Zhenotdel—of the Communist Party, run by Inessa Armand and later Alexandra Kollontai. Shishkina-Yavein was reported as being one of seven candidates of the All-Russian League for Women's Equality who stood for election to the promised Constituent Assembly in Petrograd. But the Bolsheviks dissolved it almost as soon as it finally met, in January 1918. There was no room for the moderate middle-class aspirations of Shishkina-Yavein and her kind in the new communist order. Activists like her were soon pushed aside by the far more vocal, militant, and politicized women from the ranks of the Bolshevik, anarchist, and other socialist parties.

Although Shishkina-Yavein is known to have remained president of the league until 1919, which remained affiliated to the IWSA, her activities after the October Revolution and during the upheavals of the ensuing Russian civil war until 1921 are not known. In June 1921, Chrystal MacMillan's appeal in *Jus Suffragii* revealed that Shishkina-Yavein was now a "refugee from her own country" (134). She had written asking for help from a hospital in Sofia, Bulgaria, where she was recovering from typhus. In her letter she related how she had returned to her family home in Estonia with her husband and children after the revolution, only to find it looted and vandalized. Her husband, a distinguished medical figure, had been appointed professor at the University of Dorpat, only to die before taking up his post. The Swedish mission and private benefactors had come to a destitute Shishkina-Yavein's rescue. But as a Russian, she was not allowed to practice in Estonia. She had taken an appointment as a doctor in a quarantine camp (presumably in Bulgaria) during the winter of 1920–1921 and was in desperate need of financial assistance.

It is now known that Shishkina-Yavein returned to Russia and lived in Leningrad, where she survived the terrible seige during World War II. She died sometime in the 1950s. Meanwhile, the November 1924 issue of *Jus Suffragii* testified to the loss of contact with women activists in the new Soviet Union, with the editor complaining that she no longer received "direct news from Russia."

See also Armand, Inessa; Kollontai, Alexandra.

References and Further Reading

Edmondson, Linda. 1984. *Feminism in Russia, 1900–1917*. London: Heinemann.

Jus Suffragii. 1921. (21 June): 134.

Stites, Richard. 1991 [1978]. *The Women's Liberation Movement in Russia: Feminism, Nihilism, and Bolshevism, 1860–1930*. Reprint, Princeton: Princeton University Press.

Sister Nivedita (Margaret Noble)
(1867–1911)
Ireland/India

A disciple of Swami Vivekenanda, the Hindu spiritual leader, the Irish reformer Margaret Noble was persuaded to join his mission in India in 1898. Bearing in mind the history of the Irish independence movement and Noble's Celtic blood, Vivekenanda was convinced that she would be naturally antipathetic to colonial oppression in India and would serve as a good spokesperson for Indian independence.

Born into the family of a Protestant clergyman in Dungannon, Ireland, who supported Irish home rule, Noble lived most of her young life in England, finishing her education at the Congregational College in Halifax before taking up teaching in Wrexham in the 1880s. Her social conscience was aroused by the terrible living conditions in the industrial north and the desperate poverty of women workers there. She began writing on social issues for national newspapers and took an interest in educational reform. In 1892 Noble opened a school in Wimbledon, which was inspired by the pioneering methods of the educationists Friedrich Froebel and Johann Pestalozzi. She also associated with intellectuals and socialists such as Keir Hardie and even met the Russian anarchist Pyotr Kropotkin, favoring his views on the redundancy of all governments.

As a student, Noble had studied Buddhism and later took an interest in other aspects of Asian cultures. In November 1895, she met the Indian guru Swami Vivekenanda (1863–1902) in London on one of his lecture tours. A man of considerable intellect, Vivekenanda had traveled in Europe and the United States to promote the interests of India and the wisdom and universality of the Hindu faith, as well as arguing on his pet topic—the unification of world religions. He attracted numerous followers at his many public lectures, many of them middle-class women attracted by his call to bring about India's spiritual and cultural revival. Noble became a devoted follower of Vivekenanda and his teachings, communicating his ideas through her journalism. He returned the compliment by assuring her that "you have the making in you of a world mover" (Foxe 1975, 26).

Despite her awareness of the difficulties and prejudice she would encounter, Noble initiated work for Vivekenanda's Vedanta mission at her home in Wimbledon. But she could not for long resist Vivekenanda's challenge to go to India and lead the vanguard of reform there, particularly in issues affecting the lives of Indian women. In 1897 she set off for the Indian subcontinent alone, arriving at Madras, where she was instantly filled with wonder at the glories of Indian culture. She began learning Bengali and attending lectures, as well as giving talks at Vivekenanda's Ramakrishna mission and touring in the northwestern region of India. She became a celibate novice of the Order of Ramakrishna and was renamed Nivedita—"the dedicated"—but in order to continue her secular work, she did not take her vows as a nun.

During a serious outbreak of plague in Calcutta in 1898–1899, Sister Nivedita wrote to the newspapers appealing for financial support for her plague relief activities, highlighting the bad sanitation that had exacerbated the spread of disease and calling for the education of people in standards of hygiene by practical example. In 1899–1902 she toured the United Kingdom and United States, lecturing on Indian life and Hinduism and raising funds for a school, which she opened in Calcutta on her return, adding her meager savings to buy a suitable property. Sister Nivedita's school for local girls opened in 1902. She devised her own teaching methods and taught reading, writing, and indigenous arts and crafts. She also took time out to discuss women's education and work with Vivekenanda. He was a strong believer in an idealized view of the traditional role of the Hindu woman as wife and mother. Sister Nivedita attempted to justify these beliefs in religious terms when confronted with criticism, even to the extent of condoning the practice of enforced widowhood, although she discussed with him the possibility of training Hindu child widows at her school. Although her support for Vivekenanda's antifeminist position on some issues invited criticism from sister activists, Sister Nivedita countered this with her energetic support for women's education in tandem with Indian nationalism and came out vigorously against those Indian males who considered women "no better than slaves."

Unlike her compatriot Amy Carmichael, who also worked in India campaigning vigorously against child marriage and temple prostitution, Sister Nivedita managed to sidestep these contentious issues (emphasizing, for instance, the spiritual dignity of the widow) to praise instead the positive aspects of Hinduism. The focal point of her own romanticized interpretation of "muscular Hinduism" became the worship of the goddess Kali and traditional family practices (even including child marriage and polygamy). For her, these were the cornerstone of Indian cultural and spiritual identity and the necessary foundation for the country's revival as an independent nation. In her book *Kali, the Mother* (1900), Sister Nivedita celebrated the fearsome Hindu goddess Kali who was a very popular figure in Indian mythology despite her awesome image. A metaphor for death overcoming life in spiritual terms, Kali was seen as freeing her worshippers from fear and thus empowering them, and Sister Nivedita associated this empowerment with the burgeoning Indian nationalist movement.

After the death of her guru Vivekenanda in 1902, Sister Nivedita decided to broaden her sphere of interest and influence beyond the Ramakrishna mission. She resigned from her spiritual activities and undertook more and more social work, as well as promoting Indian nationalism through her writings, discussion groups, and public lectures. In particular, she used her strong aesthetic sense to promote the qualities of traditional Indian trades and crafts at a time when resistance to imported Western goods was growing. Her school did much to encourage creativity in weaving, handicrafts, and needlework, and Sister Nivedita's objective was to extend these activities for women, as well as teach them to read and write.

Inexorably, Sister Nivedita was drawn into the nationalist movement and offered her guarded support in this to Annie Besant, despite looking on her as an outsider. She also gave her tacit support to the more militant activities of Bengali revolutionary groups after the enforced partition of Bengal in 1905 and began editing Indian revolutionary Sri Aurobindo's nationalist newspaper, *Karma Yogin*. By this time, she was lecturing and writing constantly on Indian culture, history, and education, most notably in her book *Web of Indian Life* (1904), and contributing to twenty-one different newspapers and journals. Her school was overcrowded, and she was exhausted. Her health problems, however, did not prevent Sister Nivedita from undertaking relief work during a terrible famine and flood in East Bengal in 1906. By 1907 such was her hostility to British colonial rule that she returned to England and pursued her aesthetic interests in a revival of Indian art and handicrafts. From there she embarked in 1910 on another lecture tour of the United States to raise funds for the Bengali revolutionaries.

Sister Nivedita's passionate commitment to the Indian cause was cut short when she died at age forty-four of blood dysentery. Even though her feminist critics have found her romanticization of Vivekenanda's message the product of a naive Westernized view of Hinduism that was counterproductive to the cause of Indian female emancipation, she is still revered in India, where her writings have been extensively published, for example at www.education.vsnl.com/advaita/sispub.

See also Besant, Annie; Carmichael, Amy Wilson.
References and Further Reading
Foxe, Barbara. 1975. *Long Journey Home: A Biography of Margaret Noble.* London: Rider.
Jayawardena, Kumari. 1995. *The White Woman's Other Burden: Western Women and South Asia during British Rule.* London: Routledge.
Sister Nivedita. 1967–1975. *The Complete Works of Sister Nivedita.* 6 vols. Calcutta: Ramakrishna Sarada Mission.

Sister Subbalakshmi
(1886–1969)
India

The founder of one of the first schools for high-caste child widows, Sister Subbalakshmi was educated at home before being married at the age of eleven. Her husband's premature death sent her back home to her parents, who decided to continue her education but were forced to move elsewhere because of local hostility to the education of girls.

The family moved to Madras, and Subbalakshmi's father taught her himself before sending her to a convent school. She continued her studies at Presidency College in Madras but had to run the gauntlet of constant bigotry. Finally, in 1911 she obtained her B.A. and set up a school for widows in her home. She was offered support by the Irish feminist Christina Lynch, who at that time was acting as a government inspector of female education. Lynch wanted Subbalakshmi to set up a feeder school for Brahmin child widows who could then be trained as teachers for girls' schools in Madras.

In 1912 Subbalakshmi helped found the Sarada Ladies Union to disseminate information about her project and raise funds. She eventually set up her school in an old ice storehouse on the coast and took in her first thirty-five pupils to train as teachers and then complete their matriculation at Queen Mary's College in Madras. In 1922 Subbalakshmi became principal of the Lady Willingdon Training College and Practice School and, soon after, of the Sarada Vidyalaya, a

high school for adult widows over the age of eighteen. These women boarded and lived in a strictly maintained regime of orthodox Hindu practice. As in the case of Begum Rokeya Sakhawat Hossain, Subbalakshmi was forced to compromise her beliefs in order for her school to remain open. Elsewhere, she publicly spoke out against child marriage. She supported the campaign for the Sarda Act, appearing before the Joshi Committee, which gathered evidence for it. Passed in 1930, the act raised the age of marriage for girls to fourteen and set the age for boys at sixteen. Such was the level of Subbalakshmi's devotion to her causes that she was accorded the title of reverence, "Sister," by her admirers.

See also Hossain, Begum Rokeya Sakhawat.
References and Further Reading
Felton, Monica. 1966. *A Child Widow's Story.* London: Gollancz.
Forbes, Geraldine. 1996. *Women in Modern India.* New Cambridge History of India, vol. 4. Cambridge: Cambridge University Press.
Ramanathan, Malathi. 1989. *Sister Subbalakshmi: Social Reformer and Educationalist.* Bombay: Lok Vangmaya Griha.

Sisulu, Nonsikelelo Albertina
(1918–)
South Africa

Working closely with her husband, the general secretary of the African National Congress (ANC), Walter Sisulu, Albertina Sisulu has been a major female figure in the antiapartheid movement in South Africa. She spent long periods struggling to support her five children during her husband's numerous periods of detention and imprisonment. Despite such hardship, she found time to become a forceful campaigner in her own right for improved standards of education for Bantus, the abolition of the pass laws, and the human rights of all black women.

A member of the Xhosa tribe, Sisulu grew up in a remote rural area of the Transkei and moved to Johannesburg in 1942. While training as a nurse at the Johannesburg General Hospital in the 1940s, she became increasingly aware of racial injustice and joined the ANC. In 1944, after qualifying as a nurse-midwife, she married Walter Sisulu. They lived in the township of Soweto, where Albertina joined her husband in

Nonsikelelo Albertina Sisulu (David and Peter Turnley/Corbis)

his work with the ANC, first in her activities with the Youth League and from 1948 with the Women's League. In 1954 she was a founding member of the nonracial Federation of South African Women (FSAW), which later affiliated itself with the ANC Women's League. In 1983 Sisulu became president of FSAW.

In 1958 her activities for the ANC led to arrest and imprisonment after she headed a demonstration by black women in Johannesburg against the pass laws, under which all black South Africans had to carry racial identification. Thus began a long period of her life when she was constantly under surveillance and subjected to police harassment. She was detained again in 1963 and held in solitary confinement for seven weeks, with a subsequent five-year banning order placed on her activities. A year later, her husband, who had suffered frequent arrests since 1953, and Nelson Mandela were sentenced to life imprisonment for their civil rights activities. Now the sole breadwinner with five children to support, Sisulu continued to work as a clinic nurse for the City Health Department.

In 1981 the banning order against Sisulu's activities was finally lifted after nineteen years of persecution. She took up work in the Transvaal, but within months her outspokenness at an ANC activist's funeral led once again to arrest and seven months in solitary confinement. On her release, she became copresident of the United Democratic Front, a mixed-race group fighting for social and racial justice in South Africa. In 1985 a further nine months in solitary for fomenting racial unrest still failed to crush Sisulu's spirit. She traveled to Europe to meet with political leaders such as U.S. vice president George Bush and British prime minister Margaret Thatcher and urged that they take up economic sanctions against South Africa. Upon her return, she was finally reunited with her husband, who was released from prison on Robben Island. She was elected president of the ANC Women's League in 1990–1993, in which position she came into conflict with the flamboyant, self-publicizing Winnie Mandela, who ousted her as president in 1993.

Since the dismantling of apartheid in South Africa, Sisulu has turned her energies to working for poor blacks. She has set up the Informal Business Training Trust and in collaboration with the Start-up Business Fund has been working to help unemployed blacks create their own economic independence by teaching them business skills. In East London in the Cape, Sisulu's Trust has set out to improve the 45 percent rate of unemployment.

References and Further Reading

Russell, Diana E. H. 1989. *Women for a New South Africa*. New York: Basic Books.

Uweche, Raph, ed. 1996. *Makers of Modern Africa*. 3d ed. London: Africa Books.

Villa-Vicencio, Charles. 1996. *The Spirit of Freedom: South African Leaders on Religion and Politics*. Berkeley: University of California Press.

Soewondo-Soerasno, Nani
(1918–)
Indonesia

A leading Indonesian suffragist and specialist in matrimonial law, in 1954 Nani Soewondo-Soerasno published *The Legal and Social Status of Women*, the first Indonesian-language book to deal with the position of women in that country. She used it to bolster her campaign for the recently proposed marriage law, which supported monogamy.

Born in Semarang, Soewondo-Soerasno studied law in Djakarta and took up a post in the Department of Justice. As a lawyer, she was enlisted by several women's organizations to join a commission to formulate a new marriage act in 1952 —in particular to raise the age of marriage for girls. Legislation would not, however, come into force until the 1974 Marriage Law, setting the minimum ages at sixteen for girls and nineteen for boys. At the International Federation of University Women meeting held in Manila in 1955, she acted as an Indonesian observer. Two years later in Bangkok, she was a delegate to a United Nations seminar on civic responsibilities and increased participation of Asian women in public life, at which she submitted a working paper on Indonesian women. In 1958 she was present at the Asian African Women's Conference in Colombo, Sri Lanka, joining with other delegates to call for the full enactment of the marriage law. In 1959 Soewondo won a Swedish scholarship to research the changing position of Indonesian women over the centuries. She also wrote articles for women's magazines on women's issues, supported the work of the Planned Parenthood Association as its vice president in 1957, and from 1955 led the Association of Indonesian University Women.

Like that of other women activists in this region during the same period, Soewondo-Soerasno's story suffers from a desperate lack of reliable or more detailed information.

References and Further Reading

Blackburn, Susan, and Sharon Bessell. 1997. "Marriageable Age: Political Debates on Early Marriage in Twentieth-Century Indonesia." *Indonesia* 63 (April): 107–141.

Vreede–de Stuers, Cora. 1960. *The Indonesian Woman: Struggles and Achievements.* The Hague: Mouton.

Somerset, Lady Isabella
(1851–1921)
United Kingdom

As a close colleague and devoted friend of charismatic U.S. temperance leader Frances Willard, Lady Isabella Somerset embraced Willard's "do everything" attitude toward reform work. Such

nineteenth-century women leaders turned the crusade for temperance into probably the largest reform campaign espoused by women other than suffrage. In her day a noted society figure who had access to the rich and influential, Somerset epitomized the breed of upper-class female reformer of the Victorian era whose activities, although notable, were often overpraised in contemporary hagiographies to the detriment of the contributions of many less well-known and lower-class women.

Somerset was born with the proverbial silver spoon in her mouth; the daughter of the Earl and Countess Somers, she was well placed in society by her aristocratic lineage and her father's position at court as a lord-in-waiting to Queen Victoria. A cultured and much admired society beauty, she married Lord Henry Somerset in 1872 after being educated by governesses in the required social graces. Despite the fact that the couple separated soon after the birth of a son as a result of Lord Somerset's homosexuality, Isabella's own identity would continue to be subsumed in that of her husband because of the Victorian habit of referring to her as Lady Henry Somerset (see also the writer Mary Ward).

After the scandal of her marriage breakdown, Somerset retreated to her 25,000-acre estate at Eastnor Castle in the Malvern Hills, where she turned to matters spiritual, embraced Methodism, and in 1887 encouraged her entire household to take the pledge. She took up philanthropic work, visiting the poor and nursing the sick. Her home was located in a region renowned for its cider making, and during her local ministrations, Somerset became concerned at the excessive consumption of cider by the working classes, which often led to alcoholism. Further study of the roots of poverty led her to conclude that drink was to blame for many social ills. She overcame her reticence to begin preaching the dangers of alcoholism among her tenants and at public meetings, quoting chapter and verse from the Bible on the subject of abstention and arguing the harmful effects of alcohol on the intellect.

Somerset used her own money to build a temperance mission hall on her estate for the benefit of her workers. Then she cast her net wider and began traveling around Britain, proselytizing on temperance and on respect for the temple of the human body and arguing the benefits of health, hygiene, and physical recreation. Not content with taking her message to the high-density working-class areas of Wales (where she even went to the mines to speak), the north of England, and Scotland, she also lodged with working-class families on her travels, a fact that caused considerable alarm among her family.

In 1890 Somerset was elected president of the British Women's Temperance Association (BWTA). A year later, she accepted an invitation to travel to the United States to observe the campaigning of the Woman's Christian Temperance Union (WCTU). Having already read and been moved by Frances Willard's memoir of the death of her consumptive sister, *Nineteen Beautiful Years*, Somerset quickly struck up a close and intensely emotional friendship with her that would last until Willard's death. By this time a seasoned public speaker, during her prolonged six-month stay, Somerset lectured on temperance in such major cities as Boston, Baltimore, Philadelphia, and Washington, D.C. She used her time in the United States to establish links with other activists in the WCTU and in Chicago undertook training at Mr. Moody's Training School for Christian Workers.

Exhausted by her relentless campaigning, Willard accompanied Somerset on her return to England in 1892, where she spent time recovering at Eastnor Castle. During a second, public visit later in 1892–1893, she toured with Somerset and spoke at temperance meetings. During the 1890s, Somerset coedited the WCTU journal *Woman's Herald* (later known as the *Woman's Signal*). Her high profile and combative style of leadership of the British campaign were not without their critics. Within the executive committee of the BWTA, she came up against the conservative Mary Dowcra, its chief organizer. She, along with other temperance campaigners, resisted Somerset's drive to modernize and make the organization a vehicle for other related campaigns, such as women's suffrage and what they deemed to be the unsavory social purity campaign among prostitutes. Unlike Dowcra and her cohorts, Somerset did not advocate total prohibition and did not want the BWTA to limit itself to temperance work. The conflict flared up in 1893, leading to a vote of confidence in support of Somerset but provoking the exodus from the movement of Dowcra and others, who founded the Women's Total Abstinence Union.

There was, however, more to Somerset's campaigning than the tub-thumping exhortations of the temperance crusader. She was one of the first to recognize that alcoholism was not just a social problem; it was an illness for which those addicted to drink needed proper care and rehabilitation. Intent upon doing something positive and practical for women alcoholics, in 1895 she renovated buildings on her other extensive property, Reigate Priory at Duxhurst in Sussex, as a Home for Inebriates. Later known as the Duxhurst Colony, which began operation in about May 1896, it offered a detoxification program of up to a year to forty women. Some of them, convicted of crimes relating to alcoholism, were referred to Duxhurst by the Home Office. The colony also encouraged self-help, with residents undertaking work in the home's vegetable garden and orchard and looking after the chickens. The poorest women were accommodated in a group of six cottages, each with six residents. Better-off alcoholics could pay to stay in the former manor house (now a "sanatorium") for treatment, and others with less money stayed at nearby Hope House. The home also offered accommodation to the children of inmates at a house on the estate known as the Nest. Somerset took her work seriously, dressing decorously in uniform to project the image of a nurse-cum-nun and frequently giving over time to quiet contemplation and prayer. Perhaps this was intended to contribute in part to her own social rehabilitation, suffering as she did from the stigma of a broken marriage.

After 1896, Somerset spent most of her life at Duxhurst. That year, she and Willard took time out from temperance campaigning to draw attention to the suffering of Armenian Christian refugees who had fled Turkish persecution. An enclave of these dispossessed people sprang up in Marseilles. Somerset traveled there to distribute relief supplies and set up a refuge for them in a disused hospital; funds for the purpose were raised by Willard among her rich patrons in the United States. Willard later assisted many of these refugees in emigrating to the United States.

In 1898 Willard died prematurely, her health worn down by her arduous campaigning; Somerset succeeded her as president of the World's Woman's Christian Temperance Union (1898–1906). Such was the measure of Somerset's progressive social campaigning, which had prompted

Willard to laud her as the temperance movement's equivalent of the factory reformer Lord Shaftesbury, that she too never stood still, tirelessly pursuing the allied issues of social purity (in collaboration with the Salvation Army), women's suffrage, control of the importation and use of opium, and the peace movement. In 1903 ill health and continuing conflicts over policy, including her ill-judged support for state regulation of prostitution in India (which brought criticism from Josephine Butler among others), forced Somerset to resign from the BWTA. She was succeeded by the equally able and equally aristocratic Rosalind, countess of Carlisle.

See also Butler, Josephine; Ward, Mary; Willard, Frances.

References and Further Reading
Bolton, Sarah Knowles. 1895. *Famous Leaders among Women*. New York: Thomas Y. Crowell.
Carey, Rosa Nouchette. 1899. *Twelve Notable Good Women*. London: Hutchinson.
Chappell, Jennie. 1910. *Noble Workers: Sketches of the Life-Work of Frances Willard, Agnes Weston, Sister Dora, Catherine Booth, the Baroness Burdett-Coutts, Lady Henry Somerset, Sarah Robinson, Mrs. Fawcett and Mrs. Gladstone*. London: S. W. Partridge.
Cole, Margaret. 1938. *Women of To-Day*. London: Thomas Nelson and Sons.
Eustance, Claire, Joan Ryan, and Laura Ugolini, eds. 2000. *A Suffrage Reader: Charting Directions in British Suffrage History*. London: Leicester University Press.
Fitzpatrick, Kathleen. 1923. *Lady Henry Somerset*. London: Cape.
Steward, Jane Agnes. 1906. *The Frances Willard Book*. Philadelphia: Current Syndicate.
Strachey, Ray. 1912. *Frances Willard, Her Life and Work*. London: T. Fisher Unwin.
Tyrrell, Ian. 1991. *Woman's World, Woman's Empire: The Women's Christian Temperance Union in International Perspective, 1880–1930*. Chapel Hill: University of North Carolina Press.
Ware, Vron. 1992. *Beyond the Pale: White Women, Racism, and History*. London: Verso.

Song Qingling (Madame Sun Yat-sen)
(1893–1981)
China

A patriotic Chinese figure and widow of nationalist leader Sun Yat-sen, Song Qingling was, with her two sisters Ailing and Meiling, born of a powerful dynasty of Christian converts, the Song family, into an educated and intellectual milieu. Her Americanized businessman-father provided Song and her sisters with an elite education in the United States, and after becoming the wife of Chinese nationalist leader Sun Yat-sen, she used her position to promote the cause of Chinese women and children and sponsor industrial cooperatives.

Born in Shanghai and educated at the McTyeire School for Girls before studying at Wesleyan College for Women in Georgia in the United States (where her two younger sisters also followed), Song returned to China in 1913. She became Sun Yat-sen's secretary during his exile in Japan after a failed coup. Despite her family's disapproval of the match (he was twenty-six years her senior and divorced), Song became his second wife in November 1914. The couple were able to return to Shanghai in 1916, and Sun Yat-sen became president of the provisional government in 1921 with the support of Chinese communists. In her work as secretary of the joint committee of American, British, and Chinese clubs set up to study the unhealthy factory conditions under which many women worked, Song Qingling took on the role of organizing working women's clubs in 1921. In 1924 she became one of only three women allowed to sit at the first congress of the Guomindang.

After Sun Yat-sen's death in 1925, Song, who had become a member of the Political Council of the Central Executive Committee of the Guomindang in 1926, threw her energies into running the Women's Institute of Political Training at Hankow. There, she promoted her husband's belief that all Chinese people, including women, should be involved in the regeneration of China and coordinated propagandizing among peasant and working women, encouraging them to educate themselves and develop women's trade unions. The center also gave refuge to peasant women running away from arranged marriages and helped those seeking advice on divorce. Song kept alive her husband's political ideals of equality for the masses by leading the left-wing faction of the Guomindang against the rise of Chiang Kai-shek's right wing and promoting her own high moral standards.

In 1927 she took a lead in women's emancipation by establishing party training classes for

Song Quingling (right, with Princess Axel of Denmark) (Bettmann/Corbis)

women (those in Wuhan were led by He Xiang-ning), which encouraged women activists to study their legal status and rights and disseminate reformist ideas among women at large. She founded a School for the Education of Women in Hankow, which ran up against considerable resistance for its forward thinking when propagandizing among local peasants, who were mistrustful of women activists who cut their hair short, Western style.

After a purge of communists from the nationalist party by Chiang Kai-shek, Song left for the Soviet Union and spent 1927–1929 in Moscow. Her opposition to Chiang Kai-shek created a conflict of loyalties with her own sister, Song Meiling, who in 1927 married him. Song Qingling felt Chiang had betrayed Sun Yat-sen's political ideals, but despite her calls for unity in the face of threats by Japan during the 1930s, the left and right nationalist factions frequently clashed.

Song's opposition to the dictatorship of Chiang Kai-shek led her to set up the China League

for Civil Rights in 1932, which called for freedom of speech, an end to torture, and the right of all political prisoners of the Guomindang to a proper trial. The league also founded orphanages and maintained children's nurseries and hospitals, even in communist-held Yenan in Shensi province. She also supported the Women's National Salvation Association, founded in Shanghai in 1935, in its advocacy of a united front against the Japanese and an end to civil war in China. The association set up sections for working women, professionals, teachers, and housewives and worked closely with the Young Women's Christian Association (YWCA). It also promoted women's writing through the publication of several journals. The association took a leading role during strikes by women workers in Shanghai textile mills who were protesting their long working days (often as much as eighteen hours).

Song Qingling lived in seclusion in Shanghai until 1937, when war broke out between China and Japan. At this point, many Chinese women's organizations united to form the Women's Advisory Committee. Song set up the China Defense League to coordinate the provision of medical supplies and food and the care of orphaned children and to encourage villages to contribute to the war effort by producing more food. The league's work in remote rural areas involved painstaking attempts to educate and organize reticent peasant women, many illiterate and still with bound feet, who were mistrustful of the league's objectives. Also in 1937, Song established the National Anti-Japanese United Front and once more took up her seat on the Executive Committee of the Guomindang. Having reconciled with her sister Song Meiling in 1938, she and her sister set up the Friends of the Wounded Association in 1940.

Fighting between right-wing nationalists and the communists under Mao Zedong resumed after World War II, and Song Qingling, by that time revered by the left wing, was elected honorary chair of the Nationalist Revolutionary Council in 1948. Described by the American writer Helen Foster Snow as a product of three civilizations—"American Protestant, Chinese capitalist and Chinese socialist" (Snow 1967, 151)—Song Qingling was the first woman in the world to achieve the status equivalent to vice president of a state when, in 1950, she became one of three noncommunist vice chairpersons of the People's Republic of China (PRC). In 1959 she was nominated as one of the two deputy chairs of the PRC. From this position, she continued to take an interest in child welfare and human rights as chair of the China Welfare League (which became the China Welfare Institute in 1950), and became chair of the National Committee in Defense of Children.

In 1951 the Soviets awarded Song the Stalin Peace Prize for her welfare and peace initiatives. Her major articles were collected and translated as *The Struggle for New China* in 1953. She became a friend and supporter of the first Indian prime minister, Jawaharlal Nehru, and represented China on state visits to India, Burma, and Pakistan. In 1976–1978 she served as acting head of state (chair of the National People's Congress) and in 1981 was made honorary chairman of the PRC. Shortly before her death, she became a member of the Chinese Communist Party.

A woman of considerable dignity and beauty,

Song Qingling became an iconic figure. In contrast to her sister Song Meiling, who through her promotion of Chiang Kai-shek's New Life Movement adopted a conventional attitude toward women's emancipation as a moral crusade confined to emphasizing traditional virtues of modesty, chastity, and domesticity, Song Qingling saw precisely these traditional patriarchal attitudes as being at the root of the continuing subjection of Chinese women, even into the communist era. In 1972 she wrote of the need for Chinese women to be freed from the mindset of the three obediences—to fathers, husbands, and sons—that persisted in China, a country whose peasantry still sold women into arranged marriages and denied them an education.

Despite her high political profile, Song was a shy woman and led a quiet, private life blighted by the hardship of long and bitter political struggle and the loss of many friends. Throughout, she refused to accept the idea of compromise over her social ideals. When she died in 1981, the Chinese gave her a state funeral at which her many virtues as a patriot and welfare organizer were eulogized. In 1982 the Song Qingling Foundation was established in recognition of Song's work for children and world peace. It seeks to care for the mental and physical well-being of children and promote international cooperation and friendship.

See also He Xiangning.

References and Further Reading

The Annual Obituary. 1981. New York: St. Martin's Press.

Croll, Elizabeth. 1978. *Feminism and Socialism in China.* New York: Schocken Books.

Eunson, R. 1975. *The Soong Sisters.* New York: Franklin Watts.

Fan Hong. 1997. *Footbinding, Feminism and Freedom.* Portland, OR: Frank Cass.

Gilmartin, Christina. 1995. *Engendering the Chinese Revolution: Radical Women, Communist Politics and Mass Movements in the 1920s.* Berkeley: University of California Press.

Hahn, Emily. 1943. *The Soong Sisters.* London: Robert Hale.

Jayawardena, Kumari. 1986. *Feminism and Nationalism in the Third World.* London: Zed Books.

Seagrave, Sterling. 1996. *The Soong Dynasty.* New York: Harper.

Snow, Helen Foster. 1967. *Women in Modern China.* The Hague: Mouton.

Soong Ching-ling. 1952. *The Struggle for a New China.* Peking: Foreign Languages Press.

Sorabji, Cornelia
(1866–1954)
India

Born into a cultured family of influential Parsi Christian converts, the Indian barrister Cornelia Sorabji spent her life working for the legal rights of Indian women in purdah. Together with her educator-sister Susie, she had been inspired as a young girl by the work of their mother, Francina Sorabji, who was a firm believer that education must begin at home with women "because it was the mother's influence which was strongest in molding the child's character" (Chapman 1891, 137). Francina had established several girls' schools in Poona and ensured that all seven of her daughters had a good education. These three women collectively contributed much to women's education in India at this time.

As a friend and supporter of the reformer Pandita Ramabai, Cornelia Sorabji lent a great deal of support to the movement for reform of the Hindu laws regarding child marriage and the position of widows. Like Anandibai Joshi, who traveled to the United States to earn a medical degree, Sorabji was one of the first Indian women to travel abroad to train in a profession—in her case, the law. As a child, she and her six sisters were educated at mission schools and later at the pioneering, interracial Victoria High School in Poona founded by their mother. The girls were also privately taught Sanskrit, science, and mathematics at home by their missionary father, the Reverend Sorabji Karsedji. With her parents' blessing, Sorabji went on to defy male hostility and gain a bachelor's degree in 1887, as the only female student at the 300-strong all-male Deccan College in Poona. After spending some time helping out as a teacher in her mother's schools, she was offered a fellowship in Ahmadabad at Gujarat College. There, having decided that "it would do Indian men good to be ruled for a time by a woman" (Chapman 1891, 131), she lectured on English language and literature to male students not much older than herself. Had Sorabji been male, her impeccable academic qualifications would have guaranteed her a government scholarship to continue her studies. Instead, she paid her own fare to England out of her savings, and sponsored by the National Indian Association and by a trust fund set up by Lady Mary Hobhouse (which was supported by leading

Cornelia Sorabji (Dover Pictorial Archives)

British feminists such as Millicent Garrett Fawcett and Florence Nightingale), she continued her studies. In return for an education, her sponsors appear to have expected Sorabji to metamorphose into a paragon of enlightened, reforming Indian womanhood. She did not let them down.

At the same time that Sorabji was settling in at Oxford University in the autumn of 1889, she found she was not the only Indian woman attracting attention in England at the time, and her path frequently crossed with the much-admired Rukhmabai, who had come over to study medicine. Sorabji began a two-year lecture course for an honors degree in literature but transferred to a three-year course reading law, becoming the first Indian woman to enter a British school of law. Although Sorabji was never one to shrink from entering all-male preserves, this was a bold step prompted by her overweening sense of her own mission to do something useful for India. She later acknowledged that the impetus in taking up law had come from her childhood memories of seeing women coming to her mother for advice on legal and other matters affecting their inheritance of family property.

While studying at Oxford University, Sorabji patently enjoyed the attention she aroused as the only female Indian face on campus, and that was the way she wanted to keep it. She wanted, as Antoinette Burton argues, to be "*the* Indian woman at Oxford" and positively discouraged others from following her from India (1998, 145). She soon attracted the attention of British philanthropists and social reformers, eventually meeting both Queen Victoria and Prime Minister William Gladstone. Indeed, Sorabji rapidly began displaying all the qualities of an English snob—dismissing her fellow students for their scruffy appearance at lectures and doing a lot of socializing. While resisting being made the tool of the Church Missionary Society, she did much fund-raising and speech making on their behalf. She met feminist campaigners, too, but had no truck with them or with women's suffrage. Meanwhile, her countrywoman Rukhmabai, who had been adopted by women's rights activists, became a rival in Sorabji's eyes. According to Burton, Sorabji tried to undermine her reputation and "belittled Rukhmabai's scheme for women's education in India" (1998, 142). At the root of this sense of rivalry, as Burton points out, lay Sorabji's undisguised dislike for Rukhmabai as a Hindu and for her spirit of independence.

Sorabji was awarded her bachelor of civil law degree by special decree in 1893 after her British supporters had petitioned for her to be allowed to sit for the examination. She also gained some practical legal experience working in a law firm at London's Lincoln's Inn for a year. On her return to India in 1894, Sorabji set about injecting some good British zeal into the inertia (as she saw it) of the Indian reform movement. She undertook a blue-book study of education in Baroda before engaging in social and advisory work on behalf of women in purdah who were unable, under Hindu law, to represent themselves in court cases. Through the vehicle of the *sanad*, Sorabji was able to enter pleas on their behalf, although she was unable to defend them in court.

Sorabji applied to become a barrister, but she would have to wait until 1919 before the law was changed and women were finally allowed to practice. Meanwhile, in 1902 she suggested that the India Office should provide for a female lawyer to be available in provincial courts to represent women and minors who were involved in often complex feudal disputes over their rights of succession, maintenance, property, and caste. Although there had been some reform of property laws affecting Hindu widows in the 1870s, they had no autonomy in disposing of their property and were often cheated by unscrupulous members of their husbands' families. In 1904 she was appointed legal adviser to the courts of Bengal in this capacity and took up her post in Calcutta, initially for one year as an experiment. But such was the need for female lawyers to fill this role that by 1907 Sorabji was representing women in the provinces of Bengal, Bihar, Orissa, and Assam—often for no charge. During her twenty-one years' service, she estimated she had helped 600 or so women and orphans in many intriguing and often disturbing cases, some of which she described in *Between the Twilights* (1908) and her two volumes of memoirs.

After a thirty-year delay, Sorabji finally received official recognition of her professional status when she was called to the bar at the British courts at Lincoln's Inn, London, in 1923. She moved to Calcutta to practice in the High Court until her retirement in 1929. Although Sorabji had originally linked the achievement of women's rights with the campaign for Indian independence, she later became extremely antipathetic toward the nationalist movement and developed a pronounced dislike of Mahatma Gandhi's campaign of civil disobedience. This lack of political commitment modulated the support she gained from other Indian reformers, and her attempts at organizing rural welfare schemes, such as a League for Infant Welfare, Maternity, and District Nursing, foundered because of hostility toward her pro-British stance.

In 1929 Sorabji settled in London but continued to visit India during the cold English winters. During her life, she wrote widely on numerous themes, from a colorful study of the mysteries of women's life in seclusion (*Love and Life behind the Purdah,* 1902) to short stories and newspaper articles, and memoirs of her parents (*Therefore,* 1924), her educationist sister (*Susie Sorabji,* 1932), and her own life and work (*India Calling,* 1934, and *India Recalled,* 1936).

Sorabji was a lifelong Anglophile with a deep respect for the rule of English law and made no bones about it. Nevertheless, she had no desire to see the wholesale imposition of a British legal system on Indian society any more than she sought the transplantation of other Western values in India, and she wrote vividly and with great affection in support of traditional Indian life and culture. As she saw it, education was the key to effective social change, and until the vast majority of the illiterate female population of India had access to it, she felt that universal women's suffrage would be inappropriate. It was a belief that she communicated privately to the government at the time of Lord Edwin Montagu's Joint Commission on the government of India. Her Christian upbringing undoubtedly colored her reforming activities, and she never lost an arrogant sense of her own cultural superiority as a Parsi.

The rather gushing tone of Sorabji's memoirs, punctuated as they are with much talk about the great and the good among the predominantly white elite of the British Raj with whom she personally associated ("I was the only Indian woman at English dinner parties in Calcutta," she says in *India Recalled,* 173), tend to detract at times from her real achievements as a reformer, but her courage in pursuing the difficult career of law as a lone woman among a mass of often hostile men has secured her a rightful place in both women's and Indian legal history. In 1909 Sorabji was awarded the Kaiser-i-Hind gold medal for her services to the Indian nation.

See also Joshi, Anandibai; Ramabai, Pandita
Saraswati; Rukhmabai; Sorabji, Susie.

References and Further Reading

Burton, Antoinette. 1996. "Introduction to Cornelia Sorabji's 'Stray Thoughts of an Indian Girl.'" *Indian Journal of Gender Studies* 3(2): 251–255.
———. 1998. *At the Heart of Empire: Indians and the Colonial Encounter in Late-Victorian Britain.* Berkeley: University of California Press.
Chapman, Mrs. E. F. 1891. *Sketches of Some Distinguished Indian Women.* London: W. H. Allen.
Sorabji, Cornelia. 1932. *Susie Sorabji: A Memoir by Her Sister.* London: Oxford University Press.
———. 1934. *India Calling.* London: Nisbet.
———. 1936. *India Recalled.* London: Nisbet.
Tuson, Penelope, ed. 1997. *The Queen's Daughters: An Anthology of Victorian Feminist Writings on India 1857–1900.* Reading, Berkshire, UK: Ithaca Press.

Sorabji, Susie
(1868–1931)
India

The educator Susie Sorabji epitomized the Good Samaritan of British colonial philanthropic tradition. As the archetypal cultured, Anglicized Christian convert, she lived an exemplary life of public service. The daughter of pioneer educators, she grew up in Poona in western India, where she was educated at her mother Francina's Victoria High School and where she herself helped as a teacher as soon as she was old enough. She followed up on her parents' progressive, internationalist ideas and her mother's deep commitment to women's education by setting up several schools and training establishments under the auspices of the Church Missionary Society, becoming an influential figure in education in western India.

Having helped run the Marathi and Urdu poor schools, as well as the Anglo-Gujarati school that served as feeders into her mother's Victoria High School, Sorabji set about improving their facilities and eventually set her heart on founding her own establishment. In 1904 she toured the United States to lecture and raise funds for the purchase of a permanent site for her poor schools, which became known as the St. John's Schools. She also acquired premises for the Anglo-Gujarati school and enlarged it to become the St. Helena's High School for Parsees. This latter coeducational school became a model establishment extolled by British education officials and received funds from U.S., British, and Canadian supporters, as well as injections of Sorabji's own money. Coeducational and open to children of different races, religions, and nationalities, the school was ahead of its time in its experimental approach to education and aimed for social harmony, with Sorabji taking as her inspiration the work of the newly created League of Nations. The school had its own kindergarten, and dormitories were added for boarders. After further fund-raising lecture tours in Canada and the United States in 1923–1924, new classrooms and laboratories were built. Sorabji trained her own teaching staff in English and American teaching methods, and set up her own Girl Scouts and Girl Guides groups and branches of the Red Cross and Daughters of the Empire at the school. Such was the school's reputation that eventually many Indian girls were allowed to attend rather than being kept secluded at home.

In addition to eventually running three schools, looking after their finances, and training their staff, Sorabji undertook numerous good works, visiting children's hospitals, mental asylums, widows' refuges, leper colonies, and prisons. Like her sister Cornelia, Susie was a loyal British subject who believed in the continuation of the British Empire and disliked the activities of the Indian nationalist movement and the boycotting of British goods by the Swadeshi movement. She was particularly distressed by the escalating civil unrest of the 1930s. But she was also fiercely proud of her nation and saw education as the vehicle by which its people and more particularly its women could come into their own right and give collective impetus to India taking its rightful place in world affairs.

Although her sister Cornelia paints a sugary, saintly portrait of her in her 1932 hagiography, Susie Sorabji was indeed a gentle, patient, and quietly sympathetic woman, who practiced her own deeply held Christian beliefs in peace and cooperation. Her involvement on numerous committees testifies to an honorable life in the service of others, despite problems with her health and her eyesight. Organizations such as the National Council of Women, the National Missionary Association, the Woman's Christian Temperance Union, the League of Mercy, and the All-India Educational Conference all benefited from her contributions. She also served as regent of the Kaiser-i-Hind, the Indian chapter of the loyalist organization the Canadian Daughters of the Empire. Her schools were entrusted to the Church Missionary Society before her death to ensure the continuation of her work.

See also, Sorabji, Cornelia.
References and Further Reading
Sen Gupta, Padmini. 1994. *Pioneer Women of India.* Bombay: Thacker.
Sorabji, Cornelia. 1932. *Susie Sorabji: A Memoir by Her Sister.* London: Oxford University Press.

Spence, Catherine
(1825–1910)
United Kingdom/Australia

A remarkable Australian pioneer, Catherine Spence was a successful novelist who combined fiction writing with a career as a prolific professional journalist for more than thirty years and a dogged campaign for the introduction of proportional representation. Her interests in social reform prompted her support for women's education and the care of orphaned and destitute children.

Born in Melrose, Scotland, the daughter of a banker, Spence emigrated to South Australia with her family in 1839, when her father's business ventures failed. She had resolved at the age of thirteen to be a teacher and a writer, and after taking work as a governess at age seventeen, in 1845 she opened her own school. In 1854 she published her first novel anonymously. *Clara Morison: A Tale of South Australia during the Gold Fever* is generally regarded as the first woman's novel to come out of Australia. In it, Spence provided vivid descriptions of life in Adelaide and gently satirized the preoccupations of its rapidly developing society with an ironic wit that would characterize much of her other fiction, such as *Tender and True: A Colonial Tale* (1856, again anonymously), *Mr. Hogarth's Will* (serialized in 1864 under her own name), and *The Author's Daughter* (1868). These well-observed novels have provided historians with valuable details of the colonial life of mid-nineteenth-century Australia.

During her long career in journalism for the Australian press, Spence used her writing as a vehicle for her many social interests and her often radical ideas. She traveled widely, visiting England in 1864–1865 and also touring Canada and the United States. For many years she supported improvements to the inadequate education facilities for girls in South Australia, serving on the School Board for East Torrens in Adelaide in 1877 and lobbying for the foundation of kindergartens and the first state secondary school, the Advanced School for Girls in Adelaide. Under her influence, women were admitted to teacher-training colleges and in 1881, to Adelaide University.

Spence's first philanthropic work came in 1872, when she founded the Boarding-Out Society, which worked to find homes for orphaned, delinquent, and destitute children among foster families. After serving the society with dedication for fourteen years, in 1886 she was appointed to the State Children's Council, serving on its Destitute Board from 1887. She described her work in her 1907 book, *State Children in Australia: A His-*

tory of Boarding Out and Its Developments. Although she remained single, Spence had strong maternal instincts and took three families of orphaned children into her own home.

During the years 1878–1893, Spence was a foremost woman journalist and literary critic, contributing to the South Australian *Register;* other Adelaide papers such as the *Observer, Advertiser,* and *Herald;* newspapers in Melbourne, Sydney, and Brisbane; and English journals such as the *Cornhill Magazine* and *Fortnightly Review.* In these publications, she voiced her views on history and religion and covered a comprehensive range of social and political issues relating to life in Australia, such as taxation, the prison system, education, suffrage, temperance, gambling, prostitution, and domestic violence. In 1880 she produced *The Laws We Live Under,* the first social studies textbook used in Australian schools. By this time she rarely resorted to fiction, publishing only *An Agnostic's Progress* (1884) and *A Week in the Future* (serialized in 1889).

Spence was a lifelong advocate of electoral reform and a leading voice for proportional representation, which she argued as early as her 1861 pamphlet, "A Plea for Pure Democracy: Mr. Hare's Reform Bill Applied to South Australia" (in reference to the British political reformer Thomas Hare's proposals on proportional representation). During 1892–1893, the Labour Party drew on her modification of Hare's arguments in its own campaigning. Such was Spence's deep conviction that the electoral system should be reformed before women were given the vote that she had not affiliated herself with suffrage groups. In 1891, however, conceding that the women's suffrage movement had become an unstoppable force, she joined the Women's Suffrage League of South Australia, which elected her vice president. Three years later, women won the state vote. In 1897, at age seventy-two, Spence defied a ruling that women could not sit on the South Australia Federal Convention and stood unsuccessfully for election, coming in twenty-second out of thirty-three candidates.

In 1893 Spence visited the Chicago World Fair in the United States, where she spoke at the International Conference on Charities and Correction and addressed other meetings on prison reform, proportional representation, pacifism, and women's rights. Afterwards she went on a preaching and lecture tour of the United States,

United Kingdom, and Switzerland before returning to Australia in 1894. A year later, she was the first woman in Australia to give evidence to an official inquiry, the Commissions of Enquiry into the Adelaide Hospital. In 1895 she founded the nonpartisan Effective Voting League, through which she campaigned during federal elections in 1899 and 1900 for proportional representation and supported the introduction of a succession of bills on the subject during 1902–1910. Spence's final political act came in 1909, when she became president of the Women's Political Association (established in 1902 by Vida Goldstein; later known as the League of Women Voters), another nonpartisan organization dedicated to women's political and civil rights.

Two of Spence's novels appeared posthumously: *Gathered In,* serialized in 1881–1882, was not published in book form until 1977, and the Utopian novel *Handfasted,* rejected as "too socialistic" in 1880, was not published until 1984. Spence's *Autobiography,* unfinished at her death and unreliable in places, was completed by a friend, Jeanne Young, shortly after Spence's death. In her time an admired and influential personality as well as a popular speaker and Unitarian lay preacher, Spence is still revered as the "Grand Old Woman of Australia" and is featured on the new Australian $5 note.

See also Goldstein, Vida.

References and Further Reading

Cooper, Janet. 1972. *Catherine Spence.* Melbourne: Oxford University Press.

Magarey, Susan. 1985. *Unbridling the Tongues of Women: A Biography of Catherine Helen Spence.* Sydney: Hale and Ironmonger.

Pike, Douglas Henry, ed. 1966–. *Australian Dictionary of Biography.* Melbourne: Melbourne University Press.

Sansome, Diana. 1996. *The Influence of Catherine Helen Spence on Social and Political Reform in South Australia, 1860–1910.* Medford, MA: Unitarian Universalist Women's Heritage Society.

Spence, Catherine Helen. 1975 [1910]. *Catherine Helen Spence: An Autobiography.* Edited by Jeanne F. Young. Reprint, Adelaide: Libraries Board of South Australia.

Thomson, Helen, ed. 1987. *Catherine Helen Spence.* St. Lucia: University of Queensland Press.

Young, Jean. 1937. *Catherine Helen Spence: A Study and an Appreciation.* Melbourne: Lothian.

Stanton, Elizabeth Cady
(1815–1902)
United States

A woman of enormous compassion, vision, and sensitivity, Elizabeth Cady Stanton was the undisputed theoretician and one of the most eloquent voices of the early women's movement in the United States. As the loving mother of seven children, she was never able to undertake the degree of traveling and lecturing of her close colleague Susan B. Anthony, who, remaining unmarried, handled most of the business affairs of their suffrage organization and earned more enduring fame as the public face of U.S. suffragism. The two women's talents were, however, entirely complementary, with Stanton's intellect and her distinctive voice as a writer providing some of the first and most compelling arguments for women's suffrage and their legal and civil equality with men. It was Stanton who drafted the famous 1848 *Declaration of Sentiments and Resolutions* with Lucretia Mott, which she read out at the first women's rights convention, held in Seneca Falls, New York. She would also remain a lifelong and uncompromising advocate of the liberalization of divorce laws, the protection of women from domestic abuse, and their rights to property. In later years, she risked her position as leader of the suffrage movement with her radical anticlericalism, taking a brave and independent stand to challenge sexism in the church with her controversial and iconoclastic *Woman's Bible* (1895).

Stanton was born in Johnstown, New York, the daughter of a judge and strict Presbyterian who had been elected to Congress in 1815. Her only brother died young, a fact with which her father never came to terms, forever after constantly wishing his bright and talented daughter had been a boy. Thus, Stanton enjoyed the advantage of being well educated, even studying Greek during her attendance at a boys' school, the Johnstown Academy, until the age of fifteen and then Troy Female Seminary, a progressive girls' school established in 1821 by the pioneer educator Emma Willard. Graduating in 1832, Stanton studied law privately with her father. While helping at his legal offices, she observed the distress of his women clients seeking advice over divorce and their property and custody rights and first discovered how disadvantaged women were. She became a regular visitor to the home of her

Elizabeth Cady Stanton (Library of Congress)

wealthy Quaker cousin Gerrit Smith in Peterboro, where the family campaigned for abolition and sheltered runaway slaves on their way north to Canada. It was here that Elizabeth met the abolitionist Henry Stanton, whom she married in 1840 (omitting the word *obey* from her vows and thereafter calling herself Elizabeth Cady Stanton rather than assuming the wifely anonymity of Mrs. Henry Stanton).

Stanton spent her honeymoon accompanying her husband to an antislavery convention in London, an experience that galvanized her feminism, when she and other women attending were not allowed to take part but had to listen to the proceedings from a screened-off area. There she met Lucretia Mott, who introduced her to the writings of Mary Wollstonecraft. The effect on Stanton was considerable; buoyed up by Wollstonecraft's arguments on women's equality, she resolved with Mott to hold a convention on women's rights when they returned to the United States. It would be another eight years, however, before they managed to do so. Meanwhile, Stanton was soon immersed in domesticity and the care of her first three children, born in quick succession from 1842 to 1845.

Moving to the salubrious environs of Seneca Falls in 1847 for the sake of Henry Stanton's poor health, Stanton soon found herself isolated by his frequent absences at his legal practice in Boston. She became bored with small-town life and rapidly found her domestic routine stultifying. Hungry for intellectual stimulation, she began meeting with Mott, and together with three other Quaker friends, they decided to advertise a women's convention on 13 July 1848 in the *Seneca Court Courier*. On 19 and 20 July about 300 people (including some men) gathered in the Wesleyan Methodist Church in Seneca Falls to hear Stanton read out the *Declaration of Sentiments,* composed along the lines of the U.S. Declaration of Independence of 1776. Among its list of eight "grievances," the manifesto included Stanton's resolution that "it is the duty of the women of this country to secure for themselves their sacred rights to the elective franchise" (Bolt 1993, 88). This proved to be the most controversial issue, which many of the women present considered too ambitious a demand and one that Mott, as a Quaker, would not endorse, believing abolition to be a far more pressing cause.

The Seneca Falls convention was well covered in the press, and other conventions followed elsewhere in the United States that summer and at regular intervals until the outbreak of the Civil War in 1861. Meanwhile, Stanton drew on her own domestic experiences to write articles on child rearing for Amelia Bloomer's temperance journal, the *Lily* (founded in 1849). She later wrote for the *New York Tribune* and the short-lived feminist magazine *Una* from 1853 to 1855 (where she published her notable article challenging women's complacency, "I Have All the Rights I Want"). Through her association with Bloomer, Stanton also ran the gauntlet of public derision to promote dress reform in the early 1850s by wearing the new ankle-length bloomers under a shortened skirt, which she professed to be "altogether a most becoming costume and exceedingly convenient for walking in all kinds of weather" (Stanton 1993, 201).

In 1851 Stanton established a close working partnership with the abolitionist and temperance advocate Susan B. Anthony, with whom she organized an antislavery convention at Seneca Falls in 1851. A year later, they cofounded the Woman's State Temperance Society in New York. Throughout the 1850s, constrained by the demands of family life, Stanton primarily confined herself to applying her considerable literary talents to writing an endless supply of letters, speeches, and journal articles in support of women's rights, while Anthony went out on the campaign trail. On one occasion, feeling that she was under particular pressure, Stanton jestingly told Anthony in a letter, "If you want more speeches from me, *you* must come and make the pudding and carry the baby" (Watkins et al. 1999, 45).

Although their partnership suffered from a widening divergence of views, with Stanton becoming increasingly radical during its fifty-year lifespan, it remained a respectful and affectionate one. Between them, Stanton and Anthony covered the whole spectrum of contemporary social issues: suffrage, the property rights of married women, the employment rights of female schoolteachers, dress reform, divorce, coeducation, women in the professions, temperance, and even marital violence. By 1860, Stanton was finally able to join Anthony on the lecture circuit, becoming the first woman to address a joint session at the New York state legislature that year, when she called for a new women's property bill. At the tenth women's rights convention, held that year in New York City, Stanton took the platform for an hour to speak on marriage and the difficulty for women of obtaining divorce in cases in which their husbands were drunken and abusive. Calling for marriage to be viewed as a *legal* contract and describing ten resolutions in support of a woman's right to divorce, she pointed out that "a boy can not contract for an acre of land, or a horse, until he is twenty-one, but he may contract for a wife at fourteen" (Helsinger, Sheets, and Veeder 1983, 30). Stanton's radicalism on this particular issue would remain a problem for many would-be supporters of the women's movement, but she refused to modify her views, in the belief that justice for women in marriage lay at the heart of all social progress.

In 1861, with the outbreak of the Civil War, the women's rights movement in the United States was effectively suspended. Stanton channeled her activities into the Woman's National Loyal League, collecting signatures (eventually 3 million) for a petition calling for the abolition of slavery by constitutional amendment. But she would be bitterly disappointed in the passage of the Fourteenth Amendment, which gave male blacks the vote ahead of women; she also opposed the Fifteenth Amendment, which prohibited disenfranchisement on the grounds of race or color but made no mention of sexual discrimination, a fact that galvanized Stanton's radicalism and her affirmation of suffrage as a sexual issue. She fought the wording of these amendments and tried to get a Sixteenth Amendment introduced, protesting against "the enfranchisement of another man of any race or clime until the daughters of Jefferson, Hancock and Adams are crowned with all their rights" (Evans 1977, 49). With Anthony, she founded the feminist magazine the *Revolution* (1868–1870), with funding from financier George Francis Train, who was well-known for his racist attitudes. Stanton's reluctance thereafter to push for the rights of blacks over and above those of women has led to accusations of racism and criticism of her failure to perceive suffrage as a civil liberty common to all people, not just women.

Discord in the movement for women's suffrage over the Fourteenth and Fifteenth Amendments precipitated a split in 1869, finally exacerbated by the failure of male advocates of racial equality led by William Lloyd Garrison to fulfill their promise of support for women's suffrage, partly because of their dislike of Stanton's position on marriage and divorce. Stanton and Anthony decided that women should go it alone and give up "the counsel of men" forever. They therefore excluded male officers from their new organization, the National Woman Suffrage Association (NWSA), established that year to address a range of issues under Stanton's presidency. Thus began a twenty-year division in the women's movement, with the NWSA soon finding itself in opposition to Lucy Stone's more moderate and conciliatory body, the American Woman Suffrage Association, which admitted male supporters to its ranks and dedicated itself to the fight for suffrage first and foremost.

From 1869, partly as a means of earning money to educate her children, Stanton took up paid lecturing on the Lyceum lecture circuit, where her vivacious and witty manner was greatly admired. While continuing to press for a constitutional amendment on women's suffrage, she refused to modify her position on women's right to divorce and lent her support to mavericks in the movement, such as the radical feminist Victoria Woodhull (who advocated free love and birth control)

and the English birth control pioneer Annie Besant (whom Stanton supported when she was prosecuted for disseminating birth control literature in 1877). In defending the right of dissidents such as Woodhull to speak openly, Stanton attacked the temerity of the moderates in the women's movement: "We have already women enough sacrificed to this sentimental, hypocritical prattling about purity, without going out of our way to increase the number" (Banks 1990, 58). But the moderates did not take kindly to Stanton's radical position on sexuality or her long-harbored dislike of traditional patriarchy and established religion. They resisted her attempts to incorporate these as mainstream issues in NWSA, believing that they could achieve more by exerting their moral superiority and shaming male sexual behavior through the social purity crusade, rather than attacking the institution of marriage.

In 1881, having already spent time with Anthony reviewing their vast archive of documents, Stanton retired from lecturing at the age of sixty-five, to spend the next five years producing the first three volumes of an ambitious *History of Woman Suffrage,* with the help of Anthony and the gifted feminist historian Matilda Joslyn Gage. She also began thinking about the creation of an international women's movement for suffrage, and after attending a women's conference in Liverpool in November 1883, collaborated with temperance leader Frances Willard in mounting an international women's conference in Washington, D.C., on the occasion of the fortieth anniversary of Seneca Falls in 1888, an event that prompted the establishment of the International Council of Women.

In 1890, encouraged by Anthony, who felt that the women's movement had been greatly damaged by its long division, Stanton reluctantly agreed to a merger of the two women's suffrage organizations as the National American Woman Suffrage Association (NAWSA) and served as its first president. During her tenure, she spent time in England with her daughter. Weary and increasingly estranged by the caution of the mainstream and with her eyesight failing, she returned to the United States and retired in 1892 at the annual NAWSA convention, held in Washington. It was on this occasion that she read out her haunting and elegiac speech, "The Solitude of the Self," in which, with the voice of a true poet, she urged women to overcome their traditional state of dependency and find the courage to stand alone in defense of their own sovereignty, no matter how daunting it might seem. Self-reliance had long been her own watchword, despite her years as wife and mother, and the time had come, she argued, for women to learn to live their lives, not vicariously through their husbands and children but in their own right: "So it ever must be in the conflicting scenes of life, in the long, weary march, each one walks alone. We may have many friends, love, kindness, sympathy and charity, to smooth our pathway in everyday life, but in the tragedies and triumphs of human experience, each mortal stands alone" (Ward and Burns 1999, 196).

In her years of retirement, Stanton continued to publish essays and articles on divorce, religion, and women's rights in journals such as the *New York Journal* and the *American.* She also produced a wide-ranging attack on organized religion, synthesized from numerous talks she had given from the 1870s onward and essays such as her 1885 work, "Has Christianity Benefited Woman?" In *The Woman's Bible,* published in two parts in 1895 and 1898, Stanton boldly challenged religious doctrine and its perpetuation of the traditional subordination of women, daring to reject the perceived sanctity of biblical texts by reappraising the Bible as a historical work, which had served, together with the established church, to impede women's emancipation for centuries. In her idiosyncratic reinterpretation of selected misogynist texts in the Bible, Stanton openly attacked the religious establishment's perpetuation of a traditional patriarchy that degraded women and of a set of teachings that accentuated their inequality. The work was viewed as outright heresy by many in the church but welcomed by many freethinkers and ran through seven printings in six months. Anthony, however, was alarmed, thinking it would further alienate middlebrow support for the suffrage movement; leading suffragists such as Carrie Chapman Catt and Anna Howard Shaw disassociated themselves and the movement at large from what they perceived to be a heretical work.

In 1898 Stanton also published her engaging memoirs, *Eighty Years and More: Reminiscences, 1815–1897.* They are full of affection for the many fellow feminists and campaigners she had met along the way, as are her letters and diary entries, published by her son and daughter in 1922.

These contain some penetrating insights made with Stanton's inimitable wit that are rarely matched in other suffragist memoirs. Her delightful putdown, in 1887, of Leo Tolstoy's *Anna Karenina* is a typical example: "I do not like it very much, as all the women are disappointed and unhappy; and well they may be, as they are made to look to men, and not to themselves, for their chief joy" (Stanton and Blatch 1922, 237).

By the time of her death in 1902, Stanton felt that women's suffrage, which should have been won after the Civil War, was now so long overdue that public sympathy for her advocacy of it was wearing thin: "I cannot sit on the door just like Poe's raven and sing suffrage evermore" (Lutz 1973, 296). Her campaigning spirit lived on in her daughter Harriot Stanton Blatch, who was closely involved in the suffrage movement in England during her twenty-year residency there. Blatch returned to the United States to lead the final stage of the campaign, which eventually achieved the vote for U.S. women in 1920, seventy-two years after Stanton had first inaugurated the suffrage movement. Stanton's home at Seneca Falls, as well as the Wesleyan chapel at which the first women's rights convention was held, is now part of the Women's Rights National Historical Park and open to the public. For further information, see http://www.cr.nps. gov/nr/travel/pwwmh/ny10.htm.

An excellent documentary film, *Not for Ourselves Alone: The Story of Elizabeth Cady Stanton and Susan B. Anthony,* by Ken Burns and Paul Barns, catalogues the highs and lows of their long-term leadership of the suffrage movement. In two parts, it is available on PBS video (and is also the basis of the highly illustrated book by Ward and Burns listed below).

See also Anthony, Susan B.; Besant, Annie; Blatch, Harriot Stanton; Catt, Carrie Chapman; Gage, Matilda Joslyn; Mott, Lucretia Coffin; Shaw, Anna Howard; Stone, Lucy; Willard, Emma Hart; Wollstonecraft, Mary; Woodhull, Victoria Claflin.

References and Further Reading

Banks, Olive. 1990 [1981]. *Faces of Feminism: A Study of Feminism as a Social Movement.* Reprint, Oxford: Blackwell.

Banner, Lois W. 1980. *Elizabeth Cady Stanton: A Radical for Women's Rights.* Boston: Little, Brown.

Bolt, Christine. 1993. *The Women's Movements in the United States and Britain from the 1790s to the 1920s.* London: Harvester Wheatsheaf.

Buhle, Mai Jo, and Paul Buhle, eds. 1978. *The Concise History of Woman Suffrage: Selections from the Classic Work of Stanton, Anthony, Gage, and Harper*. Urbana: University of Illinois Press.

DuBois, Ellen. 1978. *Feminism and Suffrage: The Emergence of the Independent Women's Movement in America 1848–1869*. Ithaca: Cornell University Press.

Evans, Richard. 1977. *The Feminists: Women's Emancipation Movements in Europe, America and Australasia 1840–1920*. London: Croom Helm.

Flexner, Eleanor. 1975 [1959]. *A Century of Struggle: The Woman's Rights Movement in the United States*. Rev. ed. Cambridge, MA: Belknap Press of Harvard University.

Forster, M. 1984. *Significant Sisters: The Grassroots of Active Feminism, 1839–1939*. London: Secker and Warburg.

Goldsmith, Barbara. 1998. *Other Powers: The Age of Suffrage, Spiritualism and the Scandalous Victoria Woodhull*. New York: Alfred A. Knopf.

Griffith, Elisabeth. 1984. *In Her Own Right: The Life of Elizabeth Cady Stanton*. New York: Oxford University Press.

Gurko, Miriam. 1974. *The Ladies of Seneca Falls: The Birth of the Women's Rights Movement*. New York: Macmillan.

Helsinger, Elizabeth K., Robin Lauterbach Sheets, and William Veeder. 1983. *The Woman Question: Social Issues, 1837–1883*, vol. 2, *Society and Literature in Britain and America, 1837–1883*. Manchester: Manchester University Press.

Holton, Sandra Stanley. 1994. "To Educate Women into Rebellion: Elizabeth Cady Stanton and the Creation of a Transatlantic Network of Radical Suffragists." *American History Review* 99: 1112–1136.

Kraditor, Aileen. 1981 [1965]. *The Ideas of the Woman Suffrage Movement 1890–1920*. Reprint, New York: W. W. Norton.

Leach, William. 1981. *True Love and Perfect Union: The Feminist Reform of Sex and Society*. London: Routledge and Kegan Paul.

Lutz, Alma. 1973 [1940]. *Created Equal: A Biography of Elizabeth Cady Stanton*. Reprint, New York: Octagon.

McFadden, Margaret. 1999. *Golden Cables of Sympathy: The Transatlantic Sources of Nineteenth-Century Feminism*. Lexington: University of Kentucky Press.

Melder, Keith E. 1977. *The Beginnings of Sisterhood: The American Woman's Rights Movement, 1800–1850*. New York: Schocken.

Niess, Judith. 1977. *Seven Women: Portraits from the American Radical Tradition*. New York: Viking Press.

Oakley, Mary Ann. 1972. *Elizabeth Cady Stanton*. New York: The Feminist Press.

Rendall, Jane. 1985. *The Origins of Modern Feminism: Women in Britain, France, and the United States 1780–1860*. Chicago: University of Chicago Press.

Spender, Dale. 1982. *Women of Ideas, and What Men Have Done to Them*. London: Routledge and Kegan Paul.

Stanton, Elizabeth Cady. 1993a [1898]. *Eighty Years and More: Reminiscences, 1815–1897*. Reprint, Boston: Northeastern University Press.

———. 1993b [1895, 1898]. *The Woman's Bible*. Reprint, Boston: Northeastern University Press.

Stanton, Theodore, and Harriet Stanton Blatch, eds. 1922. *Elizabeth Cady Stanton as Revealed in Her Letters, Diary and Reminiscences*. 2 vols. New York: Arno Press.

Ward, Geoffrey C., and Ken Burns. 1999. *Not for Ourselves Alone: The Story of Elizabeth Cady Stanton and Susan B. Anthony, an Illustrated History*. New York: Alfred A. Knopf.

Watkins, Susan Alice, Marisa Rueda, and Marta Rodriguez. 1999. *Introducing Feminism*. Duxford, UK: Icon Books.

Starovoitova, Galina
(1946–1998)
Russia

The assassination of Galina Starovoitova, who was looked upon as one of Russia's leading human rights campaigners and the last of a dying breed of incorruptible politicians, was a tremendous blow to hopes for a better, more democratic political climate in post-Soviet Russia. Throughout seventy years or more of communist rule, which never once saw a female member of the Politburo, outstanding women politicians (aside, perhaps, from Alexandra Kollontai) were a rarity. And Starovoitova was a woman who was never afraid to voice her views, no matter how outspoken, ever since she first openly protested the Soviet breach of civil rights in its invasion of Czechoslovakia in 1968.

Galina Starovoitova grew up in the Urals. Although her parents were members of the Communist Party, they taught her and her sister always to be skeptical about Soviet politics. After studying engineering, she transferred to social psychology and anthropology at Leningrad University. A highly intelligent and gifted woman, she could no doubt have looked forward to a long career as an eminent intellectual tucked away in the security of the Soviet Academy of

Galina Starovoitova (AP/Wide World Photos)

Sciences, where she worked for seventeen years. But Starovoitova became deeply involved in human rights, through her friendship with the distinguished scientist and dissident, Andrey Sakharov, whom she met in the mid-1980s.

Starovoitova's subsequent move into politics was partly a natural progression stemming from her deeply held belief in democracy (she never joined the Communist Party). In addition, her work as an ethnographer led her to take an interest in Soviet minority groups and to support their right to self-determination. In the late 1980s she was drawn into the bitter struggle of Christian Armenians living in the enclave of Nagorno-Karabakh in Azerbaijan, who were seeking their own political autonomy after having been forcibly incorporated into that Soviet republic under Joseph Stalin in 1936. After writing a letter to the government in support of their cause, Starovoitova became something of a heroine overnight and was asked to represent this group in elections to the Congress of People's Deputies. She took her seat in 1989 as the representative of an Armenian constituency. And once

inside Congress, she vigorously pursued her support for minority interests as a member of its human rights commission, at a time when ethnic unrest was bubbling to the surface across the Soviet Union. Starovoitova was one of several politicians who urged President Mikhail Gorbachev to defuse Russia's deepening nationalities problem by creating a voluntary commonwealth along the lines of that created by Britain.

In 1990 Starovoitova was elected to the Russian parliament as an independent candidate representing a constituency in St. Petersburg. She aligned herself with other independents in Boris Yeltsin's Interregional Group of People's Deputies. After the failed coup of August 1991 and the departure of Gorbachev, Starovoitova worked closely with Boris Yeltsin as one of his main advisers on national and ethnic issues. But in 1992 he sacked her for criticizing his policy over ethnic clashes in the northern Caucasus, when she took exception to his preferential support for the Ossetians against the Ingush.

Her action resulted in Starovoitova's political sidelining for the next three years—even more so after she took a strong moral line in 1994 on the ordering of Russian troops into Chechnya by Yeltsin. Meanwhile, she spent her time working and lecturing in the United States and the United Kingdom. In the United States she was a senior fellow at the U.S. Institute of Peace during 1993–1994—an institution dedicated to promoting the peaceful resolution of world conflicts. In 1995 she was Thomas J. Watson visiting scholar at Brown University. Thanks to her superb command of English, Starovoitova fast developed a reputation while in the West as one of the foremost media pundits on the changing Russian political scene. Late in 1995 she returned to Russia to take part in the December elections to the State Duma, where she won a seat, again representing a St. Petersburg constituency. By that time, Russian politics was rapidly disintegrating into a discordant, multiparty system, with even the democratic group succumbing to bitter infighting. Yeltsin's popularity was plummeting, and he began to regret the loss of Starovoitova's support, but she herself stood apart from the political bickering and continued to build a solid reputation as a liberal democrat, with her social concerns remaining uppermost. More and more she was speaking out against the growing domination of the Russian State Duma by nationalists and the ominous revival in Russia of anti-Semitism and fascism. She warned that after Yeltsin, if the precarious state of Russian democracy was not defended, the country was likely to slip back into either a fascist or communist-style dictatorship. Indeed, in the last few weeks of her life Starovoitova had been investigating the activities of the spurious Academy of National Security, an organization that she suspected of being rife with corruption and linked to organized crime. She had also been campaigning to put a legal stop to the anti-Semitic and ultranationalistic activities of General Albert Makashov, a leading light in the revived and increasingly xenophobic Communist Party.

At the time of her death, Starovoitova had mooted the idea of running for governor of the Leningrad region and stated her intention to stand in the presidential elections in 2000, both of which had offered new hope to many ordinary Russians who had become deeply cynical about Russia's political system. It is also known that she was planning to reveal to the Russian Duma the contents of a dossier she had been secretly com-

piling on the alleged corruption of senior Communist Party politicians. She was undoubtedly a marked woman; one piece of hate mail addressed to her had insinuated that in Stalin's time she would have been "strung up," and death threats were certainly nothing new to her. When she became the seventh deputy to be murdered in Russia since 1991, her own son, Platon Borshchevskiy, when asked to comment upon her assassination, declared that it was "utterly predictable" in light of her outspoken condemnation of right-wing extremism.

Galina Starovoitova was murdered on the staircase of her own apartment block on 20 November 1998 by two attackers—one of them a woman—using submachine guns. While her body lay in state in the Museum of Ethnography before burial at the historic Alexander Nevskiy Monastery, St. Petersburg witnessed an outpouring of popular grief not seen since the days of compulsory mass mourning for deceased political leaders. But this time the 20,000 people who patiently queued in subzero temperatures to pay their last respects were there, as ordinary citizens, to express their despair at the loss of a woman whom Boris Yeltsin himself had called "a passionate tribune of democracy."

A Galina Starovoitova Fellowship on Human Rights and Conflict Resolution has now been established by the Kennan Institute of the Woodrow Wilson Center in memory of Starovoitova, who was a visiting scholar there in 1989. For links to this and a wealth of website material on Starovoitova's politics, her life, and the circumstances of her violent death, in English and in Russian, contact Elena Leonoff's comprehensive site at www.geocities.com/Athens/2533/galina.

See also Bonner, Yelena.

References and Further Reading

Entry compiled primarily from obituaries in *The Times, Guardian, Daily Telegraph* and *Independent*, c. 20 November 1998.

McCauley, Martin. 1997. *Who's Who in Russia since 1900.* London: Routledge.

Uglow, Jennifer, ed. 1998 [1982]. *Macmillan Dictionary of Women's Biography.* Rev. ed. London: Macmillan.

Stasova, Nadezhda
(1822–1895)
Russia

Born into the Russian nobility at Tsarskoe Selo, the location of the Catherine Palace and the summer home of the czars, the Russian feminist and philanthropist Nadezhda Stasova was the daughter of one of Alexander I's court architects. Indeed, the czar was one of her godparents. She was given the usual unchallenging education at home but with her sisters secretly read works of romantic literature by Lord Byron, Alexander Pushkin, Heinrich Heine, and George Sand.

The impressionable young Stasova fell hopelessly in love but suffered a nervous breakdown after being deserted by her fiancé. She nursed her only sister Sonya through a long and incurable disease, spending much time abroad until 1858. Her profound sense of loss had by then prompted a growing concern for the welfare of the less fortunate, and the impetus for a lifetime's dedication to philanthropic work came after she met Mariya Trubnikova on her return to Russia. Stasova would never marry; she channeled all her love into what she viewed as the "universal family."

After joining forces with Mariya Trubnikova and Anna Filosova in 1859 to found the Society for Cheap Lodgings and Other Benefits for the Citizens of St. Petersburg, she worked to provide clean and sanitary affordable accommodation for destitute women and also offer them employment. In 1860 Stasova, inspired by the Sunday school movement in Europe, founded a women's Sunday school, which offered lessons in reading and writing to fifteen women ages twelve to thirty, most of them factory and shop girls. After the government closed down the Sunday Schools in 1862 (some 500 now having been established in Russia), Stasova's experiences reinforced her determination to seek better educational opportunities for women.

Meanwhile, Stasova lent her services to health care by joining the philanthropist-aristocrat Princess Dondukova-Korsava in her work running a shelter for prostitutes suffering from venereal disease. She visited sick women in the Kalinskaya Hospital for Prostitutes and organized sewing and reading classes as part of the social and moral rehabilitation of fallen women. She was shocked by the grim reality of hearing a mother remark on her daughter selling herself for as little as 50 kopecks to help feed the family (Stites 1991, 62).

Her love of literature and her desire to see women have greater access to it attracted Stasova to another new group in 1864, a women's publishing and translating cooperative. It was established by Anna and Alexander Engelhardt as a collective, not only to provide work for educated but impoverished women and aid them in becoming successful writers but also to produce suitable literature for the young as well as provide employment for women in printing and binding. One hundred women joined the collective and selected by ballot the works to be published, which included tales by Hans Christian Andersen, Louisa May Alcott, and some scientific and historical works. An official publishing firm was established in 1868 by Stasova and Trubnikova, but domestic problems forced both women to abandon the venture a year later, and the collective disintegrated.

In 1867 Stasova joined with Trubnikova in petitioning for women's higher education courses to be established at Russian universities. By this time, Stasova was beginning to comprehend the sheer numbers of working-class women longing for a better education and had opened her own home to women who wished to come and hear informal lectures given by lecturers sympathetic to the cause. Stasova also accompanied social reformer Anna Filosova on a personal mission to persuade the education minister, Count Dmitriy Tolstoy, to implement education reform, but a lack of progress in this area caused women to turn to more radical means of campaigning. Eventually, in 1869, the government allowed the first public lectures for women in St. Petersburg and Moscow, which gave women their first chance to study subjects such as chemistry, history, anatomy, zoology, and Russian literature.

Stasova was eventually appointed chair of the pedagogical council that organized the advanced courses for women, known as the Bestuzhev courses, that were introduced in St. Petersburg in 1878. But the noisy and radical element among the young students proved disruptive and attracted criticism; for her part, Stasova was accused of inefficiency and muddleheadedness by the authorities and was removed from her post.

In 1883 Stasova, Filosova, and Trubnikova founded the Society to Provide Means of Support for the Higher Women's Courses, which raised funds among the St. Petersburg elite to support needy students and also awarded scholarships. By 1886 this philanthropic society had more than 1,000 sponsors and a grant for its work from the Ministry of Education.

The final and most famous act of Stasova and her colleagues Trubnikova and Filosova—who would be immortalized in Russian feminist history as "the triumvirate"—was the founding in 1895 of the Russian Women's Mutual Philanthropic Society (RWMPS). As its name suggests, its objective was to engage in nonpolitical philanthropic work and it set out to promote educational reform, welfare for the poor, and the campaign against legalized prostitution by peaceful means such as petitioning and lobbying of officials. It left the campaign for suffrage to other organizations until the upheavals of 1905 brought with them hopes of constitutional reform and women's suffrage. By that time, the RWMPS enjoyed some successes under the leadership of Anna Shabanova (who replaced Stasova after her death in 1895), but its endorsement of only a limited form of women's suffrage tied to property ownership guaranteed that it would never win the support of working women.

See also Filosova, Anna; Sand, George; Shabanova, Anna; Trubnikova, Mariya.

References and Further Reading

Porter, Cathy. 1976. *Fathers and Daughters: Russian Women in Revolution.* London: Virago.

Stites, Richard. 1991. *The Women's Liberation Movement in Russia: Feminism, Nihilism, and Bolshevism, 1860–1930.* Reprint, Princeton: Princeton University Press.

Steinem, Gloria
(1934–)
United States

A leading figure in the second wave of U.S. feminism, Gloria Steinem was famous for her wit and incisive commentaries on women's rights, her invention of the neutral term *Ms.* for single women, and her critiques of the family and gender roles. In her day, she defined the radical overturning of society effected by the women's liberation movement of the 1970s when she pronounced the end of traditional patriarchy: "A woman without a man," she asserted, "is like a fish without a bicycle." In later years, with her well-groomed, even glamorous appearance often seen to be at odds with the widespread rejection of that image by the mainstream of the women's movement, she was accused of having sold out as a latter-day "lipstick feminist." At the age of sixty-six, she surprised critics and supporters alike by doing the one thing that she had for long vehemently opposed—getting married.

Born in Toledo, Ohio, into a family whose fortunes had declined during the Great Depression, Steinem grew up in trailer parks, and her early schooling was sporadic. During her teens, after her parents separated, she spent much time nursing her sick mother, who suffered from mental illness. In 1952 she entered Smith College to study government and after graduating in 1956 went to India, where she spent two years at Delhi and Calcutta Universities on a Chester Bowles Research Fellowship. During her two-year stay, which she further funded by writing newspaper articles on India, Steinem associated with a radical humanist group active during a period of unrest in southern India. There she was greatly influenced by the nonviolent tradition of popular protest fostered by Mahatma Gandhi. Returning to the United States in 1958, she set up her own research service in Cambridge, Massachusetts.

In 1960 she became a freelance journalist in New York, writing on the growing sexual revolution for magazines such as *Esquire, Vogue,* and *Cosmopolitan.* In 1963 she attracted attention with a powerful exposé of the sexual exploitation of women, "I Was a Playboy Bunny," which was published in *Show* magazine after she had worked undercover in one of Hugh Hefner's Playboy clubs. In 1964–1965 she worked as a scriptwriter for the satirical NBC-TV show *That Was the Week That Was.*

Steinem was drawn into radical protest from the mid-1960s, especially demonstrations against the Vietnam War and civil rights marches, and in 1968 started a political column for *New York* magazine entitled "The City Politic," in which she published powerful articles on civil rights, such as the 1968 article "Black Power, Women's Liberation." Having being introduced to feminist issues in 1968 at a meeting of the radical feminist organization Redstockings, she announced her conversion to feminism and gave much time to radical causes. In the following years, she appeared on TV talk shows and the lecture circuit, served as treasurer of the Committee for the Legal Defense of Angela Davis, and became an advocate of the unionization of migrant Chicano workers through Cesar Chavez and Dolores Huerta's United Farm Workers. She was a supporter of the Democratic politicians George McGovern and Robert F. Kennedy and worked for the latter's campaign for the presidency.

By the end of the 1960s, however, Steinem felt the time had come for women to set up their own political groups to fight sexism and campaign on issues such as women's right to have abortions. In 1971 she joined with Betty Friedan and others in founding the National Women's Political Caucus, dedicated to fighting for women's equality and encouraging women to enter politics. She was also a founder in 1970 of the Women's Action Alliance, which sought to mobilize support at the grassroots level among workers and nonwhites for campaigns against racial and economic discrimination.

In January 1972, with Patricia Carbine, Steinem founded the pioneering feminist magazine *Ms.* It had originally appeared as a supplement to the December 1971 issue of *New York* magazine but overnight became an important forum for debate on women's issues, such as child care, lesbianism, abortion, women's legal rights, divorce, and the continuing fight for passage of the Equal Rights Amendment in Congress. In a noteworthy early issue, Steinem was one of fifty prominent American women who freely admitted to having had abortions (in her case, in 1956). Within a year, *Ms.* had 350,000 subscribers and achieved a mass circulation enabling it to become an independent publication, much admired, criticized, and imitated in the years to come, for fifteen of them under Steinem's editorship. The magazine was eventually sold in 1987, but in response to popular demand was revamped and reissued (as a nonprofit publication without advertisements) from 1990, with Steinem as a consultant.

Remaining highly critical of the fact that the labor of so many women in the home went unpaid and uncredited and arguing for men to take an equal responsibility for the rearing of their children, Steinem vigorously lobbied for the passing of the Equal Rights Amendment from 1972, until it finally failed to be ratified by its deadline in 1982. Meanwhile, she had lent her support to other organizations, such as the National Organization for Women, the Coalition of Labor Union Women, Voters for Choice, and Women Against Pornography. After years of tough campaigning by the women's movement, Steinem remarked on its achievements with wry humor in a speech at Yale University in September 1981: "Some of us are becoming the men we wanted to marry." Meanwhile, she had also established, under the aegis of *Ms.,* a new organization, the *Ms.* Foundation for Women, which funds training, health and safety, and public education projects and has the objective of extending economic opportunities for women and girls of all races.

Steinem's published works include *A Thousand Indias* (1957); a collection of essays, *Outrageous Acts and Everyday Rebellions* (1983); *Marilyn,* a controversial study of Marilyn Monroe (1986); a personal, psychological memoir–cum–self-help manual, *Revolution from Within: A Book of Self-Esteem* (1992); and *Moving beyond Words* (1994).

Although sometimes belittled as the bourgeois or "glamorous" face of the feminist movement and dismissed as a political lightweight, Steinem has retained her humor and her dignity through breast cancer and into middle age. In 2000 the press had a field day over her marriage to a rich businessman, David Bale, with feminist Camille Paglia condemning the marriage as "proof of the emotional desperation of aging feminists who for over 30 years worshipped the steely career woman and trashed stay-at-home moms" (*Time,* 18 September 2000). Steinem's old friends, such as the sexologist Shere Hite, have pointed out, however, that her action is in itself a reflection of the achievements of the women's rights movement and that if feminists now choose to marry, it is because of the improved rights that women such as Steinem have fought for since the late 1960s. For further information on the *Ms.* Foundation for Women, go to http://www.ms.foundation.org/.

See also Friedan, Betty; Huerta, Dolores.

References and Further Reading

Current Biography. 1988. New York: H. W. Wilson.

Daffron, Carolyn. 1987. *Gloria Steinem.* New York: Chelsea House.

Davidson, Cathy N., and Linda Wagner Martin, eds. 1995. *Oxford Companion to Women's Writing in the United States.* Oxford: Oxford University Press.

Heilbrun, Carolyn G. 1996. *The Education of a Woman: The Life of Gloria Steinem.* New York: Ballantine Books.

Henry, Sondra. 1987. *One Woman's Power: A Biography of Gloria Steinem*. Minneapolis: Dillon Press.

Lazo, Caroline Evensen. 1998. *Gloria Steinem: Feminist Extraordinaire*. Minneapolis: Lerner Publications.

Mitchell, Susan. 1997. *Icons, Saints & Divas: Intimate Conversations with Women Who Changed the World*. London: Pandora.

Wheaton, Elizabeth. 2001. *MS: The Story of Gloria Steinem*. Greensboro, NC: Morgan Reynolds.

Stöcker, Helene
(1869–1943)
Germany

A lifelong supporter of sexual freedom and the rights of unmarried mothers and their children, Helene Stöcker never affiliated herself with a political party and worked independently for reform of traditional attitudes toward women's sexuality and the establishment of a new morality. Much of her work and her theories on free love alienated her from the mainstream of the largely conservative German women's movement. Her pioneering of the legal protection of the rights of illegitimate children and unmarried mothers and campaigning for the decriminalization of abortion, together with her theoretical writings on women's rights to self-determination and sexual freedom, had a lasting influence on sexual ethics in Germany.

Born in Elberfeld, in southern Germany, the eldest of eight daughters, Stöcker was determined to continue her education. She broke away from her strict Calvinist upbringing, rejected her religion, and in 1892 went to Berlin to train as a teacher, being one of the first women to enter the University of Berlin in 1896. After graduating, she worked as a research assistant to the philosopher Wilhelm Dilthey. A brief relationship with a German professor took her to Glasgow for a year, after which Stöcker returned to Europe to study at Berne for a doctorate on eighteenth-century German literature and aesthetics. She then traveled in Romania and Russia, as well as lecturing, writing, and becoming active in several women's organizations.

In the 1890s Stöcker began working with the feminist Minna Cauer in the radical wing of the movement for women's education and also in Cauer's Commercial Union of Female Salaried Employees. She wrote for radical journals on women's right to education and financial independence and was active in the Berlin Women's League and the movement for the abolition of state prostitution. Her interest was also captured by the ideas of Friedrich Nietzsche. Although she disliked his antifeminism, Stöcker supported Nietzsche's ideas on the assertion of the individual, women's need for spiritual independence, and the power of love. She also endorsed his call for a higher code of ethics than that perpetuated by traditional bourgeois society. She believed marriage prevented women from achieving self-fulfillment; she wanted them to break out of their narrow bourgeois existences and strive for higher education and a role in the professions.

In sexual matters, Stöcker developed her own "new morality." Having no belief in women's natural chastity, her support for female sexual permissiveness, free love, and birth control led to quarrels with moderate women within the feminist movement, which prompted Stöcker to join the League for the Protection of Motherhood and Sexual Reform (LPMSR), a group founded by Ruth Bré along utopian lines, in Leipzig in November 1904. The league was quickly taken over by a more forceful group, including Stöcker, Lily Braun, and Marie Stritt, and branches were established across Germany (ten by 1908) to offer counseling, promote welfare legislation, and petition for state benefits for unmarried mothers. Stöcker also emphasized women's right to sexual fulfillment, but by arguing for radical reform of sexual ethics and the legal recognition of sexual relations between unmarried couples, she invited criticism from right-wing feminists such as Helene Lange, who believed that such views encouraged sexual anarchy. Stöcker also set herself apart from other German feminists by supporting the rights of women to remain single and pursue professional lives, arguing that their sole role in life need not necessarily be motherhood. She believed it was essential that mothers were economically independent and protected by extensive maternity insurance.

In 1906 Stöcker published a collection of essays, *Love and Women,* in which she saw sexual love as liberating and the true basis to a higher form of marriage. She joined with Stritt in a 1908 campaign for the repeal of Section 218 of the civil code and the legalization of abortion. Together they persuaded the legal commission of the Federation of German Women's Associations to publicly support this campaign, but in 1910 the predominately right-wing membership rejected this proposal, refused the LPMSR membership in the federation, and dissociated itself from its position on sexual liberation.

Disagreements within the league over this issue and others also brought about an internal crisis, and in 1910–1912 Stöcker's colleague Adele Schreiber resigned, as did Lily Braun and other members unable to accept Stöcker's more radical views. Stöcker herself was vilified for cohabiting with the lawyer Bruno Springer. Although flagship maternity homes had been opened by the league in Frankfurt (1907) and Stuttgart (1909), these accomplishments could not counterbalance the damage done, in the public eye, by Stöcker's personal reputation as a free love advocate.

Throughout World War I Stöcker, who despised German militarism, worked as a radical pacifist, seeking to imbue the movement with the feminine values that she felt were crucial to a lasting peace. She became a leading figure in the pacifist movement, like her compatriots Lida Gustava Heymann and Anita Augspurg, finding herself at odds with the majority of German women's organizations, which became fiercely patriotic. In 1915 she joined Heymann and Augspurg at the international women's peace congress in The Hague and the following year cofounded the Center for International Law, which criticized the terms of the Brest-Litovsk peace treaty ending Germany's war with Russia in 1917.

After the war, Stöcker remained a radical campaigner for world peace, attending numerous conferences despite her failing health and becoming a member of various pacifist organizations: the German Peace Cartel, the German Peace Society, War Resisters International (which she cofounded in 1921), and the Federation for a New Fatherland. She would also support Mahatma Gandhi's nonviolent protest movement in India. During the 1920s, she was chair of the German section of the Women's International League for Peace and Freedom, calling on trade unions and pacifist groups to mount general strikes against any government seeking to mobilize for war. She joined the Pacifist Syndicate of the Left, which advocated total resistance to militarism and national service, in 1926. During the 1930s, Stöcker tried and failed to revive the

League for the Protection of Motherhood and Sexual Reform and turned to writing, editing the magazine *The New Generation* "to make human sexuality a powerful instrument not only of reproduction, but of progressive evolution, and concurrently of a heightened and cultivated joy" (Smith 1989, 429). As a believer that sexual freedom would reduce prostitution and the incidence of venereal disease rather than encourage promiscuity, Stöcker was drawn into the eugenics debate. She was convinced that the whole of the human race needed to improve the physical and intellectual quality of its children in order to achieve social progress and supported compulsory sterilization of those deemed physically and mentally "unfit."

In 1933, after a series of heart attacks, Stöcker was sent to a Czech clinic. After the 1933 burning of the Reichstag, her papers were seized and destroyed by the Nazis. She lived in Switzerland until 1938, continuing to work for the pacifist movement, and then traveled for two years, visiting Sweden, the Soviet Union, Japan, and the United States. Arriving in California in 1941, but by then terminally ill with cancer, she died in Manhattan two years later.

See also Augspurg, Anita; Braun, Lily; Cauer, Minna; Heymann, Lida Gustava; Schreiber, Adele; Stritt, Marie.

References and Further Reading

Allen, Ann Taylor. 1985. "Mothers of the New Generation: Adele Schreiber, Helene Stöcker, and the Evolution of a German Idea of Motherhood, 1900–1914." *Signs* 10(3): 418–438.

———. 1989. "German Radical Feminism and Eugenics, 1900–1918." *German Studies Review* 2: 31–56.

Braker, Regina. 1995. "Bertha von Suttner's Spiritual Daughters: The Feminist Pacifism of Anita Augspurg, Lida Gustava Heymann, and Helene Stöcker at the International Congress of Women at The Hague, 1915." *Women's Studies International Forum* 18(2): 103–111.

Bridenthal, Renate, Atina Grossman, and Marion Kaplan, eds. 1984. *When Biology Became Destiny: Women in Weimar and Nazi Germany.* New York: Monthly Review Press.

Deak, Istvan. 1968. *Weimar Germany's Left-wing Intellectuals: A Political History of the Weltbühne and Its Circle.* Berkeley: University of California Press.

Evans, Richard. 1973. *The Feminist Movement in Germany 1894–1933.* London: Sage.

Josephson, Harold, Sandi Cooper, and Steven C. Hause et al., eds. 1985. *Biographical Dictionary of Modern Peace Leaders.* Westport, CT: Greenwood Press.

O'Barr, Jean F., Deborah Pope, and Mary Wyer. 1990. *Ties That Bind: Essays on Mothering and Patriarchy.* Chicago: University of Illinois Press.

Sklar, Kathryn Kish. 1998. *Social Justice Feminists in the United States and Germany: A Dialogue in Documents 1885–1933.* Ithaca: Cornell University Press.

Smith, Bonnie G. 1989. *Changing Lives: Women in European History since 1700.* Lexington, MA: D. C. Heath.

Stone, Lucy
(1818–1893)
United States

A member of the eminent Blackwell family, Lucy Stone was a dignified campaigner for women's equality and a fine orator, like her sister-in-law Antoinette Brown Blackwell. She led the moderate suffrage group the American Woman Suffrage Association (AWSA), formed in reaction to the establishment of the National Woman Suffrage Association (NWSA) by Susan B. Anthony and Elizabeth Cady Stanton in 1869. Stone retained her own name after marriage and, although recognizing the benefits of having an enlightened partner, was nevertheless unequivocal in her belief that "marriage is to woman a state of slavery" (Rendall 1985, 305).

Stone grew up on a farm in West Brookfield, Massachusetts, where she helped herd the cows at the age of eight and developed a sense of the injustice of women's inferior position to men. She was forced to undertake her own education when her strict father refused to give her funds to attend college as he had her brothers. Objecting to her belittlement as a woman, she took work as a schoolteacher from the age of sixteen for $1 a week, using the money to study at various schools, including Mount Holyoke Female Seminary.

After working and saving for nine years, Stone had enough money only to study for one term at the first coeducational, mixed-race establishment in the United States, Oberlin College in Ohio. During her time there from 1843 to 1847, Stone worked to pay her way, teaching for two hours a day and doing domestic chores. There she found a friend and fellow advocate of women's rights in Antoinette Brown Blackwell, who joined the school in 1845 and encouraged Stone's interest in debate. However, as soon as the two women joined in debates with male students, they were banned from doing so again.

After her graduation in 1847, Stone gave her first speech on women's rights, from the pulpit of her brother's church. She had been an admirer of the abolitionist work of the Grimké sisters since her childhood, and in 1848 she became an agent of the Massachusetts Anti-Slavery Society. As a touring lecturer, traveling alone across many states, Stone fought to be allowed to devote some of her time lecturing to speaking on women's issues, arguing: "I was a woman before I was an abolitionist. I must speak for the women" (Sicherman and Green 1980, 388). Stone's physical demeanor on the podium belied her toughness as a gifted speaker. This she demonstrated in memorable speeches such as "The Social and Industrial Disabilities of Woman," "Legal and Political Disabilities," and "Moral and Religious Disabilities," all containing subject matter guaranteed to provoke an antagonistic and often aggressive response in audiences.

The passion of Stone's belief in women's rights came across particularly strongly in "Disappointment Is the Lot of Women" (1855), in which she averred that since women were forever being disappointed in their attempts to take their equal place "in education, in marriage, in religion," she had resolved that "it shall be the business of my life to deepen this disappointment in every woman's heart until she bows down to it no longer" (Stanton et al. 1881, 165). Beginning in 1853, Stone was courted by the abolitionist Henry Blackwell, whom she married in 1855 after making a private agreement with him to hold their property separately. Stone was also adamant that she retain her maiden name, an act that soon became widespread public knowledge and caused her much difficulty over the years. But no amount of hostility or intimidation or criticism would make her relent on this point: she considered it morally wrong to give up her maiden name, for to do so, she felt, would be tacitly acquiescing to her own subjugation in marriage. This decision, Leslie Wheeler argues, "marked the outermost limits of her feminist protest" (1983, 124); nevertheless, it provoked unwarranted accusations that Stone also advocated free love.

Stone lived in New Jersey and continued lec-

Lucy Stone (Library of Congress)

turing until after the birth of her only child, Alice (Stone Blackwell), in 1857. But combining motherhood with such commitments pushed her nearly to the point of breakdown. In 1858, in an act of defiance similar to that made by Abby Kelley Foster, Stone made a feminist stand on "no taxation without representation" when she refused, as an unenfranchised woman, to pay her property tax. Her household possessions were confiscated and sold but were soon after bought back and restored to her by a sympathetic neighbor.

Although no longer lecturing, Stone continued to give moral support to women's fight for economic independence and their right to pursue a professional career. In the belief that women would achieve equality with men earlier if given greater access to coeducation, she sent her own daughter to the progressive, coeducational Chauncy Hall School in Boston. Stone also supported the protection of women's health through birth control, although this belief was largely negated by her support for the Comstock Act of 1873 (which prohibited the sending of literature on birth control and sex education through the post) as part of the gathering social purity campaign. Similarly, in 1860, when Stone attended a national women's rights convention during

which the issue of marriage was vigorously debated at the instigation of Elizabeth Cady Stanton, Stone felt it was inappropriate to discuss such a topic so publicly, preferring that Stanton discuss marriage at a separate convention. Yet on the issue of her use of her maiden name, Stone retained a radically adamant but dignified tone, frequently finding herself obliged to sign documents as "Lucy Stone, wife of Henry Blackwell," determined not to jeopardize the cause of suffrage by taking a public stand against her critics (Wheeler 1983, 131). During the Civil War, Stone, like many other women activists, joined the Woman's National Loyal League in lobbying for the Thirteenth Amendment, which would abolish slavery. In 1866 she became a member of the American Equal Rights Association, which was dedicated to the emancipation of both women and blacks.

Resuming her work for women's suffrage through the New Jersey Woman Suffrage Association, in 1868 Stone also became an executive member of the New England Woman Suffrage Association. In 1869 Stone joined the executive of the American Woman Suffrage Association, a moderate group that differed on fundamental aspects of policy with the NWSA and favored the gradualist approach of working almost exclusively for the award of women's suffrage on a state-by-state basis. Stone was dismayed by the new divisiveness in the movement and continued to seek social justice through her own brand of Christian morality, in the hope of attracting a broader base of female and male support for women's suffrage. In January 1870, with Mary Livermore, she raised the money to found what would be the most influential women's rights publication in the United States, lasting until 1931, the *Woman's Journal*. Stone edited it until 1893, in addition to numerous "Woman Suffrage Leaflets" produced by the journal.

Becoming increasingly conservative in later life, Stone kept out of the political limelight and avoided controversy, chairing the executive committee of the newly amalgamated National American Woman Suffrage Association when the two rival suffrage organizations united in 1890. Stone gave her final public lecture to the World's Columbian Exposition at Chicago in 1893. Although a huge crowd turned out for her funeral, Stone was later eclipsed in the histories of women's suffrage by the more forceful and high-profile figures of Stanton and Anthony (who minimized mention of Stone in their own *History of Woman Suffrage*). Many of her speeches, given extemporaneously, did not survive, although her ideas speak loud and strong in her numerous articles and editorials for the *Woman's Journal*. After Stone's death, her daughter Alice edited the journal and also published a biography of her mother.

See also Blackwell, Alice Stone; Blackwell, Antoinette Brown; Foster, Abby (Abigail) Kelley; Grimké, Angelina Emily and Sarah Moore; Livermore, Mary; Stanton, Elizabeth Cady.

References and Further Reading
Banks, Olive. 1990 [1981]. *Faces of Feminism: A Study of Feminism as a Social Movement*. Reprint, Oxford: Blackwell.
Blackwell, Alice Stone. 1930. *Lucy Stone, Pioneer of Women's Rights*. Boston: Little, Brown.
Bolton, Sandra Knowles. 1895. *Famous Leaders among Women*. New York: Thomas Y. Crowell.
DuBois, Ellen. 1978. *Feminism and Suffrage: The Emergence of the Independent Women's Movement in America 1848–1869*. Ithaca: Cornell University Press.
Flexner, Eleanor. 1975 [1959]. *A Century of Struggle: The Woman's Rights Movement in the United States*. Rev. ed. Cambridge, MA: Belknap Press of Harvard University.
Hays, Elinor Rice. 1961. *Morning Star: A Biography of Lucy Stone*. New York: Harcourt, Brace and World.
Kerr, Andrea Moore. 1992. *Lucy Stone: Speaking Out for Equality*. New Brunswick, NJ: Rutgers University Press.
Kraditor, Aileen. 1981 [1965]. *The Ideas of the Woman Suffrage Movement 1890–1920*. Reprint, New York: W. W. Norton.
Lasser, Carol, and Marlene Deal, eds. 1987. *Letters between Lucy Stone and Antoinette Brown Blackwell, 1846–93*. Urbana: University of Illinois Press.
Melder, Keith E. 1977. *The Beginnings of Sisterhood: The American Woman's Rights Movement, 1800–1850*. New York: Schocken.
Rendall, Jane. 1985. *The Origins of Modern Feminism: Women in Britain, France, and the United States 1780–1860*. Chicago: University of Chicago Press.
Sicherman, Barbara, and Carol Hurd Green, eds. *Notable American Women 1607–1950: A Biographical Dictionary*. Cambridge, MA: Belknap Press of Harvard University.
Spender, Dale. 1982. *Women of Ideas, and What Men Have Done to Them*. London: Routledge and Kegan Paul.
Stannard, Una. 1977. *Mrs. Man*. San Francisco: Germaine Books.
Stanton, Elizabeth Cady, Susan B. Anthony, and Matilda Joslyn Gage, eds. 1881. *History of Woman Suffrage*. Vol 1. New York: Fowler and Wells.
Wheeler, Leslie. 1981. *Loving Warriors: Selected Letters of Lucy Stone and Henry B. Blackwell, 1853–1893*. New York: Dial Press.
———. 1983. "Lucy Stone: Radical Beginnings." In Dale Spender, ed., *Feminist Theorists: Three Centuries of Women's Intellectual Traditions*. London: Women's Press.

Stopes, Marie
(1880–1958)
United Kingdom

In the years separating the twentieth century's two world wars, the issue of birth control would preoccupy many feminists. In both the United States and United Kingdom, the movements that sprang up there were dominated by forceful, controversial figures: in the former by Margaret Sanger and in the latter by Marie Stopes. As the founder of the first birth control movement in Britain, Stopes was not the first woman to offer contraceptive advice—Sanger had done so before her, and they had both been preempted by the work in the Netherlands of Aletta Jacobs, who opened the world's first birth control clinic in Amsterdam in 1882, and in 1879 Annie Besant had written the first birth control pamphlet by a woman, "The Laws of Population: Its Consequences and Its Bearing upon Human Conduct and Morals." But despite the bad press she often attracted with her propensity for self-dramatization and her many personal idiosyncrasies, Marie Stopes was fearless and unstoppable in her drive not only to make the issue of contraception respectable in Britain and later worldwide but also in her mission to help women achieve sexual fulfillment and control over their own fertility. In her pioneering writings, Stopes liberated the subject of sexual pleasure from what fellow birth control advocate Dora Russell has described as "the aura of rubber-good shops and sniggering" (1975, 170).

Stopes was born in Edinburgh, but grew up in London, where she was educated at home by governesses until the age of twelve. Her mother, herself a suffragist and one of the first women to study at a university (in Edinburgh), was an important influence in her early years, and Stopes later became a member of the suffrage group the Women's Freedom League. After boarding at St. George's School in Edinburgh and attending

North London Collegiate School for Ladies, Stopes entered University College in London to study for a degree in geology, geography, and botany. Receiving her degree in 1902, she took a doctorate in botany at Munich University (1904), again specializing in fossilized plants. Now one of the first trained female palaeobotanists in Britain, in 1905 she took up a lectureship in science at University College in London.

In 1907 Stopes went on a fossil-hunting tour in Japan, based at the Imperial University in Tokyo, where she also did some lecturing. On a similar trip to Canada, she met Reginald Gates, whom she married in 1911. The couple settled in London, where Stopes returned to lecturing at University College (1913–1920), becoming a fellow and publishing her *Catalogue of Cretaceous Flora* (2 vols., 1913–1915).

Puzzled by her lack of success in getting pregnant, Stopes, at age thirty-one, began addressing her own sexual ignorance by reading medical texts. Claiming that her marriage had never been properly consummated but unable to sue for divorce, she had to wait until 1916 for an annulment. As a result of her own frustrating sexual experiences, she began to investigate marital discord provoked by lack of sexual knowledge and, mindful of the hardships encountered in large working-class families where the parents had no knowledge of effective methods of birth control, sought to promote sex education. She wrote her pioneering book *Married Love* (1918) out of a fervent desire to make marriages happier and more fulfilling for women. After some difficulty finding a publisher, the book, in the words of Mary Stocks, "broke the silence barrier which shrouded that subject [sex] with a reverberating supersonic bang" (Stocks 1970, 124). Critics were quick to condemn its frank discussion of contraception without taking into account Stopes's eloquent and sometimes poetic appeal for sexual relations within marriage to be viewed from their emotional and spiritual, not just reproductive, angles. Hers was one of the first works to offer an alternative to the dry and detached writing on sexuality by the medical establishment and neo-Malthusian proponents of social and economic control of the population. Stopes's book initiated a new era of openness about sex and a discussion of the nature of marriage that laid the foundations for women's later sexual emancipation in the 1960s. Whether the romanticized aspects of

Stopes's quasi-mystical view of the sexual "oneness" between partners had much impact on the daily lives of ordinary oppressed women with large families is, however, debatable.

The success of *Married Love* was unprecedented; it sold 2,000 copies in the first fortnight, was reprinted twenty-six times in the next five years, and was translated into thirteen languages. By the end of the 1930s, it had sold a million copies. In the United States, however, it was banned as obscene under the Comstock Act of 1873 and not published there until 1931. In 1915 Stopes had met U.S. birth control pioneer Margaret Sanger, who had fled to Britain in order to evade arrest for her birth control work. It was Sanger who introduced Stopes to contraceptive devices and inspired her to produce a second book in 1918, on contraception. In *Wise Parenthood,* with its emphasis on the need for all children to be wanted and to be born to mothers physically capable of caring for them who were not worn down by large families, Stopes argued that planned pregnancy would make for happier and healthier mothers as well as babies. Unlike Sanger, however, Stopes was not a trained nurse, and she was criticized for errors in the diagrams of the male and female reproductive organs contained in the book. In addition, Sanger's announcement of her intentions to set up a clinic in England similar to her other one in New York provoked the onset of an intense rivalry between the two women.

Stopes's detractors pilloried her books for being gushing and sentimental in tone, the medical establishment decried her lack of training, and the Roman Catholic Church condemned them for obscenity, but their publication uncovered the huge and ever-present problem in many people's lives, a problem till then never discussed in public—the right to sexual fulfillment. *Married Love* and *Wise Parenthood* provoked a huge flood of correspondence—with Stopes finding herself inundated by 5,000 letters—many from British colonies. This vast archive, which luckily was preserved by Stopes, contained letters written with the most disarming and naïve frankness, full of disturbing and often tragic stories of ignorance, abuse, stupidity, and male obduracy, and revealed women longing for more rewarding and meaningful sexual relationships with their husbands. The public, now perceiving Stopes as a latter-day guru, demanded her prognostications on a great range of subjects. As Ruth Hall observes, they "expected her to be a combination of doctor, priest, abortionist, pharmacist, nurserymaid and marriage broker" (1978, 7); by 1921, when Stopes opened her first clinic, she was receiving as many as 1,000 letters a week.

In 1918 Stopes remarried; her second husband, Humphrey Verdon Roe, was a wealthy aircraft manufacturer who, much like Sanger's second husband (the oil magnate J. Noah Slee), supported his wife in her work and funded it. On 17 March 1921 Stopes opened the Mothers' Clinic for Constructive Birth Control in Holloway, a poor district of north London. There she established a professional atmosphere, with her all-women staff wearing nurses' uniforms. Free advice, literature, and contraceptives (the Dutch cap, suppositories and sponges; Stopes rejected the condom as being "unromantic" and "unaesthetic") were offered to those in need, but the medical profession remained hostile to Stopes's work because of her lack of medical training. However, Stopes refused to offer advice on procuring abortion. (In 1926, according to Hall, articles by Stopes on birth control in the popular magazine *John Bull* brought in 20,000 letters requesting help in procuring abortions.)

In pamphlets such as "A Letter to Working Mothers" (1919), Stopes continued to direct her activities primarily at working-class women out of a genuine desire to alleviate the many stresses and strains on them as mothers, often of large families, and prevent the birth of physically impaired children. As a devout Christian who was avowedly intolerant of both masturbation and lesbianism, she slowly gained respectability and the support of the Church of England. In 1921 she also founded the Society for Constructive Birth Control and Racial Progress; originally a pressure group for greater dissemination of family planning literature, it became a vehicle for Stopes's increasingly eugenics-based arguments. By the late 1920s, she had become preoccupied with the population imbalance and shared the concern of other eugenicists that the lower classes were outbreeding the upper. She began favoring sterilization—a covert method of social control—as the best option for some working-class women.

Under Stopes's guidance, a network of independent clinics sprang up across Britain in the interwar years. The first to follow Stopes was one established by the Malthusian League in the de-

pressed London borough of Walworth in 1922; another was run in Manchester by Mary Stocks, who commented that her clientele were, for the most part, "mothers with overlarge families or sad stories of miscarriages, and deplorable health records," who were desperate to be less sexually "troubled" by their husbands (1970, 162). Clinics in Leeds, Aberdeen, and Belfast followed soon after, and in 1930 the clinics run by the Society for Constructive Birth Control and Racial Progress combined with others to found the National Birth Control Council (NBCC), which in 1939 became the Family Planning Association (FPA). Stopes also oversaw the opening of clinics affiliated with the FPA in Australia, New Zealand, and South Africa. But the concept of cooperation with the many other birth control organizations that proliferated at this time was alien to Stopes, and her dogmatism and overbearing manner made her difficult to work with, leading to her resignation from the NBCC in 1933.

Stopes's work continued to be beset by accusations of immorality, particularly from Catholics. In 1923 she sued a Catholic doctor, Halliday Sutherland, in the High Court for libeling her in his book *Birth Control.* She won the case and £100 damages, but the judgment was reversed on appeal in the House of Lords. It was the first of a succession of legal battles, which like all causes célèbres gave Stopes valuable free publicity. By 1930 opposition to Stopes had largely petered out. Both the British Medical Association and the Church of England finally conceded the relevance of her work, and the dissemination of birth control literature was permitted by the Ministry of Health through local clinics. During the 1930s, she turned her attention to India, where the practice of child marriage frequently led to pregnancy in early puberty, and with it premature prolapse of the womb.

In her private life, Stopes became ever more eccentric. She became sexually dissatisfied in her second marriage and, with her husband's agreement, took a succession of much younger lovers. After the outbreak of World War II in 1939, she turned to literary endeavors, writing romantic and often sensuous poetry, such as *The Bathe, an Ecstasy* (1946), and gushing prose, such as the now-unread novel *Love's Creation* (1928), an idiosyncratic brand of flowery rhetoric that was often pilloried. At the end of her life, dismayed by the destruction of the old social order and the arrival of a new Labour government, she became increasingly alienated from modern life and began to convince herself that her life's work had been a failure. On her death, however, she left a considerable body of seventy published works, including the comprehensive *Contraception: Its Theory, History and Practice* (1923), written primarily for the medical profession; *The Truth about Venereal Disease* (1921); *Sex and the Young* (1926); and *Sex and Religion* (1929). In 1925 Stopes's Holloway clinic was relocated to central London, where it is still in operation. An informative website on the life of Stopes and the ongoing international work of the Marie Stopes Organization can be found at http://www.mariestopes.org.uk.

See also Jacobs, Aletta; Sanger, Margaret.

References and Further Reading
Breed, Mary, and Edith How-Martyn. 1930. *The Birth Control Movement in England*. London: Bale and Danielsson.
Briant, Keith. 1962. *Marie Stopes: A Biography*. London: Hogarth Press.
Fryer, Peter. 1965. *The Birth Controllers*. London: Secker & Warburg.
Hall, Ruth. 1977. *Marie Stopes: A Biography*. London: André Deutsch.
———. 1978. *Dear Dr. Stopes: Sex in the 1920s—A Selection of Letters Written to Marie Stopes*. London: André Deutsch.
Lewis, Jane. 1980. *The Politics of Motherhood: Child and Maternal Welfare in England, 1900–1939*. London: Croom Helm.
Oldfield, Sybil. 2001. *Women Humanitarians: A Biographical Dictionary of British Women Active between 1900 and 1950*. London: Continuum.
Rose, June. 1992. *Marie Stopes and the Sexual Revolution*. London: Faber and Faber.
Russell, Dora. 1975. *The Tamarisk Tree: My Quest for Liberty and Love*. London: Elek.
Sanger, Margaret. 1931. *My Fight for Birth Control*. New York: Farrar and Rinehart.
Stocks, Mary. 1970. *My Commonplace Book*. London: Peter Davies.
Stopes, Marie. 1995 [1918]. *Married Love*. Reprint, London: Gollancz.

Stout, Lady Anna
(1858–1931)
New Zealand

The social reformer, philanthropist, and suffragist Anna Stout was a leading figure in the early women's movement in New Zealand, along with Kate Sheppard, although Stout later became critical of the preoccupation of activists such as Sheppard with political concerns over and above social issues.

Stout's father, John Logan, who had emigrated to New Zealand from Scotland in 1854, was clerk to the superintendent of Otago province. She was born in Dunedin and grew up in a Presbyterian family that was active in the temperance movement and philanthropic causes and inculcated in her a strong sense of social duty. After being educated at the Girls' Provincial School, she lived at home until her marriage in 1876 to Robert Stout, a barrister who would go on to become a leading Liberal statesman. Like the Logans, her husband was a freethinker and supporter of sexual equality and women's rights, and Anna in turn took an active interest in his political career (he had been elected to the New Zealand legislature in 1875). From 1878 to 1894, Anna had six children, but the work of child rearing did not dim her desire to take up social activism. Her support for prohibition and social purity led her into the Woman's Christian Temperance Union (WCTU), of which she was a founding member when it was established in New Zealand in 1885.

In 1884 Robert Stout became prime minister of New Zealand, which increased the many demands on Anna's time and required constant trips back and forth between Dunedin and the capital, Wellington. During her husband's three-year tenure, Stout supported his progressive reforms of New Zealand's civil service, hospitals, and charitable institutions. She became Lady Stout after her husband was knighted on leaving office.

Stout's freethinking background, with its emphasis on the fulfillment of the potential of the individual, lay at the root of her equal rights feminism; she was a lifelong patron of women's education and upheld their equal rights with men before the law, particularly in divorce. She argued that if women showed the competence to do the same work as men, including serving as members of Parliament (MPs), they should be rewarded with equal pay, but she believed that women with families had a primary duty to fulfill their domestic obligations. Stout was greatly absorbed by her welfare work. In 1897 she was a founder of the Society for the Protection of

Women and Children, which offered legal advice and help to those in distress, and as a staunch social purity campaigner, she was critical of the double sexual standard that penalized women. In 1918 she came to the defense of prostitutes put on trial after a police raid on a brothel and in 1922 led opposition to demands by the medical establishment for the compulsory notification by prostitutes of contraction of venereal disease.

Stout's suffrage campaigning began in the closing stages of the movement, when in 1892 she was elected president of Dunedin's Women's Franchise League. Women in New Zealand were awarded the franchise the following year. In 1894 she was a founding member with Kate Sheppard of the National Council of Women, New Zealand (NCW), a branch of the International Council of Women, in which she liaised with other women's groups across New Zealand. In 1896 she became one of its vice presidents but was uneasy at the high political content of NCW conventions and critical that they did not address other more pressing social issues.

In 1895 the Stouts finally moved to Wellington, where Anna founded the Southern Cross Society to promote women's political education and economic independence across all social classes and through which she fostered the education of Maori women. In 1896 she found herself on the opposing side to her husband, who was president of the Anti-Chinese League, when she voiced her objection to a new Undesirable Immigrants Bill, which sought to curb Chinese immigration. Stout considered this legislation highly unfair and responded by underlining the honesty, sobriety, and hard work of Chinese immigrants. But when her husband was appointed chief justice of New Zealand in 1897, she was obliged to keep such views to herself until she was liberated by a family visit to England in 1909. Anna remained there for three years and with enthusiasm threw herself into social and political activism. She joined the London Lyceum and the International Council of Women, becoming friendly with Emmeline and Christabel Pankhurst. As a result, she joined the Women's Social and Political Union (WSPU) during a period of increasing militancy.

During her time in England, Stout joined suffrage rallies, spoke at suffrage meetings, and wrote letters to *The Times* in support of the movement. She published articles in the WSPU journal *Votes for Women,* and the feminist journal the *Englishwoman's Review* featured her article "What the Franchise Has Done for the Women and Children of New Zealand" (1910). In 1911 the WSPU issued her pamphlet, "Woman Suffrage in New Zealand," describing the successful campaign that had given women the vote there. Her experiences of the hard-fought campaign in Britain, however, led to a certain disillusionment with women activists back in her home country. On her return, Stout found them complacent and not making full use of the vote, which she felt had come before they were politically mature enough to value it fully, despite having enjoyed it for so many years longer than other women around the world.

Stout was involved in a plethora of clubs and organizations after her return to New Zealand, including the Plunket Society, the Women's National Reserve (during World War I), the Pioneer Wellington Club, the Society of Fine Arts, and the English-Speaking Union. In the 1920s she was a member of the League of Nations Union and served on innumerable educational and charitable committees.

As a strong advocate of women's education, in 1920 she donated £500 to set up an Anna Paterson Stout Scholarship at the University of Otago and six years later provided a small bursary for women undergraduates at the Victoria University of Wellington (of which her husband had been a founder in 1897).

See also Pankhurst, Christabel; Pankhurst, Emmeline; Sheppard, Kate.

References and Further Reading

Cocker, J., and J. M. Murray. 1930. *Temperance and Prohibition in New Zealand.* London: Epworth Press.

Dictionary of New Zealand Biography. 1990. Vols. 1–5. Wellington, NZ: Allen and Unwin.

Dunn, W. H., and I. L. M. Richardson. 1961. *Sir Robert Stout: A Biography.* Wellington: A. H. and A. W. Reed.

Grimshaw, Patricia. 1987. *Women's Suffrage in New Zealand.* Auckland: Oxford University Press.

MacDonald, Charlotte, ed. 1991. *The Book of New Zealand Women.* Wellington: Bridget Williams Books.

Stowe, Emily Jennings
(1831–1903)
Canada

For long generally acknowledged as the first woman to officially be licensed as a doctor in Canada, Emily Stowe was in fact preceded by Jenny Kidd Trout in 1875. She was also a pioneer of women's rights and suffrage in that country. The Toronto Women's Literary Club, which she founded in 1876, was the genesis of the women's movement in Canada, and from the 1880s members began to petition the provincial government for women's suffrage.

Stowe came from a wealthy Quaker family and was one of six daughters born in South Norwich, Upper Canada, now the state of Ontario. Clever and thrifty, she saved for her own education and at fifteen trained as a teacher at the Provincial Normal School in Toronto. In 1854 she was appointed the first woman principal in Canada, at Brantford Public School in Ontario.

Two years later, she married and was soon the mother of three children. When her husband was struck with tuberculosis, Stowe, who had already taken an interest in healing and homeopathic medicine, decided to train as a doctor. However, she was turned away when she applied to enter the Toronto School of Medicine in 1865. She went instead to New York, to study at an institution, established in 1863 by Clemence Sophia Lozier, that taught homeopathic medicine—the New York Medical College and Hospital for Women (not to be confused with Elizabeth Blackwell's Women's Medical College in New York, set up by her in 1868).

After graduating in 1867, Stowe returned to Toronto and set herself up in practice, rapidly attracting many women patients, but was fined for practicing medicine illegally because she was not a graduate of a Canadian medical school and a member of the Ontario College of Physicians and Surgeons. Stowe took on a long battle with the medical establishment to obtain permission to attend classes, which was granted in 1871. She and the only other female student, Jenny Trout, had to contend with a barrage of derision from male students. Stowe failed her exams and went back to practicing illegally until she finally achieved recognition as a medical practitioner in 1880. Three years later, she was a founder of the Women's Medical College of Toronto. She con-

tinued to lobby for women's admission to Canadian universities, which was achieved when the University of Toronto admitted them in 1886.

As a fervent advocate of women's rights, Stowe had also been instrumental in November 1876 in the founding of the Toronto Women's Literary Club (TWLC), which was inspired by the American Society for the Advancement of Women and which behind its innocuous title was dedicated to fighting for prohibition, suffrage, and women's rights, in particular a Married Women's Property Act and the protection of women at work. Stowe lectured on women's issues in Ontario and in 1881 was in the first deputation to the Ontario government on women's suffrage. In 1882 the TWLC lobbied successfully for unmarried women property holders to be given a municipal vote in Toronto City Council. A year later, with the group now growing in confidence and increasingly involved in suffrage, it disbanded and reformed as the Toronto Women's Suffrage Association (TWSA). Between 1885 and 1893, the TWSA orchestrated nine attempts to obtain provincial suffrage for women.

In 1889 the Canadian suffrage campaign was reignited by the establishment of the new Dominion Women's Enfranchisement Association (DWEA) by Stowe, who served as its first president until her death and set up branches across Canada. She herself led a deputation to the Ontario government in February 1889 in support of a bill on women's suffrage introduced by a Liberal member, and in 1896, with her daughter Augusta, staged a mock parliament at which DWEA members debated a motion on votes for men—which they soundly rejected.

The DWEA was also a member society of the influential National Council of Women of Canada (NCWC), established in 1893 by Lady Isabella Aberdeen. Stowe organized special suffrage conferences held at the NCWC's annual meetings and also liaised closely with WCTU members. In 1904 the NCWC set up a Standing Committee on Suffrage and the Rights of Citizenship, with Augusta Stowe as president.

Stowe was forced to give up her medical practice after falling and breaking her hip in 1893. Her daughter, Augusta Stowe-Gullen, followed her into medicine and was the first woman to obtain a medical degree in Canada, in 1883. Having succeeded her mother as president of the DWEA, in 1909 Gullen was at the forefront of organizing a mass petition on women's suffrage by the combined forces of the WCTU and Canadian suffragists.

References and Further Reading

Bacchi, C. I. 1983. *Liberation Deferred? The Ideas of the English-Canadian Suffragists 1877–1918.* Toronto: University of Toronto Press.

Brown, George W., et al., eds. 1966. *Dictionary of Canadian Biography.* Toronto: University of Toronto Press.

Cleverdon, Catherine Lyle. 1950. *The Woman Suffrage Movement in Canada.* Toronto: University of Toronto Press.

Fryer, Mary Beacock. 1990. *Emily Stowe, Doctor and Suffragist.* Toronto: Oxford University Press.

Hacker, Carlotta. *The Indomitable Lady Doctors.* Toronto: Clare, Irwin, and Co.

Kealey, Linda. 1979. *A Not Unreasonable Claim: Women and Reform in Canada 1880s–1920s.* Toronto: Toronto Women's Press.

McCallum, Margaret. 1989. *Emily Stowe.* Toronto: Grolier.

Ray, Janet. 1949. *100 Years of Medicine.* Saskatoon: Modern Press.

———. 1978. *Emily Stowe.* Toronto: Fitzhenry and Whiteside.

Waxman, Sydell. 1996. *Changing the Pattern: The Story of Emily Stowe.* Toronto: Napoleon Publishing.

Stowe, Harriet Beecher
(1811–1896)
United States

In 1852, the writer Harriet Beecher Stowe produced an antislavery novel that not only proved to be a literary landmark in the development of Victorian evangelical humanitarianism but set the standard for other women writers of her time to explore social concerns in their work. Such was the unprecedented level of public debate that *Uncle Tom's Cabin* provoked that the poet John Greenleaf Whittier was prompted to proclaim that Stowe's pen had indeed proved "mightier than [the] sword" of many men. On a broader level, the novel fueled the arguments of feminists and abolitionists that there were obvious parallels to be drawn between the slavery of blacks and the domestic slavery of women.

Stowe was born in Litchfield, Connecticut, the fourth daughter of fire-and-brimstone Calvinist minister Lyman Beecher, who was himself descended from a family of Puritan clergymen. Along with her seven brothers and sister Catharine, she was brought up in an abolitionist household, where the open discussion of social justice and religious and moral issues was encouraged. Six of Stowe's brothers would eventually follow their father into the ministry. Stowe attended school in Litchfield from the ages of eight to thirteen and in 1824 joined her sister Catharine's Hartford Female Seminary, at sixteen becoming a teacher there herself.

The Beecher family moved to Cincinnati in 1832, where Stowe's father took up the post of president of the Lane Theological Seminary. She taught at another school established by Catharine, the Western Female Institute, and wrote a geography textbook. In 1836 she married one of the teachers at her father's seminary, the biblical scholar Calvin Ellis Stowe, a widower nine years older than herself. Stowe proved to be a sickly and melancholic man, prone to hypochondria and depressive moods as well as being ineffectual at earning a living. For Stowe, her marriage was the archetypal Victorian one of unflinching Christian duty as wife and mother, and, indeed, she very dutifully produced seven children in quick succession. In 1838 she began writing magazine articles to bring in money to supplement her husband's meager salary and also as a means of escape from the domestic routine. Her first literary sketches appeared in the *Western Monthly Magazine,* after she had won its writing competition in 1834. Thereafter, Stowe wrote mainly didactic and religious articles for periodicals and newspapers such as the *New York Evangelist* and published her first collection of stories, *The Mayflower: Or Sketches of Scenes and Characters among the Descendants of the Pilgrims,* in 1843. But for most of her eighteen years in Cincinnati, she wrote relatively little compared to the outpouring of her later years.

During a cholera epidemic in Cincinnati in July 1849, Stowe's favorite son and sixth child, Charlie, died. In 1850 the family moved back to New England when Calvin Stowe obtained a post at Bowdoin College. They settled in Brunswick, Maine, and Stowe set up a school in their home to supplement the family income. Dissatisfied with the modest aspirations of her literary output until then, she began seeking a way of turning her writing into a positive act of Christian service. That September the answer came with

Harriet Beecher Stowe (National Archives)

the passage of the Fugitive Slave Act, which made it obligatory for U.S. citizens to help recapture escaped slaves and threatened prosecution of those who helped them escape. The book came to her, Stowe would later claim, as a vision from God and effectively "wrote itself," to serve as a direct challenge to the conscience of all professed Christians who condoned the sinfulness of keeping slaves. Although she lacked much firsthand knowledge about slavery, during her time in Cincinnati she had been aware of the plight of slaves escaping across the Ohio River from Kentucky. Her only real experience of slavery had occurred during a brief visit to a Kentucky plantation during the 1830s. In addition, with her sense of loss still raw after the death of her baby, she sympathized with the trauma endured by slave mothers when their own children were taken from them and sold.

Uncle Tom's Cabin; or, Life among the Lowly was serialized during 1851–1852 in an abolitionist journal, the *National Era*. Appearing in book form in 1852 and hailed as the "Iliad of the Blacks," it sold 350,000 copies in the first year (Moers 1978, 15). In England alone 1.5 million copies, mostly pirated, were sold. Among its notable admirers were Queen Victoria; the poet Elizabeth Barrett Browning pronounced it the most successful book printed by man or woman (Moers 1991, 14). The Russian novelist Leo Tolstoy admired its moral tone, and the French feminist George Sand delighted in its fine characterization of women and children, notably the engaging and mischievous Topsy.

Although there were other similar works written in protest at the Fugitive Slave Act, it was Stowe's that caught the public's imagination and proved "the model for activist literature" (Moers 1978, 15). It was not, however, the first abolitionist work by a woman by any means: the little-known Cuban writer Gertrudis Gómez de Avellaneda had produced an antislavery novel, *Sab the Mulatto,* in 1841; Frances Trollope had attacked slavery in 1836 with her novel *Jonathan Jefferson Whitlaw,* as had Harriet Martineau in her 1837 critique, *Society in America.* In the United States, Angelina Grimké in 1836 and Lydia Maria Child in 1833 had both published powerful abolitionist tracts well ahead of Stowe. But *Uncle Tom's Cabin* achieved that rare thing shared by all popular books: it touched a nerve in the reading public to become nothing short of a literary phenomenon.

Such was the success of the novel that the first U.S. edition of 5,000 copies sold out in two days, and in three months alone, Stowe earned $10,000 in royalties in the United States. But so many editions were pirated abroad in translation that Stowe never received even a fraction of the royalties really due her, which no doubt would have made her the nineteenth century's first literary millionaire. What is more, even though her books continued to sell well during the remainder of her career, the money she did make was so badly invested that she was never free of financial worries. *Uncle Tom's Cabin* was eventually made available in fifty-five languages. In Germany alone, it had run to seventy-five editions in several different translations by 1910. Stowe never received royalties either from the many and regular stage dramatizations of the novel over the next eighty years or so. In 1903 the first silent film version was made by Edwin S. Porter, and *Uncle Tom's Cabin* was also bowdlerized in musicals featuring white singers as blacked-up "minstrels." Despite the novel's runaway success, not all American blacks warmed to the servility of Uncle Tom himself, prompting the use of the term "Uncle Tom" in a derogatory sense to refer to those blacks who kowtowed to white people.

Stowe later remarked that had the work been much touted before its publication, she would never have been able to write with such candor. Indeed, the vividness of the story, its narrative, and its engaging characters managed to transcend its perceived literary ineptitudes and the melodrama of the prose. The moving descriptions of the separations of black families and the observations of social customs in the South also outweighed the blatantly propagandist elements of the book's message and its paternalistic tone.

The book's publication fermented wide-reaching anger in the South and the vilification of Stowe. A flood of prosouthern novels appeared, refuting the novel's claims, as opinion further polarized between southern plantation owners determined to preserve slavery (and also those northern manufacturers whose wealth depended on it) and the liberal reformers in the North calling for abolition. Although the book's overt religiosity fanned the flames of righteous indignation everywhere, Stowe's critics accused her of factual error and inaccuracy, and a year later she responded by publishing *A Key to Uncle Tom's Cabin,* in which she listed the documentary sources and personal testimonies from which she had drawn her material.

Now firmly established as the most highly paid writer in the United States, in 1853 Stowe went on a promotional tour of England, where she was feted by Charles Dickens, William Makepeace Thackeray, Lord Palmerston, Thomas Macaulay, and Lord Shaftesbury. In 1856 she published a second antislavery novel, drawing on the mass of research she had accumulated for *Uncle Tom's Cabin* and further cataloging the moral degradation of slave owners and the deterioration of a society based on slavery. *Dred: A Tale of the Great Dismal Swamp* also depicts the conflicts provoked by the spread of slavery into Kansas and Nebraska. It was well reviewed by the writer George Eliot as a novel of "uncontrollable power . . . inspired by rare genius" (Moers 1978, 47). People were again greatly moved by its account of the slave woman Milly, whose fourteen children are taken from her and sold, as are other slaves, "to suit the phases of trade, or the fancy of the purchaser" (86). Like *Uncle Tom's Cabin,*

Dred had record sales in England. On making a second visit there in 1856, Stowe was honored with an audience with Queen Victoria, who had pronounced the novel quite as good as *Uncle Tom's Cabin.* By the time the Civil War broke out in 1861, Stowe's novel had been so influential that when she met Abraham Lincoln, he is said to have greeted her with the words: "So you're the little woman who wrote the book that made this great war!" (Sandburg 1936, vol. 2, 201).

Stowe and her husband retired to Hartford in 1864, spending their winters in Florida. She continued turning out new novels almost every year, in the course of her career producing a stream of essays, religious poetry, and popular books such as the better-known *The Minister's Wooing* (1859) and other local-color stories drawn from her New England childhood, which include *The Pearl of Orr's Island* (1862), *Oldtown Folks* (1869), and *Pogunac People* (1878). Her newfound literary status also brought an invitation to be one of the few women to write for *Atlantic Monthly.* She also contributed to the New York *Independent* and the *Christian Union,* both edited by her brother Henry Ward Beecher.

Having met Byron's widow, Lady Noel Byron, on her third visit to England in 1869, Stowe published a defense of her character in *Atlantic Monthly,* in which she attacked the late Lord Byron for committing incest with his half-sister Augusta Leigh. Published in book form as *Lady Byron Vindicated* in 1870, it provoked an extreme response in Britain to what was perceived as unfounded "scandal-mongering" by Stowe (although the emergence of documentary evidence has since vindicated her) and a defamation of the reputation of a great poet who was revered as a national icon. Sales of Stowe's books in Britain suffered as a result.

An advocate of temperance and women's suffrage, Stowe was a supporter of Lucy Stone's American Woman Suffrage Association, but she did not openly espouse women's causes. Her primary concern was to see social reform promoted through religious worship and practice, and in her essays and articles, she evangelized on women's domestic duties, health, and religious faith, which she saw as assisting them in the spiritual regeneration of others. Her discussion of women's issues can be found in works such as *A Reply on Behalf of the Women of America* (1863); *The American Woman's Home* (1869); *Pink and*

White Tyranny (1871); *My Wife and I,* in which she parodied the radical feminists Victoria Woodhull and Elizabeth Cady Stanton, with whom she had quarreled (1871); *Woman in Sacred History* (1873); *We and Our Neighbors* (1875); and *Our Famous Women* (1884).

In her last years, Stowe wrote her memoirs with the help of her youngest son, Charles Edward Stowe. In the introduction to Paxton Hibben's *Henry Ward Beecher: An American Portrait,* Sinclair Lewis remarked of Stowe that "*Uncle Tom's Cabin* was the first evidence to America that no hurricane can be so disastrous to a country as a ruthlessly humanitarian woman" (Hibben 1942, viii). For all its literary shortcomings, *Uncle Tom's Cabin* was of enormous social import and, unlike many Victorian novels of its day, has survived changing literary fashion and continuing criticism and still remains in print. The Harriet Beecher Stowe Center in Hartford, housed in Beecher's last home, contains the Stowe-Day Library and is open to the public. Go to http://www.hartnet.org/stowe/.

See also Beecher, Catharine Esther; Child, Lydia Maria; Gómez de Avellaneda y Arteaga, Gertrudis; Grimké, Angelina Emily and Sarah Moore; Martineau, Harriet; Stanton, Elizabeth Cady; Stone, Lucy; Woodhull, Victoria Claflin.

References and Further Reading
Coil, Suzanne M. 1993. *Harriet Beecher Stowe.* New York: F. Watts.
Davidson, Cathy N., and Linda Wagner Martin, eds. 1995. *Oxford Companion to Women's Writing in the United States.* Oxford: Oxford University Press.
Foster, Charles H. 1954. *The Rungless Ladder: Harriet Beecher Stowe and New England Puritanism.* Durham: Duke University Press.
Gossett, Thomas F. 1985. *Uncle Tom's Cabin and American Culture.* Dallas: Southern Methodist University Press.
Halbersleben, Karen I. 1993. *Women's Participation in the British Antislavery Movement 1824–1865.* Lewiston: Edwin Mellen Press.
Hedrick, Joan D. 1993. *Harriet Beecher Stowe: A Life.* New York: Oxford University Press.
Hibben, Paxton. 1942. *Henry Ward Beecher: An American Portrait.* New York: The Press of the Readers Club.
Moers, Ellen. 1978. *Literary Women.* London: Women's Press.
Reynolds, Moira D. 1985. *Uncle Tom's Cabin and Mid-Nineteenth Century United States: Pen and Conscience.* Jefferson, NC: McFarland.
———. 1988. *Nine American Women of the Nineteenth Century: Leaders into the Twentieth.* Jefferson, NC: McFarland.
Sandburg, Carl. 1936. *Abraham Lincoln: The War Years.* 4 vols. New York: Harcourt, Brace and Company.
Scott, John Anthony. 1978. *Woman against Slavery: The Story of Harriet Beecher Stowe.* New York: Thomas Y. Crowell.
Showalter, Elaine. 1999. *A Literature of Their Own: British Women Novelists from Brontë to Lessing.* 1977. London: Virago.
Stowe, Charles Edward. 1889. *Life of Harriet Beecher Stowe: Compiled from Her Letters and Journals by Her Son.* London: S. Low, Marston, Searle and Rivington.
Wagenecht, Edward. 1965. *Harriet Beecher Stowe: The Known and the Unknown.* New York: Oxford University Press.
Wilson, Forrest. 1941. *Crusader in Crinoline: The Life of Harriet Beecher Stowe.* Philadelphia: Lippincott.

Street, Jessie
(1889–1970)
Australia

The Australian socialist feminist and defender of Aboriginal rights Jessie Street has, until recently, been a neglected figure in Australian women's history. She was born in northeastern India, in Chota Nagpur, where her father was in the forestry branch of the Indian civil service. Her grandfather was an early settler in Australia who established a sheep station at Yulgilbar, New South Wales, in the early 1840s. When her mother inherited Yulgilbar in 1896, the family left India to settle there. The sale of the station in 1925, after her mother's death, provided Street with a comfortable income that supported her in her years of social activism.

As a young girl, Street was educated by governesses and then was sent to boarding school in England from 1903 to 1906. After attending Sydney University and gaining an arts degree in 1910, Street spent a year in Europe, where she observed women's suffrage activism in England and in 1911 attended the annual congress of the International Council of Women at Rome. During World War I, she went to New York, where she worked in a home for delinquent girls, returning to Australia to marry in 1916. Settling in Darlinghurst, she joined numerous women's clubs and was a founder of the New South Wales

Social Hygiene Association in 1916, a founding member of the Sydney branch of the League of Nations Union in 1918, and secretary of the National Council of Women in 1920.

In 1927 the Streets moved to Darling Point in Sydney, with Street concentrating on the upbringing of her four young children. In 1928 she found time to accept the presidency of the United Associations of Women (UAW), an umbrella group for white middle-class feminist organizations in New South Wales, which supported the campaign of the Council for Action for Equal Pay. As an advocate of women's economic independence, Street published several pamphlets for the UAW during the 1930s. In "Income for Wives: How It Can Be Managed or the Economic Independence of Married Women" and "Woman as a Homemaker," she decried the domestic and economic slavery of women and argued that men should assign a proportion of their earnings to their wives to ensure that they had some financial control over family spending. In "Child Endowment," she advocated state provisions for children to be paid directly to mothers, a practice that was introduced in 1941.

During the 1930s, Street became a socialist and in 1939 joined the Australian Labour Party. She was active in the Women for Canberra Movement and an unsuccessful Labour candidate in the federal elections of 1943. Also that year, she took an important role as chair of the Federal Charter Committee and prime organizer of the Women's Charter Conference, held in Sydney. The conference drew up a comprehensive document on women's social and economic position, addressing the issues of child and maternity care, birth control, legal reform, improvements to housing, and equal rights.

At the end of World War II, Street was one of only a handful of women delegates to the 1945 San Francisco Conference on International Organization, at which the United Nations was established. Taking with her a copy of the Australian Women's Charter, she lobbied in San Francisco for a similar international charter on women's rights, collaborating closely with the Brazilian feminist Bertha Lutz. Together they were instrumental in setting up the United Nations Status of Women Commission, with the objective of monitoring the political, economic, and civil status of women around the world. In 1947 Street was appointed Australian delegate to

the UN Commission and elected vice chair, where she worked on the Draft Declaration of Human Rights, proposing amendments on feminist issues, such as the rewording of statutes to take account of the female sex in place of collective masculine pronouns and nouns.

On her return to Australia in 1945, Street had resigned from the UAW to concentrate on organizing a second Australian Women's Charter Conference and to run as a Labour candidate in the 1946 election. But her high-profile communist sympathies and her pacifism, as a member of the New South Wales Peace Committee and the Russia Friendship Society, were affecting her political credibility and causing considerable public embarrassment to her husband, who was appointed chief justice for New South Wales in 1949. Although she never joined the Communist Party, with the onset of the Cold War, Street came under increasing personal attack. In 1950, with her husband's approval, she decided to spend time in England working for Anglo-Soviet friendship and the peace movement.

While living in London, Street kept close tabs on political developments in Australia and developed an increasing interest in Aboriginal issues, taking up their cause in the UN. In 1946 she joined in the defense of Aboriginal farm workers striking for the first time for better pay and conditions in Western Australia. Further strikes by Aboriginal workers in the early 1950s led to the founding of the Council for Aboriginal Rights. Street began lobbying friends and political contacts to establish a Commonwealth-wide body to fight for full citizenship for Aboriginals and for the removal of discriminatory references to them in the Australian Constitution. She became a member of the executive committee of the British Anti-Slavery Society, which was still active in the 1950s, at that time attempting to advance the welfare of Aboriginals and protect them from exploitation. She agreed to serve as patron of a new national support group, the Australian Aboriginal Fellowship, which was established during her return visit to Australia in 1956–1957.

Street became the prime mover behind a petition for a referendum on Commonwealth responsibility for Aboriginal welfare in 1957. Immediately after, she spent two months touring the country at her own expense, talking to Aboriginal civil rights leaders and urging them to play a leading role in the referendum campaign rather than leaving it to white "do-gooders." She investigated the conditions in which Aboriginals lived and worked and at the end of her trip presented a detailed report to the British Anti-Slavery Society, copies of which were sent to leading Australian officials and politicians. Street was once more back in Australia for the inaugural meeting of the Federal Council of Aboriginal Advancement in February 1958 and then returned to England until 1961, after which she resumed work for the Federal Council. Ten years of hard campaigning finally resulted in a referendum in May 1967, in which a nationwide average yes vote of 90 percent endorsed Australian Aboriginals being accorded full legal citizenship.

Energetic but notoriously disorganized, Street continued to travel and lecture into her late seventies, during which she published her autobiography, *Truth or Repose* (1966). For long underrated, her work is now beginning to attract the attention it deserves. As one contemporary of the 1930s described her, "She was before her time, that was her tragedy. She thought she could carry Australian women into the twenty-first century of international brotherhood/sisterhood. Others did not share her dream, thought her dangerous, and brought her down. It was not merely jealousy, nor envy, rather distrust of where she was leading. Such is the fate of prophets and prophetesses" (Sekuless 1978, 22).

See also Lutz, Bertha.

References and Further Reading

Lake, Marilyn. 1999. *Getting Equal: The History of Australian Feminism.* London: Allen and Unwin.

Sekuless, Peter. 1978. *Jessie Street: A Rewarding but Unrewarded Life.* St. Lucia: Queensland University Press.

Street, Jessie. 1966. *Truth or Repose.* Sydney: Australasian Book Society.

Stritt, Marie
(1855–1928)
Germany

Marie Stritt was an outstanding feminist leader, not only in Germany but in the International Woman Suffrage Alliance (IWSA), who worked for women's education and campaigned against state-regulated prostitution. As a supporter of birth control and abortion, she was a leading member of the League for the Protection of Motherhood and Sexual Reform. She also called for legal changes to the divorce laws through her Women's Legal Aid Society.

Stritt's activism began in the 1890s, after she met Luise Otto-Peters and took up the cause of women's emancipation. She joined the women's group Reform in 1891 to fight for educational equality for women, leading the group from 1895. In 1894 Stritt founded the Women's Legal Aid Society (WLAS) in Dresden, which promoted the legal protection of women, and worked closely with feminist leaders Minna Cauer and Anita Augspurg in the radical wing of the largely moderate (until 1902) Federation of German Women's Associations (FGWA), into which the WLAS was incorporated. In 1895–1896 she helped organize the federation's campaign for reform of the civil code, but it brought no significant improvement in women's rights. Stritt was elected to the executive committee of the federation in 1896 and became its president in 1899, at which time she optimistically informed the International Council of Women (ICW) that progressive German feminism would take the lead in the women's movement. But by the end of the century, she found herself forced to take a radical position in the face of the entrenched conservative majority in the German federation.

In 1899 Stritt was inspired by the work undertaken in England by Josephine Butler and other activists in the social purity movement. She met Butler in London that July and was prompted to introduce similar moral issues within the federation, setting up a German campaign against state-regulated prostitution.

Stritt became a prominent leader of the German suffrage movement from the 1900s, in 1902 lobbying the Reichstag for acknowledgment of the principle of female suffrage and urging the FGWA to formally incorporate women's suffrage in its program. From 1911 until it was disbanded in 1919, she was president of the German Association for Women's Suffrage.

In 1908 as a member of the legal commission of the FGWA and also a member by then of the League for the Protection of Motherhood and Sexual Reform (founded in 1904), Stritt was one of several women who investigated reform of Section 218 of the criminal code. She supported moral reeducation and advocated birth control, free love, and the legalization of abortion. Under the civil code, women convicted of having abortions faced sentences of six months to five years in prison. Stritt's call for the legalization of abortion prompted many long debates within the FGWA, and ended with the defeat of the proposal in 1910, engineered by moderates within the association, who inveigled the right-wing German Evangelical Women's Federation to join it, thus raising the additional votes needed to defeat Stritt at its general assembly that year. Abortion would remain in the criminal code until 1969. After the abortion debate Stritt was ousted by the right wing from the FGWA in 1910 and replaced as president by the moderate Gertrud Bäumer. It was a disillusioning experience for her to see her early hopes for a progressive movement dissolve into factional splits that would lead to the exclusion of radical feminists by the outbreak of World War I.

Meanwhile, Stritt had entered the international women's rights arena and would represent German auxiliary branches at most women's conferences and congresses until 1920. In 1896 she had been elected to the board of the National Council of Women of Germany, serving as its president from 1899 to 1901. After the national council affiliated with the International Council of Women, in 1904 Stritt, who had been elected a vice president of the ICW (until 1909), also helped organize its congress, held that year in Berlin. She became a member of the board of the International Woman Suffrage Alliance (IWSA) at its 1913 Budapest congress and during World War I attempted to revive suffrage with her German Imperial Union for Women's Suffrage, with the subject being debated in the Reichstag. But her nationalist loyalties compelled her to cancel a projected congress of the IWSA to be organized by her in Berlin in 1915; in any event, war intervened in 1914. Stritt found herself torn, as were many women in the international movement, between her loyalties to her country during wartime and the international campaigns for peace and women's suffrage. During the war, with the suffrage campaign on hold in Germany, she turned her attention to the International Neo-Malthusian League, writing the introduction to its treatise on the population problem, *Racial Improvement*. For her, the population question was also "the woman question," and it was the duty of better-off women to share the

advantages they had in terms of being able to limit their families by promoting education on birth control among overworked and exhausted working-class mothers.

After women in Germany over the age of twenty-one were finally given the vote in November 1919, Stritt retired from the board of the IWSA after its 1920 Geneva congress, where other delegates such as Carrie Chapman Catt noted how the years of war and food blockades against Germany had left her "thin and white and exhausted" (Peck 1944, 150). She entered municipal politics in Dresden, becoming a representative of the city council in 1920–1922. For the remainder of her life, she devoted herself to writing and journalism, in which she continued to raise women's issues and support the causes of pacifism and internationalism. She also translated feminist writings such as Charlotte Perkins Gilman's 1898 work, *Women and Economics*, into German.

See also Augspurg, Anita; Bäumer, Gertrud; Butler, Josephine; Cauer, Minna; Otto-Peters, Luise.

References and Further Reading
Allen, Ann Taylor. 1991. *Feminism and Motherhood in Germany, 1800–1914*. New Brunswick: Rutgers University Press.
Evans, Richard. 1973. *The Feminist Movement in Germany 1894–1933*. London: Sage.
Hackett, Amy. 1976. *The Politics of Feminism in Wilhelmine Germany 1890–1918*. 2 vols. Ann Arbor: University Microfilms International.
Jus Suffragii. October 1928. Obituary notice.
Peck, Mary Gray. 1944. *Carrie Chapman Catt*. New York: H. W. Wilson.

Suslova, Nadezhda
(1843–1918)
Russia

One of the first Russian women to qualify as a doctor, Nadezhda Suslova was an inspiration to a generation of young women eager to enter the male preserve of medicine. "I am the first, but not the last," she later wrote. "After me will come thousands" (Bonner 1995, 37). After she obtained her medical degree in Zurich in 1867, the Russian medical establishment grudgingly allowed her to practice in Russia. In the wake of Suslova's academic success and with medical training for women still proscribed in Russia, more than 100 of Suslova's compatriots would study in Zurich over the next five years, until by 1873 the Russian female student community there (of whom seventy-three entered the medical faculty) outnumbered their male compatriots by two to one.

Suslova differed from the majority of female social reformers in the second half of the nineteenth century in Russia in that she came from humble beginnings. Her father was a serf—one of the many hundreds owned by the rich and influential Sheremetev family. She was born at Panino in the province of Nizhniy Novgorod. When her father was promoted to land agent, the family moved to Count Sheremetev's estates at Makarev and then at Ostankina in Moscow. The Sheremetevs paid for Suslova's and her sister's education at Madame Penigka's boarding school, and at age sixteen Suslova transferred to a boarding school for the daughters of the nobility in St. Petersburg, where she studied French, German, English, and Latin. Meanwhile, Suslova's shrewd and hardworking father had accumulated enough capital to buy his freedom (the serfs were not emancipated until 1861) and had bought a factory near Moscow.

Suslova had been a keen reader since she was a young girl, when she had shared her father's copies of the *Contemporary,* a literary journal that had also pioneered democratic change in Russia. Fired up by the crusading social spirit of 1860s Russia, Suslova set out on her own emancipation and education. Encouraged by her enlightened parents, in 1861 she enrolled as an auditor at the Medical Surgical Academy in St. Petersburg, where some of the more forward-thinking professors allowed women to sit in on their lectures (although formal medical training for women was forbidden). She petitioned to be allowed to enter the medical school, but had only been there for two years when the government called a halt to the first tentative steps toward women's university education in 1863. Desperate to continue her medical studies, Suslova volunteered to work with Muslim women in the province of Orenburg, who would not consult male doctors, but was again turned down. The only option was to go abroad, and in 1865 Suslova enrolled as an auditor at Zurich University. She embraced her studies with a degree of commitment and dedication that condemned her to long periods of solitude and privation;

such single-mindedness would become a particular quality of Russian women medical students during that extraordinarily fertile period for women's medical education in Zurich until 1873.

In 1867 Suslova was allowed to prepare her dissertation for her medical degree at Graz in Austria, where her work with Professor Ivan Sechenov on nervous reflexes involved the endless dissection of frogs. But her determination won through, and in December 1867 she successfully defended her thesis, "The Physiology of the Lymphatic Hearts of Frogs," in German, becoming the first woman to receive a European degree in medicine in the modern era. Much attention to Suslova's achievement was given in the press in Russia, but it did nothing to soften the attitude of the Russian medical establishment when Suslova returned to Russia. She was made to sit for a special examination required of all foreign doctors applying to practice in Russia before she was allowed to set herself up in St. Petersburg in 1868. She was joined there by her husband, Frederick Erismann, a Swiss medical student she had married in Vienna that year. Together the couple made a study of standards of hygiene in the working-class tenements of St. Petersburg, publishing their findings in the *Archives of Legal Medicine and Social Hygiene.* Suslova developed a particular concern for the transmission of gonorrhea from mothers to their infants and the high incidence of eye infections among children.

In 1873 Suslova and her husband separated and later divorced. He made a career for himself as a pioneer in health and safety in Russia's factories. Suslova, who had been running her own medical practice for women at Nizhniy Novgorod, remarried in 1885 to a professor of histology, A. E. Golubev. When her husband developed glaucoma, the couple (comfortably off thanks to an inheritance) moved to an estate at Kastel in the Crimea, where they used their money to build a school and offer free medical care to the poor. Suslova nursed her husband through his increasing blindness while continuing in private practice.

References and Further Reading

Bonner, Thomas Neville. 1995. *Becoming a Physician: Medical Education in Britain, France, Germany, and the U.S. 1750–1945.* New York: Oxford University Press.

Tuve, Jeanette E. 1984. *The First Russian Women Physicians.* Newtonville, MA: Oriental Research Partners.

Suttner, Bertha Félice Sophie von (Countess Kinsky)
(1843–1914)
Austria

Eminent international pacifist, political journalist, and novelist on social issues, Suttner became a prime mover in the inauguration of numerous women's peace societies after lobbying pacifist leaders at the first peace conference in The Hague in 1899. Her life and work were driven by her conviction that war would never be prevented until women were given their full civil rights. She wrote the pioneering feminist-pacifist novel—*Lay Down Your Arms*—a huge international success that was often seen as doing for the pacifist movement what *Uncle Tom's Cabin* did for the antislavery movement. Suttner was awarded the Nobel Peace Prize in 1905.

Suttner was born in Prague into the Bohemian aristocracy. Her father was a field marshal in the Hapsburg army who died before she was born. Well educated and fluent in several languages, Suttner found herself in straitened circumstances after her reckless mother dissipated her family fortune. In 1874 she obtained a post as governess to the daughters of Baron von Suttner in Vienna and met with intense family disapproval when she fell in love with his youngest son, Arthur (seven years her junior). In 1876 she went to Paris to discuss the possibility of working as secretary and housekeeper for Alfred Nobel (the armament manufacturer and founder of the Nobel Prizes) at his home there, but after only a week returned to Vienna to marry Arthur in secret. She would, however, keep up a long correspondence with Nobel on pacifism and other issues until his death in 1896. It is said that Suttner was instrumental in Nobel's decision to institute a peace prize in his will.

The Suttners lived in Georgia, in the Caucasus, for seven years and publicized their progressive views in newspaper articles, stories, and novels. Returning to Vienna in 1885, Bertha tackled anti-Semitism, Darwinism, and socialism in works such as *Daniela Dormes* and *High Life* (both 1886). In 1883 she had written on the need for world peace in her nonfiction work *Inventory of a Soul*, a reflection of her gathering horror of war after reading about the conflicts in the Crimea (1854–1856) and Piedmont (1859) and the invasion of Austria by the Prussians in 1864.

She lived for a year in Paris (1886–1887), where she was attracted to the work of the International Arbitration and Peace Association, which sought to end conflicts by setting up international courts of mediation. She began using her writing to lobby for world détente, and this interest crystallized in 1889 with publication of her pacifist novel *Lay Down Your Arms!* The novel describes the brutalities of conflict through the personal experiences of an Austrian woman whose husband dies in the Piedmont War. She remarries, only to see her new husband go off to fight in wars in 1864, 1866, and 1870 (the Franco-Prussian War), when he is shot as a Prussian spy. The book became an international best-seller: it ran to thirty-seven editions in Germany, was translated into sixteen languages, and was exceeded in sales only by Harriet Beecher Stowe's abolitionist novel *Uncle Tom's Cabin*. The Russian writer Leo Tolstoy was so impressed that he wrote to Suttner, "The abolition of slavery was preceded by a famous novel. . . . May God grant that the abolition of war will follow on your novel" (Liddington 1989, 40–41). The book's success prompted support for Suttner's founding of the Austrian Peace Society (APS) in 1891. A year later, she took a leading role in coordinating international peace societies as vice president of the Bern Peace Bureau. Throughout the 1890s, she contributed to numerous international conferences and from 1892 to 1899 edited the pacifist journal of the APS, also titled *Lay Down Your Arms*.

Within the peace movement, Suttner entered into discourse with other leading feminist and pacifist campaigners such as Aletta Jacobs of the International Woman Suffrage Alliance, with whom she disagreed over the use of peace conferences as a platform for calls for women's suffrage. Suttner had always urged total commitment to pacifism, feeling that other social problems could only be solved in a peaceful world—and in particular a united Europe—whereas Jacobs argued that women should be fully emancipated first. They agreed to differ, with Suttner finally conceding that wars would only stop when women had more political influence over the governments that waged them. After the turn of the twentieth century, she lectured on pacifism across Europe and in the United States and became the first woman to win the Nobel Peace Prize in 1905. In 1912, she made another lecture tour to the United States. Although ill, a year before her death she attended the 1913 international peace congress in the Netherlands and, while there, also gave a memorable address to the Dutch Association for Woman Suffrage. Despite Suttner's passionate campaigning, she died just one week before the assassination of Archduke Franz Ferdinand at Sarajevo would propel Europe into a catastrophic war. It is said that her dying words were "Lay down your arms. Say it to many" (Josephson et al. 1985, 923).

See also Jacobs, Aletta; Stowe, Harriet Beecher.
References and Further Reading

Braker, Regina. 1995. *Weapons of Women Writers: Berth von Suttner's* Die Waffen Nieder! *as Political Literature in the Tradition of Harriet Beecher Stowe's* Uncle Tom's Cabin. New York: Peter Lang.

Haman, Brigitte. 1996. *Bertha von Suttner: A Life for Peace.* Syracuse, NY: Syracuse University Press.

Josephson, Harold, Sandi Cooper, and Steven C. Hause et al., eds. 1985. *Biographical Dictionary of Modern Peace Leaders.* Westport, CT: Greenwood Press.

Kempf, Beatrix. 1973. *Woman for Peace: The Life of Bertha von Suttner.* London: Wolff.

Lengyel, Emil. 1975. *And All Her Paths Were Peace: The Life of Bertha von Suttner.* Nashville, TN: T. Nelson.

Liddington, Jill. 1989. *The Long Road to Greenham: Feminism and Anti-Militarism in Britain since 1820.* London: Virago.

McDonald, Lynn, ed. 1998. *Women Theorists on Society and Politics.* Waterloo, ON: Wilfrid Laurier University Press.

Pauli, H. 1957. *Cry of the Heart: The Story of Bertha von Suttner.* New York: I. Washburn.

Suttner, Bertha von. 1972 [1906]. *Lay Down Your Arms.* Reprint, New York: Garland.

———. 1972 [1910]. *Memoirs of Bertha von Suttner: The Records of an Eventful Life.* Reprint, New York: Garland.

Suzman, Helen
(1917–)
South Africa

The eminent South African humanitarian and antiapartheid campaigner Helen Suzman, for thirty-six years a leading liberal politician, was for thirteen of those years the sole representative of the Progressive Party in Parliament. Her refusal to be intimidated by her fellow whites and her demands for investigations into the deaths of black activists in custody earned her the deep re-

Helen Suzman (Reuters/WPA/Archive Photos)

spect of the black community and nationalist leaders within the African National Congress (ANC).

Born Helen Gavronsky in Germiston in the Transvaal, Suzman was the daughter of Jewish Lithuanian immigrants. She was educated at a convent and trained as an economist and statistician after graduating from Witwatersrand University. In 1937 at the age of twenty, she married Moses Suzman and worked for the War Supplies Board during World War II.

She took up an academic career, lecturing in economic history at Witwatersrand University in 1944 and leaving in 1952 to stand for Parliament. In 1953 she became a United Party member of Parliament for the predominantly Jewish constituency of Houghton in Johannesburg and in 1959 was in a splinter group that formed the Progressive Party. From here, Suzman mounted an articulate campaign against the extension of apartheid laws in South Africa, such as the General Law Amendment Act of 1963, which allowed police to detain suspects without charging them with a crime. She visited black townships and the Bantustans (black resettlement areas) to see for herself the civil rights abuses inflicted on South Africa's blacks. She also took every opportunity to fight anti-Semitism in the South African National Party and to support the country's considerable Jewish community. In the 1960s she battled to get the South African government to investigate the conditions under which black activists were held in prison, and in 1984, in the first step on the road to democratic government in South Africa, she mediated between the government and the ANC to have the organization legalized.

Suzman retired from politics in 1989 but has continued to be a powerful force in civil rights activism across southern Africa through the work of the Helen Suzman Foundation. This organization monitors the political, educational, and employment rights of blacks throughout South Africa, Botswana, Lesotho, Zambia, Namibia, Swaziland, and Zimbabwe.

In her work for social justice, equal opportunities for both blacks and whites, and human rights throughout Africa, Suzman has received many international awards for her commitment and integrity: twenty-one honorary doctorates, the United Nations Human Rights Award in 1978, the New York Medallion of Heroism in 1980, and the American Jewish Committee American Liberties Medallion in 1984. She was named a Dame Commander of the Order of the British Empire (DBE) in 1990 and has twice been nominated for the Nobel Peace Prize. In 1994 Suzman was a member of the electoral commission that prepared the ground for the first general election at which millions of adult blacks were allowed to vote for the first time in their lives, and which elected Nelson Mandela as the country's first black president. The Helen Suzman Foundation's website address is http://www.hsf.org.za/hq/.

References and Further Reading

Lee, Robin. 1990. *Values Alive: A Tribute to Helen Suzman.* Johannesburg: J. Ball.

Strangwayes-Booth, Joanna. 1976. *A Cricket in the Thorn Tree: Helen Suzman and the Progressive Party of South Africa.* Bloomington: Indiana University Press.

Suzman, Helen. 1993. *In No Uncertain Terms: A South African Memoir.* New York: Alfred A. Knopf.

Swanwick, Helena
(1864–1939)
United Kingdom

The international pacifist and humanitarian Helena Swanwick was an unshakeable idealist who believed that British women could lead the way in the peace movement during the interwar years. The hopes she invested in women's peace campaigning were disappointed, however, as was her own campaign against militarism and in support of peace mediation during the 1930s. In her 1921 book, *A Political Pilgrim in Europe,* Ethel Snowden described Swanwick as "one of the most commanding personalities of the women's movement" and a "person of extraordinary intellectual power" (81), but Swanwick eventually fell victim to her own deeply felt and unfulfilled aspirations.

She was born in Munich, the daughter of painter Oswald Sickert, who came from a German-speaking part of Denmark. Her brother, Walter Sickert, was also a notable painter. The family moved to England in 1868, but Swanwick was educated for some of the time at a boarding school in France (1872–1876). After moving to London, where Swanwick attended Notting Hill High School, the family moved in artistic, pre-Raphaelite circles and was friendly with the Morris and Burne-Jones families, as well as Oscar Wilde and George Bernard Shaw.

As she grew up, Swanwick greatly resented the constraints placed upon her freedom of movement by her mother. She had a hard task persuading her to allow her to study at Girton College, Cambridge University, but finally succeeded, entering in 1882 to study moral sciences (psychology, philosophy, economics, and politics). After graduating in 1885, she took up a lectureship in psychology at Westfield College in London and married in 1888. She moved to the village of Knutsford outside Manchester with her husband Frederick, when he accepted a lectureship at Owens College. Taking up part-time lecturing as well as voluntary activities in local working men's and girls' clubs, Swanwick became involved with the Women's Cooperative Guild and Women's Trade Union Council, for which she gave occasional lectures. She contributed journalism to the *Manchester Guardian* and later would also write for the *Observer, Nation,* and *Daily News.*

Swanwick's socialist interests led to contact with the Pankhurst family in Manchester, but although her 1905 experience of the Free Trade Hall suffrage protest by Christabel Pankhurst and Annie Kenney impressed her and she took out a subscription to the Women's Social and Political Union (WSPU), she was a confirmed moderate and soon found WSPU militancy distasteful and detrimental to the cause of women's enfranchisement. Eventually, in 1907, she joined the North of England Society for Women's Suffrage, an affiliate of the moderate National Union of Women's Suffrage Societies (NUWSS). She became a leading figure in its activities in Manchester and one of its most regular speakers, in one year alone—1908—speaking at 150 meetings up and down Britain and advocating closer labor-suffrage alliances in the regions.

In 1909 Swanwick took up the editorship of the NUWSS's official journal, *Common Cause*. After moving back to London in 1911, she joined the executive committee of the NUWSS but relinquished the editorial post in 1912, unable to restrain her increasing criticism of WSPU militancy (this arose because the NUWSS believed its journal should show solidarity with other suffrage groups, and would not allow her to be partisan). By this time, Swanwick was drawn toward the international women's movement in preference to the single issue of suffrage; in June 1913 she attended the International Woman Suffrage Alliance congress in Budapest. Shortly after, she published her own analysis of contemporary feminism in *The Future of the Women's Movement.*

With war looming in August 1914, Swanwick organized a women's peace rally at Kingsway Hall in London. She opposed NUWSS support for the war effort and with Catherine Marshall, Isabella Ford, and Maude Royden was one of the most prominent feminist peace campaigners in Britain during the war years. In November 1914 she joined the executive committee of the Union of Democratic Control (UDC), a group of pacifists, socialists, suffragists, and intellectuals who urged more openness in governmental foreign policy and diplomatic negotiations for a lasting postwar peace. Swanwick described the work of the UDC in her 1924 book, *Builders of Peace: Being Ten Years' History of the Union of Democratic Control*. She also edited the UDC journal, *Foreign Affairs* (1925–1928).

Swanwick felt, as did her pacifist colleagues, that women's humanizing influence could help bring an end to war and make for a better post-war world. With this goal in mind, she was closely involved in the organization of (but was unable to attend) the 1915 women's peace congress in The Hague, which led to the founding of the International Committee of Women for Permanent Peace (renamed the Women's International League for Peace and Freedom, or WILPF, in 1919). In June 1915 a women's peace conference was held in England, which led to the creation of a British section of the committee, with Swanwick elected its chair (1915–1922). That December she chaired a committee branch meeting in London, where she argued against conscription, which she saw as undemocratic and a political tool of government. During the war, she threw herself into work for several different organizations, including the Women's Peace Crusade, the UDC, and the Independent Labour Party. With the suffrage movement in most countries on hold, she urged pacifists to take up relief work, which she felt would allow them to stay true to their peacemaking ideals and keep the suffrage spirit alive.

Swanwick attended the 1919 Zurich Congress of the WILPF, but peace brought her few comforts. She was deeply disillusioned by the Versailles Treaty and the draconian war reparations it imposed on Germany, which she felt might eventually provoke another war. She also became rapidly disenchanted with the newly enfranchised younger generation of women in postwar Britain in the 1920s, who she felt were too preoccupied with sex. She gave up her WILPF chair in 1922 to work for peace through the League of Nations, serving on the British delegation in 1924 and 1928–1931. She joined the huge turnout at the June 1926 Women's Peace Pilgrimage in Hyde Park in support of disarmament and throughout the 1930s continued to speak out against militarism and fascism. She advocated collective security and warned of the dangers of aerial bombardment in *Frankenstein and His Monster* (1934). But a deepening loss of faith in women's desire to lobby for peace and a growing disillusionment with international diplomacy provoked considerable spiritual unease in Swanwick and her eventual alienation from the mainstream of the pacifist movement. Such was the erosion of all her hopes for peace that on the outbreak of World War II, when she was suffering from heart disease, she took a fatal overdose.

Swanwick published an illuminating account of her early activism, *I Have Been Young* (1935). She was also the author of the prodisarmament *Collective Insecurity* (1937), laid out her arguments in support of a federal Europe in *The Roots of Peace* (1938), and contributed articles to Lady Rhondda's feminist journal, *Time and Tide*.

See also Ford, Isabella; Kenney, Annie; Pankhurst, Christabel; Marshall, Catherine; Royden, Maude.

References and Further Reading
Alberti, Johanna. 1989. *Beyond Suffrage: Feminists in War and Peace, 1914–1928*. London: Macmillan.
Banks, Olive, ed. 1985, 1990. *The Biographical Dictionary of British Feminists*, vol. 1, *1800–1930*; vol. 2, *1900–1945*. Brighton: Harvester Wheatsheaf.
Baylen, J. O., and N. J. Gossman, eds. 1979–1984. *Biographical Dictionary of Modern British Radicals*. 3 vols. Hassocks, Sussex: Harvester Press.
Caedel, Martin. 1980. *Pacifism in Britain 1914–1945: The Defining of a Faith*. Oxford: Clarendon Press.
Crawford, Elizabeth. 1999. *The Women's Suffrage Movement, 1866–1928: A Reference Guide*. London: University College of London Press.
Holton, Sandra Stanley. 1986. *Feminism and Democracy: Women's Suffrage and Reform Politics in Britain, 1900–1918*. Cambridge: Cambridge University Press.
Josephson, Harold, Sandi Cooper, and Steven C. Hause et al., eds. 1985. *Biographical Dictionary of Modern Peace Leaders*. Westport, CT: Greenwood Press.
Liddington, Jill. 1989. *The Long Road to Greenham: Feminism and Anti-Militarism in Britain since 1820*. London: Virago.
Mitchell, David. 1966. *Women on the Warpath: The Story of Women of the First World War*. London: Jonathan Cape.
Oldfield, Sybil. 1994. *This Working-Day World: Women's Lives and Cultures in Britain 1914–1945*. London: Taylor and Francis.
Snowden, Ethel. 1921. *A Political Pilgrim in Europe*. London: Cassell.
Swanwick, Helena. 1935. *I Have Been Young*. London: Gollancz.
———. 1971. *Women and War*. Introduction by Blanche Wiesen Cook. New York: Garland.
Thompson, Dorothy. 1983. *Over Our Dead Bodies: Women against the Bomb*. London: Virago.

Szold, Henrietta
(1860–1945)
United States/Israel

Henrietta Szold was a Zionist activist and worker for Jewish immigrants and refugee children through the Youth Aliyah, which rescued and resettled thousands of Jewish children from Europe during the rise of Adolf Hitler's Nazi regime. One of eight daughters of Hungarian immigrants, Szold was born in Baltimore. Her father, a rabbi, wanted her to take the place of the scholarly son he never had and ensured that she was well educated. From a young age, she spoke German, French, and Hebrew. She was educated at the Western Female High School in Baltimore until 1877 and taught classics and modern languages for fifteen years at the Misses Adams School in Baltimore. She also gave lessons in Bible history and ran a Sunday school at her father's synagogue, as well as contributing articles to the *Jewish Messenger* in New York.

An influx of Jewish immigrants fleeing from a wave of pogroms in Russia in 1882 prompted Szold to raise funds to set up a night school in Baltimore, where they and other non-Jewish immigrants could learn English and acclimatize themselves to their new American way of life. The school, which opened in 1889 and was overseen by Szold until 1893, was such a success that many similar schools were established in other cities to promote the Americanization of new immigrants.

In 1893 Szold joined the Hebras Zion, the first Zionist organization of its kind in the United States, and became full-time literary secretary of the Jewish Publishing Society of America, a post she held until 1916. In this capacity, she translated and edited Jewish scholarly works on literature, ethics, and history, such as Heinrich Graetz's *History of the Jews,* and also took on responsibility in 1899 for the annual directory, *The American Jewish Year Book.*

In 1903 Szold gave up her teaching post and moved to New York City, where she studied Judaism at the all-male Jewish Theological Seminary and became an early advocate of the Zionist cause, in 1907 joining the Hadassah Study Circle. Taking time off from her job for the Jewish Publishing Society, Szold spent 1909–1910 in Palestine with her mother and on her return became secretary of the Federation of American

Zionists. Anxious to do something to improve health care standards for both Jews and Arabs in Palestine, in 1912 Szold set up a women's group with thirty-eight others to further medical aid there as well as the ideal of Zionism. This was the Hadassah chapter of Daughters of Zion—which soon became known simply as Hadassah (the Hebrew name for Queen Esther) under Szold's presidency. A year later, Hadassah established its own medical unit and sent its first two nurses to Jerusalem.

In 1916 a group of Jewish benefactors provided funding for Szold to give up her work for the Jewish Publishing Society and work full-time for the Zionist cause, becoming the education director of the Zionist Organization of America when it was established in 1918. With the British occupying Palestine at the end of World War I, Szold organized an American Zionist medical unit, consisting of forty-four people together with considerable medical supplies and equipment, jointly funded by several Jewish groups. Soon after, the unit established the Rothschild-Hadassah Hospital in Jerusalem. Under Szold's supervision, beginning in 1920, a nurses' training school (later known as the Henrietta Szold–Hadassah School of Nursing) was established, and health programs were initiated under the new name of the Hadassah Medical Organization (1922).

Returning to the United States in 1923, Szold gave up the presidency of Hadassah in 1926 (although she continued as honorary president until her death) and a year later returned to Palestine as a member of the Palestine Executive Committee of the World Zionist Organization with a special responsibility for education and health. During the early 1930s, she continued to establish social services and health care in Palestine but in 1933 found a new and more pressing role, through Hadassah's Youth Aliyah, of helping young Jewish people aged fifteen to seventeen travel from Nazi Germany to undertake vocational training in Palestine. In the years leading up to World War II, she raised money in Europe to help bring several thousand young people to Palestine, thus saving them from almost certain death during the Holocaust. By war's end, it is estimated that up to 30,000 children had been rescued, mainly from Germany, Eastern Europe, and Russia, and resettled on kibbutzes and elsewhere in what would soon be the new state of Israel. Much of the relief work among Jewish refugees after the war was undertaken by an umbrella group, the League of Jewish Women, which Szold had also established in the late 1930s in Palestine to consolidate women's philanthropic work there.

Having settled for good in Palestine by 1937, Szold initiated a new research center there to investigate the particular problems encountered by children and juveniles at the request of the National Assembly of Palestinian Jewry, to which she had belonged since 1931. She also founded the Lemaan ha-Yeled, later known as the Szold Foundation, which was dedicated to the welfare of young Jewish people both in Palestine and the United States.

Hadassah, otherwise known as the National Women's Zionist Organization of America, is today the largest Jewish women's organization in the United States, with some 350,000 members. For further details on its work and a biography of Szold (under "archive"), contact http://www.hadassah.org/.

References and Further Reading

Current Biography. 1940. New York: H. W. Wilson.

Fineman, Irving. 1961. *Woman of Valor: The Life of Henrietta Szold, 1860–1945.* New York: Simon and Schuster.

Hyman, Paula, and Deborah D. Moore, eds. 1998. *Jewish Women in America: An Historical Encyclopedia.* New York: Routledge.

Levinger, Elma Ehrlich. 1946. *Fighting Angel: The Story of Henrietta Szold.* New York: Behrman House.

Lowenthal, Martin. 1942. *Henrietta Szold: Life and Letters.* New York: Viking Press.

Sicherman, Barbara, and Carol Hurd Green, eds. 1980. *Notable American Women 1607–1950: A Biographical Dictionary,* vol. 4, *The Modern Period.* Cambridge, MA: Belknap Press of Harvard University.

Zeitlin, Rose. 1952. *Henrietta Szold: Record of a Life.* New York: Dial Press.

T

Taleqani, Azam
(active from 1980s)
Iran

The daughter of the moderate cleric Ayatollah Mohammad Taleqani, Azam Taleqani capitalized on her father's influential position during the 1980s as the most popular cleric after Ayatollah Ruhollah Khomeini by calling on the state to acknowledge more fully the role played by women in Iranian society. She has drawn attention to women's ability to make a contribution in the workplace, but all strictly within the parameters of what she perceives as being the correct Islamicization of women's rights in postrevolutionary Iran.

A university graduate and high school teacher, Taleqani was the founder and president of the pro-establishment Women's Society of the Islamic Revolution during the 1980s and 1990s. She became a leading voice in Iran as one of the first four women elected to the first Iranian postrevolutionary consultative assembly—the *majlis*—after the revolution of 1979. In the early 1980s, she became extremely active in all aspects of political life and took part in many discussion groups on a wide range of social and political issues. Like her contemporary Mariam Behruzi, she grounds her argument in support of women's political and public roles in an interpretation of the Qu'ran, which emphasizes the traditional contribution of women to the fabric of Islam.

Taleqani is against compulsory veiling and the stoning of adulterous women and has called for a general restraint in the punishment of women involved in sex-related crimes such as prostitution (she sees the latter as a remnant of the old, hated, and Europeanized regime of the shahs).

She attempted to introduce a bill allowing women in civil and public service to work half-time, thus allowing room for other women to enter the workplace. Behruzi supported her in this call to give women a role outside the home, but both women were met with stiff opposition from conservative clerics who insist that it is the duty of Iranian women to stay at home and "raise up great Islamic leaders like Khomeini" (Afkhami and Friedl 1994, 72). The bill was finally enacted in November 1983. Despite her failure to capture a seat in parliament in the second *majlis* of 1980–1984, Taleqani found an outlet for her views through the Islamic Institute of Women of Iran and its journal *Message of Hagar,* of which she is editor; she has also contributed on a regular basis to the popular weekly woman's magazine *Zaneh Ruz.*

Originally a member of the Muslim Women's Movement, Taleqani left to found and become president of the Women's Society of the Islamic Revolution. This organization became involved in establishing a range of classes for women in literacy, religion and ideology, and crafts and vocational skills.

In the late 1980s, Taleqani suggested that female advisers should be provided in family protection courts in an attempt to regularize procedures and bring greater equanimity in verdicts, especially those relating to children. Along with Behruzi, she has also asked that the government provide welfare to "unprotected" women who do not enjoy the benefit of the family structure.

Taleqani's commitment to the basic democratic right of women to be given access to the Iranian political leadership and the right to stand for president remains the focal point of an unswerving belief that political rights are fundamental human rights that stand outside religious laws. During the 1990s she denounced the revolution for refusing to allow women a greater public role and for wishing to see them once more isolated in the purely domestic sphere. As a result, she also campaigned to have women granted greater access to a wider range of university courses, which during the 1990s were considerably circumscribed. In particular, she has emphasized the glaring anomaly that despite the fact that most Iranian women live and work in rural areas, they are not allowed to study agricultural science at the universities.

In 1997 Taleqani took her campaign for women's political rights a step further with a challenge to Article 110 of the Iranian Constitution, which states that a national leader must be "male." This came prior to the announcement of her intention to run for president as the first Iranian woman to do so. She was supported by eight other women who also stood for election, but all nine of them were rejected as candidates by the Iranian Council of Guardians.

One of only a handful of prominent, outspoken Iranian woman who have become widely known and politically active since the revolution, Taleqani has given voice to the disappointment of many Iranian women who had hoped for more political advances for their gender. For her, the government has not given them a new political voice but has concentrated its efforts on "making women stay at home, at all costs; to make them accept self-sacrifice, oppression and submissiveness" (Afshar 1998, 163). She has also argued that the imposition of *hijab* (modesty in dress) should apply equally to men and women. The changeover to a more reformist government under Mohammad Khatami in 1997 gave Iranian women hope that improvement to the traditionally inferior position of women in Iran might yet come.

See also Behruzi, Mariam.

References and Further Reading
Afkhami, M., and E. Friedl, eds. 1994. *In the Eye of the Storm: Women in Post-Revolutionary Iran.* London: I. B. Tauris.

Afshar, Haleh. 1998. *Islam and Feminisms: An Iranian Case Study.* Basingstoke: Macmillan.

Tang Qunying
(active 1900–1920s)
China

A leader of the newly emergent Chinese Women's Suffrage Alliance (WSA) in Shanghai after the collapse of the Qing dynasty, Tang was involved in petitioning the new republican government established in Nanjing after the revolution of 1911–1912. A member of the Guomindang (Nationalist Party), she was one of the first Chinese women to publicly demand women's social equality with men and their right to suffrage. Sadly, the movement was short-lived, and after its defeat in 1913 the WSA was dissolved.

Like her contemporary and fellow activist Qiu Jin, Tang went to Japan and studied at the Girls' Practical School and joined with Chinese student activists in Japan in the Restoration Alliance. During her stay, she learned the art of bomb making from Russian anarchists who had a bomb factory in Yokohama.

On her return to China, Tang took part in the growing movement for social change after the abdication of the emperor by becoming chair of the Chinese Suffragette Society in 1912. The alliance petitioned the new provisional government of the warlord Yuan Shikai when it failed to specify the rights of women in the new provisional constitution. Tang, who became a familiar speaker in Beijing and Tianjin, led a group of suffragists who stormed into the National Assembly demanding women's suffrage on three consecutive days: 19, 20, and 21 March 1912. Modeling themselves on the militant Women's Social and Political Union (WSPU) in Britain, they broke windows and threatened armed demonstrations in their demand for a meeting with nationalist leader Sun Yat-sen (who had briefly taken over as president).

With Sun Yat-sen's removal soon after, the suffrage cause lost an ally and the various women's and suffrage groups regrouped in Nanjing under the banner of the Women's Suffrage Alliance. This single body demanded equal civil rights for men and women, women's education and right to employment, women's freedom to choose marriage partners and right to monogamous marriages, improved rights within the home, and an end to footbinding, concubinage, and licensed prostitution. When the Restoration Alliance was reorganized as the Guomindang (Nationalist Party) in August 1912, it held its first conference, at which Tang Qunying and other suffragists challenged the new party's abandonment of women's equal rights with men in its program to concentrate upon the social and political transformation of China as a whole. The movement juddered on through a series of political setbacks until January 1913, when it was dissolved by the weakened government of Yuan Shikai in the wake of counterrevolution and renewed upheaval.

There was talk at the time that Tang, who had been arrested, had been secretly executed, but she reemerged to take up local activities to promote the alliance's goals on women's rights up to and during the May Fourth Movement in 1919, when women's issues were revived as part of the call for national renewal.

See also Qiu Jin.

References and Further Reading

Croll, Elizabeth. 1978. *Feminism and Socialism in China.* New York: Schocken Books.

Ono Kazuko. 1978. *Chinese Women in a Century of Revolution.* Stanford: Stanford University Press.

Wang Zheng. 1999. *Women in the Chinese Enlightenment.* Los Angeles: University of California Press.

Tarbell, Ida
(1857–1944)
United States

Renowned primarily as a pioneer of women's journalism and the dubious journalistic art of "muckraking," Ida Tarbell raised social concerns but was never a suffragist. As a single professional woman, she carved out a successful career as a journalist yet denied her fellow women's potential to do so by arguing that they were better off fulfilling a domestic role at home. Although Tarbell came to be seen as the unofficial face of antisuffragism, there is much in her thinking on women's rights that remains contradictory.

Born in Erie County, Pennsylvania, Tarbell grew up on a farm and went to school in Titusville after the family moved there in 1870. After being one of the few women to attend Allegheny College, where she developed a fascination for geology and abandoned her conventional religious beliefs for pantheism and the theory of evolution, Tarbell found herself unable to take up the career she had hoped for in sci-

ence. She was forced to settle instead for a teaching post in Ohio, spending two years at a Presbyterian school, the Poland Union Seminary. There she first witnessed the problems industry caused for farming and the environment. Tired of being overworked and underpaid, Tarbell gave up her teaching job to work as editor of the home-study magazine the *Chautauquan* (1883–1891). After studying at the Sorbonne and Collège de France in Paris, in 1894 she joined *McClure's Magazine* and worked there until 1906.

Her first published articles were on French historical subjects such as Napoleon and feminists of the French Revolution such as Madame de Staël and Madame Roland (both series of articles were subsequently published in book form). In 1900 her articles on Abraham Lincoln, originally serialized in twenty-two parts, were published as *The Life of Abraham Lincoln*. Tarbell then turned to investigative journalism with her exposé of the environmental pollution caused by the U.S. oil business in a nineteen-part series for *McClure's*, which subsequently became her best-selling book, *History of the Standard Oil Company* (1904). In its revelations of malpractice by oil magnate John D. Rockefeller, the book shook the world of big business and made Tarbell's name—and notoriety.

From 1906 to 1915, Tarbell produced numerous revelatory articles on corruption in politics and big business for the *American Magazine,* of which she was a co-owner, as well as a series of books on the U.S. economy, such as *The Nationalizing of Business* (1936). During 1909–1910, she turned to writing a series on the history of women in the United States in the *American Magazine,* covering the period from the American Revolution to the Civil War. But, believing instinctively in women's primary domestic responsibilities as wives and mothers and in their inherent lack of either the experience or the independent thought to use the vote wisely, she did not advocate women's suffrage. Women's duty, or rather their greatness, as she went so far to say, lay in a role outside professional life. As mothers, Tarbell emphasized women's essential role in setting a moral example, training their children for citizenship, and dedicating themselves to a life of service without reward (choosing as her model the selfless work of the reformer Dorothea Dix). Nor did Tarbell have much faith in women's ability to contribute significantly to civilization through arts and letters.

Throughout her life, Tarbell remained skeptical about the exclusivity of women's subjection by men and, in contrast to most antisuffragists, felt that their main problem was their economic dependence on them. Her feminist concerns were defined by her ardent advocacy of women's right to education, but training in the professions as a means of becoming self-supporting was something she seemed to advocate for herself rather than the mass of ordinary women. Tarbell discussed these and other ideas in *The Business of Being a Woman* (1912), but her argument, as Jane Camhi points out, was confused by the decisions she made in her own life regarding personal freedom and the right to remain single and celibate. Tarbell's contentious statements, such as "For the normal woman the fulfillment of life is the making of the thing we best describe as a home" (Camhi 1994, 169), laid the book wide open to attack by many suffragists, among them Harriet Burton Laidlaw, who argued that the only venues where Tarbell's concept of the "business of being a woman" applied were in fact "the Oriental harem . . . and the tolerated house of prostitution" (Camhi 1994, 161). Antisuffragists, however, looked upon Tarbell's book as a gift and an unofficial apologia for their cause. And although she never officially gave her support to the antisuffragists, Tarbell's name was associated with the New York State Association Opposed to Woman Suffrage.

After selling the *American Magazine* in 1915, the year she published *The Ways of Women,* Tarbell went on the lecture circuit for the next seventeen years, speaking on big business and disarmament. She served on the Woman's Committee of the U.S. Council of National Defense during World War I, although her opposition to women's suffrage made it difficult for her to cooperate with the many suffragists on the council, such as Carrie Chapman Catt and Anna Howard Shaw. Tarbell did not respond to Jane Addams's request in 1915 to join the efforts at peace mediation promoted by Henry Ford's "peace ship," but her support for pacifism grew in the postwar years, after she attended the Paris Peace Conference in 1919 and the Naval Disarmament Conference in Washington, D.C., in 1921. In the mid-1920s, after visiting Italy under Benito Mussolini, she wrote articles critical of fascism for *McCall's* magazine and in 1924 published *Peacemakers: Blessed and Otherwise.* Tarbell also gave her support to the social security programs of Franklin D. Roosevelt's New Deal in 1933 and was a member of the National Women's Mobilization Committee for Human Needs until 1938.

See also Addams, Jane; Catt, Carrie Chapman; Dix, Dorothea Lynde; Shaw, Anna Howard.

References and Further Reading
Brady, Kathleen. 1954. *Ida Tarbell: Portrait of a Muckraker: Ida Tarbell's Lifetime in Journalism.* New York: Putnam.
Camhi, Jane Jerome. 1994. "Ida Tarbell: The Making of an Anti." In *Women against Women: American Anti-Suffragism, 1880–1920.* Brooklyn, NY: Carlson Publishing.
Conn, Frances G. 1972. *Ida Tarbell, Muckraker.* Nashville: T. Nelson.
Jensen, Carl. 2000. *Stories That Changed America: Muckrakers of the 20th Century.* New York: Seven Stories Press.
Kochersber, Robert C., ed. 1994. *More Than a Muckraker: Ida Tarbell's Lifetime in Journalism.* Knoxville: University of Tennessee Press.
Tarbell, Ida M. 1939. *All in the Day's Work: An Autobiography by Ida M. Tarbell.* New York: Macmillan Company.

Tata, Lady Mehrbai Dorab
(1879–1931)
India

A Bombay Parsi who had married into one of the wealthiest industrialist families in India and who was a prime mover in the work of the National Council of Women in India, Lady Tata was one of its life patrons. In her day, she epitomized a particular breed of enlightened, Westernized, and wealthy Indian philanthropists who remained conservative by instinct but who was influential through her links with wealth and Indian royalty. Genteel, benign, and somewhat distanced from reality in a rather refined way (her magnificent pearls and diamonds were much admired on official occasions), Tata's generation of Indian reformers would eventually give way to Indian women working in the grass roots for social and national causes.

Tata was the daughter of an educator, H. J. Bhabba. From the Parsee community in Banglore, she had a European upbringing and was educated at home before marrying into the influential Tata family in 1898. Her husband Ratanji was the son of Jamsetji Nasarwanji Tata, who founded the industrial city of Jamshedpur in Bihar state and made numerous philanthropic gestures, such as endowing a cancer research hospital in Bombay.

In 1904 Tata went on a trip to Europe, where she observed the greater involvement of women in social causes. Inspired by this experience, on her return to India she urged a serious attempt to tackle poverty and deprivation at their source. Women could only improve their lot in India, she felt, if they were given proper education and the freedom to leave the confinement of home and purdah. In 1917 Tata led a deputation against indentured labor in the British colonies to petition the British viceroy in India. She also joined a landmark deputation of fourteen women to the secretary of state for India, Lord Edwin Montagu, requesting that women who met the same property qualifications as men be allowed to vote in India. In 1925 Tata and Lady Isabella Aberdeen were founding members of the National Council of Women (NCW), which was the Indian branch of the International Council of Women. She was a financial patron of the NCW and on its executive committee. She was also a member of the Bombay Presidency Women's Council and chair of its executive committee in 1925. In 1930, she chaired the All-India Women's Conference.

Tata was widely traveled and eventually settled in northern Wales. The Tata family tradition of enlightened philanthropy and support for reform was also exemplified in the women's rights activism by Tata's sister-in-law, Herabai Ardehir Tata, and her daughter Mithan. Both women joined a delegation sent by the Bombay Committee of Women's Suffrage, to the Joint Select Committee in London in 1919, which engendered a rare, early discussion of the suffrage movement in India in the November issue of the International Woman Suffrage Association journal *Jus Suffragii*. Their trip was financed by the family firm. Tata's niece Mithan would later study at the London School of Economics and the Inns of Court and become the first woman to pass the bar examination and practice law in India.

References and Further Reading

Tata, Lady. 1933. *A Book of Remembrance*. Bombay: J. B. Dubash.

Taylor, Harriet
(Harriet Taylor Mill)
(1808–1858)
United Kingdom

For many years the name of English feminist writer Harriet Taylor was known only in conjunction with the work of her husband, the economist and liberal philosopher John Stuart Mill. Although she worked in close collaboration with him, inspiring Mill in the later writing of his classic 1869 work, *The Subjection of Women*, because she was a woman her contribution could not be publicly credited, and for long after attempts to redress the balance were consistently challenged. Mill himself always gave Taylor credit where due, but the bias of his paeans of praise to her talents further compounded the problems for commentators of arriving at a balanced appraisal of her real contribution. That Taylor's approach to women's rights was a radical one, in her demand not just for women's equality but their economic independence from men, there is no doubt. Her advocacy of unlimited personal rights for women made clear her belief that they could and should be able to fulfill their aspirations—be they political, moral, intellectual, or material—on the same basis as men.

Taylor was born in Walworth, London, and was married at the age of eighteen to a London wholesale druggist. Within four years, she had two children and had come to loathe sexual relations with her husband. Bored and discontented with her married life and as a woman of some intellect, she sought greater intellectual stimulation among fellow radicals in the Unitarian church. Through the minister William Fox, of the South Place Chapel, she met John Stuart Mill in 1830. Discovering shared interests, an intellectual rapport, and complementary gifts—her verve and intuition and his scholarly reasoning—Taylor and Mill became closely attached. Over the next twenty years, they met regularly and exchanged letters. Whether in all this time their relationship was sexual is the subject of some debate, but unwilling to resort to separation or divorce, her husband graciously sanctioned the friendship and with it had to endure the gossip. Although it is suggested that Taylor might have been willing to act precipitately and live in sin with Mill, he was not willing to sacrifice his career and his reputation to such an extreme step. In the event, she spent increasing amounts of time apart from her husband at a house in Walton-on-Thames, where Mill was a frequent visitor.

As early as 1831–1832, Taylor and Mill began exchanging views on marriage and divorce, at a time when she was engaged in writing articles for the Unitarian journal, the *Monthly Repository* (the only writings openly credited to her). Their discussion by letter was later published; in it, Taylor expressed her own disillusionment with the institution of marriage. Women, she felt, were "educated for one single object—to gain their living by marrying" (Hayek 1969, 76). Taylor was eventually liberated from her own marriage when she was widowed in 1849. After observing the obligatory two years of mourning, in her forties, she married Mill in 1851. Before doing so, the couple drew up their own marriage contract, in which Mill undertook to respect Taylor's absolute autonomy. Having endured years of gossip, they lived quietly at Blackheath in south London, although many of Mill's erstwhile friends bemoaned his self-imposed social isolation. Thereafter, Taylor read and commented on both his journal articles and later major works, and her input is now recognized as significant, particularly in matters relating to the rights of women. She commented in detail on the draft of the *Principles of Political Economy* (1848), and it is now argued that the socialist arguments in the chapter entitled "Probable Future of the Labouring Classes" are mainly her work. She also contributed to *On Liberty* (1859) and to Mill's 1873 *Autobiography*. Although the latter was published after her death, Mill worked on it over a long period, when Taylor was still alive, and the work bears her intellectual imprint. Numerous feminist critics from the 1970s have set about reconstructing the extent of her collaboration, in so doing exposing the nineteenth-century mindset that refused to accept that a woman was intellectually capable of such work and the reluctance of commentators to dilute the power of Mill's sole authorship and with it his intellectual reputation.

One of the most contested works in terms of Taylor's contribution has been the article "The Enfranchisement for Women," published in July 1851 under Mill's name in the *Westminster Review*. Notable for giving impetus to the embryonic women's movement in Britain, it is now generally acknowledged to be mainly the work of

Taylor. The article defends the right of women to education, challenging traditional perceptions that they should be educated only sufficiently to make them more intelligent companions to men. For Taylor, women's education was not only crucial to their economic independence but also a right in itself. Equally, she dismissed the idea that maternity was the only role to which women could aspire; for too long women had lived their lives vicariously through men and allowed themselves to be subsumed in marriage and the rearing of children. Taylor controversially suggested that being wives and mothers was not a natural obligation on women and that they should have the freedom to choose not to follow this path.

With the onset of tuberculosis in the 1850s, Taylor's health rapidly failed; she began to spend the winters in the more salubrious climate of the Continent. In 1858, on one such visit, she fell ill on the way and died at Avignon in the south of France at the age of only fifty-one. Mill became a dedicated keeper of the flame; he bought a house near the cemetery where she was buried and erected an elaborate marble tomb in her memory. Harriet's daughter Helen looked after him for the rest of his life and assumed something of the role of amanuensis in place of her mother.

Although Taylor was long dead when Barbara Bodichon and other members of the Langham Place Circle began organizing a petition on women's suffrage in 1865 that was presented to Parliament a year later by Mill, her formative influence on his feminist sympathies had been a central one in the writing of *The Subjection of Women*. In this seminal text, on which Mill worked for many years, and to which his stepdaughter Helen also contributed, he presented a forceful critique of a social system that upheld the subordination of the female gender as being the chief hindrance to human progress.

See also Bodichon, Barbara.

References and Further Reading

Banks, Olive, ed. 1985, 1990. *The Biographical Dictionary of British Feminists,* vol. 1, *1800–1930;* vol. 2, *1900–1945.* Brighton: Harvester Wheatsheaf.

Crawford, Elizabeth. 1999. *The Women's Suffrage Movement, 1866–1928: A Reference Guide.* London: University College of London Press.

Hardman, Malcolm. 1991. *Six Victorian Thinkers.* Manchester: Manchester University Press.

Hayek, F. A. 1969. *John Stuart Mill and Harriet Taylor:*

Their Friendship and Subsequent Marriage.
London: Routledge and Kegan Paul.

Kamm, Josephine. 1977. *John Stuart Mill in Love.*
London: Gordon and Cremonesi.

Mill, John Stuart. 1997 [1869]. *The Subjection of
Women.* Reprint, New York: Dover.

Nicholls, C. S., ed. 1993. *Dictionary of National
Biography: Missing Persons.* Oxford: Oxford
University Press.

Rendall, Jane, ed. 1987. *Equal or Different: Women's
Politics 1800–1914.* Oxford: Blackwell.

Robson, Ann P., and J. M. Robson, eds. 1994. *Sexual
Equality: Writings by J. S. Mill, Harriet Taylor Mill
and Helen Taylor.* Toronto: Toronto University
Press.

Rose, Phyllis. 1983 [1942]. *Parallel Lives: Five Victorian
Marriages.* Reprint, New York: Alfred A. Knopf.

Rossi, Alice S., ed. 1974. *Essays on Sex Equality by
John Stuart Mill and Harriet Taylor Mill.* Chicago:
University of Chicago Press.

Spender, Dale. 1982. *Women of Ideas, and What Men
Have Done to Them.* London: Routledge and
Kegan Paul.

Te Puea
(1884–1952)
New Zealand

A much-revered Maori nationalist leader and
spiritual figure, Te Puea worked with dedication
for the social and cultural rehabilitation of New
Zealand's Maori peoples after the end of British
colonial rule, furthering in them a sense of pride
and self-respect. However, until New Zealand
ethnographer Michael King began uncovering
Maori history in the 1980s, the name of Te Puea
was virtually unknown, consigned to only passing references in major histories of New Zealand.
King's research has restored her to her right place
as undoubtedly the most significant Maori
woman since European settlement.

Te Puea was born in November 1883, in the
village of Whatiwhatihoe near the Waikato River,
the granddaughter of King Tawhiao, a member
of the Kingitanga peoples. She was educated at a
girls' school in Auckland, where she boarded
with a Maori family. Strong-willed and determined, from a young age she broke the traditional submissive mold of a Maori princess and
defiantly spoke her own mind.

Settling in Mangatawhiri, Te Puea kept her
own dairy cattle. She became a respected figure
in her community for her careful preservation of

Maori legends and songs, and after being asked
to campaign in support of Maui Pomare's election to the Western Maori electorate, she became
an increasingly influential figure.

When the Kingitanga people were devastated
by two outbreaks of disease, an epidemic of
smallpox in 1913 and another of influenza in
1918 (when the pandemic finally reached even
remote areas), Te Puea devotedly nursed the sick
on both occasions. But it was a time when Maori
people were still reluctant to accept conventional
medical care, and the diseases ravaged her people, leaving many orphaned children. Te Puea
dedicated herself to bringing them all together
into one new self-supporting community at
Mangatawhiri.

During World War I, Te Puea opposed the
conscription of Maori men and offered them
refuge in her community. This sense of solidarity
deepened during the 1920s and 1930s, when she
headed a strong movement asserting Maori
pride and independence, joining her Kingitanga
people in their work in the fields and helping
them secure employment in cutting down scrub-
land and making roads. But her main objective
was to secure a grant of land at Ngaruawahia, on
which the Maoris of the Waikato River could establish their own sacred ceremonial ground
(known as a *marae*). Formal requests to the New
Zealand government for compensation for this
land, confiscated from the Maoris in the 1860s
after the New Zealand wars, moved slowly ahead.
Eventually Te Puea and her people raised enough
money through a series of Maori concerts to buy
back their ancestral family site, Ngaruawahia,
from white farmers. She resettled her people
there, building a new meeting house that was
opened in March 1929. During the years that followed, Te Puea was at the forefront of work to re-
claim and cultivate the surrounding land in order that her people might establish their own
livelihood and constantly lobbied government
ministers over Maori issues.

The wheels of bureaucracy ground slowly on
with regard to the land issue. In 1928 a government commission had recommended compensation to the Waikato, but no money was forthcoming until the end of World War II. As always,
Te Puea was at the center of negotiations. Many
of her people rejected the idea of financial compensation, insisting on restitution of the lands
themselves; Te Puea took a more pragmatic view,

concluding that financial compensation would provide the money for economic development and better provisions for the education of Maori children.

In 1940 she took up the case of Maoris living at Orakei, who were also having disputes with the government over landownership, and set out to create a community for them similar to her own at Ngaruawahia. In 1942 she formed an Orakei Petition Committee, with backing from the General Labourers' Union and the Auckland Trades Council, requesting the return of 25 acres of land, meanwhile helping the Orakei establish a tribal *pa* (meeting house), surrounded by palisades, on the site in question.

Te Puea was married several times but had no children of her own. Instead, she adopted the orphaned children of many of her own people, including her grandniece, who later became queen of the Maoris. In 1937 she was made a Commander of the Order of the British Empire.

References and Further Reading

King, Michael. 1987. *Te Puea Herangi: From Darkness to Light.* Auckland: Hodder and Stoughton.

MacDonald, Charlotte, ed. 1991. *The Book of New Zealand Women.* Wellington, NZ: Bridget Williams Books.

Terrell, Mary Church
(1863–1954)
United States

The black educator and public speaker on civil rights Mary Church Terrell was one of the first black women in the United States to complete a college education, by studying at Oberlin College. For many years, she worked for racial justice on behalf of the National Association of Colored Women (NACW), and in the early 1950s, not long before her death, she joined the successful campaign to desegregate lunch counters and restaurants in Washington, D.C.

Born in Memphis, Tennessee, Terrell enjoyed the fruits of her parents' hard work and enterprise and grew up, by southern standards of living for blacks, in a well-off home. She studied at the model school at Antioch College in Ohio and transferred to Oberlin High School in 1875 (graduating in 1879). She completed her bachelor's degree at the abolitionist-run Oberlin College in 1884, where she studied on the classical,

or "Gentleman's Course," for most of that time as the only black woman on campus. Upon her graduation, Terrell rejected the idle life she could have enjoyed back at home (her father had made money in real estate and had become one of the South's first black millionaires). Against his wishes, Terrell took a teaching post at Wilberforce University in Ohio. In 1887 she moved to Washington to teach Latin in the Colored High School. She relented in 1888 when she finally received her M.A. from Oberlin College and accepted money from her father to travel in Europe for the next two years, where she studied French, German, and Italian.

Upon her return to the United States, Mary declined the offer of a registrar's post at Oberlin College to marry a black high school principal and lawyer, Robert Heberton Terrell, in 1891. After losing three children, Terrell finally gave birth to a surviving daughter in 1905. During these years, unable to continue teaching because she was a married woman, Terrell undertook community work as a member of the Colored Women's League, beginning in 1892, and as the first black woman appointed to the District of Columbia Board of Education (1895–1901 and 1906–1911). In 1896 Terrell became president of the National Association of Colored Women, a new self-help organization established to promote the virtues of domestic, moral, and civil life, as well as the advancement of black women. During her five-year tenure, Terrell extended existing clubs for black women (which in themselves became venues for many black suffragists and feminists) and set up kindergartens and nurseries, refuges for women and children, and relief programs for the poor and the elderly. She went on the professional lecture circuit to promote its work and her other civil rights causes, which she felt was her "duty to my race" (Bolt 1993, 223). In 1901 Terrell was elected honorary president, although in 1908 the lightness of her skin (which at times allowed her to pass for white in the South) led some members to advocate the enlistment of darker-skinned women in key roles in the NACW.

Since the 1890s, Terrell had also been active in the suffrage movement and at annual conventions of the National American Woman Suffrage Association (NAWSA), where she became a close friend of its leader, Carrie Chapman Catt, a woman she admired for her lack of racial prejudice. Terrell addressed the 1898 convention of the NAWSA on the subject of "The Progress of Colored Women," and was a key speaker at the 1908 NAWSA convention, which celebrated the sixtieth anniversary of the Seneca Falls convention. Terrell also became a familiar figure in the international women's movement, in 1904 making an impressive speech, first in German and then in English and French, at the International Council of Women's congress in Berlin. Speaking on the particular problems of black women, she made a direct comparison between the discrimination against Jews in Germany and that against blacks in the United States. In 1919 Terrell joined a delegation of American women who attended the second congress of the Women's International League for Peace and Freedom. In 1937 she was in London as a representative of black American women at a congress of the World Fellowship of Faith.

In 1904 Terrell condemned the wave of lynchings then occurring in the United States in an article in the *North American Review*. She was active in the early civil rights movement as a founding member, along with Ida B. Wells-Barnett, of the National Association for the Advancement of Colored People. She became president of Washington's Bethel Literary and Historical Association and a member of the Association for the Study of Negro Life and History and wrote articles on the subject. In her eighties, Terrell facilitated the long-overdue integration of the American Association of University Women.

There was a newfound militancy to Terrell's campaigning during her final years, after she became chair of the Coordinating Committee for the Enforcement of District of Columbia Anti-Discrimination Laws. In this capacity, she joined the first moves toward desegregation of Washington's eating places in the early 1950s. Segregated restaurants were declared unconstitutional by the U.S. Supreme Court in 1953, after Terrell brought a test case against a restaurant that refused to serve her. After women's suffrage was won in 1920, Terrell spearheaded efforts through the NACW to encourage black women to exercise their vote and to pay attention to all legislation affecting black people. Terrell published her autobiography, *A Colored Woman in a White World,* in 1940, describing her work in the black community. The book's content, however, did not fulfill the original ambition of its title and was effectively a watered-down version of what she had hoped to write.

See also Catt, Carrie Chapman; Wells-Barnett, Ida B.

References and Further Reading
Bolt, Christine. 1993. *The Women's Movements in the United States and Britain from the 1790s to the 1920s.* London: Harvester Wheatsheaf.
Hine, Darlene Clarke, et al., eds. 1993. *Black Women in America: An Historical Encyclopedia.* 2 vols. Bloomington: Indiana University Press.
Jones, Beverly Washington. 1990. *Quest for Equality: The Life and Writings of Eliza Mary Church Terrell, 1863–1954.* Brooklyn, NY: Carlson Publishers.
Lerner, Gerda, ed. 1972. *Black Women in White America: A Documentary History.* New York: Pantheon Books.
McKissack, Patricia. 1991. *Mary Church Terrell: Leader for Equality.* Hillside, NJ: Enslow.
Peebles-Wilkins, Wilma, and Francis E. Aracelis. 1990. "Two Outstanding Black Women in Social Welfare History: Mary Church Terrell and Ida B. Wells-Barnett. *Affilia* 5(4): 87–100.
Schott, Linda K. 1997. *Reconstructing Women's Thoughts: The Women's International League for Peace and Freedom before World War II.* Stanford: Stanford University Press.
Sklar, Kathryn Kish. 1998. *Social Justice Feminists in the United States and Germany: A Dialogue in Documents 1885–1933.* Ithaca: Cornell University Press.
Smallwood, Caid, Stan West, and Allison Keyes. 1998. *Profiles of Great African Americans.* Lincolnwood, IL: Publications International.
Smith, Jessie Carney, ed. 1992. *Notable Black American Women.* Detroit: Gale.
Sterling, Dorothy. 1988. *Black Foremothers: Three Lives.* Rev. ed. New York: Women's Press.
Terrell, Mary Church. 1980 [1940]. *A Colored Woman in a White World.* Reprint, New York: Arno Press.

Thomas, Martha Carey
(1857–1935)
United States

The Quaker feminist and educationist Martha Carey Thomas devoted her long career as a professor at and president of Bryn Mawr College to promoting the intellectual excellence of women. As a woman committed to the advancement of her sex, she devised an ambitious curriculum that would demonstrate women's ability to be men's equal in the professions. She also applied her considerable energies to campaigning for

Martha Carey Thomas (North Wind Picture Archives)

women's suffrage as president of the National College Women's Equal Suffrage League.

Thomas was the eldest of ten children of a Quaker family in Baltimore, Maryland. Her mother, a feminist noted for her philanthropic work, encouraged an awareness of women's rights in the young Martha and was keen to see her gain access to higher education. After attending Quaker schools, Thomas and her mother together persistently lobbied her more conventionally minded father to allow her to study at Cornell University. After obtaining her degree in 1877, she studied Greek for a year at Johns Hopkins University (but was only allowed to do so on the condition that she remain segregated from male students behind a screen). This and other continuing obstructions to women's further education in the United States prompted Thomas to travel to Europe to complete her postgraduate studies. She studied philology in Leipzig but was refused permission to sit for her Ph.D., which she finally obtained in Zurich in 1882.

On her return to the United States, Thomas discovered that thanks to a recent Quaker bequest, her father and various family members were involved in the establishment of a new col-

lege, Bryn Mawr College for Women, which opened in Philadelphia in 1885. Thomas applied for the post of president but initially was appointed dean and professor of English, being promoted to president in 1894 when the college's male president retired. At that time, she was one of four women on the staff who held Ph.D.s, which gave Bryn Mawr impressive academic credentials. With the autocratic Thomas at its helm introducing standards to match those at Harvard University, it would remain the only U.S. college where women were able to earn a Ph.D. for another fifty years.

Until her retirement from Bryn Mawr College in 1922, Thomas devoted her time not to teaching but to devising a progressive, if rigorous, curriculum for women undergraduates that included the obligatory study of foreign languages and would produce outstanding students equipped to take their place alongside men in the professions. Thomas's regime, geared as it was to academic excellence and the traditional disciplines of Greek, Latin, and mathematics, tended to neglect the liberal arts and culture and imposed a rigid discipline in a concerted attempt to preserve the reputation and high achievement levels of her students. She also became involved in establishing a feeder school for brighter potential pupils, and in 1885, she and her friend Mary Garrett established the Bryn Mawr School for Girls in Baltimore. In 1900 Thomas described her theories in *The Higher Education of Women*.

Through her activities for the Association of College Alumnae, Thomas worked not only to further the interests of women undergraduates but also to see more women admitted to postgraduate studies. In 1889 she joined with other feminists to lobby for women to be admitted to medical courses at Johns Hopkins University in Baltimore. Inevitably, she was drawn into wider issues of women's rights and was a prominent suffragist. In 1908 Thomas was elected first president of the National College Women's Equal Suffrage League (which she had cofounded in 1906 to encourage students and college lecturers to support women's suffrage) and through it came into close collaboration with the National American Woman Suffrage Association. After the winning of the vote in 1920, she was active in Alice Paul's National Woman's Party in support of an Equal Rights Amendment.

As an advocate of women's equality with men

and their entry into all professions, Thomas did not favor separate protective legislation for women, nor did she agree that women who married should abandon their careers. Such was the dedication with which she set about producing her own breed of intellectual superwomen at Bryn Mawr that she has been accused of elitism (just as her English counterpart Emily Davies, at Girton College, Cambridge, has been), even though she might have argued that her objective was for the good of social progress. Similarly, Thomas's refusal to dilute the exclusivity of female excellence at Bryn Mawr by admitting male students was also seen as excessively separatist, exaggerating the divisions between the sexes rather than eradicating them.

In 1921, the interests of working women were addressed with the inception of Bryn Mawr's Summer School for Women Workers in Industry. Bryn Mawr also established a graduate school of social science, in 1915, which was one of the first in the United States to offer such training to women and the first to offer a doctoral degree. A sizable bequest to Thomas by a female friend in 1915 led to a weakening of her social concerns; after her retirement from Bryn Mawr, she spent extended periods living in considerable comfort abroad.

See also Paul, Alice.

References and Further Reading

Dictionary of American Biography 1946–1958, and indexes to Supplements 1–10, 1981–1996. New York: Scribner's.

Finch, Edith. 1947. *Carey Thomas of Bryn Mawr.* New York: Harper.

Meigs, Cornelia. 1956. *What Makes a College?* New York: Macmillan.

Sicherman, Barbara, and Carol Hurd Green, eds. 1980. *Notable American Women 1607–1950: A Biographical Dictionary*, vol. 4, *The Modern Period.* Cambridge, MA: Belknap Press of Harvard University.

Whitman, Alden, ed. 1988. *American Reformers: An H. W. Wilson Biographical Dictionary.* New York: H. W. Wilson.

Tiburtius, Franziska
(1843–1927)
Germany

One of the first two German women to qualify as a doctor, in 1876, Franziska Tiburtius had to undertake her studies in Switzerland. Her subsequent pioneering work in private practice was dogged by official and public hostility toward women doctors. Tiburtius was also a pioneer of women's further education in Germany, working with Helene Lange in establishing the first higher education establishment for women, the Realkurse, in 1889.

Born on Rügen Island in Pomerania, Tiburtius grew up in Stralsund, where she attended school until the age of sixteen. She began life as a teacher, working at a girls' school in London during the Franco-Prussian War of 1870–1871. She had originally intended to set up a school for girls on her return to Germany but instead was encouraged by her brother Jacob, who was an army doctor, to study medicine, particularly after Jacob's wife Henriette had taken a degree in dentistry in the United States and become the first German woman dentist. However, when Tiburtius canvassed the medical faculties of German universities to be admitted, she was refused and, like many similar women in Russia, went to Switzerland to study.

In 1876 Tiburtius passed her medical examinations with distinction. She completed an internship at the Women's Clinic in Dresden that year, studying with the noted gynecologist Professor Franz von Winckel (one of the few professors prepared to accept women students). Meanwhile, an 1869 law allowed those women who had medical diplomas from abroad to take up "practical therapy." The limitations encapsulated in that phrase soon became clear when Tiburtius and her fellow student at Zurich, Emilie Lehmus, set themselves up in private practice together in a poor district of Berlin in 1877, despite being told by officials that they would not be permitted to practice. They received a rough ride from the male medical establishment, officialdom, and outraged public opinion, and their opponents obtained numerous court injunctions to prevent them from running their clinic, which pioneered health care for women and children with financial support from various women's groups. Despite the many obstructions placed in their path, including the regular removal of their brass nameplate (and its equally regular restoration), the clinic established a large clientele. By 1892 the clinic had treated 17,000 patients and also promoted women's medical education. Thanks to the work of Tiburtius, Lehmus, and other women practitioners who fought for women's medical education until 1908, when the German universities opened their doors to them, Berlin would become a major training center for women medical practitioners.

As a supporter of women's medical training and herself a former teacher, Tiburtius also embraced other feminist causes, particularly women's education, although she never actively propagandized on such issues. In 1889, together with her sister-in-law Henriette, the educator Helene Lange, and activist Minna Cauer, she set up the Realkurse, the first German institution to prepare women for university entrance, although many of its first graduates, like Tiburtius, had to study in Switzerland. Between 1896 and 1906, as a testament to the example of Tiburtius's work, 53 of the Realkurse's 111 women graduates would opt to study medicine.

Tiburtius's *Memoirs of an Eighty-Year-Old* were published posthumously in Berlin in 1929. She died in the small infirmary run by the Union of Women Physicians in Berlin, which she had founded and of which she was honorary president.

See also Cauer, Minna; Lange, Helene.

References and Further Reading
Albisetti, James. 1982. "Could Separate Be Equal? Helene Lange and Women's Education in Imperial Germany." *History of Education Quarterly* (Fall): 301–318.
Bonner, Thomas Neville. 1995. *Becoming a Physician: Medical Education in Britain, France, Germany, and the U.S. 1750–1945.* New York: Oxford University Press.
Ogilvie, Marilyn, and Joy Harvey, eds. 2000. *Biographical Dictionary of Women in Science: Pioneering Lives from Ancient Times to the Mid-Twentieth Century.* London: Routledge.

Tod, Isabella
(1836–1896)
Ireland

The Scottish-born suffragist and pioneer of Irish girls' schools and women's education Isabella Tod later became a leading light in the Northern Irish Unionist and temperance movements. A contemporary of the Irish Quaker Anna Haslam, like her Tod divided her energies among a considerable number of political and social causes as

well as wrote many pamphlets and letters to the papers, in so doing becoming one of the most well-known female activists of her time.

Tod was born in Edinburgh into a Presbyterian family but moved to Belfast in the 1860s. Little is known about her early life except that she was encouraged in self-study at home by her mother after receiving only a rudimentary schooling. In Belfast she began undertaking philanthropic work, visiting poor women, as well as writing anonymously (and thereby supporting herself) for numerous publications such as the *Dublin University Magazine, Banner of Ulster,* and *Northern Whig.* In 1867, when the National Association for the Promotion of Social Science held its first meeting in Belfast, Tod became an active member. One of the earliest outlets for women with a social conscience who wished to play a reforming role in society, the association served as a platform for Tod (as it had done for another Irish reformer, Anne Jellicoe, in 1862). Tod's first paper, "On Advanced Education for Girls of the Upper and Middle Classes," was, by polite convention, read out for her by a male friend at an association meeting in 1867. But she would later become a confident and extremely effective public speaker, according to her lifelong friend and colleague Anna Haslam, and took the debate of women's issues to a wider audience in Ireland during the crucial campaigns for women's education and suffrage.

Indeed, Tod was particularly rousing in her calls for women to be admitted into higher education, on which subject she was the first Irishwoman to speak publicly. In 1869 she added her name to a petition initiated by Queen's University for women to be admitted to examinations as one of the first steps toward their admittance to universities. In 1873 she supported a campaign that tried but failed to achieve their admittance to degree courses (they were eventually admitted in 1883). Tod held steadfast to her belief in the importance of education for middle-class women as a means of providing practical skills, thus enabling them to be more useful to society. She elaborated on this point further in another pamphlet in 1874: "On the Education of Girls of the Middle Class."

During the 1860s and 1870s, Tod was a leading personality in the Irish branch of the wider British campaign for passage of the Married Women's Property Act (eventually passed in

1882). She worked closely with other activists in the campaign, such as Frances Power Cobbe, Josephine Butler, and Lydia Becker, and gave evidence at the select committee formed to inquire into these legal changes. The long fight for the repeal of the Contagious Diseases Acts between 1869 and 1886 also drew her support as secretary of the Irish branch of the Ladies National Association that supported Butler's campaign. It underlined her strong feelings on moral responsibility, her abhorrence of the sexual double standards of Victorian society, and her advocacy of both sexual self-control and temperance. For Tod, much of the abject poverty suffered by the women and children to whom she offered help was the result of the evils of drink. She also became closely involved in other social campaigns and called for women, with their particular nurturing skills and social compassion, to be given the opportunity to work as Poor Law Guardians.

In 1874 Tod became a founding member of the Belfast Women's Temperance Association, which was primarily committed to the idea of temperance as an individual social responsibility. But the association did not confine itself to mere moralizing; Tod and other members helped establish various welfare projects to help prevent poor women from sliding into alcoholism and also to give succor to its victims. By 1889 the association, with its forty branches, had established soup kitchens for poor factory girls, a home for alcoholic women, and one for girls and gave lessons in cookery and hygiene. It also set up the Prison Gate Mission in Belfast to help alcoholics and ex-prisoners and their children. From 1877 to 1892, Tod acted as vice president of the British Women's Temperance Association. Her proselytizing on behalf of temperance went a stage further when she took over the vice presidency in 1893 of the Women's Total Abstinence Union, although she never attempted to initiate calls for the total prohibition of alcohol, as did women in the U.S. temperance movement.

As founder in 1871 of the North of Ireland Women's Suffrage Society, Tod was one of the mainstays of the early suffrage movement in Belfast. She worked tirelessly as its secretary until the 1890s, as well as being closely involved in the Belfast Ladies Institute, which she had founded in 1867 to give a course of winter lectures for women, and the Ulster Head Schoolmistresses Association. She also contributed articles to the *Englishwoman's Review,* the mouthpiece of the British women's movement. Tod was convinced that women had proven themselves a force for social good through their dedication to philanthropic work and that the ability to vote (albeit through a limited form based on property ownership) would only enhance their potential. Indeed, she considered women morally superior to men and believed that the time had come for an end to the male monopoly on education and politics. In particular, she abhorred the exploitation of working women by drunken husbands and thought that women should have greater control over the wages for which they worked so hard. She threw a great deal of energy into achieving votes for women in local, municipal elections (achieved in 1887), creating an outlet for women to implement and organize numerous social and welfare projects among Belfast's poor. In 1896 Tod's battle for women in Ireland to be able to work as Poor Law Guardians was finally won with the passage of a bill.

Tod's final crusade involved the fight to prevent Irish home rule. As a staunch Unionist, she could not compromise her views on this subject and as a result lost the support of some of her colleagues in the suffrage movement. She wrote endless letters and pamphlets against home rule and traveled to England and around Ulster, rallying female support for the cause. She also helped set up a Liberal Women's Unionist Association in Belfast. She dreaded what she saw as the inevitable religious conflict that passage of the home rule bills would provoke and felt that any ensuing conflict would also cause great damage to the economy of northern Ireland. Eventually, Tod wore herself out—this final cause was perhaps one too many for her failing strength. She struggled on for another ten years. When she died in 1896, she was given a large funeral, and many laudatory obituaries appeared in the Irish press, but, as Maria Luddy points out, like so many other female reformers of her time, Tod was so completely forgotten thereafter and her work so neglected that the facts of her personal life are almost unknown.

See also Becker, Lydia; Butler, Josephine; Cobbe, Frances Power; Haslam, Anna; Jellicoe, Anne.

References and Further Reading

Cullen, Mary, and Maria Luddy. 1995. *Women: Power*

*and Consciousness in Nineteenth-Century Ireland.
Eight Biographical Studies.* Dublin: Attic Press.

Lewis, Jane. 1987. *Before the Vote Was Won: Arguments for and against Women's Suffrage.* London: Routledge and Kegan Paul.

Luddy, Maria. 1995. *Women and Philanthropy in Nineteenth-Century Ireland.* Cork: Cork University Press.

Shiman, Lilian Lewis. 1992. *Women and Leadership in Nineteenth-Century England.* Basingstoke: Macmillan.

Torres, Elena
(active 1920s–1940s)
Mexico

Elena Torres was a leading feminist, progressive educator, and teacher and a follower of the anti-capitalist and anti-imperialist ideas of Leon Trotsky. She studied at Columbia University Teachers' College in New York City before World War I. On her return to Mexico, she joined the Socialist Party of the Yucatán and collaborated with its pro-feminist male governors, Salvador Alvarado (governed 1915–1918) and Felipe Carrillo Puerto (1922–1924), during an innovative and reformist period in local Yucatán government. She helped set up a rational education program, which focused on women and encouraged adult literacy in general, and oversaw health care programs during the 1920s. She also took steps to protect the rights of peasants and Mayan Indians.

In the first two decades of the twentieth century, Yucatán led the way in offering liberating opportunities to women. It was the first Mexican state to set out a government program on women's education and also was the venue for the first two feminist congresses, sanctioned by Alvarado, that were held in Mexico—in January and November 1916. Attendees at these meetings discussed a wide range of topics, including employment, education, suffrage, and the contentious issues of birth control and divorce. Torres was one of many Mexican women teachers who attended the second congress. In 1917, President Alvarado became so impressed with her work that he invited her to set up the first Montessori school in Mexico, in Mérida, the Yucatán state capital. The school encouraged practical skills and did not make exams the sole criterion for excellence.

In 1918 Torres became involved in the Latin American Bureau of Trotsky's Third International, which she set up with Felipe Carrillo Puerto and which aimed to promote greater cooperation between the working classes of socialist states. At the Second Workers' Congress in Izamal in 1921, Torres criticized the exclusion of women from workers' congresses and demanded they be given the right to voice their opinions. The years 1920–1924 were particularly hectic for her: in 1920 she was a cofounder of the Mexican Feminist Council in Mexico City, which set as its goals the social and economic liberation of women as well as their right to the vote. She represented the council in 1922 at the Baltimore meeting of the League of Women Voters. That same year, she also became the first woman in Mexico to be elected to a municipal post when she became president of the Mérida City Council. Her involvement in the meeting in Baltimore led her to form a delegation of Mexican women to attend the Pan-American Women's Conference, also held in Baltimore later that year, during which she was elected vice president for North America (the United States, Canada, and Mexico). In 1923 she was the guiding force behind the establishment in Mexico City of the Mexican branch of the newly founded Pan-American Association for the Advancement of Women.

As if all these activities were not enough, in 1923 Torres helped organize the Mexico Women's Congress, attended by women's groups from twenty Mexican states as well as U.S. and Cuban representatives. The congress proved to be a noisy and turbulent one, with radical motions brought by feminists from the Yucatán causing alarm in the ranks of the more conservative delegates. Torres was anxious that the congress should not be disrupted by political division and worked hard to maintain the equilibrium. In her own address, made at the last working session, she called for the repeal of the 1917 Mexican Law of Family Relations, or at least changes to some of its more undemocratic articles that allowed for double standards regarding the behavior of men and women. In particular, she wanted to see modifications to Article 97, which penalized a wife after divorce (even if she had not been the guilty party) and threatened her with loss of custody of her children if she did not abide by certain moral codes.

In 1923 Torres also found time to act as a delegate at the Second Mexican Congress on the

Child, where she gave a lecture on the importance of children in primary schools being taught their civic duties and responsibilities. Also that year, she was asked by the Ministry of Education to take charge of a free breakfast program for 12,000 malnourished schoolchildren in Mexico City. In 1924 she helped run a social welfare experiment among peasants in Mexico's more isolated rural areas.

But by the 1930s, feminist activity in Mexico went into limbo, and Torres turned to other professional activities. After the 1923 women's congress, she had, in any event, played a lesser role in the feminist movement in order to concentrate on work in progressive education in Mexico. This new field took her to a pedagogical conference in the United States in 1933. In 1940 Torres came out in support of her fellow campaigner Juana Belén Gutiérrez de Mendoza's pamphlet "Call to National Attention," which argued for women's suffrage and better employment and welfare rights, as well as criticizing the church over matters such as birth control.

See also Carrillo Puerto, Elvia; Gutiérrez de
   Mendoza, Juana Belén.

References and Further Reading
Macías, Anna. 1983. *Against All Odds: The Feminist
   Movement in Mexico to 1940.* Westport, CT:
   Greenwood Press.
Soto, Shirlene. 1990. *Emergence of the Modern
   Mexican Woman: Her Participation in Revolution
   and Struggle for Equality, 1910–1940.* Denver:
   Arden Press.

Tristan, Flora
(1803–1844)
France

A seminal figure in the history of French feminism, the utopian socialist and trade union pioneer Flora Tristan promoted the rights of workers in the craft unions (known as the *compagnonnages*), maintaining close links between the emancipation of women and the rights of working men. She was also an early advocate of the concept of the socialist workers' international organization.

Tristan was the daughter of a French mother, Anne-Pierre Laisney, and a Peruvian army officer (Tristán de Moscoso, of Incan noble background), but she was deemed illegitimate under

French law because her parents had been married in Spain by an émigré priest. She grew up in poverty after her father's early death when she was four, upon which his property was confiscated and the family denied acknowledgment as his legitimate heirs by relatives in Peru. In 1818 Tristan took work as a picture colorist to the lithographer André Chazal, whom she married in 1821 at her mother's insistence. After enduring much ill treatment, she left him in 1825 when she was pregnant with their third child. But he refused to divorce her and sued for custody of the children. This struggle and property wrangles continued until 1838. To feed her family, Tristan took the post of a ladies' companion (1825–1830) and sent her children to live with her mother. She continued to fight for custody but in 1832 was forced to hand over her son. Eventually, she regained her children after her husband was discovered (in 1837) to have sexually abused their daughter.

In 1833, Tristan made the arduous, five-month sea journey to Peru (leaving her children behind in France) to try to claim financial assistance from her father's family. Returning with only a small allowance of 2,500 francs for four years, she wrote about her experiences in *Peregrinations of a Pariah 1833–1838* (1838). The book records her deep disillusionment with married life and posits the first of her ideas on social liberation. It also contains observations on the miserable lives of women and slaves in Peru. Furious at the embarrassment caused him by this controversial account, in December 1838 her estranged husband attempted to shoot her and was sentenced to penal servitude for life. The family in Peru, also appalled by Tristan's critique of their society, withdrew her allowance. Fortunately, however, the Tristan-Chazal case had become a newspaper sensation, which helped boost sales of *Peregrinations* and Tristan's only novel, *Méphis*. Soon after publishing it, she rejected fiction as an inappropriate vehicle for her social concerns.

In Paris in 1835 after returning from Peru, Tristan had decided to turn to journalism in order to support her family, publishing her first newspaper articles in 1836–1838. She became involved with radical women's and socialist groups, including that organized by Eugènie Niboyet, editor of the *Women's Adviser,* but did not join any feminist organization. She read the work of Charles Fourier and Henri de Saint-Simon, and in 1837 she met with other radicals in England, such as Anna Doyle Wheeler and Robert Owen. In London she studied the Chartist movement and the living conditions of the urban working classes and published her observations on the four visits she made there between 1826 and 1839 in *The London Journal of Flora Tristan* (1840). Part travel writing, the book is also a pioneering sociological study that predates similar work by male writers Friedrich Engels and Henry Mayhew. Tristan presents a powerful indictment of the terrible living conditions of the English rural and urban working classes, which she considered far worse than those in France. In her view, the English worker was worse than the slave, who is at least fed by his master. The sorry lot of English working women also greatly troubled her. The *London Journal* also discussed prostitution and crime, detailed the conditions in factories where workers slaved up to fourteen hours a day in foul conditions, and described the rise of the working-class Chartist movement for political reform.

Also during this time, Tristan became familiar with the work of the French craftspeople's clubs (the *compagnonnages*), which sowed the idea for her major work of socialist theory, *The Workers' Union* (1843). An early, lengthy treatise on the position of the working classes, it made the suggestion that workers of all crafts and from all nationalities should be the makers of their own emancipation by organizing themselves into cooperatives in which women would be equal with men. All workers should pay into a fund that would finance the building of "workers' palaces," communal centers of "human unity" offering protection for the elderly and the disabled, health care, and schools and higher education facilities. Thus workers would have control over improvement of their own economic position. This book represented the first attempt at devising a workers' international organization that would unite the working classes in the struggle against capitalism.

In a chapter on rights of women, Tristan described the miseries of marriages in which the husbands drink and the wives are endlessly pregnant and stated that social change would only come when women, particularly working women, achieved improvements in their status. It was the low economic status of both women and child workers that perpetuated bad conditions for all workers and deprived them of political muscle and better pay. The only solution was for the working classes to unite in the defense of women, from which would spring economic improvements for all. For Tristan, therefore, the issue of female suffrage was not as important as the economic and educational equality of women and men.

On a lecture tour during which she was hoping to raise support for the foundation of her workers' union, Tristan fell ill with typhoid and died in Bordeaux. During her life, she had argued for reform of the divorce laws and against the death penalty. She had defended her rights as wife and mother with great strength of personality and had set out on a mission to liberate the working classes that would be carried on by others. As she said: "I have nearly the whole world against me. Men because I demand the emancipation of women, the owners because I demand the emancipation of wage-earners" (Rowbotham 1972, 55). She was also the grandmother of the French Impressionist painter Paul Gauguin.

See also Niboyet, Eugénie; Wheeler, Anna Doyle.

References and Further Reading
Beik, Doris, and Paul Beik. 1993. *Flora Tristan: Utopian Feminist*. Bloomington: Indiana University Press.
Cross, Maire. 1992. *The Feminism of Flora Tristan*. Oxford: Berg.
Desantis, Dominique. 1976. *A Woman in Revolt: A Biography of Flora Tristan*. Translated by Elizabeth Zelvin. New York: Crown.
Gattey, Charles N. 1970. *Gauguin's Astonishing Grandmother: Flora Tristan*. London: Femina.
Goldsmith, Margaret. 1935. *Seven Women against the World*. London: Methuen.
Gordon, Felicia, and Máire Cross. 1996. *Early French Feminism, 1830–1940: A Passion for Liberty*. Cheltenham: Edward Elgar.
Grogan, Susan K. 1992. *French Socialism and Sexual Difference: Women and the New Society, 1803–44*. London: Macmillan.
Moses, C. 1984. *French Feminism in the Nineteenth Century*. Albany: State University of New York Press.
Rowbotham, Sheila. 1972. *Women, Resistance, and Revolution*. Harmondsworth: Penguin.
Spender, Dale. 1982. *Women of Ideas, and What Men Have Done to Them*. London: Routledge and Kegan Paul.
Strumhinger, Laura. 1988. *The Odyssey of Flora Tristan*. New York: Peter Lang.
Tristan, Flora. 1982 [1840]. *The London Journal of Flora Tristan*. Translated by Jean Hawkes. London: Virago.

Trubnikova, Mariya
(1835–1897)
Russia

Mariya Trubnikova was one of a generation of women from the liberal intelligentsia of Russia's landed classes who worked quietly and generally without controversy for social reform—in particular, women's education—during the 1860s and 1870s.

Trubnikova's father, Vladimir Ivashev, took part in the Decembrist revolt in 1825 and was exiled to Siberia. Her French mother, Camille Ledentu, followed him there. The family lived in great hardship, and both parents died young, leaving four children. Trubnikova was taken in by a wealthy aunt and educated at home with her foster brothers, studying literature and history and learning to speak several languages. She married young, at nineteen, to a progressive landowner named Konstantin Trubnikov, who ran a school for the peasant children on his estate. He later became a stockbroker in St. Petersburg, where he lost much of Trubnikova's inheritance through ill-advised business dealings.

Trubnikova's feminist consciousness had been aroused as a young girl when she read the books in her uncle's study and became familiar with Western literature. As she grew older, she absorbed the social writings of Jules Michelet, Pierre-Joseph Proudhon, Ferdinand Lassalle, and Henri de Saint-Simon. On moving to St. Petersburg after her marriage, she helped her husband edit the *Stock Exchange News* and began meeting and exchanging ideas with other women involved in philanthropic work at a salon she established in her home.

In 1859 Trubnikova joined with Anna Filosova and Nadezhda Stasova—her lifelong collaborators in many philanthropic ventures (they were known as "the triumvirate")—in establishing the Society for Cheap Lodgings and Other Benefits for the Citizens of St. Petersburg. Through the society, they worked to alleviate the hardships suffered by working people, particularly women, offering them food, accommodation, literacy lessons, and limited forms of work—mainly sewing. Trubnikova was also involved in setting up a women's publishing and translating cooperative in 1863, which not only produced cheap and acceptable books for children but provided work for financially distressed gentlewomen in the editing, printing, and binding processes.

In the late 1860s Trubnikova became interested in Josephine Butler's campaign in England to abolish the Contagious Diseases Acts and met Butler on a visit there. She also corresponded with John Stuart Mill, author of *The Subjection of Women* (1869), who lent his support to Trubnikova's campaigning in Russia for women's higher education. She gained much inspiration in her reformist work from her personal correspondence with the French feminist Jenny d'Héricourt, who in 1860 had published a pioneer work on women's equality, *The Enfranchised Woman*.

In 1868, after female journalist Evgeniya Konradi sparked the campaign for women's admission to higher education by making an appeal at a conference of naturalists in St. Petersburg in December 1867, Trubnikova invited interested women to meet at her home to draw up a petition to be sent to the university. In it they appealed to the Ministry of Education for courses of public lectures to be set up to prepare women for university entrance. The first courses of their kind, the Alarchinsky courses, were established at a boys' school in St. Petersburg in 1869. Other similar courses sprang up that same year in Moscow, but many young students who were dissatisfied by their limited scope went to Switzerland—the only country that would admit women to universities. With the government fearful that among the notoriously radical émigré Russian community in Zurich such women would become increasingly politicized, the female students were recalled to Russia in 1873, and a reluctant Ministry of Education under Count Dmitry Tolstoy rubber-stamped the establishment of women's university courses in Russia in 1876.

In 1869 Trubnikova had left her husband and gone to live abroad. She returned to Russia but was beset by financial problems and the onset of mental illness. After joining with her old colleagues Filosova and Stasova to found the Society for Providing Means of Support for the Women's Higher Courses, in 1878 she slid toward insanity and ceased to be active.

Although Trubnikova remained cautious in her activism by the standards of the revolutionary activities of her times, and found nihilist and other radical women difficult to work with, she encouraged her own four daughters in their political and intellectual aspirations, allowing illegal meetings to take place in her home. When two of her daughters were arrested in 1881, she campaigned for their release. But the brief reformist tide in women's education in Russia was now turning, and a new era of autocratic reaction under Alexander III was setting in.

See also Butler, Josephine; Filosova, Anna; Stasova, Nadezhda.
References and Further Reading
Engel, Barbara Alpern. 1983. *Mothers and Daughters: Women of the Intelligentsia in Nineteenth-Century Russia.* Cambridge: Cambridge University Press.
Porter, Cathy. 1976. *Fathers and Daughters: Russian Women in Revolution.* London: Virago.
Stites, Richard. 1991 [1978]. *The Women's Liberation Movement in Russia: Feminism, Nihilism, and Bolshevism, 1860–1930.* Reprint, Princeton: Princeton University Press.

Truth, Sojourner (Isabella Van Wagener)
(c. 1797–1883)
United States

Sojourner Truth is one of the most celebrated nineteenth-century precursors of the black civil rights movement and an outspoken early defender of the rights of black women. As a slave, she endured backbreaking work in the fields and numerous beatings during her early life but emerged with an enormous sense of her own worth—both as a woman and as a black person—still intact. She was guided in all her activism for abolition and women's rights by her profound religious beliefs and evangelical energy. Her dignity, her Christian charity, and her great natural gifts for oratory and rhetoric despite her illiteracy have ensured that she has long been revered as an icon in black women's history.

Sojourner Truth was given the name Isabella Baumfree when she was born into slavery around 1797 in an area of Dutch-speaking settlers in Ulster County, New York. (For many years, sources were confused, if not misled, by Truth's penchant for artistic license in her accounts of her early life. For example, it was long believed that she lived to over 100.) She was first sold when still a small child and sold on again to two more masters, in 1810 becoming the slave of John Dumont in New Paltz, New York. Here she

had five children by a fellow slave named Thomas from 1820 to 1826 (although she claimed to have had thirteen). In 1826–1827 she ran away and was taken in by a Quaker family, the Van Wageners, and took their surname. The mark of Truth's mettle was demonstrated when, on learning that her son Peter had been sold into slavery illegally and taken to Alabama (in New York slavery had been outlawed in 1827), she became the first black woman to go to court in New York in order to sue for his return.

In 1829 Truth took domestic work in New York City, where she settled with her two youngest children. Wishing to celebrate her religious faith more freely in song, she left the quiet and contemplative Quaker faith to join the John Street Methodist Church, moving on to the African Zion Church. Having begun to hear voices and experience visions, Truth was drawn to charismatic and visionary groups and eventually became involved in a religious sect, the Retrenchment Society, led by Elijah Pierson, joining him and his followers in proselytizing among prostitutes at Five Points, a red-light district of New York, and urging women to repent their ways at the Magdalene Asylum, which the society had established as a refuge for fallen women.

In 1833 Truth was drawn into the cult of the self-proclaimed, bogus prophet Robert Matthews and joined his commune at Zion Hill in Sing Sing (now Ossining, New York), remaining there until it folded in 1835. In the wake of an ensuing scandal surrounding the sect in 1836, during which a newspaper libeled Truth as a "Black witch," she again went to court and won $125 in libel damages.

Truth went into retreat for several years, living quietly in New York until 1843, when, as she would later aver, God's message came to her through her spirit voices, telling her to change her name and take to the road and preach. Now traveling under the name of Sojourner Truth and often braving hostile mobs, Truth preached and sang at revival meetings in the eastern states, speaking wherever an opportunity presented itself in camps, churches, and on street corners. Wherever she went, she preached nonviolence and affirmed the brotherhood of man, opposing all idea of violent insurrection by slaves and arguing that the rule of law should prevail.

In her first winter on the road, Truth came into contact with a utopian community founded by George W. Benson in Northampton, Massachusetts. There she was introduced to the causes of abolition and women's rights. She was encouraged as a speaker by abolitionist leader William Lloyd Garrison, who also suggested she dictate her autobiography, *Narrative of Sojourner Truth: A Northern Slave Emancipated from Bodily Servitude by the State of New York, in 1828,* to an amanuensis, Olive Gilbert. The book's publication in 1850 provided a regular trickle of royalties to fund her itinerant preaching in New England and the midwestern states of Ohio, Indiana, and Kansas. Truth often spoke at abolitionist meetings with Frederick Douglass, and the large crowds that heard her speak were captivated by the force of her personality and her outspokenness.

With Truth illiterate and unable to record her thoughts on paper, history has had to rely on accounts of her speeches from observers and journalists of the time. Fortunately, her association with the cause of women's suffrage and her appearances at women's rights conventions in the 1850s and later were written down. Her most notable speech, a landmark in black women's history, was made in May 1851 at a women's rights convention in Akron, Ohio, over the noise of male hecklers doubly antagonistic toward her, both as a black and as a woman. The abolitionist Frances Dana Gage left a vivid account of Truth's appearance, first published in 1881 in volume 1 of the *History of Woman Suffrage* (also in Weatherford 1998, 50–52), in which she described Truth's commanding presence (at nearly 6 feet tall), her magnetism and passionate dignity, and recorded her inspirational qualities, saying: "She had taken us up in her strong arms and carried us safely over the slough of difficulty" (Stanton et al. 1881, 117). The account reproduced Truth's idiosyncratic speech style, in which she argued that her own physical strength was equal to any man's: "I have ploughed, and planted, and gathered into barns, and no man could head me! And ain't I a woman? I could work as much and eat as much as a man—when I could get it—and bear the lash as well! And ain't I a woman?" (116). The speech also served as a powerful reminder to white suffragists not to underrate the contributions of black women.

Truth settled in Battle Creek, Michigan, in the 1850s. During the American Civil War, she collected food and supplies for black soldiers serving as volunteers in the Union Army and also helped nurse the wounded. When the war was over, she helped freed slaves trace their children who had been illegally taken off into slavery in Maryland. In 1864 President Abraham Lincoln received Truth at the White House and appointed her counselor to the National Freedmen's Relief Association to help freed slaves adjust to their new lives. She lobbied President Ulysses S. Grant unsuccessfully in 1870 for freed slaves to be given grants of land out west on which to resettle and the implements needed to work the land. Although Truth's vision of creating a "Negro state" never materialized, nearly 20,000 emancipated slaves, or "Exodusters," took up the challenge of migrating to the Kansas frontier in the late 1870s.

Truth continued to travel the United States, preaching on civil and women's rights as well as temperance after the Civil War, and was also active in the American Equal Rights Association, which linked black civil rights with universal suffrage. She opposed the exclusion of women from suffrage under the Fourteenth Amendment, which enfranchised black males. In 1867, speaking at the first convention held by the association in New York, Truth berated the injustice of this legislation: "There is a great stir about colored men getting their rights, but not a word about the colored women: and if colored men get their rights, and not colored women theirs, you see the colored men will be master over the women, and it will be just as bad as it was before" (Stanton et al. 1881, 193). In addition, Truth argued for wage parity between women and men and also women and women, citing the fact that German women fieldworkers got paid more than black women.

In 1875 Truth retired to her home at Battle Creek, which became a place of pilgrimage for feminist and black sympathizers. Sadly, she did not live long enough to "sojourn once to the ballot box before I die" (928), but the respect accorded to her by white abolitionists and feminists alike was enduring, reflected, for example, in an 1863 article by Harriet Beecher Stowe. Entitled "Sojourner Truth: The Libyan Sibyl," it was published in *Atlantic Monthly* and did much to transform Truth into an iconic figure. Although retrospectively, some feminists have claimed that the white mainstream of the women's suffrage movement patronized Truth as a "token black," her voice raised in defense of the rights of black women was unique for its time, and her compelling message broke new ground. As she remarked in 1867, "I want to keep the thing stirring, now that the ice is cracked" (194). The life and work of Sojourner Truth are commemorated at her hometown of Battle Creek, which in 1998 opened a Sojourner Truth Institute to promote continuing work in her memory for black civil rights. For information, go to http://www.sojournertruth.org/.

See also Stowe, Harriet Beecher.

References and Further Reading

Bernard, Jacqueline. 1990. *Journey toward Freedom: The Story of Sojourner Truth*. New York: Feminist Press.

Fauset, Arthur H. 1971 [1938]. *Sojourner Truth: God's Faithful Pilgrim*. Chapel Hill: University of North Carolina Press.

Kerber, Linda K., and Jane DeHart-Mathews. 2000. *Women's America: Refocusing the Past*. New York: Oxford University Press.

Lerner, Gerda, ed. 1972. *Black Women in White America: A Documentary History*. New York: Pantheon Books.

Mabee, Carleton. 1993. *Sojourner Truth: Slave, Prophet, Legend*. New York: New York University Press.

McKissack, Patricia C. 1992. *Sojourner Truth: A Voice for Freedom*. Hillside, NJ: Enslow.

Ortiz, V. 1974. *Sojourner Truth: A Self Made Woman*. Philadelphia: Lippincott.

Painter, Nell Irvin. 1996. *Sojourner Truth: A Life, a Symbol*. New York: W. W. Norton.

Pauli, Hertha E. 1962. *Her Name Was Sojourner Truth*. New York: Appleton-Century-Crofts.

Spender, Dale. 1982. *Women of Ideas, and What Men Have Done to Them*. London: Routledge and Kegan Paul.

Stanton, Elizabeth Cady, Susan B. Anthony, and Matilda Joslyn Gage. 1881. *History of Woman Suffrage*, vols. 1 and 2. New York: Fowler and Wells.

Truth, Sojourner. 1991 [1850]. *Narrative of Sojourner Truth, a Bondswoman of Olden Times*. Reprint, New York: Oxford University Press.

Weatherford, Doris. 1998. *A History of the American Suffragist Movement*. Santa Barbara, CA: ABC-CLIO.

Yee, Shirley J. 1992. *Black Women Abolitionists: A Study in Activism 1828–1860*. Knoxville: University of Tennessee Press.

Yellen, Jean Fagan. 1989. *Women and Sisters: The Antislavery Feminists in American Culture*. New Haven: Yale University Press.

Tubman, Harriet Ross
(c. 1820–1913)
United States

Just as Moses led the Jews out of the wilderness, so in her time Harriet Tubman was looked upon as a savior by the many runaway slaves whom she helped escape the South via the Underground Railroad. As a devout Christian, she put her trust in God, never giving in to exhaustion during long hours on the road and constantly risking recapture and a return to slavery. In her later years, she took an active interest in the movement for women's suffrage.

Born on a plantation in Dorchester County, Maryland, Tubman was given the name Araminta. Like her contemporary Sojourner Truth, her early life was one of degradation and hardship. Tubman worked as a field hand from the age of seven and remained illiterate all her life. She was also given tasks as a domestic servant and cook, but when she proved recalcitrant, she was hit on the head at the age of thirteen by an overseer, causing permanent injury and prompting fits of narcolepsy during her adult life.

In 1844 she was forced to marry a freed slave, John Tubman, but had no children. In 1849, when her owner died, fearful of being sold into the Deep South, Tubman escaped from her plantation on Maryland's eastern shore. She went north on the Underground Railroad and changed her name to Harriet. Returning to Philadelphia in 1850, she joined members of the Philadelphia Anti-Slavery Society in helping other slaves escape. In December she assisted her sister and two children, and a year later her brother and his family, in making their way to the North and then to Ontario, Canada. In 1857 she returned to smuggle her parents out of Maryland in a wagon.

Like Sojourner Truth, Tubman was driven in her work by her deep religious faith and felt that she was guided directly by God. During her years working as a "conductor" on the Underground Railroad, it is thought that she made nineteen trips to Maryland, helping up to 300 slaves escape with the assistance of Quaker sympathizers. Such was her discipline and her reputation for meticulous planning and efficiency that Tubman never got caught, even though a $40,000 reward for her capture was offered by slave owners in Maryland.

In the late 1850s, Tubman began speaking in public at abolitionist meetings. She lived for a

Harriet Ross Tubman (Library of Congress)

ography, *Scenes in the Life of Harriet Tubman,* written by Sarah Bradford (1869).

In 1896, after receiving a rapturous welcome at the first convention of the National Association of Colored Women, where she had called for better care of the aged, Tubman founded the Harriet Tubman Home for Indigent Aged Negroes, built in 1908 on 26 acres of additional land next to her farm at Auburn that she had purchased in 1896 on the royalties from her biography. Denied a federal pension in recognition of her service to the army, Tubman conducted a determined campaign to secure this right for more than thirty years, until she was finally awarded $20 a month in 1897. Nevertheless, she spent her old age in relative poverty, dying at the home she had founded. The Harriet Tubman Home for Indigent Aged Negroes is now operated by the African Methodist Episcopal Zion Church, which restored the original building in 1953. For information on opening hours and Tubman's life, see http://www.nyhistory.com/harriettubman/.

See also Truth, Sojourner.

References and Further Reading

Bradford, Sarah H. 1961 [1886]. *Harriet Tubman: The Moses of Her People.* New York: Corinth (originally published as *Scenes in the Life of Harriet Tubman,* 1869).

Conrad, Earl. 1942. *Harriet Tubman: Negro Soldier and Abolitionist.* New York: International Publishers.

Heidish, M. 1976. *A Woman Called Moses.* Boston: Houghton Mifflin.

Lerner, Gerda, ed. 1972. *Black Women in White America: A Documentary History.* New York: Pantheon Books.

Niess, Judith. 1977. *Seven Women: Portraits from the American Radical Tradition.* New York: Viking Press.

Quarles, Benjamin. 1969. *Black Abolitionists.* New York: Oxford University Press.

Shea, Marian Axford. 1999. *Women Movers & Shakers.* Lincoln, NE: Media Productions and Marketing.

Smallwood, Caid, Stan West, and Allison Keyes. 1998. *Profiles of Great African Americans.* Lincolnwood, IL: Publications International.

Smith, Jessie Carney, ed. 1993. *Epic Lives: One Hundred Black Women Who Made a Difference.* Detroit: Visible Ink.

Yee, Shirley J. 1992. *Black Women Abolitionists: A Study in Activism 1828–1860.* Knoxville: University of Tennessee Press.

while with her parents in Ontario, where she first met the abolitionist John Brown, later becoming involved in the planning of his fateful 1859 raid on Harpers Ferry. Brown would recognize Tubman's organizational talents by nicknaming her "General Tubman."

In 1857 Tubman settled with her parents on a farm in Auburn, New York, sold to her by Quaker sympathizers for a nominal amount. However, she continued her activities on the Underground Railroad until 1862, and during the Civil War was a civilian volunteer for the Union Army at Beaufort on the South Carolina coast, serving as a nurse in field hospitals as well as laundress and cook. She also joined scouting parties on operations behind Confederate lines and even took command of a raiding party up the Combahee River in South Carolina.

After the war, she went home to Auburn, New York, where she took in orphans and destitute elderly blacks. In 1869 Tubman married a Civil War veteran, Nelson Davies, and with him worked to help freed slaves establish schools for their children. She raised funds by having her bi-

Twining, Louisa
(1820–1912)
United Kingdom

A guiding force in reform of Britain's work-houses through the establishment of the Work-house Visiting Society (WVS), Louisa Twining felt that women were particularly well equipped for work in the spiritual and physical rehabilita-tion of those less fortunate, and under her scheme many women took up workhouse visit-ing from the 1860s. Twining also exposed the shocking standards of health care in workhouses and lobbied for the employment of trained nurses in their infirmaries. Through the channel of workhouse visiting, she set an important precedent for women's later work in local gov-ernment, an important outlet in the years before women's enfranchisement.

The Twining family were the famous tea im-porters of the same name who had an old, estab-lished firm in the Strand in London. The family took an active part in charitable work: Twining's father played a role in the management of King's College Hospital in London and acted as super-visor of a local free public dispensary. For Louisa Twining, forty-five years of philanthropic work began in the 1840s, when she helped her father organize a local church nursing sisterhood of the Lady of Grace of the Order of St. John of Jerusalem. In 1853, having been a regular visitor to her old nurse in a slum area near her home, out of charity Twining visited one of her nurses' neighbors who had been admitted to the Strand Union Workhouse. What she encountered there appalled her: there were no washing facilities, the bed linen was filthy (it remained unchanged for sixteen weeks), and the food was inedible. The whole building was pervaded by the most nauseating smell and filled with steam from the laundry operated by inmates in the cellars. Twin-ing discovered that the sick, alcoholic, blind, and disabled were all lumped in together, with sick children who were suffering from infectious dis-eases often sharing beds with others. Those who were incurably ill were left to languish in filthy bedding and covered in bedsores, with little or no nursing care; indeed, they were usually looked after by other inmates, many of whom were themselves incapacitated physically or mentally. So high was the death rate, Twining observed, that the inmates spent much of their time in making coffins and shrouds for those who died.

When she approached the Poor Law Board for permission to visit the workhouse on a regular basis and offer small comforts—both spiritual and material—she was refused. It took a year of concerted lobbying, through letters to the papers and public lectures, to get the board to relent, during which time Twining continued visiting unofficially. After permission was granted, she began also to give sermons to the inmates at af-ternoon religious services. Twining gathered a considerable body of support for her work as a member of the National Association for the Pro-motion of Social Science (NAPSS), where she frequently gave papers on workhouse reform. Soon other women reformers, including Frances Power Cobbe, Mary Carpenter, and Florence Nightingale, visited her at the Strand Workhouse to observe her work. Publication of her pam-phlets, "A Few Words about the Inmates of Our Union Workhouses" (1855) and "Workhouses and Women's Work" (1857), contributed to the founding of the Workhouse Visiting Society in 1858. It quickly became a national organization under the aegis of the NAPSS's Social Economy Department and encouraged other women to take up workhouse visiting. Several of Twining's articles on workhouse visiting and reform reached a wider audience through publication in the *English Woman's Journal.*

After Twining was appointed secretary of the newly established WVS in 1858, she began visit-ing other workhouses around Britain, encourag-ing local boards to accept female workhouse vis-itors and lobbying for improvements to living conditions. Twining waged a concerted cam-paign for training workhouse nurses, an issue re-flected in her writings, notably *Workhouses and Pauperism,* and one that was also addressed by Florence Nightingale as well as William Rath-bone and Agnes Weston, who pioneered such re-form in Liverpool. In 1879 Twining was a founder and secretary of the Association for Pro-moting Trained Nursing in Workhouse Infir-maries and Sick Asylums, specifically for this purpose.

In her workhouse reform work, Twining also raised the issue of schools for paupers and indus-trial training for workhouse girls, giving evidence to a Select Committee on Poor Relief in 1861. That year the WVS, at Twining's suggestion, founded a hostel for poor girls as a way of preventing them from joining the workhouse population and providing a rudimentary residential training, after which the girls were encouraged to take jobs in domestic service. These positions were mainly located in the British colonies, and the society provided assistance with fares. This scheme attracted numerous patrons, including Angela Burdett-Coutts. Similarly, Twining endorsed the work of the Langham Place Circle's Society for Promoting the Employment of Women in finding suitable work for indigent middle-class women. Through contact with the circle, she also supported the campaigns for women's higher education and suffrage.

In 1880 Twining published *Recollections of Workhouse Visiting and Management during Twenty-Five Years*. She served as a Poor Law Guardian for the London borough of Kensington from 1884 to 1890, and, after her move to Tunbridge Wells, Sussex, in 1893 she served another three years as a guardian there. Retiring in 1896, she prepared her 1898 study, *Workhouses and Pauperism*. The WVS disbanded in 1878, and after overseeing the recruitment of many thousands of women to workhouse visiting, Twining lent her support to women's involvement in local government, where she soon encountered male prejudice against women's public work. In the 1880s she was chair of the Society for Promoting the Return of Women as Poor Law Guardians (a role for which she had been arguing since 1861 and which was not allowed women until 1893) and president of the Women's Local Government Society (which lobbied for the Local Government Act of 1894, which allowed women to sit on rural and parish councils).

See also Burdett-Coutts, Angela; Carpenter, Mary; Cobbe, Frances Power; Nightingale, Florence.

References and Further Reading
Banks, Olive, ed. 1985, 1990. *The Biographical Dictionary of British Feminists,* vol. 1, *1800–1930;* vol. 2, *1900–1945.* Brighton: Harvester Wheatsheaf.
Baylen, J. O., and N. J. Gossman, eds. 1979–1984. *Biographical Dictionary of Modern British Radicals.* 3 vols. Hassocks, Sussex: Harvester Press.
Hollis, Patricia. 1987. *Ladies Elect: Women in English Local Government 1865–1914.* Oxford: Clarendon Press.
———, ed. 1979. *Women in Public: The Women's Movement 1850–1900: Documents of the Victorian Women's Movement.* London: Allen and Unwin.
Pratt, Edwin A. 1897. *Pioneering Women in Victoria's Reign.* London: George Newnes.
Prochaska, F. K. 1980. *Women and Philanthropy in Nineteenth-Century England.* Oxford: Clarendon Press.
Twining, Louisa. 1893. *Recollections of Life and Work, Being the Autobiography of Louisa Twining.* London: Edward Arnold.
———. 1979 [1885]. "Suggestions for Women Guardians." In Patricia Hollis, ed., *Women in Public 1850–1900: Documents of the Victorian Women's Movement.* London: Allen and Unwin.

V

van Gripenberg, Alexandra
(1859–1913)
Finland

Little is known outside Finland of the life and work of the suffragist and feminist Baroness Alexandra van Gripenberg, a contemporary of Annie Furujhelm, in one of the first European suffrage movements to campaign successfully for votes for women, achieved in 1906. Recent research by Margaret McFadden (1999) has uncovered van Gripenberg's close association with feminists in Europe and the United States, establishing her as a founding mother of the international feminist movement who met and corresponded with luminaries such as Susan B. Anthony and Elizabeth Cady Stanton, many of whose writings she translated into Finnish.

Van Gripenberg came from a Swedish-Finnish family of some standing that was active in the Finnish nationalist movement in Kuopio; at that time, Finland was a grand duchy of the Russian Empire. The daughter of a baron and Finnish senator, she was born at Kurkijoki and educated at home, where she developed considerable literary interests as a young girl and published her first short stories in 1877. In the 1880s she acted as reader and assistant to the Finnish author Zachris Topelius; she also edited various children's journals and Finnish and Swedish periodicals. She wrote up her accounts of her travels to Germany, Hungary, England, and the United States in these publications and in Danish and Norwegian women's magazines and in 1885 published a collection of biographies of members of the Finnish Diet.

Through her travels and her literary interests, van Gripenberg monitored the development of the women's suffrage and temperance movements in England and the United States and shared her interest with other feminists in Helsinki, where she lived. She was in the United States when the first women's congress was held in 1888 in Washington, D.C., which led to the establishment of the International Council of Women (ICW) that year. Van Gripenberg served the ICW as treasurer from 1893 to 1899 and later as honorary vice president.

In 1888 van Gripenberg wrote a lively account of the congress proceedings, which was published in her travel memoir, *A Half Year in the New World* (not translated until 1954). She left a pen portrait of temperance leader Frances Willard, observing, "there is probably no other woman who is so beloved, so idolized, as she is" (1954, 17), and precisely captured what it was about the Stanton-Anthony relationship that worked so well: "Mrs. Stanton is pure philosophy, Miss Anthony pure organizing ability" (12). Van Gripenberg stayed on to tour the United States for several months, fascinated in particular by American spiritualism and fringe religions such as Christian Science and the Mormon Church. She studied women's education and suffrage and met with Harriet Beecher Stowe. In addition, she had a particular admiration for the work of the recently deceased Helen Hunt Jackson, who had been one of the first to depict Native American culture in her novel *Ramona*.

Upon her return to Finland, van Gripenberg was a founding member of the Finnish Women's Association (FWA) in 1884, serving as its second president from 1889 to 1903. During the 1890s, the moderate FWA worked for women's emancipation in education and civil and social arenas and was closely linked to the Finnish nationalist movement in its promotion of Finnish culture and language in an attempt to overcome the domination of the Swedish language. The FWA promoted higher education and entry into the professions for both men and women in a country that was still not independent. FWA members also worked among peasant women in rural areas and provided literacy classes. Activism for suffrage increased after 1897, when the Russian government refused to allow women equal eligibility with men in communal elections.

During the 1890s, while the FWA under van Gripenberg continued to emphasize work in moral reform and philanthropy (including a campaign against state-regulated prostitution), a more militant suffrage organization, the Union of Women's Societies, was established under Lucina Hagman (1853–1946) and also began to demand independence from Russia. Eventually, the two women's groups collaborated in the escalating campaign for national autonomy.

Women in Finland won the vote in 1906, a fact celebrated by van Gripenberg in "The Great Victory in Finland," published in the *Englishwoman's Review* in July. Thereafter, she worked within the ICW for the political enlightenment and enfranchisement of other women around the world, traveling to the Balkans to help establish sister branches in Bulgaria and Greece. She was a member of the Finnish Diet in 1907–1908 and a founder of the National Council of Finnish Women in 1911. At the time of her death, she was president of the Finnish Party's Women's Association.

See also Anthony, Susan B.; Furujhelm, Annie; Jackson, Helen Hunt; Stanton, Elizabeth Cady; Stowe, Harriet Beecher; Willard, Frances.

References and Further Reading

Bridenthal, Renate, and Claudia Koonz. 1977. *Becoming Visible: Women in European History.* Boston: Houghton Mifflin.

Evans, Richard. 1977. *The Feminists: Women's Emancipation Movements in Europe, America and Australasia 1840–1920.* London: Croom Helm.

McFadden, Margaret H. 1999. *Golden Cables of Sympathy: The Transatlantic Sources of Nineteenth-Century Feminism.* Lexington: University Press of Kentucky.

Moyne, Ernest J., ed. and trans. 1954. *Alexandra Gripenberg's "A Half Year in the New World": Miscellaneous Sketches of Travel in the United States.* Cranbury, NJ: University of Delaware Press.

Vérone, Maria
(1874–1938)
France

A leader of the minority of militant activists in the French campaign for women's suffrage, Maria Vérone was also one of France's first women lawyers. A daughter of lower-middle-class parents, she was drawn into radical activities at an early age by their interest in Republican politics and freethinking.

By the age of fifteen, Vérone had joined a society of freethinkers, and three years later she was giving lectures at meetings. She was also active in the pacifist movement from a young age. She had attended a communal school in a working-class district of Levallois and won a scholarship to a higher school in Paris but was forced to abandon her education when her father died. She joined her mother in making artificial flowers and feathers for ladies' hats and clothing in order to support the family.

In 1894 Vérone managed to obtain a post as a temporary teacher but was dismissed because of her political activities in 1897. She went into the music halls, singing in a chorus line, and later married a journalist and began writing articles for the *Dawn,* a pacifist newspaper.

In 1897 she joined Marguerite Durand's *La Fronde (The Sling),* contributing a regular legal column and using the earnings from this assignment and articles she published in *Peace* and *Women's Rights* to support herself while continuing with her education. She studied Greek and Latin and eventually took her baccalaureate in Paris in 1904, but her ambitions did not end there. Vérone went on to study law, graduating in 1907 to become only the fifth woman in France to be admitted to the bar.

During a high-profile career as a lawyer until 1930, she pleaded in many courts in the Palais de Justice, working for the legal rights of children and combining this with her feminist and socialist activities. She edited the journals *Work* (1908–1938), the *Syndicalist Battle* (1911–1912), and *Free France* (1916–1919), frequently writing on historical and socialist subjects. Vérone also served as founder and president of the National Union of Lawyers. She had joined the French League for Women's Rights (FLWR) in 1904 while she was studying law and served as its secretary-general until 1919, followed by another nineteen years as president. She revitalized the group in its fight for women's suffrage, keeping its activism militant but within the bounds of the law and through it establishing strong links between women's rights and pacifism. On the international level, she acted as chair of the legal section of the International Council of Women and was a loyal member of the International Woman Suffrage Alliance (IWSA), with which the FLWR was affiliated.

At a 1913 conference of the IWSA, staged in Budapest, Vérone made an impassioned plea for world peace in her speech "The War against War." At the annual congress of the International Council of Women, held in Rome in 1914 just weeks before World War I broke out, she repeated her 1913 speech, once more urging her fellow feminists to work for peace mediation. However, when war broke out she felt obliged to support the French war effort, because she considered her country to have been the innocent victim of German aggression. During the war, Vérone was one of a small group of women lawyers in France allowed to plead cases before military tribunals. She became convinced, as the fighting dragged on, that the hoped-for postwar achievement of women's rights and suffrage would facilitate a lasting international peace and developed a three-point pacifist program for the League for the Defense of Women, calling for sexual equality, pacifism, and temperance. The league also arbitrated in labor disputes and offered legal counseling for French military recruits and conscientious objectors. After the war, Vérone once more joined international pacifists in calling for international bodies to monitor military aggression; their campaigning bore fruit with the establishment of The Hague Tribunal and the League of Nations.

See also Durand, Marguerite.

References and Further Reading

Hause, Steven C., with Anne R. Kenny. 1984. *Women's Suffrage and Social Politics in the French Third Republic.* Princeton, NJ: Princeton University Press.

Josephson, Harold, Sandi Cooper, and Steven C. Hause et al., eds. 1985. *Biographical Dictionary of Modern Peace Leaders.* Westport, CT: Greenwood Press.

Sowerwine, Charles. 1982. *Sisters or Citizens? Women and Socialism in France since 1876.* Cambridge: Cambridge University Press.

Vincent, Eliska
(1841–1914)
France

Eliska Vincent was revered as one of the founding mothers of the French suffrage movement. Years after she narrowly escaped execution for her activities in the Paris Commune of 1871, Madame Vincent—as she was by then addressed by her acolytes—established the organization Women's Equality in 1888.

Born in Mézières, Vincent came from a family with a tradition of radical protest. Her father had been imprisoned because of his Republican activities in the 1848 revolution. Her activism began in 1866, when she joined the Society for the Demand of the Rights of Woman, cofounded by León Richer, Marie Deraismes, and others. She took up the particular issue of the rights of working women and was a delegate to a workers' congress in 1878 and an active member of the French Syndicalists, a trade union group that advocated direct action for social change by the working classes after the 1890s.

Vincent was also active in the suffrage campaign from 1885 and in 1888 founded the feminist group Equality of Asnières (after the Paris suburb in which she lived). When Hubertine Auclert, until then the undisputed leader of the suffrage movement in Paris, left for Algeria in 1888, Vincent took over leadership of the Paris movement through her own society, Equality. Her middle-of-the-road activism helped her succeed in establishing links with middle-class bourgeois women in the fight for women's suffrage. In 1889, when she represented Equality of Asnières at her first women's rights congress, she put forward a widely acceptable resolution for women to take part in local charity boards. Thus the dignity and respectability that Vincent emanated made her a less controversial figurehead for the movement, although Equality remained a small organization that would be overtaken later by much larger suffrage organizations, such as the French Union for Women's Suffrage.

A longtime advocate of women's admission to freemasonry, in 1893 Vincent founded the mixed lodge Human Rights with Marie Deraismes. By the turn of the century, she had become disenchanted with Equality. She resigned when it joined forces with the National Council of French Women. After she was widowed, Vincent inherited land at Saint-Ouen in Paris and became financially secure, using her money to promote the rights of women and workers. One of her last political acts was to agree to be vice president of the French Union for Women's Suffrage, founded in 1909. At her home in Saint-Ouen, Vincent built up a considerable feminist library, said to comprise more than 600,000 documents on women's history in France. She willed this unique archive to the Musée Social, which, according to Karen Offen, turned down this valuable bequest. It subsequently disappeared—either lost or destroyed.

See also Auclert, Hubertine; Deraismes, Marie.
References and Further Reading

Hause, Steven C., with Anne R. Kenny. 1984. *Women's Suffrage and Social Politics in the French Third Republic.* Princeton, NJ: Princeton University Press.

Offen, Karen. 2000. *European Feminisms 1700–1950: A Political History.* Palo Alto: Stanford University Press.

Sowerwine, Charles. 1982. *Sisters or Citizens? Women and Socialism in France since 1876.* Cambridge: Cambridge University Press.

W

Wald, Lillian D.
(1867–1940)
United States

The humanitarian and public health activist Lillian D. Wald pioneered "public health nursing," a phrase she coined, after setting up the first project to offer nursing in the community at her Henry Street Settlement in New York. In so doing, she inaugurated a system that became a prototype for nursing later adopted in rural areas across the United States by the Red Cross. Her concern for the welfare of children in particular also had a direct influence on health care policy-making by the U.S. government and prompted the establishment of the Children's Bureau in 1912.

Born in Cincinnati, Ohio, of Jewish parentage, Wald grew up in New York, where she was educated at a private boarding school. She had tried to apply to Vassar College when she was sixteen but by the age of twenty-two, desperately seeking a vocation, she decided to become a nurse. In 1889 she took up studies at the New York Hospital Training School for Nurses. Upon her graduation in 1891, she worked briefly at the New York Juvenile Asylum before entering the Women's Medical College for further training.

Her studies involved her in running nursing classes for immigrant families, and in 1893, when she finally saw for herself the terrible unhygienic conditions in which many of these families lived in New York's overcrowded tenements, she resolved to do something about it. In 1893 Wald founded a nurses' settlement house on Rivington Street with a fellow nurse, Mary M. Brewster, after fund-raising among rich friends and patrons. With a generous donation from a banking family, she was able soon after to relocate to better

Lillian D. Wald (Library of Congress)

premises at 265 Henry Street on the Lower East Side, where the nurses' settlement she established there could remain fully autonomous and not be tied to any particular charity group. By 1896, eleven nurses had joined the settlement, and they became known as the Henry Street Visiting Nurse Service. In this capacity, they visited the tenements on the Lower East Side, advising patients on personal hygiene, sanitation, and the eradication of germs. Over the years, further accommodations for nurses in the service were found in Manhattan and the Bronx, bringing their numbers to ninety-two by 1913.

In 1910 Wald persuaded Columbia University to add nursing to the university curriculum and set up a department of nursing and health with its own professor. Two years later, under her aegis, the Town and Country Nursing Service, monitored by the American Red Cross, set up a national rural nursing service along lines set out by Wald. Also in 1912, she was elected first president of a new body, the National Organization for Public Health Nursing.

Wald lived for forty years on Henry Street, in a neighborhood that she grew to love and where she oversaw a public school nursing program established in 1902 to visit New York's schools, the first public service of its kind, supported by the New York City Municipal Board of Health. Meanwhile, she also began lobbying for legal measures to protect child workers from industrial diseases and overwork, in 1902 establishing a New York Child Labor Committee and in 1904 a national body with the assistance of Florence Kelley. This organization's work gave impetus to the establishment in 1912 of the Children's Bureau under the Department of Commerce and Labor, which achieved considerable successes under the leadership of Julia Lathrop.

The work of the Henry Street Settlement, as it later became known, rapidly extended from providing a nursing service to operating as a local community center that offered advice on housing and employment as well as many educational and recreational programs, including classes in cooking, sewing, and nursing, to New York's working-class community. Wald continued to place a particular emphasis on the welfare of children in all her work. She raised funds to provide scholarships for poor children and provided specialist help to educate people with mental disabilities. In the fight to combat tuberculosis, Wald advocated the building of public parks and playgrounds in depressed slum areas. Cultural programs and a local theater were also established in 1915. From the 1900s, Wald also addressed the working conditions of women in sweatshops as a vigorous supporter of the Women's Trade Union League.

Wald's pacifism was a natural extension of her humanitarian instincts as a nurse. She worked closely in the U.S. movement with Jane Addams and helped found the American Union Against Militarism (AUAM) in 1914, serving as its first president. She supported international attempts at peace mediation during the early days of World War I, but when these failed, she joined the Women's Council on National Defense, taking responsibility for home nursing as chair of the Committee on Community Nursing of the American Red Cross. At war's end in 1918, she found herself facing the challenge of the influenza pandemic that had reached New York and hastily organized teams of volunteer Red Cross nurses as chair of the Nurses' Emergency Council. In 1919 Wald attended the women's congress in Zurich at which the Women's International League for Peace and Freedom was established and supported the work of the League of Nations by founding the League of Free Nations Association, an adjunct to the AUAM.

After joining in the final stage of the campaign for women's suffrage to 1920, Wald remained active in other causes throughout the 1920s and 1930s, representing the Children's Bureau and the American Red Cross at international conferences and serving on various state and city commissions investigating housing reform and public health. Through these commissions, she lobbied for factory inspections and for manufacturers to introduce nursing and first aid facilities in the workplace and became a personal friend of Franklin and Eleanor Roosevelt, supporting the reforms of the New Deal. She resigned from the board of directors of Henry Street in 1933 because of ill health. In 1934 she published a second volume of memoirs, *Windows on Henry Street,* to accompany her 1915 book, *The House on Henry Street.* Both books became valuable texts for social workers. Wald's Henry Street Settlement is still a venue for important work in the community; for information contact www.cr.nps.gov/nr/travel/pwwmh/ny31.htm. The Visiting Nurse Service of New York now boasts a network of 3,000 caretakers who daily service some 2,000 sick and disabled people in their homes. It can be contacted at http://www.vsny.org.

See also Addams, Jane; Kelley, Florence; Lathrop, Julia; Roosevelt, (Anna) Eleanor.

References and Further Reading

Coss, Claire, ed. 1989. *Lillian D. Wald, Progressive Activist.* New York: Feminist Press.

Daniels, Doris Groshen. 1989. *Always a Sister: The Feminism of Lillian D. Wald.* New York: Feminist Press.

Davis, Allen F. 1967. *Spearheads for Reform: The Social Settlements and the Progressive Movement 1890–1914.* New York: Oxford University Press.

Duffus, Robert L. 1938. *Lillian Wald: Neighbor and Crusader.* New York: Macmillan.

Eisemann, Alberta. 1976. *Rebels and Reformers: Biographies of Four Jewish Americans.* Garden City, NY: Zenith Books.

Epstein, Beryl. 1948. *Lillian Wald: Angel of Henry Street.* New York: J. Messner.

Kuzmack, Linda Gordon. 1990. *Woman's Cause: The Jewish Woman's Movement in England and the United States 1881–1933.* Columbus: Ohio State University Press.

Lagemann, Ellen Condliffe. 1979. *A Generation of Women: Education in the Lives of Progressive Reformers.* Cambridge, MA: Harvard University Press.

Lindenmeyer, Kriste. 1997. *"A Right to Childhood": The U.S. Children's Bureau and Child Welfare, 1912–1946.* Urbana: University of Illinois Press.

Marchand, C. Roland. 1972. *The American Peace Movement and Social Reform, 1898–1918.* Princeton: Princeton University Press.

Siegel, Beatrice. 1983. *Lillian Wald of Henry Street.* New York: Macmillan.

Wagenecht, Edward. 1983. *Daughters of the Covenant: Portraits of Six Jewish Women.* Amherst: University of Massachusetts Press.

Wald, Lillian. 1991 [1915]. *The House on Henry Street.* Reprint, New Brunswick, NJ: Transaction Publishers.

Wiseman, Alberta. 1976. *Rebels and Reformers: Biographies of Four Jewish Americans.* Garden City, NY: Zenith Books.

Wang Huiwu
(1898–?)
China

One of a handful of pioneering women involved in the first women's program started by the Chinese Communist Party (CCP), Wang Huiwu wrote about the need for wide-ranging social reforms to ameliorate the subordinate position of women. Never a formal member of the Communist Party, Wang nevertheless played a key role in the Shanghai communist organization in the early 1920s through the offices of her husband, Li Da, a CCP leader.

Born in Zhejiang province and educated at missionary schools (Jianxing Women's Normal School and the Hujun Academy for Girls), Wang converted to Christianity. She escaped the inevitability of an arranged marriage because her widowed mother was dependent upon her financial support and allowed her to take a job as a teacher. Like other Chinese feminists of this period, Wang thus benefited from a degree of intellectual and economic independence.

Wang became a leading female activist in the May Fourth Movement of 1919, a mass movement that protested the economic endorsement of Japanese exploitation of China under the terms of the Versailles Peace Treaty at the end of World War I. Wang organized protests at Hujun Academy, the school at which she taught, and embraced the opportunities for raising issues of women's oppression that the movement aroused (although it was mainly led by male intellectuals) by publishing essays in radical journals such as *Young China.* There in 1919 she published a coruscating attack on the age-old tradition of arranged marriages titled "The Chinese Woman Question: Liberation from a Trap." Like other feminists of her time, she was frustrated by the passive acceptance of their fate by the vast majority of Chinese women, long indoctrinated by the Confucian principle of the "three obediences" to their fathers, husbands, and sons. The male sublimation of the female personality was reflected in the way in which Chinese women were made economically dependent, intellectually ignorant, and socially isolated because, as Wang argued, men feared women might outstrip them if liberated from traditional roles.

In 1920 Wang moved to Shanghai, where she met and married the communist intellectual Li Da, a supporter of the Marxist interpretation of women's rights propounded by Friedrich Engels. Their marriage was not constrained by traditional role-playing, and Li involved Wang in his work in the Communist Party. During 1921–1922, Wang led a women's program in Shanghai set up by the Communist Party, overseeing the Shanghai Pingmin Girls' School, where she worked to raise literacy standards. She attempted to introduce instruction in foreign languages and invited Christian women involved in the Young Women's Christian Association (YWCA) to teach there, but the school was closed in 1922.

At this time, Wang also edited the short-lived feminist journal *Women's Voice* and cofounded the Shanghai Women's Rights League with Wang Yizhi. She collaborated with other female activists in Shanghai, which compensated for her not being given the post of director of the Communist Party Women's Bureau, which went to Xiang Jingyu in 1923. (The underlying principle was that the CCP, with typical chauvinism, would not promote Wang to a higher position in the party than that held by her husband, despite her outstanding qualities as a women's leader.) Wang lost her position of influence in the CCP when her husband was not reelected at its second congress, and the couple later divorced. In 1949 Wang became a member of the legal committee of the Chinese government.

See also Xiang Jingyu.
References and Further Reading
Gilmartin, Christina Kelly. 1995. *Engendering the Chinese Revolution: Radical Women, Communist Politics and Mass Movements in the 1920s.* Berkeley: University of California Press.

Ward, Mary
(Mrs. Humphry Ward)
(1851–1920)
United Kingdom

In her day Mary Ward, or Mrs. Humphry Ward, as she was popularly known on her book jackets, was a preeminent Victorian and later Edwardian social novelist, the author of twenty-five books—many of them best-sellers—and a notable philanthropist. Beginning in the 1870s, she had been an advocate of women's entry into higher education, but this view did not lead naturally to support for women's suffrage. On the contrary, as a conservative she was strongly opposed to women's entry into political life, believing they were most effective serving the family. In more recent times, such views have served to detract from the many positive aspects of her life and work. Nevertheless, Ward was a woman of deep religious convictions and moral purpose who, in her support for a more hands-on, practical form of Christianity responsive to the demands of modern life, advocated social reform.

Ward was born in Hobart, Tasmania, into the family that produced Thomas Arnold (her grandfather and the founder of Rugby School) and Matthew Arnold (the poet). Her early life was affected by the crises in religious faith of her father; after he converted to Roman Catholicism

in 1854, he had to relinquish his job as a school inspector, and the family returned to England in 1856. The young Mary was educated at a succession of private boarding schools. When her father returned to the Anglican church in 1865, he took a post in Oxford, where she grew up in a scholarly environment and became engrossed in the private study of theology, music, and languages, spending much time in the Bodleian Library.

In 1872 she married (Thomas) Humphry Ward, a fellow of Brasenose College, and soon after joined the movement for women's admission to universities, as secretary of the Oxford Committee for Women's Higher Education. In 1877 this became the Association for the Education of Women, which was influential in the establishment of the first women's college at Oxford, Somerville (and the second in England after Girton College, Cambridge), which Ward served as secretary from 1879 to 1881. In 1881 the Ward family moved to London when Humphry Ward became art critic and lead writer at the *Times*. Mary began publishing articles in the *Pall Mall Gazette, The Times,* and *Macmillan's Magazine.* In 1884 she brought out her first full-length work of fiction, *Miss Bretherton,* followed by a translation of Henri Frédéric Amiel's *Intimate Journal* in 1885.

In 1888 Ward became an overnight literary sensation with the publication of one of the century's most popular novels, *Robert Elsmere,* a book so widely read and discussed that there was much talk of Ward as the "new George Eliot." The novel reflected the background of religious doubt that she had encountered at home with her father and the many debates on religion to which she had been exposed during her years in Oxford at the time of the Oxford Movement. With its liberal ideas on religion and its turning away from the traditional emphasis on esoteric theological dogma and ritual, *Robert Elsmere* advocated a practical religious life guided by a sense of social mission. Its eponymous hero gives up his ministry to set up a religious community for artisans in London's East End, based on the social ideals of the Gospels. Through this New Brotherhood of Christ, Elsmere hopes to restore religious faith and with it offer a new kind of spiritual life dedicated to the service of others. The novel quickly became a best-seller in the United Kingdom, was extensively pirated in the

Mary Ward (North Wind Picture Archives)

United States, and was translated into several languages. Former prime minister William Gladstone's article, "*Robert Elsmere* and the Battle of Belief," in the May 1888 issue of the *Nineteenth Century* further boosted sales.

A stream of other didactic novels reflecting Ward's social and religious concerns and advocating service of the poor followed, including *The History of David Grieve* (1892), which was considered to be a disappointing follow-up to *Robert Elsmere; Marcella* (1894); *Sir George Tressaday,* a novel in which Ward raised public sympathy for sweatshop workers and argued for the protection of workers under an extension of the Factory Acts (1896); and *Helbeck of Bannisdale,* a study of Catholicism and a crisis in religious faith (1898). All these novels underlined Ward's awareness of urban poverty and its concomitant sufferings and the economic decline of rural communities. Ward worked at a frenetic pace, and eventually overwork, nervous exhaustion, and failing health combined to erode her talents in her post-1900 fiction. The ardors of life on the literary treadmill and writing in longhand provoked a repetitive strain injury that could only be alleviated with doses of cocaine. Although the later novels, such as *Eleanor* (1900), *Lady Rose's Daughter* (1903), *The Marriage of William Ash* (1905), and *Daphne, or Marriage à la Mode* (1909), continued to address serious topical issues such as marriage, divorce, and the sexual double standard, they also contained stronger "romantic" elements and were less successful.

But by this time, Ward was supporting an upper-class lifestyle, including a substantial house at Tring, and providing for the many hangers-on in her own family who depended on her financial support, not to mention her generous funding of many charitable enterprises.

In 1890 Ward used her own money to set up, in the spirit of *Robert Elsmere,* a religious-based settlement in Bloomsbury. Known as University Hall, it offered a social center for working-class men and women as well as instruction in history and religious topics. Her object was to teach the true qualities of public service to those volunteers who undertook social work at University Hall and inspire a respect in them for the working classes and the deserving poor that avoided the patronizing and condescending tone of many Victorian reformers of the day.

The enduring success of *Robert Elsmere* prompted philanthropist Passmore Edwards to put more money into University Hall, which in 1897 became the Passmore Edwards Settlement and offered its services to the denizens of the overcrowded tenements of Kings Cross and St. Pancras. Ward, while chained to the grueling routine of writing on demand, devoted herself in the main to publicizing the work of the settlement and fund-raising among her influential contacts. In 1898 the Passmore Edwards Settlement was granted permission to set up an Invalid Children's School to cater to the special needs of handicapped children. Later known as the Mary Ward Center, it became Ward's special project, in which she was helped by her two daughters. Originally offering care to fifteen to eighteen children under the age of fourteen, it became the prototype for twenty-three similar schools set up by the London School Board by 1906. Ward also established Saturday and evening play centers for children at the end of the 1890s. Known as the Passmore Edwards Children's Recreational Schools, they offered poor children a respite from slum life and provided the first tentative moves toward combating juvenile delinquency, like similar schemes run by Margaret McMillan in southern London. Ward's interests in the welfare of children also led her to support organizations such as the Children's Country Holiday Association and the Children's Happy Evenings Association. Her later work, which garnered cross-party support in Parliament, involved lobbying for special provisions in schools for crippled children under the 1918 Education Act.

Although Ward enthusiastically endorsed women's philanthropic work and depicted numerous independently minded women in her novels, she was a firm believer that they should operate in traditional, separate, and nonpolitical spheres, where they could be effective in setting a moral example. Women's suffrage, she felt, would debase womanhood. Women did not need or want the responsibility of power and could be far more effective in useful social service. She warned also of the dangers to women of acquiring overarching demands for self-determination that descended into selfishness and the destructive desire to seek power over men. In 1889 she drafted an "Appeal against Female Suffrage" signed by several well-known figures, which was published in the *Nineteenth Century*. In some of her later novels, notably *The Testing of Diana Mallory* (1908) and *Delia Blanchflower* (1915), she presented critical portraits of suffragettes.

In 1908, such was her sense of duty in discouraging women from political activism that Ward was a founding member and president of the Women's National Anti-Suffrage League. She found further outlet for her opposition through a reformist lobbying group, the Joint Advisory Council of Members of Parliament and Women Social Workers, which sought political changes without the need for women's enfranchisement. In 1911 her founding of the Local Government Advancement Committee further encouraged women's social and charitable work in nonpolitical ways.

During World War I, Ward was a vigorous supporter of the war effort; she visited the army in the trenches and women working in munitions factories and wrote three propagandist novels, *England's Effort* (1916), *Towards the Goal* (1917), and *Fields of Victory* (1919), aimed at galvanizing U.S. support for the war among her many readers in that country.

Although Ward's novels now have only specialist appeal, her introductions to the 1899–1900 edition of *The Works of Charlotte Bronte and Her Sisters* have frequently been commended for the quality of the writing, as has her vivid and revealing memoir, *A Writer's Recollections* (1918), which contains portraits of many of her Oxford contemporaries.

See also McMillan, Margaret.

References and Further Reading
Gwynn, Stephen Lucius. 1917. *Mrs. Humphry Ward*. London: Nisbet and Company.
Harrison, Brian. 1978. *Separate Spheres: The Opposition to Women's Suffrage in Britain*. London: Croom Helm.
Jones, E. Huws. 1973. *Mrs. Humphry Ward*. Oxford: Heinemann.
Lewis, Jane. 1987. *Before the Vote Was Won: Arguments for and against Women's Suffrage*. London: Routledge and Kegan Paul.
Peterson, William S. 1976. *Victorian Heretic: Mrs. Humphry Ward's Robert Elsmere*. Leicester: Leicester University Press.
Smith, Esther M. 1980. *Mrs. Humphry Ward*. Boston: Twayne.
Sutherland, John. 1990. *Mrs. Humphry Ward: Eminent Victorian, Pre-Eminent Edwardian*. Oxford: Clarendon Press.
Trevelyan, Janet P. 1923. *The Life of Mrs. Humphry Ward*. London: Constable.

Webb, Beatrice
(1858–1943)
United Kingdom

A leading socialist economist, political and social reformer, and writer, Beatrice Webb was a pioneer member of the Fabian Society. Together with her husband, Sidney Webb, she was an outstanding propagandist for the Labour movement in Britain in the years before World War II. However, Webb chose to serve those in need not through philanthropic work, which she considered generally ineffectual, but through her extensive writings and her political connections, in which she lobbied for legislative change. In her many publications, coauthored with her husband or written alone, she exposed the social ills of wage slavery and the exploitation of the working classes. Working closely with trade unionists, she initiated the foundation of trade boards for the regulation of wages and working conditions, particularly in unregulated industries where women workers predominated.

Webb was born into the moneyed class and grew up at Standish House near Gloucester, the eighth of nine daughters of a wealthy financier and railway magnate. She was sickly as a child and missed out on formal education, but she was widely read. Although the family lost some of its wealth in a financial crash in 1847, the young

Beatrice enjoyed the benefits of being much traveled (accompanying her father on a business trip to the United States at the age of only fifteen). A close family friend, the sociologist Herbert Spencer, who recognized in the breadth of Webb's intellect a "young George Eliot," was an early influence on her later social concerns. After her mother's death in 1882, she helped her father with his business affairs but became restless with the limitations of her life at home, without social or intellectual contact and without useful employment. After spending time nursing her father after a stroke, in 1883 Webb took up voluntary work for the Charity Organisation Society (COS) as a rent collector on Octavia Hill's housing project, Katharine Buildings, at St. Katharine's Dock. But the work did not suit her; Webb rapidly became impatient with the lack of impact on working-class apathy that this brand of social work was having, she did not find it easy to sublimate herself in charitable work in the way her female coworkers did (she would later admit to finding it much easier working with men). Jane Lewis puts it more bluntly: "Beatrice lacked the capacity for sympathetic interaction with the poor" (1991, 91).

Webb was now moving in Liberal and intellectual circles, where she met the politician Joseph Chamberlain in 1883, with whom she remained infatuated for several years. Dismayed by the impotence of the COS, she became engrossed in investigative research in 1886, when she began assisting social reformer Charles Booth (who was married to her cousin) in what would be (for Booth) a seventeen-year survey of poverty in the metropolis, published as *The Life and Labour of the People in London* (1889–1902). The work opened her eyes to the reality of working-class life in the slums. In 1888 she undertook a study of the life of dock laborers, observed the lives of immigrant Jews in the East End, and tried unsuccessfully to obtain firsthand experience of the clothing industry there by taking work sewing trousers, as preparation for giving evidence to a House of Lords Committee on the Sweating System (1888–1889).

The death of Webb's father in 1891 left her with a private annual income of £1,000 per annum, which allowed her the freedom to pursue her research interests. In 1891 Webb published *The Co-operative Movement in Great Britain,* drawn from her observations of the mill towns during a visit to relatives in Lancashire. Beatrice met Sidney Webb in 1890, at a time when she had all but resigned herself to a life of spinsterly altruism. She had always regarded marriage of mutually respecting companions as being the essential component of a happy life, and after their marriage in 1892, she and Webb found a great and enduring intellectual partnership that thrived on their complementary talents. She made a rational decision not to have a family, however, observing in her diary that childbearing would destroy the finely tuned intellect that she had now dedicated to social investigation. As political and social theorists, the Webbs worked in close collaboration on 100 books, articles, and pamphlets during their long marriage, in which they preached education reform and investigated trade unionism, the eradication of poverty through government intervention, and the development of local government. In 1894 the Webbs published their first collaboration, *The History of Trade Unionism,* and in 1897 produced *Industrial Democracy,* both works characterized by sound research and methodology based on statistical analysis.

In 1895 the Webbs were founders of the London School of Economics and Political Science, which had as its object to advance research into social and economic problems and the pedagogy of modern political economy. This project, combined with their work in support of municipal reform through the London County Council and the reorganization of schools under county borough councils, took them increasingly into public life after 1900. Their London home became a venue for socialists and social reformers, and they were much in demand as public speakers. The product of their many years researching municipal reform was published in eleven volumes as *English Local Government from the Revolution to the Municipal Corporations Act* (1906–1929), a work that finally established their preeminence as social investigators.

During 1905–1909, Beatrice served on the Royal Commission on the Poor Laws, considered to be one of the most significant social campaigns of its time, at the end of which she contributed to the preparation of a report that analyzed the roots of poverty and recommended doing away with the despised Poor Law of 1834. It had laid the blame for poverty squarely at the door of the workingman; in Victorian eyes, indigence was largely the result of idleness and lack of moral fiber. Webb despised the way in which this outmoded system stigmatized the underprivileged who received welfare. But her radical submissions were largely ignored by the commission, which ultimately recommended only minimal reforms. The commission's inaction forced Beatrice and a splinter group to draft their own *Minority Report,* calling for the abolition of the Poor Law and the introduction of a system of welfare and financial benefits for children, the old, the sick, and the poor. This report would later be drawn on by Ernest Beveridge, along with the research of Eleanor Rathbone, when he submitted his own blueprint for the welfare state in 1942. As an elaboration of the Webbs' own social philosophy, the *Minority Report* was a radical and far-reaching submission and sold better than the main report itself. In the years that followed, the practices of the Poor Law were slowly but surely done away with.

In 1912 Beatrice was elected to the executive of the Fabian Society, where she helped set up a Fabian Research Department a year later in a drive to make the society more proactive in political campaigning. In 1913 she and Sidney founded one of Britain's most successful and long-lasting left-wing journals, the *New Statesman,* which became and remains today an important forum for socialist thinking. During World War I, and by that time a member also of the Labour Party, Beatrice produced a pamphlet entitled "Wages of Men and Women—Should They Be Equal?" as a result of a study of rates of pay for women in war industries. Having been opposed to women's suffrage, she changed her opinion, although she never undertook suffrage campaigning, preferring instead to take a stand against women's exploitation as workers (for example, during 1918–1919 as a member of the War Cabinet Committee on Women in Industry) and to lobby for legislation to protect them in the workplace.

After the war, Webb served as a justice of the peace (1919–1927) and was on the Lord Chancellor's Advisory Committee for Women Justices (1919–1920). But she concentrated increasingly on research and her extensive diary (fifty-six volumes covering the years from 1873 until her death), on which she would draw for her autobiography, which was published in two parts as *My Apprenticeship,* covering her life until 1911

(1926), and *Our Partnership* (published posthumously in 1948).

In 1922 Sidney Webb was elected to Parliament, becoming a cabinet minister two years later in the first Labour government; in 1929 he was made a life peer. Beatrice hated the life of a political wife and refused to use her title, Lady Passfield, except for public engagements. In 1931 the couple retired to their home in Hampshire. By this time, they had lost faith in the socialist movement in Britain effecting real political change and had become increasingly absorbed in the Soviet Union, which seemed to offer the answers to contemporary economic and social problems. In 1932 they made an official visit, where they were feted by Joseph Stalin; Beatrice's unqualified support for the Soviet state, despite the onset of the political purges, is reflected in *Soviet Communism: A New Civilisation?,* which she and Sidney published in 1935. Many of their erstwhile socialist friends saw this book as an embarrassing apologia and a betrayal by the Webbs of their own averred beliefs in gradual and democratic social change.

Webb never exploited her intellectual gifts in fiction, but her extensive diaries have proved in themselves to be remarkable and valuable documents, which, taken with her autobiography, have provided historians with extensive insights into the rapid social and political changes going on in Britain during the first half of the twentieth century. She remained a detached figure, however, who, despite her noble intentions, lacked the warmth and compassion of grassroots social reformers. Such was her absorption in empirical research and the collation of statistics and documentary evidence that her reformist program was based on the imposition of political change by government from above, rather than on work in the field, which took into account the vagaries of the human condition.

See also Hill, Octavia; Rathbone, Eleanor.
References and Further Reading
Alexander, Sally. 1988. *Women's Fabian Tracts.* London: Routledge.
Banks, Olive, ed. 1985, 1990. *The Biographical Dictionary of British Feminists,* vol. 1, *1800–1930*; vol. 2, *1900–1945.* Brighton: Harvester Wheatsheaf.
Baylen, J. O., and N. J. Gossman, eds. 1979–1984. *Biographical Dictionary of Modern British Radicals.* 3 vols. Hassocks, Sussex: Harvester Press.

Beilharz, P., and C. Nyland. 1999. *The Webbs, Fabianism and Feminism.* Aldershot: Ashgate.

Brandon, Ruth. 1990. *The New Women and the Old Men.* London: Martin Secker and Warburg.

Cole, Margaret. 1945. *Beatrice Webb.* London: Longman Green.

———, ed. 1974 [1949]. *The Webbs and Their Work.* Reprint, Brighton: Harvester Press.

Hamilton, Mary A. 1933. *Sidney and Beatrice Webb: A Study in Contemporary Biography.* London: S. Low.

Lewis, Jane. 1991. *Women and Social Action in Victorian and Edwardian England.* Aldershot: Elgar.

Mackenzie, Norman Ian, and Jeanne Mackenzie. 1982–1984. *The Diary of Beatrice Webb.* 4 vols. London: Virago.

Marston, Kitty Muggeridge. 1967. *Beatrice Webb: A Life, 1858–1943.* London: Secker and Warburg.

Nord, Deborah E. 1985. *The Apprenticeship of Beatrice Webb.* London: Macmillan.

Radice, Lisanne. 1984. *Beatrice and Sidney Webb: Fabian Socialists.* London: Macmillan.

Seymour-Jones, Carolyn. 1992. *Beatrice Webb: Woman of Conflict.* London: Allison and Busby.

Stocks, Mary. 1970. *My Commonplace Book.* London: Peter Davies.

Todd, Janet, ed. 1989. *Dictionary of British Women Writers.* London: Routledge.

Weiss, Louise
(1893–1983)
France

A militant suffragist during the interwar years and founder of the New Woman feminist group, Weiss led the long French suffrage campaign in its final phase, ending with the winning of the vote in 1944. In later life, she became an important pacifist journalist and supporter of decolonization, European unity, and international peace mediation.

The daughter of a mining engineer who had fled the conflict in Alsace-Lorraine in the 1870s, Weiss was born in Arras. She grew up in a comfortable bourgeois household with servants, and after the family moved to Paris in 1899, she attended private school in Auteuil. She passed her baccalaureate and sat the examination for secondary school teachers, coming in first in her class and subsequently studying at Oxford and the Sorbonne.

In 1915, during World War I, Weiss set up a temporary hostel in an abandoned building in Brittany to provide shelter for refugees from northern France. The French military, however, ordered her to turn it into a field hospital for convalescent soldiers, and Weiss used her own money to obtain rations and supplies, raising money among friends and the local inhabitants to keep it going.

After the war, she visited the Soviet Union in 1921 and spent five weeks in Moscow, where she interviewed Bolshevik leaders, including Leon Trotsky. She expressed her enthusiasm for the Soviet experiment and Lenin's New Economic Policy and urged the sending of humanitarian aid to the Soviets. During the 1920s, Weiss held out great hopes for the work of the League of Nations. Turning to journalism, she published several major articles on postwar Europe, highlighting the grievances of Germany in the wake of the Versailles Treaty and urging reconciliation in Europe. She reported on foreign affairs for the magazine *New Europe*, and in 1923 she was promoted to editor in chief, a post she would retain for nine years. As a humanist and pacifist, in October 1930 Weiss founded a Peace Academy in France with the support of eminent French politicians and writers and international diplomats. This had the objective of providing a neutral forum for the discussion of major issues affecting world peace and promoting mediation by peaceful methods in international disputes. But by the 1930s, when the work of the League of Nations foundered with the rise of Nazism and fascism, the peace movement suffered major setbacks, and she turned to domestic issues.

From 1932 Weiss played an important role in the women's suffrage movement as a member of the French Union for Women's Suffrage. A believer in the moral necessity of women's struggle for their rights and the achievement of their equal civil status with men, she led the final phase of the fight for women's suffrage, for so long delayed in France. She resigned from *New Europe* and in 1932 began to channel her considerable energies and journalistic skills into women's rights issues, arguing: "We [women] are adults in our faults and liabilities, but minors in our rights" (Bess 1993, 11). In 1934 Weiss cofounded the New Woman group, which from its offices on the Champs Elysées in Paris staged numerous demonstrations and marches for women's rights during the years 1934–1939. This largely unsuccessful attempt to galvanize popular

Louise Weiss (center) (AP/World Wide Photos)

support for women's suffrage left her disillusioned by the apathy of many Frenchwomen.

In May 1935 Weiss stood unsuccessfully in the eighteenth *arrondissement* of Paris as a candidate for municipal elections. Her supporters handed out unofficial ballot papers to be inserted into hatboxes; but the French State Council, although acknowledging the validity of the claim, did not change the law. A year later in a widely publicized moment in the suffrage campaign, Weiss, dressed in a glamorous gown by top couturier Molyneux, joined with other suffragists in chaining themselves together across the Rue Royale. Despite being arrested for her activities, she was offered a cabinet post but declined the offer. She preferred to wage her own campaign for women's rights, such as organizing support for women to be allowed to participate in noncombatant forms of military service in 1938, and petitioning for the word *obey* to be taken out of the French marriage service.

As World War II approached, Weiss took up refugee work, helping Jews who had fled from Germany and eastern Europe. Tragedy struck in her private life when the man she loved (a farmer in his forties—she never named him) volunteered for the army and was killed in June 1940. Herself a Jew, she continued to take great risks during the Nazi occupation of France, although she was able to pass as an Aryan. She joined the French Resistance, ran an underground newspaper, the *New Republic,* and also went on a mission to New York and Washington to raise much-needed medical supplies. Eventually, she went into hiding to evade arrest by the Gestapo. Her home, used by the Nazis during the war, was looted and vandalized, and twenty years of Weiss's correspondence and papers were destroyed.

After the liberation of France and the final award of women's suffrage in 1944, Weiss joined the Radical Party and returned to writing. She traveled extensively in Asia, the Middle East, Africa, and the United States from 1946 to 1965, published accounts of her travels, made thirty-seven documentary films—many of them illustrating the impact of French colonialism in the Third World—and won a prestigious award from the French Academy in 1947 for her novel about the Nazi occupation, *The Marseillaise.* (In 1974 Weiss would take the academy to task for keeping its doors closed to women; in an unprecedented step, she proposed herself as a member, but her attempt at banishing discrimination against women failed.)

In 1957 Weiss founded a political journal, *Red Iron,* which tackled issues relating to French colonialism, and spent eleven years (1965–1976) writing six volumes of memoirs, published as *Memoirs of a European* (1970–1976). Still deeply committed to pacifism and disarmament, in 1971 Weiss founded the Institute for the Science of Peace in Strasbourg and spent the remaining years of her life in the international arena lecturing on her interpretation of the "European idea." In 1976, at the age of eighty-three, she embarked on a lecture tour of France and other parts of Western Europe. She acted as a French delegate to the United Nations Educational, Scientific, and Cultural Organization and became a champion of the European Union, in 1979 serving as a neo-Gaullist representative at the European Parliament. From that position she continued to promote European integration and decolonization until her death.

References and Further Reading

The Annual Obituary. 1983. New York: St. Martin's Press.

Bess, Michael. 1993. *Realism, Utopia and the Mushroom Cloud: Four Activist Intellectuals and the Strategies for Peace 1945–1989.* Chicago: University of Chicago Press.

Uglow, Jennifer, ed. 1998. *Macmillan Dictionary of Women's Biography.* 3d ed. Basingstoke: Macmillan.

Wells-Barnett, Ida B.
(1862–1931)
United States

The outstanding journalist and lecturer Ida Wells-Barnett was one of the first black women to widely and openly protest racial violence and lynching during the 1890s in the United States. A courageous individualist, she was also an early advocate of direct action in the developing civil rights movement. In her campaigning and writing, Wells-Barnett promoted a sense of dignity and pride in America's black population that

Ida B. Wells-Barnett (Library of Congress)

would result in the establishment of societies such as the Negro Fellowship League and the National Association for the Advancement of Colored People (NAACP). She also devoted considerable energy to consciousness-raising among black women, encouraging them to defend their political rights and join the women's suffrage movement.

The daughter of slaves, Wells-Barnett was born in Holly Springs, Mississippi, and educated at a local school run by the National Freedmen's Relief Society. She lost her parents and three brothers in a yellow fever epidemic in 1876. Only fourteen at the time, she lied about her age and took a job as a teacher to help support her seven siblings. She worked in rural schools in Tennessee and moved to Memphis in 1883–1884, where she continued her studies in summer school at Fisk University and the Lemoyne Institute. Her first brush with the Jim Crow laws operating in the South came when she was ordered off a Chesapeake and Ohio Railroad train for refusing to give up her seat in the first-class "Ladies' Car." This incident led to a test case in May 1884 in which she sued the railroad and won $500 in damages, only to see her case overturned on appeal in 1887 by the Tennessee Supreme Court. Meanwhile, Wells-Barnett had taken up occasional journalism for black-owned church newspapers, working on the *Evening Star* and *Living Way* and adopting the pseudonym Iola. The articles she published on local issues, such as the lack of decent educational facilities for black children and their segregation from white children, eventually brought dismissal from her teaching job in 1891. In later years she worked with Jane Addams to fight the segregation of Chicago's schools.

In 1891 Wells-Barnett bought a share in the Memphis-based *Free Speech and Headlight,* in it writing of the lynchings of three of her friends who had opened a grocery store in direct competition with one run by a white person. She urged blacks in Memphis to escape harassment by whites and migrate to frontier territory in Oklahoma, where life was safer; 6,000 took up the challenge in the ensuing months. In addition, Wells-Barnett launched her own investigation into some 728 lynchings that had taken place in the South over the previous ten years and in October 1892 published a pamphlet, "Southern Horrors: Lynch Law in All Its Phases." Here and in articles in *Free Speech,* she insisted that the lynching of her friends and of others had had nothing to do with the frequently offered explanation of fear of sexual attack of white women by black males. Wells-Barnett argued forcefully that lynching was, in many cases, a manifestation of the white fear of economic competition from blacks. As a result, her newspaper office was attacked and wrecked by a white mob.

Wells-Barnett was away in New York attending a convention of the African Methodist Episcopal Church at the time the attack took place. Worried by the escalating threats of violence in retaliation for her outspokenness, she decided not to return to the South, but to continue her campaign against lynching in the North. She did so through a new organization she founded in New York in 1892, the Women's Loyal Union. She also became a reporter on the *New York Age,* and her national articles on lynching now reached a much wider audience.

Wells-Barnett continued to found antilynching societies as she traveled and lectured in the United States and in Britain (1893–1894). Despite English support for her campaign against lynching, and the acclaim with which her speeches were received in cities such as Birmingham, Manchester, Glasgow, and London, Wells-Barnett's time there was made difficult by her open accusations of racism on the part of Woman's Christian Temperance Union leader Frances Willard, who was widely supported by the English sister movement, led by Lady Isabella Somerset. Nevertheless, by the time of her departure in 1894, sympathizers had established a British Anti-Lynching Committee.

While attending the Chicago World's Fair in 1893, Wells-Barnett protested the absence of black American culture there and the exclusion of blacks as participants in her pamphlet, "The Reason Why the Colored American Is Not in the World's Columbian Exposition," prompting further attacks on her. (The World's Columbian Exhibition was the official title of the fair, in celebration of the four hundredth anniversary of Christopher Columbus's discovery of America.) Deciding to settle in the city, in 1893 she organized the first black women's club in Chicago, the Ida B. Wells Club, which with time became a movement, originally to fight lynching but later calling for women's suffrage and the rights of black women. In 1895 she married lawyer Ferdinand Lee Barnett, who was also editor of the *Chicago Conservator,* which published many of Wells-Barnett's articles on racial injustice. That year also, she published her pamphlet on lynching, "A Red Record," in which she catalogued the history of some 10,000 lynchings that had taken place since the slaves were freed after the Civil War, including with it a statistical analysis of the occurrence during 1893–1895. In 1898 she lobbied President William McKinley for a federal antilynching law, to no avail.

In all her years of campaigning, Wells-Barnett remained outside the mainstream of both the black and white women's movements. Her uncompromising opposition to racism and sexism compelled her to fight endemic racial prejudice among conservative elements in the white suffrage movement and with it their advocacy of a restricted vote for black women based on their level of literacy. In March 1912, at a famous suffrage rally held in Washington, D.C., Wells-Barnett defied requests to stay in the back with other black suffragists (and thus not antagonize white southern suffragists) and instead proudly took her place at the front of the National American Woman Suffrage Association's parade. She remained cynical that the winning of the vote would do anything to change things for women, and black women in particular, but in 1913 she nevertheless founded the first black woman suffrage group in Chicago, the Alpha Suffrage Club. With its initial membership of 200 women, it proved an effective force in municipal politics, working hard to assist registration drives among black male voters. In 1915 Wells-Barnett was directly involved in rallying support by club members to secure the election of Chicago's first black alderman, Oscar DePriest.

Wells-Barnett encountered the same difficulty in finding a niche for herself in various black civil rights organizations because none of them seemed to her sufficiently radical in their aspirations. In 1896 with Mary Church Terrell she was one of a committee of forty that founded the National Association of Colored Women. She also served as financial secretary of the National Afro-American Council in 1898–1902, only to be promptly criticized for trying to juggle this role with rearing her four children. In the event, neither group was progressive enough for her, and she opposed all idea of compromise by black activists with white political leaders. At the Conference on the Negro in New York in 1909, she was an advocate of the formation of the NAACP, but after it was established that same year, she found it, too, insufficiently militant. She turned instead to community work, in 1910 founding the Negro Fellowship League to help black migrants from the South by providing accommodations in hostels and a community center. In 1913–1916, she worked as a probation officer for the Chicago city courts and later organized legal aid for black victims of race riots that took place in 1918 in East St. Louis, Illinois.

Wells-Barnett's autobiography, *Crusade for Justice,* was published posthumously in 1970. In it, she frequently despaired at the injustice she saw on every side and the failure of the U.S. legal system to protect its black citizens from racial violence. But she remained to the end a combative figure, whose fighting spirit would have been put to good use had she lived to see the birth of the civil rights movement in the 1950s: "I felt that one had better die fighting against injustice than to die like a dog or a rat in a trap. I had already determined to sell my life as dearly as possible if attacked. I felt if I could take one lyncher with me, this would even up the score a little bit" (Duster 1970).

See also Addams, Jane; Somerset, Lady Isabella; Terrell, Mary Church.

References and Further Reading
Duster, Alfreda M., ed. 1970. *Crusade for Justice: The Autobiography of Ida B. Wells.* Chicago: University of Chicago Press.

Flexner, Eleanor. 1975 [1959]. *A Century of Struggle: The Woman's Rights Movement in the United States.* Rev. ed., Cambridge, MA: Belknap Press of Harvard University.

Frankel, Noralee, and Nancy S. Dye. 1991. *Gender, Class, Race, and Reform in the Progressive Era.* Lexington: University of Kentucky Press.

Franklin, John Hope, and August Meier. 1982. *Black Leaders of the Twentieth Century.* Urbana: University of Illinois Press.

Giddings, Paula. 1984. *When and Where I Enter: The Impact of Black Women on Race and Sex in America.* New York: W. W. Norton.

Kerber, Linda K., and Jane DeHart-Mathews. 2000. *Women's America: Refocusing the Past.* New York: Oxford University Press.

Lerner, Gerda, ed. 1972. *Black Women in White America: A Documentary History.* New York: Pantheon Books.

McFadden, Margaret. 1999. *Golden Cables of Sympathy: The Transatlantic Sources of Nineteenth-Century Feminism.* Lexington: University of Kentucky Press.

Royster, Jacqueline Jones, ed. 1997. *Southern Horrors and Other Stories: The Anti-Lynching Campaign of Ida B. Wells.* New York: St. Martin's Press.

Sterling, Dorothy. 1994 [1979]. *Black Foremothers: Three Lives.* Reprint, New York: Feminist Press.

Thompson, Mildred I. 1990. *Ida B. Wells Barnett: An Exploratory Study of an American Black Woman, 1893–1930.* New York: Carlson Publishing.

Ware, Vron. 1992. *Beyond the Pale: White Women, Racism, and History.* London: Verso.

Wells-Barnett, Ida B. 1970. *Crusade for Justice: The Autobiography of Ida B. Wells.* Chicago: University of Chicago Press.

Wheeler, Anna Doyle
(1785–1848)
Ireland

The French-inspired radical and feminist Anna Doyle Wheeler is best known for her collaboration with the Irish socialist and feminist William Thompson on the groundbreaking tract *An Appeal of One Half of the Human Race, Women, against the Pretensions of the Other Half, Men, to Restrain Them in Political and Thence in Civil and Domestic Slavery* (1825).

A utopian socialist, Wheeler was one of a generation of fascinating and unconventional women inspired by the French *philosophes,* who espoused social causes and paved the way for the later campaign for women's suffrage. As one of the first militant feminists, she was withering in her view of marriage as a form of sexual slavery. Women were powerless to fight for their rights, in her view, because they had no economic independence from men, and Wheeler called for the equal division of property between sons and daughters. *An Appeal* is frequently compared with John Stuart Mill's better known 1869 work *The Subjection of Women,* which it predates by forty-four years, but despite in many respects being more outspoken and radical in its approach, it has been accorded far less attention than Mill's work.

The daughter of a Protestant archdeacon, Wheeler grew up in Clonbeg, Tipperary. Her family was enlightened and progressive, and she became a convinced feminist after reading Mary Wollstonecraft's 1792 work, *A Vindication of the Rights of Woman,* when she was a young woman. Her early life, however, was wrecked by a premature marriage at the age of fifteen to a drunken spendthrift, Francis Massey Wheeler, followed by numerous pregnancies and miscarriages. She sought refuge from her misery in self-education, turning to the writings of French and German philosophers such as Denis Diderot and Paul-Henri Holbach. In 1812 she left her husband and went to live in Guernsey. She then settled in Caen, in France, around 1818, where she lived for a while with a group of disciples of the French socialist Henri de Saint-Simon, who believed in the equality of the sexes and harmonious cooperation between them. Such was Wheeler's intellectual ability that they nicknamed her the "Goddess of Reason." This group collaborated closely with the followers of Robert Owen in England, who promoted his own version of feminist socialism. Wheeler translated some of the Saint-Simonian group's literature, as well as the writings of the French feminist Flora Tristan, for Owen's publication *The Crisis.*

In 1820, on her husband's death, Wheeler returned to Ireland and then lived for a while between London and Dublin, mixing and exchanging ideas with utilitarians and members of the cooperative movement (followers of Robert Owen). It was during this time that she developed her own ideas on the nature of social reform, based upon what she had learned from Saint-Simon and Owen and after meeting with Jeremy Bentham and other luminaries of the utilitarian school. She also met the social theorist Charles Fourier in Paris in 1823 and took note of his ideas on community. She appears to have held a salon in Paris, where she met many of the leading French thinkers of her day—certainly Wheeler's reputation there was far better established than in England. She also did much to encourage an interchange of ideas between Fourierists, Owenites, and Saint-Simonians.

In the 1820s, Wheeler met William Thompson, the Irish economist and theorist and follower of Owen, and in 1825 they wrote their famous treatise on sexual equality together. Whether or not Wheeler ever had a sexual union with Thompson is unclear. Certainly, they had a marriage of minds and a working partnership akin to that of Mill and Harriet Taylor. When Thompson died in 1833, he left Wheeler an annuity of £100.

A particular problem is presented by their collaborative work, *An Appeal of One Half of the Human Race,* in that it is very difficult to know how much of the content is Wheeler's own input and how much of her own thinking was subsumed within it. It would certainly appear that much of the book's sardonic tone is colored by her own miserable experience of marriage. Dale Spender, in her classic study *Women of Ideas and What Men Have Done to Them,* contends that too many historians have totally ignored Wheeler's contribution and that her creative input may in fact have been considerable. Thompson himself looked upon his collaborator as being more radical in her ideas than even Mary Wollstonecraft. Wheeler's own personal argument within *An Appeal* rings out loud and clear: women were living in a state of economic dependence that reduced their lives to domestic slavery. They could not enjoy true emancipation and happiness until they had equal rights with men with regard to property and inheritance. She argued that they had every right to be allowed into higher education and the professions and that they should be legally protected against domestic violence and be able to divorce husbands who abused them. She abhorred the subordination of women to men, but the alternative facing them in her day was a bleak one: women had either to marry or to starve. Wheeler saw women's economic dependency as a great source of disunity in society and even as the root of crime; she also was convinced that it did actual harm to women's psyches. The emancipation of women was crucial, she believed, to the regeneration of society: "though men make the law, it is women who mould the manners and morals of society; and according as they are enlightened or ignorant, do they spin the web of human destiny" (Cullen and Luddy 1995, 38).

In 1833 Wheeler became an executive member of the Grand Moral Union of the Productive Classes, a prototype of the early trade union movement, and moved in intellectual and radical circles that were pressuring government to reform the electoral system. The failure of the 1832 Reform Bill to fulfill the political expectations of many on electoral reform and universal suffrage greatly discouraged her. But far more profound was Wheeler's disillusion with her own sex, who she felt were indifferent, if not hostile, to the feminist cause and had little inkling of the extent of their own oppression. It was Wheeler's belief that they had grown too accustomed to suffering in silence, so much so that they had made a profession of it; and it was this continuing ability to endure without protest that would ensure women would remain the slaves of men. Eventually, long after Wheeler's own death, her combative spirit reappeared in her granddaughter, Constance Georgina Lytton, a leading militant suffragette from 1908 who would help win the campaign for women's suffrage, finally awarded in Britain in 1918.

See also Lytton, Lady Constance; Taylor, Harriet; Tristan, Flora; Wollstonecraft, Mary.

References and Further Reading

Banks, O. 1985. *The Biographical Dictionary of British Feminists,* vol. 1, *1800–1930.* London: Harvester Wheatsheaf.

Cullen, Mary, and Maria Luddy. 1995. *Women, Power, and Consciousness in Nineteenth-Century Ireland. Eight Biographical Studies.* Dublin: Attic Press.

Dooley, Dolores. 1996. *Equality in Community: Sexual Equality in the Writings of William Thompson and Anna Doyle Wheeler.* Cork: Cork University Press.

McFadden, Margaret. 1999. *Golden Cables of Sympathy: The Transatlantic Sources of Nineteenth-Century Feminism.* Lexington: University of Kentucky Press.

Ó Céirín, Kit, and Cyril Ó Céirín, eds. 1996. *Women of Ireland: A Biographic Dictionary.* Kinvara, County Galway: Tír Eolas.

Spender, Dale. 1982. *Women of Ideas, and What Men Have Done to Them.* London: Routledge and Kegan Paul.

Taylor, Barbara. 1983. *Eve and the New Jerusalem: Society and Feminism in the Nineteenth Century.* London: Virago.

Wickremasinghe, Doreen
(1907–2000)
United Kingdom/Sri Lanka

A socialist and progressive educator from Cheshire, Doreen Young married Dr. S. A. Wickremasinghe, a leading communist politician in Sri Lanka (then called Ceylon), and dedicated herself to human rights and women's education in her adopted homeland. In 1952 she became the first foreign woman to become a member of the Sri Lankan parliament.

Doreen Young came from a prominent socialist-pacifist family in Bristol, England. Her grandfather and father had both been active socialists, with Doreen inheriting her grandfather Robert Weare's ethical socialism, born of his work with the Bristol Socialist Society. Doreen was educated at the progressive Theosophist school, St. Christopher's. Located in Letchworth, it was one of the first to introduce coeducation and vegetarianism and was supported in its work by Theosophist leader Annie Besant. Doreen continued her education, studying economics and politics at the London School of Economics, where she became secretary of the Student Union and became active in the work of the India League. After graduating in 1929, she met Dr. S. A. Wickremasinghe, a Buddhist Theosophist and medical practitioner, at a Theosophical Society meeting. He offered to help her fulfill her dream of going to the East by finding her a job in Sri Lanka.

Doreen arrived in Sri Lanka in 1930. Now age twenty-three, she was given the post of principal of the Buddhist-run Sujata Vidyalaya girls' high school in Matara in southern Sri Lanka. Education for Buddhist girls in schools run by the Theosophical Society had started in 1889. During her two years at the school, Doreen decided that her mission was to overhaul the curriculum, divest the school of its Anglo-centrism, and promote Sri Lankan history and culture as well as world history. She also modernized methods in the school's kindergarten. She took to wearing a sari and eventually learned to speak Sinhala. In 1933 she married Dr. Wickremasinghe and was invited to become principal of the Ananda Balika Buddhist girls' secondary school. During her two years there, she instituted a relaxed and happy relationship between staff and pupils, introduced many progressive ideas in teaching methods, and emphasized the importance of social awareness and cultural identity through an encouragement of local handicrafts.

The country was at that time moving toward independence, and Wickremasinghe joined the anti-imperialist movement. As a supporter of economic reform, child welfare, and labor law reform, she became highly active in the Suriya Mal movement. It had been set up by the Colombo Youth League, originally to sell native yellow flowers (*suriya mal*) instead of the English red poppies on Armistice Day, in support of Sri Lankan rather than British ex-servicemen. It also campaigned against imperialism and fascism in the Far East in the years preceding World War II, as well as leading strikes by textile workers and taking part in relief work during a malaria epidemic. Wickremasinghe's actions were criticized in the press, as was her attack on the traditional caste system. Money made in the Suriya Mal campaign was channeled into educating a girl from the lowest caste (Rodi), who lived with the Wickremasinghe family while studying at the Ananda Balika school in Colombo. Eventually, the authorities balked at Wickremasinghe using the school as a base from which to operate the Suriya Mal movement; she was removed from her post as principal but allowed to carry on teaching there until 1935.

Finding themselves unemployed (her husband had lost his seat in Parliament), the Wickremasinghes returned to London in straitened circumstances, where Doreen's family lent them the money to set up a medical practice for her husband. During the years leading to World War II, they took part in communist-led protests against the rise of fascism, and Wickremasinghe earned a teacher's diploma in 1937. On their return to Sri Lanka in 1939, she started her own school in Colombo. Her Modern School was as progressive as the name suggests but was closed down in 1942 because of the war. The Wickremasinghes moved south and made their home

and the doctor's medical practice there a base for antifascists and social activists. After the war, Wickremasinghe went back to England with her two children and became involved in women's organizations. On her return to Sri Lanka in 1946, she became a founder of the United Women's Front, a group of communist and leftist women. This group campaigned to end discrimination against women in the workplace, the bad working conditions of women in factories, and the appalling housing conditions in the slums and stressed issues relating to natal and maternal care, in particular the high infant mortality rates.

After independence was achieved in 1948, in an essay published in the *Ceylon Daily News,* "They Preach Austerity to the Starving," Wickremasinghe castigated the new government of Sri Lanka for neglecting to aid the poor and hungry. Another essay drew attention to the iniquities of child labor. Sadly, the United Women's Front did not receive sufficient support from the male-run leftist parties, and the organization was dissolved. She returned to teaching and wrote a series of illustrated first readers based on modern teaching methods. A resurgence of leftist activity in Sri Lanka in the 1950s prompted Wickremasinghe to stand for election in 1952, and despite prejudice against her being white and British, she was elected. She became a popular member of Parliament who took a close interest in education and health care, as well as helping run her husband's medical dispensary and hospital. She also played a role in various other pacifist societies and socialist women's organizations and was a member of the Sri Lanka Federation of University Women (founded in 1941).

See also Besant, Annie.

References and Further Reading
Jayawardena, Kumari. 1986. *Feminism and Nationalism in the Third World.* London: Zed Books.
———. 1995. *The White Woman's Other Burden: Western Women and South Asia during British Rule.* London: Routledge.
"A Tribute to Doreen Wickremasinghe." www.island.LK/2000/06/07/mdwkrvw.

Willard, Emma Hart
(1787–1870)
United States

In the history of women's education in the United States, Emma Willard was one of the first to advocate high schools for girls and the establishment of women's colleges. She also promoted the idea of coeducational colleges and universities in a wider vision of women's improved social responsibilities through education, although she saw these as being confined primarily to the separate domestic sphere.

Willard was one of seventeen children born on a farm in Berlin, Connecticut. In 1802–1803 she studied at the nearby Berlin Academy and began teaching local children while continuing with her own program of self-study. In 1807 she secured an appointment as principal of a girls' academy at Middlebury, Vermont, but left in 1809 upon her marriage to Dr. John Willard.

In 1814 Willard opened a boarding school, Middlebury Female Seminary, in her own home in an attempt to supplement her husband's financial losses. She boldly offered a curriculum that included subjects never taught girls in school, such as philosophy, geometry, mathematics, and even anatomy—all intended to better prepare them for a college education. But she encountered difficulty in obtaining funding for the school and petitioned the state legislature for support in the form of "An Address to the Public, Particularly to the Members of the Legislature of New York, Proposing a Plan for Improving Female Education" (published in 1819 at her own expense), which was read out on her behalf (it was socially unacceptable for Willard to read it herself). In the address, she argued that a nation's prosperity rested in part on the good character of its citizens, especially its mothers. She therefore criticized the exclusivity of private education and called for funding from the state to establish public girls' schools and promote higher standards in women's education, which would in turn enable women to contribute to the moral reform of society. Although her proposal was rejected, Willard's ideals impressed governor De Witt Clinton, who suggested she transfer her school to Waterford, New York. She did so in 1819 but was unable to raise funding there either. Eventually, in 1821, thanks to taxes raised by local residents of Troy and donations from patrons, Willard was able to build Troy Female Seminary (which in 1895 became the Emma Willard School and survives to this day).

Emma Hart Willard (Dover Pictorial Archives)

As the first women's high school in the United States, with 300 students by 1831, Troy became the prototype for other women's establishments, such as Mary Lyon's Holyoke Seminary in Massachusetts, and a training ground for many influential teachers. Willard introduced progressive subjects such as gymnastics, improved the methodology of teaching geography and history, and wrote numerous textbooks, including the popular *Last Leaves of American History* (1849), which ran into several editions.

In 1830 Willard went to Europe. At this time, she published poetry, including her famous poem "Rocked in the Cradle of the Deep," and her *Journal and Letters from France and Great Britain* (1833). She used some of her royalties to found a training school for teachers in Athens, Greece, in 1833. Back in the United States, she established the Willard Association for the Mutual Improvement of Female Teachers to encourage further recruitment of women to the profession.

In 1838 Willard retired from Troy, leaving her son and daughter-in-law to run the seminary. A brief second marriage in 1838 to the spendthrift

Christopher Yates ended in divorce in 1843. She continued to travel and lecture on equal opportunities for women teachers and joined educator Henry Barnard in calling for improvements to public schools. During 1845–1847, Willard is said to have traveled 8,000 miles in the South and West of the United States in her crusade to encourage improvements to standards of education, school buildings, and the salaries of women teachers. In 1854 she was one of only two delegates representing the United States at the World's Educational Convention in London.

Never a suffragist and having otherwise conservative views, Willard nevertheless supported women's right to their own property and to financial independence. But for her the essential building blocks of social progress for women lay in their education, thus ensuring they would be suitably equipped to be the moral guardians of better generations of children. The Emma Willard School website has a useful biography of Willard, at http://www.emma.troy.ny.us.

References and Further Reading

Flexner, Eleanor. 1975 [1959]. *A Century of Struggle: The Woman's Rights Movement in the United States.* Rev. ed. Cambridge, MA: Belknap Press of Harvard University.

Goodsell, Willystine, ed. 1970. *Pioneers of Women's Education in the United States.* New York: AMS.

Lord, John. 1873. *The Life of Emma Willard.* New York: Appleton.

Lutz, Alma. 1983 [1964]. *Emma Willard: Pioneer Educator of American Women.* Reprint, Westport, CT: Greenwood Press.

Reynolds, Moira Davison. 1988. *Nine American Women of the Nineteenth Century: Leaders into the Twentieth.* Jefferson, NC: McFarland.

Solomon, Barbara Miller. 1985. *In the Company of Educated Women: A History of Women and Higher Education in America.* New Haven, CT: Yale University Press.

Stanton, Elizabeth Cady. 1898. *Eighty Years and More: Reminiscences of Elizabeth Cady Stanton.* London: T. Fisher Unwin.

Willard, Frances
(1839–1898)
United States

The founder of the Woman's Christian Temperance Union (WCTU), the Christian socialist and feminist Frances Willard was one of the most commanding presences in the mainstream of U.S. social reform during the second half of the nineteenth century. In enlisting American women's support for uncontroversial issues such as family values and "home protection," she mobilized large numbers of them in a plethora of organized bodies advocating a wide range of moral and social reforms. Undoubtedly the dominating presence in the WCTU and nominated as "Woman of the Century," Willard was a fine public speaker and administrator and an inveterate lobbyist, who also devoted her considerable energies to women's education and suffrage and protective measures for working women.

Willard was born in Churchville, New York, and grew up on a frontier farm in Wisconsin. She was bitterly resentful that she was denied the same educational opportunities as her brother and fought hard to change her domineering father's prejudice against women's education. She briefly attended a girls' school in Janesville, followed by a term at Milwaukee Female College, and a period at Northwestern Female College in Evanston (1857–1859). After graduation, Willard became a teacher and worked in a local school for one year and then in a succession of mainly Methodist schools in six different states, including the Pittsburgh Female College (1863–1864) and the Genesee Wesleyan Seminary (1866–1867).

In 1868 Willard went to Europe with a friend, where she studied languages and spent time at the Sorbonne and Collège de France. Upon her return, she became president of Evanston College for Ladies in 1871, which became part of Northwestern University in 1873. Willard stayed on as dean of women and professor of English and art but resigned in late 1874 after conflict with the male administration and other demands on her time made teaching difficult. By this time, she had become involved in the establishment of the Association for the Advancement of Women. This group of conservative feminists had spurned the organized women's suffrage movement when it had been tainted with scandal in the wake of the Victoria Claflin Woodhull affair of 1972. Willard also began campaigning in earnest at the local level for temperance as secretary of the Chicago Woman's Temperance Union. After becoming secretary of the Illinois Temperance Association, she gave up her teaching post.

Frances Willard (Library of Congress)

Taking on the role of organizing secretary of the newly established Woman's Christian Temperance Union, Willard found her niche at the head of a fast-growing movement. Born on the tide of evangelism sweeping across the Midwest, the WCTU had been founded in Cleveland by Annie Wittenmyer. But from the outset, Willard, who was keen to use the WCTU as the springboard for other women's rights issues, had a battle to overcome caution in the movement's leadership, with women like Wittenmyer observing that "we do not propose to trail our skirts through the mire of politics" (James 1971, 615). As a feminist and suffragist, Willard also advocated legislative protection for women workers, such as the eight-hour workday, but continuing opposition from Wittenmyer forced her to resign as corresponding secretary in 1877. She remained in the movement, however, soon discovering that she could best promote her belief in suffrage as head of the organization's publications committee and writing for its widely disseminated journal, *Our Union*.

In 1879 a liberalization of the WCTU brought with it Willard's election as president (a post she held until her death), by which time its membership had grown to 250,000 and continued to rise under her outstanding leadership. Her skills as an administrator and organizer of the WCTU's various reform activities involved liaising with thirty-nine departments of the WCTU by 1889, with their interests ranging from suffrage to women's health and hygiene to immigrant welfare and the rights of prisoners. Willard's flamboyant leadership of what became a high-profile movement was greatly admired by women such as suffrage leader Carrie Chapman Catt and effected a rapprochement of the temperance and suffrage movements by 1883.

Willard was nominated first president of the new World's WCTU in 1891, under whose banner she extended agitation against alcohol to a campaign against the narcotics trade. WCTU members collected millions of signatures worldwide calling for governments to control the use of alcohol, tobacco, and other addictive substances such as opium (Willard had campaigned against its use since seeing opium dens in San Francisco's Chinatown in 1883). Under Willard, the WCTU scored considerable success in this respect nationally, with state after state, beginning with New York in 1884, passing legislation that made instruction on the harmful effects of alcohol a mandatory part of the school curriculum. Through the international influence of the World's WCTU, similar legislation was adopted in most of Canada, Sweden, France, Ireland, and some parts of Australia and South Africa. The WCTU also became a powerful lobby in the world of publishing, seeking to control the dissemination of books on physiology and hygiene deemed inappropriate for public consumption.

The appeal of the WCTU's moral purity campaign brought many women into activism who would never have espoused the militancy of suffrage. Such recruits joined the campaign against legalized prostitution and for the protection of young girls and commended Willard's efforts to see the age of consent raised. With respect to her campaigning for suffrage, Willard's thinking was closely linked with her support for temperance. She shared the view of many other activists with a foot in both camps that women's particular moral qualities could be put to good use in reforming the male-led world once they were given the vote. Willard never fulfilled her dream of uniting the two movements, however, although she did succeed in drawing some conservative elements from the temperance movement into the suffrage one, thus diluting the radicalism of U.S. suffragism, particularly during the 1890s when the movement narrowed its objectives to concentrate almost exclusively on suffrage, thus sidelining the wider issues of women's emancipation. Having once obtained women's suffrage, Willard anticipated a massive female vote in support of prohibition. But it was precisely for this reason, as Margaret Bacon argues (1986, 134), that by drawing so many temperance activists into suffrage, Willard brought down upon the women's suffrage movement the concerted opposition of influential male business interests in the liquor trade, whose opposition to prohibition thus by association blocked the passage of suffrage.

In general, Willard's forays into politics were unsuccessful. In 1882 she helped reorganize the Prohibition Party in support of women's suffrage as the Home Protection Prohibition Party and undertook a lecture tour on its behalf in 1883, but the body was short-lived and disintegrated after the Republican Party's endorsement of its objectives on prohibition lost it the election. (This defeat was in no small part due to the widespread opposition to women's suffrage by male voters in the South.) In the 1890s, Willard laid new hopes in bringing the issues of reform, especially prohibition and suffrage, into the reform program of the People's Party, only to find her ambitions once again thwarted. But her socialist principles found an advocate in the labor leader Eugene Debs and in their inheritors in the many hundreds of women in the WCTU who graduated from prohibition to more overtly socialist activities.

During the 1890s, Willard turned her attention to the women's movement and temperance in the international arena. Having been involved in the 1888 founding of the International Council of Women, she toured England during 1892–1893 and spent much time there on and off until 1896, where she collaborated closely with her English counterpart, good friend, and leader of the British temperance movement, Lady Isabella Somerset. Willard also became more deeply drawn into the Christian socialist movement, joining the Fabian Society and becoming increasingly convinced that education was the key to overcoming alcoholism, rather than outright prohibition. The radicalism of Willard's later years and her call for women to involve themselves in all aspects of social reform was reflected in her 1895 pamphlet, which exhorted "Do Everything" and became the catchphrase forever after associated with her work.

The failure of her health resulted in Willard's premature death at the age of fifty-eight. During her life, she published many articles and books, including *Woman and Temperance* (1883) and her autobiography, *Glimpses of Fifty Years* (1889). Soon after her death, the first of several hagiographies of "Saint Frances," as she had become known, appeared. Sanctioned by the WCTU, Anna Gordon's *The Beautiful Life of Frances E. Willard* lauded her "keen prophetic eye ahead of her time" (Spender 1982, 262). A leader of the English suffrage movement, Ray Strachey, published her own tribute in 1912.

In her work for the WCTU, Willard's guiding principle had been to "make the world homelike" (Bolt 1993, 170). For many ordinary American women, this was the most comforting and reassuring of thoughts, and they lent Willard their support in droves, as "the greatest proselytizer for a distinctly feminine morality" (Buhle 1981, 293). But other, radical women saw Willard's morality as being a threat to everything they hoped to achieve. In a letter to Susan B. Anthony in July 1888, Matilda Joslyn Gage described the WCTU leader as "the most dangerous person upon the American continent today" (Gage 1980, xxxii).

Frances Willard did not live to see national prohibition in the United States, which was finally enacted under the Eighteenth Amendment in 1920. She led her troops as evangelists in the war to purify public morals, and one wonders how Willard might have reacted to the violence of gang warfare and the widespread corruption spawned by illegal liquor running that were visited on the United States in the wake of prohibition.

See also Catt, Carrie Chapman; Somerset, Lady Isabella; Woodhull, Victoria Claflin.

References and Further Reading

Bacon, Margaret Hope. 1986. *Mothers of Feminism: The Story of Quaker Women in America.* San Francisco: Harper and Row.

Bolt, Christine. 1993. *The Women's Movements in the United States and Britain from the 1790s to the 1920s.* London: Harvester Wheatsheaf.

Bordin, Ruth. 1981. *Woman and Temperance: The Quest for Power and Liberty, 1873–1900.* Philadelphia: Temple University Press.

———. 1986. *Frances Willard: A Biography.* Chapel Hill: University of North Carolina Press.

Buhle, Mari Jo. 1981. *Women and American Socialism, 1870–1920.* Urbana: University of Illinois Press.

Dillon, Mary Earhart. 1944. *Frances Willard: From Prayer to Politics.* Chicago: University of Chicago Press.

Flexner, Eleanor. 1975 [1959]. *A Century of Struggle: The Woman's Rights Movement in the United States.* Rev. ed., Cambridge, MA: Belknap Press of Harvard University.

Gage, Matilda Joslyn. 1980 [1893]. *Woman, Church and State: The Original Exposé of Male Collaboration against the Female Sex.* Reprint, Watertown, MA: Persephone Press.

James, Edward T., ed. 1971. *Notable American Women, 1607–1950.* Vol. 3. Cambridge, MA: Belknap Press of Harvard University.

Leeman, Richard W. 1992. *"Do Everything" Reform: The Oratory of Frances E. Willard.* New York: Greenwood Press.

Marilley, Suzanne M. 1996. *"Frances Willard and the Feminism of Fear": Woman Suffrage and the Origins of Liberal Feminism in the United States, 1820–1920.* Cambridge, MA: Harvard University Press.

Paulson, Ross Evans. 1973. *Women's Suffrage and Prohibition: A Comparative Study of Equality and Social Control.* Glenview, IL: Scott, Foresman.

Pivar, David. 1973. *Purity Crusade: Sexual Morality and Social Control 1868–1900.* Westport, CT: Greenwood.

Rose, Kenneth D. 1996. *American Women and the Repeal of Prohibition.* New York: New York University Press.

Spender, Dale. 1982. *Women of Ideas, and What Men Have Done to Them.* London: Routledge and Kegan Paul.

Strachey, Ray. 1912. *Frances Willard: Her Life and Work.* London: T. F. Unwin.

Ware, Vron. 1992. *Beyond the Pale: White Women, Racism, and History.* London: Verso.

Willard, Frances. 1991. *How I Learned to Ride the Bicycle: Reflections of an Influential Nineteenth Century Woman.* Edited by Carol O'Hare. Sunnyvale, CA: Fair Oaks.

———. 1995. *Writing Out My Heart: Selections from the Journal of Frances E. Willard, 1855–96.* Urbana: University of Illinois Press.

Williams, Constance. 1907. *Frances Willard: The Record of a Noble Life.* London: Sunday School Union.

Wollstonecraft, Mary
(1759–1797)
Ireland/United Kingdom

Since her rediscovery by the women's movement during the 1970s, Mary Wollstonecraft has been championed as the seminal voice in the long struggle for women's emancipation in Britain. A courageous but at times deeply troubled and unhappy woman, she rebelled against the social strictures of her time, twice choosing to live openly with the man she loved. Her short and turbulent life during the unsettling years of revolutionary change in Europe produced one of the most eloquent and impassioned pleas for a woman's right to self-determination, for her political and legal equality with men, and for her access to the formative benefits of education. *A Vindication of the Rights of Woman* is now regarded as a key text in feminist writing, one of the first to emerge after the French Revolution.

Wollstonecraft was born in Spitalfields in London, in the eighteenth century noted for its community of silk weavers. Her father, however, wasted much of his considerable inheritance in failed business schemes and abandoned a business in silk weaving. He took his family first to Barking, Essex, and then north, in 1768, to Yorkshire, where he also failed as a gentleman farmer. Mary's childhood was miserable, blighted by poverty, her father's descent into alcoholism, and his frequent tirades at her mother. She felt rejected and unloved, and the seeds of her own adult neuroses and bitterness toward men were sown there. When she was nineteen and seeking her own financial independence, Wollstonecraft took the only respectable work then available. She spent two years as a lady's companion in Bath. After her mother died, she left home again in 1780, to set up a school with her sister Eliza and her friend Fanny Blood at Newington Green, in north London. During this time, she wrote a treatise, *Thoughts on the Education of Daughters* (1787), advocating the modernization of teaching methods in girls' education in order that their intellects be more fully developed. The school was not a success, never acquiring more than a dozen pupils, and Wollstonecraft again had to find employment, this time spending a year in Ireland as a governess to the children of Lady Kingsborough. But she was not emotionally suited to the work and despised her employer for

Mary Wollstonecraft (National Portrait Gallery)

Jacobin radicalism in France. She saw his book as being a clear attempt to bolster the English monarchy against the spread of inflammatory revolutionary ideas. Her response was to defend the reformist ideas of the Enlightenment and point out the iniquities of the British political and social system, its reliance on the slave trade, and its neglect of the poor.

Wollstonecraft went on to draw parallels between the tyranny of kings over their subjects and that of men over women in her work *A Vindication of the Rights of Woman*, published early in 1792, which according to Claire Tomalin reflected "thirty years' rage distilled in six weeks' hard labour" (1985, 142), a fact reflected in its disjointed and sometimes repetitive structure. It was not the first book in English to describe the subordination of women and expound the principles of their emancipation; arguments such as Mary Astell's *A Serious Proposal to the Ladies for the Advancement of Their True and Greatest Interest* (1694) and Catherine Macaulay's *Letters on Education* (1790) predated it, as did French revolutionary Olympe de Gouges's September 1791 *Declaration of the Rights of Woman and of the Female Citizen*. But it was Wollstonecraft's work that would have the greatest impact and a wide-reaching influence.

In the *Vindication,* Wollstonecraft laid down a formal challenge that the new era of rapid social change should address the long-ignored rights of women. In so doing, she was not uncritical of women themselves. Although she recognized the enslavement—both physical and intellectual—of women to the service of men and their egos in a male world order, she also criticized women for their own foolish obedience and readiness to please and for their idle obsessions with the vanities of dress and appearance. She despised the weakness of character inbred in women by their servility and by the overemphasis on their beauty or lack of it and painted a bleak picture of the shallow, unfulfilled lives they lived, confined to the home, which brought with it the atrophying of their natural abilities and intellects. As for their economic dependence, this to Wollstonecraft was little less than parasitism; in her eyes, marriage was tantamount to legal prostitution. Men, she argued, had been brought up to believe women were at their disposal, little more than submissive, decorative toys who contributed nothing to the economic, intellectual, or

her indifference toward both her children and her poor tenants as well as for the long hours she spent in aimless preening and primping. Wollstonecraft was dismissed within a year and returned to London in 1787.

There she took up editorial and translation work (from German and Italian) for a radical publisher, Joseph Johnson, who published her early works, including *Mary: A Fiction,* based on her early life (1788); *Original Stories from Real Life,* a collection of teaching aids for children (1788); and *The Female Reader,* an anthology (1789), and printed her articles in his *Analytical Review.* Her association with Johnson brought Wollstonecraft an introduction into the literary and radical circuit in London, where she met luminaries such as Thomas Paine, Joseph Priestley, William Blake, and, in 1791, the radical philosopher William Godwin. In the wake of the French Revolution of 1789 and before that the American Revolution, Wollstonecraft published *A Vindication of the Rights of Men in a Letter to Edmund Burke* at the end of 1790 as a response to Edmund Burke's *Reflections on the Revolution in France,* published earlier that year. Wollstonecraft objected to Burke's condemnation of social life of the country. Women needed to learn greater self-respect in order to combat this belief, and only better education and intellectual enlightenment would equip them as both better wives and better citizens.

Wollstonecraft was not against the institution of marriage itself because she felt it was necessary as a stable environment for children. Instead, she sought improvement in the status of married women through the acquisition of the character-enhancing qualities of self-reliance and self-discipline. A modicum of economic independence should be guaranteed by legislation from the state, in her view. She did not speak openly of women's enfranchisement but noted their need for political representation as central to a new, utopian age that would inaugurate educational and social equality for all and do away with poverty and the class system. Alluding to her own difficulties in obtaining paid employment, Wollstonecraft advocated that certain trades be opened up to women, who had in the past pursued occupations such as midwifery, animal husbandry, bookbinding, brewing, and hairdressing, all of which were being taken over by men. Such arguments applied to middle-class women, of course, but they also begged the question of what impoverished working-class women might do to liberate themselves.

The *Vindication* enjoyed some success among radical circles and was admired by many of Wollstonecraft's friends. It was soon translated into French, and Davis records (1972, 297) that copies even reached the most remote towns of the American Midwest, making Wollstonecraft a "Tom Paine of her sex" (299) whose voice had a formative influence on feminist pioneers of the U.S. movement, such as Lucretia Mott and Elizabeth Cady Stanton. But in general, Wollstonecraft's radical ideas provoked a profound conservative reaction in a Britain uneasy that revolution might spread from France. Immune to Wollstonecraft's arguments on moral progress, the powers that be saw her demand for sexual equality as a threat to the traditional social order. She was labeled irreligious, a revolutionary who preached insurrection, condemned as a "hyena in petticoats" (by writer Horace Walpole in a letter to Hannah More, 26 January 1795) who in her private life was sexually promiscuous. Even radical women could not tolerate the extremism of her arguments; More condemned

Vindication unread, and inexorably the book was systematically discredited until it disappeared from view, to be rehabilitated by the English suffrage movement in the late 1890s.

An infatuation with Swiss artist Henry Fuseli, who was already married, took Wollstonecraft to France in pursuit of him in 1792. Johnson had commissioned her to prepare a history of the French Revolution, and Wollstonecraft arrived in Paris in December, during the height of the Reign of Terror. Her *Historical and Moral View of the Origin and Progress of the French Revolution: And the Effect It Had Produced in Europe* (1794) reflected her dismay that the ideals of the revolution were already being betrayed by the onset of arbitrary violence and executions. In Paris, Wollstonecraft fell desperately in love with an American writer and adventurer, Gilbert Imlay, an affair that resulted in 1794 in the birth of a daughter, Fanny. He soon proved to be a philanderer, and their relationship, which caused her much pain and frustration, has proven difficult territory for recent feminist biographers, who cannot square her self-demeaning and at times histrionic pursuit of Imlay with her rational condemnation of such behavior in other women on the printed page (see, for example, Janet Todd's revisionist biography of 2000). Wollstonecraft's life with Imlay was disjointed, constantly interrupted by his business ventures. In 1796 she traveled to Scandinavia on a business mission for Imlay, which resulted in her 1796 travelogue, *Letters Written during a Short Residence in Sweden, Norway and Denmark,* considered by critics such as Richard Holmes (2000) to be a gifted and underrated work.

By the time she returned to London in 1796, Imlay had installed himself with another woman. In despair, Wollstonecraft attempted suicide by jumping into the River Thames. Saved by a passerby, she went back to working for Johnson and, in the spring of 1796, resumed her acquaintance with William Godwin. After Wollstonecraft became pregnant, and despite the strong position they shared on personal freedom, the couple reluctantly married for the sake of the child in March 1797, although they continued to retain separate homes near each other. However, Wollstonecraft died of septicemia eleven days after giving birth to a daughter, Mary, in September (Mary went on to marry Percy Bysshe Shelley and was the author of the gothic classic *Frankenstein*). Wollstonecraft's collected works were published posthumously by Godwin in 1798, including *Maria, a Fiction*, a partially completed novel. Based on her early friendship with Fanny Blood, it is an exposition in fiction of many of the ideas of the *Vindication* and boldly affirms women's sexual desires. Godwin published his own *Memoirs of Mary Wollstonecraft* in 1798, also discussed in Holmes (2000), the candor of which (in its details of Mary's unhappy love affairs and her two suicide attempts) served only to add fuel to the flames of public opprobrium and with it the concerted destruction of her legacy. An informative article on Wollstonecraft, with links to other sites, can be found at http://womenshistory.about.com/library/weekly/aa092099.htm.

See also Gouges, Olympe de; More, Hannah; Mott, Lucretia Coffin; Stanton, Elizabeth Cady.

References and Further Reading
Brody, Miriam. 1983. "Mary Wollstonecraft: Sexuality and Women's Rights." In Dale Spender, ed., *Feminist Theorists: Three Centuries of Women's Intellectual Traditions*. London: Women's Press.
———. 1992. *Introduction to* A Vindication of the Rights of Woman. Harmondsworth: Penguin.
Davis, Elizabeth Gould. 1972. *The First Sex*. Harmondsworth: Penguin Books.
Eisenstein, Zillah. 1981. *The Radical Future of Liberal Feminism*. New York: Longman.
Eliot, George. 1963. "Margaret Fuller and Mary Wollstonecraft." In T. Pinney, ed., *The Essays of George Eliot*. London: Routledge and Kegan Paul (an interesting study by the English novelist, first published in 1855).
Flexner, Eleanor. 1972. *Mary Wollstonecraft: A Biography*. New York: Coward, McCann and Geoghegan.
Holmes, Richard. 2000. "The Feminist and the Philosopher: A Love Story." In *Sidetracks: Explorations of a Romantic Biographer*, by Richard Holmes. London: HarperCollins.
Hufton, Olwen. 1998. *The Prospect before Her: A History of Women in Western Europe 1500–1800*. New York: Vintage Books.
Jacobs, Diana. 2001. *Her Own Woman: The Life of Mary Wollstonecraft*. New York: Simon and Schuster.
Kelly, Gary. 1991. *Revolutionary Feminism: The Mind and Career of Mary Wollstonecraft*. Basingstoke: Macmillan.
Lorch, Jennifer. 1990. *Mary Wollstonecraft: The Making of a Radical Feminist*. Oxford: St. Martin's Press.
Moers, Ellen. 1978. *Literary Women*. London: Women's Press.
Nixon, Edna. 1971. *Mary Wollstonecraft: Her Life and Times*. London: Dent.
Rendall, Jane. 1985. *The Origins of Modern Feminism: Women in Britain, France, and the United States 1780–1860*. Chicago: University of Chicago Press.
Sapiro, Virginia. 1992. *A Vindication of Political Virtue: The Political Theory of Mary Wollstonecraft*. Chicago: University of Chicago Press.
Showalter, Elaine. 2001. *Inventing Herself: Claiming a Feminist Intellectual Heritage*. London: Picador.
Spender, Dale. 1982. *Women of Ideas, and What Men Have Done to Them*. London: Routledge and Kegan Paul.
Taylor, Barbara. 1983. *Eve and the New Jerusalem: Society and Feminism in the Nineteenth Century*. London: Virago.
Tims, Margaret. 1976. *Mary Wollstonecraft: A Social Pioneer*. London: Millington.
Todd, Janet. 2000. *Mary Wollstonecraft: A Revolutionary Life*. London: Weidenfeld and Nicolson.
———, ed. 1987. *Dictionary of British and American Women Writers, 1600–1800*. London: Methuen.
Tomalin, Claire. 1985 [1974]. *The Life and Death of Mary Wollstonecraft*. Reprint, Harmondsworth: Penguin Books.
Walters, Margaret. 1976. "The Rights and Wrongs of Women: Mary Wollstonecraft, Harriet Martineau, Simone de Beauvoir." In Juliet Mitchell and Ann Oakley, eds., *The Rights and Wrongs of Women*. Harmondsworth: Penguin Books.
Wardle, Ralph M. 1951. *Mary Wollstonecraft: A Critical Biography*. Lawrence: University of Kansas Press.
Woolf, Virginia. 1986 [1932]. "Mary Wollstonecraft." In Woolf, *The Common Reader*, Second Series. Reprint, London: Hogarth Press.

Wolstenholme-Elmy, Elizabeth
(1833–1918)
United Kingdom

The suffragist and outspoken advocate of women's sexual equality Elizabeth Wolstenholme-Elmy was a radical liberal in the early nineteenth-century mold, inspired in the individuality of her thinking by pioneer feminists such as Mary Wollstonecraft. The general consensus among feminist historians now is that this remarkable and idiosyncratic pioneer of women's activism in Britain, who addressed the subject of male and female sexuality with a candor ahead of its time, has been most woefully neglected, if not willfully underrated, particularly in British feminist history contemporaneous with her lifetime. All this occurred despite the fact that in 1865 she was a founder, in Manchester, of one of the first women's suffrage groups in Britain. Thereafter, Wolstenholme-Elmy took a leading role in campaigns for women's property and custody rights, in the fight for repeal of the Contagious Diseases Acts, and in improvements to secondary education for girls. The subsequent minimization of her role has been seen as arising in part from the discomfort among the middle-class ranks of the suffrage movement with Wolstenholme-Elmy's radical views on women's sexuality and her own unconventional private life.

The details of Wolstenholme-Elmy's early life are scant: she grew up in a Methodist family in Lancashire. Her father was a cotton spinner and Methodist minister, but both her parents died when she was young. Between the ages of fourteen and sixteen, Wolstenholme-Elmy's guardians sent her to be educated at the Moravian School at Fulneck, near Leeds, but she was, in the main, self-educated. After working briefly as a governess, at age nineteen she used her modest inheritance to establish a small boarding school for girls near Manchester.

Dedicated to improving the standards in both women's education and teaching, in 1865 Wolstenholme-Elmy founded the Manchester Schoolmistresses Association. She expressed her views publicly when she read a paper on teacher training at the National Association for the Promotion of Social Science, a society of which she would be a stalwart supporter and a regular participant at conferences (1865–1884). Along with Emily Davies, Wolstenholme-Elmy was an early advocate of women's education; in the mid-1860s, she also made submissions to the Schools Enquiry Commission. She was an early supporter of Anne Jemima Clough and Josephine Butler's North of England Council for Promoting the Higher Education of Women and was closely involved in planning its lecture program and lobbying for support, although unlike Clough, she sided with Davies in advocating women's admission to further education on the same level as men. Her essay advocating the establishment of girls' high schools in every major town in Britain, "The Education of Girls, Its Present and Its Future," was published in Josephine Butler's 1869 collection, *Woman's Work and Woman's Culture.* In it, Wolstenholme-Elmy described the lack of educational opportunities for girls as often being the result of parental complacency, which in her view condemned them to poverty and, if married, a lifetime of economic dependence.

In 1865 Wolstenholme-Elmy had become a corresponding member of the Kensington Society, an offshoot of the Langham Place Circle dedicated to the discussion of social reform and, in particular, the furthering of women's higher education. Through the society, she subscribed to the London Committee, established by the Langham Place Circle to gather petitions in support of a bill on women's suffrage. Encouraged by the group in the autumn of 1865, Wolstenholme-Elmy set up a group that became the Manchester Committee for the Enfranchisement of Women, which would in turn be replaced by the Manchester National Society for Women's Suffrage under the leadership of Lydia Becker. During 1865–1866, Wolstoneholme-Elmy enthusiastically took part in gathering 300 signatures for the huge petition presented to Parliament by John Stuart Mill.

In February 1865 Wolstenholme-Elmy transferred her school to Moody Hall at Congleton in Cheshire. She became closely involved in the campaign of the Married Women's Property Committee, serving as secretary (1867–1871 and 1880–1882), and in lobbying for the repeal of the Contagious Diseases Acts. In 1869 she contacted Josephine Butler with the suggestion of mounting a campaign against these acts in a challenge to the Victorian double sexual standard. Under the original act, passed in 1864, prostitutes were obliged to submit themselves to regular medical examinations, whereas the men who solicited their services were not. Wolstenholme-Elmy was closely involved with Butler in setting up the Ladies' National Association for the Repeal of the Contagious Diseases Acts, although her own social status, as an unmarried woman and school headmistress, precluded her from taking the lead in such a contentious campaign.

Wolstenholme-Elmy's decision to live in a free union with poet and fellow freethinker Ben Elmy in about 1874 caused considerable consternation among her colleagues. As a defender of women's autonomy and their right to be self-supporting, Wolstenholme-Elmy resented the sublimation of her own identity as a woman within marriage. At that time, under the law of coverture, a woman lost her civil status as a *femme sole* on marriage, when she became identified solely as the wife of her husband. When Wolstenholme-Elmy became pregnant in the autumn of 1874, she was persuaded by her colleagues to marry in order to preempt potential damage to suffrage and other causes for which she worked. But she allowed only a civil ceremony, kept her own surname, and refused to promise to obey. When it became clear, after her son was born in 1875, that Wolstenholme-Elmy had been pregnant before she married, there was considerable fluttering in the dovecotes of the Married Women's Property Committee. It was politely but firmly suggested that Wolstenholme-Elmy should resign as honorary secretary to save the committee from embarrassment. She reluctantly took a backseat for a year but by 1876 resumed her work for the campaign from her home in Congleton, lobbying for funds and gathering signatures for petitions in support of members' bills. At this time, she wrote regular articles on the subject for the *Englishwoman's Review* and the *Woman's Suffrage Journal,* as well as letters to the *Times.*

In 1880 Wolstenholme-Elmy read a paper at the Dialectical Society, "The Criminal Code in Its Relation to Women," in which she alluded to men's treatment of their wives as property, which in her view led to sexual abuse within marriage and what she viewed as the legalization of marital rape under existing law. She also attributed the physical wearing-down of women through too many pregnancies and childbirth as being the fault of men and argued that the many gynecological ailments suffered by women were often the result of excessive sexual demands made on them.

Between 1880 and 1886, Wolstenholme-Elmy was central to successful lobbying for the Married Women's Property Act and the Guardianship of Infants Act, which enhanced the rights of married women and gave them custody rights over their children. She again energetically organized petitions, gave public lectures, and brought out pamphlets such as "To the Wives and Mothers of Every Class," arguing not just that a mother had equal rights over her children with her husband but that men and women should have joint responsibilities in their upbringing. However, the clause advocated by Wolstenholme-Elmy, in which provisions would be made for joint

parental custody, was dropped from the Guardianship of Infants Act. In 1886 she published an account of her work in "The Infants Act: A Record of Three Years' Work for Legislative Reforms with Its Result."

Wolstenholme-Elmy now turned in earnest to the women's suffrage campaign. In 1889 she cofounded the Women's Franchise League with her husband, Ursula Bright, and Richard and Emmeline Pankhurst, serving as its secretary. But she resigned in May 1890 over personal differences, to set about creating a new organization, the Women's Emancipation Union, broadening its reform program to advocate equal political rights for married women rather than the limited form of franchise accepted by other suffrage groups. She and Ben Elmy made considerable sacrifices for her to do so, mortgaging their home to enable her to work full-time for the union without a salary (friends later raised funds to provide her with an income). Wolstenholme-Elmy continued to work long hours, lecture, and write articles for publications such as *Shafts* and the *Westminster Review.* But for all her hard work, the union was not a success and was disbanded in 1899.

During the 1890s, the Wolstenholme-Elmys published several books in close collaboration under the pseudonym of Ellis Ethelmar; the extent of each partner's input in which text is uncertain, but they bear the imprint of Wolstenholme-Elmy's strong position on women's subjugation and on the slavery of sex. In 1893 she published *Woman Free,* a discourse in verse on women's sexual abuse by men. In 1885 she and her husband cowrote books on physiology and sex education under the series title Human Flower and in 1896 cowrote *Life to Woman,* which contains the (for its time) startling view that menstruation was not a natural function but the inherited product of the sexual brutality of men. In Wolstenholme-Elmy's view, the solution to the sexual abuse of women lay in a complete reordering of society, its cornerstone being women's empowerment through the vote. In 1897 the couple published *Phases of Love,* an elaboration on the male-female ideal that further asserted woman's rights over her own body and a belief in her ability for "psychic love," which was offered as a womanly alternative to the sexual brutality of the male. Through the concept of psychic love, the Wolstenholme-Elmys advocated control of the sexual passions and the achievement of a harmonious coming-together of man and woman in a relationship of equals that was not focused solely on the sexual. Many of Wolstenholme-Elmy's ideas on sex and marriage were further discussed in a series of articles she published as "Ignota" in the *Westminster Review* in October 1897 and August 1899.

At the end of the 1890s, discouraged over whether political change would ever come, Wolstenholme-Elmy changed her position from a demand for full enfranchisement to one of limited suffrage for women, having become convinced that it was better to achieve partial enfranchisement than none at all. By the turn of the twentieth century, with the rallying of a mainstream suffrage movement by the National Union of Women's Suffrage Societies, Wolstenholme-Elmy was once more galvanized to lobby for a bill on women's enfranchisement during 1905. After it was talked down in Parliament, she published "The Enfranchisement of Women" in the *Westminster Review* in protest. As a friend of the Pankhursts, by 1905 she had opted to join the Women's Social and Political Union (WSPU). During the period 1905–1908, she published several challenging articles on women's suffrage as well as "Justice between the Sexes" (1908) and "Party Politicians and Justice to Women" (1908).

In her final years, Wolstenholme-Elmy became the "mascot" of many suffrage parades, such as that staged by the WSPU in Hyde Park in 1908, appearing at the head of the column dressed in her old-fashioned Victorian clothes, projecting an old-world, demure coziness with her corkscrew curls and dimpled smile. But she was no sweet old lady; the frailty belied a lifetime's dogged refusal to conform. And she was not afraid to withdraw her support from the WSPU when its escalating militancy finally became too much, even for her, by the summer of 1912. Wolstenholme-Elmy died only six days after Edward VII gave his royal assent to the Representation of the People Act, which gave women in Britain the vote. The breadth of her activism during a sixty-year career in social reform had been considerable and at times exhausting. Susan Kingsley Kent points out the prescience of Wolstenholme-Elmy's 1897 observation that what men most feared about the enfranchisement of women was that it would also signal the end of their sexual slavery: "No doubt their fear is justified," she remarked, "for that is precisely what we do mean" (1990, 14). And indeed, history has proved her right.

See also Becker, Lydia; Butler, Josephine; Clough, Anne Jemima; Davies, (Sarah) Emily; Wollstonecraft, Mary.

References and Further Reading

Banks, Olive, ed. 1985, 1990. *The Biographical Dictionary of British Feminists*, vol. 1, *1800–1930*; vol. 2, *1900–1945*. Brighton: Harvester Wheatsheaf.

Baylen, J. O., and N. J. Gossman, eds. 1979–1984. *Biographical Dictionary of Modern British Radicals*. 3 vols. Hassocks, Sussex: Harvester Press.

Bland, Lucy. 1996. *Banishing the Beast: English Feminism and Sexual Morality, 1885–1914*. Harmondsworth: Penguin.

Crawford, Elizabeth. 1999. *The Women's Suffrage Movement, 1866–1928: A Reference Guide*. London: University College of London Press.

Holcombe, Lee. 1983. *Wives and Property: Reform of the Married Women's Property Law in Nineteenth-Century England*. Toronto: University of Toronto Press.

Holton, Sandra S. 1996. *Suffrage Days: Stories from the Women's Suffrage Movement*, esp. chaps. 1 and 2. London: Routledge.

Jeffreys, Sheila. 1985. *The Spinster and Her Enemies: Feminism and Sexuality 1880–1930*. London: Pandora.

Kent, Susan Kingsley. 1990. *Sex and Suffrage in Britain, 1860–1914*. London: Routledge.

Pankhurst, E. Sylvia. 1977 [1931]. *The Suffragette Movement: An Intimate Account of Persons and Ideals*. Reprint, London: Virago.

Rubinstein, David. 1986. *Before the Suffragettes: Women's Emancipation in the 1890s*. Brighton: Harvester Press.

Shanley, Mary Lyndon. 1989. *Feminism, Marriage, and the Law in Victorian England, 1850–1895*. Princeton: Princeton University Press.

Showalter, Elaine. 1999 [1977]. *A Literature of Their Own: British Women Novelists from Brontë to Lessing*. Reprint, London: Virago.

Todd, Janet, ed. 1989. *Dictionary of British Women Writers*. London: Routledge.

Woodhull, Victoria Claflin
(1838–1927)
United States

The life of American feminist Victoria Woodhull was an extraordinary and eventful one. She was by turns vilified and admired for her individuality and often (for its time) outrageous outspokenness. In the history of social reform in the nineteenth-century United States, she was a maverick, undoubtedly one of its most unconventional and controversial figures. There were few issues relating to progressive reform and women's rights that she did not espouse, at one time or another, including suffrage, free love, and socialism. She even ventured successfully into the world of high finance. But whatever cause she pursued, notoriety dogged her, and stories about her flirtation with mysticism and spiritualism and a somewhat shady past during which she had on occasion resorted to prostitution prevented her from ever being taken seriously.

Woodhull was born into a most eccentric household in Homer, Ohio. Her parents, Buck and Roxana Claflin, were itinerant spiritualists and fortune-tellers who worked the traveling fairs of Ohio, offering magnetic healing and selling their quack Claflin elixir. One of a large brood of children, Victoria, as well as her sister Tennessee, were trained in psychic readings, magnetic healing, and other bogus arts in order to boost the large family's income. It was an erratic, insecure life, and when she was only fifteen, Victoria was married to Canning Woodhull. However, his alcoholism forced her to take her children and rejoin her family on the show grounds, where she once again earned a living as a clairvoyant and spiritualist.

Divorced in 1864, she took up with Colonel James H. Blood (some say they married, but no record of this survives, and Woodhull did not take his name), who introduced her to his own brand of "mystic socialism" and the reform movement. In 1868 Woodhull and the Claflin family moved to New York. Tennessee and Victoria, who were eager to enter the world of financial speculation, ingratiated themselves with millionaire businessman Cornelius Vanderbilt by obtaining spirit messages from the other world from his dead wife. In gratitude, he helped them establish a stockbrokerage, Woodhull, Claflin, and Company, and thus they became the first women on Wall Street and prob-

Victoria Claflin Woodhull (Library of Congress)

ably the first in the world to enter big business. During the "panic" of Black Friday, 1869, it is said that they made $700,000; soon after, they moved into plush new offices and installed their family in a comfortable New York mansion.

Woodhull came under the influence of the teachings of socialist philosopher Stephen Pearl Andrews and his concept of "Pantarchy," which advocated free love and legalized prostitution, the equal rights of men and women, and communal property and care of children. She announced her intention to stand for the presidency in the *New York Herald* in April 1870. In January 1871, she addressed the Judiciary Committee of the House of Representatives on the wording of the Fourteenth Amendment, arguing that its reference to "persons" implied women's right to suffrage. At the same time, she published a series of articles that she and Andrews had written on their political and social ideas (including free love) and that had first appeared in the *Herald* in 1871 as "Origin, Tendencies and Principles of Government." Nominated for the presidency in 1872 by the Equal Rights Party, Woodhull made a token attempt to vote at the polls and was, of course, blocked.

In May 1870, Woodhull and her sister had begun publishing *Woodhull and Claflin's Weekly*, notable for its quirky combination of serious articles on socialism, including publication of the first English translation of Marx and Engel's *Communist Manifesto*, with Woodhull's discussions of women's right to sexual pleasure and her demands for an end of the double standard in sexual behavior. Her candid discussion of dress reform, legalized prostitution, venereal disease, and abortion were placed alongside gutter-press exposés of political and social scandals, all guaranteed to whet the salacious appetites of scandalmongers while arousing widespread moral opprobrium. In 1871–1872 *Woodhull and Claflin's Weekly* was drawn into a huge scandal when Woodhull's involvement with suffragist supporter Theodore Tilton resulted in their publication of a defamatory article. It accused the distinguished preacher Henry Ward Beecher (brother of Harriet Beecher Stowe and Catharine Beecher) of having an affair with Tilton's wife. After the sisters published the article, they were prosecuted under the new Comstock Law of 1873, which forbade the sending of improper material (that is, copies of the *Weekly* containing the article) through the mail (this piece of legislation would also bedevil birth control campaigners such as Mary Ware Dennett and Margaret Sanger for many years).

Although Woodhull was acquitted in 1875, the scandal destroyed her finance business, and in 1876 *Woodhull and Claflin's Weekly* folded. The affair also destroyed any credibility she might have had in her presidential campaign and did considerable damage to the reputation of the suffrage movement (since Beecher and Tilton were both also advocates of women's suffrage). Many conservative women were deterred from joining the movement, and the rifts widened between the radicals under Susan B. Anthony and the moderates under Lucy Stone. Although Anthony remained impressed with Woodhull's gifts as a public speaker, the mainstream would not accept a woman who openly advocated free love. Therefore, Woodhull became part of a dissident group in the National Woman Suffrage Association that broke away in 1872 and became the Equal Rights Party.

After separating from Blood in 1876 because of his philandering and tired of the constant vilification she was receiving in the United States, Woodhull settled in England in 1877. She lived in London, where she became a society philanthropist and gave lectures, such as one on "The Human Body, the Temple of God" (coauthored with Tennessee and published in 1890), the content of which reflected an increasingly religious tone. She lent her support to the Pankhursts in the English suffrage campaign, but was never able to divorce herself entirely from fringe culture, and also published a monthly journal with her daughter Zula Maud, the *Humanitarian*, that included articles on eugenics, palmistry, and astrology alongside discussions of high finance. The English banker and landowner John Biddulph Martin proposed, but objections by his family prevented the marriage until 1883. By this time a renowned society hostess, although still something of a curiosity, Woodhull made good among the British aristocracy, as did her sister, who married an English merchant and in 1886 became Lady Cook when he received a baronetcy. Woodhull was delighted with the emancipation of women during the Jazz Age, becoming an early member of the Women's Aerial League and the Ladies' Automobile Club and living up to her own dictum that women could and should try everything. She died on her country estate near Tewksbury at the age of eighty-eight.

Beautiful and headstrong, Woodhull remains an inconsistent figure whose undoubted gift for intellectual argument was muddied by her propensity for self-dramatization. Her colorful life has spawned a great number of biographies, among which a highly entertaining account of Woodhull, her sister Tennessee, the Tilton-Beecher scandal, and their many feminist and suffragist contemporaries can be found in Barbara Goldsmith's *Other Powers*.

See also Anthony, Susan B.; Beecher, Catharine Esther; Dennett, Mary Ware; Sanger, Margaret; Stone, Lucy; Stowe, Harriet Beecher.

References and Further Reading

Flexner, Eleanor. 1975 [1959]. *A Century of Struggle: The Woman's Rights Movement in the United States*. Rev. ed. Cambridge, MA: Belknap Press of Harvard University.

Frost, Elizabeth, and Kathryn Cullen DuPont. 1992. *Women's Suffrage in America: An Eyewitness History*. New York: Facts on File.

Gabriel, Mary. 1998. *Notorious Victoria: The Life of Victoria Woodhull, Uncensored*. Chapel Hill, NC: Algonquin.

Goldsmith, Barbara. 1998. *Other Powers: The Age of Suffrage, Spiritualism, and the Scandalous Victoria Woodhull*. London: Granta Books.

Johnston, Johanna. 1967. *Mrs. Satan: The Incredible Saga of Victoria C. Woodhull*. New York: G. P. Putnam's.

Kisner, Arlene M., ed. 1972. Woodhull and Claflin's Weekly: *The Lives and Writings of Notorious Victoria Woodhull and Her Sister Tennessee Claflin*. Washington, NJ: Time Change Press.

Marberry, M. 1967. *Vicky: A Biography of Victoria C. Woodhull*. New York: Funk and Wagnalls.

Meade, Marion. 1976. *Free Woman: The Life and Times of Victoria Woodhull*. New York: Knopf.

Rowbotham, Sheila. 1992. *Women in Movement: Feminism and Social Action*. New York: Routledge.

Sachs, Emanie. 1978 [1928]. *"The Terrible Siren": Victoria Woodhull (1838–1927)*. Reprint, New York: Arno Press.

Schneir, Miriam, ed. 1972. *Feminism: The Essential Historical Writings*. New York: Vintage.

Stern, Madeleine B., ed. 1979. *The Victoria Woodhull Reader*. Weston, MA: M and S Press (includes Woodhull's major suffrage speeches).

Underhill, Lois Beachy. 1995. *The Woman Who Ran for President: The Many Lives of Victoria Woodhull*. Bridgehampton, NY: Bridge Works Publishing.

Wright, Frances
(1795–1852)
Scotland/United States

Born into a prosperous Scottish family in Dundee, Fanny Wright (as she was known) was a woman ahead of her times who suffered for her freethinking and her radicalism. Like many feminists who dared to speak out on sexual equality when prevailing attitudes sought to keep women firmly confined to the domestic sphere, she had to brave constant criticism and vilification. In her advocacy of a "national, rational and republican system of education for all" (O'Connor 1954, 47), dress reform, birth control, and other issues of sexual nonconformity, she paid no heed to social convention and went on the lecture circuit to become one of the most talked-about female radicals in the United States. Wright also experimented with a utopian scheme to liberate slaves through their own labor on land she purchased for the purpose in Nashoba, Tennessee.

Wright was brought up by progressive relatives in England after her father and mother died within months of each other when she was two.

Privileged to have been left a large fortune, she began pursuing a literary career. Wright visited the United States in 1818–1820 with her sister Camilla. In 1819 her play *Altdorf*, about the struggle for independence in Switzerland, was staged in New York but closed after three performances. On her return to England, she published her travel memoirs of the United States, *Views of Society and Manners in America* (1821), a largely uncritical panegyric full of admiration for the spirit of Republicanism and American democracy that nevertheless criticized the "pestilence" of slavery. Although published eleven years before Frances Trollope's *Domestic Manners of the Americans* (1832; a sanguine view of U.S. society by the mother of the English novelist Anthony Trollope), Wright's work was subsequently totally eclipsed by Trollope's and largely forgotten. Influenced by the romanticism of Lord Byron, Wright published a utopian discourse, *A Few Days in Athens*, in 1822.

In 1821 Wright met and developed a romantic crush on the Marquis de Lafayette (a hero of the American Revolution who refused her proposal of marriage) and returned to the United States on a tour with him in 1824. During their travels, they visited Robert Owen's utopian community in New Harmony, Indiana, where she adopted short hair as well as the pantaloons worn by female members of the community (well ahead of Amelia Bloomer's well-publicized advocacy of them in the 1850s).

After a trip up the Mississippi in 1825, Wright published *A Plan for the Gradual Abolition of Slavery in the United States without Danger of Loss to the Citizens of the South* (1825), in which she advocated her own bold social experiment, whereby the U.S. government should buy large tracts of land on which to settle and ultimately emancipate slaves. Determined to put her ideas into practice, Wright bought 640 acres of land for the purpose at Chicasaw Bluffs in western Tennessee, naming it Nashoba. After purchasing eighteen slaves, she set them up in a cooperative colony there along the lines of Owen's at New Harmony. Wright and various friends and supporters also joined the project, with the objective that the slaves, through their own hard work, would earn their own freedom after five years. As Barbara Taylor illustrates, the sexual code Wright established at Nashoba was "uncompromisingly libertarian," one in which she asserted the equal

Frances Wright (Library of Congress)

rights and responsibilities of its male and female members and stated: "No woman can forfeit her individual rights or independent existence, and no man assert over her any rights of power whatsoever beyond what he may exercise over her free and voluntary affection" (Taylor 1983, 67).

But the community did not prosper. The labor was arduous, the climate was debilitating, the crop returns were poor, and its leadership was disrupted by Wright's frequent absences on visits to New Harmony or trips to Europe. Eventually, Nashoba's notoriety was its downfall, when in 1827 a scandalmongering article appeared, accusing Wright of practicing free love and mixed-race breeding at Nashoba. This, combined with other attacks made on her for her feminism and public lecturing against organized religion, forced Wright to abandon the project, having invested and lost a good half of her fortune in it. The thirty slaves were later sent to Haiti at Wright's expense, where they were set free and helped with finding homes and jobs.

Wright took to the lecture circuit during a period of revivalism that followed, speaking out against organized religion. In 1828 she spent time at New Harmony helping Robert Owen's son edit the *New Harmony Gazette,* and in 1829 settled on a farm in New York City. She bought a disused old church in New York's Bowery and converted it into a Hall of Science, where she could hold lectures for workers and hoped to set

about educating them through a network of free state schools supported by public funds, where she could offer them a secular education as well as vocational training. With these goals in mind, she cofounded the Association for the Protection of Industry and for the Promotion of National Education. In her other lectures, Wright continued to raise the issues of women's emancipation, their rights to education and birth control (supporting Owen's 1830 tract "Moral Physiology"), and liberalization of the divorce laws. While publishing the radical newspaper the *Free Enquirer* with Owen during 1829–1830, Wright criticized the practice of imprisonment for debt and continued to argue for socialism, universal suffrage for both blacks and whites, and secular education. She once more set out on the lecture circuit along the East Coast, speaking to mixed audiences on slavery and the influence of established religion on political affairs. Some of these talks were collected in 1829 as the *Course of Popular Lectures* (expanded in 1836).

In the summer of 1830, Wright returned to Europe. Her prolonged absence saw the demise of her Hall of Science and the collapse of her national education movement. In Paris she had an affair with a fellow Owenite, the French doctor Guillaume D'Arusmont. Discovering she was pregnant in 1831, Wright kowtowed to convention and married D'Arusmont. The marriage was a disaster and led to a long legal wrangle over Wright's property and royalties, which lasted until their divorce in 1850 and beyond. Not all the issues had been resolved by the time of her death.

In 1833 Wright was back in the United States, where she took up lecturing on the evils of modern society, this time turning against banking monopolies and favoring a state banking system; she also wrote articles for the Boston *Investigator.* She campaigned for Andrew Jackson and the Democrats during the elections of 1836 and 1838, but with public interest in her arguments waning, she returned to Europe in 1839. Her existence was a restless one over the next ten years, with Wright traveling back and forth between the United States and the Continent before she finally settled in Cincinnati, where she died two years later, in 1852. Her *Biography, Notes and Political Letters* was published in Boston in 1849.

During her life, insisting that "I am not one who speaks my thoughts in whispers, nor who do [sic] things in corners" (O'Connor 1954, 49),

Wright found herself duly consigned by the moral majority to the fires of hell and damnation for her unfeminine ways. The U.S. press fanned public hostility with its denunciations of Wright as the "whore of Babylon" and the "Red Harlot of Infidelity" (Bolt 1993, 106), and her only support was among fellow male and female Owenites and radicals. Thanks to her courage and vision and those of other socialist thinkers of Wright's day, such as Anna Doyle Wheeler, a tradition of women's social criticism was established in the 1820s and 1830s that would lay the theoretical foundations of the women's movements that developed from the 1850s.

See also Bloomer, Amelia Jenks; Wheeler, Anna Doyle.

References and Further Reading

Bolt, Christine. 1993. *The Women's Movements in the United States and Britain from the 1790s to the 1920s.* London: Harvester Wheatsheaf.

Dykeman, Therese Boos. 1993. *American Women Philosophers 1650–1930.* Lewiston, NY: Edward Mellen Press.

Eckhardt, Celia M. 1894. *Fanny Wright: Rebel in America.* Cambridge, MA: Harvard University Press.

Heineman, Helen. 1983. *Restless Angels: The Friendship of Six Victorian Women.* Athens: Ohio University Press.

Kissel, Susan S. 1993. *In Common Cause: The "Conservative" Frances Trollope and the "Radical" Frances Wright.* Bowling Green, OH: Bowling Green State University Press.

Lane, Margaret. 1972. *Frances Wright and the "Great Experiment."* Manchester: Manchester University Press.

Lerner, Gerda. 1993. *Women and History,* vol. 2, *The Creation of a Feminist Consciousness: From the Middle Ages to Eighteen-Seventy.* New York: Oxford University Press.

Matthews, Glenna. 1992. *The Rise of Public Woman: Woman's Power and Woman's Place in the United States 1630–1970.* New York: Oxford University Press.

McFadden, Margaret. 1999. *Golden Cables of Sympathy: The Transatlantic Sources of Nineteenth-Century Feminism.* Lexington: University of Kentucky Press.

O'Connor, Lillian. 1954. *Pioneer Women Orators: Rhetoric in the Ante-Bellum Reform Movement.* New York: Columbia University Press.

Pease, William H., and Jane H. Pease. 1963. *Black Utopia: Negro Communal Experiments in America.* Madison: State Historical Society of Wisconsin.

Perkins, Alice J. G., and Theresa Wolfson. 1939. *Frances Wright, Free Enquirer: The Study of a Temperament.* New York: Harper Brothers.

Reynolds, Moira Davison. 1994. *Women Advocates of Reproductive Rights: 11 Who Led the Struggle in the United States and Great Britain.* Jefferson, NC: McFarland.

Spender, Dale. 1982. *Women of Ideas, and What Men Have Done to Them.* London: Routledge and Kegan Paul.

Taylor, Barbara. 1983. *Eve and the New Jerusalem: Society and Feminism in the Nineteenth Century.* London: Virago.

Waterman, William R. 1924. *Frances Wright.* New York: Columbia University Press.

Yeo, Eileen Janes, ed. 1997. *Mary Wollstonecraft and 200 Years of Feminisms.* London: Rivers Oram Press.

X

Xiang Jingyu
(1895–1928)
China

Xiang Jingyu was one of the first Chinese communist leaders to take up the cause of women workers. Looked upon as the founder of the women's movement in modern-day China, she began her activities organizing protest and resistance among Shanghai silk, cotton, and cigar workers in a series of strikes in 1922–1924. She later went on to lead the Women's Department of the Chinese Communist Party (CCP). A fervent patriot, Xiang was one of many dedicated female activists in the early communist movement in China rounded up by right-wing nationalists, often simply for having the audacity to bob their long hair. She and many hundreds of other Chinese women suffered violent deaths in the bitter fighting of 1927–1928.

Xiang was one of twelve children born into a merchant family in western Hunan province. After studying at the Changsha Girls' Normal School and the Zhunan Women's College (a progressive and fiercely nationalist girls' school, also located in Changsha), she returned to Hunan and founded a girls' primary school at Xupu.

By the time she became involved in the May Fourth Movement of 1919 (which protested the terms of the Versailles Peace Treaty, which the Chinese saw as condoning Japanese imperialism), she had already been active for some years in protesting Japanese economic and industrial involvement in China. She gave speeches and propagandized among the peasants and students in her local district and led protests in Changsha. She also attacked traditional conventions such as footbinding and ear piercing and advocated equal rights for women. She was a founder of the

Hunan Women's Association for Work-Study in 1919, which sponsored Chinese intellectuals and activists who wished to study in France.

In Paris in 1919, Xiang collaborated with French anarchists in her work-study program, studied Marxism and revolutionary ideology, and supported herself by working part-time in a rubber plant and a textile mill. She also fell in love and, having refused an arranged marriage, married fellow activist Cai Hesen. Eager to work for the reunification of their country, together they joined the Young China Communist Party. In 1920 Xiang published her first "Marxist" essay, "A Discussion of Women's Emancipation and Transformation," in the radical journal *Young China,* in which she condemned private ownership and government oppression and urged women to resist arranged marriage. She thought women were wasting their energy in the suffrage campaign and that the complete overhaul of society should precede any change in women's voting rights. When Cai Hesen was deported from France, Xiang followed him back to China. There, in 1922, she initiated her plans for achieving women's greater equality by becoming a labor organizer. She coordinated a wave of 100 or so strikes by as many as 30,000 Chinese women textile workers employed in foreign-owned mills in Shanghai, protesting their unequal pay and their twelve-hour workdays.

Xiang's organizational talents and her efforts at mobilizing women workers soon came to the attention of the CCP, and she was the first woman elected to its Central Committee, at the Second Party Congress. The party entrusted her with setting up its Women's Department in Guangzhou in 1923. In addition to being responsible for coordinating Chinese women's organizations, the department became the vehicle for

Xiang Jingyu (far right; Courtesy of Charles Monroe)

Xiang's own revolutionary plans for the emancipation of Chinese women and an attack on traditional patriarchal attitudes.

From 1923 to 1926, Xiang wrote a series of seminal articles for the journal *Woman's Weekly* in support of female emancipation and about the plight of exploited female workers in the silk and cotton industries in an attempt to raise the social and political consciousness of women. She abhorred the traditional prerogative men had of access to education and, through it, the workplace; she also criticized their lack of respect for the contributions of female workers. In a 1924 essay, she called for schools for women workers to be set up, with an improvement in their rights being a basic component of the movement for wider social change. But although she wanted Chinese women to take a role in national affairs, she had an innate mistrust of feminists and intellectuals and attacked Chinese suffrage groups, such as the Women's Suffrage Association (founded in 1921), as being bourgeois and elitist and their cause a "dead end road" because it was too narrow. Xiang set out to enlist female peasants and workers in a mass communist labor movement that would improve all women's lives. She drew other women's groups into her campaign, cooperating with Christian social groups such as the Young Women's Christian Association (YWCA) and the Chinese branch of the

Woman's Christian Temperance Union. From 1923 to 1926, Xiang expanded the activities of the Women's Department to other provinces. With the support of women from Shanghai University, she campaigned for the rights of textile mill workers in Shanghai and coordinated their activities, including a strike at the Nanyang Tobacco Company in 1924 in support of higher wages, shorter working hours, and the curtailment of physical abuse of workers.

In 1925 Xiang's activities in the Women's Department became too much for the male-dominated CCP, which remained reactionary in its views on the liberation of Chinese women. She was removed and went into exile for the next two years in the Soviet Union, where she studied Marxism-Leninism and the history of the Communist Party at the University of the Toilers of the East. She returned to China in 1927 to organize workers in the industrial districts of Wuhan and Shanghai for the Propaganda Department of the CCP.

In 1927, when Chiang Kai-shek initiated a purge of communists in the Guomindang, Xiang went underground. But in April 1928, she was arrested in the French Concession of Hankow and was summarily executed by the nationalists shortly after—just one of many hundreds of female activists rounded up and brutally murdered during Chiang Kai-shek's White Terror. The books Xiang had been working on at the time of her death were destroyed; her husband Cai was also captured in Hong Kong and executed in 1931.

As a communist leader who concerned herself primarily with the class struggle, Xiang extolled the virtues of female laborers and believed that social and political reform should be truly proletarian in nature, with women mobilized to take their part in momentous social change. Xiang led a women's department that had 100,000 members in the period 1923–1926 and established a broad base of women's support for the revolution. Her brutal public execution in 1928, at which she conducted herself with courage and dignity and called for the French revolutionary ideals of "liberty, equality, and fraternity" to prevail in China, ensured that she would be venerated in Chinese communist hagiography as the "Grandmother of the Revolution."

References and Further Reading

Croll, Elizabeth. 1978. *Feminism and Socialism in China*. New York: Schocken Books.

Gilmartin, Christina Kelly. 1995. *Engendering the Chinese Revolution: Radical Women, Communist Politics and Mass Movements in the 1920s*. Berkeley: University of California Press.

Ono Kazuko. 1978. *Chinese Women in a Century of Revolution*. Stanford: Stanford University Press.

Snow, Helen Foster. 1967. *Women in Modern China*. The Hague: Mouton.

Young, Marilyn B. 1973. *Women in China*. Michigan Papers in Chinese Studies no. 5. Ann Arbor: Center for Chinese Studies.

Y

Yajima Kajiko
(1832/1833–1925)
Japan

The Christian educator and leading light in the Tokyo Women's Reform Society, Yajima also headed the Christian Women's Society, which promoted social work among women. She came to social reform in her fifties, after being inspired by the temperance lectures of the U.S. social reformer Mary Leavitt, given when she was on a lecture tour in Japan.

Born in Kyushu, the daughter of a samurai magistrate, Yajima had been long married and was the mother of three when she left her husband and children because of his drinking. She moved to Tokyo in 1872 to join her brother, who introduced her in intellectual circles. She also came under the influence of Christian educators, which led to her own conversion in 1879. She became a teacher and at the age of forty-six obtained the post of principal of a Christian girls' high school.

Fortunate enough to be economically independent, Yajima was able to help organize the Tokyo Women's Reform Society in 1886 and acted as its first president. This Japanese equivalent of the Woman's Christian Temperance Union (WCTU) eventually affiliated itself with that body. Yajima's involvement no doubt sprang from the personal experience of divorcing her alcoholic and violent husband. The society set out to petition the Meiji government for reforms of the civil and criminal codes. In particular, it challenged old practices of concubinage and licensed prostitution as social ills. The society deemed these to be part of the still-prevailing Japanese family system that subjected women to the rule of their parents-in-law and condoned men's sexual promiscuity in order to ensure that they had sons to succeed them. The society called for the abolition of brothels and support for monogamy, which had already been achieved in part with the Meiji civil code of 1882, which endorsed monogamy but still continued to protect the legal rights of illegitimate sons over legitimate daughters. Yajima also helped organize a refuge for prostitutes fleeing licensed brothels and in 1916 led an unsuccessful campaign against the construction of prostitutes' quarters in Osaka.

In 1890 Yajima joined the swelling ranks of women activists protesting the enactment of Article 5 of the police security regulations, which forbade women from attending political meetings or even observing sessions of the Diet, and wrote on the issue in the society's journal. Her protest and that of other women may have gone some way toward achieving the lifting of the latter ban shortly after. The society also extended its concern to environmental issues, calling for a clampdown on the pollution caused by the Ashio Copper Mines and the provision of aid to people in the area affected by the mines.

In her work for the Christian Women's Society, Yajima joined in the suffrage campaign of the early 1920s. She also retained close links with the international temperance movement, representing Japan at WCTU conferences in Boston in 1906 and London in 1920. In 1921 she represented 10,000 Japanese women petitioners for peace at the Naval Arms Reduction Conference in Washington, D.C.

References and Further Reading
Mioko Fujieda. 1995. "Japan's First Phase of Feminism." In Kumiko Fujimura-Fanselow and Atsuko Kameda, eds., *Japanese Women: New Feminist Perspectives on the Past, Present, and Future.* New York: Feminist Press.

Sievers, Sharon. 1983. *Flowers in Salt: The Beginnings of Feminist Consciousness in Modern Japan.* Stanford: Stanford University Press.

Yamada Waka
(1879–1957)
Japan

The now-neglected story of Yamada Waka is an extraordinary one. Lured into prostitution in the United States, she later escaped to educate herself and become a writer and a leading voice on women's issues in Japan between the world wars. A believer in the home and family, she emphasized the positive values of the patriarchal view of women as "good wives and wise mothers," entering the feminist debate of the period 1911–1918 in Japan that contested women's education, their sexuality, and their roles both inside and outside the home.

Born in the Japanese fishing village of Kurigahama, the fifth of eight children of a farmer, Yamada attended elementary school but was thereafter obliged to look after her younger brother and help with work in the fields. At the age of sixteen, as a result of her family's ailing financial fortunes, she was married to Araki Hichijiro, a miserly man ten years her senior. Her unhappiness at this time would be reflected in her later short stories, such as "A Sullied Flower," "A Glimpse at My Youth," and "To Girls Deprived of High School." Becoming increasingly anxious to find ways to support her family when her husband refused to do so, at the age of eighteen Yamada was encouraged to seek a better life in the United States, where she hoped to make money as a seamstress or housemaid to send back home.

An ingenuous, trusting Yamada left Japan in 1895 and sailed across the Pacific. Upon arrival at Victoria, British Columbia, she was seized by Japanese pimps and sold to a brothel in Seattle. (It is likely that the woman in Japan who provided her with a phony letter of introduction was in cahoots with Japanese brothel keepers in the United States.) Held captive at the Eastern Hotel, a brothel on Seattle's King Street, Yamada somehow met a young Japanese journalist named Tachii Nobusaburo, who worked on an immigrant newspaper. He fell in love with her and engineered her escape from the second-story window of the brothel by means of a rope of bedsheets tied together.

The couple traveled 860 miles south to San Francisco where, after running out of money, Yamada was once more forced back into prostitution in 1902. Eventually, she sought refuge in the Chinese Presbyterian Mission Home there, a refuge for similar girls run by Donaldina Cameron, who taught Yamada new skills and encouraged her conversion to Christianity. Her relationship with Tachii, which had become fraught with quarrels, ended in 1903 with his suicide. Having a good knowledge of English, Yamada worked as an interpreter for the mission home and became one of its teachers. She also enrolled in an English school run by Japanese expatriate Yamada Kakichi, who encouraged her intellectual development. The couple married in about 1904, and after they lost all their possessions in the 1906 San Francisco earthquake, they returned to Japan.

Settling in Tokyo, Yamada began associating with Japanese feminists in the Bluestocking Society, founded in 1911, and wrote on a wide range of issues, including abortion and prostitution, for its feminist magazine, *Bluestocking*, between 1914 and 1916. She also undertook translations of the work of Olive Schreiner, Ellen Key, and the American sociologist Lester Ward.

In 1919 Yamada gave a speech at a summer seminar for women held in Nagoya and the following year became editor of the New Woman's Society journal, *Woman and the New Society*. During the 1920s, she accumulated a large body of work on women's issues. In essays such as "Women Bow down to Society," she discussed trade unions, the conditions under which women worked, women's suffrage, and Hull House, a settlement house founded by Jane Addams in the United States. Her work as a female critic, short story writer, and translator brought her considerable popularity, and in 1926 she was asked to write a regular column for the newspaper *Morning Sun*. Here she advised women on pregnancy, abortion, and their right to education and a profession. Mindful of her own experience of prostitution, to which poor women could be driven, she emphasized the need for them to find work that paid a decent wage. Although there was nothing groundbreaking in the way in which Yamada addressed many fundamental issues preoccupying Japanese women at that time, her column offered valued advice to masses of ordinary women. Her responses to women who wrote to her, many of them collected in two volumes, *Counseling Women* (1932) and *On Love* (1936), were prompted by a genuine concern based on her newly acquired principles of Christian charity.

Yamada became a major public figure and social critic after she accepted the chair of the Japanese branch of the Motherhood Protection League in the 1930s. Back in 1918, in her essay "The Problem of the Protection of Motherhood," she had described women's demand for independence and equality with men as erroneous: "It is an empty argument to advocate that women should ignore their husbands and children to develop self. . . . The women's movement should look forward to the perfection of the sacred mission of women, putting all the energy of the body and spirit into the home" (Bernstein 1991, 195). Thus Yamada had espoused the debate on women's maternal role begun by the Swedish reformer Ellen Key, which had attracted considerable attention in Japan, by underlining the traditional view that women's first duty was to create a happy and stable home for their children. Yamada urged the state to provide more help to women who opted to do so and in the 1930s headed a campaign for their legal protection, petitioning the Diet for legislation, which was enacted in 1937. That year she published her own study, *The Social Status of Japanese Women*. Thereafter, Yamada initiated a program to build an institution—the Hatagaya Home for Mothers and Children—and establish a nursing school on land she rented in 1938 in the Shibuya area of Tokyo.

In 1937 Yamada returned to the United States on a lecture tour to major cities that was sponsored by various Japanese associations in the United States. She revisited the brothel in San Francisco in which she had worked. (All her life, however, Yamada remained highly circumspect about her own past, making biographical research on her particularly difficult, as Tomoko Yamazaki has demonstrated.) She was received by Eleanor Roosevelt at the White House in December. After her husband's death, Yamada continued with her journalism, expanding on her views on motherhood in journals such as *Housewives' Friend*. When the Hatagaya Home was destroyed by bombing in 1945, Yamada set about

fund-raising to rebuild it as a refuge for women who wanted to break away from legalized brothels. At the newly built Hatagaya Girls' School (a misnomer since it was not run as a school), she installed her sister as principal and attempted to teach new skills to reformed prostitutes, using the methods of the Chinese Presbyterian Mission Home in San Francisco that had been her own salvation. Yamada remained active in the school until she died of a heart attack at the age of seventy-eight.

Despite being a leading public figure in the interwar years in Japan—as a member of the Japanese intellectual elite, a popular journalist, and the only female member of the committee responsible for controlling the prices of staple commodities—Yamada Waka and her work are now largely forgotten. She has been overshadowed by more radical Japanese feminists, no doubt in part because she remained largely uncontroversial for her endorsement of traditional family values.

See also Key, Ellen.
References and Further Reading
Bernstein, Gail Lee. 1991. *Recreating Japanese Women 1600–1945*. Berkeley: University of California Press.
Sievers, Sharon. 1983. *Flowers in Salt: The Beginnings of Feminist Consciousness in Modern Japan*. Stanford: Stanford University Press.
Tomoko Yamazaki. 1985. *The Story of Yamada Waka: From Prostitute to Feminist Pioneer*. Tokyo: Kodansha International.
Yamada Waka. 1937. *The Social Status of Japanese Women*. Tokyo: Kokusai Bunka Shinkokai [Society for International Cultural Relations].

Yosano Akiko
(1878–1942)
Japan

An innovative poet, essayist, and feminist in 1900s Meiji Japan who attracted much comment and vilification because of her unorthodox lifestyle, Yosano was looked upon as one of Japan's "new women." She saw the essential political and social challenges for women as lying in their absolute right to economic independence and equality of opportunity with men, both within and outside marriage.

Yosano's scholarly father, a confectioner by

trade, was a supporter of women's education and allowed her to read his books and attend the Sakai Women's School. She returned home, however, to take her place in the family business and began writing poetry and publishing it in literary magazines.

Yosano was that rarity among Japanese feminists of her time—a woman who maintained a long-lasting marriage, although it was beset by many hardships. In 1901 she ran away from home to live with leading poet and literary editor Yosano Tekkan (who was still married to his second wife). Tekkan would publish much of her poetry in his journal, *Morning Star* (1900–1908), and Akiko helped him with the day-to-day running of the journal. In 1901 her first and best-known published collection of poems, *Tangled Hair,* aroused considerable controversy for daring to express woman's enjoyment of her sexuality.

In the wake of such unanticipated celebrity, Yosano was invited to write articles for magazines and newspapers and began broaching the subject of political reform, in particular advocating women's greater access to education. She also attacked the traditional patriarchal system that remained intent on bringing girls up merely to be "good wives and wise mothers." In her view, only in a state of complete economic independence—not only from husbands but also from the state—could women fulfill themselves. The crux of Yosano's beliefs was that there should be no official legislation affording special protection to women. It was their natural right to be the unqualified equals of men.

In 1904, on the outbreak of the Russo-Japanese War, Yosano wrote a famous antiwar poem, "Die Not, My Brother," in response to the fanatical levels of patriotism being whipped up at the time. Needless to say, male politicians condemned her as a traitor. After *Morning Star* was closed down in 1908, Tekkan's literary career waned as Yosano's waxed, unleashing a long period of nervous illness and depression in him.

To support their growing family, Yosano concentrated increasingly on journalism for an income and published articles on women's rights. Her own experience of childbirth led her to refute the age-old assumption that women were physically weak and thus could never be equal with men: "It is strange that among those men who debate women's issues, there are those who view women as being physically weak. . . . I have given birth six times, borne eight children [by 1901], and have left seven new human beings in the world. Could a man suffer over and over that way?" (Bernstein 1991, 180).

In 1912 Yosano left her children in Japan to join her husband, who was visiting Europe to alleviate his depression. In Paris she took an interest in the women's movement there and compared it to the level of progress in Japan, publishing an article on the subject in the French journal *The Annals*. She returned to Japan in 1913 to support her husband's ill-judged campaign for election to the Diet in 1915. At this time, she wrote many essays and commentaries on women's issues, education, politics, and society. Meanwhile, she gave birth to two more children and, in answer to her critics who saw her pregnancies as a contradiction of her feminist beliefs, averred that her choices had been freely made within a relationship in which she and her husband considered themselves equals.

In 1915 Yosano began writing a monthly column for women, "One Woman's Notebook," in the magazine *Taiyo*. She criticized the work of the Swedish feminist Ellen Key, whose thinking had aroused great interest among Japanese feminists at that time, for asserting the physical superiority of men and the inviolable natural role of women as mothers. Despite her own large family and her obligations as a mother, Yosano rejected calls for state help or protection in that role. She defended her right to have other, independent interests outside the home. In turn, the leader of the Bluestocking Society, Hiratsuka Raicho, accused Yosano of irresponsibility in having a large family for which she could not provide sufficient food or clothing, despite her prodigious talents as a writer. In the ensuing debate between them by essay, Yosano continued to defend her belief that women had a right to work alongside men in support of their children.

From 1916 to 1921, Yosano published seven volumes of collected essays, as well as poetry and children's stories. She continued to support her unemployed husband and provide for the eleven children they eventually had together, using her many and diverse talents as a writer while still finding time to actively support the 1920s suffrage campaign. Her interest in women's education bore fruit in 1921, when she cofounded the progressive Bunka Gakuin School for Girls, where she also taught until the early 1940s. A volume of poetry, *White Cherry,* was published posthumously in 1942.

See also Hiratsuka Raicho; Key, Ellen.

References and Further Reading
Bernstein, Gail Lee. 1991. *Recreating Japanese Women 1600–1945.* Berkeley: University of California Press.

Jayawardena, Kumari. 1986. *Feminism and Nationalism in the Third World.* London: Zed Books.

Sievers, Sharon. 1983. *Flowers in Salt: The Beginnings of Feminist Consciousness in Modern Japan.* Stanford: Stanford University Press.

Z

Zakrzewska, Marie
(1829–1902)
Germany/United States

Born in Berlin to Polish parents, medical practitioner Marie Zakrzewska worked with Elizabeth Blackwell in the forefront of women's medical training and the establishment of women's hospitals in the United States. Zakrzewska was educated to the age of fourteen and began assisting her mother in her work as a midwife at the Royal Charité Hospital in Berlin. When she was eighteen, she applied to train at a midwives' school, and during her studies worked for Dr. Joseph Schmidt, who made her his teaching assistant. After qualifying in 1851, Zakrzewska began training other midwives a year later and was promoted to principal midwife at the Royal Charité Hospital in 1852.

Suffering criticism for being promoted to such a senior position at the age of only twenty-two, Zakrzewska decided to go to the United States. There, she was convinced, she would find greater opportunities for training in a medical career, particularly as she knew she would not be allowed to train as a doctor in Germany. Her father was dismayed at Zakrzewska's determination to become a doctor and, after she emigrated to New York with her sister in 1853, wrote to her: "If you were a young man, I could not find words in which to express my satisfaction and pride . . . but you are a woman, a weak woman; and all that I can do for you now is to grieve and to weep. O my daughter! Return from this unhappy path" (Bonner 1992, 140).

After a year of making a subsistence living as a seamstress, Zakrzewska approached Elizabeth Blackwell for work at her dispensary. With Blackwell's help and despite the fact that she spoke very little English, Zakrzewska obtained a place at Cleveland Medical College in Ohio in 1854 and, after graduating in 1856, set up a small private practice at Blackwell's home in New York. Together the women raised funds to open the New York Infirmary for Women and Children in 1857, the first hospital in the United States to be staffed by women, where they were joined by Blackwell's sister Emily. Zakrzewska served as the hospital's first resident physician and also as its general manager, in which capacity she set up a system of record keeping for patient histories.

In 1859 Zakrzewska set out on a fund-raising trip for the infirmary, during which time she also helped set up canteens for working women and community projects for Jewish immigrants as well as lending her support to the women's suffrage and antislavery movements. She did not return to the infirmary; instead, she accepted the post of professor of obstetrics and diseases of women at the New England Female Medical College in Boston, which had been established in 1848. There and at the college's adjacent Hospital for Women and Children, she struggled to introduce new medical practices and the use of microscopes, but finding it impossible to improve academic standards, she resigned in 1862, and the college's hospital was closed almost immediately. Zakrzewska reopened it as her own clinical hospital, the New England Hospital for Women and Children, beginning with only ten beds and an all-female staff, which she directed for the next thirty years.

With the support of many nonmedical patrons and feminists such as Ednah Dow Cheney, Zakrzewska established her own school to train nurses and give valuable hospital experience to women doctors. As the hospital grew, eventually relocating in 1872, it attracted many women pioneers in nursing and medicine, including Susan Dimock, one of the first female surgeons in the United States. Zakrzewska undertook free medical care among Boston's underprivileged, as well as running a private practice. By 1881, such were the high standards at the New England Hospital that the women training there as doctors were graduating with full credentials.

Zakrzewska's role became an increasingly administrative one as the hospital expanded, and by 1887 her role as a doctor there was only advisory. She also ran a social service program based at the hospital. In 1878 she founded the New England Hospital Medical Society and was its first president. She retired in 1899. The New England Female Medical College was eventually absorbed into the Boston University School of Medicine, but the original building of the New England Hospital for Women and Children survives as the Dimock Community Health Center in Boston.

See also Blackwell, Elizabeth.

References and Further Reading

Bell, Enid Moberley. 1953. *Storming the Citadel: The Rise of the Woman Doctor*. London: Constable.

Blake, Catriona. 1990. *The Charge of the Parasols: Women's Entry to the Medical Profession*. London: Women's Press.

Bonner, Thomas Neville. 1992. *To the Ends of the Earth: Women's Search for Education in Medicine*. Cambridge, MA: Harvard University Press.

———. 1995. *Becoming a Physician: Medical Education in Britain, France, Germany, and the U.S. 1750–1945*. New York: Oxford University Press.

Cheney, Ednah Dow. 1902. *Reminiscences of Ednah Dow Chéney (born Littlehale)*. Boston: Lee and Shepard.

Vietor, A. G., ed. 1924. *A Woman's Quest: The Life of Marie Elizabeth Zakrzewska MD*. New York: Appleton.

Walsh, Mary Roth. 1977. *"Doctors Wanted: No Women Need Apply": Sexual Barriers in the Medical Profession 1835–1975*. New Haven: Yale University Press.

Zetkin, Clara
(1857–1933)
Germany

Over a twenty-six-year period, the socialist-feminist Clara Zetkin dominated the left wing of the German women's movement and developed the official party position on the role women should play in the establishment of a socialist society. Although she remained detached from grassroots activism and philanthropy among the underprivileged, her domineering presence as party polemicist and theorist would lie at the heart of German socialism for good or ill, frequently stifling challenges to her intellectual dominance by other feminists, most notably Lily Braun.

Zetkin's inflexible, dogmatic approach for a while successfully resisted breaches in the movement by those calling for cooperation with middle-class feminists. Her leadership of women within the movement was dictated by her insistence on their primary loyalty lying with socialism and the subordination of their immediate civil and political rights to the greater and more pressing need for the emancipation of the working classes as a whole.

In placing a person's social class above all other considerations in her dealings with the various strands of the German women's movement, Zetkin was driven by her antipathy toward the despised bourgeois elements in the conservative mainstream. Unable to ally with them in furthering the cause of women's rights, Zetkin concentrated her efforts in mobilizing working-class women to achieve their own political and social emancipation through her domination of the Socialist Women's International.

Zetkin's roots were, in fact, middle-class. The daughter of a schoolteacher, she was born in Wiederau in Saxony. The family moved to Leipzig in 1872, where she followed her father into the profession, becoming one of the first women to train at the city's Teachers' College for Women, run by Auguste Schmidt. She began associating with Russian exiles who were students at the college, including a young revolutionary named Ossip Zetkin, who drew her into the emergent German socialist movement and gave her the works of Karl Marx to read. When German laws banning socialist activities were passed in 1878, Ossip was deported, and he and Clara settled in Paris, where they subsequently had two children; she took his name, but the couple never married. Over the next twelve years, the Zetkins lived in Paris and then Zurich, where they took part in clandestine activities and circulated illegal literature on behalf of the German Social Democratic Party (GSDP), which Clara joined in 1881.

In 1889, the year Ossip died, Zetkin was entrusted with the task of helping arrange the conference in Paris that inaugurated the Second Communist International. There she gave a keynote speech on women in the socialist movement, "Women Workers and the Woman Question," expounding on the urgency of women being admitted into the political arena as well as the workplace on an equal footing with men. Zetkin returned to Germany in 1890 when the laws against socialist activities were lifted, settled in Stuttgart, and soon took center stage in the left-wing women's movement there. At this time, she established her own very personal party line on women's role in the socialist movement through her editorship of the GSDP's women's paper, *Equality*; as far as she was concerned, feminist issues could only honorably be pursued by working-class women. Rejecting the ability of existing bourgeois women's groups in Germany to represent their interests for them, she urged working women to espouse socialism. As a single parent herself, she had now come to appreciate the difficulties of working mothers' lives as an area needing specific legislation and took up the protection of the legal rights of working women and children. As for suffrage, she supported the winning of universal suffrage over and above specific campaigning for women's right to vote as a separate issue.

Indeed, her opposition to any kind of separation of feminist from socialist issues was a cornerstone of Zetkin's political thinking, and she doggedly resisted all suggestions of forming separate women's organizations within the socialist movement. This brought her into conflict with the social democrat Lily Braun, who advocated the establishment of women's cooperatives. For Zetkin, participating in special activities for women was a diversionary measure that took time and energy away from the organization of the masses, and she was obsessed with achieving the right economic preconditions for the socialist revolution by strictly adhering to orthodox Marxist thinking on the subject.

Zetkin did not differentiate between men and women along traditional lines: sexual differences were, she believed, exaggerated by capitalist society, which made women choose between their role as mothers and their role as workers instead of fostering their abilities in both spheres. Women should be encouraged to develop in

Clara Zetkin (center) (Archive Photos)

both and be looked upon as fellow fighters in the struggle for socialism; for this reason, she was quick to criticize sexism within the GSDP. Zetkin believed it was essential that women workers be absorbed within a unified trade union movement in support of better wages. Lower-paid women often took work away from male workers and pushed down rates of pay, and all too often employers played women workers off against male ones. In her view, trade unionists should demonstrate solidarity with women, by uniting to achieve fair wages for both sexes. This concept of comradeship could also be translated into male-female relationships in which both partners were equal and fidelity was not a matter of a legal undertaking via a marriage certificate but was a moral ideal (a belief she lived up to in her own relationship with Ossip Zetkin).

In 1904 after the foundation of the International Woman Suffrage Alliance, Zetkin poured scorn on its membership's quest for "universal sisterhood," looking upon its program as tepid and middle-class and the international campaign for women's suffrage as being based in the main on property qualifications, which would not apply to most working-class women. She preferred to look to the establishment of women's groups within the confines of the Second International, and in 1907 Zetkin was elected secretary of its women's section. From this base, she worked to unite woman socialists in Europe by organizing an International Socialist Women's Congress that same year (also held in 1910 and 1914), of which she was elected secretary. A year later at Zetkin's suggestion, the congress adopted 8 March as International Proletarian Women's Day.

Upon the outbreak of World War I, Zetkin was ostracized in Germany as a member of the radical minority in the women's movement who opposed German militarism. She sent out an appeal to socialist women to attend a pacifist conference in Bern in March 1915 to try to bring a stop to the war and attempted to galvanize socialist support for the peace movement, believing that workers should not be fighting each other but joining together to defeat capitalism. At the Bern conference, seventy women from eight European countries passed a motion calling on working women to support an end to war—a fruitless appeal. On her return to Germany, Zetkin was imprisoned from August to October 1915 for her unpatriotic pacifist activities among working women in time of war. She was also ousted from the executive of the GSDP and the editorship of its journal, which she had edited since 1892.

After her release, such was her poor health (she suffered from a heart condition) that Zetkin was forced to give up active campaigning in the peace movement. A year later, she joined socialists supporting the war effort in the ill-fated radical socialist splinter party, the Spartacus League, led by Rosa Luxemburg and Karl Liebknecht, members of which founded the German Communist Party in December 1918. After Luxembourg's murder in 1919, Zetkin became an important figure on the German Communist Party's Central Committee and was elected as a communist deputy to the Reichstag (1920–1933). She wholeheartedly embraced the 1917 Revolution in Russia and spent much time there from 1924 onward, where she met with feminist luminaries such as Nadezhda Krupskaya and Alexandra Kollontai.

In 1920 Zetkin conducted a series of conversations with Vladimir Ilyich Lenin, a close friend and colleague, which she later published in 1929 in what remains her best-remembered work, *Recollections of Lenin* (Zetkin had encountered difficulties, however, in discussing Lenin's ambivalent position on women's emancipation). In 1921 Zetkin was elected to the presidium of the Third International. But with the death of Lenin in 1924 and the rise of Joseph Stalin, she frequently disagreed with the Soviet leadership and lost her political influence in the party. In 1932 after the burning of the Reichstag—on which occasion Zetkin denounced Adolf Hitler—she was offered sanctuary in the Soviet Union. In retirement in Moscow, she wrote numerous books on her theories of the socialist emancipation of women and attendant women's issues, which were published in East Berlin from 1957 to 1960, along with many of her political writings and speeches. She died at Arkhangel'sk in northern Russia.

See also Braun, Lily; Kollontai, Alexandra; Krupskaya, Nadezhda.

References and Further Reading

Boxer, Marilyn J., and Jean H. Quaterat. 1978. *Socialist Women: European Socialist Feminism in the Nineteenth and Early Twentieth Centuries.* New York: Elsevier North-Holland.

Evans, Richard. 1973. *The Feminist Movement in Germany 1894–1933.* London: Sage.

Foner, Philip S., ed. 1984. *Clara Zetkin: Selected Writings.* New York: International Publishers.

Frevert, Ute. 1990. *Women in German History: From Bourgeois Emancipation to Sexual Liberation.* Oxford: Berg Publishers.

Quaterat, Jean H. 1979. *Reluctant Feminists in German Social Democracy 1885–1917.* Princeton: Princeton University Press.

Slaughter, Jane, and Robert Kern. 1981. *European Women on the Left: Socialism Feminism, and the Problems Faced by Political Women, 1880 to the Present.* Westport, CT: Greenwood Press.

Thönnessen, Werner. 1976. *The Emancipation of Women: The Rise and Decline of the Women's Movement in German Social Democracy 1863–1933.* London: Pluto Press.

Ziyadah, Mai
(1886–1941)
Lebanon

A Levantine Christian born in Palestine, Ziyadah was one of the first of the area's contemporary feminist poets. She contributed to the women's cause through her writings rather than through her activities, in time becoming the writers' muse of the Cairo intelligentsia. She debated and corresponded on the emancipation of women and published biographies of other Arab feminists of her time. As a Christian, her freedom from the stultifying life of the harem allowed her to gain a broader education than most of her Muslim contemporaries. She studied at a boarding school run by the French Sisters of the Visitation in Lebanon.

She came to Cairo in 1908 but did not marry. It has been suggested that her emancipated behavior discouraged potential suitors. Writing poetry first in French, she turned to Arabic, becoming the first professional woman writer in that language. Through her articles in magazines such as *al-Jarida* and pamphlets, which she began publishing in 1911, she campaigned for women's education and their right to employment. She also asserted their freedom of choice in marriage although nonetheless advocating women's primary duty as mothers.

Beginning in 1912, Ziyadah hosted a weekly cultural salon open to both sexes in her father's house, which was frequented by literati and politicians alike of all religions and nationalities. As a Christian, she was less socially constrained from taking part in such gatherings, but she did so with a respect for Islam and without passing opinions on polygamy, the veil, and other issues that she felt were the preserve of Muslim feminists.

In 1914, Ziyadah joined with other feminists in running an intellectual group called the Women's Refinement Union and joined Huda Sha'rawi's Ladies Literary Improvement Society and contributed to her journal *The Egyptian Woman*. Ziyadah also befriended and corresponded with the Egyptian writer Malak Hifni Nasif on women's issues. The year 1914 also saw the beginning of a long correspondence and platonic love affair with the mystic and poet Kahlil Gibran, which lasted until 1931. In 1920 Ziyadah published one of her last feminist pieces, "A Discourse on Equality," in which she called for social and humanitarian reform.

As time went on, however, she became obsessive and was convinced that she was being watched by agents of the government. She had an unhappy love affair with the writer Abbas Mahmoud el-Akkad. Such was her resulting emotional distress that in the late 1930s her family committed her to an asylum. There she went on a hunger strike, but although she was allowed to leave, she seemed unable to cope with her return to society and retreated into self-imposed seclusion. She died alone in 1941, probably by her own hand.

See also Nasif, Malak Hifni; Sha'rawi, Huda.

References and Further Reading

Ahmed, Leila. 1992. *Women and Gender in Islam: Historical Roots of a Modern Debate*. New Haven: Yale University Press.

Badran, Margot, and Margaret Cooke, eds. 1990. *Opening the Gates: A Century of Arab Feminist Writing*. London: Virago.

Buck, Claire, ed. 1992. *Bloomsbury Guide to Women's Literature*. London: Bloomsbury.

"May Ziadeh." 1979. *Signs* 5(2): 375–382.

Appendix: Organizations by English and Original Names

Title in English	Founding Date	Name in Original Language	Name Change
Abeokuta Ladies' Club (Nigeria)	1942		From 1946 the Abeokuta Women's Union
African National Congress (South Africa)	1912		From 1912 to 1925 South African Native National Congress; from 1925 ANC
African National Congress Women's League (South Africa)	1943		
All-China Women's Federation	1949		
All-India Muslim Women's Conference	1914		
All-India Women's Conference	1926		
All-Russian Union for Women's Equality	1905–1908	Vserossiiskii Soyuz Ravnopraviya Zhenshchin	
American Anti-Slavery Society	1833		
American Birth Control League	1921		From 1942 Planned Parenthood Federation of America
American Civil Liberties Union	1920		
American Equal Rights Association	1866		
American Peace Society	1828		
American Woman Suffrage Association	1869		
Animal Defence and Anti-Vivisection Society (United Kingdom)	1906		
Aryan Ladies Society (India)	1882	Arya Mahila Samaj	
Association for Moral and Social Hygiene (United Kingdom)	1915		The British section of the British, Continental, and General Federation for the Abolition of Government Regulation of Prostitution
Association for the Rights of Woman (Argentina)	1919	Asociación pro Derechos de la Mujer	
Association for the Rights of Women (France)	1870	Association pour le Droit des Femmes	
Association for Women's Suffrage (France)	1871	Association pour le Suffrage des Femmes	
Association of German Women	1865	Allgemeiner Deutscher Frauenverein	

Name in English	Founding Date	Name in Original Language	Name Change
Association of Schoolmistresses (United Kingdom)	1866		
Association of Southern Women Against Lynching (United States)	1931		
Awakening Society (China)	1919		
Black Sash (South Africa)	1955		
Bluestocking Society (Japan)	1911	Seitosha	
Brazilian Federation for the Advancement of Women	1922	Federação Brasileira pelo Progresso Feminino	
British, Continental, and General Federation for the Abolition of Government Regulation of Prostitution (Int)	1875		Often referred to simply as the International Abolitionist Federation
British Union for the Abolition of Vivisection	1898		
Bureau of Women Workers (Soviet Union). *See* Zhenotdel			
Canadian Alliance for the Quebec Women's Vote	1927	L'Alliance Canadienne pour le Vote des Femmes du Québec	
Central National Society for Women's Suffrage (United Kingdom)	1888		
Charity Organisation Society (United Kingdom)	1869		
Chinese Communist Party	1921		
Commercial Union of Female Salaried Employees (Germany)	1889	Kaufmannischer Verband für Weibliche Angestellete	
Committee for Women's Suffrage (Czechoslovakia)	1905		
Congress Socialist Party (India)	1933		
Congressional Union for Woman Suffrage (United States)	1913		Often referred to simply as the Congressional Union. From 1916 the National Woman's Party
Danish Women's Association	1871	Dansk Kvindesamfund	
Danish Women's Progress Association	1886	Dansk Kvindelig Fremskridtsforening	
Danish Women's Suffrage Society	1888	Dansk Kvindelig Valgretsforening	
Daughter of the Nile Union (Egypt)	1948	al-Ittihad Bint al-Nil	
Daughters of Ireland	1900	Inghinidhe na hÉireann	
Democratic Party (United States)	c. 1828		
Democratic Suffragist Party (Cuba)	1927	Partido Demócrata Sufragista	
Dominion Women's Enfranchisement Association (Canada)	1889		
Dublin Women's Suffrage Association (Ireland)	1876		
Dutch Woman Suffrage League (Netherlands)	1907	Nederlandsche Bond voor Vrouwenkiesrecht	
East London Federation of Suffragettes (United Kingdom)	1914		
Edmonton Equal Franchise League (Canada)	1913		
Egyptian Feminist Union	1923	Jam'iyat al-Ittihad al-Nisa'i al-Misri	

Name in English	Founding Date	Name in Original Language	Name Change
Encompassing Love Society. *See* Mutual Love Association			
Equal Rights Association (United States). *See* American Equal Rights Association			
Eugenics Society			
(United States)	1926		
(United Kingdom)	1930		
Fabian Society (United Kingdom)	1884		
Family Planning Association (United Kingdom)	1939		
Federation of German Women's Associations	1894	Bund Deutscher Frauenvereine	
Federation of South African Women	1954		
Female Anti-Slavery Society (United States)	1833		Reorganized in 1866 as the American Equal Rights Association
Female Middle-Class Emigration Society (United Kingdom)	1862		
Feminist Association (Hungary)	1904	Feministák Egyesülete	
Feminist League (Mexico)	1919	Liga Feminista	
Feminist Socialist Center (Argentina)	1902	Centro Socialista Feminista	
Feminist Union (Finland)	1892	Naisasialitto Unioni	
Finnish Women's Association	1884	Suomen Naisyhdistys	
French League for the Rights of Women	1882	La Ligue Francaise pour le Droit des Femmes	
French Union for Women's Suffrage	1909	Union Française pour le Suffrage des Femmes	
General Austrian Women's Association	1893	Allgemeiner Österreichischer Frauenverein	
General German Women Teachers Association	1890		
General German Women's Association	1865	Allgemeiner Deutscher Frauenverein	
German Social Democratic Party. *See* Social Democratic Party of Germany			
German Union for Women's Suffrage	1902	Deutscher Verband für Frauenstimmrecht	
German Women's Suffrage Association	1913	Deutscher Verein für Frauenstimmrecht	
Great Circle of Indian Women	1910	Bharat Stri Maha Mandal	
Greater Japan Women's Association	1942	Fusen Kakutoku Domei/ Dai Nihon Rengo Fujinkai	
Home Rule India League	1916		
Housewives Committee of Siglo XX (Bolivia)	1961	Comité de Amas de Casa	
Humanitarian League (United Kingdom)	1892		
Hungarian Feminist Association. *See* Feminist Association			
Immigrants' Protective League (United States)	1908		

Name in English	Founding Date	Name in Original Language	Name Change
Independent Labour Party (United Kingdom)	1893		In 1900 the ILP joined with various socialist organizations to form the Labour Party
Indian National Congress Party	1885		
International Abolitionist Federation. *See* British, Continental, and General Federation			
International Alliance of Women for Suffrage and Equal Citizenship (Int)	1926		Often referred to as the International Alliance of Women; successor to IWSA
International Association of Women (Switzerland)	1868	Association Internationale des Femmes	
International Bureau for the Suppression of Traffic in Women and Children	1899		
International Committee of Women for Permanent Peace (Int)	1915		From 1919 the Women's International League for Peace and freedom
International Council of Women (national branches)			
Argentina	1901		
Australia	1899		
Austria	1903		
Belgium	1906		
Brazil	1927		
Bulgaria	1908		
Canada	1893		
Chile	1923		
Czechoslovakia	1924		
Denmark	1899		
Estonia	1921		
Finland	1911		
France	1901		
Germany	1897		
Greece	1908		
Hungary	1904		
Iceland	1920		
India	1925		
Ireland	1924		
Italy	1900		
Latvia	1922		
Lithuania	1930		
Netherlands	1899		
New Zealand	1900		
Norway	1904		
Peru	1926		
Poland	1924		
Portugal	1914		
Romania	1921		
Serbia	1911		
South Africa	1913		
South West Africa	1938		
Sweden	1898		
Switzerland	1903		
United Kingdom	1898		
United States	1888		

Name in English	Founding Date	Name in Original Language	Name Change
International Neo-Malthusian League	c. 1919		
International Planned Parenthood Federation	1953		
International Woman Suffrage Alliance (Int)	1904		
Irish Association for Promoting the Training and Employment of Educated Women	1861		
Irish Women Workers Union	1911		
Irish Women's Council. *See* Women's Council Irish Women's Franchise League	1908		
Irish Women's Suffrage and Local Government Association	1876		Successor to DWSA
Irish Women's Suffrage Federation	1911		
Irish Women's Suffrage Society	1909		
Japan Women's Patriotic Association (Japan)	1901	Aikoku Fujinkai	
Jewish Women's League (Germany)	1904	Jüdischer Frauenbund	
Josephine Butler Society (United Kingdom)	1953		Successor to the Association for Moral and Social Hygiene
Kensington Ladies Debating Society (United Kingdom)	1865		Known as the Kensington Society
Ladies' Land League (Ireland)	1881		
Ladies National Association for the Abolition of State Regulation of Vice and the Promotion of Social Purity (United Kingdom)	1870		Known as the Ladies National Association (LNA); in 1875 became a part of the International Abolitionist Federation and in 1915 was renamed the Association for Moral and Social Hygiene
Ladies National Association for the Diffusion of Sanitary Knowledge (United Kingdom)	1857		Known as the Ladies' Sanitary Association
Ladies National Association for the Repeal of the Contagious Diseases Acts (United Kingdom)	1869		Known as Ladies' National Association (LNA); the acts were repealed in 1886 and the society was disbanded
League for the Intellectual Advancement of Woman (Brazil)	1920	Liga para a Emancipaçao (Intelectual) da Mulher	
League for the Protection of Motherhood and Sexual Reform (Germany)	1904	Bund für Mutterschutz und Sexualreform	
League for the Realization of Women's Suffrage (Japan)	1924	Fusen Kakutôku Dômei	
League for the Rights of the Mother and the Child (Argentina)	1911	Liga para los Derechos de la Mujer y el Niño	
League of Nations Advisory Committee on Traffic in Women and Children (Int)	1922		
League of Republican Women (Portugal)	1909	Liga das Mulheres Republicanas	
League of Women Voters (United States)	1921		

Name in English	Founding Date	Name in Original Language	Name Change
League to Promote the Interests of Women (Italy)	1881	Liga Promotrice degli Interessi Femminile	
London Society for Women's Suffrage (United Kingdom)	1907		
Malthusian League (United Kingdom)	1879		
Manchester Committee for Women's Suffrage (United Kingdom)	1867		
Manchester National Society for Women's Suffrage (United Kingdom)	1865		
Married Women's Property Committee (United Kingdom)	1867		
Medical Foundation for the Care of Victims of Torture (Int)	1985		
Mothers of the Playa de Mayo (Argentina)	1977	Las Madres de la Plaza de Mayo	
Movement for Freedom and Popular Rights (Japan)	1874–1878	Jiyu Minken Undo	
Muhammad Ali the Great Philanthropic Association (Egypt)	1908	Mabarrat Muhammad Ali	
Muslim Women's Association (Egypt)	1936		
Mutual Love Association of Overseas Students in Japan	1904	Riben Liuxue Nüxue-sheng Gongaihui	Also known as the Encompassing Love Society
National American Woman Suffrage Association	1890		
National Association for the Advancement of Colored People (United States)	1909		
National Association for the Promotion of Social Science (United Kingdom)	1856		
National Association of Colored Women (United States)	1896		
National Association of Spanish Women	1918	Asociación Nacional de Mujeres Espanoles	
National Birth Control Council (United Kingdom)	1930		In 1931 it became the National Birth Control Association and in 1939 the Family Planning Association
National Birth Control League (United States)	1915		In 1919 changed its name to the Voluntary Parent-hood League
National Committee for Women's Suffrage (Italy)	1905	Comitato Nazionale per il Voto alla Donna	
National Consumers' League (United States)	1899		
National Council of Women (Uruguay)	1916	Consejo Nacional de Mujeres	
National Federation of Women's Associations (Cuba)	1921	Federación Nacional de Asociaciones Femeninas	
National Female Suffrage Union (Norway)	1885	Landekvinnestemmerets-foreningen	
National Feminist Alliance (Cuba)	1927	Alianza Nacional Feminista	
National Feminist League (Uruguay)	1910	Liga Feminista Nacional	
National Feminist Party (Argentina)	1920	Partido Feminista Nacional	
National Feminist Union (Argentina)	1918	Unión Feminista Nacional	
National League for Democracy (Burma)	1988		

Name in English	Founding Date	Name in Original Language	Name Change
National League of Women Freethinkers (Argentina)	1909	La Liga Nacional de Mujeres Librepensadores	
National Organization for Women (United States)	1966		Popularly known as NOW
National Revolutionary Movement (Bolivia)	1941	Movimiento Nacionalista Revolucionario	
National Society for the Prevention of Cruelty to Children (United Kingdom)	1880s		
National Union of Societies for Equal Citizenship (United Kingdom)	1919		
National Union of Women (Iran)		Ettehad-e Melli-ye Zanan	
National Union of Women's Suffrage Societies (United Kingdom)	1897		From 1919 known as the National Union of Societies for Equal Citizenship
National Vigilance Association for the Defence of Personal Rights (United Kingdom)	1881		
National Vigilance Association for the Repression of Criminal Vice and Immorality (United Kingdom)	1885		
National Woman Suffrage Association (United States)	1869		
National Woman's Party (United States)	1916		
National Women's League (Uruguay)	1910	Liga Nacional Feminista	
Nationalist Women's Party (Argentina)	1920	Partido Feminista Nacional	
National Women's Political Caucus (United States)	1971		
New Path League (Iran)	1955		
New People's Study Society (China)	1919	Xinmin Xuehui	
New Woman's Society (Japan)	1920	Shin Fujin Kyokai	
No Conscription Fellowship (United Kingdom)			
North of England Council for Promoting the Higher Education of Women (United Kingdom)	1867		
North of Ireland Society for Women's Suffrage	1871		
Norwegian Feminist Society	1884	Norsk Kvinnesaksforening	
Open Door Council (United Kingdom)	1923		
Ottoman Association for the Defence of the Rights of Women (Turkey)	1913		
Pan-American Association for the Advancement of Women (Latin America)	1922		
Patriotic Women's League (Iran)	1922		
Peronist Women's Party (Argentina)	1949	Partido Feminista Peronista	
Philippine Feminist Association	1905	Asociación Feminista Filipina	
Planned Parenthood Federation of America	1942		Successor to the American Birth Control League
Pro-Emancipation Movement for the Women of Chile	1932	Movimiento Pro-Emancipación de las Mujeres de Chile	

Name in English	Founding Date	Name in Original Language	Name Change
Progressive Party (United States)	1912		
Proletarian Committee for the Defence of Women's Suffrage (Cuba)	1926	Comité Proletario de Defensa de la Mujer	
Republican League of Portuguese Women	1910	Liga Republicana das Mulheres Portugesas	
Republican Party (United States)	1854		
Restoration Alliance (China)	1912		Precursor to the Guomindang (see below)
Rights of Woman (France)	1878	Droit de la Femme	
Royal Society for the Prevention of Cruelty to Animals (United Kingdom)	1824		
Russian League for Women's Equality	1907	Rossiskaya Liga Ravnopraviya Zhenshchin	
Russian Social Democratic Workers' Party	1898	Rossiiskaya Sotsial-Demokraticheskaya Rabochaya Partiya	
Russian Women's Mutual Philanthropic Society	1895	Russkoe Zhenskoe Zaimnoblagotvoritelnoe Obshchestvo	
Salvation Army (United Kingdom and later worldwide)	1878		Founded in 1865 as the Christian Revival Association; 1866 the East London Christian Revival Union; 1867 the East London Christian Mission; 1869 the Christian Mission; 1878 Salvation Army
Self-Employed Women's Association (India)	1971		
Sisters of Charity (Ireland)	1815		
Six Point Group (United Kingdom)	1921		
Social Democratic Party of Germany	1890	Sozialdemokratische Partei Deutschlands	Originally established in 1875 as the Socialist Workers' Party
Society for Improving the Lot of Women (Russia)	1899	Oshchestvo Uluchsheniya Uchasti Zhenshchin	
Society for Promoting the Employment of Women (United Kingdom)	1859		
Society for Providing Means of Support for the Higher Women's Courses (Russia)	1883	Obshchestvo dlya Sostav Leniya Sredstv Vyshim Kursam	
Society for the Advancement of Women (Turkey)	1909	Teali-i-Nisvan Cemiyeti	
Society for the Demand of the Rights of Woman (France)	c. 1866	Société de Revendication des Droits de la Femme	
Society for the Improvement of the Condition of Women (France)	1874	Société pour l'Amélioration du Sort des Femmes	
Society for the Mutual Education of Women (France)		Société Mutuelle d'Education des Femmes	
Society of Muslim Sisters (Egypt)	1948		
Society of Suffrage for Women (France)	1883	Société de Suffrage des Femmes	

Name in English	Founding Date	Name in Original Language	Name Change
Society to Provide Cheap Lodgings (and Other Benefits for the Citizens of St. Petersburg) (Russia)	1859	Oshchestvo Deshevykh Kvartir (i Drugikh Posobii Nuzhdayushchimsya Zhitelyam)	
Sole Front for Women's Rights (Mexico)	1935	Frente Único Pro-Derechos de la Mujer	
Southern Christian Leadership Conference (United States)	1957		
Spanish League for the Progress of Women	1920	Liga Espanola para el Progreso de la Mujer	
Student Non-Violent Coordinating Committee (United States)	1960		
Suffragette Fellowship (United Kingdom)	1926		
Swedish Women's Suffrage Association	1902	Landsföreningen for Kvinnans Politiska Rostratt	
Tax Resistance League (United Kingdom)	1909		
Tokyo Women's Reform Society	1885	Tokyo Fujin Kyofukai	
Union of Progressive Women's Associations (Germany)	1899	Verband Fortschrittlicher Frauenvereine	
United Council for Woman Suffrage (Australia)	1894		
United Farm Workers of America (United States)	1962		
Uruguayan Alliance of Women for Female Suffrage	1919	Alianza Uruguaya de Mujeres para Sufragio Femenino	
Vegetarian Society (United Kingdom)	1847		
Victoria Street Society for the Protection of Animals Liable to Vivisection (United Kingdom)	1875		Known as the Victoria Street Society
Victorian Women's Suffrage Society (Victoria, Australia)	1884		
Votes for Women Fellowship (United Kingdom)	1912		
Wafdist [Nationalist] Women's Central Committee	1920	Lajnat al-Wafd al-Markaziyah lil-Sayyidat	
War Resisters International	1921		
Weaker Sex Improvement Society (India)		Abala Abhivardini Samaj	
Woman Suffrage Association (Netherlands)	1894	Vereeniging voor Vrouwenkiesrecht	
Woman Suffrage Party (United States)	1909		New York affiliate of NAWSA
Womanhood Suffrage League (Australia)	1891		
Woman's Christian Temperance Union (United States)	1874		
Woman's Party (United States)	1916		Previously the Congressional Union for Woman Suffrage
Woman's Peace Party (United States)	1915		
Women's Anti-Suffrage League (United Kingdom)	1908		
Women's Central Committee of the Wafd Party. *See* Wafdist Women's Central Committee			

Name in English	Founding Date	Name in Original Language	Name Change
Women's Club of Cuba (Cuba)	1917	Club Femenino de Cuba	
Women's Committee for a Permanent Peace (Int.)	1915		Founded in The Hague; became the Women's International League for Peace and Freedom 1919
Women's Co-operative Guild (United Kingdom)	1883		
Women's Council (Ireland)	1914	Cumann na mBan	
Women's Equality (France)	1885	L'Egalité des Femmes	
Women's Evolution (Peru)	1914	Evolución Femenina	
Women's Federal Political Association (Australia)	1903		
Women's Franchise League (United Kingdom)	1889		Also in New Zealand 1892
Women's Franchise Union (Sri Lanka)			
Women's Freedom League (United Kingdom)	1907		
Women's Freedom Society (Iran)	1907		
Women's Indian Association	1917		
Women's International League for Peace and Freedom (Int)	1919		
Women's Labor Union (Cuba)	1930	Unión Laborista de Mujeres	
Women's Labour League (United Kingdom)	1906		
Women's League (of the African National Congress) (South Africa)	1943		
Women's National Liberal Association (United Kingdom)	1892		
Women's Organization of Iran	1960s	Sazman-e Zanan-e Iran	
Women's Prisoner's Defence League (Ireland)	1922		
Women's Progressive Party (Russia)	1905	Zhenskaya Progressivnaya Partiya	
Women's Protective and Provident League (United Kingdom)	1874		
Women's Refinement Union (Egypt)	1914	al-Ittihad al-Nisa'i al-Tahdhibi	
Women's Rights Association (Argentina)	1919	Asociación Pro-Derechos de la Mujer	
Women's Social and Political Union (United Kingdom)	1903		
Women's Society (Sri Lanka)		Mallika Kulangana Samitiya	
Women's Society of the Islamic Revolution (Iran)	1978	Jame'eh Zanan-e Enqelab-e Eslami	
Women's Solidarity (Group) (France)	1891	Le Groupe de la Solidarité des Femmes	
Women's Suffrage (France)	1883	Suffrage des Femmes	Founded in 1876 as Women's Rights
Women's Suffrage Union (Norway)	1885	Kvinnestemmeretsforeningen	
Women's Trade Union League (United Kingdom)	1874		
Women's Trade Union League (United States)	1903		
Women's Union of Chile (Chile)	c. 1933	Unión Femenina de Chile	
Women's Welfare Association (Germany)	1888	Verein Frauenwohl	

Name in English	Founding Date	Name in Original Language	Name Change
Working Women's Union (Cuba)	1930	Unión Laborista de Mujeres	
World's Woman's Christian Temperance Union (Int)	1891		
Young Women's Christian Association (United Kingdom)	1855		Established in 1858 in New York as the Ladies' Christian Association
Zhenotdel (Soviet Union)	1919	Zhenskoe Otdelenie	The Women's Department of the Communist Party

Name in English	Founding Date	Description
Other Frequently Cited Groups		
Amnesty International (Int)	1961	An international human rights organization established in London to monitor the abuse of political prisoners and the use of torture and the death penalty throughout the world.
Babists	1819	Followers of Mirza Ali Mohammad of Shiraz, Iranian mystic and prophet who claimed to be the "Bab" (gateway) to the true Islamic faith. He was the founder of the Babi religion in 1844, seen as a precursor to the Bahaist movement.
Chartists	1837–1850	Members of a popular movement that was active for social and electoral reform in Britain and that set out its demands in *The People's Charter* of 1838.
Eugenics movement		A movement that advocated the application of science in improving the human race through selective breeding. The word *eugenics* was coined by the British scientist Francis Galton (1822–1911) in 1883, but the concept goes back to Plato. It was first seriously discussed in Charles Darwin's *Origin of Species* (1859). The movement, however, soon divided into two wings: those who supported the positive benefits of its principles—better nutrition and health care for pregnant mothers and infants in avoiding the transmission of genetic diseases and ensuring that babies grew up healthy; and those who advocated the darker, negative side of eugenics—as a means of social control, by preventing the birth of children with mental and physical disabilities through pro grams of enforced sterilization and, at its worst ex treme, advocating the administration of euthanasia on the sick, mentally ill, elderly, and disabled (e.g., as the Nazis did in Germany during the 1930s).
Fabians		A socialist group dedicated to the introduction of gradual social change by constitutional means, through a program of detailed and practical reforms and state intervention in defense of the weak, the sick, and the poor.
Fourierists	1841–1846	Followers of the French social theorist Charles Fourier (1772–1837) who advocated cooperative settlements; one of the most famous experiments was set up by Transcendentalists at Brook Farm, Massachusetts (1841–1847).

Name in English	Founding Date	Description
Greenpeace	1971	An international conservationist organization founded in British Columbia, Canada, it opposes nuclear testing, the destruction of natural habitats such as the rainforest, and campaigns for the preservation of endangered species and for reductions in greenhouse gases.
Guomindang (also spelled Kuomintang)	1912	Chinese Nationalist Party, founded by Sun Yat-sen, and from 1925 led by Chiang Kai-shek. The Guomindang came to power in China in 1928. It came into open conflict with the Chinese Communist Party in 1945 and was defeated by it in 1949.
Langham Place Circle (United Kingdom)	1850s	An informal group of feminists and radicals who gravitated around Barbara Bodichon in London to discuss women's emancipation and promote their education and employment. Offshoots of the society were the all-woman Victoria Printing Press founded by Emily Faithfull, the Society for Promoting the Employment of Women, the Kensington Society, and the Female Middle Class Emigration Society.
May Fourth Movement (China)	1919	A popular movement prompted by students returning from study in Japan, which began by protesting territorial concessions to Japan in China under the terms of the Versailles Peace Treaty ending World War I. The movement attracted many Chinese women activists and promoted the debate of women's and human rights issues.
Owenites		Followers of the British social reformer Robert Owen (1771–1858), who founded a cooperative, industrial community at New Lanark in Scotland. This became the model for other communes, such as that established at New Harmony, Indiana (1825), in which Frances Wright was involved.
Saint-Simonians	c. 1826–1830s	Followers of the French social reformer and philosopher Henri Saint-Simon (1760–1825), the founder of French socialism, who advocated the reorganization of society into cooperative, communal groups. A movement flourished briefly in France in the first few years after his death.
The Society of Friends (the Quakers)	c. 1650	Founded by George Fox, this religion produced many notable women social reformers such as Elizabeth Fry, Jane Addams, Lucretia Mott, Elizabeth Heyrick, and Susan B. Anthony.
Theosophists/Theosophical Society	1875	A mystical religious and philosophical movement founded in New York by Helena Blavatsky (1831–1891) and Henry Steel Olcott (1832–1907), which was based on Hindu and Buddhist teachings, and was espoused by numerous women reformers, including Annie Besant, Margaret Cousins, and Anna Kingsford.
Transcendentalists/Transcendental Club	c. 1830–1850	A New England philosophical, religious, and literary group that gravitated around the poet Ralph Waldo Emerson and the writer Henry Thoreau at Concord,

Name in English	Founding Date	Description
		Massachusetts. Margaret Fuller and Elizabeth Peabody were among its leading women members. Inspired by Fourier (see above), the group established an experimental cooperative community at Brook Farm, Massachusetts.
Underground Railroad (United States)	1848	The escape network established by Harriet Tubman and other abolitionists to help runaway slaves escape to the North and to Canada.
Unitarians	1825	British and American dissenting groups that sprang from Calvinist Puritanism. The Unitarians in England were noted for their reformist principles. American Unitarianism developed from the Congregationalist Church in New England.
Utilitarians (United Kingdom)	late eighteenth century	Followers of the philosopher Jeremy Bentham (1748–1832) and the economist John Stuart Mill (1806–1873), who believed that the fundamental principle underlying the conduct of all citizens and governments should be that any action is right so long as it achieves the greatest happiness or good for the greatest number of people.

Note: (Int) = an international organization. Dates of establishment given where known; country of origin given where unclear.

Chronology

1789– French Revolution—the first revolutio-
1794 ary clubs (suppressed by the Jacobins 1793) for women serve as a forum for the discussion of women's emancipation. During the revolution's high point, the Reign of Terror (1793–1794), many radical women perish.

1791 Olympe de Gouges (France) publishes the *Declaration of the Rights of the Woman and Female Citizen.*

1792 Mary Wollstonecraft (United Kingdom) publishes *A Vindication of the Rights of Woman.*

Divorce and marriage laws are reformed in France.

1794 Women are banned from public meetings and political gatherings in France.

1799 Hannah More (United Kingdom) publishes *Strictures on the Modern System of Education.*

1804 The Napoleonic Code gives husbands in France full control over their wives and children and their wives' property. State-regulated prostitution is introduced.

1807 The slave trade is made illegal in Britain.

1813 Elizabeth Fry (United Kingdom) becomes a prison visitor to the women's section of London's notorious Newgate Prison and in 1817 establishes the Association for the Improvement of the Female Prisoners at Newgate with other Quaker

reformers. Fry pioneers prison reform in Britain and many of her ideas are adopted around the world.

1819 Emma Willard (United States) makes "An Address to the Public; Particularly to the Members of the Legislature of New York, Proposing a Plan for Improving Female Education."

1821 Emma Willard (United States) founds the Troy Female Seminary in New York state.

Frances Wright (United States) publishes *Views of Society and Manners in America.*

1824 Quaker abolitionist Elizabeth Heyrick (United Kingdom) publishes the landmark British abolitionist tract, "Immediate, Not Gradual Abolition of Slavery."

1825 Anna Wheeler (Ireland) and William Thompson publish "An Appeal of One Half of the Human Race, the Women, against the Pretensions of the Other Half, Men, to Restrain Them in Political and Thence Civil and Domestic Slavery."

1829 In India, the British colonial government bans *sati* (the ritual immolation of a widow on her husband's funeral pyre).

1830s Fourierist and St. Simonian communities in France are joined by many radical women eager to explore new ideas on equality between the sexes, communal living, free love, and women's rights.

1830s cont.	George Sand (France) is probably the first woman to wear trousers in public, although bloomers are said to have been worn by members of the New Harmony commune in Indiana since 1825.
1832	The First Reform Bill passes in Britain, enfranchising male but not female property holders, leading to women's support for the Chartist movement for parliamentary reform, which is active until 1848.
1833	Slavery is abolished in all of Britain's colonies. Lydia Maria Child (United States) produces the first abolitionist tract by a woman from the northern states, *An Appeal in Favor of That Class of Americans Called Africans*. The first Female Anti-Slavery Society in the United States is founded in Reading, Massachusetts; similar societies follow this year in Philadelphia and Boston. Abolitionist Theodore Weld (husband of Angelina Grimké) founds the first coeducational college that admits full-time women students, Oberlin Collegiate Institute in Ohio. Fifteen students are admitted in December; the first women graduate in August 1841.
1834	Poor Law Amendment Act in United Kingdom abolishes outdoor relief and extends the workhouse system.
1836	Angelina Grimké (United States) publishes "An Appeal to the Christian Women of the South."
1836–1865	Charles Dickens publishes his major social novels, prompting an upswing in philanthropy and charitable work in the United Kingdom undertaken by many women, along with reform of the Poor Laws and workhouse system.
1837	Queen Victoria (United Kingdom) ascends the throne.

Mary Lyon (United States) establishes the first all-women college, Mount Holyoke Female Seminary.

Caroline Norton (United Kingdom) protests her rights as a mother in "The Separation of Mother and Child by the Law of Custody and Infants Considered."

Angelina and Sarah Grimké (United States) found the National Female Anti-Slavery Society.

1838	Lucretia Mott, the Grimké sisters, Lydia Maria Child, and Abby Kelly Foster (United States) support the founding of a pacifist group, the New England Non-Resistance Society. Sarah Grimké publishes *Letters on the Equality of the Sexes* and *The Condition of Women*.
1839	In the United Kingdom the Infant Custody Act passes as a result of the campaigning of Caroline Norton in another pamphlet, "A Plain Letter to the Lord Chancellor on the Infants Custody Bill." The act gives separated wives rights of access to their children.
1840	At the first World Anti-Slavery Convention, held in London, and attended by Lucretia Mott and Elizabeth Cady Stanton, women are not allowed to participate in debates or make speeches. Feminist Amelia Bloomer (United States) omits the word *obey* from her marriage vows.
1844	The British Society for Promoting Female Education in the East sets up the first girls' school in China, at Ningbo. The Factory Act in the United Kingdom limits women's working day to twelve hours and that of children aged eight to thirteen to six and a half hours.
1845	Dorothea Dix (United States) pioneers prison reform with her *Remarks on Pris-*

ons and Prison Discipline in the United States.

Margaret Fuller (United States) publishes *Woman in the Nineteenth Century.*

1847   Elizabeth Blackwell is the first woman in the United States to be admitted to a men's medical school, The Geneva Medical Institute in New York.

1848   Amelia Bloomer introduces bloomers and promotes them in her journal the *Lily* from 1849. They are worn also by Elizabeth Cady Stanton and Susan B. Anthony in the early 1850s.

Slavery is abolished in French colonies.

Women are involved in republican struggle in Italy led by Giuseppe Mazzini; Margaret Fuller sends reports back to the United States as probably the first woman foreign correspondent. She is hired by Horace Greeley's *New York Tribune* to report on upheavals in Europe till her return in 1850.

Year of revolutions in Europe, affecting major cities—Berlin, Paris, Vienna. Many women, such as Mathilda Anneke in Prussia, are active in republican and national movements in support of change from monarchy to democratic government.

Eliza Lynn Linton (United Kingdom) is one of the first women formally employed as a journalist, on the *Morning Chronicle.*

After twelve years of dogged petitioning by Ernestine Rose (United States) and others, a Married Women's Property Act is passed in New York state.

Queen's College is founded in London to train women as governesses.

The historic first Woman's Rights Convention is held at Seneca Falls, New York, and attended by 300 people, including U.S. pioneers Bloomer, Mott, Stanton, Stone, and Truth. Its famous "Delaration

of Rights and Sentiments" is signed by 100. The convention is now seen as a defining moment in the history of the women's rights movement, and marks the beginning of its "first wave," primarily devoted to the fight for women's suffrage and property rights.

1849   Harriet Tubman (United States) organizes the Underground Railroad in the United States.

Elizabeth Blackwell is the first woman in the United States to be awarded a medical degree, by Geneva College, New York.

1850   The First National Woman's Rights Convention is held in the United States, at Worcester, Massachusetts.

Frances Buss (United Kingdom) founds the North London Collegiate School for Girls, the first public day school for girls to set higher academic standards.

1851   At a women's rights convention held in Akron, Ohio, black abolitionist Sojourner Truth makes her famous "Ain't I a Woman?" speech.

Quaker Anne Knight (United Kingdom) is a founder of the Sheffield Female Political Association, which produces an "Address to the Women of England," the first tract of its kind on women's suffrage produced by a women's group in the United Kingdom.

Women in Prussia are forbidden to join political parties.

"On the Enfranchisement of Women" is published by John Stuart Mill (United Kingdom) but is mainly the work of his collaborator, Harriet Taylor (United Kingdom), who, according to convention, has to remain anonymous.

1851–   Harriet Beecher Stowe (United States)
1852   publishes *Uncle Tom's Cabin.*

1853   Antoinette Brown Blackwell (United

1853 cont. States) is the first woman to be ordained, as minister of the South Butler First Congregational Church.

The first Whole World's Temperance Convention takes place in New York; Susan B. Anthony (United States) is a major organizer.

1854 Clara Barton (United States) is the first woman to be appointed to a civil service post, in the U.S. Patents Office.

Barbara Bodichon (United Kingdom) publishes *A Brief Summary in Plain Language of the Most Important Laws Concerning Women,* which will become the inspiration behind the campaign for the British Married Women's Property Act (not achieved until 1882).

1854–1856 Crimean War—Florence Nightingale (United Kingdom) takes charge of the British Army hospital at Scutari and the care of the wounded, but the spread of infectious disease decimates those who might otherwise have survived non-life-threatening wounds. Jamaican nurse Mary Seacole operates independently in the Crimea, running her own store and hotel for wounded officers and nursing the wounded on the battlefield.

1855 Lucy Stone (United States) insists on retaining her own name when she marries Henry Brown Blackwell.

1857 The First Matrimonial Causes Act (United Kingdom) preempts calls for a Married Women's Property Act. Under the act, wives deserted by husbands can keep the money they earn. The act also recognizes women's limited rights to divorce and right to retain their property after marriage.

Elizabeth Blackwell and her sister Emily establish the New York Infirmary for Women and Children.

1858 The *English Woman's Journal* (later known as the *Englishwoman's Review*) is founded and will promote a wide range of social and political reforms.

1859 Women of the Langham Place Circle in England found the Society for Promoting the Employment of Women to help impoverished middle-class women obtain respectable employment.

Anna Filosova, Nadezhda Stasova, and Mariya Trubnikova (Russia) establish the first major women's philanthropic organization, the Society to Provide Cheap Lodgings (and Other Benefits for the Citizens of St. Petersburg).

1860 In Italy, the Cavour Regulation licenses state regulation of prostitution. Anna Mozzoni (Italy) will lead the campaign for its repeal from 1878 to 1888, when she finally achieves her goal.

1861 The first women are admitted, as auditors only, to lectures in Russia's universities, but this right is rescinded in 1863.

The serfs are emancipated in Russia by Alexander II.

1861–1865 U.S. Civil War—women such as Clara Barton, Dorothea Dix, and Mary Livermore suspend suffrage and reformist activities to support the war effort and do pioneering work as nurses.

1862 Women property owners and rate payers in Sweden are the first to be granted the municipal vote.

1863 Marie Zakrzewska (United States) founds the New England Hospital for Women and Children.

1864 The First Contagious Diseases Act passes in the United Kingdom, introducing state regulation of prostitution and mandatory regular physical examinations of prostitutes. Josephine Butler launches a campaign for its repeal. Further acts follow in 1866 and 1869.

Anna Mozzoni publishes *Woman and Her Social Relationships.*

1865 The General German Women's Association is founded in Germany by Luise Otto-Peters.

The Thirteenth Amendment to the U.S. Constitution abolishes slavery. The Ku Klux Klan is founded the same year.

William and Catherine Booth (United Kingdom) found the Christian Revival Association in London's East End, which will lead to the foundation of the Salvation Army in 1878.

Elizabeth Garrett Anderson (United Kingdom) is the first British woman to qualify as a doctor, obtaining a Licentiate in Medicine and Surgery from the Society of Apothecaries.

1866 Elizabeth Garrett Anderson opens the St. Mary's Dispensary for Women and Children in London.

Emily Davies (United Kingdom) publishes *The Higher Education of Women,* arguing that women can achieve the same levels of academic excellence as men.

The American Equal Rights Association is founded at the Eleventh National Women's Rights Convention in New York City.

With the backing of a petition gathered by the Langham Place Circle and other feminists in the United Kingdom, John Stuart Mill submits the first bill in favor of woman's suffrage to Parliament.

1867 The universities of Paris, Berne, and Geneva allow women to attend medical lectures. From 1867 to 1873, many Russian women study in Switzerland.

Benjamin Disraeli (United Kingdom) secures the passing of the Second Reform Bill (known as the Representation of the People Bill), but this only extends the franchise among male property owners.

1868 Elizabeth Blackwell founds the Woman's

Medical College of the New York Infirmary.

The Faculty of Medicine of the Sorbonne in Paris admits women students.

Alaide Beccari (Italy) founds the influential women's journal *La Donna.*

The Fourteenth Amendment to the U.S. Constitution forbids the denial of "life, liberty, or property, without due process of law," to any person. U.S. suffragists challenge the word *person* as including women and demand their rights to suffrage, but fail to achieve legal recognition.

1868– The Meiji Restoration in Japan begins to
1912 open up education to women.

1869 The Third Contagious Diseases Act passes in Britain; the Ladies' National Association for the Repeal of the Contagious Diseases Acts is founded by Josephine Butler and others to continue fighting for repeal.

Wyoming is the first U.S. state to grant women's suffrage at the state level.

The American suffrage movement splits over the Fifteenth Amendment (ratified in 1870), which forbids deprivation of the right to vote on account of "race, color or previous condition of servitude," but not gender. Stanton and Anthony establish the National Woman Suffrage Association to concentrate on women's suffrage alone; Lucy Stone founds the more moderate American Woman Suffrage Association, which continues to advocate other issues including racial equality.

Women are admitted as auditors to lectures at the universities of St. Petersburg and Moscow.

John Stuart Mill (with considerable input during her lifetime from his wife, Harriet Taylor) finally publishes *On the Subjection of Women.*

1869
cont. Emily Davies founds the first College for Women offering university-level education, at Hitchin in Hertfordshire. In 1873 it transfers to Girton, near Cambridge, to become the first women's college at Cambridge University in 1874.

1870 Lydia Becker (United Kingdom) founds the *Women's Suffrage Journal*—the first of its kind in the United Kingdom.

The Fifteenth Amendment to the U.S. Constitution guarantees the right of all men to vote regardless of race. Suffragists challenge its wording, arguing that it should include a ruling on sexual discrimination, but their claims are rejected

The Education Act in Britain makes primary education compulsory.

The Married Woman's Property Act in the United Kingdom allows married women to keep the money they earn.

Women in the United Kingdom are allowed to stand for election to school boards: Elizabeth Garrett Anderson is elected to the London School Board for Marylebone; Emily Davies to that for the City of London.

Marie Goegg (Switzerland) founds the International Association of Women.

Utah is the second U.S. state to grant women's suffrage.

Victoria Claflin Woodhull and her sister Tennessee Claflin (United States) are the first women to enter the stockmarket, opening a brokerage office in New York (Woodhull, Claflin & Co.).

1870–
1871 The Franco-Prussian War results in the unification of Germany and the establishment of the French Third Republic.

1871 Women defend the barricades during the Paris Commune; Louise Michel (France) leads the Women's Vigilance Committee of the eighteenth *arrondissement*.

Frederik and Matilda Bajer (Netherlands) found the Danish Women's Association.

Léon Richer and Marie Deraismes (France) found the Association for the Rights of Women.

The first five young women are allowed out of Japan by the Meiji government to attend college in the United States.

1871–
1872 George Eliot (United Kingdom) publishes *Middlemarch*.

1872 The Fundamental Code of Education in Meiji Japan introduces four-year compulsory education for girls and boys.

Victoria Woodhull attempts to run for president of the United States.

The "To the People" movement in Russia prompts many idealistic young women to go out into the villages to proselytize social and political reforms in Russia among the peasants.

In Japan women are banned from bobbing their hair; all slavery is outlawed, but legalized prostitution is allowed.

1873 The Comstock Law in the United States makes it illegal to send obscene literature through the mail; this law would later be invoked to try to prevent the dissemination of birth control literature by activists Mary Ware Dennett and Margaret Sanger.

Japanese women are permitted to sue for divorce.

All Russian women students studying abroad are ordered to return home as a result of their increasing exposure to revolutionary ideas and socialism.

The Association for Married Women's Property Rights is founded in Sweden.

1874 Annie Wittenmyer (United States) founds the Woman's Christian Temperance Union in Iowa; it will become a major force for social reform campaigns by women around the world.

Sophia Jex-Blake (United Kingdom) founds the London School of Medicine for Women.

1875 British universities are allowed to grant degrees to women but all refuse except London University.

Josephine Butler (United Kingdom) and other social purity and human rights campaigners in Europe launch an international campaign against state-regulated prostitution with the establishment of the British, Continental, and General Federation for the Abolition of Government Regulation of Prostitution.

Frances Power Cobbe (United Kingdom) establishes a pionering animal-rights organization, the Victoria Street Society for the Protection of Animals Liable to Vivisection.

1876 In France, the Society for the Improvement of the Condition of Women is founded.

Queen Victoria is proclaimed empress of India.

Newnham College, the first at Oxford for women, is founded.

1877 Annie Besant (United Kingdom) is put on trial in the United Kingdom for distributing literature on birth control.

The first teachers' colleges are founded in Japan.

1878 The first International Woman's Rights Congress takes place in Paris.

The prestigious Bestuzhev women's courses in St. Petersburg admit women from all social classes to the university's faculties of history/philology and mathematics/natural sciences.

The University of London changes its charter to allow women into medical studies.

1879 Henrik Ibsen's play *A Doll's House* inspires women around the world to break out of domestic roles.

Auguste Bebel, a German Social Democrat, publishes *Women and Socialism,* which has a considerable impact on the thinking of socialist women reformers.

Annie Besant publishes a pioneering tract on birth control, "The Law of Population: Its Consequences and Its Bearing upon Human Conduct and Morals."

1880 Property-holding widows and single women on the Isle of Man are the first to be granted the vote in parliamentary elections in Britain.

The Education Act makes elementary education compulsory for children in the United Kingdom.

1881 Anna Mozzoni founds the League to Promote the Interests of Women in Milan.

Viscountess Harberton (United Kingdom) founds the Rational Dress Society.

1881–1906 The first four volumes of the *History of Woman Suffrage* are published by Stanton, Gage, and Anthony.

1882 Dr. Aletta Jacobs (Netherlands) sets up the first birth control clinic in the world in Amsterdam.

The Married Women's Property Act in the United Kingdom allows married women the right to own property and keep some of their earnings.

Women are excluded from medical schools in Russia.

1883 The Women's Cooperative Guild is established in the United Kingdom.

1883
cont.
Hubertine Auclert (France) founds the Society of Suffrage for Women.

The Contagious Diseases Acts are suspended in the United Kingdom.

Olive Schreiner (South Africa) publishes *The Story of an African Farm.*

1884   Divorce law is reformed in France.

The Finnish Women's Association, Norwegian Association for the Rights of Women, and Norwegian Feminist Society are founded.

Henrietta Dugdale (Australia) founds the Women's Suffrage Society.

1885   The first female doctor in Japan, Ogino Ginko, graduates.

The first meeting of the Indian National Congress inaugurates a nationalist movement in India, in which many women take part.

The establishment of the Woman's Christian Temperance Union in New Zealand gives impetus to a suffrage campaign that will make women in that country the first in the world to win the national vote.

The Tokyo Women's Reform Society is established.

The British journalist W. H. Stead, supported by Josephine Butler, Catherine Booth (United Kingdom) and other women social purity campaigners, publishes an exposé of the trade in child prostitutes, in a series of four articles under the title "The Maiden Tribute of Modern Babylon," in the *Pall Mall Gazette,* prompting a public outcry and the raising of the age of consent to sixteen under the Criminal Law Amendment Act.

Sweden's first major women's society, the Fredrika Bremer Society, is named after the famous author.

1886   Japanese women strike for the first time, in a Tokyo silk factory.

Finally, the Contagious Diseases Acts are repealed in Britain.

Anandibai Joshi is the first Indian woman to qualify as a doctor, at the Women's Medical College in Philadelphia.

1888   Members of the National Woman Suffrage Association found the International Council of Women at a meeting in Washington, D.C.

Married women in the United Kingdom are allowed to vote for county councils.

1889   Jane Addams and Ellen Gates Starr (United States) establish the Hull House Settlement in Chicago. Addams pioneers the movement across the country, and similar settlements will be established elsewhere in the world.

Austro-Hungarian pacifist Bertha von Suttner publishes her important antiwar novel *Lay down Your Arms!*

Elizabeth Wolstenholme-Elmy (United Kingdom) and others found the Women's Franchise League.

1890   The two major U.S. suffrage organizations unite to establish the National American Woman Suffrage Association, with Elizabeth Cady Stanton as president.

Article 5 of the Police Security Regulations in Japan prohibit women from joining political parties and organizing or attending political meetings.

1891   Germany introduces laws protecting the working hours of women and providing maternity leave.

The Womanhood Suffrage League is established in New South Wales, Australia.

1892   The British Medical Association admits women doctors.

1893   The Independent Labour Party, the first political party to support women's suffrage in Britain, is founded.

The self-governing British colony of New Zealand is the first nation to grant women's suffrage; 90,000 women vote in the first elections held in November.

Rosa Mayreder (Austria) founds the General Austrian Women's Association.

Matilda Joslyn Gage (United States) publishes *Woman, Church, and State.*

Ida B. Wells-Barnett (United States), in "The Reason Why the Colored American Is Not in the World's Columbian Exhibition," protests the absence of black culture at the Chicago World's Fair.

1894   The Icelandic Women's Association, the Association for Women's Suffrage in the Netherlands, and the Federation of German Women's Associations are founded.

The University of Edinburgh admits women to medical programs.

1895   Anna Filosova and Anna Shabanova found the Russian Women's Mutual Philanthropic Society.

Octavia Hill (United Kingdom) is a cofounder of the National Trust for Places of Historical Interest and Natural Beauty.

The Women's Institute is founded in Canada to bring together women in rural areas in cultural pursuits and social work.

mid-   The rise of the emancipated "new
1890s woman" is widely debated in the British press as the result of feminist writing on sexuality, suffrage, rational dress, and other issues affecting women.

1896   Mary Church Terrell (United States) es-

tablishes the National Association of Colored Women in Washington, D.C.

Various British suffrage societies amalgamate to form the moderate National Union of Woman's Suffrage Societies, led by Millicent Garrett Fawcett (United Kingdom), formally constituted in 1897.

1897   The Danish Women's Associations Suffrage Federation is formed.

Liang Qichao (China) advocates the abolition of footbinding, leading to the foundation of the Anti-Footbinding Society in Shanghai.

La Fronde (The Sling), one of the most influential women's daily papers in France, begins publication.

1898   Male Japanese reformer Hukichi Fukuzawa publishes *Criticism on the Great Learning for Women and Revised Great Learning for Women,* in which he argues that old moral codes subordinating women should be abolished.

Charlotte Perkins Gilman (United States) publishes *Women and Economics.*

1899   Male reformer Qassim Amin (Persia [Iran]) publishes *The Liberation of Woman,* sparking widespread debate on social reform and marking the inauguration of Arab feminism.

Carrie Nation (United States) launches her inimitable temperance crusade in the United States, smashing up saloons and bars with her brigades of "Hatchetarians."

The second congress of the International Council of Women is held in London.

The National Consumers' League is founded in the United States to lobby against the exploitation of low-paid, mainly female workers in manufacturing industries.

1900   The first medical school for women in Japan opens in Tokyo.

1900
cont.
Ellen Key (Sweden) publishes *The Century of the Child*.

Emily Hobhouse (United Kingdom) exposes the suffering of Afrikaner women and children in British concentration camps in the South African Cape during the Boer War (1899–1902).

The Anti-Saloon League campaigns for prohibition in the United States.

1900s
A period of vigorous reform activity by U.S. women ensues during the Progressive Era, under the presidency of Theodore Roosevelt.

1901
Queen Victoria dies.

The first group of Chinese women study abroad, at the Girls' Practical School in Tokyo, Japan.

1901–
1906
Gertrud Baümer and Helene Lange (Germany) publish their ambitious *Handbook of the Women's Movement*.

1902
Women in Australia win the federal vote, although Aboriginal women will not be granted it until 1962.

Anita Augspurg and Lida Gustava Heymann (Germany) found the German Union for Women's Suffrage; the Swedish Woman's Suffrage Association is also established.

1903
Emmeline and Christabel Pankhurst (United Kingdom) found the Women's Social and Political Union in Manchester.

Marie Curie (France) is the first woman to win a Nobel Prize, for physics.

The Women's Trade Union League is founded in the United States.

1904
The first congress of the International Woman Suffrage Alliance is held in Berlin by a breakaway group of more radical women members of the International Council of Women.

Helene Stöcker (Germany) founds the League for the Protection of Motherhood and Sexual Reform.

Hungarian feminist Rosika Schwimmer establishes the Council of Women and the Hungarian Feminist Association, which advocate women's rights.

Bertha Pappenheim (Germany) founds the Jewish Women's League.

1905
Bertha von Suttner is the first woman to win the Nobel Peace Prize.

Russian women are finally admitted to universities, but this ruling is withdrawn during 1909 to 1914 and not fully restored until 1916.

Annie Kenney and Christabel Pankhurst (United Kingdom) disrupt an election meeting in the Free Trade Hall in Manchester and spark the onset of a militant campaign for women's suffrage.

1905–
1907
A short-lived women's suffrage movement in Russia is led by Poliksena Shishkina-Yavein (Russia) and the All-Russian Union for Equal Rights for Women.

1906
Upton Sinclair's *The Jungle*, a gripping exposé of the Chicago meatpacking industry, leads to a major government investigation undertaken by settlement workers and other reformers, including Mary McDowell and Ella Bloor (United States) of exploitation of immigrant workers in the industry and the provision of the U.S. Pure Food and Drugs Act.

Women in Finland are the first in Europe to receive the vote.

The First All-Indian Women's Conference is held in India.

Harriot Stanton Blatch (United States) is the first woman to give a political broadcast by radio, on the subject of "Votes for Women," under the aegis of the De Forest Radio Telephone Company.

The Dowager Empress of China orders the opening up of women's education, leading to the establishment of the Beiyang First Girls' Normal School in Tinajin.

1906– Women are active in the Persian (Iranian) constitutional revolution.

1907 The militant suffrage campaign in England becomes more intense; a split in the Women's Social and Political Union leads to the foundation of the Women's Franchise League.

Women in Egypt begin unveiling.

Under the Qualification of Women Act in the United Kingdom, women can now stand for election to county and borough councils and be elected as mayoresses.

In Finland the first nineteen women members of parliament are elected to the Diet.

Maria Montessori (Italy) develops her method of preschool education among children at the Casa dei Bambini in a slum district of Rome.

1908 Jane Addams and others in Chicago establish the Immigrants' Protective League to prevent abuse and exploitation of newly arrived immigrants to the United States.

A high-profile, open-air suffrage rally in Hyde Park, London, is attended by 250,000–500,000 people.

The first national congress of Italian feminists in Rome ends in disharmony.

The First All-Russian Women's Congress is disrupted by conflict between socialist feminists led by Alexandra Kollontai (Russia) and bourgeois moderates.

1909 Alexandra Kollontai publishes *The Social Basis of the Woman Question.*

The Union for Women's Suffrage is established in France.

In Egypt, Nabawiyya Musa is the first woman allowed to sit for the state secondary school examination.

1909 Mary White Ovington (United States), Ida B. Wells-Barnett, and others found the National Association for the Advancement of Colored People (NAACP).

The escalation of hunger strikes among imprisoned suffragettes in the United Kingdom leads to the introduction of forced feeding.

1909– The Women's Trade Union League leads
1910 a major four-month strike by approximately 20,000 women shirtwaist makers in the New York garment industry.

1910 Robert Baden-Powell (United Kingdom) founds the Girl Guides (also in the United States in 1912). The movement will find an outstanding pioneer in Poland in Olga Malkowska.

Women in the U.S. states of Colorado, Idaho, Washington, Wyoming, and Utah now have the right to vote at the state level.

A Conciliation Committee of fifty-four members of Parliament in the United Kingdom drafts a women's suffrage bill for a limited form of franchise for women property holders, but it fails in debate for the next three years.

The first women's rights association in Belgium, the Feminist Union, is formed.

Clara Zetkin (Germany) nominates 8 March as International Women's Day at the Second Congress of Socialist Women in Germany.

The First International Women's Congress is held in Buenos Aires with delegates attending from Argentina, Chile, Paraguay, Peru, and Uruguay.

1911   The Triangle Shirtwaist Company fire in New York kills 146 mainly female workers and exposes the terrible working conditions in overcrowded sweatshops of many immigrant workers in the United States.

A brief flowering of the first women's rights movement in Japan occurs with the founding of the Bluestocking Society and its journal *Bluestocking* (defunct by 1916).

A women's rights movement flourishes in Mexico after the revolution that ends the dictatorship of Porfirio Díaz.

Egyptian feminist writer Malak Hifni Nasif presents ten demands on women's emancipation at the first congress of Egyptian women, held in Cairo, but the conference rejects her radicalism and her calls for women's education, professional training, and divorce reform.

Olive Schreiner (South Africa) publishes *Woman and Labour*.

The United Kingdom passes the National Insurance Act, which introduces sick benefits for workers.

1912   Julia Lathrop (United States) creates the Children's Bureau, which is later led by Grace Abbott (United States).

Muthulakshmi Reddi (India) is the first woman allowed to study and qualify as a doctor in India.

Russia reforms inheritance laws, allowing women rights to property.

The Organization of the Woman's Suffrage Alliance is founded in China but dissolves in 1913.

1913   Tokyo University is the first university in Japan to admit women (as auditors only).

Black South African women are a powerful voice in the campaign against the discriminatory Pass Laws.

Women win suffrage in Norway.

On Derby Day, militant suffragette Emily Wilding Davison (United Kingdom) throws herself in front of the king's horse and is killed.

Alice Paul (United States) founds the militant Congressional Union, which in 1916 becomes the National Woman's Party.

Rosika Schwimmer in Hungary establishes the National Council of Women.

The Cat and Mouse Act (Prisoner's Temporary Discharge for Ill Health Act) is introduced in Britain to deal with increasing numbers of suffragettes on hunger strike in prison.

1914   The All-India Muslim Women's Conference is founded in India.

The Irish Women's Council is founded.

1914– World War I—many suffrage organiza-
1918   tions around the world suspend their activities, and women work for their national war effort while others embrace the pacifist movement, oppose conscription, and form the nucleus of the postwar women's peace movement.

1915   Jane Addams and Carrie Chapman Catt call a national conference of women pacifists in the United States at which the Woman's Peace Party is founded.

Margaret Sanger publishes the first major book in the United States on birth control, *Family Limitation*. Mary Ware Dennett founds the National Birth Control League.

The Hague is the venue for women pacifists representing 150 organizations from twelve countries, who hold a peace congress at which the International Committee of Women for Permanent Peace is set up, leading to the formation after the war in 1919 of the Women's International League for Peace and Freedom.

Women's suffrage is won in Denmark and Iceland.

1916 An International Congress of Women is held in the Yucatán, in Mexico. Yucatán is the seat of radical women's activities in the early 1920s, under the government of feminist sympathizer Felipe Carrillo Puerto, resulting in a series of progressive reforms relating to birth control and sex education.

The Easter Rising takes place in Ireland.

1917 Jeanette Rankin is the first woman elected to the U.S. Congress when women in Montana are given the state vote.

Annie Besant founds the Women's Indian Association.

The United States enters World War I.

The Russian Revolutions of February and October—women's suffrage is granted and women are admitted to the civil service and public office. Alexandra Kollontai is the first woman to be appointed a government minister, as People's Commissar of Social Welfare. The Zhenotdel (women's sections of the Communist Party) are established and become a forum for the women's movement but are abolished by Joseph Stalin in 1930.

In Madras, a delegation of Indian women, led by Sarojini Naidu, meet Secretary of State Lord Montagu and call for equal franchise with men and improvements to women's education and health care.

1918 Women obtain suffrage in Austria, Canada, and Germany.

Marie Stopes (United Kingdom) publishes *Married Love* and *Wise Parenthood*.

Women in India take part in Mahatma Gandhi's *satyagraha* (civil disobedience) movement.

Hungarian suffragist and feminist Rosika Schwimmer is the first woman to be appointed an ambassador (to Switzerland).

In Britain under the Representation of the People Act, limited suffrage is granted to women over thirty. Constance de Markievicz (Ireland) is the first and only woman elected to Parliament under new electoral laws, but as a member of Sinn Féin refuses to take her seat.

1919 Eglantyne Jebb (United Kingdom) founds the Save the Children Fund.

Women take part in nationalist political protest during the Egyptian Revolution.

Women win suffrage in Belgium (very limited) and the Netherlands.

Women workers in the Shanghai textile mills go on strike.

The May Fourth movement in China encourages debate on women's issues.

U.S.-born politician Nancy Astor is the first female member of Parliament to take her seat in Britain's Houses of Parliament.

The moderate UK suffrage organization the NUWSS becomes the National Union of Societies for Equal Citizenship.

The first postwar International Congress of Women is held in Zurich; the Women's International League for Peace and Freedom is established with its headquarters in Geneva.

1919– The Turkish War of Independence brings
1923 with it the rise to power of Kamal Atatürk and a major campaign for social reform.

1920 Under the Nineteenth Amendment to the U.S. Constitution passed in 1919 and now ratified, women's suffrage is introduced in the United States.

Jane Addams, Helen Keller (United

1920 cont. States), and others found the American Civil Liberties Union.

Ichikawa Fusae, Hiratsuka Raicho (Japan), and others found the New Woman's Society in Japan.

The League for the Intellectual Advancement of Woman is founded in Brazil.

The new Bolshevik government in Russia legalizes abortion.

Austrian women gain the right to vote.

France makes the dissemination of birth control literature illegal; abortion becomes a capital offense.

Women for World Disarmament is founded.

Great Britain and Austria introduce a limited form of unemployment insurance.

1921 Women win suffrage in Sweden.

Marie Stopes open the first birth control clinic in Britain, in Holloway, London.

The Red Wave Society, the first socialist women's organization in Japan, is founded but repressed in 1925.

The Chinese Communist Party, which purports to support women's emancipation, is founded.

The Sheppard-Towner Act in the United States provides for the health care of pregnant and nursing mothers and infants and establishes 3,000 health care centers.

Eleven women's organizations in Cuba unite to found the National Federation of Women's Associations.

1922 Bertha Lutz (Brazil) heads Argentina's campaign for women's suffrage, founding the Brazilian Federation for the Advancement of Women.

The Patriotic Women's League is established in Iran.

Women's suffrage comes to the Republic of Ireland.

Chinese women establish Feminist Movement Associations and Women's Suffrage Associations.

1922–1923 The Irish Civil War takes place.

1923 The Equal Rights Amendment is proposed in the U.S. Congress by Alice Paul of the National Woman's Party.

The Matrimonial Causes Act in Britain allows women to divorce on the same grounds as men.

Huda Sha'rawi (Egypt) founds the Egyptian Feminist Union after attending the congress of the International Woman Suffrage Alliance in Rome; she symbolically unveils on her return to Egypt.

The Soviet Union is established as a nation; all traces of bourgeois women's activism have now been stifled and women are harnessed to new economic and industrial programs.

1924 Reforms of society and culture in Turkey under Atatürk include a ban on the veil.

Eleanor Rathbone's (United Kingdom) groundbreaking work *The Disinherited Family* pioneers the idea of the welfare state.

The National Council of Women is founded in India.

1925 The Guardianship of Infants Act passes in England; men and women have equal rights over their children.

1925–1941 The reformist Pahlavi dynasty of shahs in Iran brings with it improvements in the status of women.

1926 Women gain suffrage, but in provincial elections only, in India and Pakistan.

1927   Another All-India Women's Conference takes place.

U.S. journalist Katherine Mayo publishes *Mother India,* about child marriage and the lack of medical care available to Indian women, causing a public outcry.

The League of Nations publishes a report to which many women activists have contributed—the Report of the Special Body of Experts on Traffic in Women and Children.

1928   Ray Strachey publishes *The Cause,* the classic account of the women's suffrage movement in the United Kingdom.

Under the Equal Franchisement Act, the voting age for women in Britain is reduced from thirty to twenty-one (now on equal terms with men).

1929   Women gain suffrage in Ecuador.

In India, where Indian and British reformers such as Eleanor Rathbone have campaigned for it, the Child Marriage Restraint Act (popularly known as the Sarda Act) raises the age of eligibility for marriage to fourteen.

Virginia Woolf (United Kingdom) publishes *A Room of One's Own,* in which she argues for women's financial independence.

The International Association of Schools of Social Work is established in the United States.

Margaret Bondfield is the first woman cabinet minister in the United Kingdom (undersecretary of state to the Ministry of Labour).

1930   White women in South Africa are given the vote.

Abortion is outlawed in Italy by Mussolini's fascist government.

Indian women join in protest against the salt laws after Mahatma Gandhi's famous Salt March.

The first conference in Japan on women's suffrage is held.

1931   Jessie Daniel Ames (United States) founds the Association of Southern Women Against Lynching.

Women's suffrage is granted in Spain, but is repressed by General Franco with the outbreak of the Spanish Civil War in 1936 and not restored until 1975.

Women gain suffrage in Sri Lanka.

Jane Addams wins the Nobel Peace Prize.

1932   Women win suffrage in Brazil and Uruguay.

Spain reforms divorce and marriage laws.

1933   Hitler's fascist government closes down all women's organizations in Germany.

Under the "New Deal," Franklin D. Roosevelt introduces new economic measures and welfare programs aimed at countering the effects of the Great Depression. Many U.S. women reformers are active during this time, including Frances Coralie Perkins, the first woman appointed to a U.S. cabinet post, as secretary of labor.

1934   Cuba and Turkey grant women's suffrage.

The World Congress of Women Against Fascism is held in France.

Eleanor Rathbone publishes *Child Marriage: The Indian Minotaur.*

1934–   Chinese communist women join men on
1935   the Long March—9,600 kilometers—to the northern province of Shanxi.

1935   In the Soviet Union, Stalin's family laws reverse the emancipation of women introduced by the Bolsheviks.

1935
cont.
Mussolini's fascist forces invade Ethiopia (Abyssinia), prompting protests by feminists such as Nancy Cunard (United Kingdom), Una Marton (Jamaica), and Sylvia Pankhurst.

The first twelve women are allowed to enter the university in Iran; the Ladies Centre in Iran replaces the Women's Patriotic League.

Women's suffrage comes to Puerto Rico.

Alcoholics Anonymous is the first self-help group, founded in Akron, Ohio.

1936
The shah of Persia (Iran) abolishes the veil.

Abortion is made illegal and contraceptives less widely available in the Soviet Union by Joseph Stalin, in a move to put a stop to plummeting birthrates.

The first Iranian women are allowed to study at Tehran University.

1936–
1939
The Spanish Civil War ensues.

1937
Women win suffrage in the Philippines.

The League of Nations sets up a Committee of Experts on the Legal Status of Women.

1938
Japan sets up a Ministry of Health and Welfare.

Virginia Woolf's *Three Guineas* challenges sexual discrimination in the workplace.

Women gain suffrage in El Salvador.

1939–
1945
World War II takes place.

1940
Women's suffrage is finally granted to women in Quebec province, Canada.

Eleanor Rathbone publishes *The Case for Family Allowances*.

1941
The United States enters World War II and "Rosie the Riveter" posters appear everywhere, encouraging U.S. women to take on essential war work.

1942
Women gain suffrage in the Dominican Republic.

Women are active in the Quit India Movement, leading to Indian independence in 1948.

OXFAM is founded to help women and children in Greece under Nazi occupation.

Ernest Beveridge draws on the work of women reformers such as Eleanor Rathbone and Beatrice Webb (United Kingdom) for his report on the institution of a welfare state.

Ding Ling's (China) article "Thoughts on March 8" criticizes sexism in the Chinese Communist Party.

1944
Reverend Florence Tim-Oi Lee is the first woman to be ordained an Anglican minister, in Macao, as a wartime emergency measure due to lack of male priests.

Durriyah Shafiq (Egypt) founds the Daughter of the Nile Union.

Women win the right to vote in France and Jamaica.

1945
Women gain suffrage in Bulgaria, Guatemala, Indonesia, Italy, Japan, Trinidad and Tobago, and Panama; full suffrage is finally granted to women in Hungary.

At the end of World War II, the United Nations is set up with its various subsidiary organizations, including the Children's Fund (UNICEF), Educational, Scientific, and Cultural Organization (UNESCO), High Commission for Refugees (UNHCR), and World Health Organization (WHO).

The first British Labour government of the postwar era, based on the recommendations of the 1942 Beveridge Report, introduces state welfare, including provisions for illness, pensions, insurance, etc.

The first laws prohibiting female genital mutilation (FGM) pass in the Sudan, but are not enforced.

1946   Full women's suffrage is granted in Ecuador.

Legalized prostitution in Japan is banned on the orders of the Allies.

Mary Ritter Beard (United States) publishes *Women as a Force in History: A Study of Traditions and Realities.*

The U.S. Congress approves the Equal Rights Amendment, but it is defeated in 1982 for not having achieved ratification in time.

The United Nations establishes the Commission on the Status of Women to study women's rights worldwide.

Emily Greene Balch (United States) shares the Nobel Peace Prize.

1947   Women win suffrage in Argentina and Venezuela.

1948   Women gain suffrage in Israel, Burma, Chile, and Belgium (full suffrage).

India achieves independence.

The "Universal Declaration of Human Rights," written by Eleanor Roosevelt, is passed by the United Nations.

The Eugenics Protection Law in Japan allows for widespread access to abortion, contraception, and sterilization.

1949   Women win suffrage in India, Chile, and Costa Rica.

Dhanvanthi Rama Rau (India) founds

the All-Indian Family Planning Association and opens the first family welfare center in Bombay.

The United Nations holds its Convention for the Suppression of the Traffic in Persons and of the Exploitation of the Prostitution of Others.

The People's Republic of China is formed, granting women's suffrage there; women establish the All-China Women's Federation.

Simone de Beauvoir (France) publishes *The Second Sex,* considered by many feminists to be the book that inspired the worldwide "Second Wave" of the women's movement.

The Population Registration Act in South Africa classifies all South Africans as either Bantu, Coloured, or White, introducing apartheid.

1950   Women's suffrage comes to Haiti.

The Chinese communist government bans child marriage, concubinage, and female infanticide.

In India, Dhanvanthi Rama Rau founds the Planned Parenthood Federation International.

1951   Women gain suffrage in Antigua, Barbados, Dominica, Grenada, St. Kitts and Nevis, St. Lucia, St. Vincent, and the Grenadines.

Egyptian feminist Durriyah Shafiq leads a women's march on Parliament and holds a sit-in in support of women's political rights; a year later the revolution in Egypt brings an end to effective feminist campaigning.

1952   The UN Covenant on the Political Rights of Women states that women everywhere should be granted the vote and be eligible for political office.

1953 Women are granted suffrage in Bolivia and Lebanon.

The eminent Indian women's rights activist Vijaya Pandit is the first woman to become president of the UN General Assembly.

1954 Women gain suffrage in Belize and Colombia.

The U.S. Supreme Court rules in the famous *Brown v. Board of Education of Topeka* case that segregation of black and white children in southern schools is in violation of the equal protection clause of the Fourteenth Amendment to the U.S. Constitution.

The National Federation of Indian Women is founded.

1955 Women win suffrage in Ethiopia, Nicaragua, and Peru.

Sex education is now obligatory in Swedish schools.

Rosa Parks (United States) refuses to give up her seat on a bus in Montgomery, Alabama, leading to a bus boycott that marks the beginning of the U.S. civil rights movement.

1956 Women's suffrage is awarded in Egypt but the Egyptian Feminist Union and all other women's organizations are closed down by the government.

Abortion is once more legalized in the Soviet Union.

Black women in South Africa again protest the Pass Laws; 20,000 take part in a major protest march on 8 August.

Alva Myrdal, the leading Swedish social democrat, publishes *Women's Two Roles: Home and Work* with her collaborator Viola Klein.

1957 Women's suffrage is granted in Ghana, Honduras, and Malaysia.

Daisy Bates (United States) leads nine black students into the all-white Central High School in Little Rock, Arkansas. The U.S. president has to call out the National Guard to protect them from rioting whites.

African American students found the Southern Christian Leadership Conference (SCLC) in the southern United States to advocate for their civil rights.

1958 Women gain suffrage in Mexico, Paraguay, and Togo.

The Campaign for Nuclear Disarmament is founded in the United Kingdom.

1959 Women's suffrage comes to Mauritius, Morocco, and Tunisia.

The United Nations makes its Declaration on the Rights of the Child.

South African civil rights activist Helen Suzman is a founder of the Progressive Party and will be the only woman in South Africa's parliament until 1974.

The High Council of Iranian Women's Associations calls for suffrage.

1960 Sirimavo Bandaranaike is the first woman in the world to achieve the position of prime minister, of Ceylon (now Sri Lanka).

Nineteen African states win women's suffrage.

1961 Women gain suffrage in Burundi, Mauritania, Rwanda, Sierra Leone, Somalia, and Tanzania.

In Bolivia the Housewives' Committee is formed to defend the rights of miners and their families against low wages and terrible living and working conditions at the vast mining complex, Siglo XX.

Amnesty International is founded in London.

President John F. Kennedy appoints Eleanor Roosevelt to head the U.S. Commission on the Status of Women.

The Dowry Prohibition Act is passed in India but is ineffectual in eradicating the traditional practice of demanding dowries.

A Women's Strike for Peace is called by the Society Against Nuclear Energy.

1962 Women's suffrage is granted in Algeria and Uganda.

The All-African Organization of Women is founded.

Dolores Huerta (United States) and César Chavez found the United Farm Workers of America to protect the rights of many migrant, and mainly Hispanic, workers in the United States.

Many black women take part in the Voter Education Project in the southern United States to encourage black voters to register.

Rachel Carson (United States) initiates the environmental movement with her *Silent Spring*—a plea for ending the use of toxic chemical sprays in agriculture.

1963 Women win suffrage in Iran and Kenya.

Betty Friedan (United States) publishes *The Feminine Mystique,* sparking the "Second Wave" of the women's movement.

The Soviet cosmonaut Valentina Tereshkova demonstrates that no sphere is closed to women, when she becomes the first woman launched into space.

1964 Women are granted suffrage in Malawi, the Sudan, and Zambia.

The Civil Rights Act is passed in the United States, prohibiting racial discrimination in employment (Title VII of the act, which outlaws sexual discrimination, is added as an attempt to kill the bill, but to the conservatives' surprise, it passes anyway).

Fannie Lou Hamer (United States) and others found the Mississippi Freedom Democratic Party.

1965 Women gain suffrage in Botswana and Lesotho.

The United Nations passes the International Convention on the Elimination of All Forms of Racial Discrimination.

1966 Indira Gandhi becomes the first woman prime minister of India.

Betty Friedan and others found the largest women's political organization in the United States, the National Organization for Women (NOW). Modeled after the NAACP, it takes up the fight against sexual discrimination in the form of segregated classified employment advertisements.

1967 Women's suffrage comes to Iraq and Swaziland.

France legalizes the sale of contraceptives.

The Abortion Act is passed in the United Kingdom, and the government takes over providing family planning methods in 1968.

The UN Convention on the Elimination of All Forms of Discrimination Against Women (CEDAW) is the most comprehensive document on women's rights yet drawn up.

The Family Protection Law in Iran makes divorce easier for women; a further act is passed in 1975 to regulate polygyny, but both pieces of legislation are rescinded by the mullahs after the Iranian Revolution of 1979.

1968 After the disastrous Tet Offensive, women in the United States are increas-

1968 cont. ingly vocal in the mounting protest movement against the Vietnam War, leading to the withdrawal of U.S. troops in 1973.

Student unrest throughout Europe contributes to the growth of the "Second Wave" of the women's movement.

Pope Paul VI upholds the Roman Catholic Church's position on abortion in his *Humanae Vitae*.

British women sewing machinists strike for the first time, at Ford's car plant, calling for equal pay with men.

The SCLC, along with women activists including Marian Wright Edelman (United States), organize the Poor People's March on Washington.

Shirley Chisholm, a Democrat from New York, is the first black woman elected to the U.S. Congress; she takes her seat in 1969.

A major protest against sexual exploitation of women is staged by feminists at the Miss America Pageant in Atlantic City, New Jersey.

Farrokhru Parsa becomes the first woman cabinet minister in Iran (minister of education). She is executed in 1980 on trumped-up charges related to her desire to improve women's access to education.

1969 The American Convention on Human Rights is held.

Golda Meir becomes the first woman prime minister of Israel.

The first feminist group in Venezuela, the Women's Liberation Movement, is founded.

1969– 1970 The U.S. lesbian and gay rights movement begins in earnest after a protest against police harassment at the Stonewall Inn in New York City.

1970 Women in Pakistan, awarded the vote in 1956, are able to vote for the first time.

Eva Figes publishes *Patriarchal Attitudes*, Shulamith Firestone publishes *The Dialectic of Sex*, Germaine Greer publishes *The Female Eunuch*, Kate Millett publishes *Sexual Politics*, and Robin Morgan publishes *Sisterhood Is Powerful*.

Feminist demonstrators disrupt the Miss World contest in London.

The first Women's Liberation Conference is held at Ruskin College, Oxford, and is attended by 600.

1971 Women finally win suffrage in Switzerland—one of the last Western countries to grant it.

Divorce is legalized in Italy.

The United Nations passes the Declaration on the Rights of Mentally Retarded Persons.

Massive demonstrations by women in Trafalgar Square, London, demand equal pay, free contraceptives, and abortion on demand.

Erin Pizzey (United Kingdom) opens the first women's refuge for battered wives and their children, in Chiswick, London.

The National Women's Political Caucus is founded in the United States by Shirley Chisholm, Betty Friedan, Gloria Steinem (United States), and others.

In India, Ela Bhatt (India) establishes the Self-Employed Women's Association to protect the rights of impoverished women market traders.

Gloria Steinem, Robin Morgan, Letty Cottin Pogrebin, and others launch the influential feminist magazine *Ms*.

1972 Women's suffrage comes to Bangladesh.

The Black Women's Federation is founded in South Africa.

In Egypt Nawal el-Saadawi (Egypt) publishes her controversial book *Woman and Sex*, in which she confronts the issue of female circumcision in the Arab world.

The leading British feminist journal, *Spare Rib*, begins publication.

Shirley Chisholm is the first black woman in the United States to run for president.

1973   Abortion is finally legalized in the United States under the U.S. Supreme Court decision in *Roe v. Wade*, which affirms the right to privacy.

Women gain suffrage in Syria.

1974   Simone de Beauvoir founds the French League for the Rights of Women.

Ichikawa Fusae (Japan) wins the Ramon Magsaysay Award for her lifetime's work for women's rights.

Women's suffrage is granted in Guinea-Bissau and Jordan.

1975   Women win suffrage in Angola, the Cape Verde Islands, Mozambique, São Tomé, and Principe.

The United Nations declares the International Year of the Woman and the Decade for Women until 1985. A women's world congress is held in Berlin.

Elisabeth Domitien is the first woman prime minister in Africa, in the Central African Republic.

The Equal Pay Act and the Sex Discrimination Act, pioneered by Labour politician Barbara Castle (United Kingdom), become law in the United Kingdom.

In Portugal the "Three Marias" (Maria Isabel Barreno, Maria Teresa Horta, and Maria Velho da Costa) publish *New Portuguese Letters*, criticizing the government and the penal code and advocating women's sexual freedom.

Virago, the first all-women publishing house in the United Kingdom, is dedicated to publishing new works by women and rediscovering lost works of feminist literature and nonfiction.

1976   Women gain suffrage in Portugal and the Seychelles.

The first International Tribunal on Crimes Against Women takes place in Brussels.

American Women Against Violence in Pornography and Media is founded.

1977   Women are granted suffrage in Djibouti and Libya.

The new government of General Zia al-Haq in Pakistan reverts to strict Islamic law and reintroduces *hijab* (wearing the veil).

Betty Williams and Mairead Corrigan, founders of the Northern Ireland Peace Movement, are awarded the Nobel Peace Prize.

The Mothers of the Plaza de Mayo stage a protest in Buenos Aires against the military dictatorship (1976–1983) and demand news of Argentina's many "disappeared" (people kidnapped and murdered during these years).

1978   The Organization of Women of African and Asian Descent (OWAAD) is founded to combat discriminatory immigration laws.

Human Rights Watch is established in New York.

Abortion is legalized in Italy.

1979   Margaret Thatcher is the first woman to become prime minister of the United Kingdom.

1979 Nawal el-Saadawi publishes *The Hidden*
cont. *Face of Eve: Women in the Arab World,*
provoking controversy with its frank discussion of traditional practices of FGM,
child marriage, and the honor system.

The UN Convention on the Elimination of
All Forms of Discrimination Against
Women is ratified by the General Assembly.

After the Islamic Revolution and the fall
of the Pahlavi dynasty in Iran, the Family
Protection Laws of 1967 and 1975 are
abolished by the mullahs under Ayatollah
Khomeini, who announces a return to
the laws of the Qu'ran. Women must
readopt the veil and the hijab. Schools are
segregated, birth control is banned, and
the age at which girls are eligible for marriage is lowered to thirteen. Husbands
can once again divorce their wives without consent. Many university disciplines
are closed to women. On International
Women's Day on 8 March, 15,000 women
demonstrate in protest outside the Palace
of Justice in Tehran.

The first protests are held by women
against dowry murders in India.

1980 Seventy-one thousand women join the
Women Against Pornography March in
New York City.

The second UN World Conference on
Women is held in Copenhagen.

Vigdis Finnbogadothhir is the first female president of Iceland.

Women's suffrage is granted in Zimbabwe.

1980– During the Iran-Iraq War, Islamicization
1988 policies continue in Iran, reinstituting restrictions on women's right to divorce
and obtain custody of their children.

1981 Andrea Dworkin (United States) publishes *Pornography.*

A Women's Peace Camp is established
outside the U.S. air base at Greenham

Common in the United Kingdom; the
last missiles are not removed until 1991
but a feminist presence is retained at
Greenham for several years thereafter.

1982 The assassination of South African civil
rights activist Ruth First deprives the
movement of an important leader.

In the United States, the Equal Rights
Amendment fails to be ratified when it
does not achieve the required ratification
of thirty-eight states by the constitutional
deadline.

1983 Environmental campaigner Petra Kelly,
leader of the pioneering Green Party in
Germany, wins the American Peace
Woman of the Year Award and becomes
one of seventeen Green Party members
elected to the West German legislature.

1985 Wilma Mankiller (United States) becomes the first woman principal chief of
a Native American government, the
Cherokee Nation.

1986 The Band Aid concert unites the world in
consciousness- and fund-raising for the
famine in Ethiopia.

Women gain suffrage in Liberia.

1987 Diane Abbott is the first black woman in
the United Kingdom to be elected to Parliament, as Labour MP for Hackney
North and Stoke Newington.

1989 The first black Anglican woman bishop,
the Right Reverend Barbara Harris, is
consecrated in Boston.

The United Nations passes the Convention on the Rights of the Child.

The International Conference on the Implications of AIDS for Mothers and Children is held in Paris.

Women win suffrage in Namibia.

A referendum held in the Republic of Ireland on the legalization of divorce fails.

1990   A World Summit for Children is held.

Women are granted suffrage in Samoa.

1990–   President F. W. De Klerk repeals most
1991   South African laws relating to apartheid.

1991   The UN passes the Declaration on the Elimination of Violence Against Women.

1992   Rigoberta Menchú (Guatemala) is the first indigenous Latin American to win the Nobel Peace Prize.

Women gain suffrage in Yemen.

In what was called "The Year of the Woman," unprecedented numbers of women are elected to the U.S. Congress, totalling about 10 percent of the seats.

1994   The first democratic government is elected in South Africa under Nelson Mandela. Most black South Africans— male as well as female—vote for the first time in their lives.

Cairo hosts the International Conference on Population and Development, which brings the attention of the world to the increasing practice of female genital mutilation throughout Africa.

The United Nations declares the International Year of the Family.

The Church of England ordains the first women priests, bringing condemnation from the Pope. In the United Kingdom, Roman Catholic nun Lavinia Byrne (United Kingdom) challenges the right of women to become priests in her *Woman at the Altar,* despite the pope's recent "Apostolic Letter of His Holiness Pope John Paul II on Reserving Priestly Ordination to Men Alone."

1995   The UN Fourth World Conference on Women is held in Beijing. Despite attempts by the Chinese government to shut down the conference, more than 30,000 women attend.

1996   The Palestine National Authority grants full women's suffrage.

1997   In Afghanistan, a draconian clampdown on the civil liberties of women by the fundamentalist regime of the Taliban ensues. Women must now be entirely covered from head to toe. All girls' secondary schools have been closed, and adult women are excluded from higher education and vocational training as well as the professions. Strict limitations on women's employment, their modes of dress, behavior, freedom of movement, and freedom of speech are supported by medieval forms of punishment, including public execution.

An all-time record number of 120 women members are elected to Parliament, as compared to the previous record of sixty, in UK elections.

Women's suffrage comes to Eritrea.

Madeleine Korbel Albright, an immigrant from Czechoslovakia, becomes the highest-ranking woman in government in the United States, as secretary of state.

In December, four months after the death of Princess Diana, a leading advocate of the campaign against antipersonnel mines, ninety nations sign a treaty banning the manufacture and use of them by the end of the twentieth century.

1998   Russian civil rights activist and politician Galina Starovoitova is assassinated.

1999   In *The Whole Woman,* Germaine Greer reappraises the progress of the women's movement since the 1970 publication of *The Female Eunuch.*

2001   Women remain disenfranchised in the following countries: Bahrain, Kuwait, Saudi Arabia, Oman, Qatar, and the United Arab Emirates.

Female genital mutilation is still widely practiced in the majority of states in the

2001
cont.

African subcontinent, with the highest rates in Egypt (97 percent of the female population), Djibouti, Eritrea, Ethiopia, Mali, Sierra Leone, Somalia, and Sudan (all at 90 percent or over).

In May, in a chilling echo of Nazi practices, the Taliban order all Hindus in Afghanistan to wear a strip of yellow cloth on their clothing, identifying that they are not of the Muslim faith. With military strikes against terrorist groups in Afghanistan in the wake of the terrorist attack on the World Trade Center in New York on 11 September, refugees begin pouring out of the country. More than 5 million people—one-fifth of its population of 24 million—are facing starvation, and humanitarians around the world begin a massive relief effort.

Selected Bibliography

Biographical Dictionaries and Encyclopedias

Abbott, Willis J. 1913. *Notable Women in History.* London: Greening.

Adamson, Lynda G., ed. 1998. *Notable Women in World History: A Guide to Recommended Biographies and Autobiographies.* Westport, CT: Greenwood Press.

The Annual Obituary. 1980– . New York: St. Martin's Press.

Arnold, John, and Deirdre Morris, eds. 1994. *Monash Biographical Dictionary of Twentieth-Century Australia.* Port Melbourne: Reed Reference Publishing.

Ashby, Ruth, and Deborah Gore Ohrn. 1995. *Herstory: Women Who Changed the World.* New York: Viking.

Bala, Usha, ed. 1986. *Indian Women Freedom Fighters.* New Delhi: Manohar.

Banks, Olive, ed. 1985, 1990. *The Biographical Dictionary of British Feminists,* vol. 1, *1800–1930;* vol. 2, *1900–1945.* Brighton: Harvester Wheatsheaf.

Baylen, J. O., and N. J. Gossman, eds. 1979–1984. *Biographical Dictionary of Modern British Radicals.* 3 vols. Hassocks, Sussex: Harvester Press.

Bekoff, Marc, ed. 1998. *The Encyclopedia of Animal Rights and Animal Welfare.* London: Fitzroy Dearborn.

Bellamy, Joyce M., and John Saville, eds. 1982. *Dictionary of Labour Biography.* 9 vols. London: Macmillan.

Benson, Eugene, and William Toye, eds. 1997. *Oxford Companion to Canadian Literature.* 2d ed. Oxford: Oxford University Press.

Black, Helen C. 1893. *Notable Women Authors of the Day: Biographical Sketches.* Glasgow: David Bryce and Son.

Blain, Virginia, ed. 1990. *The Feminist Companion to Literature in English.* London: Batsford.

Bliss, William D. P., ed. 1898. *Encyclopedia of Social Reforms.* New York: Funk and Wagnalls.

Boyland, Henry, ed. 1998. *Dictionary of Irish Biography.* 3d ed. Dublin: Gill and Macmillan.

Brockman, Norbert C., ed. 1994. *African Biographical Dictionary.* Santa Barbara: ABC-CLIO.

Brown, George W., et al., eds. 1966. *Dictionary of Canadian Biography.* Toronto: University of Toronto Press.

Buck, Claire, ed. 1992. *Bloomsbury Guide to Women's Literature.* London: Bloomsbury.

Buhle, Mari Jo, Paul Buhle, and Dan Georgakas, eds. 1998. *Encyclopedia of the American Left.* 2d ed. New York: Oxford University Press.

Bullock, Allan, and R. B. Woodings, eds. 1992. *Fontana Dictionary of Modern Thinkers.* London: Fontana Press.

Cayton, Mary Kupiec, et al., eds. 1993. *Encyclopedia of American Social History.* 3 vols. New York: Charles Scribner's Sons.

Crawford, Anne, et al., eds. 1983. *Europa Biographical Dictionary of British Women: Over 1000 Notable Women from Britain's Past.* London: Europa Publications.

Crawford, Elizabeth. 1999. *The Women's Suffrage Movement, 1866–1928: A Reference Guide.* London: University College of London Press.

Crystal, David, ed. 1996. *The Cambridge Biographical Dictionary.* Cambridge: Cambridge University Press.

Cullen-DuPont, Kathryn, ed. 2000. *Encyclopedia of Women's History in America.* New York: Facts on File.

Current Biography. 1940– . New York: H. W. Wilson.

Davidson, Cathy N., and Linda Wagner Martin, eds. 1995. *Oxford Companion to Women's Writing in the United States.* Oxford: Oxford University Press.

Dictionary of American Biography 1946–1958, and indexes to Supplements 1–10, 1981–1996. New York: Scribner's.

Dictionary of Literary Biography. 1978– . Detroit: Gale.

Dictionary of National Biography. First published 1888–1900 in 64 vols. Supplements published every ten years, 1901–1985. London and Oxford: Oxford University Press.

Dictionary of New Zealand Biography. 1990. Vols. 1–5. Wellington, NZ: Allen and Unwin.

Dictionary of Obituaries of Modern British Radicals.
1989. Brighton: Harvester-Wheatsheaf.

Drabble, Margaret, ed. 2000. *Oxford Companion to English Literature.* 6th ed. Oxford: Oxford University Press.

Encyclopaedia Britannica. 1993. 15th ed. Chicago: University of Chicago Press and Encyclopaedia Britannica.

Encyclopedia of Social Work. 1995. New York: National Association of Social Workers Press.

Felder, Deborah G. 1996. *The 100 Most Influential Women: A Ranking of the 100 Greatest Women Past and Present.* London: Robinson.

Frost-Knappman, Elizabeth. 1994. *ABC-CLIO Companion to Women's Progress in America.* Santa Barbara: ABC-CLIO.

Gastrow, Shelagh, ed. 1995. *Who's Who in South African Politics.* Johannesburg: Ravan Press.

Golden, Kristen, and Barbara Findlen, eds. 1998. *Remarkable Women of the Twentieth Century: 100 Portraits of Achievement.* New York: Friedman/Fairfax Publishers.

Gordon, Peter, and David Doughan. 2001. *Dictionary of British Women's Organizations 1825–1960.* London: Woburn Press.

The Grolier Library of Women's Biographies. 1998. 10 vols. Danbury, CT: Grolier Educational.

Hamilton, Catherine J. 1892–1893. *Women Writers: Their Works and Ways.* 2 vols. London: Ward, Lock, Bowden.

Hannam, June, Mitzi Auchterlonie, and Katherine Holden. 2001. *International Encyclopedia of Women's Suffrage.* Santa Barbara: ABC-CLIO.

Harvey, Gayle J. 1993. *American Women Civil Rights Activists: Biobibliographies of 68 Leaders, 1825–1992.* Jefferson, NC: McFarland.

Hawkins-Dady, Mark, ed. 1996. *Reader's Guide to Literature in English.* Chicago: Fitzroy-Dearborn.

Hays, Frances. 1885. *Women of the Day: A Biographical Dictionary of Notable Contemporaries.* London: Chatto and Windus.

Hine, Darlene Clarke, et al., eds. 1993. *Black Women in America: An Historical Encyclopedia.* 2 vols. Bloomington: Indiana University Press.

Howard, Angela, and Frances M. Kavenik, eds. 2000. *Handbook of American Women's History.* 2d ed. Thousand Oaks, CA: Sage.

Hyman, Paula, and Deborah D. Moore, eds. 1998. *Jewish Women in America: An Historical Encyclopedia.* New York: Routledge.

International Who's Who of Women. 1992– . London: Europa.

Ireland, Norma Olin, ed. 1988. *Index to Women of the World from Ancient to Modern Times: A Supplement.* Metuchin, NJ: Scarecrow Press.

Josephson, Harold, Sandi Cooper, and Steven C. Hause et al., eds. 1985. *Biographical Dictionary of Modern Peace Leaders.* Westport, CT: Greenwood Press.

Logan, R. W., and M. R. Winston, eds. 1982. *Dictionary of American Negro Biography.* New York: W. W. Norton.

Low, W. A., and Virgil A. Clift, eds. 1984. *Encyclopedia of Black America.* New York: Da Capo Press.

MacDonald, Charlotte, ed. 1991. *The Book of New Zealand Women.* Wellington: Bridget Williams Books.

Marsh, James H., ed. 1988. *Canadian Encyclopedia.* 2d ed. 4 vols. Edmonton: Hurtig Publishers.

McCauley, Martin, ed. 1997. *Who's Who in Russia since 1900.* London: Routledge.

McGuire, William, and Leslie Wheeler, eds. 1993. *American Social Leaders: From Colonial Times to the Present.* Santa Barbara: ABC-CLIO.

Miller, Randall M., and Paul A. Cimbala, eds. 1996. *American Reform and Reformers: A Biographical Dictionary.* Westport, CT: Greenwood Press.

Nicholls, C. S., ed. 1993. *Dictionary of National Biography: Missing Persons.* Oxford: Oxford University Press.

Ó Céirín, Kit, and Cyril Ó Céirín, eds. 1996. *Women of Ireland: A Biographic Dictionary.* Kinvara, County Galway: Tír Eolas.

Ofosu-Appiah, L. A., ed. 1977. *Encyclopaedia Africana,* vol. 3, *Dictionary of African Biography.* Algonac, MI: Reference Publications.

Ogilvie, Marilyn, and Joy Harvey, eds. 2000. *Biographical Dictionary of Women in Science: Pioneering Lives from Ancient Times to the Mid-Twentieth Century.* 2000. London: Routledge.

Oldfield, Sybil. 2001. *Women Humanitarians: A Biographical Dictionary of British Women Active between 1900 and 1950.* London: Continuum.

———, ed. 1999. *Collective Bibliography of Women in Britain 1550–1900: A Select Annotated Bibliography.* London: Mansell.

O'Neill, Lois Decker, ed. 1979. *The Women's Book of World Records and Achievements.* New York: Doubleday.

Ousby, Ian, ed. 1993. *Cambridge Guide to Literature in English.* Cambridge: Cambridge University Press.

Parry, Melanie, ed. 1997. *Chambers Biographical Dictionary.* 6th ed. Edinburgh: Larousse.

Partnow, Elaine, ed. 1992. *The New Quotable Woman.* New York: Facts on File.

Penguin Biographical Dictionary of Women. 1998. Harmondsworth: Penguin.

Peterson, Barbara P., and He Hongfei, eds. 2000. *Notable Women of China.* Armonk, NY: M. E. Sharpe.

Pike, Douglas Henry, ed. 1966– . *Australian Dictionary of Biography.* Melbourne: Melbourne University Press.

Ploski, Harry A., and James Williams, eds. 1989. *The Negro Almanac: A Reference Work on the African American.* 5th ed. Detroit: Gale.

Rake, Alan, ed. 1992. *Who's Who in Africa.* Metuchen, NJ: Scarecrow Press.

Roberts, Frank C., ed. 1951–1960, 1961–1970, 1971–1979. *Obituaries from* The Times. 3 vols. Reading: Newspaper Archive Developments.

Saari, Peggy, ed. 1996. *Prominent Women of the Twentieth Century.* Detroit: Gale.

Sage, Lorna, ed. 1999. *The Cambridge Guide to Women's Writing.* Cambridge: Cambridge University Press.

Saxena, T. P., ed. 1979. *Women in Indian History: A Biographical Dictionary.* New Delhi: Kalyani Publishers.

Schenken, Suzanne O'Dea. 1999. *From Suffrage to the Senate: An Encyclopedia of American Women in Politics.* Santa Barbara: ABC-CLIO.

Schlueter, Paul, and June S. Schlueter, eds. 1998. *An Encyclopedia of British Women Writers.* 2d ed. New Brunswick: Rutgers University Press.

Sen Gupta, Padmini. 1944. *Pioneer Indian Women.* Bombay: Thacker.

Shattock, Joanne, ed. 1993. *Oxford Guide to British Women Writers.* Oxford: Oxford University Press.

Shukman, Harold, ed. 1988. *Blackwell Encyclopedia of the Russian Revolution.* Oxford: Blackwell.

Sicherman, Barbara, and Carol Hurd Green, eds. 1980. *Notable American Women 1607–1950: A Biographical Dictionary,* vol. 4, *The Modern Period.* Cambridge, MA: Belknap Press of Harvard University.

Smith, Jessie Carney, ed. 1992. *Notable Black American Women.* Detroit: Gale.

Sutherland, John, ed. 1988. *The Longman Companion to Victorian Fiction.* Harlow, Essex: Longman.

Sweeney, Patricia E., ed. 1993. *Biographies of British Women: An Annotated Bibliography.* London: Mansell.

Symons, Alan. 1997. *The Jewish Contribution to the Twentieth Century.* London: Polo Publishing.

Tenenbaum, Barbara A., ed. 1996. *Encyclopedia of Latin American History and Culture.* 5 vols. New York: Charles Scribner's Sons.

Todd, Janet, ed. 1987. *Dictionary of British and American Women Writers, 1600–1800.* London: Methuen.

———. 1989. *Dictionary of British Women Writers.* London: Routledge.

Trager, James. 1994. *The Women's Chronology: A Year-by-Year Record, from Prehistory to the Present.* London: Aurum Press.

Uerwey, E. J., ed. 1995. *New Dictionary of South African Biography.* Pretoria: HSRC Publishers.

Uglow, Jennifer, ed. 1998. *Macmillan Dictionary of Women's Biography.* 3d ed. Basingstoke: Macmillan.

Uweche, Raph, ed. 1996. *Africa Who's Who.* 3d ed. London: Africa Books.

———. 1996. *Makers of Modern Africa.* 3d ed. London: Africa Books.

Wasson, Tyler, ed. 1987. *Nobel Prize Winners: An H. W. Wilson Biographical Dictionary.* New York: H. W. Wilson.

Whitman, Alden, ed. 1988. *American Reformers: An H. W. Wilson Biographical Dictionary.* New York: H. W. Wilson.

Who Was Who. 1897– . London: A and C Black.

Who Was Who in America. 1943– . Chicago: Marquis Who's Who.

Who's Who in Australia. 1922– . Melbourne: Herald and Weekly Times.

Wilde, William H., Joy Hooton, and Barry Andrews, eds. 1994. *Oxford Companion to Australian Literature.* 2d ed. Melbourne: Oxford University Press.

Books and Articles by and about Individual Women

Ackroyd, Peter. 1990. *Dickens.* London: Sinclair Stevenson.

Acland, Alice. 1948. *Caroline Norton.* London: Constable.

Adams, Jerome R. 1991. *Liberators and Patriots of Latin America: Biographies of 23 Leaders from Doña Marina (1505–1530) to Bishop Romero (1917–1980).* Jefferson, NC: McFarland.

Addams, Jane. 1935. *My Friend, Julia Lathrop.* New York: Macmillan.

Adivar, Halide Edip. 1926. *Memoirs of Halide Edip.* Chicago: Century Company.

———. 1981 [1928]. *The Turkish Ordeal: Being the Further Memoirs of Halide Edip.* Reprint, Westport, CT: Hyperion.

Alberti, Johanna. 1996. *Eleanor Rathbone.* London: Sage Publications.

Albisetti, James. 1982. "Could Separate Be Equal? Helene Lange and Women's Education in Imperial Germany." *History of Education Quarterly* (Fall): 301–318.

Allen, Ann Taylor. 1985. "Mothers of the New Generation: Adele Schreiber, Helene Stöcker, and the Evolution of a German Idea of Motherhood, 1900–1914." *Signs* 10(3): 418–438.

Allen, Judith A. 1994. *Rose Scott: A Vision and Revision in Feminism.* Melbourne: Oxford University Press.

Allott, M. 1960. *Elizabeth Gaskell.* London: Longman's Green.

Anderson, Kathryn. 1997. "Steps to Political Equality: Woman Suffrage and Electoral Politics in the Lives of Emily Newell Blair, Anne Henrietta Martin, and Jeanette Rankin." *Frontiers* 18(1): 107–121.

Anderson, Louisa G. 1939. *Elizabeth Garrett Anderson.* London: Faber.

Anderson, Nancy Fix. 1922. *Margaret Fuller: A Psychological Biography.*

———. 1987. *Woman against Women in Victorian England: A Life of Eliza Linton.* Bloomington: Indiana University Press.

Andrews, Robert Hardy. 1967. *A Lamp for India: The Story of Madame Pandit.* London: Barker.

Anthony, Katharine Susan. 1954. *Susan B. Anthony: Her Personal History and Her Era.* Garden City, NY: Doubleday.

Anthony, Michael. 1997. *Historical Dictionary of Trinidad and Tobago.* Lanham, MD: Scarecrow Press.

Asbury, Herbert. 1929. *Carry Nation.* New York: Alfred A. Knopf.

Ashby, Dame Margery Corbett. 1996. *Memoirs.* Privately printed.

Ashrawi, Hanan. 1995. *This Side of Peace: A Personal Account.* London: Simon and Schuster.

Askwith, Betty E. 1969. *Lady Dilke: A Biography.* London: Chatto and Windus.

Astor, Michael. 1963. *Tribal Feeling.* London: John Murray.

Astor, Nancy. 1923. *My Two Countries.* London: W. Heinemann.

Atkinson, Linda. 1978. *Mother Jones: The Most Dangerous Woman in America.* New York: Crown Publishers.

Aubrey, Wallace, and David Gancher. 1993. *Eco-Heroes: Twelve Tales of Environmental Victory.* San Francisco: Mercury House.

Aung San Suu Ki. 1991. *Freedom from Fear and Other Writings.* London: Penguin.

———. 1997. *The Voice of Hope: Conversations with Alan Clements.* London: Penguin.

Bacon, Margaret Hope. 1976. *I Speak for My Slave Sister: The Life of Abby Kelley Foster.* New York: Thomas Y. Crowell.

———. 1980. *Valiant Friend: The Life of Lucretia Mott.* New York: Walker.

Bailey, Hilary. 1987. *Vera Brittain: The Story of the Woman Who Wrote* Testament of Youth. Harmondsworth: Penguin.

Bair, Deirdre. 1990. *Simone de Beauvoir: A Life.* London: Jonathan Cape.

Baker, Sara Josephine. 1939. *Fighting for Life.* New York: Macmillan.

Balfour, B., ed. 1925. *Letters of Constance Lytton.* London: William Heinemann.

Balfour, Lady Frances. 1918. *Dr Elsie Inglis.* London: Hodder and Stoughton.

Balme, Jenifer Hobhouse. 1994. *To Love One's Enemies: The Work and Life of Emily Hobhouse.* Cobbe Hill, BC: Hobhouse Trust.

Banks, Olive. Banner, Lois W. 1980. *Elizabeth Cady Stanton: A Radical for Women's Rights.* Boston: Little, Brown.

Banning, Evelyn I. 1973. *Helen Hunt Jackson.* New York: Vanguard.

Barlow, Tani, ed. 1989. *I Myself Am a Woman: Selected Writings of Ding Ling.* Boston: Beacon Press.

Barnes, Cyril J. 1981. *Words of Catherine Booth.* London: Salvationist.

Barnes, Gilbert H., and Dwight L. Dumond. 1934. *The Letters of Theodore Dwight Weld, Angelina Grimké Weld, and Sarah Grimké 1822–1844.* New York: D. Appleton-Century.

Barnes, John. 1978. *Evita, First Lady: A Biography of Eva Perón.* New York: Grove Press.

Barrett, Rosa M. 1907. *Ellice Hopkins.* London: Wells, Gardner, Darton.

Barrios de Chungara, Domitla. 1978. *Let Me Speak.* London: Stage 1.

Barry, Joseph. 1975. *Infamous Woman: The Life of George Sand.* Garden City, NY: Doubleday.

Barry, Kathleen. 1988. *Susan B. Anthony: A Biography of a Singular Feminist.* New York: New York University Press.

Barton, Anna. 1937. *Mother Bloor: The Spirit of '76.* New York: Workers Library.

Barton, William E. 1922. *The Life of Clara Barton, Founder of the American Red Cross.* Boston: Houghton Mifflin.

Basu, Aparna. 1986. *The Pathfinder: Dr. Muthulakshmi Reddi.* Pune: All India Women's Conference.

Bates, Daisy. 1962. *The Long Shadow of Little Rock: A Memoir by Daisy Bates.* New York: David McKay.

Baxandall, Rosalyn Fraad. 1987. *Words on Fire: The Life and Writings of Elizabeth Gurley Flynn.* New Brunswick, NJ: Rutgers University Press.

Baylor, Ruth M. 1965. *Elizabeth Palmer Peabody: Kindergarten Pioneer.* Philadelphia: University of Philadelphia Press.

Beals, Carleton. 1962. *Cyclone Carry: The Story of Carry Nation.* Philadelphia: Chilton.

Bearden, Jim, and Linda Jean Butler. 1977. *Shadd: The Life and Times of Mary Shadd Cary.* Toronto: NC Press.

Beauvoir, Simone de. 1972 [1953]. *The Second Sex.* Reprint, Harmondsworth: Penguin.

Bedell, R. Meredith. 1983. *Stella Benson.* Boston: Twayne.

Beier, Ulli. 1985. *Quandamooka: The Art of Kath Walker.* Bathurst, NSW: Robert Brown and Associates in Association with the Aboriginal Artists Agency.

Beik, Doris, and Paul Beik. 1993. *Flora Tristan: Utopian Feminist.* Bloomington: Indiana University Press.

Bell, Enid Moberley. 1943. *Octavia Hill.* London: Constable.

———. 1962 [1942]. *Josephine Butler: Flame of Fire.* Reprint, London: Constable.

Belton, Neil. 1998. *The Good Listener. Helen Bamber: A Life against Cruelty.* London: Weidenfeld and Nicolson.

Benham, Mary Lile. 1975. *Nellie McClung.* Toronto: Fitzhenry and Whiteside.

Bennett, Daphne. 1990. *Emily Davies and the Liberation of Women 1830–1921.* London: André Deutsch.

Bennett, Olivia. 1988. *Annie Besant.* London: Hamish Hamilton.

Bennett, Yvonne. 1987. *Vera Brittain: Women and Peace.* London: Peace Pledge Union.

Bernard, Jacqueline. 1990. *Journey toward Freedom: The Story of Sojourner Truth.* New York: Feminist Press.

Berry, Paul, and Alan Bishop. 1985. *Testament of a Generation: The Journalism of Vera Brittain and Winifred Holtby.* London: Virago.

Berry, Paul, and Mark Bostridge. 1995. *Vera Brittain: A Life.* London: Chatto and Windus.

Besant, Annie. 1903. *An Autobiography.* 2d ed. London: T. Fisher Unwin.

———. 1913. *Wake Up India: A Plea for Social Reform.* Madras: Theosophical Publishing House.

Bess, Michael. 1993. *Realism, Utopia and the Mushroom Cloud: Four Activist Intellectuals and the Strategies for Peace 1945–1989.* Chicago: University of Chicago Press.

Bethune, Mary McCleod. 1999. *Mary Mcleod Bethune: Building a Better World: Essays and Selected Documents.* Edited by Audrey Thomas McCluskey and Elaine M. Smith. Bloomington: Indiana University Press.

Bhushan, Jamila Brij. 1976. *Kamaladevi Chattopadhyaya: Portrait of a Rebel.* New Delhi: Abhinav.

Billington-Greig, Teresa. 1911. *The Militant Suffrage Movement: Emancipation in a Hurry.* London: F. Palmer.

Birney, Catherine H. 1969 [1885]. *Sarah and Angelina Grimké: The First American Women Advocates of Abolition and Women's Rights.* Reprint, Westport, CT: Greenwood Press.

Black, Allida M. 1996. *Casting Her Own Shadow: Eleanor Roosevelt and the Shaping of Postwar Liberalism.* New York: Columbia University Press.

Blackburn, Helen. 1971 [1902]. *Women's Suffrage: A Record of the Women's Suffrage Movement in the British Isles with Biographical Sketches of Miss Becker.* Reprint, New York: Kraus Reprint Company.

Blackburn, Julia. 1994. *Daisy Bates in the Desert.* New York: Pantheon.

Blackwell, Alice Stone. 1930. *Lucy Stone, Pioneer of Women's Rights.* Boston: Little, Brown.

Blanchard, Paula. 1987. *Margaret Fuller: From Transcendentalism to Revolution.* New York: Delacorte Press.

Bloomer, Dexter C. 1895. *Life and Writings of Amelia Bloomer.* Boston: Arena.

Blumberg, Dorothy Rose. 1966. *Florence Kelley: The Making of a Social Pioneer.* New York: Augustus Kelley.

Bodichon, Barbara. 1972. *An American Diary 1857–1858.* London: Routledge and Kegan Paul.

Bogle, Joanna. 1993. *Caroline Chisholm: The Emigrant's Friend.* Leominster: Gracewing.

Bok, Issela. 1991. *Alva Myrdal: A Daughter's Memoir.* Reading: MA: Addison-Wesley.

Bolster, Angela. 1990. *Catherine McAuley: Venerable for Mercy.* Dublin: Dominican.

Bomford, Janet. 1993. *That Dangerous Persuasive Woman: A Life of Vida Goldstein.* Carlton, Victoria: Melbourne University Press.

Bondfield, Margaret. 1949. *A Life's Work.* London: Hutchinson.

Bonner, Yelena. 1986. *Alone Together.* New York: Alfred A. Knopf.

———. 1992. *Mothers and Daughters.* New York: Alfred A. Knopf.

Bordin, Ruth. 1986. *Frances Willard: A Biography.* Chapel Hill: University of North Carolina Press.

Boyd, Nancy. 1982. *Josephine Butler, Octavia Hill, Florence Nightingale: Three Victorian Women Who Changed Their World.* London: Macmillan.

Boydston, J., et al., eds. 1988. *The Limits of Sisterhood: The Beecher Sisters on Women's Rights and Women's Sphere.* Chapel Hill: University of North Carolina Press.

Bradbrook, M. C. 1975. *Barbara Bodichon, George Eliot and the Limits of Feminism.* Oxford: Blackwell.

Bradburn, Elizabeth. 1989. *Margaret McMillan: Portrait of a Pioneer.* London: Routledge.

Bradford, Sarah H. 1961 [1886]. *Harriet Tubman: The Moses of Her People.* Reprint, New York: Corinth (originally published as *Scenes in the Life of Harriet Tubman,* 1869).

Brady, Kathleen. 1954. *Ida Tarbell: Portrait of a Muckraker: Ida Tarbell's Lifetime in Journalism.* New York: Putnam.

Braker, Regina. 1995. *Weapons of Women Writers: Berth von Suttner's* Die Waffen Nieder! *as Political Literature in the Tradition of Harriet Beecher Stowe's* Uncle Tom's Cabin. New York: Peter Lang.

———. 1995. "Bertha von Suttner's Spiritual Daughters: The Feminist Pacifism of Anita Augspurg, Lida Gustava Heymann, and Helene Stöcker at the International Congress of Women at the Hague, 1915." *Women's Studies International Forum* 18(2): 103–111.

Brammer, Leila R. 2000. *Excluded from Suffrage History: Matilda Joslyn Gage, Nineteenth Century*

American Feminist. Westport, CT: Greenwood Press.

Bramwell-Booth, Catherine. 1970. *Catherine Booth: The Story of Her Loves.* London: Hodder and Stoughton.

Breault, William. 1986. *The Lady from Dublin.* Boston: Quinlan.

Bremer, Charlotte, ed. 1868. *Life, Letters & Posthumous Works of Frederika Bremer.* Translated by Frederick Milow. London: Sampson Low.

Bremer, Frederika. 1968 [1853]. *The Homes of the New World: Impressions of America.* Translated by Mary Howitt. Reprint, New York: Negro University Press.

Briant, Keith. 1962. *Marie Stopes: A Biography.* London: Hogarth Press.

A Brief Sketch of the Life and Labours of Mrs. Elizabeth Heyrick. 1862. Leicester: n.p.

Brinkley, Douglas. 2001. *Mine Eyes Have Seen the Glory: The Life of Rosa Parks.* London: Weidenfeld.

Brittain, Vera. 1940. *Testament of Friendship: The Story of Winifred Holtby.* London: Macmillan.

———. 1963. *Pethick-Lawrence. A Portrait.* London: Allen and Unwin.

———. 1965. *Envoy Extraordinary.* London: George Allen and Unwin.

———. 1979 [1957]. *Testament of Experience: An Autobiographical Story of the Years 1925–1950.* Reprint, London: Virago.

———. 1981. *Chronicle of Youth: Vera Brittain's War Diary 1913–1917.* London: Victor Gollancz.

Brittain, Vera, and G. Handley-Taylor, eds. 1960. *Selected Letters of Winifred Holtby and Vera Brittain 1920–1935.* London: A. Brown.

Brittain, Vera, and J. S. Reid, eds. 1960. *Selected Letters of Winifred Holtby and Vera Brittain.* London: A. Brown.

Brody, Miriam. 1983. "Mary Wollstonecraft: Sexuality and Women's Rights." In Dale Spender, ed., *Feminist Theorists: Three Centuries of Women's Intellectual Traditions.* London: Women's Press.

———. 1992. Introduction to *A Vindication of the Rights of Woman.* Harmondsworth: Penguin.

Brooks, Gladys. 1957. *Three Wise Virgins.* New York: Dutton.

Brooks, Paul. 1972. *The House of Life: Rachel Carson at Work.* Boston: Houghton Mifflin.

Brownmiller, Susan. 1970. *Shirley Chisholm: A Biography.* Garden City, NY: Doubleday.

Buell, Janet W. 1990. "Alva Belmont: From Socialite to Feminist." *The Historian* 52(2): 219–241.

Bullock, Ian, and Richard Pankhurst, eds. 1992. *Sylvia Pankhurst: From Artist to Anti-Fascist.* Basingstoke: Macmillan.

Burch, Joann Johansen. 1994. *Marian Wright*

Edelman, Children's Champion. Brookfield, CT: Millbrook Press.

Burchill, Julie. 1998. *Diana.* London: Weidenfeld and Nicolson.

Burstall, Sara. 1938. *Frances Mary Buss: An Educational Pioneer.* London: Society for Promoting Christian Knowledge.

Burton, Antoinette. 1995. "Fearful Bodies into Disciplined Subjects: Pleasure, Romance and the Family Drama of Colonial Reform in Mary Carpenter's *Six Months in India.*" *Signs* 20(3), 545–574.

———. 1996. "Introduction to Cornelia Sorabji's 'Stray Thoughts of an Indian Girl.'" *Indian Journal of Gender Studies* 3(2): 251–255.

———. 1998. "From 'Child-Bride' to 'Hindoo Lady': Rukhmabai and the Debate about Sexual Respectability in Imperial Britain." *American Historical Review* 104(4): 1119–1146.

Burton, David A. 1995. *Clara Barton: In the Service of Humanity.* Westport, CT: Greenwood Press.

Burton, Hester. 1949. *Barbara Bodichon.* London: John Murray.

Butler, A. S. G. 1954. *Portrait of Josephine Butler.* London: Faber and Faber.

Butler, Marilyn. 1972. *Maria Edgeworth: A Literary Biography.* Oxford: Clarendon Press.

Buxton, Dorothy, and Edward Fuller. 1931. *The White Flame.* London: Longmans.

Byrne, Lavinia. 1994. *Woman at the Altar.* London: Mowbray.

———. 2000. *The Journey Is My Home.* London: Hodder and Stoughton.

Caird, Mona. 1896. "Beyond the Pale: An Appeal on Behalf of the Victims of Vivisection." London: Bijou Library.

Caldicott, Helen. 1997. *A Desperate Passion: An Autobiography.* New York: W. W. Norton.

Camp, Helen C. 1995. *Iron in Her Soul: Elizabeth Gurley Flynn and the American Left.* Pullman: Washington State University Press.

Campbell, Beatrix. 1998. *Diana: How Sexual Politics Shook the Monarchy.* London: Women's Press.

Candy, Catherine. 1994. "Relating Feminisms, Nationalism, and Imperialisms: Ireland, India, and Margaret Cousins' Sexual Politics." *Women's History Review* 3(4): 581–594.

Cappa, Charles. 1992. *Margaret Fuller: An American Romantic Life.* New York: Oxford University Press.

Cardozo, Nancy. 1979. *Maud Gonne: Lucky Eyes and a High Heart.* London: Gollancz.

Carey, Rosa Nouchette. 1899. *Twelve Notable Good Women.* London: Hutchinson.

Carmichael, Amy. 1903. *Things as They Are: Mission Work in Southern India.* New York: Fleming H. Revell.

Carpenter, J. Estlin. 1879. *The Life and Work of Mary Carpenter.* London: Macmillan.

Carroll, Mary Teresa Airtin. 1887. *Life of Catherine McAuley.* New York: D. and J. Sadlier.

Casgrain, Thérèse. 1972. *A Woman in a Man's World.* Toronto: McClelland and Stewart.

Castle, Barbara. 1987. *Sylvia and Christabel Pankhurst.* Harmondsworth: Penguin Books.

———. 1993. *Fighting All the Way.* London: Macmillan.

Cate, Curtis. 1975. *George Sand: A Biography.* Boston: Houghton Mifflin.

Cazamian, Louis. 1973. *The Social Novel in England 1830–1850: Dickens, Disraeli, Mrs. Gaskell, Kingsley.* London: Routledge and Kegan Paul.

Cazden, Elizabeth. 1983. *Antoinette Brown Blackwell: A Biography.* New York: Feminist Press.

Ceplair, Larry, ed. 1989. *The Public Years of Sarah and Angelina Grimké: Selected Writings, 1835–1839.* New York: Columbia University Press.

Chadakoff, Rochelle, ed. 1989. *Eleanor Roosevelt's My Day.* New York: Pharos Books.

Chapman, Mrs. E. F. 1891. *Sketches of Some Distinguished Indian Women.* London: W. H. Allen.

Chappell, Jennie. 1910. *Noble Workers: Sketches of the Life-Work of Frances Willard, Agnes Weston, Sister Dora, Catherine Booth, the Baroness Burdett-Coutts, Lady Henry Somerset, Sarah Robinson, Mrs. Fawcett and Mrs. Gladstone.* London: S. W. Partridge.

Chapple, J. B. V., and Arthur Pollard. 1966. *The Letters of Mrs. Gaskell.* Manchester: Manchester University Press.

Chattopadhyaya, Kamala Devi [sic]. 1937. *The Awakening of Indian Women.* Madras: Everyman's Press.

Chedzoy, Alan. 1992. *A Scandalous Woman: The Story of Caroline Norton.* London: Allison and Busby.

Chen, Constance C. 1996. *The Sex Side of Life: Mary Ware Dennett's Pioneering Battle for Birth Control and Sex Education.* New York: New Press.

Cheney, Ednah Dow. 1902. *Reminiscences of Ednah Dow Chéney (born Littlehale).* Boston: Lee and Shepard.

Chesler, Ellen. 1992. *Woman of Valor: Margaret Sanger and the Birth Control Movement in America.* New York: Simon and Schuster.

Chevigny, Belle Gale. 1976. *The Woman and the Myth: Margaret Fuller's Life and Writings.* Old Westbury, NY: Feminist Press.

Chew, Doris Nield. 1982. *Ada Nield Chew: The Life and Writings of a Working Woman.* London: Virago.

Child, Lydia Maria. 1843, 1845. *Letters from New York.* Vol. 2. New York: C. S. Francis and Co.

Chisholm, Anne. 1979. *Nancy Cunard: A Biography.* New York: Alfred A. Knopf.

Chisholm, Shirley. 1970. *Unbought and Unbossed.* Boston: Houghton Mifflin.

Cimbala, Paul A. 1997. *Against the Tide: Women Reformers in American Society.* Westport, CT: Praeger.

Clayton, Cherry. 1983. *Olive Schreiner.* Johannesburg: McGraw Hill.

Clements, Barbara Evans. 1979. *Bolshevik Feminist: The Life of Aleksandra Kollontai.* Bloomington: Indiana University Press.

Clifford, Deborah Pinkman. 1979. *Mine Eyes Have Seen the Glory: A Biography of Julia Ward Howe.* Boston: Little, Brown.

———. 1992. *Crusader for Freedom: A Life of Lydia Maria Child.* Boston: Beacon Press.

Clough, Blanche A. 1903. *Memoir of Annie Jemima Clough, First Principal of Newnham College.* 2d ed. London: Edward Arnold.

Cobbe, Frances Power. 1894. *The Life of Frances Power Cobbe.* 2 vols. London: Allen and Unwin.

Cochrane, Kathie. 1994. *Oodgeroo.* St. Lucia: University of Queensland Press.

Coil, Suzanne M. 1993. *Harriet Beecher Stowe:* New York: F. Watts.

Cole, Charlotte. 1989. *Olympia Brown: The Battle for Equality.* Racine, WI: Mother Courage Press.

Cole, G. D. H. 1978. "Louise Michel." *Observer Magazine* (26 November): 30–39.

Cole, Margaret. 1945. *Beatrice Webb.* London: Longman Green.

———, ed. 1974 [1949]. *The Webbs and Their Work.* Reprint, Brighton: Harvester Press.

Coles, Robert. 1987. *Dorothy Day: A Radical Devotion.* Reading, MA: Addison-Wesley.

Collett, Camilla. 1991. *The District Governors' Daughters.* Translated by Kirsten Seaver. Norwich: Norvik Press.

Collingwood, Jeremy, and Margaret Collingwood. 1990. *Hannah More.* Oxford: Lion Publishing.

Collis, Maurice. 1960. *Nancy Astor: An Informal Biography.* London: Faber and Faber.

Colman, Penny. 1992. *Breaking the Chains: The Crusade of Dorothea Lynde Dix.* White Hall, VA: Shoe Tree Press.

———. 1993. *Fannie Lou Hamer and the Fight for the Vote.* Brookfield, CT: Millbrook Press.

———. 1994. *Mother Jones and the March of Mill Children.* Brookfield, CT: Millbrook Press.

Colmore, Gertrude. 1988. "The Life of Emily Wilding Davison." In Ann Morley and Liz Stanley, eds., *The Life and Death of Emily Wilding Davison.* London: Woman's Press.

Comma-Maynard, Olga. 1971. *The Briarend Pattern: The Story of Audrey Jeffers O.B.E. and the Coterie of Social Workers.* Port of Spain: Busby's Printerie.

Conn, Frances G. 1972. *Ida Tarbell, Muckraker.* Nashville: T. Nelson.

Conrad, Earl. 1942. *Harriet Tubman: Negro Soldier and Abolitionist.* New York: International Publishers.

Cook, Blanche Wiesen. 1993, 2000. *Eleanor Roosevelt.* Vol. 1, *1884–1932;* vol. 2, *1933–1938.* New York: Viking.

———, ed. 1976. *Toward the Great Change: Crystal and Max Eastman on Feminism, Antimilitarism, and Revolution.* New York: Garland.

———. 1978. *Crystal Eastman on Women and Revolution.* New York: Oxford University Press.

Cook, Sir Edward. 1913. *The Life of Florence Nightingale.* London: Macmillan.

Coon, Anne C., ed. 1994. *Hear Me Patiently: The Reform Speeches of Amelia Jenks Bloomer.* Westport, CT: Greenwood Press.

Cooper, Janet. 1972. *Catherine Spence.* Melbourne: Oxford University Press.

Cope, Zachary. 1958. *Florence Nightingale and the Doctors.* London: Museum.

Corcoran, Teresa S. 1982. *Vida Dutton Scudder.* Boston: G. K. Hall.

Corfield, Kenneth. 1986. "Elizabeth Heyrick: Radical Quaker." In Gail Malmgreen, ed., *Religion in the Lives of English Women, 1760–1930.* London: Croom Helm.

Coss, Claire, ed. 1989. *Lillian D. Wald, Progressive Activist.* New York: Feminist Press.

Costin, Lela B. 1983. *Two Sisters for Social Justice: A Biography of Grace and Edith Abbott.* Urbana: University of Illinois Press.

Coté, Jane. 1991. *Fanny and Anna Parnell: Ireland's Patriot Sisters.* Basingstoke: Macmillan.

Cott, Nancy F., ed. 1991. *A Woman Making History: Mary Ritter Beard through Her Letters.* New Haven, CT: Yale University Press.

Cousins, James, and Margaret Cousins. 1950. *We Two Together.* Madras: Ganesh.

Coxhead, Elizabeth. 1965. *Daughters of Erin: Five Women of the Irish Renaissance.* London: Secker and Warburg.

Cranstoun Nevill, John. 1976. *Harriet Martineau.* Norwood, PA: Norwood Editions.

Cresswell, Walter D'Arcy. 1948. *Margaret McMillan: A Memoir.* London: Hutchinson.

Cromwell, Adelaide M. 1986. *An African Victorian Feminist: The Life and Times of Adelaide Smith Casely Hayford 1868–1960.* London: Frank Cass.

Cromwell, Otelia. 1971 [1958]. *Lucretia Mott.* Reprint, New York: Russell and Russell.

Cronwright-Schreiner, S. C. 1924. *The Life of Olive Schreiner.* London: F. T. Unwin.

Cross, Maire. 1992. *The Feminism of Flora Tristan.* Oxford: Berg.

Crowley, Terence Allan. 1990. *Agnes MacPhail and the Politics of Equality.* Toronto: J. Lorimer.

Cullen, Mary. 1995. "Anna Maria Haslam." In Mary Cullen and Maria Luddy, eds., *Women: Power and Consciousness in Nineteenth-Century Ireland: Eight Biographical Studies.* Dublin: Attic Press.

Cullen, Mary, and Maria Luddy. 1995. *Women, Power, and Consciousness in Nineteenth-Century Ireland. Eight Biographical Studies.* Dublin: Attic Press.

Cunard, Nancy. 1931. "Black Man and White Ladyship: An Anniversary." Privately printed.

———. 1996. [1934]. *Negro: An Anthology Collected and Edited by Nancy Cunard.* Reprint, New York: Continuum.

Cunningham, Gail. 1978. *The New Woman and the Victorian Novel.* London: Macmillan.

Curtiss, Richard H. "Shahnaz Bukhari—A Single-Minded Activist for Women's Rights." In "Washington Report on Middle East Affairs," www.washington-report.org/.

Dadson, True. 1973. *The Golden Strings.* Toronto: Griffin House.

Daffron, Carolyn. 1987. *Gloria Steinem.* New York: Chelsea House.

Dallard, Shyrlee. 1990. *Ella Baker: A Leader behind the Scenes.* Englewood Cliffs, NJ: Silver Burdett Press.

Daniels, Doris Groshen. 1989. *Always a Sister: The Feminism of Lillian D. Wald.* New York: Feminist Press.

Darley, Gillian. 1990. *Octavia Hill: A Life.* London: Constable.

Datlot, N., J. Fuchs, and D. A. Powell. 1991. *The World of George Sand.* Westport, CT: Greenwood Press.

David, Dierdre. 1987. *Intellectual Woman and Victorian Patriarchy: Harriet Martineau, Elizabeth Barrett Browning and George Eliot.* Ithaca: Cornell University Press.

Davis, Allen F. 1973. *American Heroine: Life and Legend of Jane Addams.* New York: Oxford University Press.

Davis, Mary. 1999. *Sylvia Pankhurst: A Life in Radical Politics.* London: Pluto.

Day, Dorothy. 1952. *The Long Loneliness: The Autobiography of Dorothy Day.* New York: Harper.

De Ruiz, Dana Catharine, and Richard Larios. 1992. *La Causa: The Migrant Farmworkers' Story.* Austin, TX: Raintree Steck-Vaughn.

De'Ath, Wilfred. 1970. *Barbara Castle: A Portrait from Life.* London: Clifton.

Demers, Patricia. 1996. *The World of Hannah More.* Lexington: University Press of Kentucky.

Desanti, Dominique. 1976. *A Woman in Revolt: A Biography of Flora Tristan.* Translated by Elizabeth Zelvin. New York: Crown Publishers.

Devaliant, Judith. 1992. *Kate Sheppard, a Biography: The Fight for Women's Votes in New Zealand.* Auckland: Penguin Books.

Diamond, Marion. 1999. *Emigration and Empire: The Life of Maria S. Rye.* New York: Garland Publishing.

Dickson, Donna. 1988. *George Sand: A Brave Man, the Most Womanly Woman.* Oxford: Berg.

Dillon, Mary Earhart. 1944. *Frances Willard: From Prayer to Politics.* Chicago: University of Chicago Press.

Ding Ling. 1985. *Miss Sophie's Diary and Other Stories.* Translated by W. J. F. Jenner. Beijing: China International Book Trading.

Dinnage, Rosemary. 1987. *Annie Besant.* Harmondsworth: Penguin.

Dirie, Waris, and Cathleen Miller. 1999. *Desert Flower: The Extraordinary Life of a Desert Nomad.* London: Virago.

Doig, Desmond. 1976. *Mother Teresa: Her People and Her Work.* London: Collins.

Dongre, R. K., and J. F. Patterson. 1963. *Pandita Ramabai: A Life of Faith and Prayer.* Madras: Christian Literature Society.

Dooley, Dolores. 1996. *Equality in Community: Sexual Equality in the Writings of William Thompson and Anna Doyle Wheeler.* Cork: Cork University Press.

Dorkenoo, Efua. 1992. *Female Genital Mutilation: Proposals for Change.* London: Minority Group.

———. 1994. *Cutting the Rose: Female Genital Mutilation: The Practice and Its Prevention.* London: Minority Rights Group.

Dreier, Mary E. 1950. *Margaret Dreier Robins: Her Life, Letters, and Work.* New York: Island Press Cooperative.

Dresner, Ruth Rapp. 1981. "The Work of Bertha Pappenheim." *Judaism* 30: 204–211.

Drinnan, Richard. 1961. *Rebel in Paradise: A Biography of Emma Goldman.* Chicago: University of Chicago Press.

DuBois, Ellen Carol. 1981. *The Elizabeth Cady Stanton–Susan B. Anthony Reader: Correspondence, Writings, Speeches.* Rev. ed. Boston: Northeastern University Press.

———. 1997. *Harriet Stanton Blatch and the Winning of Woman Suffrage.* New Haven, CT: Yale University Press.

Duelli-Klein, Renate. 1983. "Hedwig Dohm: Passionate Theorist." In Dale Spender, ed., *Feminist Theorists: Three Centuries of Women's Intellectual Traditions.* London: Women's Press.

Duffus, Robert L. 1938. *Lillian Wald: Neighbor and Crusader.* New York: Macmillan.

Dunn, W. H., and I. L. M. Richardson. 1961. *Sir Robert Stout: A Biography.* Wellington: A. H. and A. W. Reed.

Duster, Alfreda M., ed. 1970. *Crusade for Justice: The Autobiography of Ida B. Wells.* Chicago: University of Chicago Press.

Dutt, Guru Sadaya. 1929. *A Woman of India: Being the Life of Sarojini Nalini.* London: Hogarth Press.

Dyer, Helen. 1900. *Pandita Ramabai: The Story of Her Life.* New York: Fleming H. Revell.

Eckhardt, Celia M. 1894. *Fanny Wright: Rebel in America.* Cambridge, MA: Harvard University Press.

Edelman, Marian Wright. 1992. *The Measure of Our Success: A Letter to My Children and Yours.* Boston: Beacon Press.

Edinger, Dora. 1968. *Bertha Pappenheim: Freud's Anna O.* Highland Park, IL: Congregation Solel.

Edwards, Samuel. 1972. *George Sand: A Biography of the First Modern Liberated Woman.* New York: McKay.

Eisemann, Alberta. 1976. *Rebels and Reformers: Biographies of Four Jewish Americans.* Garden City, NY: Zenith Books.

Eliot, George. 1963. "Margaret Fuller and Mary Wollstonecraft." In T. Pinney, ed., *The Essays of George Eliot.* London: Routledge and Kegan Paul.

Elliot, Elisabeth. 1987. *A Chance to Die—The Life and Legacy of Amy Carmichael.* Grand Rapids, MI: Fleming H. Revell.

Ellsberg, Robert, ed. 1983. *By Little and by Little: The Selected Writings of Dorothy Day.* New York: Knopf.

Ellsworth, Edward D. 1979. *Liberators of the Female Mind: The Shirreff Sisters: Education as Reform and the Women's Movement.* London: Greenwood Press.

Elwood, Carter. 1992. *Inessa Armand: Revolutionary and Feminist.* Cambridge: Cambridge University Press.

Emerson, Sarah Hopper. 1896. *The Life of Abby Hopper Gibbons, Told Chiefly through Her Correspondence.* 2 vols. New York: Putnam.

Epstein, Beryl. 1948. *Lillian Wald: Angel of Henry Street.* New York: J. Messner.

Eunson, Roby. 1975. *The Soong Sisters.* New York: Franklin Watts.

Falk, Candace. 1984. *Love, Anarchy and Emma Goldman.* New York: Holt, Rinehart, and Winston.

Fancourt, Mary St. John. 1965. *They Dared to Be Doctors: Elizabeth Blackwell and Elizabeth Garrett Anderson.* London: Longman's Green.

Farnham, Eliza. 1972 [1846]. *Life in Prairie Land.* Reprint, New York: Arno Press.

———. 1972 [1856]. *California In-doors and Out.* Reprint, Nieuwkoop: De Graaf.

Fauset, Arthur H. 1971 [1938]. *Sojourner Truth: God's Faithful Pilgrim.* Reprint, Chapel Hill: University of North Carolina Press.

Fawcett, Millicent. 1924. *What I Remember.* London: T. Fisher Unwin.

Fawcett, Millicent Garrett, and E. M. Turner. 1927. *Josephine Butler: Her Work and Principles, and Their Meaning for the Twentieth Century.* London: ASMH.

Felner, Julie. 1998. "Dolores Huerta." *Ms.,* January–February, 46–49.

Felsenthal, Carol. 1981. *The Sweetheart of the Silent*

Majority: The Biography of Phyllis Schlafly. Garden City: Doubleday.

Felton, Monica. 1966. *A Child Widow's Story*. London: Gollancz.

Fennelly, Marion. 1988. *Each in Her Own Way: Five Women Leaders of the Developing World*. Boulder, CO: Lynne Rienner.

Ferrell, John. 1967. *Beloved Lady: A History of Jane Addams's Ideas on Reform and Peace*. Baltimore: Johns Hopkins University Press.

Fetherling, Dale. 1974. *Mother Jones, the Miner's Angel: A Portrait*. Carbondale: Southern Illinois University Press.

Field, Frank. 1996. "Portrait of a Great MP" [Barbara Castle]. *Financial Times,* 21 September.

Finch, Edith. 1947. *Carey Thomas of Bryn Mawr*. New York. Harper.

Fineman, Irving. 1961. *Woman of Valor: The Life of Henrietta Szold, 1860–1945*. New York: Simon and Schuster.

First, Ruth, and Ann Scott. 1980. *Olive Schreiner*. London: Deutsch.

Fisher, Dexter. 1979. "Zitkala-Ša: The Evolution of a Writer." *American Indian Quarterly* 5: 229–238.

Fisher, John. 1971. *That Miss Hobhouse*. London: Secker and Warburg.

Fitzpatrick, Kathleen. 1923. *Lady Henry Somerset*. London: Cape.

Fleming, Susie, ed. 1986. *Eleanor Rathbone: Spokeswoman for a Movement*. Bristol: Falling Wall Press.

Fletcher, Sheila. 1989. *Maude Royden: A Life*. Oxford: Blackwell.

Flexner, Eleanor. 1972. *Mary Wollstonecraft: A Biography*. New York: Coward, McCann and Geoghegan.

Flynn, Elizabeth Gurley. 1942. *Daughters of America: Ella Reeve Bloor and Anita Whitney*. New York: Workers Library.

Foner, Philip. 1967. *Helen Keller: Her Socialist Years—Writings and Speeches*. New York: International Publishers.

———, ed. 1983. *Mother Jones Speaks*. New York: Monad Press.

———, 1984. *Clara Zetkin: Selected Writings*. New York: International Publishers.

Ford, Charles H. 1996. *Hannah More: A Critical Biography*. New York: P. Lang.

Ford, Hugh D., ed. 1968. *Nancy Cunard: Brave Poet, Indomitable Rebel, 1896–1965*. Philadelphia: Chilton.

Forest, Jim. 1986. *Love Is the Measure: A Biography of Dorothy Day*. New York: Paulist.

Forster, Margaret. 1986. *Significant Sisters: The Grassroots of Active Feminism, 1839–1939*. Penguin: Harmondsworth.

Foster, Charles H. 1954. *The Rungless Ladder: Harriet Beecher Stowe and New England Puritanism*. Durham: Duke University Press.

Fowler, Robert Booth. 1986. *Carrie Catt: Feminist Politician*. Boston: Northeastern University Press.

Fox, James. 1978. "Feminists in the Firing Line" [re: Qiu Jin, Alexandra Kollontai, and Louise Michel]. *Observer Magazine* (26 November): 33–34.

———. 2000. *Five Sisters: The Langhorne Sisters of Virginia*. New York: Simon and Schuster.

Fox, Mary Virginia. 1975. *Lady for the Defense: A Biography of Belva Lockwood*. New York: Harcourt, Brace, Jovanovich.

Fox, Richard M. 1958. *Louie Bennett: Her Life and Times*. Dublin: Talbot Press.

Foxe, Barbara. 1975. *Long Journey Home: A Biography of Margaret Noble*. London: Rider.

Francis, Claude, and Fernand Goutier, trans. 1989. *Simone de Beauvoir*. London: Mandarin.

Fraser, Nicholas. 1996. Evita: *The Real Lives of Eva Perón*. London: André Deutsch.

Fraser, Nicholas, and Marysa Navarro. 1980. *Eva Perón*. London: André Deutsch.

Freedman, Russell. 1993. *Eleanor Roosevelt: A Life of Discovery*. New York: Clarion.

Friedan, Betty. 1998 [1976]. *It Changed My Life: Writings on the Women's Movement*. Reprint, Cambridge, MA: Harvard University Press.

———. 2000. *Life So Far*. New York: Simon and Schuster.

Friese, Kay. 1990. *Rosa Parks*. Englewood Cliffs, NJ: Silver-Burdette.

Fry, A. R. 1976. *Conversations with Alice Paul: Woman Suffrage and the Equal Rights Amendment*. Berkeley: University of California Press.

Fry, Ruth. 1929. *Emily Hobhouse: A Memoir*. London: Jonathan Cape.

Fryer, Mary Beacock. 1990. *Emily Stowe, Doctor and Suffragist*. Toronto: Oxford University Press.

Fuller, Edward. 1953. *Her Fighting Line: Eglantyne Jebb and the Save the Children Fund*. Edinburgh: Edinburgh House Press.

Fuller, M. L. B. 1928. *The Triumph of an Indian Widow*. New York: Christian Alliance Publishing Company.

Fuller, Margaret. *"These Sad but Glorious Days": Dispatches from Europe 1846–1850*. Edited by Larry J. Reynolds and Susan B. Smith. New Haven: Yale University Press.

Fynne, Robert John. 1924. *Montessori and Her Inspirers*. London: Longman's Green.

Gabriel, Mary. 1998. *Notorious Victoria: The Life of Victoria Woodhull, Uncensored*. Chapel Hill, NC: Algonquin.

Gage, Matilda Joslyn. 1980 [1893]. *Woman, Church and State: The Original Exposé of Male Collaboration against the Female Sex*. Reprint, Watertown, MA: Persephone Press.

———. 1998 [1893]. *Woman, Church and State.* Edited by Sally Roesch Wagner. Reprint, Aberdeen, SD: Sky Carrier Press.

García, Richard A. 1993. "Dolores Huerta: Woman, Organizer, and Symbol." *California History* 72(1): 56–72.

Gates, Joanna E. 1994. *Elizabeth Robins, 1862–1952: Actress, Novelist, Feminist.* Tuscaloosa: University of Alabama Press.

Giles, Kevin S. 1980. *Flight of the Dove: The Story of Jeanette Rankin.* Beaverton, OR: Touchstone Press.

Gilman, Charlotte Perkins. 1935. *The Living of Charlotte Perkins Gilman: An Autobiography.* New York: Appleton-Century.

Glage, Liselotte. 1981. *Clementina Black: A Study in Social History and Literature.* Heidelberg: C. Winter Universitätsverlag.

Golden, Catherine J., and Joanna Zangrado, eds. 2000. *The Mixed Legacy of Charlotte Perkins Gilman.* Cranbury, NJ: University of Delaware Press.

Goldie, Sue M. 1987. *I Have Done My Duty: Florence Nightingale in the Crimean War, 1854–1856.* Manchester: Manchester University Press.

Goldman, Emma. 1931. *Living My Life: An Autobiography of Emma Goldman.* Salt Lake City, UT: G. M. Smith.

Goldman, Harold. 1974. *Emma Paterson: She Led Woman into a Man's World.* London: Lawrence and Wishart.

Goldmark, Josephine. 1976 [1953]. *Impatient Crusader: Florence Kelley's Life Story.* Reprint, Westport, CT: Greenwood Press.

Gollaher, David. 1995. *A Voice for the Mad: The Life of Dorothea Dix.* New York: Free Press.

Gómez de Avellaneda, Gertrudis. 1992. *Sab, an Autobiography.* Translated by Nina M. Scott. Austin: University of Texas Press.

———. 2001. *Sab.* Spanish text, with notes and introduction by Catherine Davies. Manchester: Manchester University Press.

Gonzalez-Arias, Francisca. 1992. *Portrait of a Woman as Artist: Emilia Pardo Bazán and the Modern Novel in France and Spain.* New York: Garland.

Goodchild, Sophie. 1999. "Pizzey Makes a Stand for the Battered Man." *Independent* (28 March): 6.

Gordon, Ann D., ed. 1998. *Selected Papers of Elizabeth Cady Stanton and Susan B. Anthony,* vol. 1, *In the School of Anti-Slavery 1840 to 1866.* New Brunswick: Rutgers University Press.

Gordon, Felicia. 1990. *The Integral Feminist: Madeleine Pelletier 1874–1939.* Cambridge: Polity.

Gorham, Deborah. 1996. *Vera Brittain: A Feminist Life.* Oxford: Blackwell.

Gorn, Elliott J. 2000. *Mother Jones: The Most Dangerous Woman in America.* New York: Hill and Wang.

Gossett, Thomas F. 1985. *Uncle Tom's Cabin and American Culture.* Dallas: Southern Methodist University Press.

Grace, Fran. 2001. *Carry A. Nation: Retelling the Life.* Bloomington: Indiana University Press.

Graham, Abbie. 1926. *Grace H. Dodge: Merchant of Dreams.* New York: YWCA.

Graham, Frank, Jr. 1970. *Since Silent Spring.* Boston: Houghton Mifflin.

Grand, Sarah. 2000. *Sex, Social Purity and Sarah Grand.* London: Routledge.

Grant, Joy. 1987. *Stella Benson: A Biography.* London: Macmillan.

Grant, Madeline P. 1967. *Alice Hamilton: Pioneer Doctor in Industrial Medicine.* New York: Abelard-Shuman.

Grant, Mary Hetherington. 1994. *Private Woman, Public Person: An Account of the Life of Julia Ward Howe from 1819–1868.* Brooklyn, NY: Carlson Publishing.

Grassby, A. J. 1991. *Oodgeroo Noonuccal: Poet, Painter, and Elder of Her People.* South Melbourne: Macmillan.

Green, Diana, ed. 1980. *Lucretia Mott: Her Complete Speeches and Sermons.* New York: Edwin Mellen Press.

———. 1983. *Suffrage and Religious Principle: Speeches and Writings of Olympia Brown.* Metuchen, NJ: Scarecrow Press.

Green, Roger J. 1996. *Catherine Booth: A Biography of the Co-founder of the Salvation Army.* Crowborough, Sussex: Monarch.

Greer, Germaine. 1970. *The Female Eunuch.* London: MacGibbon and Kee.

———. 1986. *The Madwoman's Underclothes: Essays and Occasional Writings 1968–85.* London: Pan Books.

———. 1989. *Daddy We Hardly Knew You.* London: Hamish Hamilton.

———. 1997. "Serenity and Power." In Marilyn Pearsall, ed., *The Other within Us: Feminist Explorations of Women and Aging.* Boulder, CO: Westview Press.

Griffith, Elisabeth. 1984. *In Her Own Right: The Life of Elizabeth Cady Stanton.* New York: Oxford University Press.

Guérin, Winifred. 1976. *Elizabeth Gaskell: A Biography.* Oxford: Oxford University Press.

Gullette, Margaret Morganroth. 1989 [1894]. Afterword. In Mona Caird, *Daughters of Danaus.* Reprint, New York: Feminist Press.

Guy, Donna J. 1989. "Emilio and Gabriela de Coni: Reformers, Public Health and Working Women." In William Beezley and Judith Ewell, eds., *The Human Tradition in Latin America: The Nineteenth Century.* Wilmington, DE: Scholarly Resources.

Gwynn, Stephen Lucius. 1909. *Charlotte Grace*

O'Brien: Selections from Her Writings and Correspondence, with a Memoir by S. Gwynn. Dublin: n.p.

———. 1917. *Mrs. Humphry Ward.* London: Nisbet and Company.

Hahn, Emily. 1943. *The Soong Sisters.* London: R. Hale.

Hale, Clara. 1993. *Mother to Those Who Needed One.* Edited by Bob Italia. Edina, MN: Abdo & Daughters.

Hall, Florence Howe. 1916. *The Story of the Battle Hymn of the Republic.* New York: Harper.

Hall, Jacqueline Dowd. 1993 [1979]. *Jessie Daniel Ames and the Women's Campaign against Lynching.* Reprint, New York: Columbia University Press.

Hall, Ruth. 1977. *Marie Stopes: A Biography.* London: André Deutsch.

———. 1978. *Dear Dr. Stopes: Sex in the 1920s—A Selection of Letters Written to Marie Stopes.* London: André Deutsch.

Hallett, Mary E., and Marilyn Davis. 1993. *Firing the Heather: The Life and Times of Nellie McClung.* Saskatoon: Fifth House.

Haman, Brigitte. 1996. *Bertha von Suttner: A Life for Peace.* Syracuse, NY: Syracuse University Press.

Hamer, Fannie Lou. 1967. *To Praise Our Bridges: The Autobiography of Fannie Lou Hamer.* Jackson, MS: KIPCO.

Hamilton, Alice. 1943. *Exploring the Dangerous Trades: The Autobiography of Alice Hamilton.* Boston: Little, Brown.

Hamilton, Mary A. 1924. *Margaret Bondfield.* London: Leonard Parsons.

———. 1933. *Sidney and Beatrice Webb: A Study in Contemporary Biography.* London: S. Low.

Hannam, June. 1989. *Isabella Ford 1855–1924.* Oxford: Blackwell.

Harbison, A. W. 1981. *Evita: A Legend for the Seventies.* London: Star Books.

———. 1997. *Evita: Saint or Sinner?* London: Boxtree.

Hareven, Tamara. 1968. *Eleanor Roosevelt: An American Conscience.* Chicago: Quadrangle.

Harish, Ranjana. 1993. *Indian Women's Autobiographies.* New Delhi: Arnold.

Harlen, Judith. 2000. *Mamphela Ramphele: Ending Apartheid in South Africa.* New York: Feminist Press.

Harrison, Brian. 1987. *Prudent Revolutionaries: Portraits of British Feminists between the Wars.* Oxford: Clarendon Press.

Harter, Hugh. 1981. *Gertrudis Gómez de Avellaneda.* Boston: Twayne.

Hattenstone, Simon. 2000. "Small Wonder" [*Guardian* profile of Helen Bamber]. *Guardian* (11 March): 6–7.

Hattersley, Roy. 1999. *Blood and Fire: William and Catherine Booth and Their Salvation Army.* London: Little, Brown.

Hause, Steven C. 1987. *Hubertine Auclert: The French Suffragette.* New Haven: Yale University Press.

Hayek, F. A. 1969. *John Stuart Mill and Harriet Taylor: Their Friendship and Subsequent Marriage.* London: Routledge and Kegan Paul.

Hays, Elinor Rice. 1961. *Morning Star: A Biography of Lucy Stone.* New York: Harcourt, Brace and World.

———. 1967. *Those Extraordinary Blackwells: The Story of a Journey to a Better World.* New York: Harcourt Brace.

Healey, Edna. 1978. *Lady Unknown: The Life of Angela Burdett-Coutts.* London: Sidgwick and Jackson.

Heath, Jane. 1989. *Simone de Beauvoir.* Hemel Hempstead: Harvester Wheatsheaf.

Hedrick, Joan D. 1993. *Harriet Beecher Stowe: A Life.* New York: Oxford University Press.

Heidish, M. 1976. *A Woman Called Moses.* Boston: Houghton Mifflin.

Heilbrun, Carolyn G. 1996. *The Education of a Woman: The Life of Gloria Steinem.* New York: Ballantine Books.

Heilmann, Ann. 1995. "Mona Caird (1854–1932): Wild Woman, New Woman, and Early Radical Feminist Critic of Marriage and Motherhood." *Women's History Review* 5, no. 1: 67–95.

———. Forthcoming. *New Woman Strategies: Sarah Grand, Olive Schreiner, Mona Caird.* Manchester: Manchester University Press.

Heineman, Helen. 1983. *Restless Angels: The Friendship of Six Victorian Women.* Athens: Ohio University Press.

Hemingway, Maurice. 1983. *Emilia Pardo Bazán: The Making of a Novelist.* New York: Cambridge University Press.

Henderson, James, and Linda Roddy Henderson. 1978. *Ten Notable Women of Latin America.* Chicago: Nelson Hall.

Henderson, Leslie M. 1973. *The Goldstein Story.* Melbourne: Stockland Press.

Hendricksson, John. 1991. *Rachel Carson: The Environmental Movement.* Brookfield, CT: Millbrook Press.

Hennessee, Judith Adler. 1999. *Betty Friedan: A Biography.* New York: Random House.

Henry, Sondra. 1987. *One Woman's Power: A Biography of Gloria Steinem.* Minneapolis: Dillon Press.

Hermann, Dorothy. 1998. *Helen Keller: A Life.* New York: Alfred A. Knopf.

Hersteck, Amy Paulson. 2001. *Dorothea Dix: Crusader for the Mentally Ill.* Berkeley Heights, NJ: Enslow.

Herstein, Sheila. 1985. *A Mid-Victorian Feminist: Barbara Leigh Smith Bodichon.* New Haven: Yale University Press.

Hill, Caroline M., ed. 1938. *Mary McDowell and*

Municipal Housekeeping. Chicago: Millar Publishing.

Hill, Ernestine. 1973. *Kabbarli: A Personal Memoir of Daisy Bates.* Sydney: Angus and Robertson.

Hill, Mary Armfield. 1980. *Charlotte Perkins Gilman: The Making of a Radical Feminist, 1860–1896.* Philadelphia: Temple University Press.

Hill, William Thompson. 1956. *Octavia Hill: Pioneer of the National Trust and Housing Reformer.* London: Hutchins.

Hirsch, Pam. 1998. *Barbara Leigh Smith Bodichon 1827–1891: Feminist, Artist and Rebel.* London: Chatto and Windus.

Hoban, Mary. 1973. *Fifty-One Pieces of Wedding Cake: A Biography of Caroline Chisholm.* Kilmore, Victoria: Lowden.

Hobhouse, Emily. 1901. *Report of a Visit to the Camps of Women and Children in the Cape and Orange River Colonies.* London: Friars Printing Association.

Hoecker-Drysdale, Susan. 1993. *Harriet Martineau: First Woman Sociologist.* Oxford: Berg.

Hoefel, Roseanne. 1997. "Writing, Performance, Activism: Zitkala-Ša and Pauline Johnson." In Susan Castillo and Victor M. P. Da Rosa Porto, eds., *Native American Women in Literature and Culture.* Portugal: Fernando Pessoa University Press.

Hoffman, V. J. 1985. "An Islamic Activist: Zeinab al Ghazali." In Elizabeth Fernea, ed., *Women and the Family in the Middle East.* Austin: University of Texas Press.

Hoge, James O., and Jane Marcus. 1978. *Selected Writings of Caroline Norton.* Delmar, NY: Scholars' Facsimiles and Reprints.

Holland, P. G., M. Melzer, and F. Krasno, eds. 1982. *Lydia Maria Child: Selected Letters, 1817–1880.* Amherst: University of Massachusetts Press.

Holmes, Richard. 2000. "The Feminist and the Philosopher: A Love Story." In *Sidetracks: Explorations of a Romantic Biographer* by Richard Holmes. London: HarperCollins.

Holt, Alix, ed. 1977. *Selected Writings of Alexandra Kollontai.* London: Allison and Busby.

Holt, Rackham. 1964. *Mary McCleod Bethune: A Biography.* New York: Doubleday.

Holtby, Winifred. 1934. *Women in a Changing Civilization.* London: John Lane.

Holton, Sandra Stanley. 1990. "In Sorrowful Wrath: Suffrage Militancy and the Romantic Feminism of Emmeline Pankhurst." In H. L. Smith, ed., *British Feminism in the Twentieth Century.* Aldershot: Edward Elgar.

———. 1994. "To Educate Women into Rebellion: Elizabeth Cady Stanton and the Creation of a Transatlantic Network of Radical Suffragists." *American History Review* 99: 1112–1136.

Honig, Emily. 1992. "Christianity, Feminism, and Communism: The Life and Times of Deng Yuzhi (Cora Deng)." In Cheryl Johnson-Odim and Margaret Strobel, eds., *Expanding the Boundaries of Women's History: Essays on Women in the Third World.* Bloomington: Indiana University Press.

Hopkins, Annette Brown. 1952. *Elizabeth Gaskell: Her Life and Work.* London: Lehmann.

Hopkins, Mary Alden. 1947. *Hannah More and Her Circle.* New York: Longmans, Green.

Horowitz, Daniel. 2000. *Betty Friedan and the Making of the Feminine Mystique: The American Left, the Cold War, and Modern Feminism.* Amherst: University of Massachusetts Press.

Houghton, Frank. 1954. *Amy Carmichael of Dohnavur: The Story of a Lover and Her Beloved.* London: SPCK.

Howe, Julia Ward. 1899. *Reminiscences, 1819–1899.* Boston: Houghton Mifflin.

Howitt, Margaret. 1866. *Twelve Months with Frederika Bremer in Sweden.* London: Jackson, Walford, and Hodder.

Hughes, Kathryn. 1998. *George Eliot: The Last Victorian.* London: Fourth Estate.

Hurst, Michael. 1969. *Maria Edgeworth and the Public Scene: Intellect, Fine Feeling and Landlordism in the Age of Reform.* London: Macmillan.

Huxley, Elspeth, and Josceline Grant. 1975. *Florence Nightingale.* London: Weidenfeld and Nicolson.

"In Memoriam: Vilma Glücklich." 1927. *Jus Suffragii/International Woman Suffrage News* (27 December).

Inglis-Jones, Elisabeth. 1959. *The Great Maria: A Portrait of Maria Edgeworth.* Westport, CT: Greenwood Press.

Innis, M. Q., ed. 1959. *The Clear Spirit: Twenty Canadian Women and Their Times.* Toronto: University of Toronto Press.

Ishimoto Shizue. 1935. *Facing Two Ways: The Story of My Life by Baroness Shidzué Ishimoto.* New York: Farrar and Rinehart.

———. 1936. *East Way, West Way: A Modern Japanese Girlhood by Baroness Shidzué Ishimoto.* New York: Farrar and Rinehart.

Israel, Kali. 1998. *Names and Stories: Emilia Dilke and Victorian Culture.* Oxford: Oxford University Press.

Jack, Belinda. 1999. *George Sand: A Woman's Life Writ Large.* London: Chatto and Windus.

Jackson, Helen Hunt. 1964 [1881]. *A Century of Dishonor: A Sketch of the United States Government's Dealings with Some of the Indian Tribes.* Reprint, Minneapolis: Ross and Haines.

———. 1994. *Westward to a High Mountain: The Colorado Writings of Helen Hunt Jackson.* Denver: Colorado Historical Society.

Jacobs, Aletta. 1996. *Memories: My Life as an*

International Leader in Health, Suffrage, and Peace. New York: Feminist Press.

Jacobs, Diana. 2001. *Her Own Woman: The Life of Mary Wollstonecraft.* New York: Simon and Schuster.

Jahan, Roshan, ed. and trans. 1981. *Inside Seclusion: The Avarodhbasini of Rokeya Sakhawat Hossain.* Dakka: BRAC Printers.

Jahangir, Asma, and Hina Jilani. 1990. *The Hudood Ordinances: A Divine Sanction. A Research Study of the Hudood Ordinances and Their Effects on the Disadvantaged Sections of Pakistani Society.* Lahore: Rhotas Books.

Jahangir, Asma, and Mark Doucet. 1993. *Children of a Lesser God: Child Prisoners of Pakistan.* Lahore: Vanguard.

James, Donna. 2001. *Emily Murphy.* Toronto: Fitzhenry and Whiteside.

Jarrett-Macauley, Delia. 1998. *The Life of Una Marson, 1905–1965.* Manchester: Manchester University Press.

Jayawardena, Kumari. 1993. *Dr. Mary Rutnam: A Canadian Pioneer of Women's Rights in Sri Lanka.* Colombo: Social Scientists' Association.

Jenefsky, Cindy, with Ann Russo. 1998. *Without Apology: Andrea Dworkin's Art and Politics.* Boulder: Westview Press.

Jenkins, Ray. 1968. *Sir Charles Dilke: A Victorian Tragedy.* London: Collins.

Jex-Blake, Sophia. 1886 [1872]. *Medical Women: A Thesis and a History.* Reprint, Edinburgh: Oliphant, Anderson and Ferrier.

Jilani, Hina. 1998. *Human Rights and Democratic Development in Pakistan.* Lahore: Human Rights Commission of Pakistan.

Jinnah, Fatima. 1976. *Speeches, Messages, and Statements of Madar-i-Millat Mohtarama Jinnah (1948–1967).* London: Research Society of Pakistan.

John, Angela V. 1995. *Elizabeth Robins: Staging a Life, 1862–1952.* London: Routledge.

Johnson, B. R., ed. 1931. *Elizabeth Fry's Journeys on the Continent 1840–1841, from a Diary Kept by Her Niece Elizabeth Gurney.* London: John Lane.

Johnson-Odim, Cheryl. 1997. *From Women and the Nation: Fumilayo Ransome-Kuti of Nigeria.* Urbana: University of Illinois Press.

Johnston, Johanna. 1967. *Mrs. Satan: The Incredible Saga of Victoria C. Woodhull.* New York: G. P. Putnam's.

Johnston, Judith. 1997. *Anna Jameson: Victorian, Feminist, Woman of Letters.* Brookfield, VT: Ashgate.

Jones, Beverly Washington. 1990. *Quest for Equality: The Life and Writings of Eliza Mary Church Terrell, 1863–1954.* Brooklyn, NY: Carlson Publishers.

Jones, E. Huws. 1973. *Mrs. Humphry Ward.* Oxford: Heinemann.

Jones, M. G. 1952. *Hannah More.* Cambridge: Cambridge University Press.

Jones, Mary Harris. 1990 [1925]. *Autobiography of Mother Jones.* Edited by Mary Field Parton. Rev. ed. Chicago: Charles H. Kerr.

Jordan, Jane. 2001. *Josephine Butler.* London: John Murray.

Jordan, June. 1972. *Fannie Lou Hamer.* New York: Crowell.

Joseph, Helen. 1963. *If This Be Treason.* London: André Deutsch.

———. 1986. *Side by Side: The Autobiography of Helen Joseph.* London: Zed Books.

Josephson, Hanna. 1974. *First Lady in Congress: Jeanette Rankin.* Indianapolis: Bobbs-Merrill.

Josephson, Judith Pinkerton. 1997. *Mother Jones: Fierce Fighter for Workers' Rights.* Minneapolis: Lerner Publications.

Kahin, George. 1989. "In Memoriam: Maria Ullfah Soebadio, 1911–1988." *Indonesia* 49 (April): 119–120.

Kamester, Margaret, and Jo Vellacott, eds. 1987. *Militarism and Feminism: Writings on Women and War: Catherine Marshall, C. K. Ogden and Mary Sargant Florence.* London: Virago.

Kamm, Josephine. 1958. *How Different from Us: A Biography of Miss Buss and Miss Beale.* London: Bodley Head.

———. 1977. *John Stuart Mill in Love.* London: Gordon and Cremonesi.

Karcher, Karen L. 1995. *The First Woman in the Republic: A Cultural Biography of Lydia Maria Child.* Durham, NC: Duke University Press.

Karris, T., and G. M. Carter. 1977. *From Protest to Challenge: A Documentary History of African Politics in South Africa 1882–1964,* vol. 4, *Political Profiles.* Stanford: Stanford University Press.

Kartini, Raden Adjeng. 1964. *Letters of a Javanese Princess.* Translated and edited by Agnes Louise Symmers and introduced by Hildred Geertz. New York: W. W. Norton.

———. 1992. *Letters from Kartini: An Indonesian Feminist 1900–1904.* Translated by Joost Coté. Clayton, Victoria: Monash Asia Institute.

Kearney, James. 1968. *Anna Eleanor Roosevelt: The Evolution of a Reformer.* Boston: Houghton Mifflin.

Keller, Helen. 1996 [1902]. *The Story of My Life.* Reprint, Mineola, NY: Dover Publications.

———. 2000 [1927]. *Light in My Darkness.* 2d ed. Reprint of *My Religion.* Edited by Ray Silverman. Westchester, PA: Chrysalis Books.

Kelly, Audrey. 1992. *Lydia Becker and the Cause.* Lancaster: Centre for North-West Regional Studies.

Kelly, Gary. 1991. *Revolutionary Feminism: The Mind and Career of Mary Wollstonecraft.* Basingstoke:

Macmillan.

Kempf, Beatrix. 1973. *Woman for Peace: The Life of Bertha von Suttner.* London: Wolff.

Kendall, Katherine A. 1989. "Women at the Helm: Three Extraordinary Leaders." *Affilia: A Journal of Women and Social Work* 4(1): 23–32.

Kennard, Jean E. 1989. *Vera Brittain and Winifred Holtby: A Working Partnership.* Hanover: University Press of New England.

Kennedy, D. H. 1983. *Little Sparrow: A Portrait of Sophia Kovalevsky.* Athens: Ohio University Press.

Kennedy, David. 1970. *Birth Control in America: The Career of Margaret Sanger.* New Haven: Yale University Press.

Kenney, Annie. 1924. *Memoirs of a Militant.* London: Edward Arnold.

Kent, John. 1962. *Elizabeth Fry.* London: B. T. Batsford.

Kern, Robert. 1981. "Margarita Nelken: Women and the Crisis of Spanish Politics." In Jane Slaughter and Robert Kern, eds., *European Women on the Left: Socialism, Feminism, and the Problems Faced by Political Women, 1880 to the Present.* Westport, CT: Greenwood Press.

Kerr, Andrea Moore. 1992. *Lucy Stone: Speaking Out for Equality.* New Brunswick, NJ: Rutgers University Press.

Kerr, Laura. 1951. *Lady in the Pulpit.* New York: Woman's Press.

Kersley, Gillian. 1983. *Darling Madame: Sarah Grand and Devoted Friend.* London: Virago.

Kessler, Carol Farley. 1995. *Charlotte Perkins Gilman: Her Progress toward Utopia with Selected Writings.* Liverpool: Liverpool University Press.

Kiddle, Margaret L. 1957. *Caroline Chisholm.* Melbourne: Melbourne University Press.

King, Michael. 1987. *Te Puea Herangi: From Darkness to Light.* Auckland: Hodder and Stoughton.

Kisner, Arlene M., ed. 1972. Woodhull and Claflin's Weekly: *The Lives and Writings of Notorious Victoria Woodhull and Her Sister Tennessee Claflin.* Washington, NJ: Time Change Press.

Kissel, Susan S. 1993. *In Common Cause: The "Conservative" Frances Trollope and the "Radical" Frances Wright.* Bowling Green, OH: Bowling Green State University Press.

Kleman, Ellen. 1938. *Frederika Bremer and America.* Stockholm: Åhlén and Åkerlunds.

Koblitz, Ann Hibner. 1983. *A Convergence of Lives: Sofia Kovalevskaia, Scientist, Writer, Revolutionary.* Boston: Birkhauser.

Kochersber, Robert C., ed. 1994. *More Than a Muckraker: Ida Tarbell's Lifetime in Journalism.* Knoxville: University of Tennessee Press.

Kollontai, Alexandra. 1971. *The Autobiography of a Sexually Emancipated Communist Woman.* Edited and translated by I. Fetscher. London: Orbach and Chambers.

———. 1971. *Communism and the Family.* London: Socialist Workers Party.

———. 1971. *Women Workers' Struggle for Their Rights.* Bristol: Falling Wall Press.

———. 1972. *Love and the New Morality.* London.

———. 1972. *Sexual Relations and the Class Struggle.* London:.

———. 1977. *Love of Worker Bees.* Translated by Cathy Porter. London: Virago.

———. 1977. *Selected Writings of Alexandra Kollontai.* Edited by Alix Holt. London: Allison and Busby.

———. 1984. *Sexual Relations and the Class Struggle.* London: Socialist Workers' Party.

Kolmerton, Carol A. 1999. *The American Life of Ernestine L. Rose.* Syracuse: Syracuse University Press.

Kosambi, Meera. 1998. "Multiple Contestations: Pandita Ramabai's Educational and Missionary Activities in Late Nineteenth-Century India and Abroad." *Women's History Review* 7 (2), 193–208.

———, ed. 2000. *Pandita Ramabai through Her Own Words: Selected Works.* New York: Oxford University Press.

Kovalevskaia [sic], S. V. V. [Sofya Kovalevskaya]. 1978. *A Russian Childhood.* Translated and edited by Beatrice Stillman. New York: Springer-Verlag.

Kowaleski-Wallace, Elizabeth. 1991. *Their Father's Daughters: Hannah More, Maria Edgeworth, and Patriarchal Complicity.* New York: Oxford University Press.

Kraft, Betsy. 0000. *Mother Jones, One Woman's Fight for Labor.* New York: Clarion Books.

Kramer, Rita. 1989. *Maria Montessori: A Biography.* London: Montessori International.

Krupskaya, Nadezhda. 1970. *Memories of Lenin.* London: Panther.

Kuzwayo, Ellen. 1985. *Call Me Woman.* London: Women's Press.

———. 1996. *Sit Down and Listen: Stories from South Africa.* Claremont, South Africa: D. Philip.

La Vigna, Claire. 1991. *Anna Kuliscioff: From Russian Populism to Italian Socialism.* New York: Garland.

Lacey, Candida Ann., ed. 1987. *Barbara Leigh Smith Bodichon and the Langham Place Group.* London: Routledge and Kegan Paul.

Ladoux, Georges. 1932. *Marthe Richard, the Skylark: The Foremost Woman Spy of France.* London: Cassell.

Lamont, Corliss, ed. 1968. *The Trial of Elizabeth Gurley Flynn by the American Civil Liberties Union.* New York: Monthly Review Press.

Lane, Ann J. 1983. "Charlotte Perkins Gilman: The Personal Is Political." In Dale Spender, ed., *Feminist Theorists: Three Centuries of Women's Intellectual Traditions.* London: Women's Press.

———. 1983. "Mary Ritter Beard: Woman as Force."

In Dale Spender, ed., *Feminist Theorists: Three Centuries of Women's Intellectual Traditions.* London: Women's Press.

———. 1990. *To Herland and Beyond: The Life and Work of Charlotte Perkins Gilman.* New York: Pantheon Books.

———, ed. 1977. *Mary Ritter Beard: A Source Book.* New York: Schocken Books.

Lane, Margaret. 1972. *Frances Wright and the "Great Experiment."* Manchester: Manchester University Press.

Lanker, Brian. 1989. *I Dream a World.* New York: Stewart, Tabori and Chang.

Lansbury, Coral. 1975. *Elizabeth Gaskell: The Novel of Social Crisis.* New York: Barnes and Noble.

———. 1985. *The Old Brown Dog: Women, Workers and Vivisection in Edwardian England.* Madison: University of Wisconsin Press.

Lasch, Christopher. 1982 [1965]. *The Social Thought of Jane Addams.* Reprint, New York: Irvington.

Lasch, Joseph P. 1971. *Eleanor and Franklin.* New York: Norton.

———. 1972. *Eleanor: The Years Alone.* New York: Norton.

———. 1980. *Helen and Teacher: The Story of Helen Keller and Anne Sullivan.* New York: Delacorte/Seymour Lawrence.

Lasser, Carol, and Marlene Deal, eds. 1987. *Letters between Lucy Stone and Antoinette Brown Blackwell, 1846–1893.* Urbana: University of Illinois Press.

Laurance, Jeremy. 1991. "Sex Talks: Jeremy Laurance Talks to Erin Pizzey, the Battered Women's Campaigner Turned Steamy Novelist." *New Statesman Society* (8 February): 23.

Lawrence, Margot. 1971. *Shadow of Swords: A Biography of Elsie Inglis.* London: Michael Joseph.

Lawson, Olive, ed. 1990. *The First Voice of Australian Feminism: Excerpts from Louisa Lawson's The Dawn 1888–1895.* Sydney: Simon and Schuster.

Lazo, Caroline Evensen. 1998. *Gloria Steinem: Feminist Extraordinaire.* Minneapolis: Lerner Publications.

Lear, Linda J. 1998. *Rachel Carson: Witness for Nature.* London: Allen Lane.

Lee, Chana Kai. 1999. *For Freedom's Sake: The Life of Fannie Hamer.* Urbana: University of Illiinois Press.

Lee, Robin. 1990. *Values Alive: A Tribute to Helen Suzman.* Johannesburg: J. Ball.

Leeman, Richard W. 1992. *"Do Everything" Reform: The Oratory of Frances E. Willard.* New York: Greenwood Press.

Leighninger, L. 2001. "Frances Perkins: Champion of the New Deal." *Affilia* 16 (3), 398–399.

Leneman, Lori. 1994. *In the Service of Life: The Story of Elsie Inglis and the Scottish Women's Hospitals.* Edinburgh: Mercat Press.

Lengyel, E. 1975. *All Her Paths Were Peace: The Life of Bertha von Suttner.* Nashville: T. Nelson.

Lerner, Gerda. 1971 [1967]. *The Grimké Sisters from South Carolina: Rebels against Slavery.* New York: Schocken Books.

———. 1998. "The Feminist Thought of Sarah Grimké." In Lynn McDonald, ed., *Women Theorists on Society and Politics.* Waterloo, ON: Wilfrid Laurier University Press.

Levenson, Leah, and Jerry H. Natterstad. 1986. *Hanna Sheehy Skeffington: Irish Feminist.* Syracuse, NY: Syracuse University Press.

Levenson, Sam. 1977. *Maud Gonne.* London: Cassell.

Levinger, Elma Ehrlich. 1946. *Fighting Angel: The Story of Henrietta Szold.* New York: Behrman House.

Lewis, Gifford. 1988. *Eva Gore-Booth and Esther Roper.* London: Pandora.

Lewis, Jane. 1990. "Myrdal, Klein, Women's Two Roles and Postwar Feminism 1945–1960." In Harold Smith, ed., *British Feminism in the Twentieth Century.* Aldershort, Hants: Edward Elgar.

Liaquat, Ali Khan. 1950. *Pakistan, the Heart of Asia: Speeches in the United States and Canada, May and June 1950, by the Prime Minister of Pakistan with an Appendix by Begum Liaquat Ali Khan.* Cambridge, MA: Harvard University Press.

Liddington, Jill. 1984. *The Life and Times of a Respectable Rebel: Selina Cooper 1864–1946.* London: Virago.

Lind-af-Hageby, Louise, and Liese K. Schartau. 1903. *The Shambles of Science: Extracts from the Diary of Two Students of Physiology.* London: Ernest Bell.

Ling, Bettina. 1999. *Aung San Suu Kyi: Standing Up for Democracy in Burma.* New York: Feminist Press.

Linklater, Andro. 1980. *An Unhusbanded Life: Charlotte Despard, Suffragette, Socialist, and Sinn Feiner.* London: Hutchinson.

Linkugel, Wil A., and Martha Solomon. 1990. *Anna Howard Shaw: Suffrage Orator and Social Reformer.* Westport, CT: Greenwood Press.

Linn, James Weber. 1999 [1935]. *Jane Addams: A Biography.* Reprint, New York: Appleton-Century.

Linton, Eliza. 1899. *My Literary Life.* London: Hodder and Stoughton.

Livermore, Mary. 1897. *The Story of My Life.* Hartford, CT: A. D. Worthington.

———. 1995 [1888]. *My Story of the War.* Reprint, New York: Da Capo Press.

Long, Priscilla. 1976. *Mother Jones, Woman Organizer, and Her Relations with Miners' Wives, Working Women, and the Suffrage Movement.* Boston: Red Sun Press.

Lorch, Jennifer. 1990. *Mary Wollstonecraft: The Making of a Radical Feminist.* Oxford: St. Martin's Press.

Lord, John. 1873. *The Life of Emma Willard*. New York: Appleton.

Lowenthal, Martin. 1942. *Henrietta Szold: Life and Letters*. New York: Viking Press.

Lowndes, George. 1960. *Margaret McMillan, "The Children's Champion."* London: Museum Press.

Lowry, Bullitt, and Elizabeth Ellington Gunter, eds. 1981. *The Red Virgin: Memoirs of Louise Michel*. Mobile: University of Alabama Press.

Luddy, Maria. 1995. *Hannah Sheehy Skeffington*. Dublin: Historical Association of Ireland.

Lumpkin, Katherine Du Pré. 1974. *The Emancipation of Angelina Grimké*. Chapel Hill: University of North Carolina Press.

Lunardini, Christine A. 1986. *From Equal Suffrage to Equal Rights: Alice Paul and the National Woman's Party, 1910–1928*. New York: New York University Press.

Lundell, Torberg. 1984. "Ellen Key and Swedish Feminist Views on Motherhood." *Scandinavian Studies*.

Lutz, Alma. 1959. *Susan B. Anthony: Rebel, Crusader, Humanitarian*. Boston: Beacon Press.

———. 1973 [1940]. *Created Equal: A Biography of Elizabeth Cady Stanton*. Reprint, New York: Octagon.

———. 1983 [1964]. *Emma Willard: Pioneer Educator of American Women*. Reprint, Westport, CT: Greenwood Press.

Lutzker, Edythe. 1973. *Edith Pechey-Phipson MD: The Story of England's Foremost Pioneering Doctor*. New York: Exposition Press.

Lytton, Constance. 1914. *Prisons and Prisoners, Some Personal Experiences by Constance Lytton and "Jane Warton, Spinster."* London: William Heinemann.

Mabee, Carleton. 1993. *Sojourner Truth: Slave, Prophet, Legend*. New York: New York University Press.

MacArthur, Brian. 1998. *Requiem: Diana, Princess of Wales 1961–1997*. London: Pavilion.

MacBride, Maud Gonne. 1995 [1938]. *The Autobiography of Maud Gonne: A Servant of the Queen*. Reprint, Chicago: University of Chicago Press.

MacCurtain, Margaret, and Donnchadh O'Corrain. 1978. *Women in Irish Society: The Historical Dimension*. Dublin: Arlen House.

MacDonald, Charlotte. 1993. *The Vote, the Pill and the Demon Drink: A History of Feminist Writing in New Zealand 1869–1993*. Wellington, NZ: Bridget Williams Books.

Machel, Graça. 1996. *Impact of Armed Conflict on Children: Report of Graça Machel: Selected Highlights*. New York: United Nations Department of Public Information, UNICEF, United Nations Children's Fund.

———. 1998. *The Graça Machel/UN Study on the Effects of War on Children*. Mahwah, NJ: Erlbaum Associates.

MacKenzie, Norman. 1960. "Vida Goldstein: The Australian Suffragette." *Australian Journal of Politics and History* 6: 190–204.

Mackenzie, Norman Ian, and Jeanne Mackenzie. 1982–1984. *The Diary of Beatrice Webb*. 4 vols. London: Virago.

MacKinnon, Catharine, and Andrea Dworkin. 1997. *In Harm's Way: The Pornography Civil Rights Hearings*. Cambridge, MA: Harvard University Press.

MacLeish, Archibald. 1965. *The Eleanor Roosevelt Story*. Boston: Houghton Mifflin.

Macnicol, Nicol. 1996 [1926]. *Pandita Ramabai*. Reprint, New Delhi: Good Books.

Magarey, Susan. 1985. *Unbridling the Tongues of Women: A Biography of Catherine Helen Spence*. Sydney: Hale and Ironmonger.

Mahmoudi, Hoda. 1985. "Tahira: An Early Iranian Feminist." In A. Fathi, ed., *Women and the Family in Iran*. Leiden: E. J. Brill.

Main, Mary. 1980. *Evita: The Woman with the Whip*. New York: Dodd and Mead.

Maitland, Edward, ed. 1913. *Anna Kingsford: Her Life, Letters, Diary and Work*. 2 vols. London: John M. Watkins.

Malcolm, Tessa. 1993. "Katherine Sheppard." In *The Dictionary of New Zealand Biography*, vol. 2. Wellington, NZ: Allen and Unwin and the Department of Internal Affairs.

Malone, Mary. 1991. *Dorothea L. Dix: Hospital Founder*. New York: Chelsea House.

Mander, Christine. 1985. *Emily Murphy, Rebel: First Female Magistrate in the British Empire*. Toronto: Simon and Schuster.

Mangum, Teresa. 1998. *Married, Middle-Brow, and Militant: Sarah Grand and the New Woman Novel*. Ann Arbor: University of Michigan Press.

Mansbridge, Albert. 1932. *Margaret McMillan, Prophet and Pioneer: Her Life and Work*. London: J. M. Dent.

Mansbridge, Jane J. 1986. *Why We Lost the ERA*. Chicago: University of Chicago Press.

Manton, Jo. 1965. *Elizabeth Garrett Anderson*. London: Methuen.

———. 1976. *Mary Carpenter and the Children of the Streets*. London: Heinemann.

Manvell, Roger. 1976. *The Trial of Annie Besant and Charles Bradlaugh*. London: Elek/Pemberton.

Mappen, E. 1985. *Helping Women at Work: The Women's Industrial Council, 1889–1914*. London: Hutchinson.

Marberry, M. 1967. *Vicky: A Biography of Victoria C. Woodhull*. New York: Funk and Wagnalls.

Marcus, Jane. 1987. *Suffrage and the Pankhursts*. London: Routledge.

Marilley, Suzanne M. 1996. *"Frances Willard and the Feminism of Fear": Woman Suffrage and the Origins of Liberal Feminism in the United States, 1820–1920.* Cambridge, MA: Harvard University Press.

Markievicz, Constance de. 1934. *Prison Letters of Countess Markievicz.* London: Longman's Green and Company.

Marreco, Anne. 1967. *The Rebel Countess.* London: Weidenfeld and Nicolson.

Marshall, Helen E. 1937. *Dorothea Dix: Forgotten Samaritan.* Chapel Hill: University of North Carolina Press.

Marshall White, Eleanor. 1991. *Women: Catalysts for Change. Interpretative Biographies of Shirley St. Hill Chisholm, Sandra Day O'Connor, and Nancy Landon Kassebaum.* New York: Vantage Press.

Marsot, Afaf Lutfi al-Sayyid. 1978. "The Revolutionary Gentlewoman in Egypt." In L. Beck and N. Keddie, eds., *Women in the Muslim World.* Cambridge, MA: Harvard University Press.

Marston, Kitty Muggeridge. 1967. *Beatrice Webb: A Life, 1858–1943.* London: Secker and Warburg.

Marteena, Constance Hill. 1977. *The Lengthening Shadow of a Woman: A Biography of Charlotte Hawkins Brown.* Hicksville, NY: Exposition Press.

Martin, George W. 1976. *Madam Secretary: Frances Perkins.* Boston: Houghton Mifflin.

Martineau, Harriet. 1983 [1877]. *Autobiography, with Memorials by Maria Weston Chapman.* Reprint, London: Virago.

Martineau, Lisa. 2000. *Barbara Castle: Politics and Power.* London: Andre Deutsch.

Masarykova, Alice. 1980. *Alice Masarykova 1879–1966: Her Life as Recorded in Her Own Words.* Pittsburgh: University Center for International Studies.

Masters, A. 1981. *Nancy Astor: A Biography.* New York: McGraw Hill.

Mathes, Valerie Sherer. 1990. *Helen Hunt Jackson and Her Indian Reform Legacy.* Austin: University of Texas Press.

Matthews, Brian. 1987. *Louisa.* Melbourne: McPhee Gribble Publishers.

Matthews, Jacquie. 1983. "Barbara Bodichon: Integrity in Diversity." In Dale Spender, ed., *Feminist Theorists: Three Centuries of Women's Intellectual Traditions.* London: Women's Press.

Maurice, C. Edmund, ed. 1913. *Life of Octavia Hill as Told in Her Letters.* London: Macmillan.

"May Ziadehf: A Brief Tribute to Her Work." 1979. *Signs* 5(2): 375–382.

Mayne, Ethel Colburne. 1929. *Life and Letters of Lady Byron.* London: Constable.

Mayreder, Rosa. 1913. *A Survey of the Woman Problem.* Translated by Herman Scheffauer. London: Heinemann.

Maza, Sara. 2001. "French Feminists and the Rights of 'Man.' Olympe de Gouges's Declarations." In Ronald Schechter, ed., *The French Revolution: The Essential Readings.* Oxford: Blackwell.

McCallum, Margaret. 1989. *Emily Stowe.* Toronto: Grolier.

McClung, Nellie. 1972 [1915]. *In Times Like These.* Reprint, Toronto: University of Toronto Press.

McKay, Mary. 1993. *Rachel Carson.* Boston: Twayne Publishers.

McKissack, Patricia. 1991. *Mary Church Terrell: Leader for Equality.* Hillside, NJ: Enslow.

———. 1991. *Mary McCleod Bethune: A Great Teacher.* Hillside, NJ: Enslow.

———. 1992. *Sojourner Truth: A Voice for Freedom.* Hillside, NJ: Enslow.

McNeal, Robert. 1972. *Bride of the Revolution: Krupskaya and Lenin.* Ann Arbor: University of Michigan Press.

McPhee, C., and A. Fitzgerald, eds. 1987. *The Non-Violent Militant: Selected Writings of Teresa Billington-Greig.* London: Routledge and Kegan Paul.

McWilliams-Tullberg, Rita. 1975. *Women at Cambridge: A Men's University—Though of a Mixed Type.* London: Gollancz.

Meade, Marion. 1976. *Free Woman: The Life and Times of Victoria Woodhull.* New York: Knopf.

Mellown, Muriel. 1983. "Vera Brittain: Feminist in a New Age." In Dale Spender, ed., *Feminist Theorists: Three Centuries of Women's Intellectual Traditions.* London: Women's Press.

Meltzer, Milton. 1965. *Tongue of Flame: The Life of Lydia Maria Child.* New York: Crowell.

Menchú, Rigoberta. 1984. *I, Rigoberta Menchu: An Indian Woman in Guatemala.* London: Verso.

———. 1998. *Crossing Borders.* London: Verso.

Menuhin, Yehudi. 1964. "A Woman to Remember" [Lily Montagu]. *Times* (24 April).

Merrill, Marlene Deahl. 1990. *Growing Up in Boston's Gilded Age: The Journal of Alice Stone Blackwell, 1872–1874.* New Haven: Yale University Press.

Meyer, Alfred G. 1985. *The Feminism and Socialism of Lily Braun.* Bloomington: Indiana University Press.

Millar, Nancy. 1999. *The Famous Five, or Emily Murphy and the Case of the Missing Persons.* Cochrane: Western Heritage Centre.

Miller, William. 1974. *A Harsh and Dreadful Love: Dorothy Day and the Catholic Worker Movement.* Garden City, NY: Doubleday.

———. 1982. *Dorothy Day: A Biography.* San Francisco: Harper and Row.

Mills, Bruce. 1994. *Cultural Reformations: Lydia Maria Child and the Literature of Reform.* Athens: University of Georgia Press.

Mills, Kay. 1993. *This Little Light of Mine: Fannie Lou Hamer.* New York: E. P. Dutton.

Mitchell, David. 1967. *The Fighting Pankhursts: A Study in Tenacity.* London: Jonathan Cape.

———. 1977. *Queen Christabel: A Biography of Christabel Pankhurst.* London: Macdonald and Jane's.

Mitchell, Hannah. 1968. *The Hard Way Up: The Autobiography of Hannah Mitchell, Suffragette and Rebel.* London: Faber.

Mitchell, Susan. 1997. *Icons, Saints & Divas: Intimate Conversations with Women Who Changed the World.* London: Pandora.

Mitchison, Naomi. 1979. *You May Well Ask: A Memoir 1920–1940.* London: Flamingo.

Montagu, Eric. 1953. *Lily H. Montagu: Prophet of a Living Judaism.* New York: National Federation of Temple Sisterhoods.

Montefiore, Dora. 1927. *From a Victorian to a Modern.* London: E. Archer.

More, Hannah. 1995 [1799]. *Strictures on the Modern System of Female Education.* Edited by Gina Luria. Oxford: Woodstock Books.

Morgan, Sue. 1999. *A Passion for Purity: Ellice Hopkins and the Politics of Gender in the Late Victorian Church.* Bristol: Center for Comparative Studies in Religion and Gender.

———. 2000. "Faith, Sex and Purity: The Religio-Feminist Theory of Ellice Hopkins." *Women's History Review* 9(1): 9.

Morris, Emily, ed. 1928. *Octavia Hill: Early Ideals.* London: Allen and Unwin.

Morton, Andrew. 1997. *Diana: Her True Story, in Her Own Words,* London: Michael O'Mara.

Morton, Marian J. 1992. *Emma Goldman and the American Left: "Nowhere at Home."* New York: Twayne.

Mother Teresa. 1975. *A Gift for God.* London: Collins.

Moyne, Ernest J., trans. and ed. 1954. *Alexandra Gripenberg's* A Half Year in the New World: Miscellaneous Sketches of Travel in the United States. Cranbury, NJ: University of Delaware Press.

M'rabet, Fadela. 1969. *La Femme Algérienne suivi de les Algériennes.* Paris: F. Maspero.

Mullaney, Marie Marmo. 1990. "Sexual Politics in the Career and Legend of Louise Michel." *Signs* 15(2): 300–322.

Mulvey-Roberts, Marie. 2000. "Militancy, Masochism, or Martyrdom? The Public and Private Prisons of Constance Lytton." In June Purvis and Sandra Stanley Holton, eds., *Votes for Women.* London and New York: Routledge.

Mulvey-Roberts, Marie, and Tamae Mizuta, eds. 1994. *A Militant: Annie Kenney.* London: Routledge.

Mulvihill, Margaret. 1989. *Charlotte Despard.* London: Pandora.

Munnings, Gladys. 1993. *Canadian Women of Distinction: Emily Ferguson Murphy, Agnes Campbell, Thérèse Casgrain, Molly (Mary) Brant, Frances Anne Hopkins.* Newmarket, ON: Quaker Press.

Murray, Patricia. 1975. "Ichikawa Fusae and the Lonely Red Carpet." *Japan Interpreter* (2): 171–189.

Myrdal, Alva, and Viola Klein. 1956. *Women's Two Roles: Home and Work.* London: Routledge, Kegan Paul.

Naravan, V. S. 1980. *Sarojini Naidu: An Introduction to Her Life, Work and Poetry.* New Delhi: Orient Longmans.

Nation, Carry. 1908. *The Use and Need of the Life of Carry A. Nation, Written by Herself.* Topeka: F. M. Stevens & Sons.

Navarro, Marysa. 1977. "The Case of Eva Perón." *Signs* 3 (1), 229–240.

Nawaz, J. A. Shah. 1971. *Father and Daughter: A Political Autobiography.* Lahore: Nigarishat.

Neilans, Allison. 1936. "Changes in Sex Morality." In Ray Strachey, ed., *Our Freedom and Its Results by Five Women.* London: Hogarth Press.

Nelson, Cynthia. 1996. *Doria Shafiq, Egyptian Feminist: A Woman Apart.* Gainesville: University Press of Florida.

Nethercot, Arthur. 1960. *The First Five Lives of Annie Besant.* London: Rupert Hart-Davis.

———. 1963. *The Last Four Lives of Annie Besant.* London: Rupert Hart-Davis.

Nichols, Claudia. 1992. *Olympia Brown: Minister of Social Reform.* Unitarian Universalist Women's Heritage Society.

Niess, Judith. 1977. *Seven Women: Portraits from the American Radical Tradition.* New York: Viking Press.

Nightingale, Florence. 1978 [1928]. "Cassandra." In Ray Strachey, ed., *The Cause: A Brief History of the Women's Movement.* Reprint, London: Virago.

Nixon, Edna. 1971. *Mary Wollstonecraft: Her Life and Times.* London: Dent.

Noble, Christina, 1994. *Bridge across My Sorrows: The Christina Noble Story.* London: John Murray.

———. 1998. *Mama Tina.* London: John Murray.

Noble, Christina, and Robert Coram. 1994. *Nobody's Child: A Woman's Abusive Past and the Inspiring Dream That Led Her to Rescue the Street Children of Saigon.* New York: Grove Press.

Noonuccal, Oodgeroo. 1994. *Stradbroke Dreamtime.* New York: Lothrop, Lee, and Shepard Books.

Nord, Deborah E. 1985. *The Apprenticeship of Beatrice Webb.* London: Macmillan.

Norman, D. 1987. *Terrible Beauty: The Life of Constance Markievicz.* London: Hodder and Stoughton.

Norton, Caroline. 1855. "A Letter to the Queen on Lord Chancellor Cranworth's Marriage and Divorce Bill." London: Longman, Brown, Green.

Noun, Louise. 1985. "Amelia Bloomer, a Biography: Part I, the Lily of Seneca Falls." *The Annals of Iowa* 47(7): 575–617.

———. 1985. "Amelia Bloomer: Part II, the Suffragist of Council Bluffs." *The Annals of Iowa* 47(8): 575–621.

Nystrom-Hamilton, L. S. 1912. *Ellen Key: Her Life and Work.* New York: G. P. Putnam's Sons.

Oakley, Ann. 1983. "Millicent Garrett Fawcett: Duty and Determination." In Dale Spender, ed., *Feminist Theorists: Three Centuries of Women's Intellectual Traditions.* London: Women's Press.

Oakley, Mary Ann. 1972. *Elizabeth Cady Stanton.* New York: The Feminist Press.

Odell, Ruth. 1939. *Helen Hunt Jackson.* New York: D. Appleton-Century.

O'Faoláin, Sean. 1954. *Constance Markievicz.* London: Cape.

Offen, Karen. 2000. *European Feminisms 1700–1950: A Political History.* Palo Alto: Stanford University Press.

Old, Wendie. C. 1995. *Marian Wright Edelman: Fighting for Children's Rights.* Springfield, NJ: Enslow Publishers.

Oldfield, Sybil. 1997. "Eleanor Rathbone and India; Cultural Imperialist or Friend to Women?" *Asian Journal of Women's Studies* 3 (3), 157–168.

Ollif, Lorna. 1978. *Louisa Lawson: Henry Lawson's Crusading Mother.* Adelaide: Rigby.

O'Malley, Ida. 1931. *Florence Nightingale 1820–1856.* London: Thornton Butterworth.

O'Neill, William L. 1978. *The Last Romantic: A Life of Max Eastman.* New York: Oxford University Press.

Ortiz, V. 1974. *Sojourner Truth: A Self Made Woman.* Philadelphia: Lippincott.

Orton, D. 1980. *Made of Gold: A Biography of Angela Burdett-Coutts.* London: H. Hamilton.

Orzeskowa, Eliza. 1980. *The Forsaken, or Meir Ezofowich.* Bournemouth, UK: Delamare.

Osborne, William S. 1980. *Lydia Maria Child.* Boston: Twayne.

Otfinoski, Steve. 1991. *Marian Wright Edelman: Defender of Children's Rights.* Woodbridge, CT: Blackbirch Press.

Ovington, Mary White. 1995. *Black and White Sat Down Together: The Reminiscences of an NAACP Founder, Mary White Ovington.* New York: Feminist Press.

Painter, Nell Irvin. 1996. *Sojourner Truth: A Life, a Symbol.* New York: W. W. Norton.

Pandit, Vijay. 1979. *The Scope of Happiness: A Personal Memoir.* London: Weidenfeld and Nicolson.

Pankhurst, Christabel. 1913. *The Great Scourge and How to End It.* London: Woman's Press.

———. 1987 [1959]. *Unshackled: The Story of How We Won the Vote.* Reprint, London: Cresset Women's Voices.

Pankhurst, E. Sylvia. 1935. *Life of Emmeline Pankhurst.* London: Laurie.

———. 1977 [1931]. *The Suffragette Movement: An Intimate Account of Persons and Ideals.* Reprint, London: Virago.

Pankhurst, Emmeline. 1914. *My Own Story.* London: Eveleigh Nash.

Pankhurst, Richard. 1979. *Sylvia Pankhurst: Artist and Crusader.* London: Paddington Press.

Parker, Julia. 1988. *Women and Welfare: Ten Victorian Women in Public Social Service.* Basingstoke: Macmillan.

Parks, Rosa, with Gregory J. Reed. 1994. *Quiet Strength: The Faith, the Hope, and the Heart of a Woman Who Changed a Nation.* Grand Rapids, MI: Zondervan.

Parks, Rosa, with Jim Haskins. 1992. *Rosa Parks: My Story.* New York: Dial Books.

Pastor, Brigida. 1995. "Cuba's Covert Cultural Critic: The Feminist Writings of Gertrudis Gómez de Avellaneda." *Romance Quarterly* 42(3): 178–190.

Patterson, Clara Burdett. 1953. *Angela Burdett-Coutts and the Victorians.* London: John Murray.

Pattison, Walter Thomas. 1971. *Emilia Pardo Bazán.* New York: Twayne.

Pauli, Hertha E. 1957. *Cry of the Heart: The Story of Bertha von Suttner.* New York: I. Washburn.

———. 1962. *Her Name Was Sojourner Truth.* New York: Appleton-Century-Crofts.

Payne, Charles. 1989. "Ella Baker and Models of Social Change." *Signs* 14(4): 885–889.

Payne, Elizabeth Anne. 1988. *Reform, Labor, and Feminism: Margaret Dreier Robins and the Women's Trade Union League.* Urbana: University of Illinois Press.

Peare, Catherine Owen. 1951. *Mary McCleod Bethune.* New York: Vanguard.

Pearson, Sharyn. 1992. *The Shameless Scribbler: Louisa Lawson.* London: Sir Robert Menzies Centre for Australian Studies.

Peck, Mary Gray. 1944. *Carrie Chapman Catt: A Biography.* New York: H. W. Wilson.

Pedersen, Susan. 1996. "Rathbone and Daughter: Feminism and the Father in the Fin-de-Siècle." *Journal of Victorian Culture* 1(1): 98–117.

Peebles-Wilkins, Wilma, and Francis E. Aracelis. 1990. "Two Outstanding Black Women in Social Welfare History: Mary Church Terrell and Ida B. Wells-Barnett." *Affilia* 5(4): 87–100.

Pennington, Doris. 1989. *Agnes MacPhail, Reformer: Canada's First Female MP.* Toronto: Simon and Pierrre.

Perez, Frank. 1996. *Dolores Huerta.* Austin, TX: Raintree Steck-Vaughn.

Perkins, Alice J. G., and Theresa Wolfson. 1939. *Frances Wright, Free Enquirer: The Study of a Temperament.* New York: Harper Brothers.

Perkins, Anne. 1999. "Red Queen in the Pink." The *Guardian* profile. *Guardian,* 25 September: 6–7.

Perkins, Jane Grey. 1909. *The Life of Mrs. Norton.* London: John Murray.

Perón, Eva. 1953. *My Mission in Life.* New York: Vantage Press.

Peterson, William S. 1976. *Victorian Heretic: Mrs. Humphry Ward's Robert Elsmere.* Leicester: Leicester University Press.

Pethick-Lawrence, Emmeline. 1938. *My Part in a Changing World.* London: Victor Gollancz.

Pethick-Lawrence, Frederick. 1942. *Fate Has Been Kind.* London: Hutchinson.

Petrie, Glen. 1971. *A Singular Iniquity: The Campaigns of Josephine Butler.* London: Macmillan.

Pichanick, Valerie K. 1980. *Harriet Martineau: The Woman and Her Work 1802–1876.* Ann Arbor: University of Michigan Press.

Piehl, Mel. 1982. *Breaking Bread: The Catholic Workers and the Origin of Catholic Radicalism in America.* Philadelphia: Temple University Press.

Pinnock, Don. 1995. *Ruth First.* Cape Town: Maskew Miller Longman.

———. 1997. *Ruth First: Voices of Liberation.* Vol. 2. Pretoria: HSRC Publishers.

Pivar, David J. 1973. *Purity Crusade: Sexual Morality and Social Control, 1868–1900.* Westport, CT: Greenwood Press.

Pizzey, Erin. 1978. *Infernal Child: A Memoir.* London: Gollancz.

———. 1996. "Influences: Erin Pizzey, Campaigner for Women." *New Statesman Society,* 24 May, 21.

Plante, David. 1983. *Difficult Women: A Memoir of Three.* London: Victor Gollancz.

Playne, Caroline E. 1936. *Bertha von Suttner and the Struggle to Avert the World War.* London: Allen and Unwin.

Pollack, Jill S. 1994. *Shirley Chisholm.* New York: F. Watts.

Pollard, Arthur. 1965. *Mrs. Gaskell: Novelist and Biographer.* Manchester: Manchester University Press.

Popp, Adelheid. 1912. *Autobiography of a Working Woman.* London: T. F. Unwin.

Porter, Cathy. 1980. *Alexandra Kollontai: A Biography.* London: Virago.

Prasad, Raekha. 2000. "Lone Star of the Nile." The Guardian Profile. *Guardian,* 17 June, 6–7.

Prejean, Sister Helen. 1994. *Dead Man Walking: An Eyewitness Account of the Death Penalty in the United States.* New York: Vintage.

Pryor, E. B. 1987. *Clara Barton: A Professional Angel.* Philadelphia: University of Pennsylvania Press.

Purvis, June. 1996. "A 'Pair of . . . Infernal Queens'"? A Reassessment of Emmeline and Christabel Pankhurst, First Wave Feminists in Edwardian Britain." *Women's History Review* 5, no. 2: 259–280.

———. 1998. "Christabel Pankhurst and the Women's Social and Political Union." In Maroula Joannu and June Purvis, eds., *The Women's Suffrage Movement: New Feminist Perspectives.* Manchester: Manchester University Press.

Putnam, Ruth, ed. 1925. *Life and Letters of Mary Putnam Jacobi.* London: G. P. Putnam's Sons.

Rader, Emily. 2000. "The Indian Reform Letters of Helen Hunt Jackson, 1879–1885." *Pacific Historical Review* 69(2): 296–297.

Radice, Lisanne. 1984. *Beatrice and Sidney Webb: Fabian Socialists.* London: Macmillan.

Raikes, Elizabeth. 1909. *Dorothea Beale of Cheltenham.* London: Archibald Constable.

Ramabai, Pandita. 1981 [1887]. *The High-Caste Hindu Woman.* Reprint, Bombay: Maharashtra State Board for Literature and Culture.

Ramanathan, Malathi. 1989. *Sister Subbalakshmi: Social Reformer and Educationalist.* Bombay: Lok Vangmaya Griha.

Ramphele, Mamphela. 1991. *Bounds of Possibility: The Legacy of Steve Biko and Black Consciousness.* London: Zed Books.

———. 1993. *A Bed Called Home: Life in the Migrant Labour Hostels of Cape Town.* Cape Town: David Philip.

———. 1996. *Mamphela Ramphele: A Life.* Cape Town: David Philip.

———. 1997. *Across Boundaries: The Journey of a South African Woman Leader.* New York: Feminist Press.

Ranade, Ramabai. 1938. *The Autobiography of a Hindu Lady.* New York: Longmans.

Randall, Mercedes M. 1964. *Improper Bostonian: Emily Greene Balch.* New York: Twayne.

———, ed. 1972. *Beyond Nationalism: The Social Thought of Emily Greene Balch.* New York: Twayne.

Rathbone, Eleanor. 1924. *The Disinherited Family.* London: Edward Arnold.

———. 1934. *Child Marriage: The Indian Minotaur.* London: George Allen and Unwin.

———. 1949. *Family Allowances.* With an epilogue and new chapter on the family allowances movement, 1924–1947, by Eva Hubback. London: Allen and Unwin.

Rau, Davanthi Rama. 1977. *An Inheritance: The Memoirs of Davanthi Rama Rau.* London: Heinemann.

Ray, Janet. 1978. *Emily Stowe.* Toronto: Fitzhenry and Whiteside.

Rector, Margaret Hayden. 1992. *Alva, That Vanderbilt-Belmont Woman.* Wickford, RI: Dutch Island Press.

Reddy [I. E. Reddi], Muthulakshmi. 1964. *Autobiography of Mrs. S. Muthulakshmi.* Madras: n.p.

Reenen, Rykie van. 1984. *Emily Hobhouse: Boer War Letters*. Cape Town: Human and Rousseau.

Regan, M. Joanna, and Isabella Keiss. 1988. *Tender Courage: A Reflection of the Life and Spirit of Catherine McAuley, First Sister of Mercy*. Chicago: Franciscan Herald.

Reynolds, Larry J., and Susan B. Smith, eds. 1985. *Uncle Tom's Cabin and Mid-Nineteenth Century United States: Pen and Conscience*. Jefferson, NC: McFarland.

Reynolds, Moira Davison. 1988. *Nine American Women of the Nineteenth Century: Leaders into the Twentieth*. Jefferson, NC: McFarland.

———. 1994. *Women Advocates of Reproductive Rights: 11 Who Led the Struggle in the United States and Great Britain*. Jefferson, NC: McFarland.

Richard, Marthe. 1935. *I Spied for France: My Last Secret Missions 1936–9*. Translated by Gerald Griffin. London: J. Long.

Richards, Laura E., and Maude How Elliot. 1970 [1915]. *Julia Ward Howe 1819–1910*. Reprint, Boston: Houghton Mifflin.

Ridley, Annie E. 1895. *Frances Mary Buss and Her Work for Education*. London: Longman's, Green.

Roberts, Shirley. 1993. *Sophia Jex-Blake: A Woman Pioneer in Medical Reform*. London: Routledge.

Robins, Elizabeth. 1940. *Both Sides of the Curtain*. London: Heinemann.

———. 1980 [1907]. *The Convert*. Introduction by Jane Marcus. London: Women's Press.

Robinson, Jo Ann. 1987. *The Montgomery Bus Boycott and the Women Who Started It*. Knoxville: University of Tennessee Press.

Robinson, Marion O. 1966. *Eight Women of the YWCA*. New York: National Board of the Young Women's Christian Association of the U.S.A.

Robson, Ann P., and J. M. Robson, eds. 1994. *Sexual Equality: Writings by J. S. Mill, Harriet Taylor Mill and Helen Taylor*. Toronto: University of Toronto Press.

Romero, Patricia E. 1987. *Sylvia Pankhurst: Portrait of a Radical*. New Haven, CT: Yale University Press.

Ronda, Bruce A. 1991. *Elizabeth Peabody: A Reformer on Her Own Terms*. Cambridge, MA: Harvard University Press.

Rooth, Alice Signe. 1955. *Seeress of the Northland: Frederika Bremer's American Journey 1849–1851*. Philadelphia: American Swedish Historical Foundation.

Rose, June. 1992. *Marie Stopes and the Sexual Revolution*. London: Faber and Faber.

———. 1994 [1980]. *Elizabeth Fry*. Reprint, London: Macmillan.

Rose, Phyllis. 1983 [1942]. *Parallel Lives: Five Victorian Marriages*. Reprint, New York: Alfred A. Knopf.

Ross, Ishbel. 1956. *Angel of the Battlefield: The Life of Clara Barton*. New York: Harper.

Rossi, Alice S., ed. 1974. *Essays on Sex Equality by John Stuart Mill and Harriet Taylor Mill*. Chicago: University of Chicago Press.

Rountree, Cathleen. 1999. *On Women Turning 70: Honoring the Voices of Wisdom*. San Francisco: Jossey-Bass Publishers.

Royden, Maude. 1941. *Women's Partnership in the New World*. London: Allen and Unwin.

———. 1947. *A Three-Fold Cord*. London: Victor Gollancz.

Royster, Jacqueline Jones, ed. 1997. *Southern Horrors and Other Stories: The Anti-Lynching Campaign of Ida B. Wells*. New York: St. Martin's Press.

Rubel, David. 1990. *Fannie Lou Hamer: From Sharecropping to Politics*. Englewood Cliffs, NJ: Silver Burdett.

Rubin, S. A., and L. B. Alexander. 1998. "Regulating Pornography: The Feminist Influence." *Communications and the Law* 18(4): 73–94.

Rubinstein, David. 1991. *A Different World for Women: The Life of Millicent Garrett Fawcett*. Brighton: Harvester Wheatsheaf.

Rugoff, Milton. 1982. *The Beechers: An American Family in the Nineteenth Century*. New York: Harper & Row.

Ruser, Urusla-Maria. 1993. *Bertha von Suttner (1843–1914) and Other Women in Pursuit of Peace*. Geneva: United Nations Office at Geneva.

Russell, Jane. 1981. *Our George: A Biography of F. E. De Silva*. Colombo: Times of Ceylon.

Rye, Maria. 1987 [1859]. "The Rise and Progress of Telegraphs." In Candida Ann Lacey, ed., *Barbara Leigh Smith Bodichon and the Langham Place Group*. Reprint, London: Routledge and Kegan Paul.

———. 1987 [1860]. "On Assisted Emigration." In Candida Ann Lacey, ed., *Barbara Leigh Smith Bodichon and the Langham Place Group*. London: Routledge and Kegan Paul.

el-Saadawi, Nawal. 1980. *The Hidden Face of Eve: Women in the Arab World*. London: Zed Books.

———. 1991. *Searching*. Translated by Shirley Eber. London: Zed Books.

———. 1994. *Memoirs from the Women's Prison*. Translated by Marilyn Booth. Berkeley: University of California Press.

———. 1999. *A Daughter of Isis: The Autobiography of Nawal El Saadawi*. London: Zed Books.

Sachs, Emanie. 1978 [1928]. *"The Terrible Siren": Victoria Woodhull (1838–1927)*. Reprint, New York: Arno Press.

Saghal, Manmohini Zutshi. 1994. *An Indian Freedom Fighter Recalls Her Life*. Armonk, NY: M. E. Sharpe.

Salomon, Alice. 1937. *Education for Social Work*. Zurich: Verlag für Recht und Gesellschaft AG.

Salter, Elizabeth. 1971. *Daisy Bates: "The Great White Queen of the Never Never."* Sydney: Angus and Robertson.

Sandall, Robert, et al. 1955. *The History of the Salvation Army,* vol. 3, *Social Reform and Welfare Work.* London: T. Nelson.

Sanders, Byrne Hope. 1945. *Emily Murphy, Crusader: "Janey Canuck."* Toronto: Macmillan.

Sanger, Margaret. 1931. *My Fight for Birth Control.* New York: Farrar and Rinehart.

———. 1938. *Margaret Sanger: An Autobiography.* New York: Norton.

Sansome, Diana. 1996. *The Influence of Catherine Helen Spence on Social and Political Reform in South Australia, 1860–1910.* Medford, MA: Unitarian Universalist Women's Heritage Society.

Sapiro, Virginia. 1992. *A Vindication of Political Virtue: The Political Theory of Mary Wollstonecraft.* Chicago: University of Chicago Press.

Sarah, Elizabeth. 1983. "Christabel Pankhurst: Reclaiming Her Power." In Dale Spender, ed., *Feminist Theorists: Three Centuries of Women's Intellectual Traditions.* London: Women's Press.

Savage, Candace. *Our Nell: A Scrapbook Biography of Nellie L. McClung.* Saskatoon: Western Producer Prairie Books.

Saywell, Ruby J. 1964. *Mary Carpenter of Bristol.* Bristol: Historical Association.

Scharnhorst, Gary. 1985. *Charlotte Perkins Gilman.* Boston: Twayne.

Schlafly, Phyllis. 1964. *A Choice, Not an Echo.* Alton, IL: Pere Marquette Press.

Schlaifer, Charles, and Lucy Freeman. 1991. *Heart's Work: Civil War Heroine and Champion of the Mentally Ill Dorothea Lynde Dix.* New York: Paragon House.

Schneiderman, Rose, with Lucy Goldthwaite. 1967. *All for One.* New York: Eriksson.

Schoenbaum, Eleanora, ed. 1979. *Political Profiles: The Nixon Ford Years.* New York: Facts on File.

Schreiner, Olive. 1978 [1911]. *Woman and Labour.* Reprint, London: Virago.

Scott, John Anthony. 1978. *Woman against Slavery: The Story of Harriet Beecher Stowe.* New York: Thomas Y. Crowell.

Scudder, Vida. 1937. *On Journey.* Boston: E. P. Dutton.

Seacole, Mary. 1988 [1857]. *The Wonderful Adventures of Mrs. Seacole in Many Lands.* Introduction by William L. Andrews. Reprint, Oxford: Oxford University Press.

Seagrave, Sterling. 1996. *The Soong Dynasty.* New York: Harper.

Seaton, Helen J. "Another Florence Nightingale: The Rediscovery of Mary Seacole." Accessed at www.icml.org/Monday/hlg3/seaton.

Sebba, Anna. 1997. *Mother Teresa: Beyond the Image.* London: Weidenfeld.

Sekuless, Peter. 1978. *Jessie Street: A Rewarding but Unrewarded Life.* St. Lucia: Queensland University Press.

Sen Gupta, Padmini. 1966. *Sarojini Naidu.* London: Asia Publishing House.

———. 1970. *Pandita Ramabai Saraswati: Her Life and Work.* Bombay: Asia Publishing House.

———, ed. 1994.[1944]. *Pioneer Women of India.* Reprint, Bombay: Thacker.

Senier, Siobhan. 2001. *Voices of American Indian Assimilation and Resistance: Helen Hunt Jackson, Sarah Winnemucca, and Victoria Howard.* Norman: University of Oklahoma Press.

Severn, Bill. 1976. *Frances Perkins: A Member of the Cabinet.* New York: Hawthorn Books.

Sewall, May Wright, ed. 1894. *The World's Congress of Representative Women.* Chicago: Rand, McNally.

Seymour-Jones, Carolyn. 1992. *Beatrice Webb: Woman of Conflict.* London: Allison and Busby.

Sha'rawi, Huda. 1987. *Harem Years: The Memoirs of an Egyptian Feminist.* London: Virago.

Sharp, Ingrid, and June Jordan, eds. Forthcoming. *Diseases of the Body Politic: Josephine Butler and the Prostitution Campaigns.* 5 vols. London: Routledge.

Shaw, Anna Howard. 1994 [1915]. *The Story of a Pioneer.* Reprint, Cleveland: Pilgrim Press.

Shaw, Marion. 1999. *The Clear Stream: A Life of Winifred Holtby.* London: Virago.

Sherr, Lynn. 1995. *Failure Is Impossible: Susan B. Anthony in Her Own Words.* New York: Times Books.

Shillito, Elizabeth. 1920. *Dorothea Beale: Principal of the Cheltenham Ladies' College 1858–1906.* London: Society for the Promotion of Christian Knowledge.

Shoemaker, Adam, ed. 1994. *Oodgeroo: A Tribute.* St. Lucia: University of Queensland Press.

Shulman, Alix Kates, ed. 1971. *To the Barricades: The Anarchist Life of Emma Goldman.* New York: Crowell.

———. 1972. *Red Emma Speaks: Selected Writings and Speeches by Emma Goldman.* New York: Vintage Books.

———. 1983. "Emma Goldman: Anarchist Queen." In Dale Spender, ed., *Feminist Theorists: Three Centuries of Women's Intellectual Traditions.* London: Women's Press.

Sicherman, Barbara. 1984. *Alice Hamilton: A Life in Letters.* Cambridge, MA: Harvard University Press.

Siegel, Beatrice. 1983. *Lillian Wald of Henry Street.* New York: Macmillan.

Silcox-Jarrett, Diane. 1995. *Charlotte Hawkins Brown: One Woman's Dream.* Winston-Salem: Bandit Books.

Singer, Sandra L. 1995. *Free Soul, Free Woman? A Study of Selected Fictional Works of Hedwig Dohm, Isolde Kurz, and Helen Böhlau.* New York: P. Lang.

Sister Nivedita. 1967–1975. *The Complete Works of Sister Nivedita.* Calcutta: Ramakrishna Sarada Mission.

———. 1970s. *The Web of Indian Life: Collected Works.* 2d ed. Calcutta: Ramakrishna Sarada Mission.

Sklar, Katharine. 1976. *Catherine Beecher: A Study in American Domesticity.* New Haven: Yale University Press.

———. 1986. *The Autobiography of Florence Kelley: Notes of Sixty Years.* Chicago: Charles H. Kerr.

———. 1995. *Florence Kelley and the Nation's Work: The Rise of Women's Political Culture, 1830–1900.* New Haven: Yale University Press.

Skoglund, Elizabeth R. *Amma: The Life and Words of Amy Carmichael.* Grand Rapids, MI: Baker Books.

Small, Hugh. 1998. *Florence Nightingale: Avenging Angel.* London: Constable.

Smallwood, Caid, Stan West, and Allison Keyes. 1998. *Profiles of Great African Americans.* Lincolnwood, IL: Publications International.

Smilowitz, Erika Sollish. 1983. "Una Marson: Woman before Her Time." *Jamaica Journal* (May): 29–30.

———. 1986. *Expatriate Women Writers from Former British Colonies: A Bio-critical Study of Katherine Mansfield, Jean Rhys, and Una Marson.* Unpublished thesis.

Smith, Esther M. 1980. *Mrs. Humphry Ward.* Boston: Twayne.

Smith, F. B. 1982. *Florence Nightingale: Reputation and Power.* London: Croom Helm.

Smith, Honor Ford, ed. 1986. *Una Marson: Black Nationalist and Feminist Writer.* Kingston, Jamaica: Sistren Publications.

Smith, Sally Bedell. 2000. *Diana in Search of Herself: Portrait of a Troubled Princess.* London: Signet.

Sorabji, Cornelia. 1932. *Susie Sorabji: A Memoir by Her Sister.* London: Oxford University Press.

———. 1934. *India Calling.* London: Nisbet.

———. 1936. *India Recalled.* London: Nisbet.

Spack, Ruth. 1997. "Re-visioning Sioux Women: Zitkala-Ša's Revolutionary American Indian Stories." *Legacy* 14(1): 25–42.

Spence, Catherine Helen. 1975 [1910]. *Catherine Helen Spence: An Autobiography.* Edited by Jeanne F. Young. Reprint, Adelaide: Libraries Board of South Australia.

Spencer, Jane. 1993. *Elizabeth Gaskell.* Basingstoke: Macmillan.

Spender, Lynne. 1983. "Matilda Joslyn Gage: Active Intellectual." In Dale Spender, ed., *Feminist Theorists: Three Centuries of Women's Intellectual Traditions.* London: Women's Press.

Spink, Kathryn. 1997. *Mother Teresa: An Authorised Biography.* London: HarperCollins.

Sreenivasan, Jyotsna. 2000. *Ela Bhatt: Uniting Women in India.* New York: Feminist Press.

Standing, E. M. 1957. *Maria Montessori: Her Life and Work.* London: Hollis and Carter.

Stanley, Liz. 1983. "Olive Schreiner: New Women, Free Women, All Women." In Dale Spender, ed., *Feminist Theorists: Three Centuries of Women's Intellectual Traditions.* London: Women's Press.

Stannard, Una. 1977. *Mrs. Man.* San Francisco: Germaine Books.

Stanton, Elizabeth Cady. 1898. *Eighty Years and More: Reminiscences of Elizabeth Cady Stanton.* London: T. Fisher Unwin.

———. 1993 [1895, 1898]. *The Woman's Bible.* Reprint, Boston: Northeastern University Press.

Stanton, Theodore, and Harriet Stanton Blatch, eds. 1922. *Elizabeth Cady Stanton as Revealed in her Letters, Diary, and Reminiscences.* 2 vols. New York: Arno Press.

Steadman, F. C. 1931. *In the Days of Miss Beale: A Study of Her Work and Influence.* London: E. J. Burrow.

Steedman, Carolyn. 1990. *Childhood, Culture and Class in Britain: Margaret McMillan 1860–1931.* London: Virago.

Steel, Edward M. 1985. *The Correspondence of Mother Jones.* Pittsburgh: University of Pittsburgh Press.

———, ed. 1988. *The Speeches and Writings of Mother Jones.* Pittsburgh: University of Pittsburgh Press.

Stein, L., and A. Baxter. 1974. *Grace H. Dodge: Her Life and Work.* New York: Arno Press.

Stendhal, Brita K. 1994. *The Education of a Self-Made Woman: Frederika Bremer, 1801–1865.* Lewiston, ME: Edwin Mellen Press.

Stephen, Barbara Nightingale. 1976. *Emily Davies and Girton College.* Westport, CT: Hyperion Press.

Sterling, Dorothy. 1964. *Lucretia Mott: Gentle Warrior.* Garden City, NY: Doubleday.

———. 1991. *Ahead of Her Time: Abby Kelley and the Politics of Antislavery.* New York: Norton.

———. 1994 [1979]. *Black Foremothers: Three Lives.* New York: Feminist Press.

Stern, Madeleine B., ed. 1979. *The Victoria Woodhull Reader.* Weston, MA: M and S Press (includes Woodhull's major suffrage speeches).

Sterne, Emma Gelders. 1957. *Mary McCleod Bethune.* New York: Alfred A. Knopf.

Stevens, Doris. 1976 [1920]. *Jailed for Freedom.* Reprint, New York: Schocken Books.

Steward, Jane Agnes. 1906. *The Frances Willard Book.* Philadelphia: Current Syndicate.

Stewart, Dianne. 1996. *Lillian Ngoyi, 1911–1980.* Cape Town: Maskew, Miller, Longman.

Stewart, M., and D. French. 1959. *Ask No Quarter: A Biography of Agnes MacPhail.* Toronto: Longman's Green.

Stewart, William Rhinelander. 1911. *The Philanthropic Work of Josephine Shaw Lowell.* New York: Macmillan.

Stocks, Mary. 1949. *Eleanor Rathbone: A Biography.* London: Gollancz.

Stoll, David. 1999. *Rigoberta Menchú and the Story of All Poor Guatemalans.* Boulder: Westview Press.

Stoneman, Patsy. 1987. *Elizabeth Gaskell.* Brighton: Harvester.

Stopes, Marie. 1995 [1918]. *Married Love.* Reprint, London: Gollancz.

Stowe, Charles Edward. 1889. *Life of Harriet Beecher Stowe: Compiled from Her Letters and Journals by Her Son.* London: S. Low, Marston, Searle and Rivington.

Strachey, Ray. 1912. *Frances Willard, Her Life and Work.* London: T. Fisher Unwin.

———. 1931. *Millicent Garrett Fawcett.* London: John Murray.

Strangwayes-Booth, Joanna. 1976. *A Cricket in the Thorn Tree: Helen Suzman and the Progressive Party of South Africa.* Bloomington: Indiana University Press.

Strawn, Sonia Reid. 1988. *Where There Is No Path: Lee Tai-Young, Her Story.* Seoul: Korea Legal Aid Center for Family Relations.

Street, Jessie. 1966. *Truth or Repose.* Sydney: Australasian Book Society.

Strumhinger, Laura S. 1988. *The Odyssey of Flora Tristan.* New York: Peter Lang.

Suhl, Yuri. 1959. *Ernestine Rose and the Battle for Human Rights.* New York: Reynal.

———. 1970. *Eloquent Crusader: Ernestine L. Rose.* New York: J. Messner.

Sullivan, Mary C. 1995. *Catherine McAuley and the Tradition of Mercy.* Notre Dame: University of Indiana Press.

Sutherland, John. 1990. *Mrs. Humphry Ward: Eminent Victorian, Pre-Eminent Edwardian.* Oxford: Clarendon Press.

Suttner, Bertha von. 1972 [1910]. *Memoirs of Bertha von Suttner: The Records of an Eventful Life.* Reprint, New York: Garland.

———. 1972 [1906]. *Lay Down Your Arms.* Reprint, New York: Garland.

Suzman, Helen. 1993. *In No Uncertain Terms: A South African Memoir.* New York: Alfred A. Knopf.

Swanwick, Helena. 1935. *I Have Been Young.* London: Gollancz.

———. 1971. *Women and War.* Introduction by Blanche Wiesen Cook. New York: Garland.

Sykes, Christopher. 1972. *Nancy: The Life of Lady Astor.* London: Collins.

Tarbell, Ida M. 1939. *All in the Day's Work: An Autobiography by Ida M. Tarbell.* New York: Macmillan Company.

Tata, Lady. 1933. *A Book of Remembrance.* Bombay: J. B. Dubash.

Taylor, Anne. 1992. *Annie Besant: A Biography.* Oxford: Oxford University Press.

Taylor, Gail. 1999. *Oodgeroo Noonuccal.* Sydney: Hodder Education.

Taylor, Jean Stewart. 1976. "Raden Ajeng Kartinin." *Signs* 1(3): 639–661.

Taylor, Julie M. 1979. *Evita Perón: The Myths of a Woman.* Oxford: Blackwell.

Taylor, Robert Lewis. 1966. *Vessel of Wrath: The Life and Times of Carry Nation.* New York: New American Library.

Terrell, Mary Church. 1980 [1940]. *A Colored Woman in a White World.* Reprint, New York: Arno Press.

Tharp, Louise Hall. 1950. *The Peabody Sisters of Salem.* Boston: Little, Brown.

Thomas, Clara. 1967. *Love and Work Enough: The Life of Anna Jameson.* Toronto: University of Toronto Press.

Thomas, Edith. 1980. *Louise Michel.* Montreal: Black Rose.

Thompson, Mildred I. 1990. *Ida B. Wells Barnett: An Exploratory Study of an American Black Woman, 1893–1930.* New York: Carlson Publishing.

Thomson, Helen, ed. 1987. *Catherine Helen Spence.* St. Lucia: University of Queensland Press.

Tiffany, Francis. 1992 [1891]. *Life of Dorothea Dix.* Reprint, Salem, MA: Higginson.

Tims, Margaret. 1961. *Jane Addams of Hull House, 1860–1935: A Centenary Study.* London: Allen and Unwin.

Tipton, Elise K. 1997. "Ishimoto Shizue: The Margaret Sanger of Japan." *Women's History Review* 6(3): 337–356.

Todd, Janet. 1976. *Mary Wollstonecraft: A Social Pioneer.* London: Millington.

———. 2000. *Mary Wollstonecraft: A Revolutionary Life.* London: Weidenfeld and Nicolson.

Todd, Margaret. 1918. *The Life of Sophia Jex-Blake.* London: Macmillan.

Tomalin, Claire. 1985 [1974]. *The Life and Death of Mary Wollstonecraft.* Reprint, Harmondsworth: Penguin Books.

Tomoko Yamazaki. 1985. *The Story of Yamada Waka: From Prostitute to Feminist Pioneer.* Tokyo: Kodansha International.

Trevelyan, Janet P. 1923. *The Life of Mrs. Humphry Ward.* London: Constable.

"A Tribute to Doreen Wickremasinghe." www.island.LK/2000/06/07/mdwkrvw.

Tristan, Flora. 1982 [1840]. *The London Journal of Flora Tristan.* Translated by Jean Hawkes. London: Virago.

Truth, Sojourner. 1991 [1850]. *Narrative of Sojourner Truth, a Bondswoman of Olden Times.* Reprint, New York: Oxford University Press.

Tucker, Frederick Booth. 1893. *The Life of Catherine Booth, the Mother of the Salvation Army.* New York: Fleming H. Revell.

Turoff, Barbara K. 1979. *Mary Beard as Force in History.* Dayton, OH: Wright State University Press.

Twining, Louisa. 1893. *Recollections of Life and Work, Being the Autobiography of Louisa Twining.* London: Edward Arnold.

———. 1979 [1885]. "Suggestions for Women Guardians." In Patricia Hollis, ed., *Women in Public 1850–1900: Documents of the Victorian Women's Movement.* London: Allen and Unwin.

Uglow, Jennifer. 1983. "Josephine Butler: From Sympathy to Theory." In Dale Spender, ed., *Feminist Theorists: Three Centuries of Women's Intellectual Traditions.* London: Women's Press.

———. 1993. *Elizabeth Gaskell: A Habit of Stories.* London: Faber and Faber.

Umansky, Ellen M. 1983. *Lily Montagu and the Advancement of Liberal Judaism: From Vision to Vocation.* New York: Edwin Mellen Press.

———. 1985. *Lily Montagu: Sermons, Addresses, Letters and Prayers.* New York: Edwin Mellen Press.

Underhill, Lois Beachy. 1995. *The Woman Who Ran for President: The Many Lives of Victoria Woodhull.* Bridgehampton, NY: Bridge Works Publishing.

Urbanski, Marie Mitchell Olesen. 1980. *Margaret Fuller's "Woman in the Nineteenth Century": A Literary Study of Form and Content, of Sources and Influence.* Westport, CT: Greenwood Press.

———. 1983. "Margaret Fuller: Feminist Writer and Revolutionary." In Dale Spender, ed., *Feminist Theorists: Three Centuries of Women's Intellectual Traditions.* London: Women's Press.

Van Drenth, A., and F. de Haan. 1999. *The Rise of Caring Power: Elizabeth Fry and Josephine Butler in Britain and the Netherlands.* Amsterdam: Amsterdam University Press.

Van Thal, Herbert. 1929. *Eliza Lynn Linton.* London: Allen and Unwin.

Van Voris, Jacqueline. 1967. *Constance Markievicz in the Cause of Ireland.* Amherst: University of Massachusetts Press.

———. 1987. *Carrie Chapman Catt: A Public Life.* New York: Feminist Press.

Vavich, Dee Ann. 1967. "The Japan Woman's Suffrage Movement: Ichikawa Fusae—A Pioneer in Woman's Suffrage." *Monumenta Nipponica* 22(3/4): 401–436.

Vellacott, Jo. 1993. *From Liberal to Labour with Women's Suffrage: The Story of Catherine Marshall.* Montreal: McGill-Queen's University Press.

Vicinus, Martha, and Bea Nergaard, eds. 1989. *Ever Yours, Florence Nightingale.* London: Virago.

Victor, Barbara. 1994. *A Voice of Reason: Hanan Ashrawi and Peace in the Middle East.* New York:

Harcourt Brace and Co.

———. 1998. *The Lady: Aung San Suu Kyi, Nobel Laureate and Burma's Prisoner.* Boston: Faber and Faber.

Vietor, A. G., ed. 1924. *A Woman's Quest: The Life of Marie Elizabeth Zakrzewska MD.* New York: Appleton.

Waddell, Craig, ed. 2000. *And No Birds Sing: Rhetorical Analyses of Rachel Carson's* Silent Spring. Carbondale: Southern Illinois University Press.

Wade, Mason. 1940. *Margaret Fuller: Whetstone of Genius.* New York: Viking.

Wadsworth, Ginger. 1991. *Rachel Carson: Voice of the Earth.* New York: Lerner Publications.

Wagenecht, Edward. 1965. *Harriet Beecher Stowe: The Known and the Unknown.* New York: Oxford University Press.

———. 1983. *Daughters of the Covenant: Portraits of Six Jewish Women.* Amherst: University of Massachusetts Press.

Wagner, Sally Roesch. 1994. *Matilda Joslyn Gage: Forgotten Feminist.* Aberdeen, SD: Sky Carrier Press.

———. 1998. *She Who Holds the Sky: Matilda Joslyn Gage.* Aberdeen, SD: Sky Carrier Press.

Waite, Helen, and Elmira Waite. 1961. *Valiant Companions: Helen Keller and Annie Sullivan Macy.* London: Hodder and Stoughton.

Wald, Lillian. 1991 [1915]. *The House on Henry Street.* Reprint, New Brunswick, NJ: Transaction Publishers.

Waley, M. 1976. *Winifred Holtby: A Short Life.* Privately printed.

Walker, Martin. 2000. "Betty Friedan and the American Woman." In *America Reborn: A Twentieth-Century Narrative in Twenty-Six Lives.* New York: Knopf.

Wallace, Aubrey, and David Gancher. 1993. *Eco-heroes: Twelve Tales of Environmental Victory.* San Francisco: Mercury House.

Wallace, Christine. 1999. *Germaine Greer: Untamed Shrew.* London: Richard Cohen Books.

Walters, Margaret. 1976. "The Rights and Wrongs of Women: Mary Wollstonecraft, Harriet Martineau, Simone de Beauvoir." In Juliet Mitchell and Ann Oakley, eds., *The Rights and Wrongs of Women.* Harmondsworth: Penguin.

Wandersee, Winifred D. 1993. "'I'd Rather Pass a Law Than Organize a Union': Frances Perkins and the Reformist Approach to Organized Labor." *Labor History* 34(1): 5.

Wangari, Maathai. 1994. *The Bottom Is Heavy Too: Even with the Green Belt Movement.* Edinburgh: Edinburgh University Press.

Ward, Geoffrey C., and Ken Burns. 1999. *Not for*

Ourselves Alone: The Story of Elizabeth Cady Stanton and Susan B. Anthony—An Illustrated History. New York: Alfred A. Knopf.

Ward, Margaret. 1990. *Maud Gonne: Ireland's Joan of Arc.* London: Pandora.

Wardle, Ralph M. 1951. *Mary Wollstonecraft: A Critical Biography.* Lawrence: University of Kansas Press.

Warne, Randi R. 1993. *Literature as Pulpit: The Christian Social Activism of Nellie L. McClung.* Waterloo: Wilfred Laurier University Press.

Waterman, William R. 1924. *Frances Wright.* New York: Columbia University Press.

Watson, David. 1988. *Margaret Fuller: An American Romantic.* New York and Oxford: St. Martin's Press and Berg.

Watson, Martha. 1987. *Emma Goldman.* Boston: Twayne.

Waugh, Joan. 1997. *Unsentimental Reformer: The Life of Josephine Shaw Lowell.* Cambridge, MA: Harvard University Press.

Waxman, Sydell. 1996. *Changing the Pattern: The Story of Emily Stowe.* Toronto: Napoleon Publishing.

Webb, R. K. 1960. *Harriet Martineau: A Radical Victorian.* London: Heinemann.

Wedin, Carolyn. 1997. *Inheritors of the Spirit: Mary White Ovington and the Founding of the NAACP.* New York: John Wiley.

Weiner, Gaby. 1983. "Harriet Martineau: A Reassessment (1802–1876)." In Dale Spender, ed., *Feminist Theorists: Three Centuries of Women's Intellectual Traditions.* London: Women's Press.

———. 1983. "Vida Goldstein: The Women's Candidate (1869–1949)." In Dale Spender, ed., *Feminist Theorists: Three Centuries of Women's Intellectual Traditions.* London: Women's Press.

Wellman, Sam. 1998. *Amy Carmichael: A Life Abandoned to God.* Uhrichville, OH: Barbour Publishing.

Wells-Barnett, Ida B. 1970. *Crusade for Justice: The Autobiography of Ida B. Wells.* Chicago: University of Chicago Press.

Wergeland, Agnes Mathilde, and Katharine Merrill. 1916. "Camilla Collett: A Centenary Tribute, January 23, 1813–January 23, 1914." In Agnes Mathilde Wergeland, ed., *Leaders in Norway and Other Essays.* Menasha, WI: Banta.

West, Rebecca. 1992. "The Life of Emily Davison." In Jane Marcus, ed., *The Young Rebecca: Writings of Rebecca West 1911–17.* London: Macmillan.

———. 1992. "A Reed of Steel." In Jane Marcus, ed., *The Young Rebecca: Writings of Rebecca West 1911–17.* London: Macmillan.

Wexler, Alice. 1984. *Emma Goldman: An Intimate Life.* New York: Pantheon.

———. 1989. *Emma Goldman in Exile.* Boston: Beacon Press.

Wheatley, Vera. 1957. *Life and Work of Harriet Martineau.* London: Secker and Warburg.

Wheaton, Elizabeth. 2001. *MS: The Story of Gloria Steinem.* Greensboro, NC: Morgan Reynolds.

Wheeler, Leslie. 1981. *Loving Warriors: Selected Letters of Lucy Stone and Henry B. Blackwell, 1853–1893.* New York: Dial Press.

———. 1983. "Lucy Stone: Radical Beginnings." In Dale Spender, ed., *Feminist Theorists: Three Centuries of Women's Intellectual Traditions.* London: Women's Press.

———. 1991. *Rachel Carson.* Englewood Cliffs, NJ: Silver Burdett Press.

Whitmarsh, A. 1981. *Simone de Beauvoir and the Limits of Commitment.* Cambridge: Cambridge University Press.

Whitney, Janet. 1936. *Elizabeth Fry, Quaker Heroine.* Boston: Little, Brown.

Willard, Frances. 1991. *How I Learned to Ride the Bicycle: Reflections of an Influential Nineteenth Century Woman.* Edited by Carol O'Hare. Sunnyvale, CA: Fair Oaks.

———. 1995. *Writing Out My Heart: Selections from the Journal of Frances E. Willard, 1855–96.* Urbana: University of Illinois Press.

Williams, Constance. 1907. *Frances Willard: The Record of a Noble Life.* London: Sunday School Union.

Williams, Edwin Bucher. 1924. *The Life and Dramatic Works of Gertrudis Gómez de Avellaneda.* Philadelphia: n.p.

Williams, Gary J. 1999. *The Hungry Heart: The Literary Emergence of Julia Ward Howe.* Amherst: University of Massachusetts Press.

Williamson, Joseph. 1977. *Josephine Butler: The Forgotten Saint.* Leighton Buzzard, UK: Faith Press.

Williamson, Lori. 2001. *Power and Protest: Frances Power Cobbe and Victorian Society.* London: Rivers Oram Press.

Willis, Jean L. 1983. "Alice Paul: The Quintessential Feminist." In Dale Spender, ed., *Feminist Theorists: Three Centuries of Women's Intellectual Traditions.* London: Women's Press.

Wilson, Dorothy Clarke. 1870. *Lone Woman: The Story of Elizabeth Blackwell, the First Woman Doctor.* Boston: Little, Brown.

———. 1975. *Stranger and Traveler: The Story of Dorothea Dix, American Reformer.* Boston: Little, Brown.

Wilson, Forrest. 1941. *Crusader in Crinoline: The Life of Harriet Beecher Stowe.* Philadelphia: Lippincott.

Wilson, Francesca M. 1967. *Rebel Daughter of a Country House.* London: George Allen and Unwin.

Wilson, Howard E. 1928. *Mary McDowell, Neighbor.* Chicago: University of Chicago Press.

Winslow, Barbara. 1996. *Sylvia Pankhurst: Sexual Politics and Political Activism.* London: UCL Press.

Wiseman, Alberta. 1976. *Rebels and Reformers, Biographies of Four Jewish Americans.* Garden City, NY: Zenith Books.

Wolfe, Alan. 1999. "The Mystique of Betty Friedan—Looking Back at the Foundations of Friedan's Theory." *The Atlantic* 284(3): 98–105.

Women's Medical Association of New York. 1925. *Mary Putnam Jacobi, M.D. A Pathfinder in Medicine, with Selections from Her Writings and a Complete Bibliography.* New York: G. P. Putnam's Sons.

Woodham-Smith, Cecil. 1950. *Florence Nightingale, 1820–1910.* Edinburgh: Constable.

Woolf, Virginia. 1986 [1932]. "Mary Wollstonecraft." In Woolf, *The Common Reader,* Second Series. Reprint, London: Hogarth Press.

Wymer, Norman. 1965. *Helen Keller.* London: Macdonald.

Wynner, Edith. 1947 [1939]. *Rosika Schwimmer, World Patriot.* Reprint, New York: Degen.

Yamada Waka. 1935. *The Social Status of Japanese Women.* Tokyo: Kokusai Bunka Shinkokai (Society for International Cultural Relations).

Yeo, Eileen Janes, ed. 1997. *Mary Wollstonecraft and 200 Years of Feminisms.* London: Rivers Oram Press.

Young, Jean. 1937. *Catherine Helen Spence: A Study and an Appreciation.* Melbourne: Lothian.

Zeitlin, Rose. 1952. *Henrietta Szold: Record of a Life.* New York: Dial Press.

Zitkala-Sa. 1985 [1921]. *American Indian Stories.* Reprint, Lincoln: University of Nebraska Press.

General Works on Feminism, Social Reform, and Women's History

Accampo, Elinor, Rachel G. Fuchs, and Mary L. Stewart. 1995. *Gender and the Politics of Social Reform in France 1870–1914.* Baltimore: Johns Hopkins University Press.

Adams, W. H. Davenport. 1889. *Celebrated Women Travellers of the Nineteenth Century.* London: W. S. Sonnenschein.

Adickes, Sandra. 1997. *To Be Young Was Very Heaven: Women in New York before the Great War.* Basingstoke: Macmillan.

Afkhami, Mahnaz, and Erika Friedl, eds. 1994. *In the Eye of the Storm: Women in Post-Revolutionary Iran.* London: Tauris.

Afshar, Haleh. 1987. *Women, State and Ideology: Studies from Africa and Asia.* Basingstoke: Macmillan.

———. 1994. *Why Fundamentalism?* York: University of York.

———. 1998. *Islam and Feminisms: An Iranian Case Study.* Basingstoke: Macmillan.

———, ed. 1996. *Women and Politics in the Third World.* London: Routledge.

Ahmed, Leila. 1992. *Women and Gender in Islam: Historical Roots of a Modern Debate.* New Haven: Yale University Press.

Alberti, Johanna. 1989. *Beyond Suffrage: Feminists in War and Peace, 1914–1928.* London: Macmillan.

Alexander, Sally. 1988. *Women's Fabian Tracts.* London: Routledge.

———. 1994. *Becoming a Woman and Other Essays in Nineteenth and Twentieth Century Feminist History.* London: Virago.

Allen, Ann Taylor. 1989. "German Radical Feminism and Eugenics, 1900–1918." *German Studies Review* 2: 31–56.

———. 1991. *Feminism and Motherhood in Germany, 1800–1914.* New Brunswick: Rutgers University Press.

Anderson, Harriet. 1992. *Utopian Feminism: Women's Movements in Fin-de-Siècle Vienna.* New Haven, CT: Yale University Press.

Andors, Phyllis. 1983. *The Unfinished Liberation of Chinese Women, 1949–1980.* Bloomington: Indiana University Press.

Anthony, Katherine S. 1915. *Feminism in Germany and Scandinavia.* New York: Henry Holt.

Anthony, Susan B., and Ida Husted Harper. 1902, 1922. *History of Woman Suffrage.* Vols. 4–6. Indianapolis, IN: Hollenbeck Press (vol. 4); New York: NAWSA (vol. 5–6).

Applewhiter, H. B., M. D. Johnson, and D. G. Levy. 1979. *Women in Revolutionary Paris.* Urbana: University of Illinois Press.

Asthana, Pratima. 1974. *The Women's Movement in India.* Delhi: Vikas Publishing House.

Atkinson, Dorothy, Alexander Dallin, and Gail Warshofsky, eds. 1978. *Women in Russia.* Hassocks, Sussex: Harvester Press.

Attallah, Naim. 1998. *In Conversation with Naim Attallah.* London: Quartet Books.

Avakian, Monique. 2000. *Reformers, Activists, Educators, Religious Leaders.* Austin, TX: Raintree Steck-Vaughn.

Azari, Farah. 1983. *Women of Iran: The Conflict with Fundamentalist Iran.* London: Ithaca Press.

Bacchi, C. I. 1983. *Liberation Deferred? The Ideas of the English-Canadian Suffragists 1877–1918.* Toronto: University of Toronto Press.

Bacon, Margaret Hope. 1986. *Mothers of Feminism: The Story of Quaker Women in America.* San Francisco: Harper and Row.

Baden-Powell, Olave. 1973. *Window on My Heart: The Autobiography of Olave, Lady Baden-Powell.* London: Hodder and Stoughton.

Bader-Zaar, Birgitta. 1996. "Women in Austrian Politics, 1890–1934: Goals and Vision." In David F. Good, Margarete Grander, and Mary Jo Maynes, eds., *Austrian Women in the Nineteenth and Twentieth Centuries: Cross Disciplinary Perspectives.* Providence: Berghahn Books.

Badran, Margot. 1995. *Feminists, Islam and Nation: Gender and the Making of Modern Egypt.* Princeton: Princeton University Press.

Badran, Margot, and Margaret Cooke, eds. 1990. *Opening the Gates: A Century of Arab Feminist Writing.* London: Virago.

Bagwell, P. 1987. *Outcast London, a Christian Response: The West London Mission of the Methodist Church 1887–1989.* London: Epworth Press.

Balfour, Margaret I., and Ruth Young. 1929. *The Work of Medical Women in India.* London: Oxford University Press.

Ballhachet, Kenneth. 1980. *Race, Sex and Class under the Raj: Imperial Attitudes and Policies and Their Critics, 1793–1905.* London: Weidenfeld and Nicolson.

Balsan, Consuelo Vanderbilt. 1952. *The Glitter and the Gold.* New York: Harper.

Bamdad, Badr al-Muluk. 1977. *From Darkness into Light: Women's Emancipation in Iran.* Hicksville, NY: Exposition Press.

Banks, Olive. 1964. *Feminism and Family Planning in Victorian England.* Liverpool: Liverpool University Press.

———. 1986. *Becoming a Feminist: The Social Origins of the "First Wave" of Feminism.* Brighton: Wheatsheaf.

———. 1990 [1981]. *Faces of Feminism: A Study of Feminism as a Social Movement.* Reprint, Oxford: Blackwell.

Barr, Pat. 1976. *The Memsahibs: The Women of Victorian India.* Bombay and London: Secker and Warburg.

Barrett, James R. 1987. *Work and Community in the Jungle: Chicago's Packinghouse Workers, 1894–1922.* Urbana: University of Illinois Press.

Bartley, Paula. 1999. *Prostitution and Reform in England 1860–1914.* London: Routledge.

Basham, Diana. 1992. *The Trial of Woman: Feminism and the Occult Sciences in Victorian Literature and Society.* London: Macmillan.

Bassnett, Susan, ed. *Knives and Angels: Women Writers in Latin America.* London: Zed Books.

Bataille, Gretchen M., and Kathleen Mullen Sands. 1984. *American Indian Women: Telling Their Lives.* Lincoln: University of Nebraska Press.

Bauer, Carol, and Lawrence Ritt, eds. 1979. *Free and Ennobled: Source Readings in the Development of Victorian Feminism.* Oxford: Pergamon Press.

Bayat-Philipp, Mangol. 1978. "Women and Revolution in Iran, 1905–1911." In Lois Beck and Nicki Keddie, eds., *Women in the Muslim World.* Cambridge, MA: Harvard University Press.

Beck, L., and N. Keddie, eds. 1978. *Women in the Muslim World.* Cambridge, MA: Harvard University Press.

Beezley, William, and Judith Ewell, eds. 1987. *The Human Tradition in Latin America: The Twentieth Century.* Wilmington, DE: Scholarly Resources.

———. 1989. *The Human Tradition in Latin America: The Nineteenth Century.* Wilmington, DE: Scholarly Resources.

Beilharz, P., and C. Nyland. 1999. *The Webbs, Fabianism and Feminism.* Aldershot: Ashgate.

Bell, Enid Moberley. 1953. *Storming the Citadel: The Rise of the Woman Doctor.* London: Constable.

Berger, Iris. 1992. *Threads of Solidarity: Women in South African Industry, 1900–1980.* Bloomington: Indiana University Press.

Bergman, Emilie. 1990. *Women, Culture and Politics in Latin America.* Berkeley: University of California Press.

Berkin, Carol R., and Clara M. Lovett. 1980. *Women: War and Revolution.* New York: Holmes and Meier.

Berkin, Carol Ruth, and Mary Beth Norton. 1979. *Women of America: A History.* Boston: Houghton Mifflin.

Bernstein, Gail Lee. 1991. *Recreating Japanese Women 1600–1945.* Berkeley: University of California Press.

Berry, Dawn Bradley. 1997. *The Fifty Most Influential Women in American Law.* Los Angeles: Lowell House.

Berson, Robin Kadison. 1994. *Marching to a Different Drummer: Unrecognized Heroes of American History.* Westport, CT: Greenwood Press.

Biddle, Marcia McKenna. 1979. *Contributions of Women: Labor.* Minneapolis: Dillon Press.

Bidelman, Patrick Kay. 1982. *Pariahs Stand Up! The Founding of the Liberal Feminist Movement in France 1858–1889.* Westport, CT: Greenwood Press.

Blackburn, Susan, and Sharon Bessell. 1997. "Marriageable Age: Political Debates on Early Marriage in Twentieth-Century Indonesia." *Indonesia* 63 (April): 107–141.

Blackwell, Elizabeth. 1914. *Work for Women.* Everyman's Library series. London: J. M. Dent. Reprinted as *Pioneer Work in Opening the Medical Profession to Women* [original title]. New York: Schocken, 1977.

Blake, Catriona. 1990. *The Charge of the Parasols: Women's Entry to the Medical Profession.* London: Women's Press.

Bland, Lucy. 1996. *Banishing the Beast: English Feminism and Sexual Morality, 1885–1914.* Harmondsworth: Penguin.

Blatch, Harriot Stanton, and Alma Lutz. 1940. *Challenging Years: The Memoirs of Harriot Stanton Blatch.* New York: G. P. Putnam and Sons.

Blee, Kathleen M., ed. 1998. *No Middle Ground: Women and Radical Protest.* New York: New York University Press.

Blom, Ida. 1980. "The Struggle for Women's Suffrage in Norway, 1885–1913." *Scandinavian Journal of History* 5: 3–22.

Bolt, Christine. 1993. *The Women's Movements in the United States and Britain from the 1790s to the 1920s.* London: Harvester Wheatsheaf.

———. 1995. *Feminist Ferment: The Woman Question in the USA and Britain 1870–1940.* London: University College of London Press.

Bolton, Sandra Knowles. 1895. *Famous Leaders among Women.* New York: Thomas Y. Crowell.

Bonner, Thomas Neville. 1992. *To the Ends of the Earth: Women's Search for Education in Medicine.* Cambridge, MA: Harvard University Press.

———. 1995. *Becoming a Physician: Medical Education in Britain, France, Germany, and the U.S. 1750–1945.* New York: Oxford University Press.

Boone, Gladys. 1942. *The Women's Trade Union Leagues in Great Britain and the United States of America.* New York: Columbia University Press.

Bordin, Ruth. 1981. *Woman and Temperance: The Quest for Power and Liberty, 1873–1900.* Philadelphia: Temple University Press.

Bosch, Mineke. 1990. *Politics and Friendship: Letters from the International Woman Suffrage Alliance, 1902–42.* Columbus: Ohio State University Press.

Boxer, Marilyn, and Jean H. Quaterat. 1978. *Socialist Women: European Socialist Feminism in the Nineteenth and Twentieth Centuries.* New York: Elsevier North-Holland.

Boyd, Herb, ed. 2000. *Autobiography of a People: Three Centuries of African American History Told by Those Who Lived It.* New York: Doubleday.

Brandon, Ruth. 1990. *The New Women and the Old Men.* London: Martin Secker and Warburg.

Breed, Mary, and Edith How-Martyn. 1930. *The Birth Control Movement in England.* London: Bale and Danielsson.

Bridenthal, Renate, and Claudia Koonz. 1977. *Becoming Visible: Women in European History.* Boston: Houghton Mifflin.

Bridenthal, Renate, Atina Grossman, and Marion Kaplan, eds. 1984. *When Biology Became Destiny: Women in Weimar and Nazi Germany.* New York: Monthly Review Press.

Bristow, Edward J. 1977. *Vice and Vigilance: Purity Movements in Britain since 1700.* London: Gill and Macmillan.

———. 1982. *Prostitution and Prejudice: The Jewish Campaign against White Slavery, 1870–1939.* Oxford: Clarendon Press.

Broido, Vera. 1977. *Apostles into Terrorists: Women and the Revolutionary Movement in the Russia of Alexander II.* New York: Viking Press.

Brookes, Pamela. 1967. *Women at Westminster: An Account of Women in the British Parliament 1918–1966.* London: Peter Davies.

Bryan, Mary Lynn McCree, and Allen F. Davis. 1990. *100 Years at Hull House.* Bloomington: Indiana University Press.

Bryant, Margaret. 1979. *The Unexpected Revolution: A Study in the History of the Education of Women and Girls in the Nineteenth Century.* London: University of London Institute of Education.

Buckley, Sandra. 1997. *Broken Silence: Voices of Japanese Feminism.* Berkeley: University of California Press.

Buechler, Steven M. 1990. *Women's Movements in the United States: Woman Suffrage Equal Rights and Beyond.* New Brunswick: Rutgers University Press.

Buhle, Mari Jo. 1981. *Women and American Socialism, 1870–1920.* Urbana: University of Illinois Press.

Buhle, Mari Jo, and Paul Buhle, eds. 1978. *The Concise History of Woman Suffrage: Selections from the Classic Work of Stanton, Anthony, Gage, and Harper.* Urbana: University of Illinois Press.

Burstyn, Joan N. 1980. *Victorian Education and the Ideal of Womanhood.* London: Croom Helm.

Burton, Antoinette. 1994. *Burdens of History: British Feminists, Indian Women and Imperial Culture 1865–1915.* Baltimore: Johns Hopkins University Press.

———. 1998. *At the Heart of Empire: Indians and the Colonial Encounter in Late-Victorian Britain.* Berkeley: University of California Press.

Bush, Barbara. 1998. "Britain's Conscience on Africa: White Women, Race, and Imperial Politics in Inter-War Britain." In Clare Midgeley, ed., *Gender and Imperialism.* Manchester: Manchester University Press.

Bussey, Gertrude, and Margaret Tims. 1980 [1960]. *Pioneers for Peace: Women's International League for Peace and Freedom 1915–1965.* Reprint, London: George Allen and Unwin.

Butler, Josephine. 1869. *Woman's Work and Woman's Culture: A Series of Essays.* London: Macmillan.

Bynum, W. F., and Roy Porter. 1993. *Companion Encyclopedia on the History of Medicine.* London: Routledge.

Byrne, Lavinia. 1995. *The Hidden Tradition: Christian Women and Social Change.* London: SPCK.

Caedel, Martin. 1980. *Pacifism in Britain 1914–1945: The Defining of a Faith.* Oxford: Clarendon Press.

———. 1993. "Vida Goldstein and the English Militant Campaign." *Women's History Review* 2(3): 363–376.

Caine, Barbara. 1992. *Victorian Feminists.* Oxford: Oxford University Press.

Calabre, Marian. 1996. *Great Courtroom Lawyers: Fighting the Cases That Made History.* New York: Facts on File.

Calman, Leslie. 1992. *Toward Empowerment: Women*

and Movement in India. Boulder, CO: Westview Press.

Camhi, Jane Jerome. 1994. *Women against Women: American Anti-Suffragism, 1880–1920.* Brooklyn, NY: Carlson Publishing.

Campbell, Elaine. 1998. *The Whistling Bird: Women Writers of the Caribbean.* Boulder, CO: Lynne Rienner.

Cantarow, Ellen, et al. 1980. *Moving the Mountain: Women Working for Social Change.* Old Westbury, NY: Feminist Press.

Carlson, Narifran. 1988. *Feminismo! The Woman's Movement in Argentina from Its Beginnings to Eva Perón.* Chicago: Academy Chicago Publications.

Carson, Clayborn. 1981. *In Struggle: SNCC and the Black Awakening of the 1960s.* Cambridge, MA: Harvard University Press.

Cecil, David. 1954. *Lord M.* London: Constable.

Ceniza, Sherry. 1998. *Walt Whitman and Nineteenth-Century Women Reformers.* Tuscaloosa: University of Alabama Press.

Chafetz, Janet, and Gary Dworkin. 1986. *Female Revolt: Women's Movements in World and Historical Perspective.* Totowa, NJ: Rowman and Allanheld.

Chambers, Clarke A. 1963. *Seedtime of Reform: American Social Service and Social Action, 1918–1933.* Minneapolis: University of Minnesota Press.

Chandra, Sudhir. 1998. *Enslaved Daughters: Colonialism, Law and Women's Rights.* New Delhi: Oxford University Press.

Chaney, Elsa M. 1979. *Supermadre: Women in Politics in Latin America.* Austin: Institute of Latin American Studies, University of Texas Press.

Chattopadhay, Kamaladevi. 1983. *Indian Women's Battle for Freedom.* New Delhi: Abhinav.

Chaudhuri, Nupur, and Margaret Strobel, eds. 1992. *Western Women and Imperialism: Complicity and Resistance.* Bloomington: Indiana University Press.

Christian, Charles M. 1999. *The African American Experience: A Chronology.* Washington, DC: Civitas.

Clements, Barbara Evans. 1997. *Bolshevik Women.* Cambridge: Cambridge University Press.

Cleverdon, Catherine Lyle. 1950. *The Woman Suffrage Movement in Canada.* Toronto: University of Toronto Press.

Cocalis, Susan L., and Kay Goodman, eds. 1982. *Beyond the Eternal Feminine: Critical Essays on Women and German Literature.* Stuttgart: Akademischer Verlag Dans-Dieter Heinz.

Cocker, J., and J. M. Murray. 1930. *Temperance and Prohibition in New Zealand.* London: Epworth Press.

Cockroft, James D. 1966. *Intellectual Precursors of the Mexican Revolution, 1900–1913.* Austin: University of Texas Press.

Cohen, Marcia. 1988. *The Sisterhood: The True Story of the Women Who Changed the World.* New York: Simon and Schuster.

Cole, Margaret. 1938. *Women of To-Day.* London: Thomas Nelson and Sons.

Collette, Christine. 1989. *For Labour and for Women: The Women's Labour League, 1906–18.* Manchester: Manchester University Press.

Collopy, Michael, and Jason Gardner. 2000. *Architects of Peace: Visions of Hope in Words and Images.* Novato, CA: New World Library.

Conrad, Margaret, and Alvin Finkel, eds. 1993. *History of the Canadian Peoples,* vol. 1, *Beginnings to 1867;* vol. 2, *1867 to Present.* Toronto: Copp Clark Pitman.

Conroy, Hilary, Sandra Davis, and Wayne Patterson. 1984. *Japan in Transition: Thought and Action in the Meiji Era, 1868–1912.* Rutherford: Farleigh Dickinson University Press.

Cook, Blanche Wiesen. 1993. "Radical Women of Greenwich Village." In Rick Beard and Leslie Cohen Berlowitz, eds., *Greenwich Village.* Newark, NJ: Rutgers University Press.

Cooper, Sandi E. 1991. *Patriotic Pacifism: Waging War on War in Europe, 1815–1914.* New York: Oxford University Press.

Coulter, Carol. 1993. *The Hidden Tradition: Feminism, Women and Nationalism in Ireland.* Cork: Cork University Press.

Crawford, Vicki L., Jacqueline Anne Rouse, and Barbara Woods, eds. 1990. *Women in the Civil Rights Movement: Trailblazers and Torchbearers.* Brooklyn: Carlson Publishing.

Croll, Elizabeth. 1978. *Feminism and Socialism in China.* New York: Schocken Books.

Crosby, Christina. 1991. *The Ends of History: Victorians and "The Woman Question."* London: Routledge.

Daley, Caroline, and Melanie Nolan. 1994. *Suffrage and Beyond: International Feminist Perspectives.* New York: New York University Press.

Daly, Mary. 1978. *Gyn/Ecology: The Metaethics of Radical Feminism.* Boston: Beacon Press.

Dangerfield, George. 1936. *The Strange Death of Liberal England.* London: Constable.

Daniel, Sadie Iola. 1970. *Woman Builders.* Washington, DC: Associated Publishers.

Darling, Pam. 1994. *New Wine: The Story of Women Transforming Leadership and Power in the Episcopal Church.* Boston: Cowley.

David, Katherine. 1991. "Czech Feminists and Nationalism in the Late Habsburg Monarchy: The First in Austria." *Journal of Women's History* 3(2): 26–45.

Davies, Catherine. 1998. *Spanish Women's Writing 1849–1996.* London: Athlone Press.

Davies, Emily. 1910. *Thoughts on Some Questions*

Relating to Women 1860–1908. Cambridge, UK: Bowes and Bowes.

Davies, Norman. 1981. *God's Playground: A History of Poland.* 2 vols. Oxford: Clarendon Press.

Davis, Allen F. 1967. *Spearheads for Reform: The Social Settlements and the Progressive Movement 1890–1914.* New York: Oxford University Press.

Davis, Elizabeth Gould. 1972. *The First Sex.* Harmondsworth: Penguin Books.

Davis, Fanny. 1986. *The Ottoman Lady: A Social History from 1718 to 1918.* Westport, CT: Greenwood Press.

Deak, Istvan. 1968. *Weimar Germany's Left-wing Intellectuals: A Political History of the Weltbühne and Its Circle.* Berkeley: University of California Press.

Degen, Marie Louise, and Blanche Cook. 1939. *The History of the Women's Peace Party.* Baltimore: Johns Hopkins University Press.

Dell, Floyd. 1913. *Women as World Builders: Studies in Modern Feminism.* Chicago: Forbes and Company.

Diner, Hasia R. 1983. *Erin's Daughters in America: Irish Immigrant Women in the Nineteenth Century.* Baltimore: Johns Hopkins University Press.

Dobbie, B. M. W. 1979. *A Nest of Suffragettes in Somerset.* London: The Batheaston Society.

Dohm, Hedwig. 1976 [1896]. *Women's Nature and Privilege.* Translated by Constance Campbell. Reprint, Westport, CT: Hyperion.

Donovan, Mary S. 1994. *A Different Call: Women's Ministries in the Episcopal Church.* Ridgefield, CT: Morehouse.

Dubofsky, Melvyn. 2000 [1969]. *We Shall Be All: A History of the Industrial Workers of the World.* Reprint, Urbana: University of Illinois Press.

DuBois, Ellen. 1978. *Feminism and Suffrage: The Emergence of the Independent Women's Movement in America 1848–1869.* Ithaca: Cornell University Press.

———. 1998. *Woman Suffrage and Women's Rights.* New York: New York University Press.

Duby, George, and Michelle Perot, gen. eds. 1994. *A History of Women,* vol. 5, *Towards a Cultural Identity in the Twentieth Century.* Cambridge, MA: Belknap Press of Harvard University.

Duke, Michael S., ed. 1989. *Modern Chinese Women Writers: Critical Appraisals.* Armonk, NY: M. E. Sharpe.

Dye, Nancy Schrom. 1980. *As Equals and as Sisters: Feminism, the Labor Movement and the Women's Trade Union League of New York.* Columbia: University of Missouri Press.

Dykeman, Therese Boos. 1993. *American Women Philosophers 1650–1930.* Lewiston, NY: Edwin Mellen Press.

Edmondson, Linda. 1984. *Feminism in Russia, 1900–1917.* London: Heinemann.

Eisenstein, Zillah. 1981. *The Radical Future of Liberal Feminism.* New York: Longman.

Eldershaw, F., ed. 1938. *The Peaceful Army: A Memorial to the Pioneer Women of Australia, 1788–1938.* Sydney: A. W. Baker.

Elstain, J. B. 1981. *Public Man, Private Woman: Women in Social and Political Thought.* Princeton: Princeton University Press.

Engel, Barbara Alpern. 1983. *Mothers and Daughters: Women of the Intelligentsia in Nineteenth-Century Russia.* Cambridge: Cambridge University Press.

Engel, Barbara Alpern, and Clifford N. Rosenthal. 1975. *Five Sisters: Women against the Tsar: The Memoirs of Five Revolutionaries of the 1870s.* London: Weidenfeld and Nicolson.

Esfandiari, Haleh. 1997. *Reconstructed Lives: Women and Iran's Islamic Revolution.* Washington, DC: Woodrow Wilson Center Press.

Eustance, Claire, Joan Ryan, and Laura Ugolini, eds. 2000. *A Suffrage Reader: Charting Directions in British Suffrage History.* London: Leicester University Press.

Evans, Richard. 1973. *The Feminist Movement in Germany 1894–1933.* London: Sage.

———. 1977. *The Feminists: Women's Emancipation Movements in Europe, America, and Australasia 1840–1920.* London: Croom Helm.

———. 1987. *Comrades and Sisters: Feminism, Socialism and Pacifism in Europe 1870–1945.* Brighton: Wheatsheaf.

Evans, Harold. 1998. *The American Century.* London: Jonathan Cape.

Evans, Sarah. 1979. *Personal Politics: The Roots of Women's Liberation in the Civil Rights Movement and the New Left.* New York: Alfred A. Knopf.

Everett, Jana Matson. 1979. *Women and Social Change in India.* New Delhi: Heritage.

Falk, Gerhard. 1998. *Sex, Gender, and Social Change: The Great Revolution.* Lanham, MD: University Press of America.

Faludi, Susan. 1991. *Backlash: The Undeclared War against American Women.* New York: Crown.

Fan Hong. 1997. *Footbinding, Feminism and Freedom.* Portland, OR: Frank Cass.

Farr, Florence. 1910. *Modern Woman: Her Intentions.* London: Frank Palmer.

Fathi, A., ed. 1985. *Women and the Family in Iran.* Leiden: E. J. Brill.

Fawcett, M. G. 1912. *Women's Suffrage: A Short History of a Great Movement.* London: T. C. and E. C. Jack.

"Feminism Revisited: A Symposium." *Times Literary Supplement* 4955 (1998): 3–7.

Fernea, Elizabeth Warnock, and Basima Qattan Bezirgan. 1978. *Middle Eastern Muslim Women Speak.* Austin: University of Texas Press.

Fisher, William F., ed. 1997. *Toward Sustainable Development?: Struggling over India's Narmada River.* Jaipur: Rawat Publications.

Fitzpatrick, Ellen. 1991. *Endless Crusade: Women Social Scientists and Progressive Reform.* New York: Oxford University Press.

Fladeland, Betty. 1972. *Men and Brothers: Anglo-American Antislavery Cooperation.* Chicago: University of Chicago Press.

Flanz, Gisbert H. 1983. *Comparative Women's Rights and Political Participation in Europe.* Epping, Essex: Bowker.

Flexner, Abraham. 1916. *Prostitution in Europe.* New York: Century.

Flexner, Eleanor. 1975 [1959]. *A Century of Struggle: The Woman's Rights Movement in the United States.* Rev. ed. Cambridge, MA: Belknap Press of Harvard University.

Foner, Philip. 1979. *Women and the American Labor Movement,* vol. 1, *From Colonial Times to the Eve of World War I.* New York: Free Press.

Forbes, Geraldine. 1996. *Women in Modern India.* New Cambridge History of India, vol. 4. Cambridge: Cambridge University Press.

Ford, Isabella. 1993. "Women and Socialism." In Marie Mulvey Roberts and Tamae Mizuta, eds., *Sources of British Feminism,* vol. 2, *The Reformers: Socialist Feminism.* London: Routledge.

Forster, M. 1984. *Significant Sisters: The Grassroots of Active Feminism, 1839–1939.* London: Secker and Warburg.

Foster, Catherine. 1989. *Women for All Seasons: The Story of the Women's International League for Peace and Freedom.* Athens: University of Georgia Press.

Foster, R. F., ed. 1989. *The Oxford Illustrated History of Ireland.* Oxford: Oxford University Press.

Fout, John. 1984. *German Women in the Nineteenth Century: A Social History.* New York: Holmes and Meier.

Fout, John, and Eleanor Riemer, eds. 1980. *European Women: A Documentary History 1789–1945.* Brighton: Harvester Press.

Fox, Richard M. 1935. *Rebel Irishwomen.* Dublin: Talbot Press.

Frankel, Noralee, and Nancy S. Dye. 1991. *Gender, Class, Race, and Reform in the Progressive Era.* Lexington: University of Kentucky Press.

Franklin, John Hope, and August Meier. 1982. *Black Leaders of the Twentieth Century.* Urbana: University of Illinois Press.

Freedman, Estelle. 1980. *Their Sisters' Keepers: Women's Prison Reform in America, 1830–1930.* Ann Arbor: University of Michigan Press.

Freeman, Kathleen. 1965. *If Any Man Build: The History of the Save the Children Fund.* London: Hodder.

French, R. D. 1975. *Anti-Vivisection and Medical Science in Victorian Britain.* Princeton: Princeton University Press.

Frevert, Ute. 1990. *Women in German History: From Bourgeois Emancipation to Sexual Liberation.* Oxford: Berg Publishers.

Frost, Elizabeth, and Kathryn Cullen DuPont. 1992. *Women's Suffrage in America: An Eyewitness History.* New York: Facts on File.

Frow, Ruth, and Edmund Frow, eds. 1989. *Political Women 1800–1850.* London: Pluto Press.

Fry, Eric, ed. 1983. *Rebels and Radicals.* Sydney: Allen and Unwin.

Fryer, Peter. 1965. *The Birth Controllers.* London: Secker & Warburg.

Fujimura-Fanselow, Kumiko, and Atsuko Kameda. 1995. *Japanese Women: New Feminist Perspectives on the Past, Present, and Future.* New York: Feminist Press.

Fulford, Roger. 1957. *Votes for Women: The Story of a Struggle.* London: Faber and Faber.

Fuller, Margaret. 1998 [1845]. *Woman in the Nineteenth Century.* Norton Critical Edition, edited by Larry J. Reynolds. Reprint, New York: W. W. Norton.

Fuller, Mrs. Marcus B. 1984 [1900]. *The Wrongs of Indian Womanhood.* Reprint, New Delhi: Inter-India Publications.

Gardner, P. 1984. *The Lost Elementary Schools of Victorian England.* London: Croom Helm.

Garner, Les. 1984. *Stepping Stones to Women's Liberty: Feminist Ideas in the Women's Suffrage Movement 1900–1918.* London: Heinemann Education Books.

Gattey, Charles Neilson. 1967. *The Bloomer Girls.* London: Femina.

———. 1970. *Gauguin's Astonishing Grandmother: Flora Tristan.* London: Femina.

Gibson, Mary. 1986. *Prostitution and the State in Italy 1865–1915.* Columbus: Ohio State University Press.

Giddings, Paula. 1984. *When and Where I Enter: The Impact of Black Women on Race and Sex in America.* New York: W. W. Norton.

Gilmartin, Christina Kelly. 1995. *Engendering the Chinese Revolution: Radical Women, Communist Politics and Mass Movements in the 1920s.* Berkeley: University of California Press.

Gilmartin, Christina Kelly, G. Hershatter, L. Rofel, and T. White, eds. 1994. *Engendering China: Women, Culture and the State.* Cambridge, MA: Harvard University Press.

Ginzberg, Lori D. 1990. *Women and the Work of Benevolence: Morality, Politics, and Class in the Nineteenth-Century United States.* New Haven, CT: Yale University Press.

Gleadle, Kathryn. 1995. *The Early Feminists: Radical Unitarians and the Emergence of the Women's Rights Movement, 1831–1851.* London: Macmillan.

Goldsmith, Barbara. 1998. *Other Powers: The Age of Suffrage, Spiritualism and the Scandalous Victoria Woodhull.* New York: Alfred A. Knopf.

Goldsmith, Margaret. 1935. *Seven Women against the World*. London: Methuen.

Gollack, Georgina A. 1932. *Daughters of Africa*. London: Longman's Green.

Goodsell, Willystine, ed. 1970. *Pioneers of Women's Education in the United States*. New York: AMS.

Goodwin, Jan. 1995. *Price of Honor: Muslim Women Lift the Veil of Silence in the Islamic World*. London: Warner Books.

Gordon, Ann D., et al. 1997. *African American Women and the Vote 1837–1965*. Amherst: University of Massachusetts Press.

Gordon, Felice D. 1986. *After Winning: The Legacy of the New Jersey Suffragists, 1920–1947*. New Brunswick, NJ: Rutgers.

Gordon, Felicia, and Máire Cross. 1996. *Early French Feminism, 1830–1940: A Passion for Liberty*. Cheltenham: Edward Elgar.

Gordon, Linda. 1976. *Woman's Body, Woman's Right: A Social History of Birth Control in America*. New York: Grossman.

Grant, Joanne. 1998. *Freedom Bound*. New York: Wiley.

Greer, Mary. 1995. *Women of the Golden Dawn: Rebels and Priestesses*. Rochester, VT: Park Street Press.

Gregory Dunn, John. 1976. *Delano: The Story of the California Grape Strike*. New York: Farrar, Straus, and Giroux.

Grimshaw, Patricia. 1987. *Women's Suffrage in New Zealand*. Auckland: Oxford University Press.

Grogan, Susan K. 1992. *French Socialism and Sexual Difference: Women and the New Society, 1803–44*. London: Macmillan.

Gurko, Miriam. 1974. *The Ladies of Seneca Falls: The Birth of the Woman's Rights Movement*. New York: Macmillan.

Hacker, Carlotta. 1974. *The Indomitable Lady Doctors*. Toronto: Clarke, Irwin, and Co.

———. 1999. *Humanitarians*. New York: Crabtree.

———. 1999. *Rebels*. New York: Crabtree.

Hackett, Amy. 1976. *The Politics of Feminism in Wilhelmine Germany 1890–1918*. 2 vols. Ann Arbor: University Microfilms International

Hahner, Judith E. 1990. *Emancipating the Female Sex: The Struggle for Women's Rights in Brazil, 1850–1940*. Durham, NC: Duke University Press.

Halbersleben, Karen I. 1993. *Women's Participation in the British Antislavery Movement 1824–1865*. Lewiston: Edwin Mellen Press.

Hall, M. Penelope, and Ismene V. Howes. 1999 [1965]. *The Church in Social Work: A Study of Moral Welfare Work Undertaken by the Church of England*. Reprint, London: Routledge.

Hamilton, Mary A. 1936. *Newnham: An Informal Biography*. London: Faber and Faber.

———. 1941. *Women at Work: A Brief Introduction to Trade Unionism for Women*. London: Routledge & Sons.

Hamilton, Roberta, and Michèle Barrett, eds. 1986. *The Politics of Diversity: Feminism, Marxism and Nationalism*. London: Verso.

Hammerton, James A. 1977. "Feminism and Female Emigration 1861–1886." In Martha Vicinus, ed., *A Widening Sphere: Changing Roles of Victorian Women*. Bloomington: Indiana University Press.

———. 1979. *Emigrant Gentlewomen: Genteel Poverty and Female Emigration 1830–1914*. London: Croom Helm.

Hane, Mikiso, ed. 1988. *Reflections on the Way to the Gallows: Rebel Women in Prewar Japan*. Berkeley: University of California Press and Pantheon Books.

Hardman, Malcolm. 1991. *Six Victorian Thinkers*. Manchester: Manchester University Press

Harman, Barbara Leah, and Susan Meyer, eds. 1996. *The New Nineteenth Century: Feminist Readings of Underread Victorian Fiction*. New York: Garland.

Harmon, Rod. 2000. *American Civil Rights Leaders*. Berkeley Heights, NJ: Enslow.

Harrison, Brian. 1978. *Separate Spheres: The Opposition to Women's Suffrage in Britain*. London: Croom Helm.

Harrison, Fraser. 1977. *The Dark Angel: Aspects of Victorian Sexuality*. London: Sheldon Press.

Hartmann, Mary, and Lois W. Banner, eds. 1975. *Clio's Consciousness Raised: New Perspectives on the History of Women*. London: Harper and Row.

Hause, Steven C., with Anne R. Kenny. 1984. *Women's Suffrage and Social Politics in the French Third Republic*. Princeton: Princeton University Press.

Heasman, Kathleen. 1962. *Evangelicals in Action: An Appraisal of Social Work in the Victorian Era*. London: Geoffrey Bles.

Heilmann, Ann. 1998. *The Late-Victorian Marriage Question: A Collection of Key New Woman Texts*. 5 vols. London: Routledge Thoemmes Press.

———. 2000. *New Woman Fiction: Women Writing First-Wave Feminism*. Basingstoke: Macmillan.

Helsinger, Elizabeth K., Robin Lauterbach Sheets, and William Veeder. 1983. *The Woman Question: Social Issues, 1837–1883*, vol. 2, *Society and Literature in Britain and America, 1837–1883*. Manchester: Manchester University Press.

Hersch, Blanche G. 1978. *Slavery of Sex: Feminist Abolitionists in America*. Urbana: University of Illinois Press.

Hibben, Paxton. 1942. *Henry Ward Beecher: An American Portrait*. New York: The Press of the Readers Club.

Hibbert, Christopher. 2000. *Queen Victoria*. London: HarperCollins.

Hill, B. 1989. *Women, Work and Sexual Politics in Eighteenth-Century England*. Oxford: Oxford University Press.

Hill, Daniel G. 1981. *The Freedom-Seekers: Blacks in Early Canada*. Agincourt: Book Society of Canada.

Hine, Darlene Clark, and Kathleen Thompson. 1998. *A Shining Thread of Hope: The History of Black Women in America*. New York: Broadway Books.

Hoe, Susanna. 1991. *The Private Life of Old Hong Kong*. Hong Kong: Oxford University Press.

———. 1996. *Chinese Footprints: Exploring Women's History in China, Hong Kong and Macau*. Hong Kong: Roundhouse Publications.

Hogan, Anne. 1998. *Women of Faith in Victorian Culture: Reassessing the Angel in the House*. New York: St. Martin's Press.

Holcombe, Lee. 1983. *Wives and Property: Reform of the Married Women's Property Law in Nineteenth-Century England*. Toronto: University of Toronto Press.

Holland, Barbara. 1985. *Soviet Sisterhood*. Bloomington: Indiana University Press.

Holledge, Julie. 1981. *Innocent Flowers: Women in the Victorian Theatre*. London: Virago.

Hollis, Patricia, ed. 1979. *Women in Public: The Women's Movement 1850–1900*. London: Allen and Unwin.

———. 1987. *Ladies Elect: Women in English Local Government 1865–1914*. Oxford: Clarendon Press.

Holton, Sandra Stanley. 1986. *Feminism and Democracy: Women's Suffrage and Reform Politics in Britain, 1900–1918*. Cambridge: Cambridge University Press.

———. 1996. *Suffrage Days: Stories from the Women's Suffrage Movement*. London: Routledge.

Honig, Emily. 1986. *Sisters and Strangers: Women in the Shanghai Cotton Mills 1919–1949*. Stanford: Stanford University Press.

Howard, Judith Jeffrey. 1977. "The Civil Code of 1865 and the Origins of the Feminist Movement in Italy." In B. B. Caroli, R. F. Harney, and L. F. Tomasi, eds., *The Italian Immigrant Woman in North America*. Toronto: The Multicultural History Society of Ontario.

———. 1990. "Visions of Reform, Visions of Revolution: Women's Activism in the New Italian Nation." In Frances Richardson Keller, ed., *Views of Women's Lives in Western Tradition*. Lewiston: Edwin Mellen Press.

Huckaby, Elizabeth. 1980. *Crisis at Central High School: Little Rock 1957–1958*. Baton Rouge: Louisiana State University Press.

Hufton, Olwen. 1992. *Women and the Limits of Citizenship in the French Revolution*. Toronto: Toronto University Press.

———. 1998. *The Prospect before Her: A History of Women in Western Europe 1500–1800*. New York: Vintage Books.

Humm, Maggie, ed. 1992. *Feminisms: A Reader*. London: Harvester Wheatsheaf.

Hunt, Karen. 1996. *Equivocal Feminists: The Social Democratic Federation and the Woman Question 1884–1911*. Cambridge: Cambridge University Press.

Ingram, Angela, and Daphne Patai, eds. 1993. *Rediscovering Forgotten Radicals: British Women Writers, 1889–1939*. Chapel Hill: University of North Carolina Press.

International Council of Women. 1966. *Women in a Changing World: The Dynamic Story of the International Council of Women since 1888*. London: Routledge and Kegan Paul.

Irwin, Inez Haynes. 1964. *Up Hill with Banners Flying*. Penobscot, ME: Traversity Press. [Originally published as *The Story of the Woman's Party*. 1921. New York: Harcourt, Brace].

Isichei, Elizabeth. 1970. *Victorian Quakers*. Oxford: Oxford University Press.

Jacquette, Jane S., ed. 1989. *The Women's Movement in Latin America: Feminism and the Transition to Democracy*. London: Unwin Hyman.

Jallinoja, Riitta. 1980. "The Women's Liberation Movement in Finland." *Scandinavian Journal of History* 5: 37–49.

James, Adeola. 1990. *In Their Own Voices: African Women Writers Talk*. London: J. Currey.

Jarrett-Macauley, Delia. 1996. "Exemplary Women." In Delia Jarrett-Macauley, ed., *Reconstructing Womanhood, Reconstructing Feminism*. London: Routledge.

Jayawardena, Kumari. 1986. *Feminism and Nationalism in the Third World*. London: Zed Books.

———. 1995. *The White Woman's Other Burden: Western Women and South Asia during British Rule*. London: Routledge.

Jeffreys, Sheila. 1985. *The Spinster and Her Enemies: Feminism and Sexuality 1880–1930*. London: Pandora.

Jelin, Elizabeth. 1990. *Women and Social Change in Latin America*. London: Zed Books.

Jensen, Carl. 2000. *Stories That Changed America: Muckrakers of the 20th Century*. New York: Seven Stories Press.

Jensen, Joan M., ed. 1981. *With These Hands: Women Working on the Land*. New York: McGraw-Hill.

Joannu, Maroula, and June Purvis, eds. 1998. *The Women's Suffrage Movement: New Feminist Perspectives*. Manchester: Manchester University Press.

Joeres, Ruth-Ellen B., and Mary Jo Maynes, eds. 1986. *German Women in the Eighteenth and Nineteenth Centuries: A Social and Literary History*. Bloomington: Indiana University Press.

Johanson, Christine. 1987. *Women's Suffrage for Higher Education in Russia 1855–1900.* Kingston and Montreal: McGill Queen's University Press.

Johnson, Kay Ann. 1983. *Women, the Family and Peasant Revolution in China.* Chicago: University of Chicago Press.

Johnson-Odim, Cheryl, and Margaret Strobel, eds. 1992. *Expanding the Boundaries of Women's History: Essays on Women in the Third World.* Bloomington: Indiana University Press.

Jordan, Ellen. 1999. *The Women's Movement and Women's Employment in Nineteenth-Century Britain.* London: Routledge.

Kandiyoti, Deniz. 1991. *Women, Islam and the State.* Basingstoke: Macmillan.

Kaplan, Marion. 1979. *The Jewish Feminist Movement in Germany: The Campaigns of the Judischer Frauenbund 1904–1938.* Westport, CT: Greenwood Press.

———. 1982. "Prostitution, Morality Crusades and Feminism: German-Jewish Feminists and the Campaign against White Slavery." *Women's Studies International Forum* 5, no. 6: 619–628.

———. 1984. "Sisterhood under Siege: Feminism and Anti-Semitism in Germany, 1904–1938." In Renate Bridenthal, Atina Grossman, and Marion Kaplan, eds., *When Biology Became Destiny: Women in Weimar and Nazi Germany.* New York: Monthly Review Press.

Kaptur, Marcy. 1996. *Women of Congress: A Twentieth-century Odyssey.* Washington, DC: Congressional Quarterly.

Karam, Azza M. 1998. *Women, Islamism and the State: Contemporary Feminism in Egypt.* London: Macmillan.

Kass-Simon, G., and Patricia Farnes. 1993. *Women of Science: Righting the Record.* Bloomington: Indiana University Press.

Kaur, Manmohan. 1968. *Role of Women in the Freedom Movement.* Delhi: Sterling Publishers.

Kazantzis, Judith. 1968. *Women in Revolt: The Fight for Emancipation: A Collection of Contemporary Documents.* London: Cape.

Kealey, Linda. 1979. *A Not Unreasonable Claim: Women and Reform in Canada 1880s–1920s.* Toronto: Women's Educational Press.

Kean, Hilda. 1998. *Animal Rights: Political and Social Change in Britain since 1800.* London: Reaktion Books.

Keene, Judith. 1999. "'Into the Clean Air of the Plaza': Spanish Women Achieve the Vote in 1931." In Victoria Lorée Enders and Pamels Beth Radcliff, eds., *Constructing Spanish Womanhood: Female Identity in Modern Spain.* Albany: State University of New York Press.

Kellogg, Charles Flint. 1967. *NAACP: A History of the National Association for the Advancement of Colored People, 1909–1920.* Baltimore: Johns Hopkins University Press.

Kelly, Linda. 1987. *Women of the French Revolution.* London: Hamish Hamilton.

Kennedy, Thomas C. 1981. *The Hound of Conscience: A History of the No-Conscription Fellowship 1914–1919.* Fayetteville: University of Arkansas Press.

Kent, Susan Kingsley. 1990. *Sex and Suffrage in Britain, 1860–1914.* London: Routledge.

Kerber, Linda K. 1997. *Toward an Intellectual History of Women.* Chapel Hill: University of North Carolina Press.

Kerber, Linda K., and Jane DeHart-Mathews. 2000. *Women's America: Refocusing the Past.* New York: Oxford University Press.

Kerr, Rose. 1937. *The Story of a Million Girls: Guiding and Girl Scouting Round the World.* London: The Girl Guides Association.

Key, Ellen. 1976 [1912]. *The Woman Movement.* Translated by M. and B. Borthwick. Reprint, Westport, CT: Greenwood Press.

Kidder, Rushworth M. 1994. *Shared Values for a Troubled World: Conversations with Men and Women of Conscience.* San Francisco: Jossey-Bass Publishers.

King, Martin Luther, Jr. 1958. *Stride toward Freedom: The Montgomery Story.* New York: Harper.

Klose, Kevin. 1984. *Russia and the Russians: Inside the Closed Society.* New York: W. W. Norton.

Kraditor, Aileen. 1969. *Means and Ends in American Abolitionism: Garrison and His Critics on Strategy and Tactics, 1834–50.* New York: Pantheon.

———. 1981 [1965]. *The Ideas of the Woman Suffrage Movement 1890–1920.* Reprint, New York: W. W. Norton.

Kramer, Barbara. 2000. *Trailblazing Women: First in Their Fields.* Berkeley Heights, NJ: Enslow Publishers.

Kridl, Manfred. 1956. *A Survey of Polish Literature and Culture.* Gravenhage: Slavistic Reprintings.

Krueger, Christine L. 1992. *The Reader's Repentance: Women Preachers, Women Writers, and Nineteenth-Century Social Discourse.* Chicago: University of Chicago Press.

Krupat, Arnold, ed. 1994. *Native American Autobiography: An Anthology.* Madison: University of Wisconsin Press.

Kumiko, Fujimura-Fanselow, and Atsuko Kameda, eds. 1995. *Japanese Women: New Feminist Perspectives on the Past, Present, and Future.* New York: Feminist Press.

Kuzmack, Linda Gordon. 1990. *Woman's Cause: The Jewish Woman's Movement in England and the United States 1881–1933.* Columbus: Ohio State University Press.

Lagemann, Ellen Condliffe. 1979. *A Generation of Women: Education in the Lives of Progressive Reformers.* Cambridge, MA: Harvard University Press.

Lake, Marilyn. 1999. *Getting Equal: The History of Australian Feminism.* London: Allen and Unwin.

Lakshmi, C. S. 1984. *The Face behind the Mask: Women in Tamil Literature.* New Delhi: Vikas Publishing House.

Landes, Joan B. 1988. *Women and the Public Sphere in the Age of the French Revolution.* Ithaca: Cornell University Press.

Lasch, Christopher. 1965. *The New Radicalism, America 1889–1963: The Intellectual as Social Type.* New York: W. W. Norton.

Lavrin, Asunción. 1995. *Women, Feminism, and Social Change in Argentina, Chile, and Uruguay 1890–1940.* Lincoln: University of Nebraska Press.

———, ed. 1978. *Latin American Women: Historical Perspectives.* Westport, CT: Greenwood Press.

Law, Cheryl. 1997. *Suffrage and Power: The Women's Movement 1918–1928.* London: I. B. Tauris.

Lazarus, Morden. 1983. *Six Women Who Dared.* Toronto: CPA Publishers.

Leach, William. 1981. *True Love and Perfect Union: The Feminist Reform of Sex and Society.* London: Routledge and Kegan Paul.

Ledger, Sally. 1997. *The New Woman: Fiction and Feminism at the Fin de Siècle.* Manchester: Manchester University Press.

Leneman, Leah. 1995. *"A Guid Cause": The Women's Suffrage Movement in Scotland.* Rev. ed. Edinburgh: Mercat Press.

Lerner, Gerda. 1993. *Women and History,* vol. 2, *The Creation of a Feminist Consciousness: From the Middle Ages to Eighteen-Seventy.* New York: Oxford University Press.

———, ed. 1972. *Black Women in White America: A Documentary History.* New York: Pantheon Books.

Levin, Beatrice. 1988. *Women and Medicine.* Lincoln: Media Publishing.

Levine, Philippa. 1987. *Victorian Feminism 1850–1900.* London: Hutchinson.

———. 1990. *Feminist Lives in Victorian England: Private Roles and Public Commitment.* Oxford: Blackwell.

Lewenhak, Sheila. 1977. *Women and Trade Unions: An Outline History of Women in the British Trade Union Movement.* London: Ernest Benn.

Lewis, David. 1965. *From Newgate to Dannemore: The Rise of the Penitentiary in New York, 1796–1848.* Ithaca: Cornell University Press.

———. 1994. *The Portable Harlem Renaissance Reader.* New York: Viking.

Lewis, Jane. 1980. *The Politics of Motherhood: Child and Maternal Welfare in England, 1900–1939.* London: Croom Helm.

———. 1987. *Before the Vote Was Won: Arguments for and against Women's Suffrage.* London: Routledge and Kegan Paul.

———. 1991. *Women and Social Action in Victorian and Edwardian England.* Aldershot: Elgar.

Liddell, Alix. 1970. *The Girl Guides 1910–70.* London: Frederick Muller.

Liddington, Jill. 1989. *The Long Road to Greenham: Feminism and Anti-Militarism in Britain since 1820.* London: Virago.

Liddington, Jill, and Jill Norris. 2000 [1978]. *One Hand Tied behind Us.* Rev. ed. London: Virago.

Lind, Mary Ann. 1988. *The Compassionate Memsahibs: Welfare Activities of British Women in India 1900–1947.* Westport, CT: Greenwood Press.

Lindenmeyer, Kriste. 1997. *"A Right to Childhood": The U.S. Children's Bureau and Child Welfare, 1912–1946.* Urbana: University of Illinois Press.

Litwack, Leon, and August Meier. 1988. *Black Leaders of the Nineteenth Century.* Urbana: University of Illinois Press.

Li-Yu-ning, ed. 1992. *Chinese Women through Chinese Eyes.* Armonk, NY: M. E. Sharpe.

Longford, Elizabeth. 1981. *Eminent Victorian Women.* London: Weidenfeld and Nicolson.

Lovejoy, Dr. Esther Pohl. 1957. *Women Doctors of the World.* New York: Macmillan.

Lovell-Smith, Margaret, ed. 1992. *The Woman Question: Writings by the Women Who Won the Vote.* Auckland: New Women's Press.

Luddy, Maria. 1995. *Women and Philanthropy in Nineteenth-Century Ireland.* Cork: Cork University Press.

———. 1995. *Women in Ireland, 1800–1918.* Cork: Cork University Press.

Luddy, Maria, and Cliona Murphy, eds. 1989. *Women Surviving: Studies in Irish Women's History in the Nineteenth and Twentieth Centuries.* Swords: Poolbeg.

Luker, Ralph, ed. 1995. *Black and White Sat Down Together: The Reminiscences of an NAACP Founder.* New York: Feminist Press.

Lvov-Rogachevsky, V. 1979. *A History of Russian Jewish Literature.* Ann Arbor: Ardis.

MacEwan, Grant. 1975. *And Mighty Women Too: Stories of Notable Western Canadian Women.* Saskatoon, SK: Western Producer Prairie Books.

Macías, Anna. 1983. *Against All Odds: The Feminist Movement in Mexico to 1940.* Westport, CT: Greenwood Press.

Mackenzie, Midge. 1975. *Shoulder to Shoulder.* London: Penguin.

Macnicol, John. 1980. *The Movement for Family Allowances 1918–1945.* London: Heinemann.

Malgreen, Gail, ed. 1986. *Religion in the Lives of English Women.* London: Croom Helm.

Marchand, C. Roland. 1972. *The American Peace Movement and Social Reform, 1898–1918.* Princeton: Princeton University Press.

Marcus, Jane. 1985. *Art and Anger: Reading Like a Woman.* Columbus: Miami University of Ohio Press.

Marcus, Julie, et al., eds. 1993. *First in Their Field: Women and Australian Anthropology.* Melbourne: Melbourne University Press.

Massey, Mary E. 1966. *Bonnet Brigades: American Women and the Civil War.* New York: Alfred A. Knopf.

Matthews, Glenna. 1992. *The Rise of Public Woman: Woman's Power and Woman's Place in the United States 1630–1970.* New York: Oxford University Press.

Maynes, Mary Jo. 1986. *German Women in the Eighteenth and Nineteenth Centuries: A Social and Literary History.* Bloomington: Indiana University Press.

Mba, Nina Emma. 1982. *Nigerian Women Mobilized: Women's Political Activity in Southern Nigeria, 1900–1965.* Berkeley: University of California Press.

McCann, Carole R. 1994. *Birth Control Politics in the United States, 1916–1945.* Ithaca, NY: Cornell University Press.

McCrone, Kathleen E. 1988. *Sport and the Physical Emancipation of English Women 1870–1914.* London: Routledge.

McDermid, Jane, and Anna Hillyar. 1999. *Midwives of the Revolution: Female Bolsheviks and Women Workers in 1917.* London: UCL Press.

McDonald, Lynn, ed. 1998. *Women Theorists on Society and Politics.* Waterloo, ON: Wilfrid Laurier University Press.

McFadden, Margaret. 1999. *Golden Cables of Sympathy: The Transatlantic Sources of Nineteenth-Century Feminism.* Lexington: University of Kentucky Press.

McFeely, Mary Drake. 1988. *Lady Inspectors: The Campaign for a Better Workplace 1893–1921.* Oxford: Blackwell.

McHugh, Paul. 1980. *Prostitution and Victorian Social Reform.* London: Croom Helm.

McLaren, Eva Shaw, ed. 1919. *A History of the Scottish Women's Hospitals.* London: Hodder and Stoughton.

Meigs, Cornelia. 1956. *What Makes a College?* New York: Macmillan.

Melder, Keith E. 1977. *The Beginnings of Sisterhood: The American Woman's Rights Movement, 1800–1850.* New York: Schocken.

Melnyk, Julie. 1998. *Women's Theology in Nineteenth-Century Britain: Transfiguring the Faith of Their Fathers.* New York: Garland.

Meyer, Donald. 1987. *Sex and Power: The Rise of Women in America, Russia, Sweden, and Italy.* 2d ed. Middletown, CT: Wesleyan University Press.

Middleton, L. 1977. *Women in the Labour Movement.* London: Croom Helm.

Midgely, Clare. 1992. *Women against Slavery: The British Campaigns 1780–1870.* London: Routledge.

———. 1998. *Gender and Imperialism.* Manchester: Manchester University Press.

Milani, Farzaneh. 1992. *Veils and Words: The Emerging Voices of Iranian Women Writers.* London and New York: I. B. Tauris.

Mill, John Stuart. 1996 [1869]. *The Subjection of Women.* Reprint, New York: Dover.

Miller, Francesca. 1992. *Latin American Women and the Search for Social Justice.* Hanover, NH: University Press of New England.

Minault, Gail. 1981. *The Extended Family: Women and Political Participation in India and Pakistan.* Delhi: Chanakya Publications.

Mioko Fujieda. 1995. "Japan's First Phase of Feminism." In Kumiko Fujimura-Fanselow and Atsuko Kameda, eds., *Japanese Women: New Feminist Perspectives on the Past, Present, and Future.* New York: The Feminist Press.

Mitchell, David. 1966. *Women on the Warpath: The Story of Women of the First World War.* London: Jonathan Cape.

Mitchell, J., and Ann Oakley, eds. 1976. *The Rights and Wrongs of Women.* Harmondsworth: Penguin.

———. 1986. *What Is Feminism?* Oxford: Blackwell.

Moers, Ellen. 1978. *Literary Women.* London: Women's Press.

Mogadam, Valentine M. 1993. *Modernizing Women: Gender and Social Change in the Middle East.* Boulder, CO: Lynne Rienner.

———, ed. 1994. *Identity, Politics and Women: Cultural Reassertions and Feminisms in International Perspective.* Boulder, CO: Westview Press.

Moghissi, Haideh. 1994. *Populism and Feminism in Iran.* Women's Studies at York. London: St. Martin's Press.

Morin, Isobel V. 1994. *Women of the United States Congress.* Minneapolis: Oliver Press.

Morris, Aldon D. 1984. *The Origins of the Civil Rights Movement.* New York: Free Press.

Mort, Frank. 1987. *Dangerous Sexualities: Medico-Moral Politics in England since 1830.* London: Routledge.

Morton, Ward D. 1962. *Woman Suffrage in Mexico.* Gainesville: University of Florida Press.

Moses, Claire Goldberg. 1984. *French Feminism in the*

Nineteenth Century. Albany: State University of New York Press.

———. 1993. *Feminism, Socialism, and French Romanticism.* Bloomington: Indiana University Press.

Mowat, Charles Loch. 1961. *The Charity Organisation Society, 1869–1913: Its Ideas and Work.* London: Methuen.

Mulhern, Chieko Irie. 1991. *Heroic with Grace: Legendary Women of Japan.* Armonk, NY: M. E. Sharpe.

Mulvey-Roberts, Marie, and Tamae Mizuta, eds. 1994. *The Militants: Suffragette Activism.* Perspectives in the History of British Feminism. London: Routledge.

Murphy, Cliona, ed. 1989. *The Women's Suffrage Movement and Irish Society in the Early Twentieth Century.* London: Harvester Wheatsheaf.

Murray, Janet Horowitz. *Strong-Minded Women: And Other Lost Voices from Nineteenth-Century England.* Harmondsworth: Penguin.

Nanda, B. R., ed. 1976. *Indian Women: From Purdah to Modernity.* New Delhi: Vikas Publishing House.

Nashat, Guity, ed. 1982. *Women and Revolution in Iran.* Boulder, CO: Westview Press.

Neff, W. F. 1966. *Victorian Working Women.* London: Frank Cass.

Newsome, Stella. 1957. *The Women's Freedom League 1907–1957.* London: Women's Freedom League.

O'Barr, Jean F., Deborah Pope, and Mary Wyer. 1990. *Ties That Bind: Essays on Mothering and Patriarchy.* Chicago: University of Chicago Press.

O'Connor, Lillian. 1954. *Pioneer Women Orators: Rhetoric in the Ante-Bellum Reform Movement.* New York: Columbia University Press.

Offen, Karen. 2000. *European Feminisms 1700–1950: A Political History.* Stanford: Stanford University Press.

Oldfield, Audrey. 1992. *Woman Suffrage in Australia: A Gift or a Struggle?* Melbourne: Cambridge University Press.

Oldfield, Sybil. 1984. *Spinsters of This Parish: The Life and Times of F. M. Mayor and Mary Sheepshanks.* London: Virago.

———. 1989. *Women against the Iron Fist: Alternatives to Militarism 1900–1989.* Oxford: Basil Blackwell.

———. 1994. *This Working-Day World: Women's Lives and Cultures in Britain 1914–1945.* London: Taylor and Francis.

O'Leary, Margaret Hayford. 1993. "Norwegian Women Writers." In Harald S. Naess, ed., *A History of Norwegian Literature.* Lincoln: University of Nebraska Press in cooperation with the American-Scandinavian Foundation.

Olson, Lynn. 2001. *Freedom's Daughters: The Unsung Heroines of the Civil Rights Movement from 1830 to 1970.* New York: Scribner.

O'Neill, William L. 1969. *The Women's Movement: Feminism in the United States and England.* London: George Allen and Unwin.

———. 1989. *Feminism in America: A History.* 2d ed. New Brunswick, NJ: Transaction.

Ono Kazuko. 1978. *Chinese Women in a Century of Revolution.* Stanford: Stanford University Press.

Orleck, Annelise. 1995. *Common Sense and a Little Fire: Women and Working-Class Politics in the United States, 1900–1965.* Chapel Hill: University of North Carolina Press.

Orr, Clarissa Campbell, ed. 1996. *Wollstonecraft's Daughters: Womanhood in England and France, 1780–1920.* Manchester: Manchester University Press.

Owen, David. 1965. *English Philanthropy 1660–1960.* Oxford: Oxford University Press.

Owens, Rosemary Cullen. 1984. *Smashing Times: A History of the Irish Women's Suffrage Movement 1889–1922.* Dublin: Attic Press.

Paidar, Parvin. 1995. *Women and the Political Process in Twentieth-Century Iran.* Cambridge: Cambridge University Press.

Palmieri, Patricia. 1995. *In Adamless Eden: The Community of Women Faculty at Wellesley.* New Haven, CT: Yale University Press.

Paulson, Ross Evans. 1973. *Women's Suffrage and Prohibition: A Comparative Study of Equality and Social Control.* Glenview, IL: Scott, Foresman.

Pearl, Cyril. 1980 [1955]. *The Girl with the Swansdown Seat: An Informal Report on Some Aspects of Mid-Victorian Morality.* Reprint, London: Robin Clark.

Pearsall, Ronald. 1969. *The Worm in the Bud: The World of Victorian Sexuality.* London: Weidenfeld and Nicolson.

Pearson, John. 1978. *Facades.* London: Macmillan.

Pease, William H., and Jane H. Pease. 1963. *Black Utopia: Negro Communal Experiments in America.* Madison: State Historical Society of Wisconsin.

Pedersen, Susan. 1993. *Family, Dependence, and the Origins of the Welfare State: Britain and France, 1914–1945.* Cambridge: Cambridge University Press.

Perkin, Joan. 1993. *Victorian Women.* London: John Murray.

Peterson, Carla L. 1995. *Doers of the World: African-American Women Speakers and Writers in the North (1830–1880).* New York: Oxford University Press.

Pharr, Susan J. 1981. *Political Women in Japan: The Search for a Place in Political Life.* Berkeley: University of California Press.

Pierson, Ruth Roach, ed. 1987. *Woman and Peace: Theoretical, Historical and Practical Perspectives.* London: Croom Helm.

Pivar, David J. 1973. *Purity Crusade: Sexual Morality and Social Control, 1868–1900.* Westport, CT: Greenwood Press.

Poovey, Mary. 1989. *Uneven Developments: The Ideological Work of Gender in Mid-Victorian Britain.* London: Virago.

Porter, Cathy. 1976. *Fathers and Daughters: Russian Women in Revolution.* London: Virago.

Pratt, Edwin. A. 1897. *Pioneering Women in Victoria's Reign.* London: George Newnes.

Prelinger, Catherine M. 1980. "The *Frauen-Zeitung* (1849–1852): Harmony and Dissonance in Mid-Century German Feminism." *History of European Ideas* 11: 245–251.

———. 1987. *Charity, Challenge, and Change: Religious Dimensions of the Mid-Nineteenth Century Women's Movement in Germany.* Westport, CT: Greenwood Press.

Prochaska, F. K. 1980. *Women and Philanthropy in Nineteenth-Century England.* Oxford: Clarendon Press.

Pugh, Martin. 2000. *Women and the Women's Movement in Britain 1914–1999.* 2d ed. Basingstoke: Macmillan.

Pujol, M. A. 1992. *Feminism and Anti-Feminism in Early Economic Thought.* Aldershot: Edward Elgar.

Purvis, June. 1991. *A History of Women's Education in England.* Milton Keynes: Open University Press.

———, ed. 1995. *Women's History: Britain, 1850–1945.* London: UCL Press.

Purvis, June, and Sandra Stanley Holton, eds. 2000. *Votes for Women.* London and New York: Routledge.

Pushkareva, Natalia. 1997. *Women in Russian History: From the Tenth to the Twentieth Century.* Stroud: Sutton Publishing.

Quarles, Benjamin. 1969. *Black Abolitionists.* New York: Oxford University Press.

Quaterat, Jean H. 1979. *Reluctant Feminists in German Social Democracy 1885–1917.* Princeton: Princeton University Press.

Radzinsky, Edvard. 1997. *Stalin.* London: Sceptre.

Raeburn, Antonia. 1973. *The Militant Suffragettes.* London: Michael Joseph.

Ramelson, Marian. 1967. *The Petticoat Rebellion: A Century of Struggle for Women's Rights.* London: Lawrence and Wishart.

Ramusack, Barbara N. 1981. "Catalysts or Helpers? British Feminist, Indian Women's Rights, and Indian Independence." In Gail Minault, ed., *The Extended Family: Women and Political Participation in India and Pakistan.* Delhi: Chanakya Publications.

Rasmussen, Janet E. 1982. "Sisters across the Sea: Early Norwegian Feminists and Their American Connections." *Women's Studies International Forum* 5(6): 647–654.

Ray, Janet. 1949. *100 Years of Medicine.* Saskatoon: Modern Press.

Reed, James. 1978. *From Public Vice to Private Virtue: The Birth Control Movement and American Society since 1830.* Princeton: Princeton University Press.

Rendall, Jane. 1985. *The Origins of Modern Feminism: Women in Britain, France, and the United States 1780–1860.* Chicago: University of Chicago Press.

———, ed. 1987. *Equal or Different: Women's Politics 1800–1914.* Oxford: Blackwell.

Reynolds, Sian, ed. 1986. *Women, State and Revolution: Essays in Power and Gender in Europe since 1789.* Brighton: Wheatsheaf.

Roberts, E. 1984. *Woman's Place: An Oral History of Working Class Women 1890–1940.* Oxford: Blackwell.

Roberts, Marie Mulvey, and Tamae Mizuta, eds. 1993–1995. *Sources of British Feminism.* Vol. 1, 1993: *The Pioneers: Early Feminists;* vol. 2, 1993: *The Reformers: Socialist Feminism;* vol. 3, 1993: *The Disempowered: Women and the Law;* vol. 4, 1993: *The Exploited: Women and Work;* vol. 5, 1993: *The Suffragettes: Towards Emancipation;* vol. 6, 1994: *The Campaigners;* vol. 7, 1995: *The Educators.* London: Routledge.

Robertson, Priscilla. 1982. *An Experience of Women: Pattern and Change in Nineteenth-Century Europe.* Philadelphia: Temple University Press.

Robin-Mowry, Dorothy. 1983. *The Hidden Sun: Women of Modern Japan.* Epping, Essex: Bowker.

Roessler, Shirley E. 1996. *Out of the Shadows: Women and Politics in the French Revolution, 1789–1795.* New York: P. D. Lang.

Roosevelt, Eleanor, and Lorena A. Hickok. 1954. *Ladies of Courage.* New York: Putnam.

Rose, Kalima. 1992. *Where Women Are Leaders.* London: Zed Books.

Rose, Kenneth D. 1996. *American Women and the Repeal of Prohibition.* New York: New York University Press.

Rosen, Andrew. 1993 [1974]. *Rise Up, Women! Militant Campaign of the WSPU 1903–1904.* Reprint, London: Routledge.

Ross, Ishbel. 1965. *Charmers and Cranks: Twelve Famous American Women Who Defied the Conventions.* New York: Harper & Row.

Rossi, Alice S. 1988. *The Feminist Papers: From Adams to de Beauvoir.* Boston: Northeastern University Press.

Rothblatt, Sheldon. 1968. *The Revolution of the Dons: Cambridge and Society in Victorian England.* London: Faber and Faber.

Rover, Constance. 1967. *Women's Suffrage and Party Politics in Britain 1866–1914.* London: Routledge and Kegan Paul.

———. 1970. *Love, Morals and the Feminists.* London: Routledge and Kegan Paul.

Rowbotham, Sheila. 1972. *Women, Resistance, and Revolution.* Harmondsworth: Penguin.

———. 1973. *Hidden from History: 300 Years of Women's Oppression and the Fight against It.* London: Pluto Press.

———. 1992. *Women in Movement: Feminism and Social Action.* New York: Routledge.

———. 1999. *Threads through Time: Writings on History and Autobiography.* London: Penguin.

Rubinstein, David. 1986. *Before the Suffragettes: Women's Emancipation in the 1890s.* Brighton: Harvester Press.

Rupke, Nicolaas A., ed. 1987. *Vivisection in Historical Perspective.* London: Routledge.

Rupp, Leila J. 1997. *Worlds of Women: The Making of an International Women's Movement.* Princeton: Princeton University Press.

Russell, Diana E. H. 1989. *Women for a New South Africa.* New York: Basic Books.

Russell, Dora. 1975. *The Tamarisk Tree: My Quest for Liberty and Love.* London: Elek.

Sadleir, Rosemary. 1994. *Leading the War: Black Women in Canada.* Toronto: Umbrella Press.

Sadlier, Darlene J. 1991. "The Struggle for Women's Rights in Portugal." *Camões Center Quarterly* 3(1–2): 32–36.

Sakharov, Andrei. 1990. *Memoirs.* London: Hutchinson.

Sanasarian, Eliz [*sic*]. 1982. *Women's Rights Movement in Iran: Mutiny, Appeasement, and Repression from 1900 to Khomeini.* Praeger Special Studies. New York: Praeger Publications.

Sandburg, Carl. 1936. *Abraham Lincoln: The War Years.* 4 vols. New York: Harcourt, Brace and Company.

Sanders, Valerie. 1996. *Eve's Renegades: Victorian Anti-Feminist Women Novelists.* London: Macmillan.

Sarah, Elizabeth, guest ed. 1982. "Reassessments of First Wave Feminism." *Women's Studies International Forum* 5(6).

Sayder, A. 1972. *Dauntless Women in Childhood Education, 1856–1931.* Washington, DC: Association for Childhood Education International.

Schneir, Miriam, ed. 1972. *Feminism: The Essential Historical Writings.* New York: Vintage Books.

Schofield, Mary Anne, and Celia Macheski. 1986. *Fetter'd or Free? British Women Novelists, 1670–1815.* Athens: Ohio University Press.

Schott, Linda K. 1997. *Reconstructing Women's Thoughts: The Women's International League for Peace and Freedom before World War II.* Stanford: Stanford University Press.

Schreiber, Adele, and Margaret Mathieson. 1955. *Journey towards Freedom: Written for the Golden Jubilee of the International Alliance of Women.* Copenhagen: International Alliance of Women.

Schupf, Harriet Warm. 1974. "Single Women and Social Reform in Mid-Nineteenth Century England: The Case of Mary Carpenter." *Victorian Studies* 17(2): 307–319.

Scott, Anne Firor. 1970. *The Southern Lady: From Pedestal to Politics, 1830–1930.* Chicago: University of Chicago Press.

Scott, Joan. 1974. *The Glassworkers of Carmaux.* Cambridge, MA: Harvard University Press.

———. 1996. *Only Paradoxes to Offer: French Feminists and the Rights of Man.* Cambridge, MA: Harvard University Press.

Service, Robert. 2000. *Lenin: A Biography.* London: Macmillan.

Shah, A. M., B. S. Baviskar, and E. A. Ramaswamy. 1996. *Social Structure and Change,* vol. 2, *Women in Indian Society.* New Delhi: Sage.

Shanley, Mary Lyndon. 1989. *Feminism, Marriage, and the Law in Victorian England, 1850–1895.* Princeton: Princeton University Press.

Shea, Marian Axford. 1999. *Women Movers & Shakers.* Lincoln, NE: Media Productions and Marketing.

Sheehy-Skeffington, Andrée, and Rosemary Owens, eds. 1975. *Votes for Women: Irish Women's Struggle for the Vote.* Dublin: Skeffington and Owens.

Shiman, Lilian Lewis. 1992. *Women and Leadership in Nineteenth-Century England.* Basingstoke: Macmillan.

Shirley, Ralph. 1920. *Occultists and Mystics of All Ages.* London: W. Rider and Son.

Showalter, Elaine. 1999 [1977]. *A Literature of Their Own: British Women Novelists from Brontë to Lessing.* Reprint, London: Virago.

———. 2001. *Inventing Herself: Claiming a Feminist Intellectual Heritage.* London: Picador.

Sievers, Sharon L. 1981. "Feminist Criticism in Japanese Politics in the 1880s: The Experience of Kishida Toshiko." *Signs* 6(4): 602–616.

———. 1983. *Flowers in Salt: The Beginnings of Feminist Consciousness in Modern Japan.* Stanford: Stanford University Press.

Simey, Margaret B. 1951. *Charitable Effort in Liverpool in the Nineteenth Century.* Liverpool: Liverpool University Press.

Simon, Rita J., and Gloria Danziger. 1991. *Women's Movements in America: Their Successes, Disappointments and Aspirations.* New York: Praeger.

Sinclair, Upton. 1986 [1906]. *The Jungle.* Reprint, Harmondsworth: Penguin Books.

Siu, Bobby. 1982. *Women of China: Imperialism and Women's Resistance 1900–1949.* London: Zed Books.

Sklar, Kathryn Kish. 1998. *Social Justice Feminists in the United States and Germany: A Dialogue in Documents 1885–1933.* Ithaca: Cornell University Press.

Slaughter, Jane, and Robert Kern. 1981. *European Women on the Left: Socialism, Feminism, and the Problems Faced by Political Women, 1880 to the Present.* Westport, CT: Greenwood Press.

Smith, Bonnie G. 1989. *Changing Lives: Women in European History since 1700.* Lexington, MA: D. C. Heath.

Smith, Harold L., ed. 1990. *British Feminism in the Twentieth Century.* Aldershot: Edward Elgar.

Smith, Jessie Carney, ed. 1993. *Epic Lives: One Hundred Black Women Who Made a Difference.* Detroit: Visible Ink.

Smyth, Ethel. 1987. *Memoirs of Ethel Smyth.* Abridged and introduced by Ronald Crichton. London: Viking.

Snow, Helen Foster. 1967. *Women in Modern China.* The Hague: Mouton.

Snowden, Ethel. 1921. *A Political Pilgrim in Europe.* London: Cassell.

Sochen, June. 1972. *The New Woman: Feminism in Greenwich Village 1910–1920.* New York: Quadrangle.

Soldon, Norbert C. 1978. *Women in British Trade Unions 1874–1976.* Dublin: Gill and Macmillan.

Solomon, Barbara Miller. 1985. *In the Company of Educated Women: A History of Women and Higher Education in America.* New Haven, CT: Yale University Press.

Soloway, Richard Allen. 1982. *Birth Control and the Population Question in England, 1877–1930.* Chapel Hill: University of North Carolina Press.

Soong Ching-ling. 1952. *The Struggle for a New China.* Peking: Foreign Languages Press.

Soto, Shirlene. 1990. *Emergence of the Modern Mexican Woman: Her Participation in Revolution and Struggle for Equality, 1910–1940.* Denver: Arden Press.

Sowerwine, Charles. 1982. *Sisters or Citizens? Women and Socialism in France since 1876.* Cambridge: Cambridge University Press.

Spence, Jonathan D. 1982. *The Gate of Heavenly Peace: The Chinese and Their Revolution, 1895–1980.* London: Faber and Faber.

Spence, Jonathan, and Annping Chin, eds. 1996. *The Chinese Century.* London: HarperCollins.

Spender, Dale. 1982. *Women of Ideas, and What Men Have Done to Them.* London: Routledge and Kegan Paul.

———, ed. 1983. *Feminist Theorists: Three Centuries of Women's Intellectual Traditions.* London: Women's Press.

Spink, Kathryn. 1991. *Black Sash: The Beginning of a Bridge in South Africa.* London: Methuen.

Stacey, Judith. 1983. *Patriarchy and Socialist Revolution in China.* Berkeley: University of California Press.

Stanton, Elizabeth Cady, Susan B. Anthony, Matilda Joslyn Gage, and Ida Husted Harper. 1881. *History of Woman Suffrage.* Vols. 1 and 2 1882, vol. 3 1886. New York: Fowler & Wells; Vol. 4 1902. Indianapolis: Hollenbeck Press; Vols. 5 and 6 1922. Harper, NY: National American Woman Suffrage Association. (Also reprinted in 1985 in 6 vols. Salem NH: Ayer Publishers.)

Stites, Richard. 1991 [1978]. *The Women's Liberation Movement in Russia: Feminism, Nihilism, and Bolshevism, 1860–1930.* Reprint, Princeton: Princeton University Press.

Stock, Phyllis. 1978. *Better Than Rubies: A History of Women's Education.* New York: Putnam.

Stocks, Mary. 1970. *My Commonplace Book.* London: Peter Davies.

———. 1973. *Still More Commonplaces.* London: Peter Davies.

Stoner, K. Lynn. 1991. *From the House to the Streets: The Cuban Woman's Movement for Legal Reform 1898–1940.* Durham, NC: Duke University Press.

Stott, Mary. 1978. *Organization Woman: The Story of the National Union of Townswomen's Guilds.* London: Heinemann.

Stowell, Sheila. 1992. *A Stage of Their Own: Feminist Playwrights of the Suffrage Era.* Manchester: Manchester University Press.

Strachey, Lytton. 1971 [1918]. *Eminent Victorians.* Reprint, Harmondsworth: Penguin.

Strachey, Ray. 1936. *Our Freedom and Its Results by Five Women.* London: Hogarth Press.

———. 1978 [1928]. *The Cause: A Brief History of the Women's Movement.* Reprint, London: Virago.

Strong-Boag, Veronica. 1987. "Peace-Making Women: Canada 1919–1939." In Ruth Roach Pierson, ed., *Woman and Peace: Theoretical, Historical and Practical Perspectives.* London: Croom Helm.

Strumingher, Laura S. 1979. *Women and the Making of the Working Class: Lyon, 1830–1870.* St. Albans, VT: Eden Press.

Stuart, James. 1911. *Reminiscences.* Privately printed.

Subido, Tarroso. 1955. *The Feminist Movement in the Philippines 1905–1955.* Manila: National Federation of Women's Clubs.

Tabari, Azar, and Naihd Yeganeh. 1982. *In the Shadow of Islam: The Women's Movement in Iran.* London: Zed Books.

Talhami, Ghada Hashem. 1996. *The Mobilization of Muslim Women in Egypt.* Gainesville: University Press of Florida.

Tax, Meredith. 1980. *The Rising of the Women: Feminist Solidarity and Class Conflict 1880–1917.* New York: Monthly Review Press.

Taylor, Barbara. 1983. *Eve and the New Jerusalem: Society and Feminism in the Nineteenth Century.* London: Virago.

Taylor, Clare. 1974. *British and American Abolitionists: An Episode in Transatlantic Understanding.* Edinburgh: Edinburgh University Press.

Terrot, Charles. 1959. *The Maiden Tribute: A Study of the White Slave Traffic of the Nineteenth Century.* London: Frederick Muller.

Thébaud, Francoise, ed. 1994. *A History of Women: Toward a Cultural Identity in the Twentieth Century.* Cambridge, MA: Belknap Press at Harvard University.

Thomis, Malcolm, and J. Grimmett. 1982. *Women in Protest 1800–1850.* New York: St. Martin's Press.

Thompson, Dorothy. 1983. *Over Our Dead Bodies: Women against the Bomb.* London: Virago.

Thönnessen, Werner. 1976. *The Emancipation of Women: The Rise and Decline of the Women's Movement in German Social Democracy 1863–1933.* London: Pluto Press.

Tickner, L. 1987. *The Spectacle of Women: Imagery of the Suffrage Campaign 1907–1914.* London: Chatto and Windus.

Tobey, James A. 1925. *The Children's Bureau: Its History, Activities and Organization.* Baltimore: Johns Hopkins University Press.

Tobias, J. J. *Crime and Industrial Society in the Nineteenth Century.* London: Batsford.

Todd, Janet. 1983. *Women Writers Talking.* New York: Holmes & Meier.

Trattner, Walter I. 1970. *Crusade for the Children: A History of the National Child Labor Committee and Child Labor Reform in America.* Chicago: Quadrangle Books.

Tucker, J. E., ed. 1993. *Arab Women.* Bloomington: Indiana University Press.

Tuson, Penelope, ed. 1997. *The Queen's Daughters: An Anthology of Victorian Feminist Writings on India 1857–1900.* Reading, Berkshire, UK: Ithaca Press.

Tuve, Jeanette E. 1984. *The First Russian Women Physicians.* Newtonville, MA: Oriental Research Partners.

Tyler, Helen E. *Where Prayer and Purpose Meet: The WCTU Story, 1874–1949.* Evanston, IL: Signal Press.

Tyrrell, Ian. 1991. *Woman's World, Woman's Empire: The Women's Christian Temperance Union in International Perspective, 1880–1930.* Chapel Hill: University of North Carolina Press.

Usborne, Cornelie. 1992. *The Politics of the Body in Weimar Germany.* Ann Arbor: University of Michigan Press.

Varikas, Eleni. 1993. "Gender and National Identity in *Fin de Siècle* Greece." *Gender and History* 5(2), 269–283.

Vasilieva, Larissa. 1994. *Kremlin Wives.* London: Weidenfeld and Nicolson.

Vicinus, Martha. 1972. *Suffer and Be Still: Women in the Victorian Age.* Bloomington: Indiana University Press.

———. 1977. *A Widening Sphere: Changing Roles of Victorian Women.* Bloomington: Indiana University Press.

———. 1985. *Independent Women, Work and Community for Single Women, 1850–1920.* London: Virago.

Villa-Vicencio, Charles. 1996. *The Spirit of Freedom: South African Leaders on Religion and Politics.* Berkeley: University of California Press.

Volkogonov, Dmitri. 1994. *Lenin: Life and Legacy.* London: HarperCollins.

Vreede-de Stuers, Cora. 1960. *The Indonesian Woman: Struggles and Achievements.* The Hague: Mouton.

Vyvyan, John. 1969. *In Pity and in Anger: A Study of the Use of Animals in Science.* London: Michael Joseph.

———. 1971. *The Dark Face of Science.* London: Michael Joseph.

Wagner, Gillian. 1979. *Children of the Empire.* London: Weidenfeld and Nicolson.

Wagner, Sally Roesch. 1992. "The Iroquois Influence on Women's Rights." In Jose Barreiro, ed., *Indian Roots of American Democracy.* Fairfax, VA: Falmouth Institute.

Walker, Cheryl. 1990. *Women and Gender in Southern Africa to 1945.* Cape Town: David Philip.

———. 1991. *Women and Resistance in South Africa.* 2d ed. Cape Town: David Philip.

Walkowitz, Judith. 1980. *Prostitution and Victorian Society: Women, Class and the State.* Cambridge: Cambridge University Press.

———. 1992. *City of Dreadful Delight: Narratives of Sexual Danger in Late-Victorian London.* London: Virago.

Walsh, Mary Roth. 1977. *"Doctors Wanted: No Women Need Apply": Sexual Barriers in the Medical Profession, 1835–1975.* New Haven: Yale University Press.

Walton, Ronald G. 1975. *Women in Social Work.* London: Routledge and Kegan Paul.

Wang Zheng. 1999. *Women in the Chinese Enlightenment: An Illustrated History.* Berkeley: University of California Press.

Ward, Geoffrey C. 1990. *The Civil War: An Illustrated History.* New York: Alfred A. Knopf.

Ward, Margaret. 1983. *Unmanageable Revolutionaries: Women and Irish Nationalism.* London: Pluto Press.

———. 1996. *In Their Own Voice: Women and Irish Nationalism.* Dublin: Attic Press.

Ware, Vron. 1992. *Beyond the Pale: White Women, Racism, and History.* London: Verso.

Waters, Kristin. 2000. *Women and Men Political Theorists: Enlightened Conversations.* Malden, MA: Blackwell.

Watkins, Susan Alice, Marisa Rueda, and Marta Rodriguez. 1999. *Introducing Feminism.* Duxford, UK: Icon Books.

Weatherford, Doris. 1998. *A History of the American Suffragist Movement.* Santa Barbara, CA: ABC-CLIO.

Wells, Susan. 2001. *Out of the Dead House: Nineteenth-Century Women Physicians and the Writing of Medicine.* Madison: University of Wisconsin Press.

Wertheimer, Barbara M. 1977. *We Were There: The Story of Working Women in America.* New York: Pantheon Books.

Whittick, A., with Frederick Muller. 1979. *Woman into Citizen.* London: Atheneum, with Frederick Muller.

Wieringa, Saskia. 1995. *Subversive Women: Women's Movements in Africa, Asia, Latin America and the Caribbean.* London: Zed Books.

Williams, Juan. 1987. *Eyes on the Prize: America's Civil Rights Years, 1954–1965.* New York: Viking.

Williams, M. 1984. *Women in the English Novel 1800–1900.* London: Macmillan.

Willis, Chris, and Angelique Richardson, eds. 1999. *The New Woman in Fiction and in Fact.* Basingstoke: Macmillan.

Wilson, Edmund. 1960. *To the Finland Station.* London: Collins.

Wilson, Francis. 1989. *Uprooting Poverty: The South African Challenge.* Report for the Second Carnegie Foundation Inquiry into Poverty and Development in Southern Africa. New York: W. W. Norton.

Wiltsher, Anne. 1985. *Most Dangerous Women: Feminist Peace Campaigners of the Great War.* London: Pandora, and Westport, CT: Greenwood Press.

Wingerden, Sophia A. van. 1999. *The Women's Suffrage Movement in Britain.* London: Macmillan.

Winks, Robin. 1971. *The Blacks in Canada: A History.* Montreal: McGill-Queen's University Press.

Woodruffe, Kathleen. 1962. *From Charity to Social Work in England and the United States.* Toronto: University of Toronto Press.

Woodsmall, Ruth Frances. 1936. *Moslem Women Enter a New World.* London: George Allen and Unwin.

Yee, Shirley J. 1992. *Black Women Abolitionists: A Study in Activism 1828–1860.* Knoxville: University of Tennessee Press.

Yellen, Jean Fagan. 1989. *Women and Sisters: The Antislavery Feminists in American Culture.* New Haven: Yale University Press.

Yeo, Eileen. 1998. *Radical Femininity: Women's Self-Representation in the Public Sphere.* Manchester: Manchester University Press.

Young, Marilyn B. 1973. *Women in China.* Michigan Papers in Chinese Studies no. 5. Ann Arbor: Center for Chinese Studies.

Journals
The following journals are all a rich source on women's history and many contain articles on lesser-known women, especially *Signs,* which is indexed for the period 1975–1995. Please note, however, that most journals are indexed on an annual, not a cumulative, basis, if at all.

Affilia (Journal of Women and Social Work) (1986–)

The Common Cause (1909–1920), journal of the National Union of Women's Suffrage Societies

English Woman's Review (1866–1910)

European Journal of Women's Studies (1994–)

Feminist Forum

Feminist Review (1979–)

Gender and History

Hypatia: A Journal of Feminist Philosophy (1986–)

Journal of Victorian Culture (1996–)

Journal of Women's History (1989–)

Signs: Journal of Women in Culture and Society (1974–)

Social Service Quarterly (United Kingdom, 1930–1979)

Social Service Review (United States)

Studies on Women Abstracts (1983–1999)

Victorian Studies (1957–)

Votes for Women (1907–1918), journal of the Women's Social and Political Union

Woman's Journal (1870–1931) (United States, 1870–1931, edited by Lucy Stone and Alice Stone Blackwell)

Women's History Review (1992–)

Women's Studies (1972–1992)

Women's Studies International Quarterly (1978–1981), from 1982 known as *Women's Studies International Forum.*

For abstracts of articles and book reviews on women's history, see:

Studies on Women Abstracts (1883–1999)

Studies on Women and Gender Abstracts (2000)

For the history of the international suffrage movement and many rare photographs of women activists, as well as some obituaries, the following is an essential and engrossing source, particularly for the years 1913–1940:

Jus Suffragii (1906–1925), after which it was known as the *International Woman Suffrage News* (1926–1930) and then *International Woman News* (1931–). A reprint is forthcoming in 2003 as *Jus Suffragii: An International Suffrage Journal during World War I.* 6 vols. Edited by Sybil Oldfield. London: Routledge.

Index

Abbott, Edith, **1–2**, 5, 389
Abbott, Grace, **2–3**, 5
Abella de Ramírez, María, **3–4**
Abeokuta Ladies' Club (Nigeria), 572
Aberdeen, Lady Isabella, 97, 683, 703
Abernathy, Ralph, 214
Abolitionists, 137–138, 266
  in UK, 294, 295–296, 454
  in U.S., 17, 18, 19, 85–86, 151–152, 220, 232, 233,
    254–255, 279–281, 399, 461–462, 665, 676,
    684–687, 716–717, 718–719, 769
  writings of, 684–687
Aboriginal peoples, 52–53, 495, 688–689. *See also*
  Indigenous peoples; Native Americans
Abortion, 20, 54, 60, 235, 540, 541, 542, 556, 585, 622,
  673, 674, 680, 690
Abzug, Bella, 235
Addams, Jane, 1, 2, **4–7**, 43, 44, 212, 229, 257, 287,
  288, 293, 301, 317, 331, 358, 388, 429, 430, 437,
  504, 505, 548, 570, 587, 611, 612, 626, 627, 728,
  738
Adivar, Halide. *See* Edip, Halide
Adoption, 290, 392
Adult Suffrage Society (UK and Canada), 97, 450,
  451, 466
Adultery, 272, 273, 497, 699
Afghan women social reformers, **7–9**
Africa Prize for Leadership for the Sustainable End of
  Hunger, 411
African Americans, 137, 739
  economic condition of, 76, 214–215, 286, 438, 505
  and education, 75, 76, 83, 112, 137, 138, 151, 403,
    622
  voting rights of, 19, 84, 286, 462, 594, 665–666,
    717
  See also Abolitionists; Anti-lynching movement;
    Civil rights; Racial justice; School desegregation
African cultural tradition, 138–139, 170, 412, 424,
  425, 438
African National Congress (ANC), 345, 431, 432, 484,
  567, 652, 653, 693, 694
Agnes McPhail Award, 415
Agrarian reform, 341, 414, 415, 527

AIDS (acquired immunodeficiency syndrome), 192,
  285, 460, 620
Albert Einstein Peace Award, 471
Albert Schweitzer Prize for Animal Welfare, 137
Alcohol, ban on, 386, 746. *See also* Temperance
  movement
Alcoholism, education and rehabilitation for,
  102–103, 134, 655, 745
Alcott, Bronson, 535, 537
Alice Hamilton Science Award for Occupational
  Safety and Health, 289
All-Arab Federation of Women, 640
All-Asia Women's Conference, 168, 582
All-Ceylon Women's Conference, 601
All-China Democratic Women's Federation, 126
All-China Women's Federation, 182, 184, 398, 399
Alliance des Femmes (France), 78
All-India Child Marriage Abolition League, 577
All-India Family Planning Association (AIFPA), 578
All-India Muslim League, 480
All-India Muslim Women's Committee and
  Conference, 341–342, 480
All-India Women's Central Food Council, 609
All-India Women's Conference (AIWC), 146, 147,
  168, 313, 352, 353, 476, 508, 575, 577, 578, 581,
  582, 610, 703
All-Pakistan Women's Association, 363
All-Russian League for Women's Equality, 445–446,
  648, 649
All-Russian Union for Women's Equality, 445–446,
  552
All-Russian Women's Congress, 226, 369, 446, 635,
  648
Alma Dolens, **9–10**, 284
Alpha Suffrage Club (U.S.), 739
Alvarado Rivera, María Jesus, **10–11**
American Academy of Arts and Letters, 311
American Academy of Arts and Sciences, 137
American and Foreign Anti-Slavery Society, 233
American Anti-Slavery Society (AASS), 19, 151, 232,
  233, 461
American Association of University Women
  (AAUW), 707

857